Arming for Armageddon

Arming for Armageddon

John Wesley White

MOTT MEDIA

ARMING FOR ARMAGEDDON

Copyright © 1983 by Mott Media, Inc.

Edited by Carolyn Stanford Goss and Leonard George Goss
Cover designed by Jetzer Design Center, Inc.
Typeset by Frieda Bohn and Joyce Bohn
Printed by BookCrafters

Manufactured in the United States of America

ISBN 0-88062-109-5

Introduction

ARMAGEDDON, AHR muh GED un, is a word which comes from the Hebrew *Har-Megiddo*, which means Hill of Megiddo. Armageddon is named in Revelation 16 as the place where the rulers of the world will fight the last great battle between good and evil.

Armageddon is located in the mountains of central Palestine, across the Plain of Esdraelon from Nazareth. Many battles were fought here in Bible times, near the town of Megiddo. In 1918, the British under General Allenby defeated the Turks at Armageddon. Archaeologists from the Oriental Institute in Chicago have found temples, jewelry, art objects, and other valuable archaeological items at Armageddon.

Contents

Foreword

The Scriptures exhort us to pray for peace, seek peace, pursue peace and hope for peace. Jesus said, "Blessed are the peacemakers!" So as another New Year rings in to the sound of peace bell aspirations from Buckingham Palace, from the Vatican, from the Kremlin, from the Heavenly Gate in Peking, and from the White House in Washington, we are to join in the effort in the words of the Pope: "Peace . . . we must want it at any cost!"

However, whether you read the literature of diagnosis or prognosis, it seems that in the frightening world of today, as the syndicated pundit Jack McArthur puts it, you encounter "almost solid gloom and disaster." Good men throughout the ages have tried admirably to avoid an impending Armageddon. The great Jewish scholar, Rabbi Reuben Slonim, notes incisively that for centuries organized religion has sincerely "promised to abolish war, establish the equality of all men, prohibit the exploitation of human beings, and transform the City of Man into the City of God. Despite the collective efforts of all cults and creeds, the sword is still the sword, not a ploughshare." Today nearly a trillion dollars is being earmarked this year for weaponry, armaments, and death machines. Rabbi Slonim's point is well made.

"Everybody would like to think that a god is going to come out of somewhere and lead us out of our troubles," said the Chairman of the Democratic National Committee on network television. The fact of the matter is that God's Son is going to come back from heaven and fulfill His disciples' prayer through the ages: "Thy Kingdom come. Thy will be done on earth as it is in heaven." The apostle Paul defined a Christian as one who has "turned to God from idols to serve the true and living

God and to wait for His Son from heaven." A scrutiny of current events demonstrates that we could very well be living close to what the Bible calls the "time of the end."

To those who are Christians, I hope that a reading of this book will rouse you, in the words of the ancient prophet Joel, to "put ye in the sickle, for the harvest is ripe: come, get you down; for the press is full . . . Multitudes, multitudes in the valley of decision: for the day of the Lord is near in the valley of decision." Let's go everywhere, as Jesus exhorted, and preach the Gospel in all nations and "then shall the end come." If you are not a Christian, my prayer is that your reading this book will cause you to "prepare to meet your God." Remember God's promise: "Whosoever shall call upon the Name of the Lord shall be saved."

Billy Graham
Montreat, North Carolina

Preface

Laments Barbra Streisand in *Esquire*, as Brezhnev passes the Soviet torch to Andropov, "I do believe the world is coming to an end. I just feel that science, technology, and the mind have surpassed the soul—the heart. There is no balance in terms of feeling and love for fellow man."

Entering 1983, despite the profuse rhetoric "peace, peace", the war clouds worldwide are definitely darkening. Ann Landers carries in her column, read daily by 84 million, the resolution of the World Association for Social Psychiatry as written by Dr. Jules Masserman, Honorary Life President: that currently "acknowledged experts in international and military affairs [calculate that] unless present trends are reversed, chances are 4 in 5 that a nuclear war will destroy civilization in the next decade." The Dean of Behaviorists, Harvard's B. F. Skinner at 78, shocks The American Psychological Association Convention by pleading "Why are we not acting to save the world? Is there to be much more history at all?" Asked afterwards "Has the observer of social conditioning lost his optimism?" His reply was "I have . . . when I wrote *Beyond Freedom and Dignity* I was optimistic about the future. A decade ago there was hope, [but] today the world is fatally ill . . . it is a very depressing way to end one's life . . . the argument that we have always solved our problems in the past and shall, therefore, solve this one is like re-assuring a dying man by pointing out that he has always recovered from his illness."

I wish it were not so, but as I watch Dr. Carl Sagan, the world's highest profile astrophysicist on the Tonight Show with Johnny Carson, state that the armaments bill, if all accounts were in, would this year total up to a trillion dollars, I had the feeling that really, mankind is in fact *Arming for Armageddon*.

John Wesley White, D.Phil. (Oxon)
Toronto, Canada
January, 1983

Chapter One

"WARS AND RUMOURS OF WARS"

"Armageddon!" That final tragic triumph of "Evil" over "Good!" That's the irreversible direction modern man persists in traveling, sirens Harvard's Professor of Psychiatry Robert Coles in his cover story "The Psychology of Armageddon" (*Psychology Today*, May, 1982). In June, President Ronald Reagan solemnizes before the British House of Lords and Commons to hundreds of hearers—and to hundreds of millions worldwide on television—that everywhere "we see around us today the marks of our terrible dilemma—predictions of doomsday." Daily we struggle desperately to co-exist with "nuclear weapons" beckoning the "extinction of mankind."

This ever-present "threat of global war! No president, no congress, no prime minister, no parliament can spend a day entirely free of this threat" (*New York Times*, June 9, 1982). In July, in the wake of a month of hand-wringing rhetoric from the heads of states and their deputies before the United Nations Debate on Disarmament, an exercise in seeming futility that had editors universally lamenting that it entered with a roar and trailed off in a whimper, United Nations Secretary General Javier Prerez de Cuellar agonized that the whole affair seemed to be a balloon full of sound and fury signifying nothing. Man, he agonized, is hell-bent on a blind "drift towards World War III." The President of the United Nations General Assembly, Ismat Kittani, angrily asked, "What have the governments of the world done to respond to the fervent demand of the people of the world that this insane arms race be stopped?" He gave his own reply: "You and I know that answer, but I want to state it for the world to hear—nothing! Not a single weapon was destroyed over the past four years." In fact, Assessor A. LeBlanc calculates that the worldwide armaments bill adds up to a perilous 775 billion dollars for 1982. Who could argue that we are not veritably "Arming for Armageddon!"

Before his death a generation ago, H. G. Wells sounded the knell that "human history becomes more and more a race between education and catastrophe." Today man himself seems to have capitulated to the lemming syndrome: being locked into a date with disaster. Poll after poll indicates resignation to impending Armageddon. According to a 1982 CBS News poll of Americans, 70 percent of the people believe that a nuclear war is a real possibility at any moment. A combined AP-NBC News poll reveals that 68 percent of Americans believe it is likely that the U.S. will become involved in a war during the next few years and that the use of nuclear weaponry in such a hecatomb is a tragic likelihood. In Canada, our Department of National Defense, in polling our people, discovers that a majority expect we'll be involved in a nuclear war within this decade, Carroll Allen rationalizing, "Murphy's law is constant, and what can go wrong, sooner or later will." All of this is despite the fact that, as *The Wall Street Journal* carefully reasons, (Apr. 10, 1982) "there is no protection" from the extermination of man from this planet "except the prevention of nuclear war." Seventy-five percent of Britishers actually reply to George Gallup that despite these woeful odds, they'd prefer a nuclear war to being conquered by the communists (*Montreal Gazette*, July 13, 1982). They really would "sooner be dead than red."

War! World War! Nuclear War!—is certainly the obsessive preoccupation of peoples' minds as man journeys into the 'Eighties. Hollywood's "World War III" captures an even larger prime-time viewership than Monday night football. "Thinking the Unthinkable: Rising Fears About Nuclear War" is a 1982 *Time* cover story, captioned over an exploding mushroom assuming a grim human face. *Maclean's* of

Canada—in huge yellowish letters of fire—demands on its cover, "Is World War III Inevitable?" Editor Peter Newman, just back from a tour of European capitals, is convinced that it is. Those who are indifferent to the threat of terminal war are definitely "drowsing toward oblivion," remonstrates Jonathan Schell in his funereal *Fate of the Earth*, which currently is being lauded by the liberal intellectual establishment as "The new Bible of our time, the White Paper of our age."

Reckons Phil Surguy of *Today*, "Everybody who's anybody believes that global war is imminent." Gwynne Dyer writes from London that currently there are 23 wars in progress—most of them to the southwest or northeast of Israel, and several of them capable of triggering Armageddon. Who could witness the wars between the Argentines and the British in the Falklands, or the Israelis and the P.L.O. in Lebanon, or the heating up of the Iran/Iraqi conflict into the largest land battle since World War II, without wondering which fingering of the hair-trigger will ignite World War III?

We pick up the newspaper and read yet another headliner: "How Close Is Doomsday?" and we feel compelled to turn to the warning words of Jesus Christ to His disciples, who had asked Him their edition of that same question. They inquired: "What shall be the sign of thy coming and of the end of the world? And Jesus answered ". . . ye shall hear of wars and rumours of wars . . . nation shall rise against nation, and kingdom against kingdom" (Matthew 24:3,6,7). As we open our Bibles to the prophetic passages relating to the end times, we read a great deal that would lead us to believe that Armageddon is now beckoning. In the Book of Daniel, whom Jesus quoted as an authority on the final age prior to the coming of His Kingdom, the prophet assures us ominously, "War will continue until the end." In the concluding book of the Bible, the Revelation of Jesus Christ, which deals with things yet to come to pass, the eleventh, thirteenth and sixteenth chapters delineate the advent of "the beast"—that is, the Antichrist—[he] shall make war" (11:7). And it's asked, "Who is able to make war with [the Antichrist]?" (13:4). The answer is obvious three verses later, "And it was given unto him to make war . . . and to overcome . . . all kindreds, and tongues, and nations. And all that dwell upon the earth" (vss. 7, 8). And after 42 months of horrific holocaust, we read that the Antichrist will be surrounded and supported worldwide by "the spirits of devils, working miracles, which go forth unto the kings of the earth and of the whole world, to gather them to the battle of that great day of God Almighty. Behold . . . he gathered them together into a place called in the Hebrew tongue Armageddon" (16:14-16). The Bible is clear. The world is on a tear, hell-bent and headed for a final showdown, a rendezvous with doomsday.

Putting the mood of our times into perspective, Ellen Goodman reckons that myriads are "sure" this time around "that Armageddon" is indeed just "around the corner . . . we are living literally on a deadline . . . [we] wrap ourselves in mourning sheets and wait for the end . . . we are not talking about death, but extinction. Not about our future, but about any future: [as long as we have this] incompatible couple: the human being and the nuclear bomb" (her syndicated column, August 10, 1982). Goodman writes on another occasion (in *The Boston Globe)* about "this long-term deepening pessimism about the possibility of any lasting peace. Once there was a generation that believed in wars to end all wars . . . today we have a generation that believes in a war to end all life." Goodman concludes that "when you see 9 percent more, expecting war currently, than there were eight months previous, you've got to conclude that people are already numbed for war . . . because of all the war talk, the war charts, the war papers . . . a new outfit of nuclear weapons. 'Us Against Them,' 'Ours Against Theirs,' are written as if the United States and Russia were already in combat. If the enemy is here, can the war be far behind?" The question may be asked: Do Americans feel that a U.S.A. - U.S.S.R. war could be localized? *Newsweek* (Oct. 5, 1981) affirms, "A majority of Americans think that any war between the United States and the Soviet Union would ultimately lead to an all-out nuclear

holocaust." One of our most visible and vocal Canadian media-
men, Pierre Berton, has little doubt that man is spoiling for war,
reasoning that whenever, and wherever, in history two superpowers have armed themselves to the teeth—and are head to
head, as the U.S. and U.S.S.R. are currently—inevitably, they
eventually go to war. Berton suggests that the trigger man may
well be a Qadhafi or an Ayatollah Khomeini. The irony of
Berton's observation is that if he were to turn to Ezekiel 38:5
in the Bible in which he professes to place no special faith, he
might discover how right he might very well be!

Turning to the heads of state, former Japanese Prime
Minister Zenko Suzuki was a pilgrim to the United Nations in
mid-1982 to implore all governments to embark immediately
"to realize a world without nuclear weapons—a world where
nuclear catastrophe will never be repeated. [We] alone have
experienced atomic bombs, [the] unprecedented horror of
nuclear weapons." All mankind must "pledge . . . never to go
to war again" (U.P.I. June 10, 1982). But Suzuki's neighbor,
China's Deng Xiaoping is sure peace is well beyond man's reach.
The Los Angeles Times quotes him in a most un-atheistic sounding utterance, insisting on "the inevitability of world war. This
is independent of man's will." This came at a time when a million
Europeans had taken to the streets to "demonstrate for peace,"
something Aleksandr Solzhenitsyn puts down to their being
[unwittingly—or perhaps all too often, wittingly] "dupes of the
Soviets. Today's European pacifists, in their spiritual devia-
tions, hasten to [these] foggy negotiations with the communists" without the slightest hope of success.

As the Ground Zero and Nuclear Freeze marchers were peak-
ing in intensity, Mark MacGuian, our Canadian Minister of External Affairs, observed, "There is nothing the Soviets would
like better than for things to be frozen in the way that gives
them a permanent advantage, not just in terms of quantity but
in quality." The score in 1982? The Soviets have 7,868 megatons
of nuclear destructive capacity; the Americans, 3,505. It went

almost unreported in the Western press that when seven an-
tiwar activitists unfurled a 10-foot banner in Russia that read,
"Bread, life and disarmament," they were pounced on and
imprisoned before they could hand out one pamphlet. And that
when a million demonstrated for peace in Western Europe, a
strictly applied law was passed in East Germany which ruled
that it was illegal to wear a button stating, "Swords Into
Plowshares" (*Washington Post*). It was rather ironic that at the
height of these "demonstrations," former President Leonid
Brezhnev traveled to West Germany for "Peace Talks." His
high-handed hypocrisy—as the Chinese news service (*Xinhua*)
commented—his "honeyed words," were surely proven hollow
as a culvert, when the Russians got caught red-handed in a most
"crude violation." Their beached submarine was shown to be
carrying nuclear weapons in the restricted military zone of
Sweden's Karlskrona naval base. All the world saw the pictures.
It provided the incident for the usually neutralist former
Socialist Prime Minister of Sweden, Olof Palme, to observe acidly, "It is inconceivable why Soviet military authorities" could
engage in such shocking duplicity. It is yet another terribly
"frightening reminder how close we are to the precipice, how
great the risk is for nuclear war." Nor did former Chancellor
Helmut Schmidt let the moment pass, as he bemoaned, "The
demonstrators are blind to the huge Soviet arms buildup. They
make no contribution to securing peace on the basis of military
balance. Instead, they weaken the West's position and thus indirectly strengthen the East's position." A predecessor of
Schmidt's, Willy Brandt, within a few weeks pointed to the
ominous portent of a U.S.S.R. which he had discovered in a personal tour of the Soviet Union to "have a 'fantastic' lead over
the West in rocket numbers ranging from 10 to 100 times
more." President Francois Mitterand of France laments the present situation to a *Time* correspondent as being "tragic"—the
world everywhere being devoid of peace. Prime Minister
Margaret Thatcher in the throes of her war with the Argentines
over the Falklands agonized that the 'Eighties is surely the

most dangerous decade in human history. She borrowed a phrase from St. Paul, calling ours a "perilous time." Prime Minister Trudeau looks at the world in an armaments race and warns truly, if rather helplessly, "Disarmament is no less than the survival of humanity on this planet," while, at the same time insisting that the West must match the Soviets "gun for gun" (*Toronto Globe and Mail*, Mar. 20, 1982).

Which brings us again to President Reagan, who was in Houston in late 1981 where at the time I happened to be in a Crusade with Billy Graham. The President flew back to Washington in his "Doomsday Plane," the huge aircraft packed with the best electronic and communications gear made. It would be the flying command post for the President in case of an attack on the United States. Officially known as the E-4-A-B National Emergency Airborne Command Post, the big plane is kept ready for instant duty around the clock. Its "multiple decks contain radar, communications, jamming, detection and countermeasure facilities that would allow the President to make decisions aloft, in case of war" (*The Houston Chronicle*, Nov. 13, 1981). The "Doomsday Plane" is itself a service of notice to whom it may concern, that the real war could envelop this planet in flames at any given moment.

President Reagan reckons that the U.S. and the U.S.S.R. may very well go to war. *The Los Angeles Times* comments, "In a significant break with Presidents from Harry Truman to Jimmy Carter, the emphasis of [President Reagan's] administration seems to be less one of preserving a delicate post-World War II peace and more that of preparing for a possible World War III. President Reagan does not trust the Soviets." Rather, he insists their "leaders have a low regard for human life, and therefore would find a nuclear holocaust 'acceptable.' " The President reckons, "The Kremlin's design, first under Joseph Stalin, later under Nikita Khrushchev and now under Leonid Brezhnev has always been that of world domination, and to think otherwise is naive." President Reagan fears, that *if* the

U.S.-U.S.S.R. arms gap—in favor of the latter—is not closed, at some point, the Russians "will be able to take us with a phone call." Meanwhile he is extremely pessimistic, reasoning, "Man has used every weapon he has ever devised . . . it takes no crystal ball to perceive that a nuclear war is likely." This is based on the assumption, as *Time* (Nov. 2, 1981) quotes Mr. Reagan, "I do have to point out that everything that has been said and everything in their manuals indicates that unlike us, the Soviet Union believes that a nuclear war is possible, and they believe it is winnable." Reagan's own contention, however, is, "In a nuclear war, all mankind would lose."

On this point, that same edition of *Time* quotes the late President Leonid Brezhnev: "Only he who has decided to commit suicide can start a nuclear war." Brezhnev—whatever he believed privately, or argued domestically—contended that "any nuclear conflict would develop into a world war. Once it has broken out—in Europe or elsewhere—a nuclear war would inevitably and inescapably acquire a worldwide character." Addressing the Supreme Soviet, Brezhnev cautioned, "The very nature of modern weapons has become such that, if used, the future of all mankind would be at stake." Not impressed with Brezhnev's statements, which he reckoned to be wholly cosmetic, Aleksandr Solzhenitsyn observed, "One has to be blind to expect salutary results from talks with a heartless adversary." Does the American will have the resolve to resist communism? If "necessary" would its leader push the button? Replied Rosalyn Carter for the current President in the heat of the 1980 election campaign, "I can tell you that my husband would not be afraid to declare nuclear war." Perhaps in this agonizing dilemma, the most sobering observation of all, insofar as a head of state is concerned, was made by Poland's imposer of martial law, President Wojciech Jaruzelski who, stone-faced, warned we are, "on the edge of the abyss. Achievements of many generations raised from the ashes, are collapsing into ruin." "The people of Poland," contends a Roman Catholic Priest on network T.V. in the spring of 1982, "believe that

World War III began on December 13, 1981." Only the cancellation of Martial Law would soften this view.

Jaruzelski is an Army General. So is English General Sir John Hackett, a former Commander of NATO's Northern Army Group. Hackett wrote that startling best-seller, *The Third World War.* He argues convincingly that it could happen at any moment. As we turn to other heads of the military, we hear similar remarks. Cousin to Queen Elizabeth, Lord Mountbatten of Britain, before he was killed by the I.R.A. toured the U.S. lecturing on "The Third World War"—warning that, yes, it will be "fought with nuclear weapons." Hundreds of millions last saw the late General Omar Bradley as he participated in President Reagan's Inauguration. Asked if he thought man would emerge alive from the twentieth century, he expressed grave doubts, "Ours is a world of nuclear giants and ethical infants. We know more about war than we know about peace, more about killing than we know about living. We have grasped the mystery of the atom, and rejected the Sermon on the Mount" (*Quote* Nov. 1981).

Assesses U.S. General Robert Schweitzer, "The Soviets are superior to the U.S. on land, on sea, and in the air. And it is my belief that the Soviets will start a nuclear war." The top ranking Soviet General, Valentin Varennikov answers back, that America's military effort at playing catch-up in armaments is "doomed to failure" because "the Kremlin would never allow the military balance to shift against the Soviet Union." When Yuri Andropov succeeded Brezhnev, one of his first statements was to re-affirm this position. In short, the Soviets will take action if the Americans persist in closing the gap. And if it did, General David Jones, Chairman of the U.S. Joint Chiefs of Staff, calculates, "A Soviet nuclear attack on North America would kill" hundreds of millions of people, in what would be "the greatest catastrophe in history by many orders of magnitude."

Sometimes we in Canada wonder about the words "duels of the superpowers." But our own Minister of Defense Gilles Lamontagne laments that currently there is "a dreadful

imbalance" in both "nuclear and conventional military power,"
in favor of the Communist world over the Free, which causes
Lamontagne to remonstrate, "A nuclear war could result if the
Soviet Union perceives it has gained a war-winning capability,
or a technological breakthrough convinces Moscow it is invulnerable" (*Toronto Star*, Jan. 15, 1982). Our Chief of Staff,
General Ramsey Withers, agrees that one of the most unnerving phenomena of our times are these "peace marches," which—
while purporting peace—make war more likely. To quote again
our Secretary of State for External Affairs, Mark MacGuigan,
"These [peace march] movements seem to be more a product
of fear than logic. We must convince our publics that unilateral
disarmament increases, rather than reduces, the risk of war."
The American director of the Arms Control and Disarmament
Agency, Eugene Victor Rostow, counsels President Reagan that
"our posture today is comparable to that of Britain, France,
and the United States during the 30's. Whether we are at the
Rhineland or Munich watershed remains to be seen. There is
no difference between the Soviets now and Hitler then, except
that the Soviets are stronger. We are living in a pre-war and
not a post-war world." The U.S. Secretary of State scared the
world exceedingly with his suggestion that the West, to stop
the Soviets' aggression have "contingency plans in the NATO
doctrine to fire a nuclear weapon for demonstrative purposes,
to demonstrate to the other side that they are exceeding the
limits of toleration." When someone argued with him that with
Russia's third back-to-back crop failure, and with their economy
in serious trouble, surely they'd ignore war as an option, and
concentrate on their domestic needs, his reply was, "Internal
problems historically lead to 'foreign diversions.' And with the
Soviets in such deep trouble at home, they are doubly
dangerous, because they are armed to the teeth."

A former U.S. Secretary of State is the incomparably astute
Henry Kissinger. He has gone so far as to calculate that indeed
"Moscow has . . . plans to fight a nuclear war rather than simply
to defer such a conflict. For example, substantial resources have

been devoted to a civil defense program to protect the population in a nuclear exchange." He reckons that these are years "of maximum danger, insofar as the Soviets are concerned, because of their serious economic problems at home, the restlessness in such of their satellites as Poland, and their own military superiority over the West. All are a nudge for them to engage in daring ventures of conquest, perhaps deliberately provoking a major war."

One of the last Canadians I expected to speak as he has on this theme is our former Cabinet Liberal, Walter Gordon. Now an old man, he laments that every year into the 'Eighties "the threat of nuclear war is increasing and Canada should set up a royal commission to conduct a full-scale debate and re-examination of our defense policy." For if we are thrown into another World War, "the holocaust resulting from such a nuclear contest would mean that a large portion of the Canadian population would be annihilated."

Turning to the military, the evaluation of the world's armed forces carronades a coming theomachy. *The Toronto Sun* satirizes that our Canadian "military has become so threadbare that there is hardly a Third World country that couldn't whomp us." As Aleksandr Solzhenitsyn says of Western Europe, we prefer that the Americans bite the bullet: "Europe does not want to count on its own forces" (*Kansas City Times*, Jan. 23, 1982). But according to *Jane's Handbook* (London, 1982), *Armies of the World*, "The United States has (only) the world's fifth largest standing army." Not only does the Soviet Army have 170 divisions, it has four million reserves. And they are still building rapidly. According to the U.S. Defense Intelligence Agency, "The Soviet Union built more than four times as many tanks [they now have 50,000] and aircraft as the United States last year." *Jane's Fighting Ships* ('82) states that the Soviets are dramatically widening the gap of their already superior navy—in the last year building over twice as many warships and submarines as the U.K. and the U.S.A. combined.

While this is not the place to assess the size of the Soviet lead in armaments, it does show how really crucial is their superiority, when it is pointed out that they already have some 400 SS-20 Nuclear Missiles in Eastern Europe—deploying new ones every week. NATO is not even scheduled to begin its installation of 108 land-based Pershing II missiles until 1983—these supposedly to offset the SS 20's. *Macleans* (Feb. 15, 1982) in their cover story article, "Is World War III Inevitable?" grieves that the Soviets will have 700 in position before the Americans will get to put one Pershing II in place. Each 36-foot-long SS-20 missile carries three 500-kiloton warheads—each of which can be directed at a separate target with a force roughly 30 times more powerful than the bomb that leveled Hiroshima. Most are pointed at targets in Western Europe. The Soviet Intercontinental Strategic Arsenal [the long-range biggies, mostly pointing at targets in North America] includes 7,000 nuclear warheads and is rising rapidly. A cartoonist expressed it well, if it weren't so tragically terrifying. He pictures the Soviet leader complaining to his defense chief: "I liked the arms race better when we were the only ones in it" [a situation his current propaganda is seeking to re-establish]. With the expenditure of arms worldwide from 1980 to 1985 rising from 350 billion to a trillion annually, according to the projection of a U.S. T.V. Network President, the Soviets are currently spending three times as much of their GNP on armaments as the Americans. Jacques Soppelsa, President of the Sorbonne in Paris, head of the Institute of Strategic Studies and France's delegate to the United Nations on disarmament is one of the world's best informed and most neutralist experts on the war possibilities of the Superpowers. Asked in August of 1982 if he thought the Soviets in the future were expecting to go to war, he replied that when Brezhnev is off the scene "there is a very strong chance the new leaders will look around for a war to fight as an alternative to the economic crisis."

Turning to the computer scientist, the evidence is highly unnerving. Petra Kelly notes, "A mere computer error could start a war that would obliterate us." A *Grand Rapids Press* headliner reads, "Computer Error Could Start War." The UPI article beneath states, "For the second time in seven months, a computer at the nation's missile warning center erroneously put U.S. strategic forces on alert against a Soviet missile attack on the United States, the Pentagon disclosed. Overdependence on computer warning systems for nuclear weapons—that are subject to inevitable false alarms—could possibly lead to a real nuclear war, the Union of Concerned Scientists said in a statement." The Soviet leader frequently has warned that world war could very well result from an accident or a miscalculation.

Turning to the medical profession, we do not receive consolation. The Soviet leader's personal physician, Dr. Eugeni Chazov traveled across the Atlantic to intimate the cheerless fact that "the onset of nuclear war would inevitably mean destruction of the U.S.S.R. as well as the west." Any number of psychiatrists and doctors warned the Convention of the International Physicians for the Prevention of Nuclear War meeting in Toronto in December 1981 of how close man is to the edge of the precipice. Dr. Elizabeth Gold summed up, "Nuclear war is an incurable disease and the biggest single health hazard faced by every inhabitant of the planet. Therefore, the physician has no choice but to work for a cessation of the arms race, and the elimination of nuclear weapons from the face of the earth."

It's perhaps one of the most pathetic ironies of all that even our entertainment industry features wars. A leading counter attraction to the Baseball Allstar Game in Montreal in 1982 was the Papa Dee Allen-led American-Afro-funk-jazz-rock group calling themselves "War" and packing them into Le Club. The music critic Peter Goddard says that among the 40 top rock songs of our generation, you've got to place the Talking Heads with their "Life During Wartime" near the top, with its grim reminders of what war will really be like. Stevie Wonder, speaking of World Peace Sunday, reflected out loud in a statement that was anything but reassuring: World War III? Yes, I "think it's going to happen" (*L.A. Times*, quoted in *Boston Globe*, June 5, 1982).

Finally, we turn to some of the world's foremost contemporary writers. Margaret Atwood is our most read Canadian authoress. She asks, "Why do we make war? Why do we behave like rats and ants, which are the other creatures that do that? What has made us this way and how do we stop being like that? That would be my top priority, because unless somebody finds out pretty soon, we are going to blow ourselves up." Oxford Professor Michael Howard, in a lecture at UCLA to the "Committee on the Present Danger," is not so far to the left that he cannot refer to the Soviet Union as "an implacably aggressive power, quite prepared to use nuclear weapons as an instrument of its policy." This he says, in referring to "the brutal momentum of the massive Soviet strategic arms buildup—a buildup without precedent in history." Harvey Cox of Harvard, the high profile social activist, says all men today, whether or not they know it, are in a "plummeting plunge toward nuclear oblivion." "Today's right-wingers in politics," complains columnist Sydney Harris, "strike me as the mirror-image of the radical 'Barn Burners' of the last century, who were said to be willing to burn the barn down in order to get at the rats."

Answering from the right, there's Lawrence Beilenson (his book is *The Treaty Trap*), President Reagan's longtime counselor. At 82, he believes that "nuclear war with the Soviet Union is inevitable because of their 'Leninism.' " And there's Simon Ramo, in his *National Will and Nuclear War* (quoted in *The Wall Street Journal*), in which a scenario is presented "of the Soviets taking a surprise surgical strike against America's nuclear weaponry—concurrently all over the world. The U.S. would be faced with an immediate decision, either to surrender, or to face total destruction by remaining Soviet nuclear forces." Richard Nixon takes the position in his thoroughly researched *The Real War* that World War III has already begun and that the other side is winning. He not only points to Afghanistan, but to the other 14 countries where the banners bearing variations of the Hammer and Sickle have been unfurled since the post World War II settlements. Aleksandr Solzhenitsyn writes in 1982, [we're all] "heading toward disaster. It is too late to avoid the Third World War."

I was personally amazed to see *The Atlantic Monthly* (June, 1982) devote a cover story to "Apocalyptic Prophecy," which begins, "The world as we know it is coming to an end." On the first of a seven-page article, it justifies its treatment of such a theme to its elitist readership by stating, "The number-one non-fiction volume of the 1970's was not a revolutionary diet plan or a manual on sexual fulfillment but Hal Lindsey's *The Late Great Planet Earth* (over 15 million copies sold), one of five successful prophecy books by Lindsey that led *The New York Times* to name him the best-selling author of the decade. The book was also the basis of a 1977 movie narrated by Orson Welles." About as far as one could get across the philosophic and theological spectrum from *The Atlantic Weekly* is *Christianity Today*. Its editor, Ken Kantzer (Apr. 9, 1982), levels, "we live in an increasingly dangerous world. Planet earth has become a spaceship about to explode with little room for human survival . . . one day someone will push a button that will set off a chain reaction among nations. As each seeks to defend its allies, the whole world will go up in flames. Does the Christian faith have anything to say about this?" That last question is a handle on the most burning pot on the stove of human history.

Certainly the secular humanist is finding that pot too hot to handle. Harry Bruce, executive editor of *Atlantic Insight*, in an incisive review of the possibility soon of World War III breaking out, sums up, "I smell a kind of mind-poisoning fog that's creeping into the public consciousness and slowly, but ever so surely, making us resign ourselves to the imminence of the most ghastly event in human history. The unthinkable is becoming thinkable . . . but I have no answers. A newspaper publisher once told me never to end an editorial without proposing a solution. Well, I can't."

Harry Bruce, there is an answer! It's Jesus Christ! He said

to His followers: "Blessed are the peacemakers for they shall be called the children of God." Every child of God should be a peacemaker. But Jesus also said, as we've noted, that before He came back to this earth to set up His Kingdom of peace and prosperity, the world would go to war.

We ask why? "From whence come wars?" Jesus' questioner, James, wrote a generation later, "Come they not hence, even of your lusts that war in your members? Ye lust, and have not: ye kill, and desire to have, and cannot obtain: ye fight and war, yet ye have not" (James 4:1,2). What a commentary on man today! The human psyche has never changed, apart from the grace of God. Thousands of years ago, the Psalmist spoke of the warmonger, "The words of his mouth were smoother than butter, but war was in his heart" (Psalm 55:21). He "hateth peace. I am for peace: but when I speak, they are for war" (Psalm 120:6,7). War is God's permitted judgment on man when he ignores his Maker, and corporately refuses to walk according to His Word. Take one example: Asa, the ancient King of Judah. The first half of his reign, he put away the idols that his fathers worshiped, restored the Word of God, and the priests to their place of ministry. And we read that in prayer, "Asa cried unto the Lord His God, and said, Lord, it is nothing with thee to help, whether with many, or with them that have no power: help us, O Lord our God; for we rest on thee, and in thy name we go" (2 Chronicles 14:11). For half a lifetime, King Asa lived wholly for the Lord. Then, alas, he lapsed. And to him came a prophet of whom we read, "The Spirit of God came upon Azariah the son of Oded. And he went out to meet Asa, and said . . . the Lord is with you, while ye be with Him; and if ye seek Him, He will be found of you; but if ye forsake Him, He will forsake you" (2 Chronicles 15:1,2). Well, for years King Asa sought and served the Lord and had incredible peace and prosperity. Then he forsook the Lord's Word and became surly and disobedient. So God sent to Asa another of His prophets, Hanani the seer, who told him, "Because thou hast . . . not relied on the Lord thy God . . . therefore from henceforth thou shalt have wars" (2 Chronicles 16:7,9). And for the rest of King Asa's life he had terrible wars, and a tragic downhill skid to a pathetic death. God had said to his forefather David, "Come, behold the works of the Lord . . . He maketh wars to cease unto the end of the earth" (Psalms 46:8,9).

To us today, Jesus assures, as He did to His disciples—and He was talking about conditions in the world preceding His return, "In the world ye shall have tribulation"—there'll be war, terrible war!—but "in Me" ye shall "have peace." "I believe," stated President Reagan before the German Bundestag, that in a world on the brink, there is everywhere a widespread longing for "inner peace," for "spiritual well being." People are in a quest "to find their own personal peace" (*New York Times*, June 10, 1982). Such peace is to be found only in Christ.

Early in 1982, in the Midwest, I was speaking of confessing Jesus Christ as Lord and Savior. Coming forward to make her decision for Christ was a very beautiful immigrant from Belfast, Ireland, Carol Oldrich. She was a teacher. Belfast is a city of war. Carol had married and had two wonderful children—Morin, 16, and Dane, 11. But she had no peace in her heart. As St. Paul wrote to the Romans (7:23) she could "see a law in my members, warring." Within her was conflict, and she had war in her marriage. She and her husband had divorced, and she had left a city embroiled in war these many years. So when Carol was brought to the meeting, and saw all those faces full of love for Christ and effulgent with peace, she longed for the same. I presented Christ, and that night Carol came and entrusted herself to the Savior. Nights later, she came up looking serene and secure—her countenance aglow—to testify that she indeed had been "justified by faith" and had "peace with God through our Lord Jesus Christ." On the concluding night, Carol's face was shining even brighter. Both Morin and Dane had come forward, and now through commitment to Jesus as Lord, all three had been endowed with that peace that the world can't give and that it can't take away—come nuclear war or a new world!

Chapter Two

"ALL SORTS OF ARMOUR"

The New York Times labels Isaac Asimov as today's most-widely-credible-and-read science writer. No international convention of eminent illuminati is considered complete without his presence. It was hard science Asimov was writing when he published his best-seller, *A Choice of Catastrophies*. He expects man to do himself in sooner or later, probably sooner. And he presents several worldwide scenarios as to how it will happen. It is common consensus universally that man is most likely to do himself in through the weapons he himself is shaping. In Ezekiel 38:4 it is prophesied that the Soviets would fight what we're calling World War III with "all sorts of armor." A walk through Red Square on May Day reveals to any unbiased observer that never in human history has there been such a display of "all sorts of armor." Red Square on May Day is only the tip of the iceberg. One catastrophe Asimov poses as a distinct possibility and indeed billions feel they're being shoved into backwards, is nuclear annihilation. Two millennia ago, St. Peter forecast that in "the day of the Lord . . . the elements shall melt with fervent heat," (2 Peter 3:9,10). Peter used a Greek word, translated "elements" which means "the letters of the alphabet." Scientists describe a nuclear explosion as "the radiation of alpha, beta, gamma, delta rays"—letters of the Greek alphabet.

George B. Kistiakowsky, known as "the father of the nuclear trigger" for the crucial role he played in the Manhattan Project of 40 years ago, which produced the Atomic Bomb, currently heads the Boston-based Council for a Livable World. Longtime Chairman of the chemistry department at Harvard, he was born and brought up in the Russian Ukraine. A close friend of John Kenneth Galbraith and Arthur Schlesinger, Jr., he was science adviser to President Eisenhower. In mid-1982, he does not hestitate to warn, "Nuclear war is becoming inevitable . . . the threat is real and . . . the devastation [will be] unbelievable." To the apathetic, he cautions, "Don't kid yourself, you will be one of the victims . . . nuclear weapons will be used somewhere between now and the end of the century" (*Atlanta Constitution*, June 7, 1982). Adds Kistiakowsky's current colleague and former collaborator on the Manhattan Project, Jerrod R. Zacharias: the use of nuclear weapons will spell "extinction" of the human species from this planet. Sums up the third member of the Harvard/MIT/Manhattan Project Troika, Victor F. Weisskopf (who currently serves as advisor to the Vatican on nuclear issues, because he fears that the nuclear threat is something only God can be trusted with anymore), "With the discovery of fission, mankind entrained cosmic forces with human irrationality." Only "a miracle" from God can save man from nuclear "holocaust" (*Atlanta Constitution*, June 7, 1982.)

An estimated 60,000 nuclear bombs are currently allocated throughout the continents and oceans of the world, and according to *Time*, ten new ones are being made every day. One of these hydrogen bombs when detonated would produce heat of 150 million degrees Fahrenheit, and in one-millionth of a second would unleash more destructive energy than all the weapons in all the wars of history combined. It's hardly to be wondered at that Dr. Allan Bromley, the Yale physicist who presided over the 5,000 scientists who met in Toronto for the American Association for the Advancement of Science Annual World Convention should have deplored profoundly "the treat of nuclear war" as that blackest of hecatombs hanging over the world. He was followed by another member of the Manhattan Project, Prof. Philip Morrison of M.I.T., who bewailed the gigantesque "sword of Damocles" hanging over man. He insisted passionately that the only hope would be if the nations could get together and hang an all-seeing monitor in the skies—that from that satellite, every nuclear device would be seen and eliminated by mutual agreement. That is, of course, about as likely as unscrambling eggs, or as our being able to turn the calendar back to 1910. Bromley and Morrison were followed by physicist Amory B. Lovins, of London, who lamented, "It's likely we'll all be blown up by nuclear wars in my lifetime," adding plaintively, "Before I die, I'd like to see a magic wand or some sort of scientific device that would make nuclear fission impossible." That, of course, was wishful thinking, a fantasizing sophistry which Lovins was stating in a time of shifting sands, to reaffirm his own humanity. Broods Volkmar Deihe, a German, "There is an increasing feeling that like drug addicts" the nations today "are hooked" on nuclear death weaponry. And to quote a Russian—the father of the Soviet H. bomb—Andrei Sakarov (who in the 1980's is never out of the news very long), "The pulling of a few levers, the pushing of a few buttons, and the throwing of a few switches, would result in the complete annihilation of every living thing on the earth."

The crucial weapon in today's world wide armaments race is the hydrogen bomb. U.S. Secretary of Defense, Caspar Weinberger claims that the Soviets are currently spending three times as much of their GNP on nuclear bombs in particular and on armaments overall as the Americans, and in his 99-page booklet on "Soviet Military Power" he concedes the Russians an unnerving lead in virtually every vital area of the arms race (*New York Times*, Sept. 30, 1981). So the Americans are currently going from a defense expenditure of 146 billion dollars in 1981, to 222 billion in 1982, to 255 billion in 1983, (*Washington Post*, Feb. 3, 1982). Israel's defense budget is 30 percent of its GNP, and is currently edging over the 3 billion dollar mark.

Looking at the American nuclear forces, their capacity for destruction is mind boggling, especially when President Raegan announces that the U.S. is in the process of adding 17,000 new nuclear bombs to its already formidable force (Ellen Goodman's column, August 10, 1982). The American defense system against nuclear attack from the Soviets is based on TRIAD (land, air and sea forces), which means the deployment worldwide of a network of land-based ballistic missiles which are classified as short range, medium and intercontinental. Then there are the bombers deployed to U.S. strategic bases throughout the world and poised to carry nuclear warheads into any potential enemy target area, and thirdly, there are nuclear submarines, which circle the oceans and seas of the world with rocket power poised to unleash a nuclear holocaust into any country. While it is conceded that the Soviets have a big lead in nuclear submarine strength (*"Jane's Fighting Ships,"* 1981-82 edition), American submarines can rain 9,632 nuclear bombs on Soviet soil. As Greer Boyce points out, "One U.S. Poseidon submarine carries 16 missiles, each with 10 warheads [which] could destroy 160 targets, more targets than there are cities in the Soviet Union." A Trident submarine dives into the oceans of the world in late 1982 with 24 warheads able to destroy 500 separate targets (*Toronto Star*, July 25, 1982).

But the Soviets, notes the *Los Angeles Times*, have titanic nuclear submarines—behemoths almost as big as the American Essex-class aircraft carrier—with a displacement of 30,000 tons, equipped with 20 tubes for ballistic missiles that have a range of 4,000 miles. We no longer need to wonder at the credibility of Revelation 8:8,9, where we read that a terrible "burning with fire was cast into the sea" and "the third part of the creatures which were in the sea, and had life, died; and the third part of the ships were destroyed." And for the two-thirds that remain? We read in Revelation 16:3 that when "the second angel poured out his vial upon the sea . . . every living soul died in the sea."

Turning to the land-based missile system, according to *Chemical and Engineering News* based on U.S. Defense Department reports, the Soviets have 78% of the land-based missiles—5,500 warheads, compared to 2,152 for the Americans.

Currently in Europe, "the Soviets have a 6-1 advantage," helped by deployment so far of 280 triple-headed SS-20's" (*Toronto Star*, Feb. 7, 1982). And will a halt be called through negotiations between the U.S. and the U.S.S.R. in their current talks? On the contrary, Chancellor Schmidt laments that from all objective observations that it seems only to be speeding the Russians up (*Toronto Star*, Feb. 6, 1982), while NATO experts predict the talks will drag on for years, much like those in Vienna on reducing conventional forces in Europe. The U.S. and Russia are, of course, only two of the total cacophony of 212 "un-united" nations on earth, each one trying to find its place in the sun and get its voice heard on the international scene. In terms of exporting armaments, the U.S. is currently tripling its annual exports of arms, up from 8.5 billion in 1981 to a current 23 billion. So immense is the current stockpiling of weaponry worldwide, according to Robert Soboff in *The Boston Globe*, that "there are now four tons of explosives for every man, woman and child in the world." "Arming the world," according to the Overseas Press Club, was the year's most thoroughly written and read article in any American magazine (*Time*, May 10, 1982), and is indicative of how high a priority man is putting on nuclear death weaponry in the decade of the eighties.

One would do well to ask how many nations currently have nuclear bombs. Writes Jack Cahill in the *Toronto Star* (May 5, 1982), "Forty-four countries of the world already have the capability to detonate a nuclear device, and the ever increasing number is causing grave concern to military analysts and disarmament experts." According to the International Atomic Energy Agency as cited in *The New York Times*, 50 nations currently are jockeying, dabbling and dancing on the fringes of the nuclear club. France has jumped up its expenditures in this area by 17.6% this year over last and, like Britain and Canada, provides nuclear reactors for third world countries around the world. It now has to be conceded that the Israelis knew very well what they were doing when they bombed out the Iraqi reactor in 1981— which the Iraqis doubtless were fully intending to develop into bombs with which to destroy the state of Israel. Canada's Candu Reactor, of course, provided India with know-how to produce its first nuclear bomb, which it felt it had to have to match Red China. *The New China News Agency* looks back on 1981 as a year when through the help of the Americans, Red China took a giant leap forward (or backward) by currently going into the mass production of "both strategic and tactical missiles." Presently it has some 300 of the current 60,000 poised nuclear warheads in the world. While playing its cards extremely close to the chest, Israel a decade ago let it be known that she had 13 nuclear bombs assembled and emplaned. The *Jerusalem Post* (Dec. 6, 1981) reports 40 new nuclear bombs being mounted on missiles at Jericho in Israel. In a published report by an Israeli authority in May 1982, Israel had 200 nuclear bombs poised for action (*Toronto Star*, May 16, 1982). In addition to South Africa's nuclear arsenal (CBS Evening News), a host of nations, like Pakistan, Libya, Brazil, and Argentina are at least on the verge. "If we had had the atomic bomb" rigged and ready, grumbled an Argentine authority, "the British fleet would not have begun its war in the Atlantic" (*The Globe and Mail*, May 7, 1982). Steve Weissman and Herbert Krosney's new book, *The Islamic Bomb*, makes frightening reading, reasoning that what the 40 nations of Islam are saying—with their vast oil fortunes—is, "Nice Doggie! until you can find a rock. Then when you can get your hand on that ultimate nuclear weapon, you turn and deal with that teethy growl in whatever way you feel is in your own best interests!"

Complicating the handling of the Qudhafis, the Khomeinis or the Colonel Mariams, and the good possibility that they might use nuclear blackmail, is the matter of nuclear "accidents" or "miscalculations," as the late Brezhnev often said. One has frequently felt that Brezhnev, in airing his views on this matter, was attempting to say far more than seemed apparent. If the Soviets had nuclear accidents—if they were to occur, say, in a submarine off the North Atlantic Coast, like their nuclear submarine beached on Swedish shores in 1981—would such an accident trigger an all-out nuclear war? That's surely one of the world's "heavies"! We do know that the American Pentagon admits to having had some 32 serious nuclear accidents, the more open-mouthed Center for Defense Information in Washington insisting there have been at least 96. I was close to one near Cambridge, England, when a B-47 bomber crashed into a nuclear bomb storage center. And 1,800 times the nuclear detonation of Hiroshima was prevented only by some kind of uncanny "miracle," which—when the information first leaked out in 1981—it was said, would have killed perhaps twenty million and "a large part of eastern England would now be a desert." An even closer call occurred when "a crashing B-52 bomber jettisoned two nuclear bombs over Goldsboro, N.C. A parachute deployed on one bomb, while the other broke apart on impact. The parachute cords of the first bomb caught in a tree, and five of the six interlocking safety switches were released when the bomb jolted. Only one switch prevented the explosion of a 24-megaton bomb, 1,800 times more powerful than the one dropped on Hiroshima in 1945. The Pentagon immediately bought all the farmland in the area where the second bomb broke apart, but they never have been able to find all the pieces." When one reads such accounts in the press, one cannot but turn to the Bible to such prophecies of the last days as in Joel 2:3, "A fire devoureth before them; and behind them a flame burneth [into] desolate wilderness; yea, and nothing shall escape"; or again, "The fire hath devoured the pastures of the wilderness, and the flame hath burned all the trees of the field" (Joel 1:19). Isaiah makes the broader expression that "the inhabitants of the earth are burned and few men left" (24:6). Perhaps the only nuclear accident to hit the publicity fan in a widespread way was the "Three-Mile-Island" incident in Pennsylvania in 1978. There is still a highly volatile argument about how far the meltdown got, how much radio activity got out, and how close the accident came to taking the Northeastern

United States to the brink of a nuclear inferno (*Toronto Star*, July 22, 1982). This discussion leads us to state that among the proliferating "kinds" as well as "degrees" of new fires being invented by scientists, coming up for world attention in the '80's has been the neutron bomb, which President Carter put on a back burner, but President Reagan and President Mitterand of France have decided to go ahead and manufacture in large numbers. They are "designed to produce far more radiation and far less blast and heat than other tactical nuclear weapons, so that they kill people without severe damage to their surroundings" (*New York Times*, Aug. 9, 1981). Some scientists have observed that Zechariah 14:12 is a precise description of the effects of the neutron bomb: "Their flesh shall consume away while they stand . . . and their tongue shall consume away in their mouth." *The Globe and Mail* editorializes that the decision to go ahead with the neutron bomb was the biggest step taken toward "Armageddon" since 1961. Why? Because, as it reasoned, it augured "theater" war—and, of course, this was the triggering issue which produced the huge "peace" marches in Western Europe.

It is contended by President Reagan's network of intelligence forces that the Soviets, for all their cosmetic peace propaganda, are indeed making ready for such venturesome pickoffs as Afghanistan and further forward forays into Europe, and that they are preparing for nuclear theatre war involving surgical thrusts. For while they talk peace, their military postures worldwide are poised for offense, not defense, and at home they are spending 16 times as much (*The Los Angeles Times*, Jan. 17, 1982) as the Americans on Civil Defense—provisions such as bomb shelters, indicating that they seriously entertain "the hope not only of surviving but, indeed, winning nuclear war against the United States." Their SS 4's, SS 5's, SS 18's, and SS 20's are in place for this purpose.

In Europe, there is a Catch 22 situation. According to Dan Rather in his prime-time series, "CBS Reports," there are 7,000 nuclear warheads in West Germany, and to a people well aware of the terrible ravages of war, this could spell doom. The fear that the neutron bombs strike is one that sets up a scenario whereby a regional nuclear war breaks out, and as is almost universally felt, who—or what—would indicate that this would not escalate into World War III? A Reuter report (Feb. 6, 1982) states, "The North Atlantic Treaty Organization's arsenal of conventional anti-tank weapons is so deficient that it makes early recourse to nuclear weapons . . . more likely, otherwise a Soviet attack would be absolutely devastating."

Then there's the matter of chemical warfare. It seems now to be reasonably well proven that the Soviets have a huge arsenal of chemical warfare weapons. And, despite the fact that they were outlawed by an international agreement in 1925, their agents used them in Cambodia and Laos (see *Atlanta Constitution*, June 7, 1982). According to a U.S. State Department report, "the death toll from so called 'Yellow Rain' and other chemical weapons was 6,310 in Laos, 981 in Cambodia, and 3,042 in Afghanistan" (A.P., Mar. 23, 1982). The U.S. Secretary of State states "firmly that the United States has evidence the outlawed weapons were used in Afghanistan and Laos." To be prepared, Harvard's molecular biologist Matthew Meselson revealed at the Washington Conference of the American Association for the Advancement of Science in 1981 "that the United States had more than 100,000 poison gas artillery shells," while Professor Arthur Westling remarked that with the Soviets' conduct and the recrudescence of "interest in producing chemical weapons, the world finds itself on the threshold of a chemical arms race" (*Toronto Star*, Jan. 5, 1982). On Feb. 8, 1982, President Reagan announced publicly that after a 13-year halt, the U.S. was resuming openly "the manufacture of two new chemical binary weapons," and that during the next year 705 million dollars would be spent on the manufacture of chemicals for warfare. A whole section of the Washington Conference (AAASC-1982) was given over to a discussion of biological warfare. I was riding on a plane with a Jewish government official recently. He assured me that the simplest way to destroy a continent of population in a matter of two or three days is with biological or bacteriological warfare. He contended that the technology in this is so sophisticated and so ready that either of the Americas—or both—or EuroAsia could witness their total populations exterminated in less than a week. It needs to be kept in mind that Jesus predicted not only "famines" but "pestilences" (Matthew 24:7).

Another means of wreaking holocaust on humanity to which we have not yet alluded is with the laser beam. The term LASER stands for "Light Amplification by Stimulated Emission of Radiation." Lasers are incredibly powerful instruments and they have a variety of constructive uses. For purposes of destruction they can be mounted on jets and satellites and have already been used "to knock airplanes from the sky" (*Indianapolis Star*, Sept. 15, 1981). Huge lasers, it is envisaged, can be placed "in space to shoot at enemy missiles coming up though the atmosphere." A British scientist sees the Soviets functioning from "fortresses" in outer space from which with laser beams they could paralyze the U.S. intercontinental missile installations on which they so totally depend before ever they could get up out of their silos. Robert Waters writes, "A space-based laser beam mirror" is envisaged by the U.S. State Department, a weapon "capable of destroying Soviet nuclear missiles up to 5,000 miles away in outer space."

Aviation Week and Space Technology claims that "the Soviet Union has a new killer satellite in earth orbit capable of destroying several orbiting U.S. satellites. It's an anti-satellite battle station equipped with clusters of infrared-homing guided interceptors that could destroy multiple U.S. spacecraft. The podded miniature attack vehicles provide a new U.S.S.R. capability for a sneak attack on U.S. satellites." Robert Moss writes of all this in his new book, *Death Beam.*

Gerald Utting argues that the first battle of the future World War is likely to be fought in outer space by robot-controlled satellites using long-range missiles and lasers. The aim? To "blind" the other side to a surprise attack, to gain perhaps a couple of minutes during which an enemy would have to guess what an aggressor was doing with his intercontinental missile strike force. Utting quotes *Aviation Week and Space Technology*: that we can now be sure that the Soviets have succeeded in breakneck speed to having "developed a new and much more sophisticated variety of sputnik that makes a war in which satellite kills satellite much more possible."

Another catastrophe scenario emerged in the news early in 1982. Val Sears, Science editor of *The Toronto Star*, in a feature article (Feb. 7, 1982) quoting German scientists writes: "On the day the world ends, a Soviet Cosmos satellite—supposedly on its routine picture-taking mission—is crossing the United States at a height of about 450 kilometers. Suddenly over the Great Plains, a few pounds of enriched plutonium in the fake satellite explode, blanketing the United States and Canada with a shower of gamma rays. In one-billionth of a second all electrical power and transmissions in North America are blanked out. Cars, trucks, and machinery stop. Nuclear power plants go dark. Radio and television stations go off the air. Planes crash. Missile systems fail, and, in any case, the President of the United States has no way to communicate with the silo crews and set the missiles off on a retaliatory strike. This effect is called a Nuclear Electromagnetic Pulse, and even in an age of increasingly horrifying weapons, it is giving the Pentagon and NATO nightmares. In January 1982, the prestigious German newspaper *Die Zeit* devoted two pages to a description of this "satanic weapon that can cripple the total nervous system of civilization." American scientific and military journals are paying more and more attention to a doomsday scenario that begins with a Nuclear Electromagnetic Pulse. *Science* Magazine recently ran three articles on it in a row." Val Sers sums up, "The 'Satanic' nuclear pulse has made it peace . . . or Doomsday."

As we ponder what posture to adopt in the face of the overwhelming odds against the human race, were I not a Christian, I simply do not know what I would think or do! I sympathize with Dr. Frank Sommers—of the University of Toronto Medical faculty—who insists that man is on a direct collision course with nuclear annihilation. He feels that we must escalate the grass roots support for all disarmament agitation. Margo Raudsepp in conceding the same—that man currently is headed straight for doomsday—says that "we must all get angry and take out our righteous indignation on the leaders of the world, by insisting they make love, not war." Frank Showler, of the Canadian Friends Service Committee affirms, "We do not believe that the way to peace is to prepare for war." William F. Buckley insists on the reverse, that "the way *to* peace *is* to prepare for war." Everyone supposedly yearns for peace, while we are drifting straight into the barracuda jaws of war.

I have no personal doubt about what a Christian is to do and think. He is to seek peace and make peace—whenever and wherever he can. But he must always remain aware that Jesus prophesied that man is headed for war—terrible-but not terminal war. There is hope, blessed hope! Man would burn himself up, but for the advent of Christ. Dealing with this theme St. Peter writes, "The Lord is not slack concerning His promise, as some men count slackness; but is longsuffering to usward, not willing that any should perish, but that all should come to repentance" (2 Peter 3:9). St. Jude urges, "Save [them] with fear, pulling them out of the fire" (Jude 23). And St. Paul wrote to the Thessalonians, "To you who are troubled rest with us, when the Lord Jesus shall be revealed from heaven with His mighty angels, in flaming fire taking vengeance on them that know not God, and that obey not the Gospel of our Lord Jesus Christ: who shall be punished with everlasting destruction from the presence of the Lord, and from the glory of His power" (2 Thessalonians 1:7,9). These are strong words.

Last autumn, I was preaching out west in a large arena. There were 106 who came forward to give their lives to Christ one night, and among them was a doctor. He had lived for years as a secular humanist, but he was unfulfilled. In addition, his city was situated in the center of one of the world's heaviest concentrations of nuclear missiles, routinely maintained and in their silos, ominously poised and pointed toward the annihilation of a sizable percentage of the human race. Dr. Trosper had saved many lives by his medical expertise, but he had done nothing about the salvation of his own soul. There was a clergyman in that city whose physical health had been saved by that doctor. So the clergyman, to return the compliment, invited him to the crusade. That night, he came forward to give his life to Christ. That is the only salvation there is from the inevitable destruction to which this world is destined. As Lloyd George ended up saying: now it's either Christ or chaos!

Chapter Three

"THERE SHALL BE SIGNS IN THE SUN, AND IN THE MOON, AND IN THE STARS"

As men and women, arming for Armageddon scan the skies, Jesus assures them "there shall be signs in the sun, and in the moon, and in the stars . . . for the powers of the heaven shall be shaken. And then shall they see the Son of man coming in a cloud with power and great glory" (Luke 21:25-27).

The ancient Daniel (12:4) foresaw at "the time of the end" that "many shall run to and fro", which could be translated "will move at incredible speeds." In the 1980's, passengers cross the Atlantic in a Concorde at 1,500 miles per hour, and a dozen astronauts have gone to the moon and back at speeds of 25,000 miles per hour. And there's the sensational spectacle of the Columbia taking space explorers up into the celestial for a week at a time, and now the Challenger. And there's the potential demonstrated by a Pioneer 10, which in 1982 is two billion miles from earth, soaring out of the solar system with nearly all of its 570 pounds of equipment functioning as well as it did ten years ago when it was launched. It demonstrates how man himself will one day travel out of the solar system into his celestial home which Christ has gone to prepare for a people ready to meet their God.

Certainly the space race is not unrelated to people's yearning to escape the "Great Tribulation" ahead—to which Jesus so clearly alluded, and the omens of which the great and small of our times are feeling strongly. John Schlessinger was quoted on network T.V. that "the Space Program marked the end of when man would feel at home on this earth."

Isaac Asimov's *ExtraTerrestrial Civilizations* probes with credible scientific measurements into whether or not there are other extant civilizations similar to ours on earth around the universe. By the process of examination and elimination, he reckons there should be 390 million technological civilizations! But then he asks acidly, "Where is everybody? If they're out there, why don't they show up? Or at least, why don't they send us a message?" *Time* magazine's 1982 scientific release *Discover* notes that "for years, scientists have assumed that the universe teemed with life. Now there's a growing consensus that we may indeed be alone."

This leads us to Asimov's writings—best-sellers all—on human colonization of other worlds, starting with the moon, so that they can escape "Catastrophies," as he calls them. Asimov sees, within a century, 50,000 people living in Luna City on the moon. While earthlings war and threaten to exterminate each other, Lunarians, as he calls them, set up a whole new celestial civilization.

Asimov is a writer. U.S. and Soviet space scientists are doers. A Reuters report (July 6, 1982) indicates that according to the last U.S. intelligence source, the Soviets are currently preparing to launch the world's first permanent space village housing 100 cosmonauts. The space base would be assembled from modules carried aloft by a new rocket booster. How does this relate to arming for Armageddon? U.S. sources claim the Soviet space station, with a continuous human presence, would serve "as a base for an anti-ballistic missile laser weapon, reported under development (and nearly ready to go) in the Soviet Union. What is considerably more unnerving are reports in *The Los Angels Times* (July 1982) that the Soviets have already actually tested "the world's first fighter spacecraft," a delta-winged vehicle capable of carrying "five or six people to a space station," a "purely military mission." This machine was actually launched from a site near the Caspian Sea and dropped by parachute into the Pacific Ocean, below the equator, where a Soviet fleet waited to recover it. It is an alarming reality, laments Daniel Deudney, researcher for Worldwatch Institute in Washington, that "the two superpowers today spend fifteen percent or more of their space research funds on military activities." In short, they're spending three times as much to promote death on earth as life in space.

There is, of course, much more cheerful news in the whole matter of the race into space. "We're not too far—the human race—from going to the stars," exclaimed Commander John Young exultantly, when he emerged from the ten-billion-dollar spaceship Columbia after looping the earth 36 times. He had the look in his eye, it was said, which historians and artists have associated with Christopher Columbus when he made his maiden voyage to the New World five centuries ago. Walter Cronkite says he would just about give anything if he could fly out into space aboard Columbia. *The Los Angeles Times* reckons that Cronkite and George Plimpton's special, "The Future: What's Next?" in which "space colonies" are featured, was a "T.V. highlight." Morris Sneiderman contended at the 1982 Washington Conference of the American Association for the Advancement of Science that "we live in interesting times. We'll see it happen in our lifetime—the establishment of permanent communities (and factories) in outer space. The era of tentative probing is over." In fact, one of the 160 symposia at that Conference, and one which evoked enormous interest, was on "industry in space." Among the "exciting technological achievements of the future," Billy Graham is quoted as saying, will be "food factories orbiting in outer space."

The Biblical reason I would credit such a conclusion is that when Christ comes—and I believe it to be the "second" phase of His return—"immediately after the tribulation of those days (i.e. Armageddon) He shall send His angels with a great sound of a trumpet, and they shall gather together His elect from the four winds, from one end of heaven to the other" (Matthew 24: 29,31). Note: "He shall send His angels." A great deal has been written in the world press in the early '80's including UPI reports from both Spain and Red China on whether or not UFO's are sometimes angels. Is this fact or fiction? I do not know. I've found it best, in my case, to believe the Word of God totally, and the word of man where it is consistent with the Word of God and credibly demonstrated by honest competent scientists.

God has so many laws that we have not yet detected or harnessed to fulfill His will. "When the Son of man cometh, shall He find faith on the earth?" (Luke 18:8) asked the Son of God of sons of men, who by faith could become sons of God. We're hearing a lot about solar power! In mid-1981 Pilot Stephen Ptacek took the solar-powered plane Solar Challenger from California to France and flew—solely on solar power—for five hours and 23 minutes, traveling 230 miles to England including a crossing of the English Channel. If a son of man can soar toward the sun and thus travel on sunpower, can't a son of God soar beyond the sun—to heaven powered by the Son of God at His coming?

We read the words of Jesus that there'd be signs in the moon. *The Jewish Chronicle* reports that there is currently a team of experts working on a project to place giant aluminum mirrors on the moon. These, says *The Chronicle*, would be used for lighting at night and provide a vast saving in electricity and power. "After that tribulation," Jesus said, "the moon shall not give her light" (Mark 13:24). Does that mean, someone asks, that the big aluminum mirrors will be bombed? We do not know. What we do know is that when Christ comes again, He is going to take us eternally to be with Himself—at which time He will issue to us new, glorified, celestial bodies. The astronauts were able to go to the moon and back because they wore space suits which had to be tailored exactly according to long-studied and precise specifications so that they would operate without the slightest malfunction. Then, and only then, could they rocket at the speed of 25,000 miles per hour to a distance of a quarter of a million miles from the earth and after walking around heaven—howbeit the moon is only the "second heaven"—return safely to earth again. "Behold, the days come, saith the Lord"—it was Jeremiah (51:47,53) who told us about its possibility— when men will actually "mount up to heaven." Wrote St. Paul to the Philippians (3:20,21), "Our [citizenship] is in heaven; from whence also we look for the Savior, the Lord Jesus Christ; who shall change our vile body, that it may be fashioned like unto His glorious body, according to the working whereby He is able even to subdue all things unto himself." Yes, He, Jesus Christ, "is able." So we won't just put a space suit on our mortal bodies. We'll be issued immortal bodies. Actually, our terrestrial bodies will be dissolved. And we'll be issued celestial ones. St. Paul wrote to the Corinthians of "bodies terrestrial" and of "celestial bodies" (1 Corinthians 15:40) affirming that "we know that if our earthly house of this tabernacle were dissolved, we have a building of God, an house not made with hands, eternal in the heavens. For in this we [do] groan, earnestly desiring to be clothed upon with our house which is from heaven. If so be that being clothed we shall not be found naked" (2 Corinthians 5:1-3).

So how will it happen? St. Paul explained: "Behold, I show you a mystery; we shall not all sleep, but we shall all be changed, in a moment, in the twinkling of an eye, at the last trump: for the trumpet shall sound, and the dead shall be raised incorruptible, and we shall be changed. For this corruptible must put on incorruption, and this mortal must put on immortality. So when this corruptible shall have put on incorruption, and this mortal shall have put on immortality, then shall be brought to pass the saying that is written, Death is swallowed up in victory" (1 Corinthians 15:51-54). With a promise like that how can a *Toronto Globe and Mail* reporter allude to the "irrelevant evangelist, praying in [his] psychological fallout shelter for the

Second Coming"? Why, as C. I. Scofield wrote nearly eighty years back: "Nothing brings us into such molding intimacy with God as the believing study of prophecy." And nothing, I must add, makes us so earthly good, for heaven's sake. So let's say, "Hats off to the past and coats off to the future." With the Second Coming of Christ to look forward to, how could we ever have a stronger motivation to live constructively? After all, the highest born are those who are born from on high. To be heaven-born is to be heaven-bound. As Carlyle the philosopher exhorted, to have a true vision of eternity is to get a true hold of time.

To return to some lessons from the space race relating to the return of Christ, it seemed to me a sharp irony which took place at the 5,000-strong 1982 Conference of the American Association for the Advancement of Science. After passing a resolution supporting the elimination of all positive allusions to the teaching of Creationism—even as a theory—alongside Darwinian evolution in the American secular school classroom, they stated that it's alarming that the sorts of people who subscribe to Biblical creationism are astronauts in particular and those in the space industry generally. This, to any objective observer, is puzzling indeed, in the light of the fact that astronauts put their lives on the line, based on the hardware of exact science— science based on precise performance according to pre-planned prescription. Too many of those who call themselves "scientists" are soft hardware types who engage in polemical sophistries in which theory is upgraded into alleged fact and pseudoscience bantered about by conjecturing eggheads who never want to level with exact, eternal truth. And let it be known that it's not just astronauts and obscurantists who believe the teaching of creationism belongs back in the classroom. According to *The New York Times* (Feb. 15, 1982): "Seventy-six percent of the American people favor teaching creationism alongside evolution in science classes."

Darwinian evolution has contended for a century and more that the universe has no fixed origin or edge. Theists believe the material universe has both an origin and an edge, basing their thinking on the Old Testament. So that whether they're Jewish, Christian, or for that matter Moslem, they maintain that there was a fixed origin and that there is an edge. Genesis 1:1 states, "In the beginning [a specific time] God created the heaven and the earth [a specific universe]."

A U.P.I. report in the spring of 1982 states that British scientists Alan Wright, David Fauncey, and Ann Savage, and Australian Bruce Petersen, have discovered through the world's most sophisticated telescope the Quasar PKS-2000-330—which is 18 billion light-years from the earth, and yields the most conclusive evidence yet forthcoming that the material universe had a "Big Bang" origin about 18 billion years ago, and that the above Quasar represents the outer "edge of the known physical universe."

Perhaps the most revealing article I've seen recently on this absolutely fascinating theme was in *The New York Times* in March 1982, written by physicist Heinz Pagels of Rockefeller University, author of *The Cosmic Code*: *Quantum Physics as the Language of Nature*. He begins by affirming, "Most physicists agree that the universe began as an immense explosion—a hot 'Big Bang.' . . . Our universe could have been created by God . . . Not so long ago, this remarkable creation story was unknown. But in the last two decades, scientists have learned more about the origin of the universe than in previous centuries—a consequence of two major developments. The first has been advances in instruments used in astronomy—large optical and radio telescopes, computers and artificial satellites—a technology that has extended human consciousness deep into space. The second is the arrival of the long-sought unified-field theories of sub-nuclear quantum particles. Only by understanding the laws obeyed by the smallest things—quantum particles—are physicists able to reconstruct the origin of the largest thing—the entire universe."

This is the view of perhaps the world's most credible astrophysicist, Fred Hoyle. It was Hoyle, of course, who gave the title and credence to the widely held "Big Bang" theory. Hoyle, as Dr. Gary Parker stated on network television, was converted from agnosticism to at least theism—purely, he says, from the scientific evidence. So what relevance has the "Big Bang" to the second coming of Christ, to Armageddon, and to "the end of all things" (1 Peter 4:7)? It is almost unanimous among astrophysicists that as physical creation came into existence with a "Big Bang," so it will go out of existence with a "Big Bang"—to be succeeded by "New heavens and a new earth" (2 Peter 3:13). Which leads us straight to 2 Peter 3:10, "The day of the Lord will come as a thief in the night; in which the heavens shall pass away with a great noise" (a Big Bang!). Recently, I was reading Terence Dickinson's treatment of the "Black Hole" theory, which had been so fully discussed at the 1982 plenary conference of the American Association for the Advancement of Science in Washington. Reduced to laymen's language, Dickinson notes that the whole planet earth could be compressed to the size of a grape. My mind went to the twin passages in Isaiah 45:11, 12, "Thus saith the Lord, the . . . Maker . .. my hands have stretched out the heavens, and all the host of heaven shall be dissolved, and the heavens shall be rolled together as a scroll." When it comes time for God to pronounce "the end," scientists are simply explaining, willingly or unwittingly, what He can do.

I remember at the circus, as a child, I couldn't figure out how 20 big clowns could get out of one small car—and then get back in. But I saw it happen, so seeing was believing. Today it boggles my mind as to how God can roll out the universe like a scroll. And then He will roll it together again. The Lord's coming again, which St. Peter said would involve a thousand-year period, will spell the end of the world and the first and second heavens, which will be replaced by new ones (2 Peter 3:8-13).

Finally, as we look at Outer Space, and more specifically the lessons taught us by the astronauts, it's necessary for those going into Outer Space to prepare meticulously for their missions. The Bible tells us: "Prepare to meet thy God" (Amos 4:12); and to "prepare ye the way of the Lord" (Luke 3:4). No space shot is ever made without mammoth and meticulous preparation, and even then, sometimes an accident or miscarriage occurs. How do we prepare for Christ's coming again? By repenting of our sins, and turning in full trust to Jesus Christ as Lord. I recently heard a space scientist on national TV on "Meet the Press" state that man today can achieve "infinity in space, and eternity in time." With Jesus Christ we're assured that time and eternity one day will be one, and we'll go to the furthest reaches of infinity in space, by a fulfilled faith in Jesus Christ as Lord.

During one of the Columbia's launchings, Charlie Brown asks his 85 million comic strip readers, "How can I get transferred to another planet?" That happens for the believer in Christ when the Lord comes again. During the network TV coverage of one of Columbia's launchings and later landings, one of the commentators turned to his colleague and asked, "Have you booked space for space?" That's what I'd like to ask you. Have you made your reservations for heaven? Have you prepared for Christ's coming again?

When I'm going from Toronto Airport to the United States, I always make my reservations ahead of time. Then I just turn up and get on the flight, room having been reserved for me in advance. Have you called on Jesus Christ for your spiritual reservations? He assures, "Whosoever shall call upon the name of the Lord shall be saved" (Romans 10:13). To go to the United States from Toronto, I clear customs and immigration, right in Toronto Airport. Then I board the plane. And I never really notice when I cross into the United States. I've already been admitted. That's the way you do with the Lord. You clear with Jesus Christ ahead of time, asking Him to take you to heaven. And He assures, "Him that cometh to Me I will in no wise cast out" (John 6:37). He never rejects those who come to God by Him. He takes you all the way through life, with its often bumpy passage, and on into heaven and eternity, forever to be with the Lord. Neil Armstrong insists that he did not say—as the world thought, because of what the TV commentators intimated—when he strode out on to the moon, "That's one small step for man, one giant leap for mankind." What he did say was, "That's one small step for *a* man, one giant leap for mankind." Each of us just must take the initial, single step individually for Christ if we would one day go forever to be with the Lord. It's an individual decision, not a group, corporate, universal or surrogate one.

Early in 1982, I was speaking on this theme in the Midwest. A medical doctor, Dr. Darren Wicoff came to give himself to Christ. He told me that he had married a lovely woman and they had a beautiful daughter, but living apart from the church and being away from God, they did not know Christ. Darren asked me to pray for them, as a family. What a thrill it was on the last night of that Crusade to see his wife, Jane, and daughter, Leanne both come forward to give themselves to Jesus Christ and thereby be prepared to meet their God.

Chapter Four

"UNDERSTANDING SCIENCE"

No one utilized the quantum leaps forward of science more than Winston Churchill. But in his sunset years he sighed: "the Stone Age may return on the gleaming winds of science and . . . may even bring about its total destruction. Beware, I say: time may be short . . ."

As Jesus answered His disciples concerning omens of Armageddon, He paralleled the last days with antediluvian times, prophesying that "as the days of Noah were, so shall also the coming of the Son of man be" (Matthew 24:3,37). We turn back to Genesis 6:4 and read, "There were giants in the earth in those days"—not just physical giants, but mental giants! Daniel, the Hebrew prophet, lived in Babylon, where science and technology had achieved incredibly lofty plateaus. It is significant that in Daniel we find the only use of the word "science" in the Old Testament. Young Jewish scholars who served in the Court of Nebuchadnezzar were, as Daniel indicated, "skillful in . . . understanding science" (Daniel 1:4). But Daniel insisted their knowledge and understanding of science was primitive compared to what would happen at "the time of the end" when "knowledge shall be increased" (Daniel 12:4); or as it may more literally be translated, "There will be a knowledge explosion." In the New Testament, as in the Old, science is only mentioned once. It's in St. Paul's writings to Timothy, and it's in those same writings that He prophesies: "This know also, that in the last days" people will be "ever learning" (2 Timothy 3:1,7).

Time magazine, in publishing its new brainchild *Discover* in 1982, expostulates: "It's no exaggeration. You're living in the middle of an age of exploration like nothing that's ever happened before in the whole long history of mankind: genetic engineering, artificial organs, laser surgery . . ."

It's as ironic as it is tragic that it is in the matter of "learning war" that humans currently are most energetic in science and technological research. Dr. George Keyfort, science adviser to President Reagan, stated to the Washington Conference of the American Association for the Advancement of Science that the Reagan administration is spending 21 percent more on defense research in 1982 than in 1981, and this at a time when nearly all other federal budgets are being drastically cut back due to a recession in the economy. It is being done, it is contended, because the Soviets are spending three times as much of their GNP on armaments as the Americans. And what, understandably, annoys President Reagan is the fact that the Russians use most of their immense armaments monies to manufacture war machines. "The Reagan Administration is trying to stanch," observes *The New York Times* (April 12, 1982) "the 'hemorrhage' of militarily useful technology to the Soviet Union," because "the Soviet Union is building its military machine" (notes *Time*, January 25, 1982) almost entirely on "Western technology." Following is a case in point: Four high-ranking Japanese nuclear experts rode the Soviets' Red Arrow express train from Moscow to Leningrad in 1982. While they slept in the night, their highly secret documents were rifled and doubtless the contents confiscated for reproduction. The Soviets' explanation? "A burglary"! (*Los Angeles Times*). Why should the Soviets bother to duplicate research, when espionage is a Russian ace?

The fact of the matter is that man universally, as the Bible predicts, talks peace while he walks with his arms full of arms for Armageddon. We're familiar, very familiar with how the Bible prophesies that our swords will be turned into plowshares and our spears into pruning hooks. But sometimes we overlook the clear fact of scripture that Joel prophesies, that in the approach to the last days you'll "beat your plowshares into swords, and your pruning hooks into spears" (Joel 3:10). That's happening on a tragic scale today. Notes George Will in *The Washington Post* (May 12, 1982): "In East Germany, a new law makes it a crime to wear a button saying 'Swords into Plowshares.' " The Soviets are much more concerned about converting "Plowshares in Swords" than vice versa. President Reagan made this point before the German Bundestag when he quoted Frederick Schitler who observed that no man, however peace loving he may be can stay in peace unless it please his evil neighbor. And so out of one side of their mouth certain world leaders are saying "peace, peace," while out of the other side they say "make war, make war!"

Robert Sobel in his impressive new book on IBM, *Colossus in Transition*, makes the point that, always, "war has been for IBM a significant catalyst for innovation." One only needs to look back at the half decade when World War II was being fought to realize that during that brief span more crucial inventions were achieved, including antibiotics, radar, jet planes and nuclear bombs, than during the whole of the rest of the first half of this century combined. Since World War II, we're told that knowledge is doubling every 10 years. But, laments Walter Cronkite, it's often information without wisdom, and head knowledge without that heart judgment which made our fathers great. Real knowledge begins when you come to know Christ as Savior and Lord. St. Paul's great aspiration was: "that I may know Him (Christ) and the Power of His resurrection" (Philippians 3:10). This leads us to state that it is the usage to which these inventions are put that determines whether or not they contribute in the final analysis to progress or impending disaster.

Just prior to the attempt on his life in 1981, Pope John Paul visited Hiroshima. The priest who served as his Japanese host bore glaring scars from the heat and radiation of that landmark nuclear flash. Others in the crowd suffered from anemia, blood diseases, and sterility inflicted by that haunting holocaust. Remonstrated the Pope: "Technological development for its own sake" is one of the tragedies of modern times. *The Wall Street Journal* asks reflectively whether "the American dream that technology can cure all ills will ultimately prove to be a Utopian solution, or a Frankenstein monster." It is surely one of the bittersweet dilemmas of all time.

More than any other in this century, the brain that opened this Pandora's box was Albert Einstein. As the centennial of his birth was celebrated, someone recalled asking him what weapons would be used for World War III. He hesitated on that one. But he did feel that he knew what weapons would be used for World War IV. "Rocks!" Einstein made other apt observations that were to prove ominously prophetic: that great spirits are too often dwarfed by small minds, and that "the splitting of the atom has changed everything save our mode of thinking, and thus we drift towards unparalleled catastrophe." Einstein's awareness that his inventions could well spell the eventual extinction of the human race were evident to him in 1933 when his correspondence with Sigmund Freud, *Why War*, was published in which the admission was acknowledged: "owing to the perfection of instruments of destruction a future war might involve the extermination of one or perhaps both of the antagonists." Einstein's pupil and acknowledged father of the atomic bomb, Robert Oppenheimer, lamented, "The physicists have known sin, and this is a knowledge they cannot lose." This was an obvious allusion to Adam and Eve's experience in the Garden of Eden, when, to indulge in the fruit of the tree of the knowledge of good and evil, they jeopardized their access to the tree of life.

It may be recalled that Jesus, in reply to His disciples' questions about "the end" that would be the means to a new age, explained that humankind ineluctably would be like a pregnant woman in terrible travail with believers waiting for the delivery, which event for them would augur joy unspeakable. Meanwhile, the world around would grovel in anguish. The late

Eric Hoffer, the labor leader turned pop writer, expressed tren-
chantly: "Everywhere we look at present we see something new
trying to be born. A pregnant swollen world is writhing in labor,
and everywhere untrained quacks are officiating as obstetri-
cians. These quacks say that the only way the new era can be
born is by Caesarean operation. They lust to rip the belly of
the world open." All of this causes such people as our Canadian
Anglican Primate, Archbishop Ted Scott, to decry "the fantastic explosion of knowledge in the last two decades [an in-
felicitude which] has brought us more questions than answers."
The final word from the last World Council of Churches General
Assembly over which Scott presided as moderator was a
remonstrance which decried "technological giantism" as being
a monstrous menace to man's survival on this planet.

Yet when we come to dealing with the pre-Armageddon
scenario, there are some salient inventions springing up in a
host of research fields which are too relevant to ignore. There's
no doubt that man universally finds himself in a rat race to pursue what the Toronto Conference of the American Association
for the Advancement of Science took as their theme: "Science
and Technology: Bridging the Frontiers." "The next five to ten
years will produce more dramatic changes than the last 50,"
projected futurist Dr. Emil Gaverluk as we stumbled stub-toed
in 1982.

Alvin Toffler, author of *Future Shock*, in his more recent *The
Third Wave* reasons that man is moving from the Industrial
Society, in which the labor force uses their hands, to the
"electronic cottage family" in which they stay home with their
computers and use their heads. "We are going from an energy
system based on fossil fuels to one based on multiplicity. Diver-
sity will replace uniformity." He points to the highly in-
dustrialized Northeastern United States with cities like Detroit
that are in decline and even depression while the specialized
computer and communication industries of the Sunbelt flourish.
Larry Solway, the Toronto pundit, projects, "Home computers
are going to come down in price very dramatically. Companies

dealing in personal computers like Atari, Apple, Radio Shack
. . . what happened with calculators is going to happen with
computers." Sydney Harris claims "computer circuits today are
10,000 times more reliable than they were 25 years ago" (Harris
Syndicated Column - June 29, 1982).

It was only ten years ago that the revolutionary computer-
on-a-chip replaced bulky transistors, which in turn had been
replaced by the miniaturized slices of etched silicon. Now
Newsweek (Jan. 25, 1982) does a feature article on Bell
Laboratories. As the world's electronic leaders Bell can place
on a single chip, a wafer the size of a fingernail, 150,000 of the
old transistors. These chips can hold 262,000 separate items
of information—four times the capacity of anything previously
manufactured. A whole library can be placed in your shirt
pocket. In terms of speech transactions, an MIT computer can
perform 100 billion transactions in a second. Jack Miller tells
us that with a low-cost home computer, by the pushing of a few
key punches, the pulling of a lever or two, in a split second we
will soon be able to retrieve from a data bank information we
require on our own visual display unit from the libraries, stock
exchanges, and supermarkets of the world. And we'll be able
to make decisions and punch them back in with the flick of our
fingers. Literally we'll let our fingers do the walking, rather than
becoming embroiled in those life shortening freeway traffic jams
in our gas-guzzling tanks, the wheeled prisons we've been com-
muting in for what has been too long.

Certainly more and more workers in the 1980's are staying
home from the assembly lines in the factories, and making their
living at the panel of a computer terminal. The American
Association for the Advancement of Science projects that by
the late 1990's the labor force will have been reduced in the West
from 25 to 5 percent, with 95 percent of those who work functioning in the emerging "information society."

That "there will be a knowledge explosion" in "the time
of the end" is evident in the fact that 70 percent of all the
scientists of history are alive today. There are currently 40,000

scientific journals being published regularly, and a half million new books annually. In a single generation, Canada, a typical Western democracy, has increased its numbers of annual university graduates by 700 percent; India, a third-world country, a thousand percent. In the field of medicine, Dr. Malcolm Todd, an American Medical Association President, reckons that "about half of medical knowledge is outdated every ten years." Seventy-five percent of the current medicines in use are ones which have been developed in this generation. And the mental capacities of moderns themselves are being improved by biological breakthroughs. Dr. Stephen Rosen in *Future Facts* reckons you will eventually be able to "swallow a knowledge pill that teaches you Spanish." Since 1975, led by two Scots at Aberdeen University, brain scientists—including Canadian biologist Dr. Michel Cluetien and several Americans from the University of California at Berkley—have been working with a substance in the brain called: "Beta-h-P.H." They are asking,"Is this a key to the learning processes of the mind?"

Automation takes over more and more from the labor force at the workbench, the switchboard, the assembly line and—in the future, we're told—at cooking in the kitchen and cleaning in the livingroom. Robots are to the blue collar worker what computers are to the white collar worker. Billy Graham surmised late in 1981 that the future holds out hope for robots that "will be capable of almost any household chore—including cooking and cleaning." Even now, there are 70,000 of them on the factory floors of Japan. Val Sears, reporting from the Washington Conference of the American Association for the Advancement of Science writes of how cyberneticists—robotic scientists—can already imitate the behavior of men. Robots can "exhibit curiosity, learn from their mistakes, be creative in the sense that they can look for purposes which they can fulfill, reproduce themselves, and have an unlimited life span through a capacity for self-repair." "In short," says cyberneticist D. Rorvik, "a generation of robots is rapidly evolving, a breed that can see, read, talk, learn, and even feel emotions." The "groundwork has been laid," adds Lehman Wilzig, "for the arrival in the not too distant future of artificially intelligent machines—'humanoids'—which will exhibit all the important qualities and traits characteristic of man." Isaac Azimov even reckons we'll have to institute firm legislation which he labels *"Laws of Robotics."* Val Sears cautions that we have on our hands "the Frankenstein horror of a creature turning on its creator." St. Paul warned the Romans of the perils attendant when sophisticates "changed the glory of the uncorruptible God into an image made like to corruptible man . . . and worshipped and served the creature more than the Creator, Who is blessed forever. For this cause God gave them up" (Romans 1:23, 25, 26). We're getting more and more to the place where we program men to act like machines, and machines like men, to the place where we're deifying humans and humanizing machines. Mrs. Ghandi of India regrets that the fine line between life and machine, between the animate and inanimate, is so thin that man is scarcely able to recognize where one ends and the other begins. It's the new Pantheism. *The New York Times Book Review* critiques Tracy Kidder's *The Soul of a New Machine*, in which two humans "West and Alsing sign on to a new project, a gaggle of maniacs from Cal Tech with IQ's of 200 who think that life has nothing to show more fair than two weeks of Dungeons and Dragons hooked into a computer for companionable advice." It comes close to fulfilling Aldous Huxley's prophecy in his *Brave New World*, as an obsessed generation of technocrats pursuses macro-minded machine pleasures, as earlier collegians had pursued "girls, booze or drugs. In fact," concludes Kidder, "only an actual engagement in War could top it." War could top it? War would not be a "topping"! It would be a bottoming out!

Time runs a cover story on the new annual five-billion-dollar video-game business in America. It's but another sortie into idolatry, surely. It's why Jesus Christ must come again to be Lord of the world of technology, as well as to sort out men from machines and humans destined for immortality from humanoids destined for the material scrap heap "where moth and rust doth corrupt" (Matthew 6:19). Most of these video games—from Pac Man to Space Invaders—are played on television screens! Probably no technological invention has more revolutionized modern society in a single generation than television. By the mid-'Eighties a ring of satellites orbiting the equator will beam T.V. shows directly from any part of the globe to every part of the world. A NASA scientist on the CTV network describes how ready-to-be-manufactured T.V. sets, the size of a large wrist watch and costing very little, will be bought and worn by peoples around the world, bringing in programs directly from the orbiting satellites. How about China, the last frontier for the masses to be able to see television? Coming into the 'Seventies they had one set to every 30,000 people. Today virtually all have access to T.V. sets. U.P.I. notes of the "three-million-plus" people of one Chinese city, "They're just glued to them."

How does this relate to impending Armageddon? For one thing, it's conditioning the minds of the masses for World War III. In May 1982, a comprehensive study of ABC, NBC, and CBS-TY network programs indicates that violence on television is, tragically, still on the increase! Currently T.V. depicts an average of eight violent acts per hour. Graduating high schoolers have watched 19,000 hours of T.V., and have attended school 11,000 hours. They've seen 136,000 violent acts—20,000 of which have been killings! Add to this the fascination of wars dominating the T.V. news, day in and day out, year after year, in Vietnam, in Afghanistan, in the Falklands, in Lebanon, in the Persian Gulf. It's where the real action is: not just fun and games like sporting events. Why, it's more exciting than the Superbowl! It's the real thing! As Malcolm Muggeridge adjudges, yes, there's handwringing and knee jerking alright, and exclamations of "isn't it awful!" But it's a narcotic! It's got people unwittingly hooked. It's the red herring, the deathtrap set for all mankind! Though no one would admit it, overall, the masses love it. Television as the inadvertent sponsor of war world-wide becomes a set of polished mirrors, seducing the public ineluctably toward Armageddon!

Another relevance of television to Armageddon is, as Billy Graham notes in a national magazine article, that it will surely be on T.V. that the Antichrist will be seen as well as heard throughout the world. And there are those two witnesses in Revelation 11:9,10. In the middle of the Great Tribulation, they're to be killed in the streets of Jerusalem where their Lord was crucified, and "for three and a half days men from every people, tribe, language and nation will gaze on their bodies." A hundred years ago that sounded ludicrous, like some fantastic pipe dream. Today T.V. makes such an event just another breaking news scoop.

Then there's the use of television in fulfilling the Great Commission. Jesus insisted that preceding Armageddon "this gospel of the kingdom shall be preached in all the world for a witness unto all [peoples]; and then shall the end come" (Matthew 24:14). My friend Pat Robertson transmits my T.V. program weekly via satellite. One day on the 700 Club, he and I discussed that prophecy in Revelation 14:6: "And I saw another angel fly in the midst of heaven, having the everlasting gospel to preach unto them that dwell on the earth, and to every nation, and kindred, and tongue, and people." In that angels in the Bible are emissaries of God—and not always living creatures—might not this angel be a satellite which flies through the heavens transmitting the everlasting Gospel? An interesting observation has been made by Dr. Charles Taylor. He points out that videotape is made out of ground stone! So in proclaiming the Gospel to the world on television, might we not be—in a sense— fulfilling our Lord's prophecy that the stones will cry out that Jesus Christ is Lord?

The following illustration describes even further possibilities. I was eating with the Vice-President of an American T.V. network recently, and he apprised me of computers that are on the verge of being able instantaneously to translate a human speaker into several languages—with the same intensity decibels and tone of voice used by the person giving the address. Imagine that Billy Graham is preaching on T.V. Watching him could be the people of a dozen countries, each hearing him in their own language, *a la* the Book of Acts chapter 2! What would eventually prevent this phenomenon in 3,000 to 5,000 languages of the world? The ominous side of this invention, of course, is the use to which the future Antichrist may well put it.

It's important at this point to re-focus on the fact that Bible prophecy keeps revolving around the Middle East, with primary attention to Israel. Although only one in 270 people throughout the world is Jewish, I would venture to say that at least one in three of the crucial inventions and improvisations in science and technology of the twentieth century has been made by Jews of various countries. How about tiny Israel, where only one in 1,100 of the world's population lives? A recent edition of the *Jewish Gazette* pertinently points out that "Israel's achievements in the technological field include the most sophisticated computer systems in the world . . . the most advanced vehicle performance testers" and "surgical lasers." Numerous other firsts and frontiers of research are named.

For the Christless person, the prospect of Armageddon and what follows spells the judgment, as a great number of scriptures indicate. All impenitent people will be judged from records of their words and deeds. Nothing is hidden. Every secret thing comes out. This didn't make as much sense a century, or even a decade ago, as it does today. God has an all-seeing eye and all-hearing ear, and His own special brands of computer chips to record your life in the minutest and most comprehensive detail. The Russians, we read, have satellites on a clear day so sensitive that they can take a picture from outer space of a baseball being pitched in Yankee Stadium and tell whether or not it's a Spalding. American telescopes can isolate an object the size of a postage stamp on the moon. And something else! Million-dollar medical scanners are currently being installed in metropolitan hospitals in North America, with X-ray, computer, and video technologies so sophisticated that a specialist can glance at a cross section of your body and then on the computer readout can tell you approximately what ails you! If man can do that by machine, what could the Omniscient Maker not hear in your conversation or see in your sub-conscious mind that He won't be in a position to reveal at the judgment?

Finally, we read that in the "new heaven and new earth . . . God shall wipe away all tears from their eyes; and there shall be no more death, neither sorrow nor crying, neither shall there be any more pain" (Revelation 21:1,4). How our Lord will accomplish this we don't completely comprehend. We frequently hear medical scientists say that man is going to live longer. In spite of their promises, we still average the proverbial "three score years and ten," though a few years ago there lived a man with a purported age of 137, and today the oldest known person is 117 years old. A clue to what law God may utilize in His economy is the fact that for the last few years many "thousands of scientists—neurobiologists, biophysicists, pharmacologists— around the world are feverishly competing to find the key that will unlock the mystery of endorphins" (*Toronto Star*, Jan. 17, 1982). Endorphins comprise the brain's own narcotics system which control pain, addiction, mental illness—and who knows— perhaps aging itself. Says Montreal psychiatrist and endorphin researcher Dr. Heinz Lehmann, "We are discovering bits and pieces of a complex mechanism we knew nothing about until recently. Erdorphins promise a panacea to man's ills." In that the Bible indicated there will be a millennium beyond Armageddon in which man may again live nearly a thousand years, might such research not lead to laws God will engage to restore longenity?

Man longs, not just to live a thousand years, but as the Rich Young Ruler revealed in his question to Jesus: "Good Master, what shall I do to inherit eternal life?" Man longs to live forever! And Jesus has the key to eternal life. He assures: "My sheep hear my voice, and I know them, and they follow me: And I give unto them eternal life, and they shall never perish." (John 10:27,28). And the same Jesus Christ is "the key of knowledge"

(Luke 11:52). Indeed, He holds both of these keys in His hands.

On a Saturday night in 1982, I presented Christ. Into the back row of the meeting came a brilliant M.I.T. student, Mark Copp. He had been an all-star baseballer and footballer at both the high school and university levels. But he was not committed to Christ. As I gave our Lord's invitation for the Crusade crowd to respond, many did. And I saw this impressive young man swaying physically back and forth like the pendulum of a grandfather clock. Finally, he came! And Mark became like the Gospel writer after whom he was named—a follower of Jesus Christ, having decisively "turned to God from idols to serve the living and true God; and to wait for His Son from heaven" (1 Thessalonians 1:9,10).

Chapter Five

"EARTHQUAKES IN DIVERS PLACES"

In the twilight of civilization, "potholes" will deeply fissure the descending broadway on which humankind winds its way into the darkening valley of the shadow, Jehoshaphat. Forecasts Jesus, "Great earthquakes shall be in divers places" (Luke 21:11) as well as the "wars and commotions" mentioned in the same passage (vss. 9-10). As we've been noting, there will be pandemonium throughout the world, but the final Waterloo of the age will be in the Middle East. It's also true that there will be antichrists worldwide, but that the real Antichrist will set up his headquarters in Israel itself. And so with earthquakes! Jesus said they would be in "divers places"—that is, here and there throughout the world! And they would be getting more and more destructive. When that's happening, in fact when it begins to happen, Jesus said, "Look up, and lift up your heads; for your redemption draweth nigh" (Luke 21:28).

But then, He said there'd be that time of Great Tribulation. And to read about it, we could turn to several pertinent passages, but the one which is accepted by Jew and Christian alike is Zechariah 14:1-9 (N.E.B.): "Watch, for the day of the Lord is coming soon! On that day, the Lord will gather together the nations to fight Jerusalem; the city will be taken, the houses rifled, the loot divided, the women raped; half the population will be taken away as slaves, and half will be left in what remains of the city. Then the Lord will go out fully armed for war, to fight against those nations. That day His feet will stand upon the Mount of Olives to the east of Jerusalem, and the Mount of Olives will split apart, making a very wide valley running from east to west, for half the mountain will move toward the north and half toward the south. You will escape through that valley, for it will reach across to the city gate. Yes, you will escape as your people did long centuries ago from the earthquake in the days of Uzziah, King of Judah, and the Lord God shall come, and all the saints and angels with Him . . . life-giving waters will flow . . . and the Lord shall be King over all the earth." The only telling difference in the New Testament is that the Lord Who comes at the nadir of that deracinating Battle of Armageddon will be Jesus Christ. So we read in The Revelation, in chapter 16, that the rulers of the world were gathered "for the great day of battle . . . that is the day when I come as a thief . . . so they assembled . . . at the place called in Hebrew Armageddon . . . and there was a great earthquake, such as was not since men were upon the earth, so mighty an earthquake, and so great. And the great city was divided . . . and the cities of the nations fell . . . and every island fled away, and the mountains were not found" (Revelation 16:14-20).

That kind of macrocosmic earthquake, however, as we noted, is not due until it's been preceded by increasingly "great earthquakes . . . in divers places." Early in 1982, I was riding on an airplane when I picked up *The New York Times*. It read, "Sharp earthquake that 'sounded like thunder' jolted residents of eastern Canada awake yesterday morning, rattling dishes and shaking furniture through New England as far south as Connecticut. It was the first significant quake in the area in more than a century. The National Earthquake Center said the quake measured 5.9 on the Richter Scale." *The Times* reckoned that it was the first significant earthquake in that Halifax—Montreal—New York triangular area since Feb. 8, 1855. This earthquake was followed by three more comparable ones and a host of aftershocks. And on the national CTV evening news Lloyd Robertson, Canada's best known newscaster, intimated that there were many who suspected that the earthquakes might well be related to John Gribbin's predicted "Jupiter Effect: 1982."

The Jupiter Effect was a controversial book which became a best-seller during the seventies. At that time, the nine planets of the solar system moved into conjunction with the sun. This was the order: the Sun, Mercury, Venus, Earth, Mars, Jupiter, Saturn, Uranus, Neptune, and Pluto—Mercury and Venus being between the earth and the sun. According to the theory, this created considerable gravitational pull on the Earth imposing pressure on the crust, a phenomenon which poses the question: Will this contribute further to the triggering of massive earthquakes and tidal waves? A Chinese scientist, in a calculation which is not unchallenged by his colleagues, predicts in a widely publicized report that this grand alignment will tend toward 25 years of increasing natural disasters and lowering temperatures in the northern hemisphere. He bases his predictions on data which, he claims, go back 5,000 years.

The case is taken up in *Pole Shift* by John W. White, published by Doubleday. The reasoning is that all nine planets are only on one side of the sun every 179 years, but never in astronomical recorded history have they been grouped to as near as 98° of each other as in 1982. What is known is that the gravitational pull of each planet has a slight effect on the surface of the sun, so that all in such close proximity at once would have some delayed effects, altering slightly the sunpot patterns and stimulating solar storms. These in turn may eventually emit solar winds that will affect long range the crusts of the planets, including Earth. How much, and how soon? These are moot questions for which the jury is still out. What is sure is that earthquakes are like the mills of God—they grind slowly.

Seismologists have now developed the theory of "plate tectonics" to help explain the occurrence of earthquakes. The crust of the earth consists of about a dozen giant 70-mile-thick rock plates, which float on the earth's semi-molten mantle. Where they engage, high pressure friction generates tremendous stress. Eventually, they break loose and the rock fractures allow the plates to resume their motion. That's when earthquakes occur. But eventually what happens—as such eminent seismologists as Don Anderson of Cal Tech and Don Leet of M.I.T. reason—is that once one earthquake takes place in a region, it's like the breakup of ice on the Great Lakes in the spring thaw. It's the beginning of more to follow. An example cited by *The New York Times* is that until 20 years ago there had not been a solitary measurable earthquake in Colorado. Since then, over three thousand earthquakes have been registered.

Time states that there have been more macroearthquakes in the past ten years than in the previous hundred. A network TV newsman observes that there have been 25 macroscopic earthquakes since 1958, compared to 24 during the whole previous period of history known as A.D. Seismology historians have calculated that megalithic earthquakes have increased over 2,000 percent since Columbus discovered the New World. What is more readily verifiable is that as many have died in earthquakes during the last dozen years as had perished in the previous 120. Certainly a great many more people have been slain in this quarter of the century in earthquakes than on battlefields.

Iran was again traumatized in late 1981 when 8,000 reportedly died in a 7.3 Richter Scale blockbuster, an estimated 3,000 having been dealt death blows the previous June. Greece, that same autumn, was hit by a 2-billion-dollar devastater. In 1980, Italy lost 3,000 lives and Algeria 20,000 to ravaging flatteners. Back in the seventies, earthquakes slaughtered almost 67,000 people in Peru, 22,000 in Guatemala, 25,000 on another occasion in Iran, and according to the *Hong Kong View*, it was a million-killer crust cracking crusher that wrecked Tangshan, China, in 1976. It was perhaps to be history's most lethal natural disaster, at least since Noah's flood. *Time* (Mar. 1, 1982) quotes the late Nelson Rockefeller as having complained about the breadth of his duties as Vice-President: "I go to funerals. I go to earthquakes."

In the United States, California's San Andreas Fault has elicited for years predictions from seismologists that there could occur a million-massacring leveller there between now and the end of the century. It has also been the basis of the best-seller *The Late Great State of California*, and the BBC TV documentary: *"The City That Waits to Die"* (San Francisco). In December 1981, Professor Raymond Arvidson of Washington University revealed that a fault-line twice as long as San Andreas (l,650 miles and as wide as 50 miles) runs diagonally across the United States from Washington State to the southern tip of the Appalachian Mountains in North Carolina. It was seen from space by a newly developed geo-scanner, and it could eventually be one of the world's most gaping continental rifts, and the fault-line of a multi-million decimator macro-quake in the future.

But Bible prophecy was written from a Middle Eastern perspective and that's where the highest per capita losses in earthquake disasters, with some exceptions, have been concentrated during the last few years: places like Greece, Iran, and Turkey, where, of course, all the churches of Revelation 2 and 3 were located. Judith Perera, political editor of *The Middle East Magazine* for January 1982, writes, "So far this century, earthquakes have killed nearly 200,000 people in the Middle East and North Africa." The seismic belt reaches down from Southern Europe and Southeast Asia through Israel and the Arab world into Northern Africa. Since mid-century, 800 villages have been obliterated. The danger is escalating. "Only Israel has sufficiently sophisticated seismography to caution where to build and where not to build," contends Perera. For example, the Hilton Hotel chain wanted to build its premier luxury showpiece to the world on the Mount of Olives. But the seismology engineers made a thorough investigation and came back with their report: Don't build. It's on a fault-line! That, as we've already noted from Zechariah 14, is precisely where, when Messiah comes, the mountain will split to the North and to the South. The outcome is described in Ezekiel 47:1-12. A waterway resulting from the greatest earthquake in human history will open a river between the Mediterranean and the Dead Sea, which is 1,500 feet below sea level.

In the light of this, it was indeed amazing that the Israeli Cabinet in 1981, led by an inspired President Begin, gave final approval to the digging of a 50-mile canal to carry Mediterranean water across the occupied Gaza Strip to the Dead Sea, and among other things, to provide Israel with 16 percent of its electrical power. Digging having begun, digging that would last eight years at least, *The Jerusalem Post* in late August 1981 carried several euphoric statements by Begin. Whether or not that canal reaches completion as envisaged by Begin remains to be seen. What is sure is that when Messiah comes to terminate Armageddon, destroy the Antichrist, and set up His Millennial Kingdom, His advent will coincide with the greatest earthquake since the advent of man, in which the river—the river of God—will flow from the Mediterranean through Jerusalem to a Dead Sea which, after thousands of years of being a symbol of death, will be a waterway of life.

Meanwhile, if there is any natural disaster which has to be thought of as an "Act of God"—as insurance companies or governments throughtout most of the Western world designate them—it's earthquakes! In Isaiah 29:5-6, we read from the Word of God, "At an instant suddenly, thou shalt be visited of the Lord of hosts . . . with earthquake and great noise." Certainly the blockbuster which shook the Philippian jail where Paul and Silas were imprisoned did more to the jailor than merely awaken him physically. It awakened him spiritually with one of history's sharpest jolts, causing him to implore the apostles—in what H. G. Wells has labeled man's most basic and univeral question—"What must I do to be saved?" And they replied, "Believe on the Lord Jesus Christ and thou shalt be saved" (Acts 16:30,31). What we have to do is to keep in mind that Jesus assures, "Behold I stand at the door and knock. If any man hear My voice and open the door, I will come in, and will sup with him, and he with Me!" (Revelation 3:20). So that whatever earthshaking experiences you've had in your life, you can be sure that they are sent directly by, or allowed of, God to awaken you to the call of Christ.

Central America has dominated world news for whole months at a time the last few years. First to gain world headlines with its 22,000-casualty-earthquake was Guatemala. Five years later, we began hearing that the number of evangelical Christians had doubled since the disaster. And in April 1982, *Time* carried a three-page feature article on the spiritual miracle steps that have brought "Born-again General Jose Efrain Rios Montt" to power as Guatemala's Prime Minister. *Time* traces his remarkable conversion to Christ, his practice of fasting and prayer, and his becoming "an active member of the Christian Church of the Word, teaching Sunday School, preaching and serving as academic director of the school. So complete was his transformation that he often manned a broom and swept out the large green and yellow revival tent in the church compound ... Rios Montt's rise to power was nothing less than a miracle." God—and history—will judge what kind of a head-of-state Rios Montt will make.

God shakes nations! He also knocks heavily at the hearts of individuals! Early in 1982, I was preaching in a Presbyterian Church on a night when there was a howling blizzard. But through that blinding snowstorm had come a very beautiful woman. In fact, Jane was a beautician, but her life had not recently been beautiful. Her husband Ric had been a lapsed Roman Catholic. Then he came to one of our Crusades four years earlier and gave his life to Christ. Jane thought and thought about her life. Then she went through a human heartbreak as her seven-year-old son developed muscular dystrophy. So that night, Christ having knocked on her heart's door for months and even years, she came through the blizzard and forward to give her life to Christ. She went home with the peace Jesus promised on her face, and the river of God flowing in her life!

Chapter Six

"THERE SHALL BE FAMINES"

When the disciples of Jesus came asking Him what would be the prevailing conditions at the time of His coming again and the end of the world, they presented their questions in a noteworthy order. They did not ask Jesus, "What will be the sign of the end of the world and of Your coming again," but rather, "of Your coming again and the end of the world." Jesus replied that there would be "wars." Yes! And there "shall be famines" for starters: "these are the beginnings of sorrows." Conditions worldwide will then rapidly deteriorate into "affliction, such as was not from the beginning of the creation which God created unto this time, neither shall be. And except that the Lord had shortened those days, no flesh should be saved" (Mark 13:7,8,19,20).

Dr. Robert Evans of France points out that the world is capable of growing enough food for the nutritional needs of its present inhabitants, but that the bottleneck is a matter of distribution. And here is precisely where the problem lies. Jesus said because of wars, there'd be famines. And famines would lead to more wars, until the affliction deepens into a worldwide crisis. Then agriculture and transport become more and more complicated as whole nations scrape for a scrap of bread for each of their peoples. The ancient Hebrew prophet Joel (1:15-20) foresaw that when "The day of the Lord is at hand . . . the barns are broken down; for the corn is withered . . . the beasts groan!

The herds of cattle are perplexed . . . the rivers of waters are dried up."

As political anarchy threatens and economies collapse in today's world, we read that prior to the return of Jesus Christ to this world to set up His Kingdom, "I beheld, and lo a black horse; and he that sat on him had a pair of balances in his hand. And I heard a voice in the midst of the four beasts say, A measure of wheat [which is about a quart] for a penny, [that is, for a day's wages]" (Revelation 6:5,6). The black horse, as Bible teachers have agreed, is famine. You can look at Lamentations 4:8,9, or Jeremiah 4:28; and in such instances, black is indicative of famine scourging as a blighting plague striding through the land. In January 1982, Poland was into its second month of martial law, and by a single stroke of General Jakuzelski's dictatorial pen the price of food was trebled, and in some instances quadrupled. Dr. Philip Johnston pointed out, "If an average pensioner were to have an egg a day for a month, at least half of his income would be gone" (Reuters, Jan. 12, 1982). *Newsweek* (Jan. 25, 1982) characterizes Poland as "a nation awash in black." For Poles "awash in black," they were already being visited by "the black horse." Further depressing the food crisis in Poland, by the autumn of '82 was the "extreme draught" withering "farm crops across Poland" (Reuters, Aug. 6, 1982).

As the United Nations' Food and Agicultural Organization met in Rome in November 1981, the hunger needs of the world were in mounting crisis. They noted that ten years earlier, there were an annual ten million earthlings starving to death. By 1981, the numbers had rocketed up to 62 million—that's up 620 percent in a decade. Pope John Paul, addressing that Rome Conference, stated that "the persistence of . . . degrading poverty and especially the lack of the absolutely basic minimum of food is the scandal of the modern world." Opined the leader of the World Food Council, "Food consumption will rise faster than output over the next decade, and the number of people starving will double to more than one billion." Jack Denton Scott, in a new publication from McGraw-Hill in New York, receives widespread reviews on his contention that we simply must level with the facts—that by the year 1990 the majority of our populated planet will be ravaged by rampant famine. And when nuclear war strikes, as Desmond Ball reported to the International Institute of Strategic Studies in London recently, within weeks man can reckon to lose 100 million to starvation, apart altogether from the incalculable others who will be killed (*Los Angeles Times*, Jan. 17, 1982).

World-renowned biologist Dr. Paul Erlich of Stanford University, who was on Johnny Carson early in 1982, notes that there are whole areas of the globe where people alive today will die tomorrow from starvation. "There is not the slightest hope of escaping a disastrous time of famines," for from this moment onward, "it is shockingly apparent that the battle to feed man will end in a rout."

Lester Brown notes *The Washington Post*, is "one of the world's most influential thinkers" of 1982. As President of Worldwatch Institute, "he heads one of the most respected and independent think tanks in the world." His newest study being so intensely scrutinized currently is "the most excerpted and reviewed new book in the U.S. this season," despite its being such a depressingly "gloomy report." Ross Howard's critique suggests that we "forget about using the word 'crisis' when talking about the world production of food." Crisis "suggests a severe but temporary shortage. The correct word now is 'climax,' meaning a final—and irreversible—shortage." As Brown puts it, "Planet Earth is no longer a sustainable society." With "world population doubling twice in this century, the world's land is being worked so hard for food that one-quarter of the topsoil is turning sterile or eroding away. Thirty-four percent of U.S. cropland is losing its long-term productivity due to topsoil erosion. Iowa alone lost 260 million tons of topsoil last year (something that could be said of Saskatchewan or Kansas). The Sahara Desert has moved 60 miles further south into Africa in the last decade—100 since 1960. Florida, source of half of the world's grapefruit and a quarter of all the oranges, will lose virtually all of its prime farmland to towns, cities, and other uses by 1995, if current trends continue. The world's fishing ponds are in irreversible trouble." Brown insists that they simply cannot produce any more than the "maximum 50 million tons they yielded ten years ago." They have since been tapering off. Over-fishing and pollution have turned the Black and Azov Seas from prosperous fishing grounds to dead waters in the last 20 years."

What else has been happening to lower the food supply? In addition to the crisis in Poland, "Romania became the second Soviet Bloc country after Poland to ration food" (*Wall Street Journal*); and then according to *The Los Angeles Times*, the Soviet Union itself has serious food problems. In 1982, *The New York Times* (June 27, 1982) notes that Russia is undergoing its fourth crop failure in a row, this year's being its smallest harvest since 1975, despite the fact that its 1981 harvest was a disastrous 21.6% below its needs and expectations—a crop which Brezhnev himself admitted on world TV was "a disaster." Nor is this about to reverse itself. David Dyker of the University of Sussex in England projects, as a researcher for NATO in April 1982, that the Soviets "will have zero growth in farm output over the next four years." An A.P. article (Apr. 15, 1982) quotes a Kremlin report that in the last five years the per capita meat and fat consumption for Russians has been reduced from 207 to an estimated current 125 pounds. President Reagan raised eyebrows when he stated before the German Bundestag that the Soviets were "on the brink of famine" (*The New York Times*, June 10, 1982). Credibility, however, was added to this statement by the assessment of John Burns in *The New York Times* (June 27, 1982) that whereas in 1970 Soviet food imports amounted to 4 million metric tons of grain, in 1981 they escalated to 43 million metric tons.

The Soviet Union, of course, has been undergoing shocking changes in its weather. The summer of 1981 was the hottest in the western Soviet Union in at least a century. It complains that it's now experiencing drought where it once had sufficient moisture, while in other areas there is unpredictable and uncontrollable flooding which throws off crop planning. This, as Val Sears points out, is not unique to the Soviet Union. "There is something awesome happening to the weather. Those rolling cold snaps, one behind the other" have brought on what serious meteorologists are calling "Little Ice Age II." The National Academy of Science in the United States calls it a "serious worldwide cooling" (*Toronto Star*, Jan. 18, 1982), with "profound social and economic implications." What I found unnerving was that Toronto's average temperature for 1975 was 50 degrees; for 1981, 47 degrees! "If the average annual temperature in Western Canada dropped by one degree Celsius" notes the *Toronto Globe and Mail* (Mar. 15, 1982), "it would no longer be possible to grow wheat." By the same token, insists *The Globe*, if it were to happen in India, they would have a major drought every four years; if in China, a major famine would occur every five years.

During the winter of 1982, cold records were registered in a great number of North American states and provinces. For example: Chicago -29ºF., Atlanta -5º. In January 1982, the U.S. heat bill was up 1.4 billion dollars over January '81. It was so cold in Scotland that the sea froze. In Florida, *Newsweek* (Jan. 24, 1982) noted that, for the second year running, 30 percent of the citrus crop was destroyed. The year previous, the temperature in the Yukon was warmer on January 15 than in Tampa, Florida.

Might not this just be a temporary thing? Dr. Richard Willson of the Jet Propulsion Laboratory in Pasadena, a Nobel Prize winner, calculates that it is not. He documents his findings from the myriad of new sophisticated studies of the sun's behavior, affirming that currently there is a "drop in the sun's energy of one-tenth of one percent" each 18 months. At this rate, as Val Sears points out, the reduction in output of solar energy in 150 years "would freeze the earth;" and it "can be predicted that the sun will disappear in 960 centuries"—not the ten billion years physicists formerly had projected (*Toronto Star*, May 5, 1982).

The St. Paul Dispatch quotes the "CIA's World Weather Forecasts: Pictures of Major Disasters" and editorializes, "No nation anywhere in the world, especially Russia, China, India, and the United States, can afford to take lightly the ominous" warnings of this "century weather forecast covering the entire planet." It is truly a "chilling and scholarly meteorological study, pointing to such radical changes in the climate as to cause its authors to warn" all and sundry that "the consequences in political and economic upheaval and international violence will be 'almost beyond human comprehension.' "

Following the news the last two or three years, we can all recollect the sweltering heat and drought wave over Texas and the lower Midwest in 1980 with the damage running into the billions. England six years ago experienced its severest drought in modern times. In East Africa, a United Nations' official reported from Nairobi that from the Red Sea to South Africa's Natal province is "a disaster area. No matter what we do, millions will die." Gary Collins has said in *Hour Magazine* that this has penetrated Ethiopia and Somalia, where the deaths from starvation may yet run to several million. Dr. Stan Mooneyham in his "World Vision" appeal for help said recently on national television that "five of Ethiopia's 30 million are starving to death." *Action News*, in one of those cheerless assessments, documents how in Mali, 2 million; in Niger, a million; in Chad, a million; in the Sudan, 2 million; in Ethiopia, 5 million; in Somalia, 2 million; in Kenya, 2 million; in Tanzania, 2 million; in Zambia, a half million; in Botswana, 200,000; in Gambia 100,000; in Djibouti, 100,000; in Mauritania, 200,000; and in Senegal, 250,000—are currently starving to death. The new CBC-TV news program, "The Journal," highlighted in sickening detail some of these calamitous facts in its "Uganda, Land of Famine."

Where the population explosion is sharpest, of course, is in the Third World, where the hunger is most acute. With the human family adding 90 million per year, being projected to reach a total of 6.35 billion by the end of the next decade, according to the Global 2000 Report to the President of the United States, 90 percent of this increase will take place in the poorest countries of Asia, Africa, and Latin America. China's population rose to one billion, one million people in May, 1982. In seven of Europe's countries, there are only five births per thousand people annually—similar to North America—whereas India's rate is 34, and Ethiopia's 48. American and Canadian mothers currently have—on average—just over two children; in Kenya, it is 8.1; throughout black Africa, the average is six. One of the pathetic outcomes, of course is, as Major Eva Den Hartog orates after returning from her Third World trek, "Fifty million children alone, die annually in the world from starvation."

I sat at the same table with the Tanzanian Ambassador to the U.N. at the Presidential Prayer Breakfast in Washington on February 4, 1982. He feels that it could be in a matter of two or three months that "Tanzania's 20 million poeple face famine . . . unless the country gets immediate food aid." The U.N. Food and Agriculture Organization reports critical food shortages in 29 countries, 22 of these in Africa, and it's getting worse. In 1962, Africans produced 98 percent of their own food, and today that's down to 90 percent.

"It's when you hear of tragedies like this that you feel badly that according to a current Gallup polling of Canadians, "only half as many of our people offer grace before their meals, as did so in 1962" (down from 52 percent to 26 percent). This in itself is a fulfillment of St. Paul's forecast that "in the last days perilous times shall come. For men shall be . . . unthankful" (2 Timothy 3:1,1).

It is a tragic irony, as *Time* notes (Jan. 4, 1982), that "The Soviet Union's largesse seems inexhausible in the form of the wherewithal for armed struggle. It has remained almost the exclusive purveyor of violent goods and services to customers on the left." Yet its record in granting foreign aid for peaceful purposes is abysmal. Africans are getting the message. Leaders in Mozambique and Zimbabwe are saying to the Russians, "We can't eat guns." And to the Americans, "When you're always at war, you cannot shoot grain, or fight tanks with tractors. You can't repel cross-border raiding parties with Peace Corp volunteers."

The West itself, of course, can neither afford, nor does it have the will, to feed the world's hungry with the altruism that it once had. M.I.T. economist Lester Thurow marshalls facts on how fragile the financial infrastructure of the West is currently: "The world economy is in a very dangerous situation—walking along the edge of a cliff" with "the U.S. economy [having] endured zero growth for three years." Much more of the same will "court disaster." *The New York Times* (Feb. 20, 1980) laments that the percentage of those below the poverty line in the U.S. in the year past has gone up from 11.6 percent to 13 percent. Bill Moyers gave a very convincing CBS-TV special in April 1982 on the new "Proverty in America." In Canada, a *Globe and Mail* headliner cries, "Economic woes worst since '47 . . . when detailed records were first kept" (Apr. 6, 1982).

This brings us to the glaring matter of rearmament in a hungry world. As Lance Taylor points out in *The New York Times* (Dec. 22, 1981), with away and by far the largest famine toll in the world, India develops and manufactures nuclear weapons (initially from a Canadian Candu nublear reactor, which was negotiated on the basis of its being strictly for the production of electricity). And in addition, they're into a multi-billion dollar annual armaments build-up. Ethiopia is another of these desperately poor countries which are into the billion or multi-billion dollar annual armaments build-up. It "devotes 30 percent of its gross national product to weapons." But do they just stockpile them? Adds *The Times*, since Vietnam, "The list in the third world was long: countries in Indo-China, the Indian Subcontinent, Southwest Asia, the Horn of Africa,

Southern Africa, West Africa and Central America all fought full-scale wars."

It was President Eisenhower (who had seen more of war than any of his predecessors) who rightly said, "Every gun that is built, every warship launched, is a theft from those who hunger and are not fed." As United Church of Canada clergyman John Guy states, "It's pathetic that 97.9 percent of the people [of the world] want all arms banned, but are forced instead to a posture of 'sitting and waiting for the final bang.' " It is! It's terribly pathetic. Our world seems to be obsessed with war. Armaments have jumped during the eighties from an annual 350 billion to 775 billion, and by 1984, to a trillion a year. Yes, it is a fact that those 775 billion dollars would abundantly feed, and adequately clothe and house the world's famishing family of a billion. Especially when it's known that the people of Bangladesh have an annual per capita income of $94—approximately what a middle-class North American makes in one workday. So, should the West unilaterally disarm? And the Soviets take the world for communism?

I'm sure most Canadians felt the vibrations from Prime Minister Trudeau's appeal in our House of Commons on behalf of the world's peoples living in stark poverty, as he remonstrated, "The prospect of a new arms race at a time when billions of people are dying of hunger, is a veritable scandal. If we were to set aside for peaceful uses, just two-weeks worth of global military spending it could be used to turn life around for tens of millions of people." With his analytical mind, the Prime Minister was able to elaborate on this highly commendable but hypothetical aspiration. The question is: "Who is going to bell the cat?" And as Mr. Trudeau himself insists—the West must indeed match the Soviets "gun-for-gun."

One thing is sure—a hungry man is going to fight for food. When Australian Prime Minister Malcolm Fraser hosted world leaders in the North-South dialogue late in 1981, a part of the Melbourne Declaration, as it has come to be known, alluded to "the protracted assault on human dignity; and the deprivation from which many millions in developing countries suffer must inevitably lead to political turmoil." Such turmoil, Fraser added, would be used "to extend the realm of dictatorship in the world." The American President was similarly advised in "Global 2000 Report" that there is simply no arguing that the current "shrinking resources and soaring populations will see a world in which the widening gap between rich and poor nations will ineluctably "lead to economic disasters and open conflict." The well-known former World Bank President McNamara agrees, "Many of the poorest countries of the world are . . . doomed to economic and political chaos in the decade ahead."

And, of course, evangelicals are to go all out to do their utmost to feed, medicate, house, and clothe the poor of the world. Compassion, World Vision, World Concern, World Relief, Food for the Hungry, MAP International and Samaritan's Purse are some of the organizations who are doing this—but not any of them with the announced intent of ushering in a social millennium. It is incumbent upon every prophet of God to exhort Christians—who are too fat, rich and uncaring, for the most part—to be much more sacrificing, giving and compassionate. Major Eva Den Hartog is right, in her crusades across North America and Western Europe, to exhort us to shed the fat of overindulgence. Sixty percent of us are overweight, she states. Actually, Americans weigh a billion pounds too much, and Canadians a hundred-million. Here in North America, we spend an annual 15 billion dollars on diet formulas and 22 billion on cosmetics. Those expenditures alone would be the difference between life and death to those who will starve to death, worldwide, this year.

But when all is said and done—and we're to do all we can do—Jesus said plainly that there would be ever-worsening famines in divers places. Of course, much of the world is living sumptuously. And as Robert McNamara says, the rich are getting richer and the poor, poorer. Currently the number of millionaires in North America is rising ten percent per year. But it's a clear sign of the end of the age, when there are famines in divers places.

When people are Christless previous to our Lord's return, Jesus said their hearts would collapse for fear of those things coming to pass on the earth. *Time* (Nov. 2, 1981) notes that as holocaust threatens through the horror of impending nuclear war, or pandemic "disease or radiation or some vague Apocalypse Now that everyone fears but cannot give a face to, 'myriads,' prepare for anarchy by retreating to the hills with automatic weapons, radiation detectors and the 'Royal Canadian Air Force Exercise Plans for Physical Fitness'; a few have taken to storing freeze-dried survival foods in their garages for a well-fed Armageddon."

The cleanest prophetic picture of what the world faces biologically in any secular writings that I have read recently appeared in "Canada's National Newspaper": *The Globe and Mail* (Mar. 15, 1982). It featured a near full-page article under the headliner, "Nuclear Holocaust" by Dr. Donald G. Bates, Professor of the History of Medicine and Chairman of the Department of Humanities and Social Studies in Medicine, McGill University. He does not deal with the nuclear holocaust itself, but with what would follow in its wake. He begins by quoting Nikita Khrushchev's comment that "The survivors will envy the dead." Bates assumes that the nuclear exchange of the future by the U.S.S.R. and the U.S.A. may annihilate all North Americans—or if a restricted one, it may leave a residue of survivors. Of these, "80 percent to practically everybody" will be seriously affected by "the catastrophe . . . The greatest damage of a nuclear war is not just death and material destruction . . . but the creation of chaos. The chaos would be natural as well as social. The highest expression of organization in nature is the living cell. Its molecules are arranged with such exquisite precision that it can perform unbelievable chemical feats, including self-repair and handing on its know-how to daughter cells. But bombing this delicate machinery with radiation . . . creates disorder . . . for practically everybody . . . Exposed adults would suffer damage to their genes that is passed on to later offspring." It would produce "premature aging . . . deaths from leukemia" would be legion. "Radiation also disrupts the body's defenses against infection. If this were combined with social disintegration, the result would be devastating epidemics . . . plague." Though Bates makes no allusion to the Bible whatsoever, you'd think he was writing a modern footnote to the Revelation of Jesus Christ, or to Luke 21, where our Lord assured that when superpower rises up against superpower there'll be "plagues" (vs. 11, N.E.B.)—also translated "epidemics" (L.B.).

Bates goes on, "Whatever happened, one thing is certain: bacteria, viruses and insects are highly resistant to radiation. In an all-out nuclear war, a heavy dose of this primitive energy could tilt the favorable balance of nature from humans to bugs. If the meek don't inherit the earth, the cockroaches will." In Revelation 9, we read that in the wake of what I believe to be the first holocaustic nuclear exchange between the Soviets and the West "there came . . . locusts upon the earth" (vs.3).

Bates insists that in "the natural order . . . current scenarios of a nuclear war postulate the release of . . . dust thrown up by these outsized explosions which would remain in the stratosphere for long periods . . . dense enough to reduce the sun's light." St. Peter assured, "before that great and notable day of the Lord's coming" the earth will be struck with" a fire and vapour of smoke: the sun shall be turned into darkness" (Acts 2:19, 20: see also Matthew 24:29). Bates says that the reduction in "the sun's light will tragically affect surface temperatures and all terrestrial life. And significant cooling of the earth's surface from such a dust blanket would be catastrophic."

Bates also explains, "Despite the virtuosity of the twentieth century, it is really the domestication of nature by social order that is fundamental. Destroy that order, and technology and know-how will not save us." He elaborates, "Human rights and democratic freedoms . . . would be the first social institutions

to go . . . With no police, probably no military at home, governments at all levels decimated, who will preserve law and order?
Will the legitimacy of a government that is not perceived to
have done everything possible to prevent nuclear war go
unchallenged after such a disaster? . . . Martial law will be
immediately declared and ruthlessly enforced. If not, society
will dissolve into marching bands of desperate people. It will
be a choice between Orwell's *1984* and the Dark Ages." Bates
asks, "And what of economic ruin? The essential ingredients
of our affluence—social order, capital investment in resource
and manufacturing industries, and a trained and educated labor
force—would be far more devastated in a few hours than Europe
was in the five years of the Second World War."

This is not the place to elaborate further on what will happen biologically during the Great Tribulation. It is amazing how
close Bates comes to reflecting what the Bible prophesies conditions will be like. This is the place to plead that the rational
thing to do is to turn to Christ, Who warned us not to let our
hearts be troubled in the face of such present or impending
catastrophe. In fact, the ancient prophet Amos explained that
when man's final "days come, saith the Lord God, that I will
send a famine in the land, not a famine of bread, nor a thirst
for water, but of hearing the words of the Lord" (Amos 8:11).

Everywhere I go, in a hundred countries of the world, I encounter this spiritual hunger. During the second quarter of
1982, it was my privilege to hold crusades in New England,
where as many as 235 a night would come forward to decide
for Christ. One night in May, in Maine, among those who responded was a beautiful blond lady. Berrie had been brought
up in a fashionable home in New York. She was a professional
woman, and out of college she married her high school
sweetheart, but he proved untrue. Divorced, she tried a second
marriage to an Arab who had oil money. Two-and-a-half years
later, that marriage too was on the rocks, and up in Maine she
was in a hospital working with Dr. Yeow Tan, who had earned
her M.D. in London, during which time she had received Christ.

Dr. Tan had come from Southeast Asia where her experience with non-Christian religions had left her hungering and thirsting for the bread and water of life that she found now in Christ. When Berrie shared her problems with Dr. Tan, the latter knew where to bring her—to our Crusade where Christ was being presented as the Savior and satisfier of longing souls. As Berrie made her decision for Jesus, she went away with that same joy and assurance that she had seen and desired in Dr. Tan's life. She had found the Christ!

Chapter Seven

"ALWAYS LEARNING AND YET NEVER ABLE TO GRASP THE TRUTH"

What will be the preoccupation of the minds and moods of the masses, as man rounds the bend into the last lap leading to Armageddon? Jesus left no doubt: There will be signs in the human psyche, like terminal "dismay . . . and bewilderment" (Luke 21:25, Phillips). St Paul wrote similarly to Timothy that he "must realize that, in the last days, the times" will be characterized philosophically by people with "morbid cravings—who are always learning and yet never able to grasp the truth. These men are as much enemies to the truth as Jannes and Jambres were to Moses. Their minds are distorted, and they are traitors to the faith." Eventually "their folly will become as obvious to everybody as did that of Moses' opponents" (2 Timothy 3:1, 6-9, Phillips). So Paul counseled, "See to it that no one makes a prey of you by philosophy and empty deceit, according to human tradition, according to the elemental spirits of the universe, and not according to Christ" (Colossians 2:8, R.S.V.).

Thinking people everywhere have never in human history admitted so unanimously that ours is a day in which people are "always learning and yet never able to grasp the truth." Moans Mary McGrory, in the wake of the Ground Zero and Nuclear Freeze campaigns, "Have you ever seen so many thinkers

openly agonizing over 'the end of the world' on street corners?"
One of the earlier intellectual gurus whose castles had come
crashing to the ground, razed by the growth of a post-World
War II nuclear terror which completely demolished his own
nineteeth century roseate idealism, was George Bernard Shaw.
Near the end, he openly opined that the philosophy and "the
science to which I pinned my faith is bankrupt ... Its counsels,
which should have established the millennium, led directly to
the suicide of Europe . . . In their name, I helped to destroy
the faith of millions of worshipers in the temples of a thousand
creeds. And now they look at me and witness the great tragedy
of an atheist who has lost his faith." Some of his
contemporaries—such as H. G. Wells, Bertrand Russell, the
Huxleys, and his earlier mentor Charles Darwin—all sighed
similar lamentations. Their successors are such neo-intellectuals
as Oxford's Professor Michael Howard, who says the whole
climate of the thinking world today is obsessed with the Ares
syndrome, with "the possibility that, in a lethal mixture of
hubris and despair we might one day feel ourselves compelled
to initiate a nuclear war. Such a war might or might not achieve
its object, but I doubt whether the survivors on either side
would very greatly care" (*L.A. Times*, Sept. 28, 1981).

Prime Minister Trudeau alludes to the countless Canadians
currently who simply retreat into "a corner where we can hide
our faces from the future." This funereal "sense of disaster, of
gloom" seems to be all "around in 1982," remarks our Ontario
Premier William Davis. Former Prime Minister Joe Clark
apologizes to our immigrants that everywhere presently, we're
seeing "people who came to Canada (who) thought of it as a
country of hope. Now Canada is becoming a country of despair."
"The tragedy of Canada," notes our Governor General Ed
Schreyer, is our unmitigating "pessimism and . . . undisguised
sadness." American best-seller Alvin Toffler, in commenting
on his *Third Wave*, warns that as a world "we've hit a
dangerous level of pessimism"—a capitulation to the paralysis
that "there is no way out." As Archbishop Runcie stated in his

wedding sermon to Prince Charles and Princess Diana, "Much of the world is in the grip of hopelessness. Many people seem to have surrendered to fatalism about the so-called inevitabilities of life: cruelty, injustice, poverty, bigotry and war." Perhaps our most-known Canadian merchant is John Craig Eaton. In addressing the world's prominent newspapermen, he wondered out loud whether there is no other news than the current diet we get of "economic gloom, VIP scandal, rapes, fires, murders, mugging, crime and suicide." Peter Truman, anchor newsman for the Global TV Network, admits that crime and impending war are the core of today's hard news. And he quotes a polling that 12 percent more Canadians are deeply dissatisfied with life this year than last. A Gallup poll of people in 29 countries confirms that in 1982 the vast majority are looking both in the political and economic arenas to a bleak rather than a bright future. In Canada, pessimism about our economic prospects outweighs optimism by more than ten to one. Sums up Leonard Shurm in *The Toronto Star*, "people's basic confidence . . . and expectations show both at all-time lows . . . The best thing that can be said for 1981 is that it could have been worse. And the worst thing that can be said about 1982 is that it may well be."

If the public is so pessimistic about what the future holds, how about the philosophic intellectuals? Entering the 1980's, Jean-Paul Sartre died—his doctors said—because "He didn't want to live any longer!" As the most-read philosopher in the world, Sartre, a French existentialist, wrote in his novels, such as *Nausea*, his plays, such as *No Exit*, and his tracts, such as "Being and Nothingness," that God is dead, and so is man. In reality, "there is no escape from the present dilemma." This philosophic posture being fashionably espoused by so many deans of academies and perpetrated upon our public has much more to do with impending Armageddon than we might ostensibly realize. David Manvel writes to the editor of *Time* in mid-1982 that: "Anthony Burgess' essay (on "The Freedom We

Have Lost") is easily the most articulate, lucid and compelling estimate of the failing art of democracy yet published in the news media. But it is a blinkened point of view. Mr. Burgess laments the passage of a sense of individual responsibility for perpetuating integrity, without considering its source. When this country was being settled, and later when it was founded, nearly everyone in it believed in God . . . But once the psychologists and educators were able to convince enough people that God was passe' our democracy became a shell. Long after the life had withered, the shell survived. But now it has begun to crumble, and brilliant agnostic writers like Mr. Burgess are wondering why."

Someone who seems to see the handwriting on the wall, and who warns us often that with democracy dying we are being tragically conditioned for a coming world dictator, is Christopher Lasch. In his work, *Narcissism in an Age of Diminishing Expectations*, he sees current man as "plagued by anxiety, depression, vague discontents, a sense of inner emptiness," capable of achieving "neither individual self-aggrandizement nor spiritual transcendence." The newest darling of the intellectuals among the Nobel Prize winners for literature is the Jewish writer, Saul Bellow, who has just published his most sombre novel, *The Dean's December*. It is the first of Bellow's literary works to almost completely bypass humor. As *Time* (Jan. 28, 1982) notes, Bellow reckons that the vast majority of current writers hold "the view that existence is meaningless." It's based on "nihilism" and "the death of God, and descending to the last detail of one's wretched biology." Bellow depicts his "Dean" as typical of "hopeless man with his back to the decayed city," with "emptiness behind him and in front of him. He knows there will be no moral revolution, no rebirth of the spirit."

Psychiatrist Viktor Frankl, who popularized the phrase "meaningless existence," sees even the inveterate sex obsession of our times as modern man trying to fill up the vacuum, which seems more and more to be a bottomless pit. Psychiatrist

Bruno Bettelheim in his best-seller *Survival and Other Essays*, deplores our fun-oriented Miracleland, our Disney World-dominated plastic "existence", as a cop-out; as a desperate expression of endeavoring to deny our mortality. Margaret Atwood, in her *Bodily Harm*, laments that ours is a deeply disappointing and disintegrating world, tearing apart at the seams because the threads have rotted.

Reflective of classical thought in the world of Islam is U.S. Naipaul, who—critic Robert Fulford reckons—is one of the diminishing number of engaging intellectuals of our time. Coming from the East to the West, he is disillusioned, deeply disillusioned! For he discovers in the U.S.A., as in the U.S.S.R., in the U.K. as in the U.A.R.—from Arabia to America—"Wherever he goes in the world, he finds chaos and brutality." A European whose brilliant works have now penetrated the North American mind is the Swiss writer Fritz Zorn. At 32 years of age, in his just-published best-seller, *Mars*, he writes as much a biography of all men as an autobiography on himself. "My parents' neuroses were responsible for producing my lifelong despair; my despair is responsible for my being ill with cancer; and my cancer will be the cause of my death." Such, sums up *Time*, is Zorn's angst as he rides the rapids in a capsizing canoe, in a river red with human casualties. Examining recent Far Eastern literature, we find that perhaps the most dazzling and representative novel to come out of Japan in the eighties is entitled *Somewhat Crystal*, by Yasuo Tamaka. It demonstrates the canyon of emptiness amidst the "hollow standards that have been mindlessly taken up by a vapid generation of Japanese" (A.P., Nov. 12, 1981).

Perhaps the most practical handbook on current American philosophic moods is Daniel Yankelovich's *New Rules: Searching for Self-Fulfillment in a World Turned Upside Down.* Yankelovich reckons that in the late 1960's and through most of the 1970's some fundamental and widely shared cultural views changed in the United States. With the economy booming many Americans were liberated from old anxieties about

material success. The belief that hard work, self-denial, and
moral rectitude were their own rewards gave way to the notion,
held fervently and misguidedly by some, that the "self" and
the realization of its full "potential" were all-important pursuits.
This phenomenon was characterized by Tom Wolfe as the "me"
decade. But alas! "The people came to believe they could have
it all—wealth without work, sexual freedom without marital
problems, self-absorption without loss of community. Then
came the shortages and the new austerity, and suddenly there
was the effect on the corporate ego that a spoiled child experiences the first time he or she is critically denied." Frankly,
one wonders if with all this dumping of pessmism on the public
how much people will really want to engage further in the good
fight to avoid Armageddon! Could the masses eventually, if inadvertently, will Armageddon? Might man, left to himself, as
a hostage joins his captor, perhaps join the march to
Armageddon?

Jesus said clearly that with the mounting pressure of the end
times, we'd see "men's hearts failing them for fear." Why?
Because they'd be clever enough to "realize what is threatening the world, for the very powers of [the heavens] will be
shaken" (Luke 21:26, Phillips). It used to be that the less people knew, the more likely they were to be brooders on, and
brokers of, gloom and doom. Today it's the more they know!
For example, consider the woman who wrote to Ann Landers
about how to handle her highly intellectual husband, who is
chronically worried about neclear war and, overall, "extremely
pessimistic about the future." It is well known that heart
disease is North America's number one killer and costs us 22
billion dollars annually to try—often in vain—to medicate.
Stress, often caused by fear of the future, costs us 133 billion
dollars annually. Currently 52% of North Americans die from
heart failure, and 66% of this number are adult men.

There's a new phrase around which is relevant: "Burn-out!"
Gail Smith groans, "There's enough pressure in a travel agent's
job these days to pump up a truck tire." We're told that 25%

of teachers in Britain, Sweden, and North America suffer "battle fatigue" from stress in their jobs. In sports, a head coach of one of our slumping Toronto professional teams, when summoned before a press conference of reporters, snaps: "I wish you guys had some answers instead of questions."

Professional athletes in all sports are increasingly breaking down under the pressure. A case in point is the contention of a national magazine that 67% of the National Basketball Association players occasionally or regularly take illegal drugs to "get up" for a game, or "get down" afterwards. *Sports Illustrated* (June, 1982) quotes a player source that as many as half of the National Football League players use or have used cocaine. The stress is just too great. Former Toronto Mapleleaf Jim McKenney was supposed to be a Bobby Orr in the National Hockey League. But he wasn't! He told Mike Anscon on Global Network TV why he beat a retreat to Switzerland, "My life was a shambles. I'd go to the juice . . . had a lotta trouble with the bottle . . . I couldn't deal with myself, let alone my family. You're in a void." *The Los Angeles Times* (Jan. 10, 1982) carried a comprehensive critique on the traumatic tumble most superstars take when they're shipped from the gladiatorial mumbo-jumbo and hurly-burly of the arena and the attendant magical "highs" associated with being idolized to the place at which their playing days suddenly end. They must decompress and adjust from being the object of emperor worship to being a peon. Once a "Who's Who", the athlete is now a "Who's He?", and must awake daily to grey dawns and the rueful realization that the glory days are past. Too often it's alcoholism, drugs, manicdepression, divorce, jail, even suicide. Bill Bradley, Princeton basketball superstar and NBA'er, who came to Oxford as a Rhodes scholar while I was there, writes in his *Life On the Run*, "The pro athlete must eventually live all his days never able to recapture the feeling of those few years of intensified youth." Valery Kharlamov, the Russian hockey rocket, was quite possibly the most glamorous rightwinger ever to lace on skates. To see him streak from center ice to the slot, and fire that shot like a pistol bullet into the top corner of the net had to be a hockey high for any purist fan! When in 1981 he was denied the thrill of traveling to North America to play in the Canada Cup, he simply drove his car into a truck at high speed, in what only the most naive deny to have been a deliberate suicide. In a full page article on Muhammed Ali *The Washington Post* concludes in 1982 that "The Greatest" is now just another dispirited has-been who's "lost."

The philosophic and psychic hypochondria on the entertainment center stage circuit of the 1980's is epidemic. A headliner confides: "Star of Happy Days! Unhappy!" Rakish Jill Robinson tattles on TV of Jane Fonda, currently perhaps Hollywood's most celebrated and glamorized film star. Throughout much of 1982 *Jane Fonda's Workout Book* topped bestseller lists. Fonda is a godling. To some who know her personally, she seems to be always looking, longing, never satisfied, never fulfilled. She seems to have absolutely everything, yet to feel totally deprived and denied. The world sees her as a golden calf. But beneath the idolmania is a melancholic moper, a piqued person, full of angst and anxiety.

Margot Kidder's new film is entitled *Heartache*, reminding one of Elvis Presley's song, "Heartbreak Hotel," where too many millions hole up. Mendelson Joe writes of Elvis that he was one of those blackdog souls, "just another mortal who got lost on his journey", like fellow celebrants Mick Jagger and Keith Richards, whom *Newsweek* labels "the lost boys" (July 20, 1981). Yoko Lennon recalls John on the anniversary of his being shot: he had become "a recluse . . . he was depressed"— not for a day or two, but for years! Yes, he was fantasizing of himself when he sang, "I'll give you everything I've got for a little peace of mind."

For too many in the '80's, the peace won't come. Trent Lehman, the 20-year-old actor who had become famous as Butch Everett in "Nanny and the Professor," strings himself up with his own belt. And he was hardly cold in his grave before 33-year-old John Belushi of Saturday Night Live took the pipe with an overdose of combined cocaine and heroin. And there seemed so little time for the public to pause before Super-Soap star Brenda Benet of *Days of Our Lives* cried that marriage to the Incredible Hulk was not enough. So at 35, she shut the bathroom door and blasted a bullet through her head.

Has all this an effect on our young? The chairman of Suicide Anonymous, speaking on national television, assesses that the suicide rate among 8- to 14-year-olds in the United States in the '80's has already quadrupled. Has this trend a link to impending war? It has! *The Chicago Tribune* (June 21, 1982) publishes a poll of teenagers which revealed: "65 per cent of the kids thought a nuclear war would happen in the next 10 years and that they could not survive it."

Linda Perger of the Distress Center in Toronto dirges that in 1982 call-ins from teenagers on the brink have jumped 30% this year over last. *The Vancouver Province* (Oct. 5, 1981) reports that suicide among adolescents has rocketed up 317% in a decade. Canadian statistics show that over the last 20 years teenage suicides have multiplied tenfold. Adrian Waller, in pointing up this shocker, fingers the musicians. Not only have the Janis Joplins, the Jimi Hendrixes and the Sid Viciouses committed suicide, but there is even a pop group calling themselves "The Grateful Dead." Elton John sings, "I Think I'm Gonna Kill Myself," Elyse Wineberg whines "I'm Mortuary-Bound" and Tin Lizzy, the British rock group, belt out: "Suicide." Self-esteem is reduced to zero. Don Summers, the Britisher, saw a youth with hand-stitched lettering on his back which screamed "No Future." So they just put an end to it all by taking the pipe. It's Armageddon: one at a time, in which the warmonger and victim is the same person. Human annihilation is self destruction multiplied by four and a half billion. Thank God Armageddon won't go that far!

Of the thousand a day who commit suicide worldwide, all too many are those from society's top echelons. Pushed into a global village where there's more and more neighborhood, and less and less brotherhood, and being shoved toward nuclear war, too many simply ask: what's the use? In November 1981, 29-year-old Princess Maria de Bourbon, cousin of King Juan Carlos, did herself in with an overdose of heroin. Ravishingly beautiful but bugged with bewilderment, she just couldn't cope with the fatuous inanimities in her circle of debutantes. In *Princess Margaret, A Life Unfulfilled*, Nigel Demspter wrote that the royal lady is frequently suicidal. On the occasion of one of her romantic breakups, Dempster sirens, "The Fleet Street grapevine had it that the Princess had taken an overdose."

Margarret Trudeau did not leave her story to be told by a biographer. She confides in her own autobiography, *Consequences*, "Pierre often used to say to me: 'Margaret, you must face the consequences of your actions. Your scatty behavior is going to come back at you. You must take heed of what you do' . . . no one could have made me feel worse than I already did: a traitor to Pierre, a slut in the eyes of the world. I knew then that I had reached my lowest point and that there was no going back . . . I felt lost. However hard I looked for them, I couldn't find any roots. Alone with myself late at night or first thing in the morning, I cried. All my guilt and recrimination at my excessive life-style would surface . . . cocaine . . . to get me up, valium to bring me down again. Only valium did more than bring me down. It made me low and depressed—far lower and more depressed than I had been . . . My escapades, my drug-taking, were no more than outbursts of despair at how profoundly I failed, wretched attempts to kick back at what I could not handle . . . I'm sick of Margaret Trudeau's traumas. More than anything in the world, I want to get away from myself." Margaret Trudeau is a pathetic figure, a morose example of flower power gone sour. Is Margaret Trudeau's hedonism relevant to the bursting dyke that will unleash Armageddon? Yes! When the closest relatives of world leaders live such blue devil lives, their example depreciates the dignity and worth of human life.

Making an observation relevant to our discussion, Wisconsin Sociology Professor Ray Short testified in the spring of 1982 before a U.S. Senate Committee that the incalculable escalation in current teenage permissive sex can be put down to their—often unconscious—expectation "of nuclear war." Notes *The New York Times* (April 13, 1982), with divorces now soaring to half as many as there are marriages, "Over a million additional children have had their homes disrupted by divorce each year since 1972 . . . one-third of the nation's children will go through this experience before they reach 18." One only needs to study the sexual breakdown in the North of Ireland over the last two decades to realize how closely and tragically a constant war consciousness and moral breakdown are intertwined. Perhaps Margaret Thatcher summed it up best in the *Sunday Times of London*, "We are reaping what was sown in the sixties: The fashionable theories and permissive claptrap! . . . Our children are fed on a daily diet of violence unparalleled in our history. That diet can numb the sense of shock and render acceptable those things which we should reject." Take the matter of abortion, which is war to the death on the unborn. In 1982, 40 million unborn babies are murdered in the womb. It's all a philosophic softener for the barking dogs of war. It means that our hopes have to be from a vertical dimension. The horizontal hails holocaust!

Dr. Carl Sagan, writer of the best-seller, *Cosmos*, and star of the TV series "Cosmos Galactica" noted as Christmas was approaching, "It's hardly out of the question that we might destroy ourselves tomorrow." Taking us via TV on another of those astronomical interstellar tours of the stars, Sagan mused, "Today we are searching for a message from the stars. As yet, we don't have one! Is there a cosmic Rosetta Stone? Can science bring us a message? Someday a message from distant space may arrive on our earth. The receipt of a message from a civilization in outer space would be one of the most significant events in human history."

Actually we do have that Rosetta Stone! It's the Bible, a Message indeed from outer space—from heaven! And more than a Message, we have had the Messenger—the Messiah from heaven come to earth—Jesus Christ the Son of God! He came to bring us life and love and hope. As Bishop Handley Moule used to say, in almost every case where the word "hope" appears in the New Testament, there is a reference, explicit or implicit, to the Lord's Return.

Paul in Titus 2:13 refers to it as "blessed hope"; Peter in his first epistle (1:3) as "a lively hope"; John as a "purifying hope" (1 John 3:3); and the Hebraist (in Hebrews 6:19), "This hope we hold" (Phillips). Yes, and it's a hope that holds up! As Professor Tasker writes in *The New Bible Dictionary*, "Hope is not a kite at the mercy of the changing winds, but 'an anchor of the soul, both sure and steadfast,' penetrating deep into the invisible and eternal world."

So in a world of philosophic despair, turn to Christ, "in hope of eternal life, which God, that cannot lie, promised before the world began" (Titus 1:2). I read in a newspaper column recently about how to beat depression—"visit a florist and breathe inward." But that's like taking aspirin for cancer. Christ treats causes, not symptoms.

Many of our Billy Graham Team are residents of the Carolinas where Mark Goodger lives. He makes it a weekly practice to hand out tracts from door to door. One day he stopped at a house and rang the bell. Because he heard movement inside, he knew someone was there; so he felt an inner urge to keep ringing, though it almost seemed futile. Eventually a man, rather upset, appeared, took the tract and quickly closed the door. But Mark was a man of God, and he knew the power of the Word of God. A week later he felt constrained to return to that house. He rang the bell. The man answered almost immediately. Cheerfully inviting him in, he asked him to follow him to the attic. There he saw a sturdy rope dangling from the rafters with a box below it. The man said, "Friend, when you rang my doorbell last week my head was in that noose! I was ready to jump! But you were so persistent that I decided to go down and see who it was. After receiving your tract, I read it because its title interested me. And through it God spoke to me. Instead of jumping off that box, I knelt beside it and gave my heart to the Lord."

If you're in an intellectual state of "always learning and yet never able to grasp the truth," I urge you right now to trust the Jesus Christ, Who, immediately after assuring us that He would come again to take believers to mansions of glory declares, "I AM the truth . . . come to the Father . . . by Me" (John 14:6).

Chapter Eight

"ANTICHRIST SHALL COME"

Oxford scholar Alex de Jonge in his newly published *The Life and Times of Grigori Rasputin* characterizes the pre-Revolution Russia of 70 years ago: the whole country seemed possessed by demons and redeemers. And who could tell the difference? Queried by Peter and Andrew, James and John, about what was on the agenda to precede Armageddon, it's important that the very first sign Jesus pointed to was, "Take heed that no man deceive you. For many shall come in my name, saying, I am Christ; and shall deceive many" (Matthew 24:4,5). He gave this sign previous to His allusion to "wars and rumors of wars," and all the other signs Jesus identifies as following these two. I think it is significant that it was not until ten verses later that our Lord alluded initially to the Antichrist himself (vs. 15 "abomination of desolation"). But substantially in advance of the appearance of the actual Antichrist, who will precipitate Armageddon, will be this matter of many masquerading messiahs whom we cannot mistake recognizing because they will themselves claim to be christs. Everyone of these antichrists will harden hearts to Jesus Christ, and soften up the way for the revelation of the actual Antichrist.

Later in Matthew 24, Jesus prophesied clearly that when scavengering saviors and roving redeemers inflict themselves on the world scene, the craze will not be an ephemeral one. He made plain that during the Great Tribulation as civilization is dragged down to its lowest nadir ever, there'll be a worsening rash of christ-pretenders. As deceived masses, desperately grasping for a straw, gasp, "Lo, here is Christ, or there; believe it not. For there shall arise false Christs, and false prophets, and shall shew great signs and wonders; insomuch that, if it were possible, they shall deceive the very elect. Behold, I have told you before. Wherefore if they shall say unto you, Behold, he is in the desert, go not forth: behold, he is in . . . secret chambers; believe it not" (Matthew 24:24-26).

Among those who listened closely to our Lord was the Apostle John. In the Revelation of Jesus Christ he would later characterize in astonishing detail what the reign of the Antichrist would be like. But prior to that, he wrote three epistles, and in them he made clear that while we are to keep in mind definitely that the "Antichrist shall come," we will be able to detect when he's actually about to appear by his precursors. There will be "many antichrists; whereby we know that it is the last time" (1 John 2:18). Intertwined with these evil "antichrists" will be a "spirit of antichrist" (1 John 4:3); and "a deceiver and an antichrist" (2 John 7), which is a description of much which passes for religion in our world today.

The "spirit of antichrist" (1 John 4:3) is certainly ubiquitous in the 1980's. I think it's pretty obvious in the movies that people go to see in the cinema or watch on T.V., or even in the soap operas. *General Hospital* recently featured Elizabeth Taylor, inserted by ABC to "play the widow of a man who was thwarted in his attempt to take over the universe by the show's hero, Luke Spencer." This scenario is, of course, familiar to the movie-going fans of *Star Wars*, *Battle Star Galactica* and any number of other fantasy-feeding fictionalizers of space-dominating messiahs. The whole Western world today is featuring such films as *The Idolmaker*, *The Possessed*, and *The Windwalker* with the sub-description: "He walks the winds of eternity." The Antichrist is referred to frequently in both Daniel and Revelation as "The Beast" and certainly Hollywood is on to this with *The Raging Bull*, *The Elephant Man*, and yes, believe it or not, *The Beast* and *The Little Beast*. *Time* (January 11, 1982) ran a cover story recently on "Children of War," and it quoted from

William Golding's *Lord of the Flies*, a book which later was made into a movie, where the hero, a fictional messiah, says to the victims of war, "There isn't anyone to help you. Only me. And I'm the Beast." On network television in prime time in mid-1982, *The Phoenix* is featured starring Bennu, "being from another time who has been cast adrift in the 1980's and possesses astounding powers"—yet another humanly contrived messiah offering deliverance!

But, of course, every romance involves two. And the response of the mesmerized masses to these masquerading messiahs is quite incredible. I was driving into St. Petersburg, Florida, last year when I heard a pop singer crooning, "Come and get me, Mr. Jones." Is it any wonder that the Jim Jones' have such cakewalks? Laurie Anderson, in 1982, sings for 15 minutes non-stop her new hit, "O Superman," which tops the charts on both sides of the Atlantic. And so high is "Superman's" profile that the movie is on prime time T.V. across North America twice in 1982—it being the first non-sports program in some months to come in first for the week atop the Nielson ratings. And with the church lagging as a force for moral reform in Britain, Superman is placed on a huge poster exhorting like some super-savior, "With my amazing x-ray vision, I can see the harm cigarettes do inside people's bodies. That's why I don't smoke." Seventy thousand kids order the poster, or perhaps some are parents. The fact that the end is in this instance good does not justify the means. Christopher Reeve is currently acting for "Superman III" (*Time*, May 10, 1982), and asked how he copes with the armies of young people plaguing him for his autograph, he replies that he simply rushes away from them insisting that "I've got to save somebody." He's graduated from "hero" to "saviour."

It is my belief that these movies and T.V. series which feature christ figures from outer space definitely are conditioners, preparing the human psyche for an Antichrist who can solve the problems that have stumped man on his own. We've seen them come and go: the Purple Monster from Mars in *The*

Purple Monster Strikes; Mota the Martian in *The Flying Disc Man from Mars*, Klaatu in *The Day The Earth Stood Still*; *The Phantom from Space*; *Devil Girl from Mars*; Kreton in *Visit to a Small Planet*; *The Man Who Fell to Earth*; *Unearthly Stranger*; *I Married A Monster From Outer Space*; *Invasion of the Body Snatchers*; and the current biggie at the box offices, *E.T.*

This messiah imaging is ever becoming bigger in sports. When ace Canadian Grand Prix race driver Gilles Villeneuve was killed in May 1982, Maurice Moyrond wept, "For me, he was a god." "Hockey is my religion," oozes Gary Jones in *The Toronto Star* (Jan. 3, 1982) and Wayne Gretzky his god. At the time of a Gretzky visit to Maple Leaf Gardens, scalpers reportedly got up to $400 a ticket for people who insisted, "I want to see him!" His General Manager, Bob McGregor exults that this "Super-duper, superstar . . . 'belongs in a higher league.' "

What is the effect on "The Crown Prince," "the Great Gretzky"? "What bothers Wayne is that many people don't realize that he's just a human being. They phone and say, 'You mean you have to eat? And you have to sleep?' " Comments *MacLeans*, "In a nation admittedly starved for heros" Canadians have found in the Great Gretzky a godlike figure.

What effect does all this have on the heroes themselves? It's a yo-yo thing. They go from the apogee to the nadir. At the top is self-deification. At the bottom is suicide. As I sit here writing, a frontpage features yesteryear's flashy rightwinger for the Buffalo Sabres found yesterday in his car, parked in his house garage—gassed to death.

One also recognizes christ posturing in the professions. One of my closest friends says of his brother, who is a surgeon, "When he buttons on those white togs, up and down those hospital corridors, he's like a god." *Time* in an article on physicians and suicide—the rate is from three to seven times as high as the general public—comments that there are those times when "they believe themselves to be omnipotent." And it can also happen to social workers. *The Los Angeles Times* (Jan. 10,

1982) quoted Bette Lee, the founding administrator of "Angel's Haven Nursery for Severely Handicapped Children," who disclosed what fuels her energy engines: "Where else can you feel like God?"

No scene, of course, is so dominated by this blowing up of personality balloons into messiah-assuming head halos as that of pop music. Peter Goddard, the rock music critic, writes of KISS (initials stand for Knights In Satan's Service) as they release *The Elder*, their top new album—[which] "is concerned with a group of god-like figures who've watched over the planet since its beginnings in primordial ooze." Now appears *The Elder*, "an orphan boy who, through a succession of events, comes to save the world" (*Los Angeles Times*, Jan. 10, 1982). It's not only the content of the lyrics but the performers themselves who come off as messiah pretenders. The Rolling Stones performed coast to coast in North America during the latter part of 1981 to crowds as large as 90,000. Forty-year-old Mick Jagger, son of a professional academic and certainly no fool himself, would have his band do "Jumping Jack Flash" while he would pass over the audience at about 40 feet above them in a huge cherry picker crane tossing flowers to these frenzied fanatics as they threw their hands up to him in simulating embraces. It would have made Hitler green with envy.

It was not so much the Rolling Stones or KISS who initiated this antichrist posturing, however, as it was the Beatles, when they claimed that they were more popular than Jesus, and that Jesus would soon be reduced to a footnote. Their manager Derek Taylor said of them as they peaked in popularity world-wide, "They are completely antichrist. Sick people rushed up. It was as if some savior had arrived. The only thing left for the Beatles to do is to go on a healing tour. I'm antichrist, but these boys even shock me."

The successors to the Beatles in the '80's emanating out of Britain's rock world have been the Punk Rock groups. Most notorious was Sid Vicious, who killed his girl friend and then himself. Their theme song was "Anarchy," which goes: "I am antichrist, I am an anarchist. Don't know what I want, but I know how to get—I wanna destroy." Rivaling the Royal Wedding for press coverage in 1981, both inside Britain and throughout the world, were the British "skinheads," who were the punk rock street people. In addition to their antichrist, anarchist songs, they roused riots in the streets involving so many right-wing youths that the British army had to join the police to try to quell their rumbles. Their heads shaven, most of them out of work, they waved the banner of the latest *Sounds* magazine (a Nazi-Facist organ that sets up the kind of power vacuum that would be tailor-made for a coming antichrist). In the end, they brought the proud British establishment to its knees in a plea for peace.

To what extent are some of these Rock groups, who are high on drugs and low on morality and social stability, Satan-inspired? *The Boston Globe* (Apr. 30, 1982) carried a front page article, which quoted "The Rolling Stones" featuring "Sympathy for the Devil": "Pleased to meet you. Hope you guessed my name. But what's puzzlin' you is the nature of my game. 'Sympathy for the Devil'!" *The Globe* goes on to quote from a prominent legislator, Phillip Wyman, and a neuroscientist, William Yarroll, who claim that hard rock is filled with subtle Santanic messages. For example, Led Zeppelin's "Stairway to Heaven" has six such, three of which when unscrambled state, "I live for Satan," "The Lord turned me off," and "Here's to my sweet Satan." In the song, "Snowblind," by Styx, the message is "Satan moved through our voices." On the Black Oak Arkansas album, *Raunch 'n' Roll*, the words are "Satan, Satan, Satan, Satan, Satan . . . he is God." The messages were recorded backwards through a process called "backward masking." Yes, writes Sonja Beal to *The Bangor Daily News* (May 7, 1982), "Teenagers like me who care about what goes into their heads are victims of 'Satanic cultures' expressed through chants and praises" . . . with "our subconscious minds [we] kids in the rock culture are being drawn into cults, etc., without realizing what's actually going on." Is this freedom? No, it isn't. It's the masses surrendering, to Satan, to the spirit of antichrist.

This spirit is in the language of the street, the media, academia, and sports. It's up with Satan, and down with Jesus Christ! A thesis researcher tells us that Jesus Christ's name is used 50 times as often in cursing as in prayer and adoration. *Time* (Dec. 14, 1981) has a feature article on "Profanity," which quotes Los Angeles Dodger Manager Tommy Lasorda as unleashing 144 curse words in a brief pep talk to his championship winning team. A different but nonetheless still frightening use of language involves words the media sometimes uses to describe politicians. I felt that *Time* could have better described its Man of the Year, Lech Walesa, by some other comparison than to say he was a "Christlike figure." Right over the page, Anwar Sadat was likened to a teacher and forgiver like "Christ." When the antichrist does come, of course, he's going to simulate Christ-likeness as a deception ploy. He'll be "a deceiver and an antichrist"(2 John 7).

Dick Cavett remarked recently that he had just interviewed a prominent politician who "actually thought he was God." John Fraser writes in *The Toronto Globe and Mail* (Jan. 8, 1982) of a certain Canadian politician and his inability to rise to earlier projected expectations (both his own and others), "We place ridiculous faith in government to solve everything. The investment of such expectations not only devalues individual responsibility, it also makes potential monsters out of good people. If we tended reality and our duty as citizens in a more intelligent and committed fashion, our politicians might be spared their current incarnations as latter-day messiahs who inevitably find themselves presiding over our fate on the very throne of Satan." This is such a fascinating phenomenon that some experts are coming out with studies in depth on what it is that tends to make leaders megalomaniacs. Are they, like the maniac of Gadara, actually demon-possessed? Dr. Frank Elliott, former British army neurologist, who currently is consultant to the Elliott Neurological Center at Pennsylvania hospital, personally observed both Stalin and Hitler, and is convinced that the Neros and Napoleons have been made monsters by their crazed followers, who have exploited some strange weakness in the man. He lets the weakness grow into an uncontrollable malignancy until he becomes an incorrigible psychotic, who loses his capacity for normal "emotion . . . he lies, steals, blames others and has a strange inability to feel guilt or shame." Elliott claims that early in his relationship with Stalin, he and others ". . . saw a man who was paranoid, but none of us realized what was happening. He always seemed such a reasonable guy."

This is indicative of what strong and totally unique pressures our leaders are put under. I think it is profane to headline President Ronald Reagan as "a savior who will put America back on the proper track." We read regrettably of Premier "Begin's more extreme supporters, who have taken to referring to their leader as a 'messiah' " (*Time*, June 29, 1981). That kind of labeling might tempt even the best of leaders. It's what may, in part, have happened in Watergate—and any number of similar situations, to which much less attention has been paid.

It is, however, the stuff out of which antichrists are made. To wit, the "many antichrists; whereby we know it is the last time" (1 John 2:18). Harvey Cox of Harvard sees ours as a time when there are some 2,000 masquerading messiahs prowling— more than any other territory—the University campuses of North America. Cox reckons that for anyone who may be unemployed, if he announces his own divinity, snap! The devotees crawl out of the woodwork. Billy Graham notes that currently there are a least 500 such christs in California alone. The late Fulton Sheen ventured that there was seldom a day in which a new one didn't surface in Greater Los Angeles. Timothy Foley in his *The Cults: Signs of New Times* (1982) explains that today, more than ever, in human history "There is a spiritual void that needs filling." A TV network does a program on this theme, stating that apart from accepted Christian denominations and such other major faiths as Judaism, Islam and Buddhism there are fully 4,000 cults in North America, a shocking number having their own pseudo-messiah;

and that attached to these cults are some 28 million people. Moishe Rosen writes from Israel itself, where surely all Bible prophecy is most directly relevant, that "young Israelis are seeking spiritual meaning, either by becoming very religious Jews, or by delving into cults."

Jim Jones was a product of the '70's, and his 913 suicide volunteers, like Jones himself, are dead. But the spirit of Jim Jones is very much alive. Christopher Lasch warns us on a network television documentary, "Lest We Forget," that unless we can do something to restore a threadbare democracy, we'd better be scanning the horizons for a dictator who will be a blown-up edition of Jim Jones. Another egomaniac, who, like Jones, claimed to be Christ was Charles Manson. His trial attorney for the prosecution, Vincent Bugliosi (his book is *Helter Skelter*), keeps popping up in the news to remind us that this man's emulators may well be the wave of the future.

"Ticket to Heaven" starring Nick Mancuso is a film which is built on this current craze. It demonstrates how devotees are recruited with typical standard brainwashing techniques including "therapy, food deprivation, sleep deprivation, isolation, touching, holding, feeling, chants and games that involve hyperventilation and spacing out, and digging into the person's personal life. This leads to nervous breakdown after two or three days, the first successful sign of brainwashing." Mancuso was himself into a cult from which he was deprogrammed. Director Ralph Thomas researched heavily into the "2,200 cults in North America." He reckons "millions of young people are involved, and even more millions of friends and parents out there who have someone involved. It's almost impossible to turn around without encountering someone who has a niece, a nephew, a friend, a child in cults."

Nick Mancuso, of course, was a "Moonie" prior to his deprogramming. Into the eighties, we still have the Maharajs, the Maharishis (T.M.), the Hare Krishnas, the various campus gurus, and such militant and highly visible cults as the Scientologists and the Children of God. Rev. Sun Myung Moon of

Korea, perhaps more than any other, however, has demonstrated that the messiah movements are escalating rather than passing. A Korean clergyman of sorts, Moon moved to the U.S. a decade ago. George Cornell, in an AP release (Oct. 17, 1981), points to the fact that according to his American organizational president (former New York College Professor Mose Durst) Moon now openly claims to the the "second messiah. Jesus failed in His mission because He was crucified instead of marrying and starting a perfected human lineage"— something Moon proposes, as the new true christ himself, to do. During the summer of 1982, Moon arrogates on national television that he has just conversed with Buddah, Moses and Jesus Christ!

Many laugh! *The Wall Street Journal* (Feb. 3, 1982), however, insists that Moon and his movement are no laughing matter! Indeed his organization is veritably "a present-day curiosity of the business world in a spreading network of companies with interests in publishing, entertainment, fishing, food retailing, and banking." The Unificationalists are "spreading rapidly in many countries . . . brainwashing . . . impressionable young recruits" with "30,000 members in the U.S." and realizing an income of "20 to 25 million annually. Mr. Moon's ambitious dream [is the] unifying [of] business, politics, culture and religion into a global theocracy that he would control." He's aiming for "5,000 stores to take $750 million" annually—something that "would put his church members in touch with 5 million people daily." *The Journal* points to their *News World Communications* paper and states that they almost pulled off a purchase of *The New York Daily News*. It sums up that people had better start looking at the Moonies for what they indeed are—a conspiracy in our midst. A full expose of the movement can be seen in J. Allan's new *The Rising of the Moon* (InterVarsity Press). *Time* (July 5, 1982) estimates that currently there are 3 million Moonies worldwide.

Another antichrist movement is Rastafarianism. In the late

summer of 1982, Rastafarians held their "First International Rastafarian Conference" in Toronto. Launched by Marcus Garvey, he rallied his worldwide following to "look to Africa for the crowning of a black king; he shall be the redeemer." It's just another hoax to give impetus to oppressed people who yearn for a deliverer.

While it is true that christ crouchers are currently poised chiefly as vultures on the fringes of our culture, waiting for their chance to pounce, they are definitely penetrating more and more toward the center of society. And they get monumental coverage in the media. In mid-1982 Emory Lamb of Arkansas was a headliner as the "Jesus Christ" of the Foundation of Ubiquity ("the state of being everywhere at the same time"). Did he get his "fame" by some noble deed? No indeed. It was through the infamous act of his two late desciples Keith and Kate Haigler who took a busload of hostages and then shot themselves dead before their would-be arresting police. Loud but hollow followers claimed that in 3½ days their "Jesus Christ Ron Lamb" would raise them from the dead. It didn't happen. Ron Lamb is of course, just another "false christ."

The nefarious and ubiquitous presence in our midst of antichrists and antichrist movements is a huge and problematic study, but there is an answer. Jesus promised that "where two or three are gathered together in My name, there am I in the midst of them" (Matt. 18:20). Jesus, wherever His word and invitation to "Come unto Me" are presented, receives people. Instead of brainwashing, He heartwashes them. Instead of turning them into weirdos, He makes them workers, doers, real people—sons and daughters of God, and heirs of His everlasting Kingdom.

Laura Done, first-year student at the University of Missouri, near to where I was recently presenting Christ in a Crusade, came forward to give her life to Christ. She had spent several years going in and out of cults. Born in a large eastern city, she had lived in the Midwest and in Florida. She had spent part of her life with her father, who had divorced three times, and

part of her life with three of her so-called mothers. She had had
no exposure to the message of the Word of God whatsoever
until she was 17. Consequently, she had been in and out of
several of those religious antichrist movements and in and out
of various life-styles. She tried drugs, sex, everything for fulfillment but God. Then she came to where we were presenting
Christ, and that night she committed herself to Jesus Christ
as Lord. The unqualified answer to antichrists and eventually
to the Antichrist is Jesus Christ. About that, there can be no
doubt!

"AND SO ALL ISRAEL SHALL BE SAVED"

When Israel returns to her ancient homeland and is re-established as a nation, let it be known, presaged Jesus, that this is the *sine qua non* of the beginning of the Final Conflict: "Know that it is near, even at the doors." He spoke through the parable of the fig tree, "When his branch is yet tender, and putteth forth leaves, ye know that summer is nigh" (Matthew 24:33,34). It is in the announcement of Jesus in verse 34 that the meaning is fraught with such crucial import for our times. The King James version reads, "This generation shall not pass, till all these things be fulfilled." The word "generation" here should be rendered "nation." Jesus was saying that restored Israel—as a nation again—definitely "shall not pass, until all these things be fulfilled." Link this to the Psalmist's statement, "When the Lord shall build up Zion, He Shall appear in His glory" and note, "This shall be written for the last generation" (Psalm 102:16,18, literal translation). This is strong and plain language.

New Testament commentators are nearly unanimous in their agreement that Jesus' use of the fig tree refers to Israel as a people, as a nation under God. Repeatedly in the Old Testament and consistently in rabbinical literature, Israel is symbolized by the fig tree. Christ Himself on a former occasion alluded to Israel as a fig tree (Luke 13:1-10). Early in the week in which our Lord was crucified, as He and His disciples went from

Bethany to Jerusalem, they paused and took note of a solitary fig tree which was flush with leaves but barren of figs. Jesus, having the previous day wept over Jerusalem in particular, and Israel generally, for their impenitence and rejection of His Messiahship, and alerting them that judgment was impending because of their outward piety but inward spiritual barrenness, cursed this wayside fig tree. We read that "when the disciples saw it, they marveled, saying 'How soon is the fig tree withered away!'" (Matthew 21:20). So it was later during that week that our Lord picked up on the same analogy and "spake to them a parable; Behold the fig tree, and all the trees" (only St. Luke, the Greek physician, includes this fascinating statement "all the trees"); "when they now shoot forth, ye see and know of your own selves that summer is now nigh at hand. So likewise ye, when ye see these things come to pass, know ye that the kingdom of God is nigh at hand" (Luke 21:29-31). Jesus is saying that as the barren fig tree was a picture of Israel, about to be cut off, so the fig tree which shoots forth new leaves is a picture of a restored Israel in the era when "the times of the Gentiles be fulfilled" (vs. 24).

Taking a look at St. Luke's inclusion, "and all the trees," I believe that this refers to the proliferation of new nations which sprang into existence in the wake of World War II, joining in the formation of the United Nations, all with highly nationalistic aspirations, seeking their own place in the sun. But amidst "all the trees" there was to be a special tree, "Israel!" So Jesus assured His disciples, that before He came back to the earth, amidst the carnage of Armageddon, Israel would have returned to her ancient homeland and become a nation again.

God's fulfillment of His promise to restore the Jews to their ancient homeland has its roots in His promise to Abraham four thousand years ago. We read in Genesis 12:1-3, "Now the Lord has said unto Abram, Get thee out of thy country, and from they kindred, and from thy father's house, unto a land that I will shew thee: and I will make of thee a great nation, and I will bless thee, and . . . bless them that bless thee." It is significant to notice that God specified the boundaries of the promised land (Genesis 15:18). Lebanon was a part of the parcel of land God allotted to Abraham. It's also important to note that God insisted that the land would belong to Abraham's seed as "an everlasting possession" (Genesis 17:8). Furthermore, the Lord enunciated that the promised land would be specifically passed from Abraham to Isaac's seed (see Romans 9:7), and from Isaac's sons, to the seed of Jacob (vs. 13). By now, we're wondering, "on the basis of human merit?" Not really, declared Moses to the Israelites, who were about to enter the promised land for the second time—a promised land that Moses himself, during his illustrious 120-year-long life, never entered—"The Lord did not set His love upon you, nor choose you, because ye were more in number than any people . . . but because the Lord loved you" (Deuteronomy 7:7,8).

One more thing! When Christ as God the Son came to earth, lived in Israel, was rejected by the majority of Jews, and crucified just outside Jerusalem—and with the inception of His Church, had His disciples turn to the Gentiles—this did not entail God's abandonment of the Jewish people as His chosen nation. St. Paul deals with this theme in Romans, chapters 9 to 11, asking, "Hath God cast away His people [Israel]?" He replies with unmistakable clarity, "God hath not cast away His people which He foreknew" (Romans 11:1,2). Yes, they would be set aside while Christ called out a people for His name—the Church. Paul puts it this way, "I would not, brethren, that ye should be ignorant of this mystery . . . that blindness in part is happened to Israel, until the fullness of the Gentiles be come in. And so all Israel shall be saved: as it is written, There shall come out of Zion the Deliverer, and shall turn away ungodliness from Jacob: for this is My covenant unto them" (Romans 11:25-27). This, of course, refers to the coming again of Christ, as Israel's Messiah, at the time of Armageddon. "A nation," prophesied Isaiah (66:8) shall "be born at once . . . as soon as Zion [travaileth]." As Israel corporately receives her Messiah, Jesus Christ, all her surviving peoples will experience spiritual rebirth. *Christianity Today*, dealing with this theme, cites Dr. David Martyn Lloyd-Jones, who notes, "I have a feeling that we are in the period of the end." He points to Paul's arguments to the Romans, especially in the eleventh chapter, regarding the remarkable "return among the Jews before the end-time," prophesied unmistakably to precede "the return of Christ."

U.S. General S.L.A. Marshall was an astute observer of modern Israel from early in this century until their repossession of Jerusalem in the 1967 war. He was convinced that there was only one word to describe their restoration to their ancient homeland, and re-occupation of Jerusalem, against all human odds—but in undeniable fulfillment of scriptural prophecy—as long predicted by both Orthodox Jewish scholars and devout Evangelical Christian expositors. The only suitable word, from a military or any other point of view, was "miracle", insisted Marshall. Harvard Ph.D. Charles Malik, the Lebanese statesman who served as President of the United Nations General Assembly, concedes that to ignore the promises of God in His prophetic Word concerning the restoration of Israel to their ancient homeland, and instead to put it all down to a mere humanistic "politico-enonomic struggle, is to have no sense whatsoever of the holy and ultimate in history."

It was another Harvard scholar, from another era, Increase Mather, perhaps the most distinguished President Harvard University has ever had (1685-1701), who wrote in his *The Mystery of Israel's Salvation Explained*, at a time when Palestine was a barren wilderness ruled by the Turks and with scarcely any Jews in residence, that "the Scripture is very clear and full in this, that you see not how it can be justly denied or questioned." He not only held out emphatically that Israel would return from the four corners of the earth and become a nation again in her ancient homeland, he wrote, quoting from Isaiah 31:5, that "the Israelites at their return, shall even fly." English divine John Owen is thought by many to have been the foremost of all Congregationalist clergy. In 1673 he insisted, "The Jews shall be gathered from all parts of the earth where they now are scattered, and brought home into their homeland" before "the end of all things," prophesied by St. Peter (1 Peter 4:7) can occur.

So where is Israel's return to its ancient (and present) lands prophesied in the Bible? The Scriptures are so many, that if quoted in full on this subject, they would fill a small book. Isaiah 11:11,12 states that "it shall come to pass in that day, that the Lord shall set His hand again the second time to recover the remnant of His people." (The first time, of course, was when they were brought home from Babylonian captivity during the sixth century, B.C.) And where would the Lord bring Israel from? "From the islands of the sea." Indeed, He'd "assemble the outcasts of Israel, and gather the dispersed of Judah from the four corners of the earth." Not until modern times could the Jewish people have been found in "the four corners of the earth." The ancient Middle East was but one of the four corners of the earth.

When Jesus was on earth, Israel had been an occupied country for six centuries (from 586 B.C.). Our Lord predicted that within a generation of His crucifixion the land would be overrun by Gentiles in an *en masse* massacre and not one stone of the then-resplendent temple would remain upon another. In 68 A.D., 20,000 Jews were killed by the Romans in Caesarea, and in 70 A.D., Jerusalem was conquered and the temple completely demolished. Not one stone was left upon another. More than 100,000 bodies of Jews were thrown over the wall of the city, having for the most part, been crucified; and another 100,000 were sold as if they were animals in an auction, to slave traders from near and far. In one day, the people of Damascus cut the throats of 10,000 Jews. An estimated one million were mercilessly murdered at this time. Under Emperor Hadrian (117-138 A.D.), the Romans destroyed another 985 towns (in what by then had been re-named Palestine), and killed 580,000 men. In particular, the Jews were banished from Jerusalem, a policy which succeeding Roman emperors pursued relentlessly. Then there was that valiant last stand—the Masada massacre. *The*

Boston Globe (May 12, 1982) features Prime Minister Menachem Begin addressing an emotional commemoration of Masada, the Jewish rebellion led by Bar-Kochba in 132-135 A.D. During that historical period there occurred "the death of a half million Jews and the exile of the rest." Remembering Masada highlights, orated Begin, "our glorious fathers. We have tidings for you. We have returned to the place from whence we came. The people of Israel live, and will live in its homeland, the land of Israel."

As history continued, the second to the sixth centuries, A.D., Palestine was again occupied, desolated and—yes, decimated by the Romans. Then for a thousand years—with brief breaks from such invasions as those conducted by the Crusaders—Palestine was overrun by Islam. From the sixteenth century to 1917 it was in the hands of the Turks, at which time it became a British Mandate.

True evangelical Christians and Orthodox Jews, throughout the centuries, never for a minute doubted that Palestine would, one day, be re-occupied by a restored Israel. Both communities clung to such clear passages as Jeremiah 16:15: "But, the Lord liveth, that brought up the children of Israel from the land of the north, and from all the lands whither He had driven them: and I will bring them again into their land that I gave unto their fathers"; and Ezekiel 36:24: "For I will take you from among the heathen, and gather you out of all countries, and will bring you into your own land." Isaiah (60:21) prophesies for how long: "They shall inherit the land forever." This return will be a final one, without there being another dispersion. Prophesied Amos (9:14,15), "And I will bring again the captivity of my poeple of Israel, and they shall build the waste cities, and inhabit them . . . they shall also make gardens, and eat the fruit of them. And I will plant them upon their land, and they shall no more be pulled up out of their land which I have given them, saith the Lord thy God."

As one looks at a promise like "They shall also make gardens, and eat the fruit of them," one cannot help but think of

Jerusalem Mayor Teddy Kollek's current allusions to how modern Israel carved their fruit orchards and flower gardens out of a 2,000-year-old wilderness. And despite the fact that their Jewish population has escalated to 3½ million, 80% of their fruit is in excess of their domestic needs. So they export it. And in what might even be a more amazing fulfillment to prophecy, as Kollek aptly notes, "Our second biggest export is roses." "The desert" the ancient prophet Isaiah (35:1,2) prophesied, shall "blossom as the rose. It shall blossom abundantly"; but, as Isaiah went on, it would mean "strengthen ye the weak hands, and confirm the feeble knees." And God's reward would be that "the parched ground shall become a pool, and the thirsty land springs of water" (vss. 3,7). How more vividly could the overpoweringly impressive irrigation schemes of modern Israel—implemented by their faith and hard work— be expressed! What is not widely known is the fact that Israel is only one of six countries in the world which grows more food than its people consume, and is, therefore, a net exporter of food.

How did all this come about, insofar as the last hundred years is concerned? A combination of Orthodox Jews and Evangelical Christians believed in claiming the promises of God in His Word that Israel was destined to become a restored nation with Jerusalem as its capital. When these two communities combined in faith, God Almighty performed a great number of incredible miracles—some of them judgments—without which modern Israel simply would not exist.

In all honesty, liberal Protestants have not felt any reason to support Israel as a nation. For example, *The Toronto Globe and Mail* reported (Jan. 8, 1981): "400 U.S. Clergymen, including several bishops" are "calling for the United States to reduce its aid to Israel." This is because it is not a conviction of liberal Protestants that the Bible assures that Jews will return to their ancient homeland as a fulfillment of scriptural prophecy. Nor is this a belief officially of Roman Catholicism, hence "the Vatican has never recognized Israel as a state" (*Toronto Globe and Mail*, Jan. 8, 1982). This is not to imply that there are not tens of millions within the respective memberships of liberal Protestant and Roman Catholic churches who accept the concept of modern Israel being an unmistakable fulfillment to Biblical prophecy.

Indicative of the intense interest of worldwide Jewry in the restored nation of Israel and its prophesied destination in the Old Testament, is such a quote as the following: "Rabbi Erwin Schild, spiritual leader of Adath Israel Congregation, says the response to adult study sessions has surprised officials, due to the large attendance. Instead of the expected handful of participants, there have been crowded classes of hundreds, a pleased Schild reported to his congregation. He said there appears to be 'a genuine hunger,' for knowledge about the Bible and Jewish affairs" (*Toronto Star*, Jan. 16, 1982). Majorie Hyer writes in *The Washington Post* that whereas a perusal of the 1982 Yearbook of American and Canadian Churches reveals that mainline Protestant churches are suffering severe and even critical losses, "Jews and conservative evangelicals are registering remarkable, and in many places dramatic, gains." There's no other description for "Reform Judaism in North America" complains Religion Editor Tom Harper than to use the characterization "Fundamentalism." A doctor friend of mine tells me that his Jewish patients are constantly complaining that "our children are becoming so fanatically Orthodox! What's hitting them to make them this way?" Of course it is God putting it into their hearts to fulfill His promises to Abraham.

Theodor Herzl, in 1897, masterminded the first Zionist Congress, in Basel, Switzerland, where it was resolved "to create for the Jewish people a home in Palestine secured by public law." At this time, there were only 50,000 Jews in Palestine (up from 10,000 in 1839), of a total population of 625,000. By December 11, 1917, when British General Edmund Henry Allenby walked reverently into Jerusalem (he refused to ride, as Christ had done) and declared Palestine a British Mandate, free from the Turks, there were 100,000 Jews to 700,000 non-Jews. Allenby was a remarkable Evangelical Christian. As a child, he had adopted the daily prayer, "Lord, forget not Thine ancient people. Hasten the day when they shall be restored to Thy favour and to their land." On the evening of December 10, Allenby felt a deep constraint to pray and search the Scriptures—which he did all night. He was led to Isaiah 31:5, "As birds flying, so will the Lord of hosts defend Jerusalem; defending also, He will deliver it; and passing over He will preserve it." So on the morning of December 11, moving his army in from Egypt, he issued strict orders to his British air force to fly low and in waves over Jerusalem, and without firing a solitary shot, to invoke the Turks to surrender. His plan was a complete success. The Turks retreated wtihout any resistance whatsoever. And later, when the familiar Allenby Bridge over the Jordan was completed and being officially opened, Allenby stated humbly for the world to hear, "I never knew that God would give me the privilege of helping to answer my own childhood prayer."

Complementing this amazing conquest of Jerusalem by Allenby was the Zionist factor which, in cooperation with Bible-believing churchmen, produced the crucial Balfour Declaration of 1917 in Great Britain. It declared: "His Majesty's Government view with favour the establishment in Palestine of a national home for the Jewish people, and will use their best endeavors to facilitate the achievement of this object." The prime mover by now was an Orthodox Jew, a Manchester chemist, Chaim Weizmann. He had given to the world the crucial formula for synthetic acetone. Weizmann had taken over from Herzl as the head of the Zionist movement and had worked for a dozen years to influence Lord Balfour, Lloyd George, Winston Churchill, and indirectly even on President Woodrow Wilson, all of whom were sympathetic, being intimately familiar with the Biblical promises relating to a restored Israel in their ancient homeland.

This could not be said of Neville Chamberlain, who began the reneging, and of Clement Atlee, the British Socialist Prime

Minister from 1945 onwards, who were both thorns in the flesh
of a determined world Jewry—by that time, of course, newly
inflamed and fused by the Hitler Holocaust in which 6 million
Jews had perished. A colleague of Atlee, who was to serve as
Socialist Prime Minister in the 1960's and 70's, is Harold
Wilson. In his *The Chariot of Israel: Britain, America and the
State of Israel* (London, 1982), Wilson states convincingly that
Ernest Bevin, Atlee's foreign secretary from 1945 onwards was
the "anti-Zionist" who did the most to influence Atlee and "to
revoke the principles and ideas of the Balfour Declaration." This
is the place also to state that Wilson, a socialist, candidly concedes that when it comes to giving credit to whom credit is due,
it was the Conservative Winston Churchill who was the powerful "spokesman of rare eloquence for the Zionist cause and his
speeches about the squalid retreat from Balfour's promise" were
decisive. Churchill was specially harsh on "Malcolm Mac-
Donald, the British Foreign Secretary who issued the infamous
white paper of 1939 which doomed European Jewry to Hitler's
death camps." Wilson points to the Britains overall strong
Zionism during the 1910-1939 era, as reflective of a population
which for a century had been strongly evangelical and "nur-
tured on Protestantism."

Doubtless Wilson's work on this crucial theme is a classic.
But not nearly enough is being made in the current secular press
of this occasionally trespassed but ever-strengthening bond
between true Evangelicals and Orthodox Jewish believers. It's
important to keep in mine that Israeli Prime Ministers have
all reiterated that Jews are back in their "Land" to await the
coming of Messiah. Menacheim Begin and George Otis were in
conversation in June, 1982. The Prime Minister, holding the
Bible open to several passages, pointed to one of the many
which refers to "the last days." His remark was: "See here
where this speaks about 'the last days?' Now that doesn't mean
the end of the world. 'The last days' means the time just before
our Messiah comes. You know we could be coming to that
sometime in the near future." Is it any wonder that Menacheim

Begin was referred to in *Time* (July 26, 1982) as that "thundering prophet of the Old Testament." And every Israeli and every Jew worldwide (there are 17 million, nearly 4 million being in Israel) probably gets an emotional and spiritual high when they go to the theatre and hear that line from "Fiddler on the Roof": "We have been waiting all our lives for Messiah. Wouldn't this be a good time for Him to come?" Seven-hundred-thousand of Israel's current Jewish population is mildly if not militantly Orthodox, the others being Conservative or Reformed (liberal).

The 1982 Oscar-winning film, *Chariots of Fire* (proclaimed before a T.V. audience of 300 million as Best Picture), is a typical joint project of Evangelical Christians and Orthodox Jews, featuring the Olympian winners at Paris in 1924—Eric Liddell, the Evangelical "Flying Scotsman," who died prematurely two decades later in China in a squalid internment camp; and Harold Abrahams, the Lithuanian Jew from Cambridge. I suppose one could say that the Carter/Begin, or the Reagan/Begin relationships have reflected these two theological positions. Other examples of Evangelical and Jewish cooperation would include Billy Graham films *The Hiding Place* and *His Land*.

Another example of a joint project between these two communities as reported in *Time* (Nov. 2, 1981), is the annual International Christian Celebration During the Feast of Tabernacles (Sukkoth) which brings Christians and Jews together to Jerusalem under the current Chairmanship of Rev. Johann Lukoff of the Dutch Reformed Church. *Time* reported that this Conference represents "tens of millions of Evangelicals around the world" who believe that the Messiah is coming to the world to install universal peace and prosperity, initially appearing at Jerusalem. "As the end of the world nears, according to the biblical prophet Zechariah, visitors from many nations gather each year in Jerusalem 'to worship the King, the Lord Almighty, and to celebrate the Feast of Tabernacles.'" In the October 1981 Conference "3,000 people from 35 countries [gathered] with parades, cookouts, and musical services in one of the Holy City's most spectacular religious events. In a welcoming speech, Prime Minister Menachem Begin declared, 'I would like to tell all [to] come to Jerusalem [and see that] Israel is not alone.' Among those applauding were Christians from Kenya, Ghana, Nigeria, and India—none of which even have diplomatic relations with Israel. At a time of dwindling religious and secular support for Israel, it acts [to] rally friendship for the Jewish state, [trumpeting that] Zionism is part of God's design for the days preceding the Second Coming of Jesus Christ.''

I find in the writings of the Hebrew scholar Arthur W. Kac a most empathetic exposition of why God in His Sovereignty permitted the Holocaust. Kac points out that previous to the Balfour Declaration in 1917 the vast majority of Jews lived in Europe, and that this was still true up to World War II. Many of them were secular humanists and deeply attached to the countries of their adoption, which had been their domicile for a thousand years and more. Kac points out that the Holocaust and the establishment of the State of Israel in 1948, with the hugh exodus of the surviving Jews from European and Arab lands, marked the end of "The Great Dispersion"—the longest era in Jewish history. It is a remarkable fact that history knows of no other instance of a people which, while separated from the country of its national origin for some nineteen centuries, not only retained its ethnic and theological identity but also, at the end of these two millennia, returned from far (both culturally and geographically) and near to its ancient homeland.

The Scriptures give the only rationale for this national phenomenon. And they also point plainly to the fact that the Jewish people are returning often despite themselves. Let us look at one of many passages which Kac, along with many others, insists deals with this fact. In Ezekiel (20:32-37) God warns Israel that just when their dispersed think they are a permanently settled and integrated part of the Gentile community among whom they reside and say, "We will be as the heathen," it's then "saith the Lord God, surely with a mighty hand, and with a stretched out arm, and with fury poured out

I will bring you out from the people, and will gather you out of the countries wherein ye are scattered, with a mighty hand, and with a stretched out arm, and with fury poured out. And I will bring you into the wilderness of the people . . . and I will cause you to pass under the rod, and I will bring you into the bond of the covenant."

That "bond of the convenant"—when did it take place? Promised four thousand years ago, when Jehovah covenanted with Abraham, and reiterated repeatedly since, that "bond of the covenant" was surely affirmed in May 1948, when Israel became a sovereign unoccupied nation for the first time in 2,500 years. The circumstances were filled with convulsions and trauma. The Holocaust had massacred 6 million Jews. Hundreds of thousands escaped to a desolate Palestine, many fleeing in abject poverty, but with their unprecedented professional and industrial skills intact. In 1948, when the new (renewed) nation was born, there were some 650,000 Jews "in the land."

But for the Grace and Sovereignty of God, the plan for the nation would have aborted. As we've already noted, Winston Churchill, who was so consistently supportive of Zionism, was voted out of power in 1945, replaced by British Prime Minister Clement Atlee. Atlee and his Foreign Secretary Ernest Bevin tried to fudge on Lord Balfour's earlier commitment—as Menachem Begin has so faithfully reminded the world. But this was providential, because it caused Britain simply to turn the whole matter of Palestine over to the newly formed United Nations. Turmoil ensued. On November 29, 1947, the General Assembly of the United Nations passed a resolution stating that "the Mandate for Palestine shall terminate . . . not later than August first, 1948 . . . Independent Arab and Jewish States, and the specific international regime for the City of Jerusalem . . . shall come into existence." But this almost didn't happen. A fierce war between the Arabs and the Jews broke out in Palestine, in which the Israelis were grossly outnumbered (53-1) and underequipped. Against all known odds, they prevailed sufficiently to proclaim themselves a nation with

Chaim Weizmann as President and David Ben Gurion as Prime Minister.

Scrambling both militarily and politically, on May 13, Weizmann addressed a letter to President Truman imploring immediate American recognition of the newly constituted State of Israel. By the next day, Truman's official reply from the White House was read before the United Nations General Assembly: "This Government has been informed that a Jewish State has been proclaimed in Palestine, and recognition has been requested by the Provisional Government itself. The United States recognizes the Provisional Government as the *de facto* authority of the new State of Israel." The timing was just right! Even the Soviets followed Truman's precedent and recognized the newest nation!

While Britain generally, and Balfour in particular, must receive large credit for laying the groundwork for the emergence of the modern State of Israel, the single non-Jew who must be highlighted as the one who did most to pull the lever that established Israel as a nation on that momentous, historic date of May 14, 1948, was President Harry Truman. Harold Wilson makes this clear in his book. And Henry Kissinger, whose family had nearly all perished in the Holocaust, writes in *Time* (March 8, 1982) that without a doubt the strongest and most strategic Gentile supporter of modern Israel was President Harry Truman. In turn the greatest political upset in a post-World War II democracy was in November 1948, when—against all predictions by pundits—Truman was elected U.S. President ahead of heavily favored Thomas Dewey. It is inarguably a vindication of God's ancient promise to Abraham, "I will make of thee a great nation" and "I will bless them that bless thee, and curse him that curseth thee" (Genesis 12:2,3).

Hitler's terrible end was a corroboration of this promise. And I believe that it was the prime factor in Stalin's sudden and unexpected death. Not only had Stalin eliminated some six million Jews, it has been widely reported that it was when he screamed in rage in early 1953 that his next move would be to massacre the Jews of Russia—wholesale—that he was struck with a stroke, and his death was immediate! And this is the place, in a book like this, to state that the terrible nuclear destruction of the communist regime will occur as God's judgment on the Soviets, not only for their militant atheism, but for their treatment of the Jews.

In contrast, one of North America's keys to peace and prosperity has been its magnanimous treatment of the Jewish people. Thomas Jefferson insisted two hundred years ago that the new Republic receive with open arms Jewish people into all walks of life to which they might aspire. Before his death, included in his exposition of his "Fourteen Points," Woodrow Wilson was a strong supporter of Israel's right to evolve into a sovereign nation. From Truman to Reagan, this has been true more or less of all American presidents in the latter half of the 20th century. In 1982, amidst turmoil and controversy in the Middle East, Reagan reaffirmed "an unshakable American Commitment to Israel," it being pointed out that Reagan "was one of the original supporters of the creation of the State of Israel." His views on this issue are widely heralded: "I believe that our nation has a moral obligation and commitment to the preservation of the nation of Israel. Beyond that . . . we should help and protect Israel as the one who is the great deterrent to the spread of godless communism."

Writes Walter Gerzin in *Time* (Jan. 18, 1982), that but for "the American Eagle . . . the Russian Bear will gobble [Israel] up." What price do Americans pay? A high one indeed! To an Israel, which has only four million of the world's 4½ billion peoples, the U.S.—as the Vice-President has pointed out—metes out over half of its foreign aid. It flows at the rate of 7 million dollars a day. *U.S. News and World Report* reckons that Americans have invested 15 billion dollars in Israel's military, not to mention the many times that amount in the other aspects of building up the State of Israel. And during the highly controversial Israeli invasion of Lebanon to eliminate the P.L.O. during the summer of 1982, according to George Gallup: "52

percent of the survey respondents" said their support was with
Israel. "10 percent sided with the Arab" cause. This was put
down to the combined forces of Evangelicalism and the way
Jewish people stick together politically. Gale McVay writes in
The Idaho Statesman (August 9, 1982) "The State of Israel
effectively controls the U.S. government. If a politician is a
strong supporter of Israel, he has it made."

People understandably ask, "Where does Israel get so much
clout?" The media of both the United States and Canada, in
particular, and much of the Western world in general. It is
estimated currently that seventy percent of the upper executive
echelons of the media are Jews. To quote Henry Kissinger again
(*Time*, Mar. 8, 1982), Jews in the United States have "control
of the media." This, in itself, makes them away and by far
America's most "powerful cohesive group".

Indeed, supposed Jewish control of the media gets peoples'
backs up! According to *The New York Daily News* (Jan. 6,
1982). "Anti-Semitic vandalism, assualts and harrassments
increased sharply in the United States last year. The Anti-
Defamation League of B'nai B'rith reports . . . anti-Semitic
incidents were up 250%." This itself is the beginning of the
fulfillment of Jesus' prophecy that prior to His advent to earth
Jewish believers would be "hated of all nations" (Matthew 24:9).
The last vote on an Israeli issue in the United Nations General
Assembly that I noted was 127 to 2 (June 26, 1982), something
too typical to attract much notice.

This leads me to state why I find it essential to deal so fully
with this matter of the modern State of Israel in a book on
Arming For Armageddon. A crucial passage, and one which has
many others to support it, is Zechariah 12:3, "In that day will
I make Jerusalem a burdensome stone for all people: all that
burden themselves with it shall be cut in pieces, though all the
people of the earth be gathered together against it." David
Shipler writes in *The New York Times* (Apr. 14, 1982) of this
"burden": "Israelis increasingly are feeling the terrible 'burden
of their modern nation.' " This "terrifying sense of loneliness,

always the affliction of Jewish people!" Back to Zechariah, "I will make Jerusalem a cup of trembling unto all the people round about, when they shall be in the siege . . . against Jerusalem." Writes James Reston of *The New York Times* that we have come today to look upon "Jerusalem, of all places, [as] not a symbol of spiritual reconciliation, but of division, hostitity and potential war." So when we refer to Jerusalem, we're on to the most volatile subject in both the Jewish and Arab worlds. We must keep in mind here that Jesus assured—leading up to Armageddon—that Jerusalem would be compassed about with "armies," and that Jerusalem would be "trodden down of the Gentiles, until the times of the Gentiles be fulfilled" (Luke 21:24).

To date, while not ignoring the others of the four Middle East Wars over the last generation, the crucial one—in addition to the one in 1948—was in June 1967, when the Israelis took over Jerusalem. Only Mecca and Medina are more sacred cities to Moslems than Jerusalem. The conquest and repossession of Jerusalem by Israel, has to be the most explosive single issue in the world today. To quote Dr. David Martyn Lloyd-Jones from *Christianity Today*, "We are in a dissolving world. All my life I've opposed setting 'times and seasons,' but I feel increasingly that we may be in the last times. What undergirds that conviction? To me, 1967, the year that the Jews occupied all of Jerusalem was very crucial. Luke 21:24 is one of the most significant prophetic verses. 'Jerusalem,' it reads, 'shall be trodden down of the Gentiles until the times of the Gentiles be fulfilled.' It seems to me that that took place in 1967—something crucially important that had not occurred in two thousand years." Special attention to Jerusalem was highlighted again recently when the Israeli Knesset passed into law the declaration of an undivided Jerusalem as the country's eternal capital. Prime Minister Menachem Begin worded it thusly: "Jerusalem, City of David, is the eternal capital of Israel and of the Jewish people, and will remain undivided for all future generations."

Coming to the matter of the fierce hatred for Israel and the

resolve to exterminate these peoples as a nation, we read in
Zephaniah (2:2,1) that ere "the day of the Lord" come, Israel
is to "gather yourselves together, yea, gather together, O nation
not desired." We deal elsewhere, in this light, with the Soviet
Union, the Arab world as a whole, Western Europe, Africa, and
the Far East. Let's say something here about Poland, where
a priest notes in March 1982 (on U.S. TV) that the people feel
"World War III broke out on Dec. 13, 1981." *Time* (Jan. 4, 1982)
refers to "Poland's notorious anti-Semitism." Writes Leon
Offman (*Toronto Star*, Jan. 4, 1982), "Nowhere, not even in
Germany, has the eradication of a Jewish population been so
vicious and complete. Poland had the greatest percentage of
Jews of any country outside Israel—nearly ten percent, com-
prising nearly three million Jews out of a pre-World War II
population of around 30 million. Now there are a mere 6,000."
As Danile Karmazyn wrote of his former kinsman: "Jews were
shot, gassed, cremated, tortured, buried alive, used as guinea-
pigs in medical experiments, converted into lampshades,
pillows, eiderdowns and soap" (*Toronto Star*, Jan. 13, 1982). So,
as Rabbi Jordan Pearlson points out (*Toronto Star*, Jan. 16,
1982), it was expedient for the impacting Martial Law regime
to target this existent handful of "Polish Jews, mostly aged"
with the onus of having roused Solidarity into an insurrectionist
movement against the Communist Government.

Slogans quickly went up throughout Poland pointing an
accusing finger at these Zionists for having initiated the trouble. So up went Anti-Jewish signs showing the Solidarity union
emblem, a dollor sign and the Star of David. Simon Wiesenthal
of Vienna pointed out that the Martial Law leadership were
sinister enough to incite "a wave of anti-Semitism" which would
appeal to many Poles. Writer Michelle Lansberg, of the
celebrated political Lewis family, insists that evidence that the
Poles were as cooperative as the Germans—if not more so—in
gassing Jews to death could be seen in the fact that 200,000
Jews still resided in Poland after World War II, but that
this was down to a current 6,000 through fierce continuing

persecution of these people who had been in Poland in large numbers for a thousand years. Lansberg's final blast was reserved for the Martial Law leaders who, "among their 20,000 political prisoners, have included 2,200 Jews of a total of 5,000, most of them old. That's like imprisoning 14 million Poles, if the percentage of non-Jews and Jews were handled in an even-handed selection." *Christianity Today* (Mar. 5, 1982) notes that the Jews again have been fingered as scapegoats, by the Poles' trumped-up charges of "wrecking the economy by hoarding goods, stirring up unrest in universities and collaborating with International Zionism."

Of course, millions of Poles are sincere friends of Israel. But the official posture of the current Martial Law Government of Poland is as militantly anti-Jewish as it is anti-Democratic. "The Warsaw Pact" is the Communist Military Umbrella into which even Syria is now admitted in membership. As we will see later, Syria will be a part of the route where the Soviet military will be decimated in their attempt to overrun Israel. President Assad has been aligned with the Soviets since the sixties. As *Time* (Jan. 12, 1982) notes, he has vowed that neither he nor his country will "talk to Israel for the next 100 years."

While the Soviet clash with the State of Israel will be dealt with later, we can now state that the paranoia that they have for Jews is sharpening every year. Notes Bert Raphael, chairman of the Canadian Lawyers and Jurists for Soviet Jewry, there is this "terrible irony. [Jews] are not wanted within the Soviet Union, [yet] they are kept against their will." While in 15 years, "250,000 have emigrated"—51,320 in 1979—last year, less than one-fifth of that number got out, and currently it's as few, according to Jack Anderson, as 283 a month (March '82).

Abba Eban says of the United Nations that whereas it "was established as an anti-Nazi alliance; it's now acting like a Ku Klux Klan." The new U.N. Secretary General, Perez Cuellar—a South American—affirms that of all the insoluables in the world of 1982, the constant number one "problem that needs our most concern is the Middle East." *World Press Digest* points out the crucial point that "the Arab Muslim countries regard the Israeli occupation of Jerusalem and the West Bank . . . as a more heinous and long-standing aggression than the Soviet threats." It's basic to grasp this fact—something many Westerners don't seem to apprehend. Yasir Arafat maintains that "Jerusalem is an Arab city. Sooner or later, my armies and I will enter Jerusalem." He is totally committed, "politically, socially, economically and culturally," to the demolition of Israel (*MacLeans*, Jan. 25, 1982). For Jordan, and really for the more moderate Arabs, King Hussein serves notice that Arabs definitely will "settle for nothing less than total withdrawal from the territories occupied in 1967—first and foremost Jerusalem" (*Jerusalem Post*, July 11, 1981). As the battle lines are being drawn and withdrawn, year in and year out, there are few illusions. Writes the U.S. Secretary of State in his "private notes"—made public by that paper which frequently specialized in such investigative revelations, *The Washington Post*: "Egypt will go back into [the] Arab world with [the] U.S. isolated as Israel's sole defender." This, to many Jews, is extremely disheartening, especially in the light of the fact that Israel's final withdrawal from the Sinai in April 1982, "is estimated to be worth $10 billion."

On the other hand, God's ordinances are often both costly and crucial. Tom Harpur writes from Jerusalem (*Toronto Star*, Dec. 23, 1981), "History has been forged here [and] in the opinion of many, the fate of the peace of the world always hangs in the balance here." It's well known that the huge paw of the Russian Bear is hanging over the Middle East ready at any time arbitrarily to strike. Every Israeli Prime Minister has reiterated that the real enemy they fear in the Middle East is the Soviet Union. And the future will surely vindicate that those fears are valid.

Is it any wonder that—in addition to the enormous weaponry Israel is "given" by the U.S. and others, including Western Europe—she is currently spending six billion dollars annually on her military? At 18, young men—and women— must enter the army for three years, and thereafter serve every 12th month; in fact, virtually every Israeli over 18 is a trained soldier. One in four of Israel's labor force (300,000) work in defense-related jobs (*Calgary Herald*, Aug. 24, 1981). It's important to note that Israel's army is not just for the protection of modern Israel. As an A.P. (May 15, 1982) story stresses, "Prime Minister Menachem Begin's uncompromising doctrine dictates that any terrorist action designed to spill Jewish blood anywhere in the world merits Israeli military retaliation." So a death attempt on Israel's Amassador to Britain ignites the Lebanon thrust. Indeed goings-on in all Arab countries are monitored especially closely. And Israel's Ambassador to the United Nations, Yehuda Blum, is alert and vigorous to remind everyone who will listen that the Arab states "have today 500,000 more men under arms that has NATO, and three times the artillery of the combined NATO forces."

Will Israel's defenses be enough? Not on their own! A recent poll indicated that 40% of Israelis are fed up with the war syndrome and, were the right seeming strong man to come along, would give him a hard look. "Democracy isn't perfect and dictatorship isn't all bad," said Yossi Sarid, Member of the Knesset, adding, "they say dictatorship has its advantages. It solves economic problems. It weakens inflation, puts the trade unions in their place . . . why not try it?" Concludes James Reston in a *New York Times* assessment of Israel's dilemma in the Middle East, "Perhaps then, if we listen attentively, we shall hear, amid the uproar of empires and nations, a faint flutter of wings, the gentle stirring of life and hope. Some will say that this hope lies in a nation; others in a man." "A man?" Exactly! Israel is looking for a man! A man who will offer them peace! "Israel does have a rapacious appetite—not for land but for peace," writes Helen Aminoff in *Time* (Jan. 18, 1982). President Francois Mitterand, in whose France the European Parliament sits, paid an official visit to Jerusalem in March 1982. Israelis were euphoric ("electric with excitement"), as Mitterand "standing beneath a Marc Chagall fresco depicting the Jews' return to Israel" exulted, "Rest assured that a true friend has come to you today, and I say this in the name of everyone in France." He had come "to stress France's unwavering commitment to Israel's security" (*Time*, Mar. 15, 1982).

Such will be the undertaking of the Antichrist when he signs a Peace Pact with Israel immediately after the rapture of the Church. Yes, Israel's euphoria will be enormous. But they'll be betrayed. Then seven years thereafter, the real Redeemer will come to Zion to introduce a world wide kingdom of peace and prosperity. Jerusalem will be the capital!

Meanwhile, Israel is on exact schedule for their reception, first of the antichrist, then of the True Christ. Hebrew was a dead language a century ago. Then Eliezer Ben Yehuda became a fanatic to revive it—if that were possible. Today, Orthodox Jews are more strict about Hebrew in Israel than any Francophone zealot ever has been about French in Quebec. It's definitely a fulfillment to Zephaniah's prophecy (3:9): "For then will I turn to the people a pure language, that they may call upon the name of the Lord, to serve Him with one consent." And with the Hebrew Old Testament, the chief intellectual occupation of Israelis today, the world is reading again and again of their dreams and visions of the Coming Messiah.

When Jesus prophesied, "Ye therefore shall see the abomination of desolation, spoken of by Daniel the prophet, stand in the holy place (whoso readeth, let him understand:)" (Matthew 24:15), He was speaking of a Temple in Jerusalem during the "Great Tribulation." St. Paul elaborated that The Antichrist would surely come, "That man of sin shall be revealed, the son of perdition; who opposeth and exalteth himself above all that is called God, or that is worshipped; so that he as God sitteth in the temple of God, showing himself that he is God" (2 Thessalonians 2:3,4)

Will the Millennial Temple be built before, during or after the Great Tribulation? That is a moot question. There certainly will be a Temple in use during the Great Tribulation, and certainly Christ will have the most Glorious Temple of all, during His

Millennial reign. Meanwhile, in August, 1982 "Israeli Prime Minister Menachem Begin took time off from the Lebanese war to dedicate what has been called "the world's most beautiful synagogue, a soaring $14.5 million building in the heart of Jerusalem. The Jerusalem Grand Synagogue . . . took 10 years to build . . . Some 1,700 oak seats encircle the marble ceremonial area" (Reuters, August 5, 1982). Many Orthodox Jews as well as studious Evangelicals avow this will be Israel's Temple shortly. Certainly it provides for the restoration of sacrifices on an altar.

On the other hand, there are those who believe the Tribulation era Temple must be in the place of where currently the most sensitive building on earth stands. All the world witnessed the events of Easter Sunday 1982, when Alan Harry Goodman, 37, an American-born Israeli soldier with an automatic rifle, shot his way into the Dome of the Rock—Islam's third holiest shrine, killing two and wounding nine. The Mosque of Omar (another name for the Dome) was built first, in the seventh century around the protrusion of bedrock where the prophet Mohammed, according to Moslem tradition, ascended to heaven on his horse. In Goodman's possession was literature from the Kach movement of extremely orthodox Jews, led by ultra-nationalist Rabbi Mei Kahane. *The New York Times* (April 12, 1982) makes the point that they contended uncompromisingly that Bible prophecy promises that the Mosques of Omar and Al Aksa (adjacent) must be replaced with a New Temple because this is "the site of the original Jewish temple built by Solomon, and of the second temple which was destroyed by the Romans in A.D. 70." *The New York Times* noted further that Rabbi Kahane's group placed a bomb at the entrance of the Al Aksa Mosque on Good Friday (April 8, 1982), serving notice, "Wait for more operations against you."

When the Church has been raptured to heaven, there will be 144,000 Jewish evangelists during the Great Tribulation, going to the whole world amidst horrific holocaust and persecution, presenting the Gospel of the Kingdom of Jesus Christ. It will be they in particular who will be "hated of all nations" for Jesus' Name's sake. Jews in unprecedented numbers will become Christians. Many will become martyrs, while other millions are making their way toward Jerusalem to await the coming "Man on the White Horse"—these paralleling those hundreds of millions of heathen who will be heading toward Israel for Armageddon.

Sid Roth, the Hebrew Christian who shares Christ regularly on a worldwide radio network, has computed that for the first time in 1,900 years of church history there is a larger percentage of Jews being born again in today's world than Gentiles. So, joyfully he reaffirms the Pauline text, "I am not ashamed of the Gospel . . . for it is the power of God unto salvation to every one that believeth; to the Jew first, and also to the Greek" (Romans 1:16).

One Saturday afteroon in the spring of 1982, I received a phone call from the West Coast. It was from a Jewish friend with whom I've been very close for thirty years. He told me that his cousin Stan had just come from the funeral of his son Gary, who had been crushed to death atop a truckload of hay bales when it tried to go under a low bridge. Gary was 17. Stan who earlier had led Gary to Christ was himself 17, when, in Belfast, Ireland, he came into the Curzon Theatre, where I was presenting Christ. The previous week I had been at my mother's funeral, so that night I spoke on the second coming of Christ, when He will take home to heaven the dead in Christ, resurrected along with those of us who are alive and remain, forever to be with the Lord. The same Christ Who will appear from heaven to earth as the Man on the White Horse to be proclaimed by Israel as their Messiah, and a nation shall be born [again] in a day. That night—at 17—Stan had come forward and given his life to Jesus Christ. He was forever changed! As we met again in the autumn of 1982 on the occasion of my addressing 1,200 ministers in Spokane, Washington, Stan's faith and face were radiant with hope and expectation!

Chapter Ten

"GOG, THE LAND OF MAGOG"

Recently, I was on an escorted tour of Canada's most celebrated castle—Casaloma in Toronto. On the top floor is a room full of guns, ballistics and a vast collection of other lethal war weapons. Over this ominous array of death instruments hangs a plaque, on which appears George Orwell's dictum, "It is unfortunate, but the history of civilization is largely the history of weapons."

Jesus clearly prophesied that men would "see Jerusalem compassed with armies; then know [that the end] is nigh" (Luke 21:20). One doesn't have to look far in the 1980's to see many armies, mobilized in the Middle East for the most part, for the sole reason of driving Israel from the face of the earth. They are the Islamic armies—of 40 countries, representing 100 million militant Arabs and another half billion peoples, who are chronically obsessed with a passion to obliterate the Jewish people. There is more war paranoia, editorializes the prestigious *Christian Science Monitor* (Jan. 2, 1982) in a classic understatement, in the Middle East than in any other part of the world. They, of course, keep cancelling themselves out, by internecine battles among themselves such as the Iran/Iraqi war, or the Jordan/Syrian skirmishes, or the Libyan/Egyptian fusillades.

But when we think of a modern army, we think of the Soviet Union, who have assembled by many orders of magnitude the most potent military force in human history. Notes Paul Robinson, U.S. Ambassador to Canada in 1982, the Soviet edge over the West is "two times in tactical air, three times in submarines, four times in artillery, and five times in tanks." Experts in both Europe and America, according to *U. S. News and World Report*, estimate the Soviet army has a 2-1 advantage over the West. The Soviets outnumber the U.S., for instance, in armed men by 4.84 million to 2.09 million; and in such a modern battlefield necessity as tanks by 50,000 to 12,000. Currently, the most exhaustive and accurate evaluation of the military strengths of the superpowers can be read in U.S. Defense Department Consultant James F. Dunnigan's *How to Make War* (1982). Dunnigan calculates that the Soviets in 1982 are spending 14 percent of their GNP, and the U.S. 7 percent of theirs on armaments. The bill for the world has already doubled in the '80's from an annual 350 billion to a reported 725 billion dollars.

With this built-up lead (Canadians know what a Russian lead in hockey does), as Henry Kissinger points out, they have already achieved their longtime aim to get into a position where they could call the shots. That's militarily, where currently they very much are! Indeed, a usually self-confident U.S. is polled by the *L.A. Times* (Jan. 10, 1982), and its people "believe, by a 2-1 ratio, that Reagan will not be able 'to halt the spread of Russian influence around the world.' " President Reagan has warned again and again that he has no doubt that the Soviets intend to conquer the world, and that "the only morality they recognize is what will further their cause, meaning they reserve unto themselves the right to commit any crime, to lie, to cheat in order to attain" their objective: to wit the subjugation of all peoples to their authority.

Marxism extended into Russia in 1917, to the Ukraine in 1919, into Azerbaidzhan and Armenia in 1920, into Georgia in 1921, Mongolia in 1924; Estonia, Lapland and Lithuania in 1939; Carelia, Tannu and Tuwa in 1944; North Korea, Manchuria and the Kuril Islands in 1945; Bulgaria and Albania in 1946. By 1949, Marxism extended into all of China, Poland, Romania, Hungary, Czechoslovakia and East Germany; in 1959, Cuba; in 1969, South Yemen; in 1973, all of Vietnam; 1974,

Guinea; 1975, Angola, Laos, Mozambique; 1977, Ethiopia; 1978, Cambodia; and in 1980, Afghanistan. In 1982, three Marxists hold the balance of power in the new Irish parliament (*Toronto Star*, Feb. 22, 1982), and according to a UPI report (July 24, 1982), it was an I.R.A. recruit, trained in Libya, who masterminded the assassination of Lord Mountbatten in 1979, and the bombings that killed 10 British soldiers in London in July 1982. It is also commonly conceded that through the Soviet support for the Argentines in the Falklands War, definite gains were scored for them throughout Latin America. The price of these communist takeovers and gains has been monstrous. Nikolal Tolstoy, in her new *Stalin's Secret War*, reckons that in the Soviet Union Stalin sent as many as one-tenth of the population to the prison camp of the Gulag. Aleksandr Solzhenitsyn estimates that Stalin murdered 67 million in cold blood. In Cambodia, the toll in lives lost in the '70's was the extermination of 3½ million of a 9 million population.

But we're focusing here on Israel. How are the Soviets relevant? Notes Andrei Sakharov, father of the Russian hydrogen bomb, "The Soviet Union has raised anti-Semitism to the level of religion in a godless society." Jesus said that a sure sign of His return would be that the Jews would be hated, and nowhere has this despicability been more an obsession than among the Soviets. Stalin exterminated six million Jews. But the hatred is no longer something the Russians are content to direct at the 3 million Jews left within their borders. They are chafing to eliminate the State of Israel. And the consequence, Arnold Handeleman points out in *The Globe and Mail*, is that "Russia in the Mideast is as innocent as a fox in a henhouse."

We turn to Ezekiel, chapters 38 and 39 for an account that not only Evangelicals, but Orthodox Jews have no doubt applied to the Soviets. Rabbinic literature dealing with this is both massive and definitive, and is an integral basis for current Israel Government policy. Of the Israeli Prime Ministers, none have been as diligent to search the Scriptures daily as Menachem Begin and Ben Gourion. Ezekiel is surely the most

familiar and dramatic passage in Scripture relating to the return
of Israel to their ancient homeland, culminating in verses 21
and 22: "Behold, I will take the children of Israel from among
the heathen, whither they be gone, and will gather them on
every side, and bring them into their own land: and I will make
them one nation in the land." Then we proceed into chapter 38
where we're told, in verse 8, "in the latter years"; and in verse
16, "it shall be in the latter days" at which time worldlings will
hear it asked, "Art thou he of whom I have spoken in old time
by My servants the prophets of Israel?" (vs. 17). And chapter
39—verses 1, 7 and 8—make unmistakably plain the purpose
of what we are about to explore: "Thus saith the Lord God . . .
So will I make my Holy Name known in the midst of My
people Israel; and I will not let them pollute My Holy Name
any more: and the heathen shall know that I AM the Lord, the
Holy One in Israel. Behold, it is come, and it is done, saith the
Lord God; this is the day whereof I have spoken."

What is come? What is done? What day is this? We go back
to the beginning of chapter 38, where Ezekiel recounts: "The
word of the Lord came unto me, saying, Son of man, set they
face against Gog, the land of Magog, the chief prince of . . .
Tubal, and prophesy against him. And say, Thus saith the Lord
God; Behold I AM against thee, O Gog, the chief prince of
Meshech and Tubal," (vss. 1,2). Volumes have been written by
Jewish as well as Christian scholars to establish that Gog and
Magog (first referred to in Genesis 10:2) here refers to Russia,
and Meshech to its capital, Moscow. In addition to the historical
and linguistic clues, we note that they come from their "place
out of the north parts" (38:15), (39:2). The Soviet Union of
course, is precisely north of Israel, from which this prophecy
was written. And they are supplemented by "a great company"
(38:4); by "all thy bands" (39:4), which could be translated
"satellite nations." And as we've noted earlier, they'd have
"all sorts of armour" (38:4). No nation in the history of the
world has put such emphasis on armaments as the Soviets.
It is claimed that they spent 23 percent of their GNP in war

preparations (14 percent on materials, 9 percent on militarily training and manuevering their men and machines of war).

In Ezekiel 38:5 and 6, we're told who comes with them: There's "the house of Togarmah of the north parts." "Of the north parts" is significant. Professor of Assyriology at the University of London, D. F. Wiseman identifies "Togarmah" as Armenia, and while southwestern Armenia lies in modern Turkey, the "north parts" half is in the Soviet Union. located precisely where the Soviets would assemble for a southward march through either Iran or Turkey and Syria toward Israel. On the occasion of the Armenian terrorists killing nine and wounding many others in Ankara, Turkey in August, 1982, the Associated Press (August 9, 1982) reported how presently "political extremists plague Turkey," and its questionable how long Turkish "martial law" can contain them.

Then Ezekiel 38:6 refers to Gomer coming against Israel. Certainly the Orthodox Jew has no doubt but what this refers to East Germany, since in the Talmud Gomer is spoken of as "Germani." While Russia has kept East Germany severly in tow, the Germans' achievements in the West could be seen in their dominance at the Olympics. And those who have known the inner workings of the infiltrations and revolutions effected by the Marxists in Africa and West Asia are aware of what a powerful influence they've had in subversion and communist takeover, probably most specifically in Ethiopia.

Ethiopia, we notice in Ezekial 38:5, is one of the nations joining the Soviets in their march on Israel. *The U.S. News and World Report* (Oct. 19, 1981) points out that the "East German" presence in Ethiopia was crucial in its conversion to Marxism. This event took place in 1974, when Emperor Haile Selassie, a Christian whose name meant "Lion of the Tribe of Judah," was overthrown by a hardline Communist Lt. Col. Mengistu Haile Mariam. *The Toronto Star* (Jan. 3, 1982) assesses he "has turned Ethiopia upside down politically." Former Ethiopian journalist Dereje Denessa writes in the *The New Republic* that the present regime "propped up by Soviet, East German and

Cuban forces has unleashed a reign of terror that has taken the lives of over 500,000 Ethiopians." Haile Selassie addressed The World Congress on Evangelism in 1966 in Berlin, at which time I met him. I recall vividly wondering how Ethiopia would ever come to be a surrogate of the Soviets. It has happened with wicked rapidity. *Church Around the World* (March, 1982) reports that Mariam currently is closing down completely the 500,000 membership Ethiopian Evangelical Church. And so totally is Ethiopia committed to the aggrandizement of world communism that in March, 1982, its trainees were reportedly to be found fighting alongside the guerrilla forces in El Salvador and Nicaragua, half a world away. And when, the following July, Ethiopia undertook a war to conquer Somalia for communism, Cuban and Libyan troops and East German advisors were a part of the attack force (U.P.I., July 13, 1982; *Time*, July 26, 1982). That they'd move with the Soviets in a future war to obliterate Israel is now a universally accepted assumption.

And with Ethiopia, Iran is named (Ezekial 38:5 "Persia"). The West had no more loyal ally—it seemed—in Europe, Asia, or Africa, than the Shah. But Iran had to change sides, because the Bible prophesied it would. The Ayatollah Khomeini has to be the biggest enigma—and largest single news story over the last four years. There are many in government and in the media who are convinced that Khomeini is a communist plant. The Former Polish espionage chief, Colonel Michael M. Goleniewski, a defector to the West, has no doubt that the Ayatolla is a Russian agent. "A picture of Khomeini (the one who left Iraq for France in 1976) showed him with a finger missing, but present photos show him with all his fingers intact," notes an English paper. And according to reliable sources, "on the basis of a secret treaty dating from January 15, 1979, the Soviet Union was to be appealed to by Khomeini under the hypocritical pretext of 'help for the weak and oppressed' to march into the country. In a lightning-like campaign, for which preparations had long been made, the Red Army would have occupied Iran." Obviously the idea is that the Soviets and the Khomeini were in collusion. And what has since happened would tend to bear out this fact. Yes, thousands have been slaughtered; but to a dedicated communist, blood is as cheap as lies are expedient. After all, it is a Marxist maxim: "the end justifies the means."

Time reports that on November 18, 1981, a secret cooperation pact was signed between Iran and Russia, whereby the Soviets would supply Iran with intelligence and security forces, bolster the Islamic Guard (how could atheists do this for religious fundamentalists?) and assist in rebuilding the country's devastated economy. On Febrary 16, 1982, Iran "signed new economic agreemeents with the Soviet Union" declaring, "We want to have good relations . . . we consider the Soviet Union a friendly country." By March 1982, "Iran and the Soviet Union [had] concluded an agreement for 'accelerated economic and political' cooperation." This complete turn-around, commented *Time* (Mar. 1, 1982), has Ayatollah Ruhollah Khomeini . . . an apostate." And as if this weren't enough, the following week the American intelligence community was shocked to turn up evidence of not only "Soviet officers" but "Cuban troops" in Iran—and also a network of Russian intelligence collecting stations (*Time*, Mar. 8, 1982). In its cover story on Iran (July 26, 1982) *Time* notes that Iran has now moved its "eight divisions away from its border with the Soviet Union [it being] the first time since World War II [that] the Iranians had left their 1,090-mile border with the Soviet Union virtually unguarded." Amazingly Iran has no interest in Afganistan. *The Christian Science Monitor* (May 15, 1982) put down the turn-around in the Iraqui-Iran war, in Iran's favor, to the new infusion of Soviet military might into the Iranian army.

In March 1982, Maurice Farqhauson reports that the Soviets consider that within five years their current oil pumping sources will no longer be able to cope with their needs, and that their cheapest source would be either a conquest or takeover of Iran's oil industry to supply their requirements, especially those of their war machines. An alienated and realigned Iran would also tighten the oil tourniquet on the West.

Canadian hero and former Ambassador to Iran, Ken Taylor, says frankly that he reckons "Iran's current chaos could tempt the Soviet Union to move into that country, a move that would be too much for the West." Would this kind of current bond on its own automatically cause Iran to join the Soviets in a war of conquest? Perhaps not! But with the hatred fundamentalist Moslems have for Jews, if that attack were to be on Israel, who would deny that Iran would not collaborate with total abandon? Notes *Newsweek* (May 24, 1982): "Iran launched its latest offensive, 'Operation Holy City of Jerusalem,' on April 30 . . . using a Russian-type mass attack." How could anything be more plain? Iran—destined according to Ezekiel 38:5 to join with the Soviets in an eventual war on Israel—calling its assualt on Iraq "Operation Holy City of Jerusalem." A *Reuters* (May 11, 1982) report notes that as millions of orchestrated Iranians hit the streets on command from the Ayatollah Khomeini to celebrate the third anniversary of their Revolution, their chorus was, "Death to America and Israel." By July of '82, the Jewish synagogue in Tehran was shut down, 2,000 militant Iranian Shi'ites had been sent to Lebanon to fight the Israelis there (called the 'Zionist Demon') while the Khomeini rationalized his launching of "the largest land war since World War II" (A.B.C. TV news) against Iraq on the basis that Inman (The messiah the shi'ites are expecting soon to appear on the world scene to vindicate Islamic fundamentalism) will soon be returning to the earth. The Iranian slogan with which Khomeini aroused his martyr-minded military—including thousands of children—was "Tariq-al-Quds" (—"The Road to Jerusalem"). And old as Khomini is, he has chosen as heir apparent Ayatollah Hossein Montazeri who hopes to mobilize a Muslim army of 20 million men that "would liberate Iraq and Jerusalem in a single victorious march."

The third country named in Ezekiel 38:5 is Libya. "Syria and Libya," notes *The Christian Science Monitor* (May 15, 1982), are "the only Arab countries supporting Iran in its war with Iraq." *Newsweek* cover stories refer to Colonel Mu'ammar

Qadhafi as, "the most dangerous man in the world"; and *Time* says that he's "the world's most notorious supporter of international terrorism." Former U.S. President Carter said on ABC TV, "He's an unscrupulous animal who has no morals of his own and believes in murder . . . as a natural course." President Reagan has felt compelled to surround himself with double security forces to prevent Qadhafi's assassins from killing him—as apparently they killed Sadat—who had called him, "demon possessed." What is Qadhafi's foulest obsession? In proposing merger with Syria, he pledged, "I will declare myself, Mu'ammar Qadhafi, a member of the fedayeen and will go join them to fight Israel. I am going to fight and die in Galilee." "Galilee!" It is both ironic and significant that Qadhafi says Galilee, not Judea, where Jerusalem is located. For if Qadhafi joins with the Soviets in a war to obliterate Israel it would indeed be where the mountains of Northern Galilee rise to merge with the Golan heights and the Lebanon Mountains that the holocaust is to take place. Furthermore, when the 6,000 PLO troops under Arafat were holed up in West Beirut, Qadhafi urged them to die rather than relocate. He would!

Newsweek contends that Qadhafi "bought so much Soviet hardware that he can use less than half of it. Some of it isn't even uncrated . . . Qadhafi is building up an Arab arsenal for a war with Israel." He boasted belligerently during his celebrated visit to Austria that he expects to face "Israel" in "a third world war" in which he will not "hesitate to turn to the Soviet Union" (*Toronto Star*, Mar. 12,13, 1982). Israel and the West are "particularly concerned about Libyans' effort to develop a nuclear capacity." Qadhafi says that with his money "the atom will [soon] have no secrets for anybody; [shortly] we will be able to buy an atomic bomb and all its parts."

The Soviets and their satellites, including East Germany (the most westerly) and North Armenia (the most southerly), plus Libya, Ethiopia and Iran in—till that time—the most mad rage and rampage of human military history are to make a thrust on Israel, with the avowed intent to once and for all obliterate

her from the face of the earth. It is significant that as of this
writing the Soviets have signed military agreements with
Ethiopia, Libya, Iran and Syria. Syria, of course, is a militant
member of the Warsaw Pact. Orthodox Jews link passages from
Isaiah 13, 17, 18, 19 and 24; Joel 1 and 2; Ezekiel 25; and Daniel
11:40-44 to this terrible "Battle of Gog and Magog" as they
call it. Evangelical scholars believe they can see it prophesied
also in Revelation 6 and 8. U.P.I. triggered the media of the
whole Western World into giving very widespread coverage to
the dreams—on the same night—of three distinguished Jewish
Rabbis that "the Battle of Gog and Magog" was not far away.
Noted the U.P.I. report, "The chief Rabbi of the Wailing Wall
in Jerusalem's old city is sure Israel will confront the Soviet
Union in a battle over the holy city. 'And it will be a nuclear
war,' they contended, drawing in both superpowers." As Henry
Kissinger sat half-way up a tree outside Moscow with the late
Leonid Brezhnev, he received the unmistakable impression that
the Soviets will not hesitate to initiate war when they think the
timing is right, and it is in their own interests. Kissinger became
convinced that "the much maligned domino theory turned out
to be correct" after all. For the Soviets, Detente, Salt, and the
Helsinki Accord were all "a ruse to lull us while the Kremlin
prepared a geopolitical offensive . . . when we build weapons,
they build; when we stop, they nevertheless continue to build
. . . Our policy toward the Soviets was based on a balance between the carrot and the stick. But a combination of Watergate
and the new liberal positioning "destroyed the carrot" and "we
were not given a bigger stick" (See *Time*, March 1,8,15, 1982).

Kissinger contends that by the time America recovered from
the setbacks of Vietman, Watergate, and another liberal fling
in the late '70's, the Soviets had moved militarily into a 2-1 lead.
And playing catch-up is usually as hopeless an undertaking in
the military theater as it is in the sports stadium. As the darling liberal of the intellectuals, Susan Sontag shocks her fellow
liberals in 1982, "Like many people on the democratic left, I

did not understand the essentially despotic nature of the Communist system" (*Time*, Mar. 15, 1982).

It needs to be pointed out that Brezhnev himself (not Marx, Lenin, Stalin or Khrushchev) stated candidly "We consider it our prime international task to consolidate and develop the world Socialist system. Detente does not in the slightest abolish and connot abolish or alter [that intent]. None should expect that, because of detente, Communists will reconcile themselves with capitalism [so let it be clear. There] is no place for neutrality or compromise," (*Charlotte News*, May 13, 1982). It is important to point out that: "the most important play in theatres [in the Soviet Union] this year is Tak Pobedim! Thus we will win" (AP, July 24, 1982).

MacLean's editorializes that we are beginning to wake up—hopefully not (but, perhaps) too late—to the realization that even "the reborn European peace movement" (a million marchers) is playing the role of "naive machinations of Soviet dupes." Charles Leroyer wrote concerning a cover story in *MacLean's* on "Is World War III Inevitable?": "The Soviets are locked into a program of massive build up in the belief that they will eventually wear down the will of the Western democracies" (*MacLean's*, Jan. 18, Feb. 15, Mar. 15, 1982).

Turning to Ezekial 38 and 39, we need to keep in mind that the prophet was an ancient. He must have been boggled by what he was about to describe. Less than forty years ago, when the first atomic bomb was detonated, its producers and beholding journalists wondered what to call it. So they labeled it "a mushroom cloud"!

People ask, "But how could the Soviets instigate a nuclear war?" Ezekiel 38 puts it this way: at that "time shall things come into thy mind, and thou shalt think an evil thought" (vs. 10). Ilya Gerol, a former Soviet journalist who now lives in Canada, wrote early in 1982 (*Toronto Star*, Jan. 23, 1982) that Brezhnev, Kirilenko and Pelske, who were presently in power, are between 75 and 81. The real hard-liners are Grigory

Romanov, 58, and Mikhail Gorbachev, 50. They believe "contacts with the West should be cut, even though it might endanger technological progress," and the Soviets must ruthlessly return "back toward the hard-line doctrines of the Stalinist era." (See also *Time*, Mar. 15, 1982). So the Soviets shall "think an evil thought: and thou shalt say, I will go to the land of unwalled villages; I will go to them that are at rest, that dwell safely, all of them dwelling without walls, and having neither bars nor gates, to take a spoil, and to take a prey; to turn thine hand upon the desolate places that are now inhabited, and upon the people that are gathered out of the nations, which have gotten cattle and goods, that dwell in the midst of the land" (vss. 10-12).

Israel today, is exceeding rich in "spoil" (natural resources) in a hungry world. We're told that there's enough potash in the Dead Sea bottom to fertilize the present aricultural lands of the Soviet Union—a country where the crop failures, back to back, now number four—for a thousand years. The President of a University told me that one of the largest untapped deep pools of underground oil in the world is under the Dead Sea. And another is under the old land of Asher, Moses having prophesied, "Let Asher ... dip his foot in oil" (Deuteronomy 33:24). It is exceedingly important to note that Sidon and Tyre are in Asher where, according to *The Toronto Globe and Mail* (July 14, 1982), the Soviets had stockpiled equipment and outfits for as many as a million soldiers (the P.L.O. forces in Lebanon at most were 10,000).

Jewish ownership of "goods" worldwide is legendary. Thus, "in the latter years thou shalt come into the land that is brought back from the sword, and is gathered out of many people, against the mountains of Israel, which have been always waste: but is brought forth out of the nations" (Ezekiel 38:8). "The mountains of Israel"! We wonder if there was any real significance to Begin's annexation of the Golan Heights, in the middle of the Polish crisis? Indeed there was! Dr. Roy Gustafson of our Billy Graham Team told me that an Orthodox Jew in gesturing toward those Golan Heights muttered to him soberly, "On those mountains will lie, one day, the corpses of the Russian armies, thrown back in their attack on our land."

When Eric Meyer wrote in *The Toronto Star* (July 22, 1982) that the Lebanon War is just the type of conflict "which has the potential of drawing the U.S.A. and Russia into a conflict that could result in a nuclear confrontation," I wondered if he was really aware of how tragically true his warning is! One of such Mideast wars is going to do just that! And what makes the Lebanon War of 1982 so significant is the fact that it is a country of north/south mountains in two ranges with two valleys between, connecting Western Syria and modern Israel. It is the logical path that a Soviet led attack on Israel would take. It's vitally relevant here to point out that Lebanon was a part of God's promised land to ancient Israel. In Deuteronomy (1:8) we read: "Behold I have set the land before you: go in and possess [it, including] Lebanon unto [the] Euphrates." Moses, due to his loss of temper never entered the promised land: Joshua died before undertaking the conquest of Lebanon, and neither in the days of the Judges, nor of the kings of Israel was Lebanon taken. (Lebanon and its cities or territories have no less than 174 references in the Scriptures).

Prophetically, it is my belief that Lebanon will be a massive crematorium during the Great Tribulation and a restored paradise during the Millennium. Its mountains will largely be where the Soviets corpses and their war machines will fall. Habbakuk 2 is dealing with leadup events to the Day of the Lord (Hebrews 10:37 clarifies this) where we read: "the violence of Lebanon shall cover thee" (vs. 17). Zechariah 11:1 declares: "open thy doors, O Lebanon, that the fire may devour." And there's Isaiah 10 which refers to the times of the Great Tribulation: "He shall cut down the thickets of the forest with iron, and Lebanon shall fall by a mighty one" (vs.34). When the Millennium is ushered in by the Messiah Jesus, as Israel shall "blossom as a rose" the "glory of Lebanon shall be given unto it" (Isaiah 35:l,2).

Now back to Ezekiel 38:9, where we read that Soviets and their above identified satellites "shall ascend and come like a storm, thou shalt be like a cloud to cover the land, thou, and all thy bands, and many people with thee." If the Israeli armies in the past Middle East wars, with a population of 3 million or less, where able to repulse the armies of a hundred million and more, is it conceivable that the Soviets with 250 million population would take half measures in their assault on Israel? And Qadhafi, with his passion to die in Galilee, just might! And the Ethiopians, and the Iranians—Iraq has found that the Iranians, after all, were too much for them! They'll all be there.

Will the Western Europeans and the Americans just stay home? Doesn't the U.S. have a mutual defense pact with Israel? Won't the insurgent Antichrist have already signed a Peace Covenant with Israel, ensuring the backing of his ten-nation federation? Indeed! And I believe that's who Ezekiel identifies in verse 13: "Dedan, and the merchants of Tarshish, with the young lions thereof" (These I believe are North Americans, and Australians, etc.). And they'll be asking, "Art thou come to take a spoil? Has thou gathered thy company to take a prey? To carry away silver and gold and goods to take a great spoil?" Things will happen so fast!

But immediately "it shall come to pass at the same time when Gog shall come against the land of Israel, saith the Lord God that My fury shall come up in My face. For in My jealousy and in the fire of My wrath have I spoken, Surely in that day there shall be a great shaking in the land of Israel" (vss. 18,19). And God will see to it that He rains upon "him, and upon his bands, and upon the many people that are with him" (vs. 22). Among the things God will arrange to rain down on them will be: "fire, and brimstone." What man-induced shaking in the history of the world has ever matched nuclear explosions?

God can do this by means of miracles utterly beyond our comprehension. Or He may choose to use neutron bombs. Certainly, the Israelis themselves, a decade ago, according to *Time*, readied 13 nuclear bombs for deployment should the necessity arise. An Israeli Government-endorsed book was published May 20, 1982, *Two Minutes Over Iraq*, which reveals that the Israelis currently have 200 nuclear—including neutron—bombs with cruise missiles capable of carrying them to every Arab and Soviet Union capital, and posing a threat which alters considerably the current balance of power. Even as I write, the news is that satellites can be armed with laser beams or death-ray bombs, triggered from halfway around the world, but dropping in from space and literally raining down nuclear "fire, and brimstone." *Time* (Mar. 15, 1982) reports that by the end of the decade the Soviets are planning "a large, permanent, manned, orbital space complex capable of attacking ground, sea and air targets from space." When you read articles like that you literally wonder how close we may well be to the final apocalypse of human history!

I have frequently wondered if God will repeat the pattern of 2 Chronicles 20, where King Jehoshaphat was attacked by three formidable enemies. But instead of Jehoshaphat having to fight, the foreign forces got completely confused and disoriented, and killed each other. Under a *Toronto Star* headliner: 14 Nations Have Nuclear Know-how, two of those powers are Libya and Iran. I frankly wonder if the Libyans, Ethiopians, and Iranians, unable to handle their nuclear weaponry, will not fall into a tragic theater of the absurd and themselves inflict the release of nuclear death engines on the Soviets. This occurred to me when I was reviewing James Dunnigan's *How To Make War*, in which he noted that in the 1973 Yom Kippur War the Arabs fired 2,100 Russian-made antiaircraft missiles. But of the 85 jets shot down, 45 or them—over half—where their own. God has a changeless principle that what men sow, they reap (Galatians 6:7).

We are given two clues about what happens, which are highly revealing. The first is that five-sixths of the Soviet Army involved will perish on the mountains of Israel (Ezekiel 39:2). One-sixth will be turned back to go home and tell about it, apparently! This implies to me that the effect would be of neutron bombs—the troups dead, but their bodies intact. "And seven months shall the house of Israel be burying of them, that they may cleanse the land . . . and there shall they bury Gog and all his multitude: and they shall call it the Valley of Hamon-gog"(Ezekiel 39:12,11). It is a terrible thought: it is now known (A.P. Report: Oct. 14, 1981) that the Russians buried 20,000 Afghans alive as they conquered that country. In the coming war of Gog Magog, the Soviets will at least apparently be dead when they're buried. The further reason I'd be inclined to feel this requires neutron bombs is that they can be used surgically—theater warfare—as confined nuclear warfare is being referred to currently. That's how the Israeli people themselves would have been preserved.

Secondly the Soviets will have used equipment that can be burned, and the Israelis, frugal and fiercely practical as they've always been, will utilize them as fuel for seven years. Ezekiel 39:9,10 reads, "And they that dwell in the cities of Israel shall go forth, and shall set on fire and burn the weapons . . . with fire seven years. So that they shall take no wood out of the field, neither cut down any out of the forests; for they shall burn the weapons with fire." The Soviets for years have been making weapons out of a substance which is harder than steel, but burns like wood—chiefly because it's immune to radar detection. This may or may not be what is meant here. Indeed in 1982, a Swedish bicycle was put on the market, made exclusively of highly inflammable plastic, and General Motors announced that they would shortly be manufacturing car motors made exclusively of the same substance.

However, what is strinkingly significant to me is that I think I see the clue here that this war will be almost immediately after the rapture. Indeed, the rapture may trigger it. American's ranks—with her multitudes of born-again people suddenly gone, would make an opportune moment for the Soviets to make their move. And what may have angered the Soviets would be the Antichrists's having signed a Peace Covenant with Israel. It would certainly rile the Libyans, Ethiopians and Iranians. The Camp David accord is evidence of that!

But the big point that affects terribly the Soviet Union itself, and I fear North Americans, is made in chapter 39:6, "And I will send fire on Magog, and among them that dwell carelessly in the isles (translated "coastlands"); and they shall know that I AM the Lord." I fear that what is meant here is that the U.S.S.R. and the U.S.A. may very well engage in an awful nuclear exchange. For we read that not only will there "be a great shaking in the land . . . all the men that are upon the face of the earth, shall shake" (38:19,20). And linking this passge with its parallels in the Revelation, there will occur the first of the great earthquakes, which will cause mountains and islands to shift. Peoples universally will flee for cover to caves and mountains, and I believe that with "the third part of men killed by the fire [the nuclear bombs], and by smoke [radiation, etc.]" most of these will be Russians and North Americans. Russians to whom God says deliberately, "I am against thee, O Gog" for their unprecedented imposition of atheism upon hundreds of millions; and North Americans, because with the Rapture having taken place, those left behind will be the impenitents— who had "dwell(ed) carelessly," who knew they should repent and turn to God, but didn't. So what does the Bible say? They'll know it's God's judgment, but "the men which were not killed . . . repented not of the works of their hands, that they should not worship devils, and idols of gold, and silver, and brass, and stone, and of wood . . . neither repented they of their murders, nor of their sorceries, nor of their fornication, nor of their thefts" (Rev. 9:20,21).

Professor Edward Teller, father of the American H-Bomb warned, "In a nuclear war, the United States would be wiped from the earth, because the Soviet Union has nuclear weapons which are far more advanced." Isaac Asimov, recently lamented, "The jockeying for nuclear superiority is merely a race to arrange the precise details of the world's suicide." Both of those warnings have awesome relevance. But the first nuclear war will not annihilate all people. Only "a thind" will die. Haward Silverman wrote recently in the *Toronto Star*, "I, along with millions of others, am becoming increasingly disturbed by the seemingly almost certain expectation of a nuclear war within the near future." Haward is right. It is not just a "certain expectation." It's a certainty.

"How shall ye escape, if ye neglect so great salvation?" asked the Hebraicist. There is no escape outside of Christ. In Christ, He delivers from the wrath to come!

Recently I was holding a Crusade in the beautiful Four Seasons Arena in Great Falls, Montana, a city that is surrounded with the huge nuclear warheads of the SAC Minuteman Missiles. A Colonel recalled that ten years before, I had held a Crusade in a large gymnasium in Cheyenne, Wyoming. Into the meeting came the Chief of Operations of the SAC Base there, the very distinguished and highly responsible Colonel Gerald McIlmoyle. Mrs. McIlmoyle had given her life to Christ. On Thursday, Gerald resolved to take time off and attend. He did! He thought about his life. In trying to save millions from nuclear war, might it happen despite his best efforts? And was he really doing anything, let alone the ultimate in life, if he wasn't Christ's? So, that night Colonel McIlmoyle came forward and confessed Jesus as his Lord and Savior. Thereafter, come peace or war, health or illness, life or death, he was Christ's. And today he's a vigorous Christian, worshiping and serving our Lord both in society and in the fellowship of His Church.

Chapter Eleven

"ABOMINATION OF DESOLATION"

Crossing North America during 1982, going from radio studio to TV station to newspaper office to lecture theater, in city after city after city, as if driven by a firey furnace within, was the Scot Benjamin Creme. Professorial, pontifical, and with a mesmerizing mystique, he was a precursor, he said, of a Christ who already is groomed and primed and about to appear to the world. Sixteen metropolitan newspapers including *The New York Times*, *The Washington Post*, and *The Los Angeles Times* had placed in them full page ads, announcing:"THE CHRIST IS NOW HERE." Throughout the text, it was stated that "The world has had enough of hunger, injustice, war." Today "Christians await the Second Coming. Jews await the Messiah, the Buddhists the fifth Buddah, the Moslems the Imum Mahdi, and the Hindus await Krishni. These are all names for one individual. His presence in the world guarantees there will be no third World War . . . Look for a modern man concerned with modern problems—political, economic and social. [Shortly] the Christ will announce his identity and . . . will speak to humanity through a worldwide television and radio broadcast. His message will be heard inwardly, telepathically by all people in their own language. From that time . . . we will build a new world. [The Christ's] task will be to show you how to live together peacefully as brothers." Creme highlights his ad:

"Since July, 1977, the Christ has been emerging . . . in a well-known modern country." A generation or two ago, Creme would have been dismissed as a kook. The tragedy of the 1980's is that he was not dismissed. He was on a roll. And the buzz which gathered around him was frightening. I thought of the words of Jesus, recorded in John 5:43, "I AM come in my Father's name, and ye receive Me not." But alas, "Another shall come in his own name; him ye will receive."

The most mysterious and perhaps misunderstood phrase Jesus ever uttered was "abomination of desolation." It's found in Matthew 24:14,15, where we read, "Then shall the end come. When ye therefore shall see the abomination of desolation, spoken of by Daniel the prophet, stand in the holy place, (whoso readeth, let him understand)." When we turn back to Daniel, we read about the most evil man of all history, leading the world into history's most horrible holocaustic epoch. John's recording of the Revelation of Jesus Christ reads in many places as though it were half exposition of Daniel and half an elucidation of today's most *avant-garde* science journals. St. John used the word "Antichrist" several times in his epistles, assuring his readers that "Antichrist shall come" (1 John 2:18). St. Paul also dealt with the coming Antichrist, devoting most of 2 Thessalonians 2 to "the man of sin," as he labels him.

They said of Hitler, "You wouldn't believe the number of names by which he was called!" Why? Because he was so evil. The Antichrist in the Bible is called by many names—for the same reason. Daniel, to whom Jesus refers, referred to him as "the willful King," "the prince that shall come," "the King of fierce countenance" and "the little horn." St. John labels him "the Beast," "666" as well as "the Antichrist"; and St. Paul—in addition to "the man of sin"—calls him "the son of perdition," "the man doomed to destruction," and "that wicked one."

Why is the Antichrist to be the most wicked man in all history? The answer is in his name: Antichrist. The Antichrist is the very antithesis of Jesus Christ! Looking at the two in Scripture, the contrast is total. Jesus Christ is "God manifest in the flesh—the mystery of godliness" (1Timothy 3:16). Antichrist is "the mystery of iniquity" (2 Thessalonians 2:7,9). Jesus Christ is the truth (John 14:6), the Antichrist "the lie" (2 Thessalonians 2:11); Jesus Christ came to save (Luke 19:10), the Antichrist to destroy (Daniel 8:24); Jesus Christ is the Good Shepherd (John 10), the Antichrist, the evil shepherd (Zechariah 11:16,17). Jesus Christ came in His Father's Name, the Antichrist in his own (John 5:43); Jesus Christ came to do His Father's will (John 6:38), the Antichrist, his own will (Daniel 11:36). Jesus Christ humbled Himself (Phillippians 2:8), Antichrist exalts himself (2 Thessalonians 2:4); Jesus Christ was despised and afflicted (Isaiah 53), the Antichrist will be admired and lauded (Revelation 13:3,4). Jesus Christ was from heaven, to which He returns (John 6:38), the Antichrist from hell, to which he'll be returned (Revelation 20:10).

The predictions of the Antichrist are worldwide today. Hollywood's Harvey Bernhart, a producer, states candidly that his *The Final Conflict* which is the third of a series (the two previous ones in the sequel being: *The Omen* and *Damien— Omen II*) is definitely a deliberate effort to capitalize on the universal fascination the people of our times have for the Antichrist. The lead character, Damien, is cast as a 32-year-old business tycoon. Named United States ambassador to Britain, he goes on to coerce his way by guile and military conquest to become a world dictator. In the end he is overcome by the Second Coming of Christ. Bernhart makes the point that he had not been a religious man. But he sought counsel from "Jess Moody, past president of 35,000 Baptist churches" and many "enthusiastic Roman Catholic clergy, including 'The Brothers of Notre Dame.' " Bernhart said that irreligious as he was he found himself unable to "avoid a certain involvement when dealing with this subject. Look, the prophecy is set according to the Book of Revelation, and I can't say for sure whether or not the antichrist is here. But take a look at the disarray of the world today. It certainly is following what Revelation said. I think we are living "awfully near to Armageddon now" (*Can. Press*, Apr. 8, 1981).

And in 1982, augurs of the Antichrist keep firing shrill sirens through the new corridors. The most blasphemous shocker came in 1982. It was widely publicized in the press, and in lead stories on our evening TV newscasts. It was no great surprise that after the kind of "hype" it got, *The Holy Blood and the Holy Grail* was soon a best-seller.

Henry Lincoln is a veteran BBC TV writer and filmmaker. A decade ago, he did a British Broadcasting Corporation documentary on a 19th-centry French priest, Berenger Sauniere, who purportedly amassed great wealth after discovering and deciphering four parchments hidden in a hollow pillar of his church at Rennes-le-Chateau, a hilltop village in the south of France. Lincoln co-researched and co-authored the newly published book with U.S. novelist Richard Leigh and New Zealander Michael Baigent. The authors contend that "a secret society called Prieune de Sion" still exists "to guard the Holy Grail—according to medieval legend, the cup used by Jesus at the Last Supper." They allege that Jesus staged and survived His crucifixion, married Mary Magdalene and has living descendants among Europe's nobility. They purport that "Prieune de Sion" exists to protect alleged royal descendants of Jesus and prepare the way for their accession to world power. The authors allege that patrons of this sinister secret order have included Isaac Newton, Victor Hugo, and Charles De Gaulle.

Lincoln, Leigh, and Baigent report that they have held several secret meetings with the order's wary present grand master, Pieurne Plantard, a librarian, a French Resistance hero, and former associate of Charles De Gaulle. The authors allege that Plantard is a lineal descendant of Jesus Christ, and the Prieune is working to establish one of Christ's descendants on the throne of a united Europe. Another purported descendant, Alain Poher, a former French interim president (1969 and 1973) may be the candidate in question.

What, of course, brings this fantastic and completely

apocryphal fabrication into relevance here is that authors Lincoln, Leigh, and Baigent hold that "the present-day Prieune is working to a precise timetable, and that Prieune expects France to have a king on the throne by 1990. Prieune members are said to wield quiet influence in France, Switzerland, and the European Parliament. Its members—or close associates— include politicians, financiers, religious leaders, and one of the foremost writers of our time, the Mexican novelist (and former ambassador to France) Charlos Fuentes . . . The authors mention that the Prieune de Sion claims to possess the treasure of the Temple of Jerusalem, lost since Roman legions sacked the city in 70 AD and rediscovered by the Knights Templar, the Prieune's former military arm."

My view of all this is expressed in the words of one of those listed in the book as a "descendant of Jesus," the Duke of Devonshire: it's "absolutely obnoxious." I am acquainted with the Duke, as I am with the Right Reverend Hugh Montefiore, Anglican Bishop of Birmingham, who dismisses it with righteous indignation as "worthless" going from "howler to howler." Montefiore points to 79 "inconsistencies . . . of gross errors, vital omissions, gravely misleading statements" in fact totally obscene and profane "hypotheses." Why do I discuss the above? Obviously not because I put any credit whatsoever in its validity; but rather, to show just how ready millions are to pursue an Antichrist, who will indeed ascend the throne of Europe. Then eventually—for 42 months (Revelation 13:5)—he will have the rulership of the whole world.

The coming of the Antichrist will certainly be auspicious. He'll emerge as a nice guy—someone who could have dictated to the late Dale Carnegie his *How To Win Friends and Influence People*. Yet Jesus intimated that he'll be the worst of wolves in sheep's clothing. He'll be not unlike the burglar who was caught in a break-in, wearing a President Reagan mask. St. Paul, writing to the Thessalonians, made unmistakably clear that the "man of sin" would arrive on the scene with "power and signs and lying wonders" (2 Thessalonians 2:9); as it were "transformed into an angel of light," appearing as a "minister of righteousness" (2 Corinthians 11:14,15). Let us take Jesus' instruction to His disciples to turn back to the prophecy of Daniel—to chapter 9. There we learn that when the times of the Gentiles are complete, which I personally take to be the rapture of the church, the Antichrist will make his move and "confirm the covenant with many [the context indicates the Jews] for one week [that is, one heptad, or period of seven years]. And in the midst of the week he shall cause the sacrifice and the oblation to cease, and for the overspreading of abominations he shall make it desolate, even until the consummation, and that determined shall be poured upon the desolate" (Daniel 9:27). St. Paul teaches, as I read it, that the Antichrist will not be "revealed" until this present age of the Holy Spirit is complete and the Church is "taken out" (2 Thessalonians 2:6-8; 1 Thessalonians 4:16-18).

Ripening Western Europe for the Antichrist's take over, more than any one other factor is spiritual apostasy. While millions are turning to Christ in Asia, Africa and the Americas, one seldom hears of any such wide spread wakenings in modern Europe. The evangelical churches are tiny, and the conventional churches are sparsely attended. The radio and TV media have been mysteriously closed to the Gospel for two generations. The percentage of the population which profess to be born again is only a small fraction of Christians in North America. A remark in *Church Around the World* (March, 1982) is typical: "In 30 years of TV broadcasting, the people of France have never seen an evangelistic program." The fundamental reason why Europe will be taken over by the Antichrist is because of the tremendous lack of spiritual committment.

Currently, two dramatic fulfillments of prophecy converge, indicating that the Antichrist could well be trained and in the wings, making ready for his revelation. The first is that the entry of Greece into the European Economic Community in 1981 brings their number of nations to ten. Originally, this prophecy was made by Daniel, who interpreted the dream

Nebuchadnezzar had of a metallic colossus bottoming out into the ten toes. Daniel declared the ten toes represented ten nations, emerging where the old Roman Empire once stood, at the end of secular history. Jerome wrote 1,600 years ago, "All ecclesiastical authors have handed down that, in the consummation of the world, when the Kingdom of the Romans is destroyed, there will be ten rulers in the Roman world." A hundred years ago, F. C. Bland, basing his prediction on the Bible—as seen by a consensus of his expository contemporaries—said, "Ten kingdoms will be on the scene in the last days, the kingdoms designated by the ten toes of the image and by the ten horns of the Beast in Daniel." Robert Middleton wrote 65 years ago, when it couldn't have looked more unlikely, that the Antichrist "will have the international federated army of the United States of Europe at his command, the military might of ten great powers."

Men as separated as Friedrich Neitzsche, Aristotle Briand, Winston Churchill, and John Kennedy dreamed of such a European Confederacy; and 25 years ago, it was formed. A decade ago its original six nations became nine, with the intent of one day stabilizing with ten "inner circle" members, something which happened in 1981. The ECC formed a Parliament with 410 members, thereby going into the eighties with political intent. Its President is Jewish—Simone Veil, an Auschwitz survivor with fierce allegiance to Israel. The newscaster on the CKO-radio network in March, 1982, remarked of the President of the European Parliament that you think of this person as a sort of "political messiah."

Most of the countries in the ECC, of course, belong to NATO, and the news of the last year has been dominated by their efforts to galvanize a defense system to resist a potential attack from the East. The official organ of the ECC, *Europe Magazine*, contends regularly that the ECC must not only politicize but militarize. Professor Robert Neild of Cambridge, and director of the Stockholm International Peace Research Institute, in an article in *The New York Times* (Feb. 17, 1982) contends that the countries of Western Europe are becoming increasingly wary of leaving their defense in the hands of the Americans. He points to the fact that when NATO was formed, Western Europe's GNP was scarcely half of that of the U.S. Today it exceeds it, and as they are "face-to-face ready to resort to nuclear weapons" with the Soviets and Warsaw Pact countries, there has never been such a ground swell of resolve to take their defense into their own hands.

So there is definitely a centripetal force at the center of Western Europe today. With 10.7 million (9.5 percent) of its work force unemployed, by far the highest since World War II, its members are talking constantly of closing ranks economically. The SS-20 Missiles—now numbering 275—pointing at them from the U.S.S.R. have them terrified of nuclear war, and dropping their former pride to unify. "We" affirms the Iron Woman Margaret Thatcher going into 1982, "will stick together." Asserts Italy's President Sandro Pertini, no one will "destabilize" our position. And politically, one of the latest to speak up was the British Foreign Secretary. "You must not expect," he served notice, Europeans "to sing in unison, but in harmony." That harmony in the Falklands crisis was certainly stretched, but strengthened for the long road ahead.

It's now official. "The ten European Common Market countries" have decided "to issue a common passport." And militarily there's increasing "standardization" of their armaments (*New York Times*, Feb. 20, 1982). It should be stated here that the present "ten" may not be the eventual "ten." Spain, Portugal, and Austria have applied for membership; and currently there are gathering contentions in Greece and Denmark to secede, with Ireland—not a member of NATO—perhaps withdrawing. There are strongly held interpretations of Daniel 7:8 and 24 that whoever is the military leader of the eleventh nation to join the ten nations may well be the Antichrist.

While it is my belief that the Antichrist will not be revealed until the Church is raptured, the first question Pat Robertson asked me on a recent 700 Club program was whether I thought

King Juan Carlos of Spain might turn out to be the Antichrist. I had just the day before been reading about him in *Time* and *The New York Times*. A direct descendant of both Queen Victoria and Louis XIV, he certainly has ample royal blood in his veins. At 44, he just might be the most highly trained military leader Europe has ever seen. He graduated from the academies of all three branches of Spain's armed services—the army, navy, and airforce—training for 27 years prior to his inauguration as King. *U.S. News And World Report* (Oct. 19, 1981) says he definitely leans toward European membership "as a means of ending decades of Franco-forced isolation—and as a way to turn the military away from internal politics and coups, toward international affairs and defense." In the summer of 1982 Washington pledged two billion dollars to Spain to build up its military.

How the move of the emerging Antichrist into leadership of the ECC will be precipitated is not something that it is my view we can—or need—know now. But there is certainly a power vacuum in our world, and the trend is toward dictatorship, not democracy. Observes columnist Sydney Harris: "At heart, we are largely totalitarians masquerading as democrats." Freedom House in its *Freedom at Issue* for January 1982, a 44-page assessment comparing 1982 with 1981 appraised: "Almost 325 million people worldwide saw their human rights decline or vanish . . . losses greatly outnumbered the gains." Laments Margaret Atwood, "Total up the number of countries in which there is anything resembling what we think of as democracy. There are really a very few. It's shrinking." Kurt Waldheim retired from the United Nations, which showed such hope a generation ago, groaning: "This place is a depository for insoluble problems." *Time* quoted one of Britain's leaders during the Skinhead Street riots of 1981, "There is panic and there is fear, because they know that this country is very, very close to being completely out of control." And as was reported, it was not the leftist but neo-Nazi types who were the chief agitators—as is the current situation in West Germany. In fact, in an A.P. analysis (Feb. 20, 1982) it is stated that definitely "Fascism is on the rise in Italy, West Germany, Britain, France, Belgium, and Spain; and police have found links . . . between several ultra-right wing groups. Certainly, this is the issue which has been at stake in the British-Argentina war over the Falklands."

So an Antichrist wielding actual *authority* will take over the reins of Western Europe, precipitated by an economic collapse, or a military foray (perhaps a nuclear theater war-thrust by the Soviets). *Maclean's* (Feb. 15, 1982), in a cover story by Editor-in-Chief Peter Newman, entitled: "Is World War III Inevitable?" is convinced that a war escalating into a nuclear exchange—perhaps a "nuclear theater war" confined to Europe—is a distinct possibility in the near future. Or it may be through a political power vacuum. Meg Greenfield asks in *Newsweek* (Jan. 25, 1982) of an imploding Europe, "What variation on the Alliance (NATO), or substitution for it, can fill the void?" Certainly, militarizing the ECC is one probability. *European Community* asserts, "The statesmen who proposed and negotiated the (ECC) saw a politically united Europe as the ultimate goal of their endeavors." On the other hand, former U.S. Defense Minister James Schlesinger reckons currently that Europe is surely the most likely place in the world for World War III to break out: "The far greater danger is miscalculation and escalation in Western Europe."

And the first *augmentation* of the Antichrist's power beyond "the ten" will be to sign a peace pact with a desperately questing Israel. *Newsweek* (May 24, 1982) reports, "The European Economic Community [has] undertaken a peace initiative in the Mideast." Already they're acting in concert. President Francois Mitterand is incomparably friendlier toward Israel than his predecessors, D'Estang or De Gaulle. And this is also true of Margaret Thatcher and Helmut Schmidt. In a little-known effort, back in the '70s, Israel sought membership in the ECC—more for military security than economic gain. Now Eric Moonman, a former ECC Monitor, writes, "Israel should

pursue its earlier application to become a member of the ECC."
At a time when the press is reporting a hardening of U.S. policy
toward Israel, *The New York Times* (Feb. 1, 1982) reports how
finally, amazingly, "Britain, France, Italy and the Netherlands"
with the support of the whole "Common Market" have agreed
to send a peace-keeping force of 2,500 to Sinai, to help maintain the peace in the Middle East. Whatever impressions
accrued from the Israeli war in Lebanon during the summer of
1982, few objective observers could doubt that what Israel
craves most, currently, is peace and security on her borders.
The first act by the Antichrist will be to provide that kind of
a pact for them. In April 1982, I was addressing a Rotary Club
in Halifax on this theme. Afterwards a prominent Jew told me
that he was just back from Israel, where a government leader
assured him that currently many in Israel feel that to maintain peace they'll have to opt for a military dictatorship.
Antichrist will one day be just that.

The Antichrist then moves into Israel and becomes their
guarantor of peace. Jesus, Paul, John, and Daniel all distinctly
allude to how he moves from the political into the ecclesiastical,
and becomes involved in the rebuilt Temple worship. It is to
this that Jesus alludes in His already cited quotation from
Daniel, regarding the Antichrist standing in the Holy Place performing the "abomination of desolation." He turns from
political protector to spiritual desecrater. St. Paul writes that
"that man of sin [shall] be revealed, the son of perdition; who
opposeth and exalteth himself above all that is called God, or
that is worshipped; so that he as God sitteth in the temple of
God, shewing himself that he is God" (2 Thessalonians 2:3,4).

We have already looked at the matter of the rebuilding of the
temple, currently the most politicized place of worship in the
world. Will the Moslem Dome of the Rock sitting atop the old
Solomon Temple foundation be blown up, as almost happened
by the hand of a zealous Australian in 1980? Will it come down
in an earthquake? Will it collapse in the terrible holocaust—
which some of us believe will take place, perhaps immediately

after the rapture, when 5/6ths of the Soviet Army will be destroyed on the mountains from the Golan Heights northward?

Many think that the Temple will be built at the beginning of the Millennium, after Armageddon, and that during the Great Tribulation the Jerusalem Great Synogogue, completed in 1982 and located on King George Street next to Hechal Shlomo (Rabbinical Headquarters), will be the scene of the "Abomination of Desolation." The two buildings share a common open plaza, large enough to have an altar of sacrifice. There are a great number of Orthodox Jews who anticipate the reinstituting of animal sacrifice in the near future. Thousands of Levites have been trained, and many are descended from the faithful priest Zadok, his descendants having been trained as high priests. An actual majority of Jews, of course, have been—and are—going back to Israel as secularists, just as St. Paul predicted they would. Romans 9-11 states that they will return in unbelief and then a nation will be born [again] in a day! It is important to keep in mind that the current Begin Government owes its paper-thin majority to its strictest orthodox Jewish sects on the extreme right.

We have already dealt with the Soviet invasion of Israel, which biblically is one of the most clearly prophesied events of the future. Once Soviet Communism, with all its satellites, is defeated, the Antichrist strikes out to conquer the world, which he orchestrates from Jerusalem. It is the mid-point in the Seven-Year Tribulation—the latter half being, as Jesus called it, the "great tribulation, such as was not since the beginning of the world to this time, no, nor ever shall be" (Matthew 24:21).

Since Jesus referred us to Daniel, let's look at his projection in prophecy of what the Antichrist will be like as he goes out and conquers the world: "And the king shall do according to his will; and he shall exalt himself, and magnify himself above every god, and shall speak marvelous things against the God of gods, and shall prosper till the indignation be accomplished: for that that is determined shall be done. Neither shall he regard the God of his fathers, nor the desire of women, nor regard any god: for he shall magnify himself above all. But in his estate shall he honour the God of forces: and a god whom his fathers knew not shall he honour with gold, and silver, and with precious stones, and pleasant things" (Daniel 11:36-38).

One is boggled just to think of the Antichrist conquering the world. One thing that the Falklands War between Britain and the Argentine shows is just how fragile the hold of democracy is in the 1980's. India is depicted in 1982 in *The Los Angeles Times* as a land of "mushrooming corruption, declining law and order, and growing public desquiet about the government's apparent inability to cope." The Antichrist will make short shrift there. The [Willy] Brandt Commission on World Development reports that in the Third World instead of there being an improvement, there's been further tragic "deterioration in the two years" (of the '80s). *The New York Times* assures that much of the Third World—through voices like Castro's castigations of the West in the U.N.—"Advocate" a "New International Economic Order." Certainly, the Antichrist will promise them this. *Consensus* for August 1981, points to how ripe Canada is: "Mark MacGuigan [currently our Foreign Secretary] on November 9, 1979 . . . as the Chairman of the World Federalist Parliamentary Association, which consisted then of some 100 MPs and senators . . . proposed, among other things, that Canada commit itself to transferring agreed national powers to world authorities when this would facilitate world peace." This doubtless was well intended. But as the late John Diefenbaker pointed out, it will play into the hands of some future brute of a dictator, who will come as a peace-pretender, and switch into the most traitorous warmonger the world has ever known.

The *authorization* of the Antichrist's power is from the Devil himself. St. John—in Revelation 13—saw how "the dragon gave him his power, and his seat, and great authority. And I saw one of his heads as it were wounded to death; and his deadly wound was healed: [the Antichrist dies and rises from the dead] saying, Who is like unto the beast? Who is able to make war with him? And there was given unto him a mouth speaking great things and blasphemies; and power was given unto him to continue forty and two months. And he opened his mouth in blasphemy against God, to blaspheme His name, and His tabernacle, and them that dwell in heaven. And it was given unto him to make war with the saints, and to overcome them; and power was given him over all kindreds and tongues and nations. And all that dwell upon the earth shall worship him, whose names are not written in the Book of Life of the Lamb slain from the foundation of the world. If any man have an ear, let him hear" (Revelation 13:2-9).

This is one of the great understatements of the Bible, "If any man have an ear, let him hear!" We have already noted how ubiquitous drugs, worldwide, are opening up the younger generation especially to demonization; how the whole pop rock music scene is brainwashing the young to worship the devil. "A warning to the youth" is issued in *The Toronto Star* (Apr. 29, 1982) under a headline: "Hidden Satanic Mess", which reads, "Those rock 'n roll records you're listening to may be turning you into a *Satanic fiend.* And you may *not* even know it." Example? "I sing because I live with Satan. The Lord turns me off. There's no escaping it. Here's to my sweet Satan." Add to this the Satan worship and devil emphasis in current novels and movies, and it can be seen how conditioned the consciousness of the masses is becoming to pave the way for a demonized dictator to move in and take over.

So the Dragon, which the Revelator indentifies as the Devil, *authorizes* or *empowers* the Antichrist. And he really does turn into a beast of a man. Some people understandably will argue that a Juan Carlos or any number of other prospective candidates for the Antichrist could never sink to those depths. Could he not? I think the Falklands war tells us what a war-mongering Junta can do. It's often quoted, "Power corrupts; total power totally corrupts." We've often seen it. I have a friend, who is an old man now. For a generation he has been

one of the strongest Christians I've ever known. He's German.
The irony is that he was nominally a Christian fifty years ago.
In my friend's Drawing Room, Hitler made many of his plans
for the Nazi Party. "The streets of our country are in turmoil;
the universities are filled with students rebelling and rioting;
Communists are seeking to destroy our country, and the
Republic is in danger—yes, danger from within and without.
We need law and order! Without law and order, our nation cannot survive!" Was that an excerpt from a President Reagan
address to the American Police Convention in 1982? No, it was
a statement by Adolf Hitler in 1932!

As a Bishop often has an auxiliary bishop, the *antichrist* will
have an *auxiliary*: "a Junta" arrangement, if you will! John in
Revelation 13 goes on, "And I beheld another [the word means
another of a similar kind] beast coming up out of the earth; and
he had two horns like a lamb, and he spake as a dragon. And
he exerciseth all the power of the first beast before him, and
causeth the earth and them which dwell therein to worship the
first beast, whose deadly wound was healed. And he doeth great
wonders, so that he maketh fire come down from heaven . . .
in the sight of men."

The devil has always been an imitator. Here we see him
counterfeiting the Triune God: Father, Son and Holy Spirit—
with himself as the Dragon corresponding to the Father; the
Antichrist aping Jesus Christ, wounded, dead and resurrected,
at which time his powers become supernatural to a new degree;
and now "the false prophet," copying the Holy Spirit. This
second beast focuses attention on the first beast, the Antichrist.
St. Paul wrote to the Thessalonians of this Antichrist "whose
coming is after the working of Satan with all . . . deceivableness
of unrighteousness in them that perish" (2 Thessalonians
2:9,10).

This brings us to universal man's *awe* for the Antichrist. Let's
pick up from Revelation 13 where we read that for forty-two
months the false prophet seizes supernatural power and "in the
sight of men" (Satellite TV, as we've already seen) "deceiveth

them that dwell on the earth by the means of those miracles which he had power to do in the sight of the beast; saying to them that dwell on the earth, that they should make an image to the beast, which had the wound by a sword, and did live. And he had power to give life unto the image of the beast, that the image of the beast should both speak, and cause that as many as would not worship the image of the beast should be killed" (Revelation 13:13-15).

To go back and quote from self-styled precursor Benjamin Creme, when the coming "Christ" to whom he alludes—the Bible calls him the Antichrist—arrives, he will not emerge as a religious leader "but as a superman: mentally, physically and psychologically, He'll appear as the master of wisdom. And his breadth of view, his inclusiveness, [his] grasp of human problems and ability to indicate the solutions to man's dilemma, political and economic, religious and social," will set him apart from all others. "One day soon, men and women all over the world will gather around their radio and television sets to see and hear the Christ: to see his face, and to hear his words dropping into their minds—in their own language. In this way they will know that he is truly the Christ." In short, it's not mere allegiance, but worship the Antichrist will elicit.

Therefore, the false prophet causes man to worship the Antichrist, including a huge image to the beast, which might well be the chromascope over which all world television programming is shown. Fedor Dostoevski, the Russian, was right to insist that men universally are worshiping creatures. H. L. Mencken's dictum, "Democracy is a form of religion. It is the worship of jackals by jackasses," might be adjusted at mid-tribulation to read that as fleas gravitate to a dog, so the adulations of the people of the world will be magnetized by the Beast. And "the Image"! I was watching on TV that Halloween Appeal, showing desperately poor African children looking up at a big image of UNICEF, with the moving music and lyric, "The only friend they have is UNICEF!" That's a tiny reflection of the kind of focus there'll be on the Antichrist. Clement

Rogers bemoans, "Life has become so complicated that world government cannot be carried on by one man unless he is omnipresent." The Antichrist can have that kind of presence through television. As we have already noted, it is extremely technologically feasible for today's futurists.

One increasingly powerful force which is militating inscrutably in this direction is the media. And surely it needs to be pointed out, as *The Chicago Tribune* tells us from a polling, that whereas 42 percent of Americans go to church or a synogogue, only 8 percent of the media people do, which means—as the article makes clear—that already they tend to be more than five times as irreligious as the general public. And while the TV networks are crying about the greed of the oil companies, NBC made a bigger profit last year than all the oil companies combined. Billy Graham has said that the president of a major TV network, in fact, has more power than the U.S. President. All dictators know that to control the masses, it's imperative that they control the media. And do the masses read papers, watch television and listen to radios? Yes, as we've pointed out elsewhere—very much so. Colonel Qadhafi of Libya brags that "in ten years we have imported 90 transistors per person."

Progressively, as he tightens his grip on the world, the *autocracy* of the Antichrist will become more and more totalitarian. The chameleon of the ages, he'll have turned from peace promoter to warmonger; from fraternizing friend to fierce foe, as he unsheaths his sword with a worldwide vengeance. And he'll have all the modern mechanisms and electronics at his disposal. Daniel, in the verse in which he intimates that he may be at least part Hebrew, observes, "In his estate shall he honour the God of forces: and a god whom his fathers knew not shall he honour" (Daniel 11:38). Bert Raphael, Chairman of the Canadian Lawyers and Jurists for Soviet Jewry, writes in *The Toronto Star*, "The point our leaders continue to miss is that with the ever-shrinking number of democracies in the world, there may soon be no one left to protest." The Antichrist will not tolerate a million marchers in Europe—or anywhere—against his regime. *The Toronto Sun* is unwittingly prophetic in forseeing "a time in the future when no one questions the dictator," and reprisals "will be ubiquitous." He'll back his moves with immediate military force. *Time*, referring to Poland (Jan. 25, 1982), could have been alluding to the future Antichrist: "Napoleon was correct when he declared that morality belongs to the country with the largest artillery." The Antichrist will go all out to gain complete military control of the planet— something which has been denied the Alexanders, the Charlemagnes, the Napoleons, the Hitlers and the Stalins. Of course, he won't have forewarned the avant-garde intellectual communities of the West of his intentions, at least not when initially he's pursuing power.

This leads to the *austerity* and the Antichrist. There are so many passages on this, both in the Old Testament and the New. In Revelation 6:15,16, we read that "the kings of the earth, and the great men, and the rich men, and the chief captains, and the mighty men, and every bondman, and every free man, hid themselves in the dens and in the rocks of the mountains; and said to the mountains and rocks, Fall on us, and hide us from the face of him that sitteth on the throne, and from the wrath of the Lamb: for the great day of His wrath is come; and who shall be able to stand?" (Revelation 6:15-17). The masses under the suppression of a ruthless dictator have always hated it, but what can they do? Sofia Berchanowski (65) arrived in Toronto, having miraculously gotten out of Poland, to say that the Poles she knew "sank into listless despair when military rule was imposed. People just stay quiet—they pray for God to help them. They walk around the streets with their faces long and thin. My relatives pray to die, instead of living in this situation." This sounds very much like what Jesus said in the verses linked to His depiction of what life would be like when "the abomination of desolation," the Antichrist, was ensconced for his 42 months in the "Great Tribulation." "Then let them which be in Judea flee into the montains: let him which is on the housetop not come down to take anything out of his house: neither let him which is in the field return back to take his clothes. And woe unto them that are with child, and to them that give suck in those days! But pray ye that your flight be not in the winter, neither on the sabbath day: for then shall be Great Tribulation, such as was not since the beginning of the world" (Matthew 24:16-21).

I thought of this passage when I read the *Reuters* report (Mar. 31, 1982) that "President Ronald Reagan has proposed a seven-year buildup of the nation's civil defense program that would relocate up to 80 percent of the country's population if a nuclear war was imminent. The $4.2 billion program calls for residents of large cities "to rush for shelters in the country: preferably in the mountains."

Which leads to the *auditing* of the Antichrist. It's one thing for the world to see the Antichrist on TV, or hear him on the radio. It's another thing for him to see them, and to impose total control over them. Revelation 13:16-18 characterizes the regime of the Antichrist, when "he causeth all, both small and great, rich and poor, free and bond, to receive a mark in their right hand, or in their foreheads: and that no man might buy or sell, save he that had the mark, or the name of the beast, or the number of his name. Here is wisdom. Let him that hath understanding count the number of the beast: for it is the number of a man; and his number is Six hundred threescore and six."

A hundred years ago, Cecil Rhodes predicted, "In one hundred years all the world trade will be conducted by one man." The world currently is in deep financial trouble— something we didn't think, even ten years ago, could happen. The U.S. has just gone over a trillion dollars in debt, and Canada a hundred billion. West Germany's former Chancellor Helmut Schmidt complains that interest rates are higher than they've been since Christ was born. Many are wondering if there's some super financial wizard out there on the horizon somewhere who can economically intervene and save us. For years we've been hearing about "Big Brother," the idea being initially popularized by George Orwell's *1984*.

Doubleday has just published Alix Granger's *Don't Bank On It*, in which he contends that today's "ubiquitous computer . . . will change banking more in the next five years than it has changed in the last 100." World banking is introducing Electronic Funds Transfer System (EFTS), whereby each citizen will be issued with what today we call a Credit Card. But the wave of the future is to eliminate all other cards and get us down to one plastic card on which will appear our SIN (Social Insurance Number)—in the U.S., Social Security Number. Even now when we go, for instance, to the supermarket, we bring our groceries to the counter, the automatic scanner then checks them out, and we pay by placing our card in the slot. Money as we know it, under the Antichrist will likely be eliminated. Employers will not issue paychecks to workers. Their wages will have automatically been placed in their account, the banking systems all having been made uniform. At home, there'll be the computer terminal. It's already almost obsolete to talk about this, as the five-billion-dollar computer game business is not only a cover story in *Time*, but the story of living room games. They are practice drills for the times up ahead. In fact, as Alvin Toffler points out in *The Third Wave*, the totally computerized society is now upon us. The Bank of Montreal, according to William Mulholland, "is no longer a Canadian bank with Canadian appendages. It's an international bank that happens to be based in Canada." This is terribly relevant here, because it shows how close we really are to a World Bank.

It might not be difficult to imagine a sort of electronic world phone book—which holds information on every individual on earth. We've heard a great deal about the "Beast" computer in Brussels. Most significant was the recent unveiling by Mme. Simone Veil, the President of the European Parliament in Strasbourg, of the Direct Information Access Network for Europe-known popularly already as DIANE. It's the official computerized information system, consisting of twenty-five

European services, with access to one hundred and eight data bases and data banks.

We are only about two steps away from the world control system the Antichrist might well use: i.e., the "mark in their right hand, or in their foreheads and . . . no man might buy or sell, save he that had the mark, or the name of the beast, or the number of his name . . . his number is 666." Certainly, most of us have had a micro-electronic impression imposed on our hand—or where else would be so handy as the forehead—say at Disney World, so that we could go in and out unobstructed, the scanner picking up whether or not we had paid. So this prophecy is already fulfilled. Insofar as the masses going grocery shopping are concerned, it's just waiting to happen. It is significant that 666 is the best functioning number for a prefix for international banking. It is widely reported that the American Internal Revenue Service already have 666 on the W2 and W2p forms for widespread use in the near future, some having actually already come out with an instruction written on the back, "Do Not Cash Unless Bearer Has Mark on Hand or Forehead."

As men act more and more like machines, machines act more and more like men. The cover story of *The Journal* for January 1982, was by Sylvia Scott who wrote that her husband had more or less abandoned her and become married to his TRS-80-Computer—"an omen of trouble ahead" of her becoming a "computer widow." Alarm clocks awaken us by talking to us. And our cars have computer voices to tell us when we're low on fuel, or exceeding the speed limit, or what to do and what we shouldn't be doing when we're driving.

Some say that the Antichrist will be besieged by such wars that electronics will be destroyed. Hardly! There were many more inventions during the five awful years of World War II than during the previous 40. I have no doubt that the Antichrist as "king of the world" will press every frontier to impose his total control. And violators will pay with their lives. As we'll note in the next chapter, the martyrs will be into the millions;

the human slaughter, into the billions. It will be as Jesus assured, the lowest level to which the world has ever sunk. And the galling thing will be that the masses will be abysmally unhappy, but until the ground swell worldwide rises up into Armageddon itself, they'll just have to take it. Some have humorously suggested that "If computers get too powerful, we can organize them into committees that'll do them in." The trouble with that idea, up ahead, is that the Antichrist won't function on the basis of committee recommendations, but by fiat.

I published my *Coming World Dictator* just over a year ago. A copy fell into the hands of Roy Michael Cline, in a jail. I received a letter from Roy. For him, life had been rough. The way of the transgressor has always been hard. And now to be imprisoned for his crimes had been a terrifying experience. Could life ever, on this planet, be worse? Yes, as we've noted, life under the Antichrist would be incomparably worse. And then hell would be falling out through the bottom into eternal woe. But before I closed out the *Coming World Dictator* I explained to all readers without Christ that no matter how far down they might be, they could call upon the Name of the Lord Jesus Christ and be saved. Roy wrote to say that as he concluded reading the book, he came upon the prayer, "God, be merciful to me a sinner. I wholeheartedly turn away from my sin. Save me now, for Christ's sake!" Then and there Jesus Christ came into his life and Roy has been forever changed!

Chapter Twelve

"A PLACE CALLED
IN THE HEBREW TONGUE
ARMAGEDDON"

Billy Graham notes that the devil "will bring to power a counterfeit world ruler" who "will establish a false utopia for an extremely short time. The economic and political problems of the world will seem to be solved. But after a brief rule, the whole thing will come apart. During the reign of Antichrist, tensions will mount, and once again the world will explode—with a gigantic world war of overwhelming ferocity involving conflict and massacre on an unparalleled scale. Even the iron grip of the Antichrist will be unable to prevent it. This massive upheaval will be the world's last war—the Battle of Armageddon."

We may do well to pause at this point and ask how in the world could the people of the world go so beserk as to accept such a world tyrant as the Antichrist? Will rationality be completely replaced by insanity? More and more people today realize that with a patchwork world of wobblong democracies, warped, wierd dictatorships and nuclear weaponry all thrown into the same boiling pot, eventually the mix is going to erupt or explode. So we have Allan Fotheringham writing in *MacLeans* (June 14, 1982) on "The Lessons of Modern War" and Ross Smyth replying (July 12, 1982) "Disarmament is an illusion without world government. Effective disarmament requires enforceable world law and limitations on national sovereignty." It's into this understandable vacuum that the Antichrist will step. But as Harvard Professor of Psychiatry, Robert Coles, intimates in his "Psychology of Armageddon" (*Psychology Today*, May, 1982), the triumph of "Evil" will have prevailed. The gamble man will have taken will be the worst in all human history. The Antichrist will be a monstrous imposter: the incarnation of iniquity. And poeple the world over will lament "We've been had!"

Jesus, forecasting to His disciples the very worst times of the Tribulation, stressed that conditions worldwide would sink to their lowest in human history—since creation's dawn! Nature itself, by this time, is convulsed as "there shall be signs in the sun, and in the moon, and in the stars; and upon the earth, distress of nations, with perplexity; the sea and the waves roaring; men's hearts failing them for fear, and for looking after those things which are coming on the earth: for the powers of heaven shall be shaken. And then shall they see the Son of man coming in a cloud with power and great glory" (Luke 21:25-27).

Religion editor Tom Harpur laments that in 1982 people seem obsessed with "when the Battle of Armageddon is to be fought." The Bible gives us many leads. In both Daniel and Revelation, it is clear that the Tribulation is divided into two parts. In Revelation 12:14, we read of "time, and times, and half a time," in 11:2 and 13:5 of the 42 months; and in 11:3 and 12:6, of 1,260 days—which on the Jewish calender is 3½ years. This period Jesus designated as the "Great Tribulation." An ancient Jew, the Apostle Paul, prophesied that "in the last days" the world would "wax worse and worse" (2 Tim. 3:1,13).

Jesus said many things about Jerusalem in particular, and the Middle East in general, at the time of the end. There would be huge armies surrounding Jerusalem. Then it would be beleaguered, beseiged, and overrun. The earth beneath, generally, would be rocking as if solid land were liquid waves of the ocean, with people thinking they were living on a giant, half-filled water bed; and the sun, moon and stars blacking out.

Masses, mobs—whole marauding migrations of people—will be fleeing to the mountains! The powers of the heaven will be shaken—with obvious nuclear warfare, for the word used by our Lord in Luke 21:26 for heaven (*ouranos*) is the one from which we derive the word uranium. Myriads will be dropping dead from heart failure. During this last half of the tribulation, people will enter a depression in which they feel like they're in a snake's belly in the bottom of a prairie depression-time, rural road rut, being run over by a steel-wheeled tractor with lugs. Tim Bawden writes in "Prime Time" (July 30, 1982) that "the picture of the world" everyone who watches TV in the 1980's gets is one of terrifying shots of murders and disaster." Thank God things are not that bad yet. But as the Antichrist corrals man toward Armageddon, the world really will be that way. Americans currently complain that they are each paying an average annual $5,138 to Uncle Sam. The Antichrist will exact everything: all people have, their lives, and in most cases, their souls.

In the previous chapter, we looked at conditions in the world under the Antichrist. He's the coming world dictator. But he doesn't have as two-fisted a grip on his world as he'd like to have. He's walking on logs in a roaring river, red with human blood. There's regional mutiny from four blocs of the nations of the world, indicated by a host of passages to which we could turn. But perhaps we can get the clearest picture from a look at Daniel 11, and then at Revelation 16 and 19. Daniel 11:40 informs as that "at the time of the end shall the king of the south push at him." In verse 41, the Antichrist is in "the glorious land, and many countries shall be overthrown." And in verse 42, "he shall stretch forth his hand also upon the countries: and the land of Egypt shall not escape." Who are these countries from the Southern Bloc? The Egyptians lead, and the Libyans and the Ethiopians are again activated. While Sadat was alive, there was great euphoria over the Camp David accord. Now that scene is shifting back, and the Arab bloc of 41 nations and the Organization of African Unity, formed in

Ethiopia in 1963, binding most of the African Continent together in a bloc, accounts for the nations of "the South." Egypt is prominent in both! Notes an *A.P.* article (May 15, 1982), "Because of the 1973 Middle East War, to show their support of the Arab bloc in the Third World movement, there is near total isolation of Israel by black African countries."

In addition to the bloc of nations in the West—which is, of course, the Antichrist's original Kingdom—and now the bloc to the South, there's the bloc to the North. Daniel 11:40 states that the rulers of "the north shall come against him like a whirlwind . . . and with many ships." The Soviets will have undergone that earlier nuclear destruction, in which 5/6ths of their armies were slain! And great nuclear destruction will have been wrought on their cities, and their satellites. After five or six years again, they're sweeping down—and with a vengeance. We read that they "enter into the countries, and shall overflow and pass over" (vs. 40). What a description of land, sea and air forces! An article in *Newsweek* entitled "Prophets in Jerusalem" points to a future, inevitable "conflict between the Soviet Union and Israel, the emerging Battle of Armageddon [involving] the King of the North and the King of the South— the apocalyptic adversaries described in the Book of Daniel."

But there's one other section of the world to account for— the East! In Daniel 11:44, we read that "tidings out of the East shall trouble him: therefore he shall go forth with great fury to destroy, and utterly to make away many." When we turn to Revelation 9:16, we read that this bloc of nations to the East are a massive mobilized army of 200 million. Assured the late Mao Tse-tung: "In the battle for the world, China will field an army of 200 million." And in August, 1982, Fane's of London announced that the Chinese now have the world's third largest submarine fleet (*U.P.I.*, Aug. 5, 1982). An insight into the Chinese mind can be clearly seen by the late Mao Tse-tung's remarks to Henry Kissinger a decade ago. He urged Kissinger to keep contending that America simply must build a bulwark of defense against the Soviets, warning "against a fake detente that would sap resistance to [their] expansionism and confuse the peoples of the West." He underlined that the Chinese despise with a vengeance those who "bully the weak" (*Time*, Mar. 15, 1982). In the West, many liberals have felt that if we just settle down with the Russians, through cooperation and coexistence, we'll survive nicely. The Chinese do not share this rose-tinted optimism. They exhorted Kissinger that the greatest concentration of nuclear weaponry, which is now ready to go, is in the Balkans and they insist *"it will move."* In the eighties, Deng Xiaoping has said again and again that WW III is "inevitable. This is independent of man's will." What is true of the present Chinese posture toward the Soviets will be true of their future refusal to knuckle under to the Antichrist. But it is my belief that under the oppression of the Antichrist, alignments for obvious pragmatic reasons will shift, and peoples of differing ideologies will galvanize themselves together to take on a common foe. I believe that India, Japan, the Philippines and the whole of the Far East will all be banded together. Why? Because repeatedly we're assured that "all nations" will assemble for Armageddon! The world knows well what a militarized Japan can do. For a generation they've been out of it. But on July 23, 1982 Prime Minister Zenko Suzuki announced "approval" of a "64 billion dollar program to build up its military."

In Zechariah 14, we read that "Behold, the day of the Lord cometh and . . . I will gather all nations against Jerusalem to battle; and the city shall be taken . . . then shall the Lord go forth, and fight against those nations" (vss. 1-3). Pope John Paul used the prophecy from Joel, "The day of the Lord cometh . . . a day of darkness and of gloominess, a day of clouds and of thick darkness . . . I will also gather all nations, and will bring them down into the valley of Jehoshaphat . . . multitudes, multitudes in the valley of decision: for the day of the Lord is near in the valley of decision" (Joel 2:1,2; 3:2,14).

Turning to Revelation 16, we read that the false prophet is working all kinds of occult "miracles". Principal J. S. Wright

of Tyndale Hall, University of Bristol, points out that the Greek
word *pharmakos* and cognates translated 'sorcerer', 'sorcery',
and 'witchcraft' carries "the root idea of drugs, potions,
poisons" (Rev. 9:21; 18:23; 21:8; 22:15 and Galations 5:20). So
we read: "by the sorceries (demonized by drugs) were all nations
deceived." It could well be the drug pandemic which will have
much to do with inciting the peoples of the world to Armageddon. The last year or so, masses of people have been disillusioned to hear of their heroes in the athletic and acting worlds
being hooked on drugs. Harvard's Timothy Leary coined the
slogan: "The best hope is dope." In the end, it will fuel man's
march to Armageddon. According to *Time*, illicit drugs—
especially cocaine, heroin, and marijuana—devoured 80 billion
dollars of Americans' income last year. It is the biggest single
business in the country. The CTV news in Canada reckons an
incredible 31% of Canadians have tried cocaine. And according
to the *Toronto Sun*, LSD use has doubled in the last two years.
Milton Silverman has just published *Prescriptions for Death:
The Drugging of the Third World.* Universally man is getting
hooked. And the higher the echelon of society is, the more likely its peer-leaders are to be on drugs. An Associated Press
release (July 14, 1982) reckons seven members of the U.S. Congress are being investigated for their being hooked on cocaine.
It will be government leaders who will lead their peoples to
Armageddon.

In addition to drug addiction demonizing man for
Armageddon, Psychiatrist Cole in his "Psychology of Armageddon" article already cited, quotes Sigmund Freud who "Kept
on emphasizing the 'death instinct' " in man. This too, *en masse*,
will come to bear on a worldwide scale, driving the masses
instinctively to Armageddon. So, returning to Revelation
16, we read of "the spirits of devils, working miracles, which
go forth unto the kings of . . . the whole world, to gather them
to the battle of that great day of God Almighty" (vs. 14).
Among them (Verse 12) are "the [rulers] of the east," where the
waters of the Euphrates are dried up so that 200 million troops

might make their way toward Armageddon. The Soviets have already built a dam at the headwaters of the Euphrates, to make this possible, though it may or may not be what God uses to implement their way. The Soviets may hate the Chinese today, but by then I suspect they'll hate the Antichrist more. After all, he will have caught them when they were devastated four or five years earlier, and occupied their borders.

Sorcerized through drugs, demonized and under the sway of evil spirits who performed "miracles, which go forth unto the kings of the earth, and of the whole world, to gather them to the battle of that great day of God Almighty [the Antichrist] gathered them together into a place called in the Hebrew tongue Armageddon." "Armageddon" according to the *New Catholic Encyclopedia* will be the place where the Antichrist will summon the Kings of the earth for the final battle of mankind. Some people get very angry that a comparatively tiny plot of land like Armageddon, in Israel, should so dominate the news. The fact of the matter is, it will more and more do so rather than less and less! President Reagan, in addressing the Joint House of Lords and Commons in London stated that in the Middle East, war is an ever present threat. The long and short of the matter is that one day it will not merely be "an ever present threat": it will be "present" tense, and the involvement will be total, worldwide.

Armageddon dominates the news today, as cancer dominates the consciousness of someone whose biopsy indicates malignancy. Does Armageddon, as a geographical site, exist? It does indeed! It is a 14-by-20 mile plain in Northern Israel stretching out eastward from the foot of Mount Carmel, where Elijah invoked the fire of God to fall from heaven, thousands of years ago. But would it make a battle field for Armageddon? Napoleon conquered part of Palestine in early 1799 and stayed for five months. He is thought by many to have been the foremost military strategist in modern history. As he gazed across the length and breadth of Armageddon on a sunny day he gasped, "[it's] the most natural battleground of the whole earth." Previous to Napoleon, Richard the Lion Hearted of England, Louis of France, Pompey and Titus of Rome, Rameses of Egypt, Sargon, Sennacherib, Nebuchadnezzar, Antiochus Epiphanes, and David had all fought wars in Armageddon!

But will that be the only place where they'll fight? No, as Joel prophesies, there'll be multitudes in the Valley of Jehoshaphat, and throughout—and beyond—the Jordan Valley. And they'll be in Jerusalem. With millions overrunning the length and breadth of Israel, they'll overflow into what is now Lebanon, Syria, Jordan, and the Sinai. And everywhere there will be fighting to the death between these demonized, death deifying, bloodletting hordes and the Satan possessed forces of a devil-dealing Antichrist. The slaughter! The bloodshed! The carnage! Jesus said there would be nothing like it in the annals of man. It would be as though Hitler, Nero, Idi Amin, Attila the Hun, the Genghis Khan and Jack the Ripper were locked into solitary in Sing Sing with half a loaf of bread and half a dozen hatchets with ignited passions to fight it out to the death. Multiply that by a few million and spread it over 200 miles as we read in Revelation 14:20 it will be. There'll be blood in pools as deep as the bridle of a harnessed or saddled horse.

No, war is not hell. But its the worst condition a human can sink to in this life when it reaches its nadir. General George C. Marshall calculated that truly "there is no pay scale that is high enough to buy the services of a single soldier during even a few minutes of the agony of combat, the physical miseries of the campaign or the extreme personal inconvenience . . . and danger."(*Newsweek*, July 12, 1982). Armageddon will be that one soldier's miseries multiplied by millions. Lehman Strauss calculates that in human history 600 million people are known to have been killed in wars. During the Tribulation period, if it were to occur in the 1980's, you could treble that, in that very first nuclear exchange at the beginning of the Tribulation where one-third of the population of the earth is wiped out. Another quarter of those surviving will be killed, which means that half are slaughtered. And those who survive till the Battle of

Armageddon? Jesus said plainly, "Except those days should be shortened, there should no flesh be saved: but for the elect's sake, those days shall be shortened" (Matthew 24:22).

The nuclear arsenals, which obviously will have been restrained some seven years earlier, when the Soviets and the U.S. unleashed enough to wipe out that first third of the population of the earth, will be unleashed again in a total disregard for human life. All thought of detente, Salt agreements, and nuclear freeze will be flung to the winds. It will be ground zero worldwide. Man at his worst will uncork the whole bottle of lethal nuclear poison. Even an ancient man's description in King James English is vivid, "The seventh angel poured out his vial into the air . . . and there . . . [were] thunders, and lightnings; and there was a great earthquake [this means earth shaking—which could be seismic from beneath, or nuclear-induced from above], such as was not since men were upon the earth, so mighty an earthquake, and so great." And such was the effect on the earth's crust—the sea is already devastated—that "every island fled away, and the mountains were not found, and there fell upon men [destruction] out of heaven" (vss. 17-21). There are several passages in the Old and New Testaments that say that the sun ceases shining, and the moon turns to blood. Does that mean the sun, or moon, are themselves affected? Not necessarily. When we say the sun sets, it means the world revolves so as to cut off sunshine for a night. What's here implied, I feel, is that the whole atmosphere is so polluted with nuclear explosives that the sun ceases to shine through—the moon and stars virtually being blacked out. One could take a cursory glance at any number of science journals as to what would be the effect if all the submarines unleashed their nuclear arsenals, the air forces of the world dropped all their stockpiled bombs and all the shortrange, middle, and intercontinental ballistic missiles were triggered to travel to their targets and be detonated. It used to be that Bible students of prophecy couldn't conceive of man *ever* having his hand on these massacring monsters.

Today, most are becoming aware that only God's intervention can, in the end, save man from his own internal commitment of universal suicide. Thomas J. Watson, former U.S.
Ambassador to the Soviet Union, in lamenting in *The New York
Times* (Dec. 22, 1981) that today's superpowers "are on a collision course . . . " said that "thermonuclear weapons are good
for two things—for deterrence or for suicide." Watson is right
from man's perspective. And so is Representative A. M.
Thompson of Maine, who takes to the streets to crusade during "Ground Zero" week in the U.S. (April 1, 1982)—to highlight
the fact that a nuclear bomb in Portland would heat things up
to 130 million degrees Fahrenheit. If the bombs are used, "We
are talking about the horror of an end to our species." Writes
Russel Clark (in the *Toronto Star*, April 27, 1982), "I am a
veteran of World War II, and well remember August 1945. Since
that time I have lived with a feeling of near certainty that I
would, indeed, see the end of civilization during my lifetime.
The feeling has grown stronger and more pervasive in recent
years, and I have really wondered whether there is any possible way out, short of a direct intervention by God." I have good
news for Russel Clark. God *does* enter the scene, and as Jesus
assured, "as lightning cometh out of the east, and shineth even
unto the west; so shall also the coming of the Son of man be"
(Matthew 24:22,27). The late Albert Schweitzer's lament: "Man
has lost the capacity to foresee and to forestall. He will end by
destroying the earth," would be right, except that Jesus Christ,
as God the Son, is going to step in and implement His own program of peace and prosperity, "for the elect's sake." Arnold
Toynbee of Cambridge reckoned: "I believe the human race will
not commit suicide—it will stop just short of that." The fact
is that it likely would annihilate itself, except that Jesus Christ
will step in. John Kennedy was quoted by the Pope during his
visit to the United States that "Mankind must put an end to
war, or war will put an end to mankind." In fact it will be Jesus
Christ who will terminate Armageddon. Otherwise Armageddon would exterminate our race.

And how does God intervene? The passages illustrating this are many! In addition to Matthew 24, there's Mark 13, Luke 21, 2 Thessalonians 2 and Zechariah 14. But as we earlier intimated, let's go to Revelation 19:11-15: "And I saw heaven opened, and behold a white horse; and He that sat upon him was called Faithful and True." Let's stop here a moment. There are prophetic students who insist that armies will ride to Armageddon on horses. Will this white horse from heaven be a white Clydesdale, or a white quarter-horse—born and bred in Kentucky and brought up on bluegrass? Of course not! I only state this to demonstrate that Bible writers, while literalists whenever and wherever possible, encountered those occasions when they had to use the best language at their command to describe future events that would be far removed from the technology and techniques of their own times. Jesus Christ is the Man on the white horse. Johnny Carson asks: is Ronald Reagan the man in the White House, or the Man on the White Horse? Definitely, Mr. Reagan is the man in the White House. And the Man on the White Horse is "called Faithful and True, and in righteousness He doth judge and make war. His eyes were as a flame of fire, and on His head were many crowns; and He had a name written, that no man knew, but He Himself. And He was clothed with a vesture dipped in blood: and His name is called the Word of God. And the armies which were in heaven followed Him upon white horses, clothed in fine linen, white and clean. And out of His mouth goeth a sharp sword, that with it He should smite the nations."

Is that a multiple podded laser beam? I don't know. Is it enriched plutonium? It could be! Is it an emission of nuclear or neutron bombs? Only God knows. What the Scriptures do teach us is that our God is a consuming fire—just as He is light. And He is love! "And He shall rule [the nations] with a rod of iron." Prime Minister Margaret Thatcher is called "The Iron Lady" because, in contrast to her immediate predecessors, she presides over Britain with command and authority. Jesus

Christ's ruling with a "rod of iron" means He'll reign and rule over the world with total authority.

When Nazism was vanquished, the whole world wanted to know what had finally happened to Adolph Hitler. What was his end? So everyone wonders about the Antichrist! What happens to him? St. Paul tells us about his body; St. John, about the total person. Paul writes to the Thessalonians (2 Thessalonians 2:8) that our "Lord shall consume [him] with the Spirit of His mouth, and shall destroy [him] with the brightness of His coming." John wrote (Revelation 19:19,20) that he saw the Antichrist "and the kings of the earth, and their armies gathered together to make war against Him and sat on the horse, and against His army." And the Antichrist was "cast alive into a lake of fire burning with brimstone."

Jesus Christ baptizes the world with fire, and thoroughly purges His floor, as John the Baptist announced that He would. And He sets up His Judgment of the nations, as recorded in Matthew 25, and ushers in the Millennium. From history's nadir, the story of God the Son, as the Son of God among men— to make the sons of men the sons of God by faith—rises to its highest point ever, as Jesus sets up His Kingdom of peace and prosperity, with Jerusalem as its capital. And as St. Paul taught, a nation, the surviving Jews, are a people accepting their Messiah—a nation born again in a day. Prophesied Zechariah (12:10; 14:9) of the outcropping of Armageddon, "And I will pour upon the house of David, and upon the inhabitants of Jerusalem, the spirit of grace and of supplications: and they shall look upon Me whom they have pierced." Yes, "and the Lord shall be King over all the earth: in that day shall there be one Lord, and His name one." Ezekial put it as a climax to that glorious 37th chapter: "one King shall be King of them all" (vs. 22). When Jesus was here on earth, on the occasion of His triumphant entry, He was hailed: "Hosannah to the King." But His time was not yet come. In fact a week later a superscription was hung over His cross in derision: "This is Jesus of Nazareth the King of the Jews." He would be King but not then, not till He comes to turn Armageddon into a Coronation. And then as Handel wrote in that greatest of modern musical compositions: "The Messiah", Jesus Christ will indeed be crowned "Kings of Kings and Lord of Lords!" In Tel Aviv on July 17, 1982, a reported 200,000 Israelis took to the streets to demonstrate their support for Menachem Begin and his policies. They went into chants of "Begin, King of Israel! Begin, King of Israel! Begin, King of Israel!" But no one knows better than Begin himself that he is not the King of Israel. As the Gaithers have inspired evangelicals all over the world to sing "The King is Coming," indeed the King—Jesus Christ—is surely coming! And the saints of all the ages? St John wrote, "And they lived and reigned with Christ a thousand years" (Revelation 20:4).

The Kingdom of Christ is made up of believers who have been redeemed to God by His Blood "out of every kindred and tongue, and people and nation" (Revelation 5:9). Fifteen years ago I was presenting Christ on another continent, and an Egyptian physician, Dr. Mehat Girgis and his wife, were born again. They had since immigrated to the United States. In 1981, I was holding a Crusade in a 6,000-seat field house. Dr. and Mrs. Girgis invited our Team to their home. There we met their daughter, Moyra; and sons, Mickey and Kamal. During that Crusade, all three came forward to give their lives to Christ. And on the concluding night, Dr. Girgis asked me to join hands with that beautiful, beautiful family of five and commit them in prayer and praise to God, and to the Word of His grace! For them, a wonderful spiritual armistice through Christ saved them from the outreaching arms of Armageddon!

Chapter Thirteen

"THE THOUSAND YEARS"

"Ring out the thousand wars of old, Ring in the thousand years of peace!" Engaging this quote from Alfred Lord Tennyson's *In Memorium* as a sort of euphoric euphemism in a grim world, Senator Ted Kennedy brought to a tumultuous climax the National Convention of the American Democratic Party in 1982. With wars roaring in full rage in Iran, Iraq, the Falklands and Lebanon, it was a highly laudable if seeming near impossible aspiration.

Adolf Hitler's grandiose notion of Nazism was to aggrandize his imperialist empire into the entire earth and that it would "last a thousand years." It didn't happen! *Time* (Jan. 4, 1982) points back to Mao Tse-tung's "global-export of revolution" as an obsessive vision to "hasten the Communist millennium." Already communism is crumbling. The Antichrist's craze for a millennium will be comparable. It won't happen! His ascendancy will collapse in chaos after 42 months (Revelation 13:5).

The true Millennium, in which Christ Himself will reign in peace and prosperity, is on the way; just as President Reagan boldly and rightly affirmed before the United Nations Second Special Session on Disarmament in mid-1982: "The Bible tells us there will be a time for peace" (*The New York Times*, June 18, 1982). He was referring to the Millennial reign of the Messiah over the world. Regrettably, as the late Dag Hammerskjold noted, even when in the present there is a pause from war, at best it is "a time of peace, which is no peace." But, as the pop song enthuses, "There's a New World Comin!"

Jonathan Schell's new "Bible" of the secular humanists, *The Fate of the Earth* envisages a day when "existing institutions must give way to some sort of transcendent sovereignty and security, presumably by a government that embraces all mankind, in fact 'world government'." (See *Time*, April 19, 1982). That will happen, when Christ comes again. *The Fate of the Earth* will be: "Faith on the Earth" (Luke 18:8) with Christ as King over all the earth. Yes and the world's "government shall be upon His shoulder: and His name shall be called Wonderful, Counselor, the Mighty God, the Everlasting Father, the Prince of Peace" (Is. 9:6).

Turning back to our Lord's Word, Matthew 24 is primarily concerned with the "Great Tribulation" (Matthew 24:21) plummeting man to his nihilistic nadir at Armageddon. But that is not Jesus' last word. The oldest authentic literary quotation extant is in Jude (14,15) where the Second Coming of the Lord is highlighted. "Enoch, who lived seven generations after Adam, knew about" what would occur and prophesied, "See, the Lord is coming with millions of His [saints]. He will bring the [nations] of the world before Him in judgment, to receive just punishment, and to prove the terrible things they have done in rebellion against God, revealing all they have said against Him" (LB).

This coincides with Matthew 24:21,22,27,30,31 where we read that just when the Great Tribulation sinks man into a cataclysmic carnage—"there will be persecution such as the world has never before seen in all its history, and will never see again. In fact, unless those days are shortened, all mankind will perish. But they will be shortened for the sake of God's chosen people . . . for as the lightning flashes across the sky from the east to west, so shall My coming be, when I, the Messiah, return . . . and the nations of the world will see Me arrive in the clouds of heaven, with power and great glory. And I shall send forth My angels with the sound of a mighty trumpet blast, and they shall gather My chosen ones from the farthest ends of the earth and heaven."

Matthew 25 (31-40, LB) picks up the action: "When I, the Messiah, shall come in My glory, and all the angels with Me, then I shall sit upon My throne of glory. And all the nations shall be gathered before Me. And I will separate the [nations] as a shepherd separates the sheep from the goats and place the sheep at My right hand, and the goats at My left. Then I, the King, shall say to those at My right, 'Come, blessed of My Father, into the Kingdom prepared for you from the founding of the world. For I was hungry and you fed Me; I was thirsty and you gave Me water; I was a stranger and you invited Me into your homes; naked and you clothed Me; sick and in prison, and you visited Me.' Then these righteous ones will reply, 'Sir, when did we ever see you hungry and feed you? Or thirsty and give you anything to drink? Or a stranger, and help you? Or naked, and clothe you? When did we ever see you sick or in prison, and visit you? And I, the King, will tell them, 'When you did it to these my brothers you were doing it to Me!' "

First of all, note (vs. 32) that it is the "nations" that Christ—now crowned King of the world—judges: nations that are the survivors of Armageddon. Their leaders have all come (Revelation 16:14). It will be history's foremost summit, only it will be summoned in a valley—a valley newly created by the all-time blockbuster earthquake. Projects Zechariah, the nations that day will stand before Him whose "feet will stand upon the Mount of Olives, to the east of Jerusalem, and the Mount of Olives will split apart, making a very wide valley running from the east to the west, for half the mountain will move toward the north and half toward the south." And just prior to when "the Lord shall be King over all the earth. In that day there shall be one Lord—His name alone will be worshiped" (Zechariah 13:3,4,9). There the judgment of the nations will take place. It will be based on how the nations have treated those of Israel who have received Christ as their Messiah, along with those redeemed and discipled by the 144,000 Jewish evangelists during the Great Tribulation. Of course, "two-thirds of all the nation of Israel will be cut off and die, but a third will be left

in the land. I will bring the third that remain through the fire
[the Tribulation holocausts including Armageddon] and make
them pure, as gold and silver are refined and purified by fire.
They will call upon My name and I will hear them; I will say
'These are My people,' and they will say, 'The Lord is our God' "
(Zechariah 13:8,9).

The hammer of history will have come down on the anvil at
Armageddon and the crushing of the nations, at the behest and
beckoning of Christ, will determine who goes to hell from this
judgment of the nations (Matthew 25:41,46) and who goes into
the Millennial Kingdom. Notice that Jesus decreed that the
determining factor of who goes "into the Kingdom" will be
those who shared their allegiance to their Lord with the
persecuted, hungry, thirsty, and martyred believers of the earth
during those ghastly times of "Great Tribulation": the awful
era of "Jacob's Trouble" (Jeremiah 30:7). These will be joined
at Christ's installation of the Millennium by the newly resurrected tribulation saints (a sizable percentage of whom will have
been martyred) along with the Old Testament believers up to
the time of the inauguration of the Church—who also will be
resurrected at this time. The Church will consist of those who
come with Christ in His Second Coming. Those saints from
before Christ, to whom St. Paul refers in 2 Timothy 4:1, as those
who'll be included in His resurrecting and judging "When He
appears to set up His kingdom" (2 Timothy 4:1, LB). There is
no Scriptural basis to believe that any of these groupings will
receive glorified bodies at this point. Rather they will be resurrected as Lazarus was, or as the Old Testament believers were
on the occasion of Christ's resurrection. They will, however, live
a thousand years, because Satan and the Adamic curse on
nature will be removed.

We might pause here to quote from *The Atlantic Monthly*
(June, 1982). The returning Christ with "the raptured saints"
having defeated "the Antichrist and the false prophet" at
Armageddon will "cast (them) into a lake of fire, and Satan will
be bound in a bottomless pit, to remain for a thousand years.

With Satan out of the way, at least temporarily, the saints will enjoy the marvelous Millennium—an age characterized by good weather, peace, an end to crime, advancements in knowledge and the absence of fear."

This sends us scurrying for our Bibles to read in Revelation 20:1-6 that the ancient apostle John foresaw, as Christ came back to the earth and defeated the Antichrist at Armageddon, "an angel come down from heaven with the key to the bottomless pit and a heavy chain in his hand. He seized the dragon—that old serpent, the devil, Satan—and bound him in chains for 1,000 years, and threw him into the bottomless pit, which he then shut and locked, so that he could not fool the nations . . . Then I saw thrones, and sitting on them were those who had been given the right to judge [these will be the Church, the Bride of Christ who are in their glorified bodies]. And I saw the souls of those who had been beheaded for their testimony about Jesus, for proclaiming the Word of God, and who had not worshiped the creature [the Antichrist] or his statue, nor accepted his mark on their foreheads or their hands. They had come to life again and now they reigned with Christ for a thousand years. This is the First Resurrection . . . blessed and holy are those who share in the First Resurrection. For them the second death holds no terrors, for they will be priests of God and of Christ, and shall reign with Him a thousand years." The "first resurrection" refers to a "who" rather than a "when": i.e., those who are Christ's—from whatever era—are assumed His "first resurrection." Those who are not Christ's will be resurrected to the Great White Throne Judgment and sentenced to their eternal destiny (Rev. 20:11-15).

For those of us who anticipate reigning as His Bride and presiding with Christ for a thousand years over this earth, perhaps as soon as beginning seven years from now, the Millennium is certainly one of the most underwritten and underproclaimed of themes. Since Adam and Eve were ejected from the Garden of Eden, the original Paradise of God on earth, prophets, poets, musicians, political philosophers, theologians, and artists have dreamed of an eventual "Golden Age," a Utopia on this earth when—under the benevolent reign of an all-seeing, all-knowing, all-powerful Ruler—man could live in harmony with his or her Maker, family, society, and world. The dream schemes of the Platos, Owens, and Bellamys have proven to be just that—dream schemes. So for millennia, man has kept his fingers crossed—waiting, eager, expectant for someone from outer space to come riding in on His white horse and introduce to a souring society of men perfect peace and plenty for all. Whatever else man wants in the 1980's, observes Edward Cornish, President of the World Future Society, two salients are stable in the aspirations of all: to live in a "peaceful, prosperous" world.

A "peaceful" world! Father Theodore Hesburgh, President of Notre Dame, remonstrates on national T.V., "We've got to get rid of the nuclear monster—the murderer of all mankind." "The possession of nuclear weapons by dozens of countries," adds Billy Graham, means veritably that "the world is on the brink of calamity." However, warns Pope John Paul, who has lived most of his life under Communism, desperate as we are for a "totally and permanently peaceful human society" idealized too often as "a Utopia" we must not heed empty promises which would lead "straight to the false peace of totalitarian regimes." Genuine hope is in short supply currently. Professor A. F. P. Taylor, one of the world's leading historians, revealed recently how impossibly situated the secular humanist is today: "The only hope of avoiding a catastrophic world war which would end civilization was for somebody to create a world empire." When journalist Gwynne Dyer "objected that any attempt to unite the world under a single political authority by force would almost certainly cause exactly that kind of devastating war, he merely agreed. It was not a solution that offered much real hope, he said—just the only 'alternative that offered any hope at all.' " Alas, Jesus Christ will come again to restore hope and to rule the world in peace. And He'll provide not only a "peaceful" world but a "prosperous" world.

Author A. LeBlanc mourns, "It is obscene that the nations spend billions a year on arms for destruction. This money spent for construction could solve all our problems." The Berrigan brothers, Father Daniel and Philip, are right that our swords should become plowshares. But man does not have the muscle or mind to wield them on to the anvil and swing the hammer. Only Christ can. Just think of what the transferred funds from one Trident submarine—at a cost of 2 billion dollars a throw—could do to turn proverty to prosperity in the Third World. What Christ won't do in the Millennium with the reported 775 billion dollars currently being annually wasted on armamemts!

And, yes, it will happen! Polish underground leader of Solidarity, Zbigniew Bujak yearns for a Poland free from "war . . . a Poland without prisons and internment camps, a Poland without police roundups and without fear" (*Time*, Jan. 4, 1982). It will happen! Canadian Dona Cauchon cries out for a fully rehabilitated and united world that will give us all "a sense of global identity," for "it is the gnawing emptiness of spirit that comes without such a goal that is our greatest affliction." It will happen! Shirley Chisholm is featured in *Quote*: "We Americans have a chance to become someday a nation in which all racial stocks and classes can exist in their own selfhoods but meet on a basis of respect and equality and live together, socially, economically, and politically. We can become a dynamic equilibrium, a harmony of many different elements, in which the whole will be greater than all its parts and greater than any society the world has seen before. It can still happen." It will happen when Christ comes again to set up His kingdom in this world, and it won't just be in the United States, but throughout the whole earth. Everywhere British Columbians advertise their province as "supernatural." It isn't today! But one day it will be—along with our whole world.

Indeed, the Bible has assured us that a golden age lies just beyond Armageddon—an age of unprecedented peace and prosperity. The word "Millennium" comes from the Latin words "mille" meaning "thousand" and "annus"meaning "year."

According to the church historian H. Mosheim, "The prevailing opinion that Christ was to come and reign one thousand years among men before the final dissolution of the world met with no opposition previous to the time of Origen."

Which leads us to ask: just what will the Millennium be like? The Scriptures have a great deal to say about this coming idyllic age. It will not be a democracy, a monarchy, or socialist state. It will be a theocracy! Christ, as we've already noticed, will be Lord and King over all the earth. And what the Antichrist will have failed to do with militaristic might and computer surveillance, Jesus Christ will do by His Omniscience, Omnipotence, and Omnipresence. Prophesied Isaiah (9:6,7, LB), "And the government shall be upon His shoulder. These will be His royal titles: 'Wonderful,' 'Counselor,' 'the Mighty God,' 'the Everlasting Father,' 'The Prince of Peace.' His [will be an] ever-expanding, peaceful government . . . He will rule with perfect fairness and justice from the throne of His father David. He will bring true justice and peace to all the nations of the world. This is going to happen because the Lord of heaven's army has dedicated Himself to do it!"

Yes, the angel's prophecy to Mary, mother of Jesus, will be fulfilled, "And the Lord God shall give Him the throne of His ancestor David. And He shall reign over Israel" (Luke 1:32,33). It will be in the Millennium that Christ the King will assume that throne to which He is legally appointed by His Father (Matthew 1:20; Luke 1:27).

Israel, a tiny land, struggling desperately, militarily for space these days, will be expanded from the Nile to the Euphrates, with the future regathering of Israel being vastly expanded over what we've seen during the last hundred years. Today, four million of the world's seventeen million Jews are in Israel. And what of the "ten tribes"? God knows who and where they are, and just how He'll arouse them to "return." And in the Millennium, Israel will be divided according to the ancient twelve tribes (Ezekiel 47, 48 gives the precise divisions). Under Christ, the reigning and ruling King of the world, will be David, whose principality will be Israel (Hosea 3:5; Ezekiel 34:23,24; Isaiah 55:3,4). He will also lead Israel in worship (Ezekiel 45:22; 46:2,16). What a wealth of Psalms he'll have to call on, and he'll do so from Christ's Millennium Temple in Jerusalem (Ezekiel 40-47).

All nations and peoples will worship the true King Jesus, God's "Anointed One" (Psalm 2:2). Yes, they'll "go up to Jerusalem each year to worship the King, the Lord of Hosts, to celebrate a time of thanksgiving. And any nation anywhere in all the world that refuses to come to Jerusalem to worship the King, the Lord of Hosts, will have no rain" (Zechariah 14:16,17). And who will rule over the flourishing twelve regions of Israel? "Jesus replied, 'When I, the Messiah, shall sit upon My glorious throne in the kingdom, you My disciples shall certainly sit on twelve thrones judging the twelve tribes of Israel' " (Matthew 19:28).

With supra-metropolitan Jerusalem as the Capital, and an ultra-modern, vastly expanded Israel as the flag center of the earth, the Millennium will be resplendent with a flourishing world in the worship and service of Christ the King, as the Abrahamic Covenant will be fully realized. The worldwide dominion of our Lord will include the multitudinous tongues of the Gentile nations (Amos 9:12; Micah 7:16,17; Zechariah 14:16-19; Isaiah 66:18). What a contrast will prevail, compared to current events! There will be a total transformation of the geopolitical configuration of the whole Millennial world as "In that day the Lord will make Himself known to the Egyptians. Yes, they will know the Lord and give their sacrifices to Him . . . in that day Egypt and Iraq will be connected by a highway, and the Egyptians and the Iraqi will move freely back and forth between their lands, and they shall worship the same God. And Israel will be their ally; the three will be together, and Israel will be a blessing to them. For the Lord will bless Egypt and Iraq because of their friendship with Israel. He will say 'Blessed be Egypt, My people; blessed be Iraq, the land I have made; blessed be Israel, my inheritance" (Isaiah 19:21-25). Only a miracle could bring about such a change. It will happen through the Messiah's Millennial reign.

Recently the world paused for the rhetoric of the U.N. Debate on Disarmament from New York. In the surrounding streets were 700,000 demonstrators for the abolition of nuclear warfare and the institution of universal peace. The banners read, "Peace Now, No More Wars!" "No More Bombs!" "You Can't Hug Your Children with Nuclear Arms!"—and "Mushrooms Are For Quiche, Not Clouds." The theme song was: "Some day they'll join us and the world will be one!" That's a wonderful aspiration, but it's beyond the capacity of secularists to establish. It *will* happen when Christ comes to set up His theocratic kingdom.

The East German government has illegalized even the wearing of the lapel button "Swords Into Plowshares" in public. But, in the Millennium, "the whole world will be ruled by the Lord from Jerusalem! He will issue His laws and announce His decrees from there. He will arbitrate among the nations, and dictate to strong nations far away. They will beat their swords into plowshares and their spears into pruning-hooks; nations shall no longer fight each other, for all war will end. There will be universal peace, and all the military academies and training camps will be closed down. Everyone will live quietly in his own home in peace and prosperity, for there will be nothing to fear. The Lord Himself has promised this" (Micah 4:2-4, LB). On a statue across from the United Nations building in New York there is an inscription: "They shall beat their swords into plowshares." That really will happen—but not just yet. There are still too many who insist that peace is not something which comes down from God, but rather is something worked out by men of good will. "Good will" to men is the bequest of the coming Christ. Pope Paul VI exhorted, "If you want to be brothers, let the arms fall from your hands." Men today are only brothers when they've been born again into God's kingdom. Therefore, they're not dropping their arms.

One day they will—when Christ comes again to establish His

kingom. And so transformed will the world be that even the beasts will be tamed. "In that day the wolf and the lamb will lie down together, and the leopard and goats will be at peace. Calves and fat cattle will be safe among lions, and a little child shall lead them all. The cows will graze among bears; cubs and calves will lie down together, and lions will eat grass like the cows. Babies will crawl safely among poisonous snakes, and a little child who puts his hand in a nest of deadly adders will pull it out unharmed. Nothing will hurt or destroy in all My holy mountain, for as the waters fill the sea, so shall the earth be full of the knowledge of the Lord" (Isaiah 11:6-9, LB).

Additionally, sickness will be removed by Christ, the Great Healer of nations. And He will remove all deformities and handicaps. There will be no blindness, deafness, dumbness, nor paralytics; no need for glasses, hearing aids, speech therapy, wheelchairs or crutches (Isaiah 29:18; 33:24; 35:3-6; Jeremiah 30:17; Ezekiel 34:16). Ann Landers ran a fascinating column (Sept. 29, 1981) in which she quotes Dr. George Hatern. By rigid totalitarian controls, he was able to eliminate V.D. from China's billion people. He claims it could happen worldwide today, if there were a strict one world government. Concludes Ann Landers, "I believe him." It will happen in the Millennium. And we're informed that childhood will be extended. Yes, "the streets will be filled with boys and girls at play"; while with the world in a state of "peace and prosperity" there "will once again be aged men and women" (Zechariah 8:4) as, like Adam and Methuselah, people may well live for a thousand years.

And how will the earth support such a flowering, flourishing, proliferating population? The Lord will remove the ancient curse upon agriculture (Genesis 3:18) as "even the wilderness and desert will rejoice in those days; the desert will blossom with flowers. Yes, there will be an abundance of flowers and singing and joy! The deserts will become as green as the Lebanon mountains, as lovely as Mount Carmel's pastures and Sharon's meadows; for the Lord will display His glory there, the excellency of our God. With this news," rhapsodizes Isaiah (35:1-3), there'll be perpetual "cheer to all discouraged ones." In short, there'll be no need for psychiatrists or "uppers" to lift hypochondriacs from their depressions. St. Paul wrote to the Romans (8:23, 19-22) of how in this age "even we [as] Christians, although we have the Holy Spirit within us as a foretaste of future glory, also groan to be released from pain and suffering." For "all creation is waiting patiently and hopefully for that future day when . . . thorns and thistles, sin, death, and decay— the things that overcame the world against its will at God's command—will all disappear, and the world around us will share in the glorious freedom from sin . . . For we know that even the things of nature, like animals and plants, suffer in sickness and death as they await this great event." For millennia, man universally has craved for such an era of perfect peace and prosperity on this earth. The wonderful assurance of God's Word is that it's coming.

While I was preparing this chapter, I received a letter from Allan Emery, President of the Billy Graham Evangelistic Association. He told me of a lawyer whose name is Steve. He is President of his State's Bar Association. Three months ago it was my privilege to preach in a crusade in the chief city in Steve's state, where a thousand came forward to give themselves initially or in renewal to Christ. Steve "had lived a flagrantly wild life and came to know salvation." His girl friend, Lynda, had been raped at gunpoint, and manager of a furniture store as she was, had preferred not to be married. She lived in fear: fear of herself, fear of men, fear of the future. It was with the greatest of reluctance that Steve got her to attend the final service of that crusade. But she came. And when it was my privilege to extend the invitation to all present to come and give themselves to Christ, Lynda came forward, accompanied by Steve. A month later, they both met me in a Billy Graham crusade, with plans to be married, and happily to live the life of Christian victory in a world that seems everywhere to be fraught with omens that the days of the present order are definitely numbered.

Chapter Fourteen

"DEPART FROM ME YE CURSED INTO EVERLASTING FIRE"

There's an old saying: "All good things must come to an end." Will the Millennium end in triumph or tragedy—in jubilation or judgment? The answer is that it will, as all other preceding eras of human history, end in a downer, a downhill plunge that leads not only to tragedy but to the physical dissolution of the world and heavens around it, and straight on to the Great White Throne Judgment. The account is in many Biblical passages, but let us turn back to Revelation 20:2,3,7-9 (LB) where we read that Christ will have incarcerated Satan in "the bottomless pit . . . bound [and] in chains for 1,000 years . . . so that he could not fool the nations anymore until the thousand years were finished. Afterwards he would be released again for a little while." I pray that a little while will be a *very* little while. John picks it up, "When the thousand years end, Satan will be let out of his prison. He will go out to deceive the nations of the world and gather them together, with Gog and Magog, for battle—a mighty host, numberless as sand along the shore. They will go up across the broad plain of the earth and surround God's people and the beloved city of Jerusalem on every side. But fire from God in heaven will flash down on the attacking armies and consume them."

"Satan" and "Gog and Magog" again? That's what St. John

foresaw! History does repeat itself! In his U.N. address, President Reagan looked back on the 1970's: "The decade of so-called detente witnessed the most massive Soviet buildup of military power in history. They increased their defense spending by 40 percent, while American defense actually declined in the same real terms." And currently, "at the very time the Soviet Union is trying to manipulate the peace movement in the West, it is stifling a budding peace movement at home. In Moscow, banners are scuttled, buttons are snatched, and demonstrators arrested wherever a few people dare to speak about their fears." And the Bible teaches that it will happen again.

There will be residual unbelief and rebellion throughout North-Central Euro-Asia in particular, and the earth generally, surfacing during the final days of the Millennium, as the "world and the flesh"—which will not pass off the scene during the Millennium—will be joined by the devil fresh out of hell. This malevolent recrudescence of latent evil will be pounced upon by a briefly released Satan, who will obviously go berserk, because his time will be so short. Like the Judas he possessed to betray our Lord, what he does he'll feel compelled to do quickly—very quickly!

In the really ultimate conflagration of history, St. Peter's prophecy (2 Peter 3:8-13) will be fulfilled. Before quoting it, let us clear up one or two unwitting descrepances which have arisen around this passage, due to its not being looked at carefully and in perspective. The passage actually interprets itself, the key being that "the day of the Lord" in length is "a thousand years." Note that Peter is careful to remind us that this "day is with the Lord as a thousand years, and a thousand years as one day" (vs. 8). With that in mind, the Apostle Peter assures us that the finale to "the day of the Lord is surely coming, as unexpectedly as a thief, and then the heavens will pass away with a terrible noise and the heavenly bodies will disappear in fire, and the earth and everything in it will be burned up. And so since everything around us is going to melt away, what holy, godly lives we should be living! When God will set the heavens on fire, and the heavenly bodies will melt and disappear in flames" they'll be replaced with "God's promise of new heavens and a new earth afterwards, where there will be only goodness."

Did Jesus make allusion to this in Matthew 24? Yes, in verse 35, "Heaven and earth will disappear, but My words remain forever." Is the world to go up totally in nuclear flames at any time now? No! But it will eventually do so, and with it the whole of the physical interstellar universe. We keep asking if the 60,000 current hydrogen bombs were to go off all at once, what would happen? Only God knows! We're told that our nearly 5 billion humans would be annihilated 100 times over. Twenty years ago Canadian Prime Minister Lester Pearson reckoned upon receiving his Nobel Peace Prize, that every man, woman and child in the world is only 30 minutes from potential annihilation. We think: 60,000 H. bombs! What if one or two go off? Senior Physicist David Inglis of the Argonne National Laboratory in Washington, in his *Unless Peace Comes*, warns that a hydrogen bomb wrapped in cobalt can exterminate all life in the Northern Hemisphere. That would mean 3½ billion humans right there! Veteran Milton Burton, an Oak Ridge nuclear scientist who helped produce the first atomic bomb, has informed a U.S. Senator that the distinct "possibility exists of lighting the nitrogen chain, in which event the whole world would go up in flames." Burton went on to say, "Should other planets be inhabited, they would look and cry, 'Ah, a Nova, a new star.' " What in fact will happen—more than a thousand years in the future—is that the whole physical universe will go up in flames at once!

The distinguished writer Gwynne Dyer reckons in 1982 that a cold hard assessment of the facts currently would lead an objective observer to conclude that the cosmos is physically "doomed" with the "weapons of mass destruction" there are today. But he goes on thoughtfully to reason that it may not be "World War III" that will issue in the "eventual collapse which is inevitable." It well "might take World War IV, or even World War V." Dyer might in fact be correct—if WW III is the U.S.S.R./Israeli/U.S.A. nuclear war; WW IV, Armageddon; and WW V the final war at the end of the Millennium between Satan with his re-assembled forces, largely from Gog and Magog, taking on those of Christ the King. And at that point, St. Peter prophesied, not only the earth but the heavens will decompose in flames. An enormous literature can be culled from the current 40,000 science journals worldwide, on how the physical cosmos may well collapse in a "Big Bang" consummation: very much as it allegedly came into existence at creation's dawn—some conjecture 18 billion years ago. That will surely be the signal for the Great White Throne Judgment!

The Great White Throne Judgment will be summoned out in space. St. John in the Revelation of Jesus Christ writes about this consummation of all things, this culmination of human history. In chapter 20:9-15, he records how Satan has seduced the residue of the rebellious in the Millennial world as concentrated in Gog and Magog, and "God in heaven will flash down on the attacking armies and consume them. Then the devil who had betrayed them will again be thrown into the Lake of Fire" where the Antichrist "and false prophet are, and they will be tormented day and night forever and ever." That's it!

Satan's gone—everlastingly! "And I saw a great white throne and the One who sat upon it, from whose face the earth and sky fled away; but they found no place to hide. I saw the dead, great and small, standing before God; and The Books were opened, including the Book of Life. And the dead were judged according to the things written in The Books, each according to the deeds he had done. The oceans surrendered the bodies buried in them; and the earth and the underworld gave up the dead in them. Each was judged according to his deeds. And Death and Hell were thrown into the Lake of Fire." This is the Second Death—the Lake of Fire. And if anyone's name was not found recorded in the Book of Life, he was thrown into the Lake of Fire. I'm sure this was the consummation judgment to which St. Paul alluded when addressing the Athenians, whom he urged "to repent: because He hath appointed a day, in the which He will judge the world in righteousness by That Man whom He hath ordained; whereof He hath given assurance unto all men, in that He hath raised Him from the dead" (Acts 17:30,31).

Jesus assured that when He judges the impenitent, He will issue their sentence: "Away with you, you cursed ones, into the eternal fire prepared for the devil and his demons" and "they shall go away into eternal punishment" (Matthew 25:41,46). This is the "second death" to which St. John alludes in the above quoted Revelation 20:14; and to which he refers again in the following chapter, verse 8, which reads, "But the fearful, and unbelieving, and the corrupt, and murderers, and the immoral, and those conversing with demons, and idol worshipers and all liars—their doom is in the lake which burneth with fire and brimstone: which is the second death." "The Second Death" is the title of chapter 2 of Jonathan Schell's *The Fate of the Earth*, in which he projects beyond nuclear annihilation of all life on this planet—"beyond the end, as it were, into the void. Death lies at the core of each person's private existence, but part of death's meaning is to be found in the fact that it occurs in a biological and social world that survives. Were that world to perish, it would be the 'second death'—the death of the species, not just of the earth's population on doomsday, but of countless unborn generations" (*Time*, April 19, 1982). This "Second Death" lifting of this phrase out of the Bible is yet another example of how reliant modern thinkers are on ancient theologians. But this is not what St. John meant. He meant that Christ-rejecters would be everlasting occupants of hell.

With that kind of sentence, we need to look at what our Lord had to say about hell. General Sherman reckoned a century ago: "War is hell." If that was true then, what could be said today! But war is not hell! Simply put, war puts an end to life. Hell perpetuates existence in torment forever. If this is believed by a Christian, his or her concern about war versus hell should be the difference in attention an astronomer gives to the total cosmos over a single atom. And that's an inestimable understatement.

When He [Jesus] was demanded of *the Pharisees* when the Kingdom of God should come, He answered *them*—note carefully that it was not His disciples this time asking Jesus "when the Kingdom of God should come," but the Pharisees. They were the religionists of their day—actually strictly orthodox people—people who, unlike the Sadducees, believed in the coming of the Messiah, and in resurrection from the dead. And they were asking Jesus when the Kingdom of God would come (Luke 17:20). But those who asked were overtly rejecting him as their Messiah. Jesus told them that it would be: "As the lightning, that lighteneth out of the one part under heaven . . . so shall also the Son of man be in His day" (vs. 24). And Jesus said that it would be "as it was in the days of Lot; they did eat, they drank, they bought, they sold, they planted, they builded; but the same day that Lot went out of Solom it rained fire and brimstone from heaven, and destroyed them all. Even thus shall it be in the day when the Son of man is revealed." And then He gave that terribly solemn warning: "Remember Lot's wife" (vss. 24,28,29,32). It must be kept in mind that the unregenerate are reserved in Hades from the time of their death until the Great White Throne Judgment (Rev. 20:5).

Several sobering points stand out here. Jesus was addressing people who were devoutly religious, but poeple who were rejecting Him as their Messiah. Immediately when they asked Him, the first part of His answer was that "the kingdom of God cometh not with observation" (vs.20). People didn't enter the kingdom by speculation. Christ's next statement is, "Behold the kingdom of God is within you" (vs. 21). In short, you have to ask Christ to come into your heart, for you to be inside His kingdom. Then, after telling them that there'd be a time when they'd desire to see the day of Christ's kingdom, He said that there was a "must" on which the kingdom door swung open or closed. It was: "The Son of man . . . first must . . . suffer many things, and be rejected of this generation" (vss. 22-25).

Then He completed His answer with the warning that as Lot was saved from the fire of Sodom, and Lot's wife almost was, except she turned back, so He warned them to "Remember Lot's wife."

When we think of Queen Elizabeth, we think of Buckingham Palace. When we think of President Reagan, we think of the White House. When we think of Jesus Christ, we think of heaven. But what most of us have not realized is that Jesus Christ spoke thirteen times as much about hellfire as He did about heaven! Why did He do this? Was it because He was angry? Was He an intimidator? Was He an ignorant bigot? No, indeed! It was because He was God and he knew the total truth! And it was because He totally loved people! It was because He wanted people, who He loved so much that He came from the glories of heaven to the gates of hell to die for them, to stay out of hellfire!

Here He warns, "Remember Lot's wife!" The first atomic bomb to kill one person in modern times, killed one-hundred-thousand. That was in Hiroshima, Japan. Scientists note that there is a substantial resemblance between the ashy soils on the site where Sodom and Gomorrah were incinerated and those where Hiroshima and Nagasaki were vaporized. It was said that some who were fleeing Hiroshima and Nagasaki turned back to see them going up in mushrooming flames. But alas, in exposing themselves frontally to the nuclear quietus, they were turned into saltlike—or ashy—pillars resembling burnt, unsnuffed cigarettes! It is not insignificant that Moses used the same word for salt, used in Genesis 19:26, where we read that Lot's wife "looked back . . . and she became a pillar of salt" (Hebrew: "Melach"). Moses—in Deuteronomy 29:22,23—was prophesying. And he warned of "the generation to come" that would see "brimstone, and salt, and burning." So the pillar of salt may have been a pillar of ash. We may assume that Jesus in prophesying hellfire may well have been referring to a form of fire and brimstone which was not the oxidation fire familiar to His earthly contemporaries. It was a kind of fire not known then, and perhaps not known yet, but nevertheless, fire; real and terrible fire.

Jesus said something else about Christ rejecters and hellfire. He said they'd be "cast into hell, into the fire that never shall be quenched: where their worm dieth not and the fire is not quenched" (Mark 9:45,46). People imply that that was a slip of Jesus' tongue. But was it? He said it three times over, back to back! Read verses 43-48. Impenitents will "be cast into hellfire where their worm dieth not and the fire is not quenched." And as if this weren't enough, after saying it three times, He adds to the fact that the unrepentant shall "be cast into hellfire: where their worm dieth not, and the fire is not quenched. For everyone shall be salted with fire" (vss. 47-49). So what does salt do? It preserves! Back on the farm in Saskatchewan we'd rub salt into hams—and they'd hang on the wall in the summer heat for weeks without spoiling. Hellfire is not as alien a phrase to modern sophisticates as once it was: Nick Toches writes in *The New York Times* (June 20, 1982) on Hellfire! Jesus said what He meant! And He meant what He said. He said that if you're impenitent you'll go to hell. And there'll be hellfire. And you'll be in that hellfire forever.

I know that in a theater it's illegal to yell with a loud voice, "Fire!" It seems to me at this moment in history that it's perilous to be in church, the Church of Jesus Christ—the church where Jesus Christ saves people from hellfire through repentance and faith—and not to shout, "Fire!" There's hellfire! Turn or burn, if you will! Despite the ridicule and social ostracism you'll absorb from such activity, it's the message of the Bible. So don't ever engage lightly in the profanity, "Go to hell!" It's a million times worse than saying, "Get cancer." Cancer is also a form of mysterious fire that medical scientists don't understand. If they did, they'd have a cure. And better to threaten, "I'll commit suicide!" than to say, "I'll be damned!" And it's kinder to exclaim, "I'll kill you!" than to yell, "Damn you!"

One of the great tragedies of our time is the travesty on the truth of hell made by the pop songs. The Meatloaf Album

features "Bat Out of Hell" and AC-DC acid rocks "Highway
to Hell." Cliff Edwards asks in his country western lyric of 1982:
"What's Forever For?" One thing's for sure! It's not for spending it in hell. The song that followed on my radio dial lamented:
"He's going to hell, and this he knows too well!" No one needs
to go to hell, while Jesus Christ invites us to heaven.

Let us ever keep in mind that it is the most loving person
who ever lived, Jesus Christ Himself, who eventually in judgment will say to "them on His left hand, depart from Me, ye
cursed, into everlasting fire, prepared for the devil and his
angels . . . and these shall go away into everlasting punishment"
(Matthew 25:41,46). So it will be everlasting punishment in
everlasting fire!

We turn to modern revelations of actual kinds of fire, and the
disbeliever objects with the argument that surely Jesus said
that hellfire would be a place of darkness! How could there be
hellfire and darkness? Let me confirm that Jesus preached
hellfire again and again. And indeed He did say that hell would
be a place forever dominated by darkness, as heaven would surely be a place of light; light, day and night forever. Matthew 8:12
reads that the impenitent would be "cast out into outer
darkness. There shall be weeping and gnashing of teeth." How
can there be fire and darkness? I asked Dr. James Kennedy,
minister of the Coral Ridge Presbyterian Church of Fort Lauder-
dale, Florida, this question. He replied soberly that in their
house, they cook their meals most frequently in a microwave
oven. It's ten times as fast. It cooks from the inside out, rather
than the outside in, and inside a microwave oven, it is, if
possible, blacker and darker than it would be if the oven were
a sealed steel safe, with no flame or light in it whatsoever! The
Apostle Jude (13) clarified that, for unbelievers, there "is reserved the blackness of darkness forever."

In 1982, Dr. Patrick Osmer, the American astronomer, looking through the most powerful telescope in the Southern
Hemisphere, located in Chile, has found what he says may be
"the edge of the universe . . . looking for light sources called

quasars, the most distant objects ever detected." Omar "found only darkness."

And Jesus said hellfire is forever! Its victims are preserved rather than consumed. No, I don't understand it, any more than I understand microwave ovens. I don't understand what we've been seeing on television, reading in our newspapers, or hearing on the radio about neutron bombs—that when detonated they destroy people, while preserving property. I may not understand it, but my physicist friends—at least some of them—do understand it. And I believe what they say. Oppositely, I don't understand how the visible heavens and earth will be burned up with fire but the human inhabitants of earth will be preserved by fire, to burn forever. The ancient Isaiah asked, "The sinners in Zion [who] are afraid . . . who among us shall dwell with everlasting burnings?" Short of the question, "What then shall I do with Jesus who is called Christ?" I suspect the most important question I could ask of you is, "Who among us shall dwell with everlasting burnings?" No, I don't understand it, any more than I understand chronic insanity, or incurable terminal herpes simplex. But how could I love people without asking it, when God's Word declares it? The atheist purports that the earth beneath us and the skies and stars above us will last indefinitely, but we will die and that's it! The Bible teaches the exact opposite. It tells us unmistakably that we'll edure forever, while all that's seen will pass away in a terrible universal fire, to make place for new heavens and a new earth.

While I have been writing this solemn chapter, I've been in New England holding crusades in such places as the great John F. Kennedy Coliseum where some ten percent of those overflowing gatherings would surge forward to commit themselves to Christ. An Ivy League-trained reporter attended and was amazed, asking why it's happening. One of the reasons has been that the doomsday jeremiads, flooding the classical magazines and media with their scarey warnings, have been the Harvey Coxes, the John Kenneth Galbraiths, and the Henry

Kissingers—even more than the Billy Grahams and Ronald Reagans. One of those who responded was Dr. Dennis Moore, Principal of a huge high school. He had nearly forgotten the descriptions of hellfire he had heard the priests propound in the churches of his childhood. Now the ground-zero, the nuclear freeze, and the peace marchers had stirred up the embers of memory by piling nuclear fuel onto the fire. They thundered of the flames that one of these days would burst out into a huge holocaust: hell on earth! And if hellfire were worse than that, what must it be like? "U-turn from doom," screamed the headlines. And I recalled, it being New England, that John Kennedy's most oft-quoted admonition was a quote from Dante, "The hottest place in hell is reserved for those who take no stand at all." In the face of the facts, Dr. Moore decided to take his stand for Christ, so he was a part of the ten percent of the crusade crowd to come forward and give himself to the Savior. And the next night, it was his wife, Anne! Jesus as their Lord assured Dr. and Mrs. Moore as He did Nicodemus, "There is no eternal doom awaiting those who trust Him to save them" (John 2:18, LB).

Chapter Fifteen

"I WILL COME AGAIN"

The television series which has received the biggest "hype" in a decade in Canada has been the prime-time CBC TV news week nightly magazine, "The Journal." Assembling an all-star cast, it's Executive Producer Mark Starowicz was asked in the wake of its 1982 debut what he thought of his massively touted brainchild. Reflecting a moment, he leveled, "I know we didn't have the Second Coming!" Starowicz was referring, of course, to the Second Coming of Jesus Christ. For a generation and more, the largest conceivable heeadlines that newspapers can engage are known as "Second Coming" headlines. George Gallup tells us that four times as many North Americans believe in the Second Coming of Jesus Christ as voted for President Reagan's and Prime Minister Trudeau's Governments combined. "Second" Coming is a phrase which derives from Hebrews 9:28, where we read that "unto them that look for [Christ] shall He appear the second time without sin unto salvation."

A clergyman friend of mine was given a Rubik's Cube for Christmas, and starting uninitiated to play with it, spun it into chaos. Trying to turn it back into its original uniformity, the more he expended himself, the more exasperated he became. As he later learned, his hope for success on the basis of chance was one in 43 quintillion. Finally, totally frustrated, with proud reluctance, he was about to give up, when he noticed that a book came in the gift package with the Rubik's Cube. To his delight, it provided the key for him to restore the Cube to its original pattern. And so, with forgivable exaggeration, he claims his sanity and honor were saved—by the book!

Our world is headed for worse war than history has ever witnessed. The only escape for believers in Christ is to turn to His Word where Christ assures us He's coming back. James Reston of *The New York Times* writes that in this age of horrible holocaust hanging over us, "If we listen attentively, we shall hear, amid the uproar of empires and nations, a faint flutter of wings, the gentle stirring of life and hope. Some will say this hope lies in a nation; others in a man." The Bible definitely assures us that the only true hope lies in The Man: The God-Man, God the Son, Jesus Christ, returning as the Son of man to take home His own.

Dr. Leonard DuPree, a Plains, Georgia, native, and relative of former President Jimmy Carter, said to me in mid-1982 that with the signs of the times as they are, it's as one of his southern brothers exhorted: "Gabriel's licking his lips." One of these days, "the trumpet shall sound, and the dead shall be raised incorruptible, and we shall be changed" (1 Cor. 15:52). Millions long for Christ's coming again. Billy Graham was saying last year that when he was in Moscow in the Baptist Church, to accommodate the crushing crowds there were five services, back to back. And the theme in every one, was the hope of the second coming of Jesus Christ. In the most familiar paragraph in the New Testament, one that we hear recited at nearly all funerals, Jesus warns of coming persecution. Then He warns, "Let not your heart be troubled: ye believe in God, believe also in Me. In my Father's house are many mansions: if it were not so, I would have told you. I go to prepare a place for you. And if I go and prepare a place for you, I will come again, and receive you unto Myself; that where I AM, there ye may be also" (John 14:1-3).

The disciples reflected a moment, then Thomas responded, "Lord, we know not whiter thou goest; and how can we know the way? Jesus saith unto him, I AM the way, the truth, and the life: no man cometh unto the Father, but by Me" (John

14:5,6). Not long after, Peter, James, John and Andrew asked Jesus privately what would signal "the end" of life here and the ascent to the life hereafter with Christ forever (Mark 13:3; Matthew 24:3). "The end" was very much in the minds of Biblical believers. Daniel (8:19) was given to "know what shall be in the last end." Habakkuk (2:3) was assured of his vision, "at the end it shall speak, and not lie." Jesus made quite plain to His disciples, "so shall it be in the end of this world." As for life with Christ, "of His kingdom there shall be no end" (Luke 1:33). St Paul warned impenitents indulging iniquities, "The end of those things is death." But for the redeemed who yield "fruit unto holiness," the end is "everlasting life" (Romans 6:21,22). While St Peter rejoiced for those "receiving the end of your faith, even the salvation of your souls" (1 Peter 1:9), he agonized, "What shall be the end of them that obey not the Gospel" (1 Peter 4:17)? The Psalmist (39:4) prayed, "Lord, make me to know mine end, and the measure of my days, what it is; that I may know how frail I am."

The End is the title of a prime-time movie on T.V. MacMillan Publishers advertises their "End Times" in *The New York Times*. Theologian Carl Henry, founding editor of *Christianity Today*, features the eighties as a decade when we're propelled into the "End Time"—"the Final End," "the End of all Ends" when suddenly "trumpet sound" expectations cause us "to revise our perspective, to shift to a last-day theology, a theology of the last hour, a theology of 'the moment,' of the twinkling of an eye, a theology that sees Christ the King . . . coming in great power and glory, a theology of full consummation." Certainly, the world around us has no realistic substitute for the Savior's promise to return and usher in a new age. Della Reese belts out on TV, "Don't Bring Me No Bad News!" George Gallup polls North Americans, asking them, in looking at 1982, do they expect deepening trouble worldwide, or a protraction of peace. Four times as many Americans expect trouble as expect peace, and seven times as many Canadians. "War, famine and disaster" asseverates Global TV Network newscaster Peter

Truman, whether or not we like it, is what constitutes the news in 1982. Mickie Moore on her TV program, "You're Beautiful," interviews an eminent sleep therapist, who diagnoses that what keeps most insomniacs awake is the chronic terror that if they do get to sleep, they might not wake up prior to doomsday. Andy Rooney editorializes in *The Indianapolis Star*, "As I always do, this morning I got up early and turned on the radio to make sure the world hadn't come to an end during the night." Pundit Dick Beddoes ruminates glumly in *The Globe and Mail*, "Bookmakers in this town will lay you no better odds than eight to five that there will be such a thing as the year 2000. And if you win, you can't collect."

Without hope in Christ, people not only despair, some turn sordid, and even downright mean. Burt Saxton, denominating himself and his followers "The Survivalists," comes out of his Arkansas cave, where the "survivalists" are ensconced with a year's supply of food, and an arsenal of guns, to prognosticate on the Evening TV news that when economic collapse, nuclear war, and political anarchy have devoured the democracies he's at least got "Eleven Steps to Survival." It will involve killing off the few other stragglers who many emerge from the impending apocalypse, and subsist on the spoils in a torpedoed world which at best would be a Neanderthal milieu. One can hardly blame people for desperately questing for corners into which to back, especially when they're barraged with such headlines as: "Global Outlook Extremely Bleak" and "In the Pentagon's Halls; Visions of Apocalypse."

"Forever" for the Christian is reality. The Lord "will preserve me unto His heavenly kingdom," wrote St. Paul to Timothy, "forever and ever" (2 Timothy 4:18). Bob Dylan currently enthralls halls full of listeners with his "Forever Young," because he was born again and looks, as his song goes, for Christ's soon coming again. It's calculated currently that a 70-year-old Christian has slept 23 years, worked 19 years, played 9 years, eaten for 6 years, traveled for 6 years, had 4 years of leisure, but only one year in the house of the Lord. "I will dwell in the house of the Lord forever" (Psalm 23:6), contemplated King David.

The Archbishop of Canterbury, Donald Coggan, in retiring exclaims that to aspire for Christ's coming again is "the spur of the eschatological hope." As the old Welsh preacher assured, "When the Lord Jesus left the world at the Ascension, He took a return ticket. He's coming back!" Led Zeppelin tops the charts with "Stairway to Heaven," but only Jesus Christ can actually be that stairway. *Heaven's Gate* is a film. The real gate to heaven is Jesus Christ. Emil Brunner, writing before his death on the return of Christ, made plain, "It is clear that this thought of the future coming is anything but a piece of mythology which can be dispensed with. Faith in Christ without the expectation of His Parousia is a voucher that is never redeemed, a promise that is not seriously meant." Dr. Ted Randall puts it so well in his *Prairie Overcomer*, "Our conviction that the end of the world is in sight must never create irresponsibility on our part resulting in a withdrawal from society. On the other hand, our commitment to God's work in the world must not create indifference to the fact that it is three minutes to midnight. We must learn to live with the tension created by the world around us and the Word within us. A world in flames around us warns us that the end cannot be far off. The Word within us exhorts us to keep working and witnessing for Christ."

So St. Peter wrote that he lived to make "known unto you the power and coming of our Lord Jesus Christ" (2 Peter 1:16). John addressed his spiritual children, "Abide in Him; that, when He shall appear, we may have confidence, and not be ashamed before Him at His coming" (1 John 2:28). James counseled, "Be patient therefore, brethren, unto the coming of the Lord . . . stablish your hearts: for the coming of the Lord draweth nigh" (James 5:7,8). St. James wrote of the "early" and "latter" rain. When the ancient prophet Joel wrote so profusely of the "last days" he assured (Joel 2:28,32) that it would be accompanied by a great outpouring of God's Holy Spirit: Yes, "I will pour out My spirit upon all flesh" and "it shall come to pass that

whosoever shall call on the name of the Lord shall be delivered."
Dr. Leighton Ford causes the Christian world to rejoice with
the finds of his Lausanne Continuation Committee on World
Evangelism: in 1982—on average—65,000 daily are becoming
Christians, 27,000 of these being in Africa, and astonishingly
large numbers being in Red China and the Soviet Union. *The
Church Around The World* (March, 1982) points to such
remarkable assemblies as the Seoul National Central Church,
pastored by the Rev. Paul Yo Cho, which has a current "congregation of 200,000 members [and] has increased its membership by at least 50,000 this past year." How many born again
people are there in the entire world? God only knows! But
according to British Anglican David Barrett in his newly
published *World Christian Encyclopedia*, there are 420 million
who so signify. So when Christ comes again—if it were today—
we might hypothesize that one in ten would rise from earth to
heaven to be forever with the Lord.

There is nothing more important for us as believers to do,
in the light of Christ's promise to come again at any moment,
than to evangelize: "Watch [for] souls as they that must give
account," wrote the Hebraicist (13:17). Coming into the 1970's
there were 37,000 Christian missionaries worldwide. Today
there are 53,000. So let's keep up the increase. "Put ye in the
sickle, for the harvest is ripe . . . multitudes, multitudes in the
valley of decision. The day of the Lord is near in the valley of
decision" (Joel 3:13,14).

While there are 1,845 unmistakable references in the Bible
to the Lord's return, there are not less than 90 New Testament
verses which signify that Christ's coming again could occur at
any moment. It will happen "in a moment, in the twinkling of
an eye, at the last trump: for the trumpet shall sound, and the
dead shall be raised incorruptible, and we shall be changed,"
wrote St. Paul to the Corinthians (1 Corinthians 15:52).

It is interesting that an enterprising San Francisco mortician
has devised an ingenious scheme whereby he advertises that
for as little as $3,000 he will project deceased loved ones

atomically into space, so that the ascended corpses will hurtle into orbit and go into perpetual gyrations around the planet. This would certainly be a parody of the parousia, and it's indicative of man's inherent longing to ascend to the heavens. Ray Bradbury, the premier science fiction writer on space spectaculars, told Walter Cronkite that the whole space race has to do with man yearning to rise to immortality into the stars. Jesus made clear that when He comes there will be innumerable beds from which one will be taken, and one left; farmers in fields in pairs, one of whom will be taken and the other left; factory workers with two at a machine, one being taken, and the other left. So get right or you'll be left, when Christ returns. A new film is entitled "Missing." Will you be "missing", or "missiling" heavenward, when Christ comes back to take home His own, forever to be with Him?

We're constantly to be "looking for that blessed hope, and the glorious appearing of the great God and our Savior Jesus Christ" (Titus 2:13) exhorted St. Paul to Titus; and to the Philippians (Philippians 3:20) we're to "look for the Savior, the Lord Jesus Christ," from heaven, for it's "unto them that look for Him shall He appear" explained the Hebraicist (Hebrews 9:28). Jesus Christ Himself urges us to "look up, and lift up your heads." When? "When these things begin to come to pass." He clearly did not say that when the apocalyptical events to which He points in Matthew 24, Mark 13, and Luke 21 have reached their worst, that's when believers are to look up. He rather states, "When these things *BEGIN* to come to pass, then look up, and lift up your heads; for your redemption draweth nigh" (Luke 21:28). I cannot agree with distinguised columnist Ellen Goodman (August 10, 1982) that "the bomb [hangs] over us like some apocalypse without the promise of redemption." There is promise of "redemption"—in Christ's coming again! He urges "lift up your heads; for your redemption draweth nigh." But thats not all. He further exhorts: "watch ye therefore, and pray always, that ye may be accounted worthy to escape all these things that shall come to pass, and to stand before the Son of man" (Luke 21:36).

In the words of St. Paul's writing to the Thessalonians: "I can tell you this directly from the Lord: that we who are still living when the Lord returns will not rise to meet Him ahead of those who are in their graves. For the Lord Himself will come down from heaven with a mighty shout and with the soul-stirring cry of the archangel and the great trumpet call of God. And the believers who are dead will be the first to rise to meet the Lord. Then we who are still alive and remain on the earth will be caught up with them in the clouds to meet the Lord in the air and remain with Him forever. So comfort and encourage each other with this news" (1 Thessalonians 4:15-18, LB). The Thessalonians desperately needed comfort, as they shortly fell into terrible tormenting persecution. Paul heard about it and wrote them a second letter, the second chapter of which begins: "How we beseech you, brethren, by the coming of our Lord Jesus Christ, and by our gathering together unto Him, that ye be not soon shaken in mind, or be troubled, neither by spirit, nor by word, nor by letter as from us, as that the day of [the Lord] is at hand. Let no man deceive you by any means: for that day (of Great Tribulation) shall not come, except there come a departure" (—as a ship departs). What is that departure? The departure of believers in Christ to heaven: The evacuation of Christians from this earth at the return of Christ in the clouds. As I write I'm looking at a front page, topline, headliner: one word: EVACUATE! The paragraph indent reads "President Reagan in March signed an order allocating $4.2 billion for . . . 380 nuclear attack risk areas . . . the Federation Emergency Management Agency [has earmarked] to develop nuclear 'crisis relocation' plans." The EVACUATION to which the believer looks forward is the coming again of Christ to take us home to heaven, just prior to the most awful time of holocaust the world has ever known.

On the much more positive and pleasant side, Jesus said that the homegoing of the church would be like a wedding, and St.

John described it as the Marriage Supper of the Lamb to which believers in Christ are invited. Centuries ago the tenderhearted Scot, Samuel Rutherford, who was martyred for Christ in the Aberdeen Prison, wrote in one of his celebrated letters, "God has booked your heaven and your happiness, if you are called to the Marriage Supper of the Lamb." *The China Daily* carries a news story announcing how 304 young couples had been married in one super ceremony. That's nothing compared to the numberless saints of the ages, who will rise at Christ's coming again to bring His bride to the Marriage Supper of the Lamb. It seemed pathetically sad to me to read that periodically Marlon Brando talks to the ashes of his late roommate Wally Cox. When Christ comes again, the saints of all the ages will rise from the ashes of cemeteries in innumerable burial grounds to be forever with the Lord. St. Paul promised that when Christ comes for His bride, ash corpes may arise, but He "shall change our vile body, that it may be fashioned like unto His glorious body, according to the working whereby He is able even to subdue all things unto Himself" (Philippians 3:21). Scottish martyr James Graham wrote on the window of his jail cell the night before his execution 333 years ago: "Open all my veins that I may swim to thee my Maker! In that crimson lake. Then place my parboiled head upon a stake—scatter my ashes—strew them in the air; Lord! since thou know'st where all these atoms are, I'm hopeful thou'lt recover my dust, and confident thou'lt raise me with the just."

Richard Glover of China read from his Bible and took heart: "No day is named in connection with the Second Coming of Christ, so that every day may be hallowed by the sense of the possibility of its being the day of His Advent." Oh, I know there are those who defy Jesus' firm word that "ye know neither the day nor the hour wherein the Son of man cometh" (Matthew 25:13). Bill Maupin and his handful of followers in Tuscon, Arizona, received press coverage around the world that Jesus Christ would return on June 28, 1981; and when it didn't happen, reproach and aspersions were cast upon the doctrine of the second coming. Quebecer Roch Moses Theriault predicted February, 1982, as the month in which the world would end. It didn't happen! Dr. Walter Martin, researching for CBS, points out that the Jehovah Witnesses have announced 14 different dates for the end of the world, each turning out to be yet another trespass against Christ's caution "of that day and hour knoweth no man" (Matthew 24:36). Is this to throw us off track, in announcing that Christ Jesus is indeed coming again, and perhaps soon? No! St. Peter assured that Christians must know surely "that there shall come in the last days scoffers, walking after their own lusts, and saying, Where is the promise of His coming? For since the fathers fell asleep, all things continue as they were from the beginning of the creation. For this they willingly are ignorant of" that "the day of the Lord will come as a thief in the night" (2 Peter 3:3-5,10).

Recently at our home we had our first burglary in a generation. The fact the thief got away with so much, so easily, partially reflected our total non-preparedness for such an event. I held a Crusade in Oregon recently. Into the concluding meeting was brought a distinguished Jewish surgeon, Dr. Burt Seligman. He had been able to cope with life's ups and downs until a lawyer ran off with his wife. Completely shattered and feeling no hope in his future, he heard Jesus Christ proclaimed as the Messiah who came and took his place on the cross, shedding His life blood to cleanse him from his guilt and save him. Also, he heard of Jesus Christ the Messiah who is coming again, forever to receive him home. That night Dr. Seligman came forward and made his decision for Jesus Christ. He prepared to meet his God, as the Ancient Hebrew prophet, Amos, urged (Amos 4:12).

The whole upshot of Jesus Christ's teaching was that we should "be . . . ready: for in such an hour as ye think not the Son of man cometh" (Matthew 24:44). I believe that our late Governor-General Georges Vanier was a committed Christian, his son today being a very effective evangelist. Said our former number one citizen, as quoted by Prime Minister Trudeau, "The best time is always the present time, because it alone offers the opportunity for action, because it is ours; because on God's scale it is apocalyptic, a time when the lines between good and evil are clearly drawn, and each of us must choose his side, a time when there is no longer room for either the coward or the uncommitted." President Reagan is quoted in *The Saturday Evening Post*: "Our responsibility begins with 'the peace the world cannot give,' the peace of spirit." This, of course, is what St. Paul wrote to the Romans, "Therefore being justified by faith, we have peace with God through our Lord Jesus Christ" (Romans 5:1). It's the salvation which Martin Luther described: "When by the Spirit of God, I understood the words, 'the just shall live by faith,' I felt born again like a new man; I entered through the open doors into the very paradise of God." Father Dr. Robert McDougal of Toronto had a similar experience, recalling his previous Christian commitment as being merely a theological knowledge which "occupied me from my Adam's apple to my skull." Now, as he tells the whole world, "It's Christ in me, all of me, from the soles of my feet to the crown of my head! And it's forever!"

Should you, the reader, be a church insider who needs a vital re-dedication of your life to Christ; a backslider, who needs to return to the Lord with your whole heart; or an outsider, who needs to begin with Christ, and go with Him forever—I'm going to urge you without delay to confess your sin to Christ. Do so right now, in the assurance that "if we confess our sins, He Jesus Christ is faithful and just to forgive us our sins and to cleanse us from all unrighteousness" (1 John 1:9). Don't conceal any of your sins for "he that covereth his sins shall not prosper but whoso confesseth and forsaketh them shall have mercy" (Proverbs 28:13). When you confess your sins, what happens to them? "The blood of Jesus Christ God's Son cleanseth us from all sin (1 John 1:7). Hence they're gone—as far as the East is from the West—into "the sea of God's forgetfulness," never to be remembered against you forever.

And having confessed your sins to Christ, you have the

guarantee from God's Word that you're saved. "That if thou shalt confess with thy mouth [Jesus as Lord] and shalt believe in thine heart that God hath raised Him from the dead, thou shalt be saved. For with the heart man believeth unto righteousness, and with the mouth confession is made unto salvation" (Romans 10:9,10).

So you're saved! But you'll only enjoy the assurance of salvation when you confess, not only your sins to Christ Jesus as Lord with your mouth, but when you share Christ with others. For it was Jesus Himself who insisted, "Whosoever therefore shall confess Me before men, him will I confess before My Father which is in heaven. But whosoever shall deny Me before men, him will I also deny before My Father which is in heaven" (Matthew 10:32,33).

Perhaps you'd like me to word a confession for you to pray to the Lord, one which I've prayed with well over a hundred thousand people who have professed Jesus Christ as Lord. Just pray, out loud, from your heart to Jesus Christ, "God, be merciful to me a sinner. Receive me now for Christ's sake. Cleanse me from my sin by your Precious Blood, shed on the cross for me; and fill me with Your Holy Spirit. Teach me to pray each day; to read Your will for my life from Your Word, the Bible; and help me to worship and serve You in the fellowship of Your Chruch. I thank you, Lord Jesus Christ. Amen!"

If you've made that your prayer, write to me and tell me about it. And I'll send you a letter of encouragement along with literature to help you on your way. Write to: Dr. John Wesley White, Billy Graham Association, Minneapolis, Minnesota 55440, U.S.A.

Praise for *Annelies*

"Gillham is a powerful storyteller, and *Annelies* is marbled with spare eloquence that captures the absurdity of life after the camps. . . . A novel that reminds the world to remember Anne Frank is most welcome."   —*USA Today*

"A tour de force."   —Historical Novels Society

"In this haunting what-if, David Gillham asks us to reflect on the quandary of how one learns—in the unimaginable wake of the Holocaust—to live again, shedding a powerful, human light on the tragedy of lost potential."

> —Georgia Hunter, *New York Times* bestselling author
> of *We Were the Lucky Ones*

"To imagine the could-have-been life of Anne Frank, one of the real-life pillars of our understanding of the Holocaust, is a risky undertaking, but David Gillham delivers his story with sensitivity and grace. The result is not only a poignant reminder of all that was lost during the war but a vivid, searching exploration of what it meant to exist in the aftermath."

> —Jessica Shattuck, *New York Times* bestselling
> author of *The Women in the Castle*

"I had to slow down reading *Annelies* to better absorb the beauty and power of David Gillham's words. His depth of understanding of human resilience and our capacity to survive and find the light after unimaginable darkness is a gift. A stunning evocation of the human spirit and its ability to inspire across borders, languages, and decades."

> —Kathleen Grissom, *New York Times* bestselling author
> of *The Kitchen House* and *Glory Over Everything*

"In *Annelies*, David Gillham not only explores what might have happened if Anne Frank had survived but also draws an intimate portrait of life as a Jewish survivor in postwar Amsterdam. By turns a coming-of-age novel and a story of survival, redemption, and family, *Annelies* is a meticulously researched, emotionally resonant what-if."

—Jillian Cantor, author of *Margot* and *The Lost Letter*

"Gillham has given Annelies Marie Frank the life so brutally taken from her, in the process honoring all the 'Annes' who were lost in the Holocaust. . . . Gillham's beautifully crafted novel is a respectful tribute to the creative and passionate writer who died so young. . . . Frank's life thereafter is so vividly realized that readers will have to keep reminding themselves this is fiction. Highly recommended for admirers of literary historical fiction such as Kristin Hannah's *The Nightingale* and Martha Hall Kelley's *Lilac Girls*."

—*Library Journal*

PENGUIN BOOKS

ANNELIES

David R. Gillham is the *New York Times* bestselling author of *City of Women*. He studied screenwriting at the University of Southern California before becoming a novelist. After moving to New York City, Gillham spent more than a decade in the book business. He now lives with his family in western Massachusetts.

ANNELIES

David R. Gillham

PENGUIN BOOKS

PENGUIN BOOKS
An imprint of Penguin Random House LLC
penguinrandomhouse.com

First published in the United States of America by Viking,
an imprint of Penguin Random House LLC, 2019
Published in Penguin Books 2019

Title page photograph: ilolab/shutterstock.com

ISBN 9780735215313 (paperback)

THE LIBRARY OF CONGRESS HAS CATALOGED THE
HARDCOVER EDITION AS FOLLOWS:
Names: Gillham, David R., author.
Title: Annelies / David R. Gillham.
Description: New York City : Viking, [2019] |
Identifiers: LCCN 2018025172 (print) | LCCN 2018026671 (ebook) |
ISBN 9781101601280 (ebook) | ISBN 9780399162589 (hardcover) |
ISBN 9780525561781 (export)
Subjects: LCSH: Frank, Anne, 1929–1945—Fiction. | Holocaust survivors—Fiction. |
Psychic trauma—Fiction. | Amsterdam (Netherlands)—History—20th century—Fiction. |
GSAFD: Alternative histories (Fiction)
Classification: LCC PS3607.I44436 (ebook) | LCC PS3607.I44436 A85 2019 (print) |
DDC 813/.6—dc23
LC record available at https://lccn.loc.gov/2018025172

Printed in the United States of America
1 3 5 7 9 10 8 6 4 2

Set in Haarlemmer MT Pro

This is a work of fiction based on actual events.

To all the Annes

I want to go on living even after my death!

—Anne Frank, from her diary, 5 April 1944

ANNELIES

I

THE HEATH

We thought we had seen it all.
Until Belsen.

—J. W. Trindles
"Until Belsen"
1945

1945

Konzentrationslager (KL)
BERGEN-BELSEN
Kleines Frauenlager
The Lüneburg Heath

THE GERMAN REICH

She lies sprawled among the dead who carpet the frozen mud flats, time slipping past, her thoughts dissolving. The last of her is leaking away as the angel of death hovers above, so close now. So close that she can feel him peeling away her essence. Her body is baked by fever and ripped by a murderous cough; her mind is more animal now than human. She is numb to the bitter cold that has penetrated her bones. Thirst is gone, and so is hunger. She has passed through them on her way out of her body.

But from somewhere there is a loud pop, the anonymous discharge of a rifle or a pistol, and she can feel the darkness above her hesitate. The sound of the gunshot has grabbed its attention, and instead of collecting her final breath, death, in its forgetfulness, passes over her. And in that fractured moment, the world that would have been takes a different path: a flicker of the girl she once was makes a last demand for life. A breath, a flinch of existence. A small, tentative throb of expectation dares to flex her heart. A beat. Another beat, and another as her heart begins to work a rhythm. She coughs viciously, but something in her has found a pulse. Some vital substance. She feels herself draw a breath and then exhale it. Slowly. Very slowly, she pries open her gluey eyelids till the raw white sunlight stings.

She is alive.

2

HER ONE TRUE CONFIDANTE

Writing in a diary is a really strange experience for someone like me. Not only because I've never written anything before, but also because it seems to me that later on neither I nor anyone else will be interested in the musings of a thirteen-year-old schoolgirl.

—Anne Frank,
from her diary,
20 June 1942

... all Dutch Jews are now in the bag.

—Dr. Hans Böhmcker,
Beauftragter des Deutschen
Reiches für die Stadt Amsterdam,
2 October 1941

1942

Merwedeplein 37
Residential Housing Estate
Amsterdam-Zuid

OCCUPIED NETHERLANDS
Two years since the German invasion

Anne gazes out the open window of their third-story flat in the Merwedeplein, her elbows braced against the windowsill. The sun is cradled in a sharp blue sky. The grass of the common is a lush green. It's a Sunday midday. Down below, a stylishly dressed wedding party is off to the magistrate's office, and Anne is absorbing the details with excitement because she positively adores fashion. The bride is modeling a well-cut suit with a tapered skirt and a felt hat. A wartime look for a bride, sleek and smart without the frills. She carries a generous bouquet of white roses. People peer from their balconies as the bride and groom process down the steps and pose for a movie camera as if they were film stars.

"Anne, get away from the window, please," her mother calls out. Unwilling to budge, Anne calls back over her shoulder, "In a minute!" She imagines herself in front of the camera one day, as a famous film star. Like Greta Garbo, or Priscilla Lane. She loves the films and film actresses, and it angers Anne more than almost anything that the Nazis have seen fit to ban Jews from the cinemas. After the war, though, who knows? She could become another Dorothy Lamour, followed everywhere by eager photographers.

Her mother grows adamant, correcting her in her normal singsong reprimand. "You should be setting the table for lunch. And besides, it's simply too unladylike for you to be there with your head stuck out the window like a nosy giraffe." Though Mummy herself cannot resist a discreet giraffe's peek, followed by a shallow sigh. "When I married your father, I wore a beautiful white silk gown with a long, long train," she reminds herself. "Decorated by the most charming little filigree of Belgian lace, specially imported."

"I'm never going to marry," Anne decides to announce at that instant, which leaves her mother blinking, utterly appalled. Really, Anne was just irritated and wanted to strike back at Mummy in some way she knew would sting. But her mother's expression is positively stricken, as if Anne has just threatened to jump out the window.

"Anne, but you *must*," she insists. "Your papa and I must have grandchildren."

"Oh, Margot can handle that," Anne assures her casually. "That's what firstborn daughters are for."

"*Anne,*" her sister, Margot, squawks from the chair where she is paging through the book of Rembrandt plates, a gift from their omi in Basel. Her hair is combed back with a single silver clip holding it in place. Lovely as always, which makes Anne even madder. "What a thing to say!"

Anne ignores her. "I'm going to be famous," she declares. "A famous film star, probably, and travel the world."

"So famous film stars don't have *children*?" her mother asks.

Anne enlightens her, trying not to sound too superior. "They do if they want, I suppose. But it's not expected. Famous people live a completely different existence from most people, who are *happy* to live boring lives."

"Happy lives are not boring, Anne," her mother instructs her. Anne shrugs. She knows that Mother was sheltered by her upbringing. That the Holländers of Aachen were a religious family who kept a kosher household, were bent on respectability, and that any ambitions beyond marriage and family she might have harbored were eclipsed by the diktats of tradition. So she tries not to condescend too much when she says, "Maybe for *some* people that's true, Mummy. But for those who devote themselves to great achievements, it's different."

That's when her papa appears from the bedroom. Anne's dear Pim. Her dearest Hunny Kungha. Tall and lanky as a reed, with intelligent, deeply pocketed eyes and a pencil-thin mustache. Only a fringe of hair remains of the crop from his youth, but the loss has exposed a noble crown. He's so diligent that he's even been out tending to business on a Sunday morning. He still wears his skinny blue necktie but has changed into his around-the-house cardigan. "Hard work and dedication. That's how *lasting* fame is achieved," he informs all assembled.

"And talent," Anne replies, feeling the need to counter him in some way, but not unpleasantly. Pim, after all, is on her side. That's the way it's always been. Margot and Mother can grouse, but Pim and Anne understand. They understand just what kind of fabulous destiny awaits Miss Annelies Marie Frank.

"Yes, of course. *And* talent." He smiles. "A quality both my girls possess in great abundance."

"Thank you, Pim," Margot says lightly before sticking her nose back into her book.

But Mummy doesn't look so pleased. Maybe she didn't appreciate being left out of Pim's accounting of talented girls. "You'll spoil them, Otto," she sighs, a favorite anthem of hers. "Margot has a head on her shoulders at least, but our petite chatterbox?" She frowns, referring to who else but Anne? "It only makes her more insufferable."

Inside, daylight whitens the lace of the tablecloth as the adults cluck over their coffee cups and slices of Mummy's chocolate cake, eggless, baked with flax meal instead of flour, surrogate sugar, surrogate cocoa, and two teaspoons of precious vanilla extract, but still not so bad. Nobody has ever said Mummy isn't a resourceful cook. Anne has already gobbled up her slice and is sitting at the table hugging her beloved tabby, Moortje, while her parents converse in the muted, apprehensive tone they've adopted since the occupation.

"And what about those poor souls who have been sent to the east?" Mummy wonders. "The horrible stories one hears over the English radio."

Anne holds her breath and then exhales. For once she is only too happy to be left out of the adult discussion. She's often informed about how terribly unreasonable she can be, but would it be *so* unreasonable at this moment to go hide in her bedroom and stick her fingers in her ears? She does not want to hear any more about the conquering Hun and his atrocious behavior; she wants to pick out her birthday present.

She feels the excitement twitching in her body, so it's hard to keep still and sit up straight at the supper table. "Mother, can we use Oma Rose's sterling ware for my party?"

"Excuse me, Anne," her mother answers, frowning, "please don't interrupt. It's rude. Your father and I are having an important conversation. Unpleasant, perhaps, but necessary."

Pim, however, seems to be happy to remind them all in his gently pointed manner that one should not believe every rumor one hears. One must recall that there were stories of all manner of atrocities fabricated by the English about the kaiser's army in the last war. "Propaganda," he calls it. And shouldn't Mummy admit that he's the expert on this subject? He was, after all, a reserve officer in the kaiser's field artillery.

Mummy is not dissuaded. She is not convinced that the talk she has heard is all English fabrication. She believes that the Nazis have made Germans into criminals. "Look how Rotterdam was bombed," she offers. A defenseless city. And must she continue to enumerate the horrid slew of diktats imposed upon Jews since that Austrian brute Seyss-Inquart was installed as Reichskommissar, the high, almighty governor of the German occupation?

Anne's father shrugs. Certainly it's no secret that since the occupation, Germans have been happy to treat Jews abominably. Decrees are enshrined weekly in the *Joodsche Weekblad,* the mouthpiece of the Nazi invader, published by what the Germans call the Jewish Council. Within its pages are the details of their persecution. Jews are forbidden *this* and Jews are forbidden *that.* Jews are permitted to do their shopping *only* between such and such times. Jews must observe a curfew; they are forbidden to walk the streets from this hour to that hour. Jews who appear in public are required to wear a yellow star of explicit dimensions sewn to their clothes. Pim, however, harbors sweeter memories of the good old Fatherland and makes allowances for Good Germans as opposed to Hitler's hooligans. "Edith," he says to his wife, pronouncing her name with a calm, intimate authority. A standard tone. "Perhaps we can table this," he wonders, indicating the children. But Pim is incorrect if he thinks that the mere presence of the children is enough to dissuade Mummy from her favorite subject: how she was robbed of the life she once led. She wants to know if it has slipped her husband's mind how much she was forced to give up, and she doesn't just mean visiting Christian friends in their homes. She means how much she's been forced to leave behind. The lovely furniture made from fruitwoods. The velvet drapes. The carpets handwoven in the Orient. The collection of Meissen figurines a century old.

According to the story she's so fond of repeating, their family once had a big house in the Marbachweg in Frankfurt and Mummy had a housemaid, though Anne remembers none of it. She was just a toddler when fear of Hitler caused them to flee Germany for Holland. To Anne their flat here in Amsterdam South is her home. Five rooms in this perfectly well-respected bourgeoisie housing estate in the River Quarter, occupied by perfectly well-respected bourgeoisie refugees of the deutschen jüdisches variety. The children have started gabbling away in Dutch, but for most of the adults settled here German is still the daily conversational vernacular. Even now the Frank household speaks it at the table, because heaven forbid Mummy be required to learn another word of Dutch, even though German has become the language of their persecutors.

Mother is seldom happy, it seems, unless she's unhappy. Anne suspects that when Oma Rose died, she took something of Mummy with her. A piece of her heart that connected her to the world of her childhood, a comfortable world of affection, warmth, and safety. But after Oma passed, Mummy seemed to lose all resilience. Perhaps the loss of a mother can do that to some people. At least Anne can pity Mummy for this. Anne, too, still mourns the loss of her sweet grandma, so she can try to imagine her mother's pain. But she doesn't dare imagine what it would feel like if she were to *ever* lose her papa. Her one and only Pim.

"Aren't we going to the shop?" Anne inserts this question with a quick, prodding tone.

"*Please,* Anne," her mother huffs. "Put down the cat. How many times must I remind you that animals do not belong at the table?"

Anne rubs her tabby's fur against her cheek. "But he's not an *animal.* He's the one and only Monsieur Moortje. Aren't you, Moortje?" she asks the little gray tiger, who mews in confirmation.

"Anne, do as your mother asks," Pim instructs quietly, and Anne obeys with a half sigh.

"I just wanted to know how much longer I have to sit here being bored."

"Bored?" her mother squawks. "Your father and I are discussing important matters."

"Important to *adults,*" Anne replies thickly. "But children have a different view of the world, Mother. Based on having *fun.*"

"Oh, *fun,* is it? Well, isn't *that* important news," her mother mocks her sternly, the line of her mouth going flat. "It's too bad that children like you don't run the world."

"I'll agree with *that,*" Anne says. "Don't you agree, Margot?"

"There are other things more important than fun," her sister informs her." Now, *that's* Mummy.

"Your sister is sixteen," their mother explains approvingly. "She's not a child any longer."

Margot gives her sister a quietly dismissive shrug. "You just don't understand, Anne."

"I understand plenty, thank you very much. What I *don't* understand is why grown-ups take such pleasure in chewing over the worst of the world like gristle."

"Finish your brussels sprouts," her mother says, frowning.

Anne frowns back, her voice fizzling with dejection as she says, "I don't like them."

"Finish them anyway."

Pim breaks in gently. "Edith. Perhaps she can have more carrots."

Mummy quite definitely disapproves, but she shrugs. "Of course. By all means. Let her do as she pleases. It appears that children rule the world after all, Anne." To her husband she says, "It's only that one must *wonder,* Otto. It may all just be 'propaganda,' as you like to suggest, but one must wonder how many hungry Jewish girls there are right now in terrible circumstances who would give *quite a lot* for a plate of healthy food."

No answer to this. How could there be? Mummy takes a grim sip from her coffee cup as Anne quietly scoops a small helping of carrots onto her plate, isolating them from the abominable choux de Bruxelles. Pim exhales, releasing a breath of smoke from his cigarette. Again he suggests a change of subject.

Poor Pim thinks he can shield his daughters from the ugly realities. Impossible. It's obvious that things are not good for the Jews since the Hun occupied the city. It's even obvious to a child that terrible things are happening. Anne is not so oblivious as everyone believes. But why in the world should they dwell on it so? If Anne confined her thoughts each morning to the lurking menace of the German hordes billeted in her lovely Amsterdam, she would be paralyzed, hiding under her bed, refusing to budge. She *must* believe that tomorrow will come unimpeded. That the sun will rise at dawn in spite of the old Herr Six-and-a-Quarter Seyß-Inquart on his high Nazi perch. Margot calls her childish when she says this, but who cares what sisters think? And really, whether there are crimes against Jews in progress a thousand kilometers away or in the center of Amsterdam, what can *she* do about it? Crimes against Jews are as ancient as Scripture. And doesn't she have a duty to God to enjoy the life he has given her? She is about to turn thirteen, and the entire German Wehrmacht has not been able to prevent *that* from happening. Besides, she has an ultimate, unshakable faith that Pim will figure things out for all of them, as he always has. Mummy isn't completely wrong—there are plenty of Jews in much, *much* worse circumstances than the family Frank, and there is only one reason for that: Pim is too smart to allow them to be caught in the Hitlerite net. Surely even Mummy must recognize that fact. It's only too bad she cannot see past her own fear and give her husband the credit he deserves, instead of always moaning about the past. One would think a wife would do as much for the man she's wed. As for Anne, there is no one on earth who can make her feel as safe and loved as her papa. And though it may hurt Mummy when Anne chooses Pim to listen to her prayers at bedtime, she cannot help it. She knows that as long as God and Pim are on the job, she is protected.

After the dishes are cleared, her father bends down to her and whispers the good news. "Go get your coat. It's time to put our troubles aside."

Anne claps her hands together and hooks Pim with a hug, inhaling the zesty scent of his cologne. Her parents are allowing her to choose a present for herself in *advance* of her birthday party. There are still hours before the Jewish curfew begins, so they all visit the stationery shop a few blocks away. Blankevoorts Subscription Library at Zuider Amstellaan 62. One of Anne's favorite spots. She loves the inky smell of the place. The neat boxes of thick writing paper tied with ribbons. The sleepy orange tom lounging on one of the shelves, purring when she strokes his fur. At least Jews are still allowed to pet cats!

Mummy tries to draw her attention to a flower-pressing kit and then a scrapbook with a Moroccan leather binding, but Anne knows precisely what she wants. She has picked out a red tartan autograph album with a lock that snaps shut, because her favorite writer is Cissy van Marxveldt and she has been absolutely captivated by the adventures of the author's plucky young heroine, Joop ter Heul. Joop keeps a secret diary and addresses her many entries to her friends: Phien, Loutje, Conny, and especially her very best friend for all time, Kitty. Anne thinks this is a breathtaking idea, and she intends to have loads of fun keeping her *own* diary of adventures. When it's time to leave, Pim's cheery voice separates Anne from her mother. "So the young lady has made her choice?"

The lilt of disappointment colors Mummy's response. "This is what she wants," she says, and shrugs.

Joods Lyceum
Stadstimmertuin 1
Amsterdam-Centrum

The so-called Jewish Lyceum, where it has been decreed that *all* Jewish children attend classes, is housed in a decaying cavern of sandy red brick west of the Amstel. In the classrooms paint peels from the ceiling. The hallways stink vaguely of moldering plumbing. Her mathematics teacher is a bespectacled old bird who speaks passable Dutch with a sharp, clip-clop Berliner's accent. The rumor is that he had been a member of the Royal Prussian Academy of Sciences until the Nazis purged all Jews. His pupils call him "the Goose," because his name is Gander and because of his habit of honking into his handkerchief.

As the Goose opens his lesson that Monday morning, drawing down a clean blackboard, he glances about the room, and when he spots the newest vacancy among the desks, he waits for the silent explanation. It's a code that's developed between teacher and pupils. The teacher's glance is the question. Another empty desk—what has become of the former occupant? The pupils answer with subtle hand signals. The clenching of a fist means arrested, a small downward swooping motion means gone into hiding. "Diving under," it's called. Onder het duiken. This time the Goose pauses slightly and then goes about chalking an equation onto the board.

Anne, though, catches the tart scent of the river breezing through the open windows. It's not that she doesn't want to pay attention to the teacher, but she can be so easily distracted—by a breeze, by a scent, by a slant of light—and her mind veers off into another direction. Outside, the beauty of nature beckons her. If she had her way, she would be sitting in the grass watching the river flow by. It's a secret she keeps to herself, but being with nature allows her to sink into herself, not in a lonely way, mostly, but in a private way that permits her to ponder the Anne on the inside, who is not always so bold or confident. Not always so wonderfully cheerful or impervious. She thinks about what a good time she had with Mummy and Margot last Saturday, baking macaroons. They were laughing and joking with one another, and when Anne used too much coconut, Mummy wasn't critical at all but instead started singing a ditty about the little monkey who steals too many coconuts from the coconut palm.

"Miss Frank?"

It's in those moments that Anne wonders if she is completely wrong about her mother. If Mummy is *not* a faultfinder at heart but is generous and loving and appreciates Anne for who she is. For who God made her to be.

"Miss Frank?"

She looks over at the sound of her name, only to find the Goose glaring at her under his bushy eyebrows, a wry expression on his face. "Are you in dreamland again, Miss Frank?"

The class titters.

"No, sir," she replies, doing her best to gather her dignity, though she can feel her face flush.

"Then please," the Goose says, "solve the equation for x."

"Oh, Mr. Gander," Anne replies, "I'm sure we both know that's not very likely to happen."

And this time when the class titters, she feels a lift. Victory.

On the playground she shows off with her favorite trick, displacing her shoulder from its socket and then, like magic, popping it back into place. A performance guaranteed to draw a crowd of admirers. Even the boys leave their football to come watch. She likes the attention. Especially from the boys. Her many beaux, as her mother would call them, with her favorite overtone of criticism. Mummy always warns her about flirting. The *dangers* of it. "Look at Margot," she insists. "Do you see her behaving in such a way?"

There's a boy whom everyone calls Hello, who's much closer to Margot's age. A Good Jewish Boy, excruciatingly polite, with only a hint of playful devilishness. He once took Anne for a gelato at Oase on the Geleenstraat, one of the last ice-cream parlors to serve Jews, and it made her feel grown-up. She liked his attention. She likes the attention of boys in general, it's true. It makes her feel bright and adored.

The name of her friend, her *very best* friend, is Hanneli, but Anne often calls her by her nickname, Lies. She lives in the Amsterdam South, too, with her parents and baby sister. Her father was once an underminister and a press secretary in the Prussian government, but the Nazis took care of that, purging Jews from the civil service, so now the family has made their adopted home here in Amsterdam, just like the Frank family. Anne finds Lies to be sweet and thoughtful, and shy enough to make for a good counterpoint to Anne's bravado.

"But wouldn't you rather have a surprise?" Hanneli wants to know. They are soldiering on with their book satchels after leaving school. They walk now because no Jews are permitted the use of bicycles. Or streetcars. Or public parks. No more swimming in the Amstelparkbad pool for Jews, or ice-skating, or tennis at the Apollohal, because that's all for gentiles only now. But today who cares? These are the final days of school before the summer holiday. And on a fresh, cloudless afternoon like this one, Anne can inhale the briny-sweet drift of the Amstel and listen to the chatter of the gulls. She feels light in her body, as if she could easily fly away on a breeze, and she might just do so.

"I'm mad about surprises," Lies declares wistfully. "I mean, for me, half the fun of birthdays is the surprises."

Her chestnut hair is woven into braids, which swing lightly as she walks. They make Anne jealous sometimes, those braids, but in a delicious way. Sometimes she'd just love to give them a good yank. Instead, Anne delivers her opinion. "For me surprises are overrated. I'd rather get what I know I want," she says with conviction, and then her heart tightens in her chest. An angry gust of thunder invades the street as a German motorcycle squadron blasts past with their steel helmets and goggles, polluting the air with their fumes. Anne grimaces, clutching her school satchel against her breast, concealing her yellow Judenstern, though she knows it's illegal. But Lies just stares at them with a blank kind of terror, her hands clapped over her ears and her star on perfect display as the squadron roars down the street, uninterested in two scrawny Jewish schoolgirls on the sidewalk. "They're such beasts," Anne breathes.

Lies has lowered her hands from her ears, but her expression is racked by anxiety. "I asked Papa if we were going to go into hiding."

"Really?" This interests Anne. "And what did he say?"

"He said, 'Hiding from *what*?'" she answers vacantly.

Anne shakes her head. "I don't want to talk about this," she suddenly decides. Instead she has a swift desire to misbehave. She tastes it like spice on the back of her tongue.

Up ahead there's a clot of older boys loitering on the sidewalk. They are congregated in a slump at the corner of the Uiterwaardenstraat by a tobacconist shop that has a reputation as a black-market hangout, run by a Galician Jew who trades in Jewish valuables. At least that's the story from Mr. van Pels, Pim's business partner.

"These sorts of operations are a growing concern," Mr. van P. had insisted while visiting their flat for coffee. "So you've been hiding the jewelry under a floorboard to keep it from the Germans? Your heirloom set of silver is under the bed? Your great-great-granny's gold-plated menorah's at the bottom of the laundry hamper, and in the meantime you're wondering how to feed your family? Why not resign yourself to the inevitable and sell off the lot to the Galician? It's better than handing it over to the robbery bank. You'll only get a pittance, but at least it's a pittance from another Jew."

"The *robbery* bank? What is *that*?" Anne had wanted to know, because she likes to know everything. No harm in that. Mummy had shushed her, but Pim had explained it in his quiet way. Along with all the other indignities, Jews have been ordered to deposit any assets of worth with the Sarphatistraat branch of the Lippmann, Rosenthal & Company. Now run by the Nazis, of course.

At this point Mrs. van Pels, who's anything but retiring, puffed herself up to declare, "I don't care how hungry I get, Putti. I'm never going to let you sell off my furs. I'll be buried in them first," causing her husband to hoot out a laugh.

"And she's not joking!" he assured all assembled with a fat grin.

One of the boys up ahead is kicking at a crack in the sidewalk, sending pebbles flying. Another laughs suddenly, sounding like a mule braying. Who knows *what* boys think is funny? Yellow stars are stitched onto their pullovers and jackets. Maybe Mummy likes to believe that if they must wear the Magen David in public, then they should do so with pride, but these boys wear their stars like what they are: badges of exclusion. Of rejection. Badges that assert their status as outsiders, as rough cuts on the edge. Their clothes ragged at the seams, their hair poorly groomed, the boys examine the two approaching girls with the kind of sullen interest common to street-corner troublemakers.

"Don't look at them," Lies warns. She has already cast her eyes downward to the uneven pavement of the sidewalk, tracking the progress of her feet. But Anne cannot quite follow Hanneli's example. She knows that Hanneli thinks she's overly obsessed with boys, but this isn't about silly flirting with their well-mannered schoolmates. Anne cannot help glancing at the wild challenge of their eyes.

"Wanna smoke?" one of them inquires, offering his cigarette butt. His clothes are unkempt, and he looks poorly cared for.

"*No,*" Lies replies firmly.

But Anne has stopped.

"*Anne,*" her friend prods with a scandalized whisper.

"It's just a *cigarette,*" Anne insists. "I've never tried one."

Only for an instant does she catch the curious smirk on the boy's face when she plucks the cigarette from his fingers. The butt is damp from his saliva as it touches her lips, and she inhales with what she believes is a certain aplomb. But her body quickly convulses and her breath contracts as she chokes on the gritty smoke. Garbo she is not. The boys laugh as she coughs it out, her face flushing, her eyes tearing up. She drops the cigarette without thought as Lies seizes her by the arm, dragging her away. "*Anne,*" she says with both reproach and sympathy.

"Don't tell your mother," Anne manages to beg as they leave the sniggering boys.

"What? My *mother*?"

"Don't tell her, please," Anne begs, smearing tears from her eyes. "I don't want her to think I've gone boy-crazy. She already thinks I'm a know-it-all."

"She *does not* think you're a know-it-all, Anne," Lies replies in a tone that suggests she is defending her mother as much as defending Anne.

"She *does,*" Anne insists. "You heard her: God knows everything, but *Anne* knows everything else."

"That was a joke."

"No it wasn't. It was true. I *am* a know-it-all."

"All right," Hanneli concedes. "And you're boy-crazy, too. But we still love you."

And now Anne laughs. She sniffs back her tears, flinging her arm around Lies's shoulder. Darling Lies. But then she says, "Oh, *no*."

"Oh, no?"

"Good *morning,* Mrs. Lipschitz," Anne sings, properly polite, at the approach of a matronly mitteleuropäische specimen with the star on her coat.

"Good morning, child," the gnädige Mrs. Lipschitz replies with disapproval, a shopping bag looped over her arm and a scowl stamped onto her face as she passes.

"Oh, now I'm really in for it," Anne predicts with dread when they're a safe distance away.

"Who was *that*?"

"*Mrs. Lipschitz.* I call her Old Mrs. Snoop. She's always looking for something to criticize me over. If she saw me taking a puff off that cigarette, she'll go straight to Mummy about it," Anne huffs. But there's nothing to be done about it now. "I want a pickle," she announces.

She's spotted an old fellow with a pushcart across the street. "The town's most delicious pickle!" he claims, calling out to all who pass. The girls laugh as their pickle halves crunch satisfyingly in their mouths, tasting nutty-sweet from a hint of mace. Anne parts with Lies at the Zuider Amstellaan, indulging a sudden urge to hug her good-bye for no other reason than just because. Lies does not seem to mind.

But traveling up the Deltastraat with her schoolbag on her shoulder, Anne feels the light flush of joy drain from her heart as a stinging loneliness, unbidden and enigmatic, creeps over her. She tries to cheer herself with another crunching bite of her pickle, but she really only wanted it to mask the smell of tobacco on her breath, so she tosses it down a storm drain when she crosses the street. It's this loneliness that often makes her cry for no reason. If her parents catch her, she pretends to have a stomachache, because they'll readily fall for that one. Mummy is always saying how sickly she is. What a weak constitution she has, catching everything there is to catch. But really it's an ache like a hook that threatens to drag her into a dark hole. Maybe it was the puff on the cigarette. The dizziness that seized her and the bitter choking. She stops and hugs a lamppost, her breath rising. This is the Anne she keeps secret from others. The panicked Anne. The helpless Anne on the edge of a lonely void. It would not do for such an Anne to show up in the world. Grabbing her wrist, she thumbs her pulse and tries to calm its speed. Mummy will say she's just a nervous child, like so many girls, and dose her with valerian. But Anne knows it's something more than a twitch of girlish nerves. When it arrives in force, she feels as if there's a black fog coming for her. It's a fear that has clutched at her since she was too young to define it. A fear that beneath her smiles and jokes and know-it-all antics, she is simply a fraud. That she will live her life with nothing to offer but her shadowboxing frolics and leave not a single lasting mark, because no one will ever truly love her or truly know her, and that her heart is nothing but dust that will return to dust.

She has taught herself tricks when the panic overtakes her. Focusing on the clouds floating above like grand barges. Counting backward from a hundred. Or simply bawling her eyes out. She could easily do that now, but she does not wish to sob in public, so instead she chooses to concentrate on the progress of a long-legged spider up the lamppost. Spinning his silky filament, Mr. Longlegs. Higher and higher on a silvered thread. Anne breathes in deeply and exhales slowly. She swallows hard, and the clutch of dread begins to loose its grip. Her pulse retrieves its usual tempo. Wiping a clammy sheen from her brow, she slings her schoolbag back over her shoulder. Like the clouds above her head, she is on the move, herself again. The emptiness safely locked away.

The rows of modern sandstone apartment buildings radiate in symmetry from the central star of a tall yellow tower called the Wolkenkrabber. The Cloud Raker. A twelve-story jut of concrete masonry, steel, and glass scraping the cloud bellies as it anchors a commons of well-groomed turf. The afternoon smells of the bread in the ovens of the Blommestein bakery with a trace of pithy river air. This is the Merwedeplein, which Anne likes to call "the Merry."

Her home is number 37. Four rooms, a kitchen, a bath, and a water closet, plus a room upstairs, which they rent to a bachelor tenant. It's an airy flat, with a wonderful little platje—their narrow, tar-pebble terrace that's as good as any lakeshore for sunbathing in the summer. Anne bounds up the stairwell from the doorway and meets her mother, who's dressed in her housecoat, a look of glum disappointment on her face. She is a stolidly built lady, her mother, with a broad brow and the easy smile of the Holländer family, though she seldom smiles these days. *"Anne."* Mummy frowns. "I need to speak to you for a moment. Come sit down."

The sea-green French doors of the living room are open. Plunking her book satchel down on her mother's camelback sofa without argument, she plunks herself down as well and exhales her annoyance, head tilted toward the more arrogant side of obedience. Old Mrs. Snoop must have absolutely *sprinted* home to telephone Mummy and inform on Anne. She watches her mother seat herself in the club chair opposite, ankles crossed, and waits for it, the downpour of scorn and criticism.

But instead her mother says simply, "You're growing up."

Anne blinks.

"I know that," her mother tells her. "Only days away from thirteen, and how that happened so soon I can't begin to guess. But it's clear; you're becoming a young lady. You think I don't understand," she says, "but you're wrong. I understand very well. I was once thirteen, too, believe it or not, and I thought that your oma Rose, bless her name, didn't understand a single fig's worth about me. At that age I wanted to try new things. I wanted to be like your uncles and get in trouble once in a while. Break a rule or two. But since I was the girl, well . . ." Mummy releases a breath. "It was unacceptable at the time. My mother watched me closely to make sure I stayed firmly within the limits of what was proper."

"Really?" Anne says. She must admit that she is surprised. Oma Rose, may she rest in peace, always liked to tease Mummy over her addiction to propriety. Anne's mother shakes her head with a wry smile, pursing her lips.

"Oh, I know. You think that your oma was always on *your* side, that she liked to have her jokes about how Her Majesty Edith must have everything just so, but believe me, she was much, *much* stricter than I have ever been. I wasn't even permitted to *speak* in the company of adults unless spoken to first. Can you imagine *that,* my dear daughter?"

Anne must admit, "No, I *can't,* Mummy. I think I would explode."

"*Yes,*" her mother agrees, still with her dry smile. "I think you *would.* So I am not that way. I try, Anne, I *do try* to allow you and your sister as much latitude as I am able. And it's not as if I haven't suffered plenty of criticism as a result. Many of the other ladies think that I'm far too modern with you, far too permissive. But *I* say time passes, the world changes. So when you tell me that you simply cannot tolerate brussels sprouts, I let you have another helping of roasted carrots. When a boy rings our doorbell and asks to take you for a walk or for an ice cream, I hold my breath and don't object. When you want privacy, I try to give it to you. And when you have something you think is important to say, I *do* try to listen, regardless of what you choose to believe. *But,*" Anne's mother says finally, "I am still your mother, and I am still responsible for your well-being. That, my dear girl, will never change, no matter how grown-up you become."

Anne gazes from the sofa. She is trying to figure this out. Her mother's eyes are moons. She tries to imagine Mummy evolving someday into a sweet grandmother, just like Oma, but her mother's face has thinned since the moffen have come, and her skin is rumpled around her chin. There is no sweetness in her face. Her thick head of lustrous caramel-colored hair, of which she's always been so proud, is pinned neatly with an amber comb and threaded with silver. Her mother's hands have been folded in her lap all this time, in the proper position, but now they fidget. She strokes her hair as if to smooth an errant strand, a sure sign that Mummy is either about to say something that will start an argument or is deciding *not* to say something that she knows will start an argument. "I don't want to be harsh," she tells Anne. "As I said, I know that you are growing up. But for now I must insist on this: You cannot *smoke,* Annelies. After all the illnesses you've suffered since you were small, you must realize how harmful smoking will be to your respiration."

"So Mrs. Lipschitz reported," says Anne heavily. Finally they are at the root of the matter, and she can barely keep herself from rolling her eyes. At least it's the smoking she's in trouble over and not, amazingly enough, the boys.

But there's a tick in her mother's expression, and she looks a bit confused. "Mrs. Lipschitz?"

Glaring at the sofa's velvety upholstery. "She told you I took a puff off that boy's cigarette on the way home from school."

"Anne." A frown immediately collapses her mother's expression. "I'm sure I don't know what you're saying. I'm talking to you because I found *these* in your desk cubby," she says, removing one of the thousands of blue, red, and white Queen's Day cigarette packets dropped over Holland by the British Royal Air Force. A map of the Dutch Colonial East Indies on the front of the packet and on the back the Dutch tricolor. VICTORY APPROACHES, the slogan proclaims. Anne suddenly laughs, slapping the knobby knees poking out from her skirt.

"What?" her mother demands, her expression tensing. "What's funny?"

"Oh, Mummy, those are Papa's. He gave them to Margot as a souvenir."

Her mother's eyebrows knit together when she frowns, causing her eyes to look beady and too close-set. "Margot?"

"Yes, the *good* daughter," says Anne. "Don't you know that she's collecting cigarette cards of the royal family?"

"No. I didn't know that."

"Well, she is. Mr. Kugler is always saving them for her," Anne says, the relief of her laughter losing steam. "Ask her if you don't believe me. Ask Pim."

"No. No, I believe you, Anne."

"Though, I might note that you automatically assumed that *I* was the criminal."

"I didn't," says Anne's mother. "I didn't. It's just that . . ." But her mother doesn't seem to be able to finish this sentence, so Anne finishes it for her. Helpfully.

"It's just that you can't imagine *Margot* ever doing anything against the rules, and it's just that you *always* assume that *Anne* is at fault."

Her mother blinks. Then her face sharpens. "So you took a ciga-rette from a boy on the *street*?"

Anne huffs lightly. "It was only a puff, Mummy." Frowning at the strands of hair she is twirling around one of her fingers.

"A *puff* from a strange boy's *cigarette*?" Her mother's voice is ris-ing. "First of all, think of the diseases he may have transferred to you."

"Oh, *diseases*," Anne repeats, emphasizing the ridiculousness of the word.

"Not to *mention*," her mother adds, "the *appalling* lack of good judgment on your part to be consorting with a strange boy."

"I wasn't 'consorting.'"

"With a strange boy, *on the street*."

"Oh, that's what's *really* worrying you, isn't it? Not the *diseases*."

"You were endangering your reputation."

"Mine or yours, Mother? You're not worried about *me*. Not really. You're just worried about what gossip that busybody Mrs. Lipschitz is going to spread about Mrs. Frank's little troublemaker."

"You don't understand, Anne. You're still so young."

"I'm old enough to know that things are changing, Mummy." She slants forward to emphasize her point. "Girls my age simply aren't *accepting* the old rules that our mothers bowed to. We intend to make our *own* decisions."

"And that will include acting like . . . like a *strumpet*?"

Anne recoils as if she has just been slapped. She can feel her eyes heat with tears. Snatching her book satchel, she darts from the room. She can hear her mother calling after her. "*Anne!* Anne—*please!* That was too harsh. I'm sorry, I just lost my temper. Please come back." These are the last words Anne hears before she slams shut the door to her room.

Bedtime. Anne is dressed in her silky blue pajamas. She had begged for these pajamas after seeing a magazine picture of Hedy Lamarr in a pair, but now her legs are too long for them. Her mother complains that she won't stop growing.

In the lamplight the room's wallpaper is warmed to a pale honey color. Beds were too difficult and expensive to transport from

Frankfurt and were a scarce and pricey commodity in Amsterdam, a city flooded by waves of immigrants fleeing the Reich. So they don't have regular beds, Margot and she, not really. Anne sleeps on a davenport with an upholstered back and Margot sleeps on a bed that folds up into the wall! Still, Anne appreciates the room for its coziness. Her prized swimming medals, her schoolroom paintings, and the pictures of royal families and film stars that she's pinned onto the wall give her a sense of proprietorship over her space. Mummy's mahogany-veneered secretaire, where they do their homework, stands in the corner like a friendly sentry. And thanks to their lovely tall window, she can look out at the trees. She stares for a moment at the dark branches rustling under the clouded night.

Margot is still busy with her ablutions in the washroom, but Anne has hurried through hers and has wrapped two curlers in her hair in the continued hope of obtaining wavy bangs. Now, though, lying in bed, she feels a heavy silence resting on her chest. She barely glances up when Pim knocks on the doorframe.

"Do you want to hear my prayers, Pim?" she assumes.

"Yes. But in a moment." He enters and sits on the corner of her bed. "We need to talk first."

Anne moans dully and stares blankly at the ceiling. *"Fine."* She sighs.

"Your mother is very upset," Pim tells her quietly.

"Well, she should be," Anne insists self-righteously.

"She's very distraught," says Pim.

"Did she tell you what she *called* me? Did she tell you the *word* she used?"

"Yes, she did. And she regrets it deeply."

"So she sent you in to tell me that?"

"Well. Quite honestly, Anne, I think she is ashamed to tell you herself."

"She would never have called Margot a name like that. *Never.*"

"Your mother's relationship with Margot has nothing to do with this. Mummy made a mistake. A dreadful mistake. She hurt your feelings, and she is very, very sorry for it."

Anne says nothing.

"But it is *also* true, Annelies, that you have a talent for provoking your mother in unnecessary ways."

A gleam of tears appears. "So it's *my* fault as usual."

"I'm saying it takes two to argue. Mummy lost her temper and said something she didn't mean. But she was also looking out for you. Trying to teach you about certain behavior that, as a child—"

"Of course! I'm *such* a child."

"That as a child," her father repeats, "you are still quite uninformed about."

"Don't be so sure, Pim. I may be a child, Pim, but *children* are quite well informed these days."

"In that case you should have known better."

"I accepted a *puff*, Pim." She frowns, pushing herself up on her elbow and glaring into her father's face. "A *single puff* from a boy's cigarette. That's all. I didn't even like it. And yet in *her* eyes that was enough to make her daughter a *strumpet*."

Pim breathes in and exhales slowly. "You must understand that your mother's nerves are stretched. You must remember what she was forced to leave behind when we came to Holland. She had a life in Frankfurt. A lovely house. Lovely things."

"I know all about it, Pim. We've all heard it a hundred times. The big house, the maid, everything. But may I point out that *you* left a life behind in Germany as well, and yet *you* don't hate me."

"Your mother doesn't *hate* you," Pim corrects her firmly. "She *loves* you. She loves you and Margot more than anything."

Anne drops back down onto her pillows, wiping her eyes on her pajama sleeve. "Well. Margot maybe."

"*Anneke.*" Pim sighs forlornly, shaking his head. "You can be so hard on her. And she can be hard on you, too, I know this," he concedes. "But she is sorry. *Sincerely* sorry. And when a person's regret is sincere, then the only decent thing to do is to forgive them."

Anne frowns at the air. "All right," she agrees thinly. "All right. For your sake I'll forgive her. I'll pretend it never happened. But you're wrong about one thing," she tells him. "Mummy will never love me. Not like you do. You're the one who truly loves me." She pushes herself up and embraces him, arms around his neck and her ear pressed to his chest so she can hear the tick of his heart.

"Your mother loves you," he insists quietly, patting her back. "We both love you, and there's nothing you can *do* about it, young lady. Now, let's forget all about tears and angry words. It's your birthday coming. Sleep tight and dream about what a marvelous day it's going to be."

But as her father rises to leave, she calls out to him, "Pim, are we going into hiding?"

Her father stiffens as if he has just stepped on a tack but wants to keep it a secret. "Why do you ask such a thing?"

"Because I wonder where Oma Rose's sterling-silver set has gone." One hundred and thirteen pieces from Koch & Bergfeld of Bremen, and one of her mother's prized possessions. "I was hoping that I would be allowed to use it for the party, but when I looked for it in the cabinet, it was missing. I even looked under the beds. The entire case has vanished."

"And did you ask your mother about this?" Pim wonders.

"No. I'm asking you. Did you have to turn it over to the robbery bank?" Anne asks, worried to know the answer if it's yes.

But Pim's expression remains calm. Rational. "Your mother's silverware is quite valuable to her," he explains. "We thought it would be safer to ask some friends to hold on to it for the time being."

"Friends who aren't Jewish," says Anne.

"That's right," her father admits without embarrassment.

"So the silverware has gone into hiding, but not us?"

"This is nothing you need to worry about tonight, my dear," her father tells her. He returns to her bedside long enough to give her forehead a kiss. "Now sleep."

"Pim, wait. My prayers." Anne closes her eyes. Sometimes when she prays, she pictures God listening. A colossal, snowy-bearded bompa, the contented Master of the Universe, who gladly sets aside the governing of the cosmos long enough to listen to Anne Frank's small recitation. Her prayers are in German still, just because they always have been so, and she ends them as she always has, with her closing message to the Father of Creation. Ich danke dir für all das

Gute und Liebe und Schöne. Her thanks for all the goodness and love and beauty in the world. Amen.

"Very nice," her father says with quiet satisfaction.

She gazes for a moment at the misty image of the divine in her head but then blinks it away. "Do you think that God can protect us, Pim?"

Pim appears surprised by this question. "Can he? Well. Of course he can, Anne."

"Really? Even when the enemy is all around?"

"Especially then. The Lord has his plan, Anneke," Pim assures her. "No need to worry yourself. You should simply have a good night's sleep."

Anne settles. He kisses her again on the forehead as Margot enters from her toilette.

"Good night, my dear Mutz," he tells Margot.

"Good night, Pim," Margot answers, and stops for a kiss on the head before their father exits into the hallway. Anne's tabby has pranced into the room behind her sister, slinking around Margot's ankle, but when he hops up to the end of Anne's bed, Anne seizes him, gazing at her sister closely. Margot does not bother with curlers. She never talks about cosmetics, like Anne does, or begs Mother to let her wear lipstick, as it's generally agreed that of the two of them Margot is the Naturally Pretty One. Anne is all gawky elbows and limbs, with a too-pointy chin and therefore in need of some cosmetic improvement. She stares as her sister says her prayers alone in an intimate whisper into God's ear, too old to require Pim to watch over her. *"What?"* Margot demands thickly when she finishes.

Anne squeezes Moortje like the little bag of stuffing he is. "I didn't say a thing."

"Maybe not." Margot fluffs her pillow with a spank. "But I could hear you anyway."

"I asked Pim if we were going into hiding."

"Yes?" Margot faces her, now alert.

Anne lifts the cat up under his front legs so that his paws dangle loosely. "He said they have given Oma Rose's silverware to Christian friends for safekeeping. But that's it."

Margot expels the breath she has been holding. "Good."

"Good?"

"I don't want to go into *hiding*," she says as she slips into her bed. "Do *you*?" she asks, as if Anne might be harboring some silly desire on the subject.

"No, of course not." Anne returns her attention to Moortje, who mews lightly when she lowers him enough to press his nose against hers. "You think I want to be stuck in a smelly old farmhouse somewhere and lose all my friends?"

"I never know with you," her sister says, settling her head on the properly fluffed pillow. "Anyway, you told me that Pim said there's nothing happening."

"*No,*" Anne must point out, letting Moortje loose on the blanket. "In fact, he *didn't* say that. Not in so many words. He said I should go to sleep."

"What a tremendous idea," Margot replies with sisterly sarcasm.

Anne huffs but says nothing further, settling under her bedclothes as Moortje finds his spot at the foot of her davenport. Hiding. A frightening prospect, but also slightly exciting. Can she be forgiven for feeling a certain sly thrill at outsmarting the Nazis? Diving under. Onder het duiken! Farewell, Boche! Auf Wiedersehen! May we never meet again.

The rumor at school is that the whole Lowenstein family is paying a Christian farmer in Drenthe to let them live in a hayloft. Could *she* live in a hayloft? Surely not. She draws her knees up under the covers and rolls over toward the wall. Certainly, if the day comes, they will do better than a hayloft. If. *If* the day comes. Until then she will rely on Pim and God, as always, to make the right decisions.

<hr>

Prinsengracht 263
Offices of Opekta and Pectacon
Amsterdam-Centrum
The Canal Ring West

When Anne was still a toddler, Pim had purchased an Amsterdam franchise of the Opekta pectin company to cover their exit from

Germany, opening the office with Mr. Kugler, selling products for quick jam. Mr. Kleiman had come aboard soon after to keep the books, and then came Miep, who had quickly been promoted to senior secretary, though, as Miep tells it, Pim had her in the kitchen for her first month making batch after batch of ten-minute jam so that she'd learn *everything* that could possibly go wrong with every recipe. "Too much fruit," says Miep. "That was the main problem. People didn't follow the recipe. They put in too much fruit and not enough sugar."

Dearest Miep. She was sent to a foster home in Holland as a child because her parents in Vienna were too poor to feed her. It's difficult for Anne to imagine such a thing, but it happened, though Miep is not the least bit bitter about it. She is such a trustworthy and understanding soul, Anne thinks. And even if she still speaks with a ghost of a *wienerisch* accent, she can be forgiven that, because in every other way she is completely Dutch.

A Dutch husband. Dutch fortitude. Dutch honesty and stubbornness. Miep possesses them all.

The window glass rattles. Another squadron of Luftwaffe Junkers grumbles through the sky from its air base north of Arnhem. Eyes rise for as long as it takes the buzz of the bombers to drift away, but no one has much to say about it. The German occupation is a fact of life, like a chronic bowel problem.

There's a German, in fact, in the private office. A Herr So-and-So from the Frankfurt office of the Pomosin-Werke that oversees all Opekta franchises. He is cloistered in there with Mr. Kleiman, but the managing director of the franchise, Mr. Frank himself, is in the kitchen washing out dirty cups and saucers.

Anne has abandoned her after-school office duties, sorting invoices and such, out of boredom, and also out of a kind of nervous curiosity. "So what are you doing in *here*?" she asks Pim, hanging in the kitchen's threshold.

A glance and a half smile. "What would you guess I'm doing?"

"Well, you're washing dishes, but *why*?"

"Because they are dirty."

"You know what I'm asking," Anne says, and she captures Pim by the arm. "Why is there a mof in your office?"

"I don't appreciate that term, Anne," he tells her.

"So why is there a *Hun* in your office?"

Pim sighs. Shakes a few drops from the cup he has just rinsed. "He's going over our books."

"Not with you."

"No," Pim admits, "with Mr. Kleiman."

"But not with *you*."

"Mr. Kleiman is our bookkeeper."

"And you're the owner of the company."

There's a small lesion in her father's composure, as if he's trying to swallow a nail.

"You *are* still the *owner,* Pim, aren't you?" Only now does Anne drop her prodding tone and betray a note of the fear she so often tries to conceal. Even from herself.

"It's business, Anne." Pim's voice softens, perhaps in response to the slip of anxiety in Anne's tone. "We've had to make some adjustments to the company's organization," he explains.

"Because we're Jews."

Pim places a cup on a towel to drain. "Yes," is all he says.

"But you are still the *owner,* correct?"

"Of course," says Pim. "Nothing has *really* changed, Anne. It's only paperwork. Speaking of which, don't you have a job to finish for Miep? Filing invoices?"

"Maybe," Anne mutters, and she allows herself to collapse girlishly against her father. "But it's absolutely boring me to pieces."

"Well, life cannot always be electrifying, can it? We'd be worn to a frazzle." Pim hugs her shoulder. "You must go and see to your responsibilities, yes? What is our motto?"

"I don't remember," Anne lies.

"You *do*. 'Work, love, courage, and hope.' You know this, I'm sure. Now go. Miep needs all the help she can get with the paperwork. You and Margot are essential to the operation here."

"Ha," says Anne glumly. "Essential as well-trained monkeys."

"Would you like to come down to the warehouse with me instead? You can say hello to Mr. van Pels."

"No. I'll return to the salt mines." She sighs, surrendering to her fate. She likes to watch the grinder at work, milling spices, even though it's loud, but today she can comfortably skip an opportunity to visit with Hermann van Pels, who's often as loud as any grinder while expressing his opinions. Also, he tells the worst jokes in the world and thinks they're hilarious. Better that she returns to the front office. The business has only recently moved from the Singel to this roomy canal house in the Prinsengracht, and the room still smells of newly applied floor wax. Mr. Kugler's desk is vacant, but she and Margot are squished into sharing Mr. Kleiman's desk across from where Miep and Bep toil as secretaries—though, *where is* Bep anyway? Her chair is empty. "Where's Bep?" she asks curiously.

Miep is on the telephone, but when she covers the mouthpiece for a moment, all she says is, "She'll *be* here, Anne."

Margot is matching up invoice copies with numbers in a large ledger. "And where have *you* been?" she wants to know.

"To the moon," answers Anne.

"I believe it. That's where you live most of the time." Margot is dressed in a short-sleeved blouse and a skirt she has sewn herself. Another of the Amazing Margot's talents. Anne gazes at her sister. They're only three years apart, but since Margot turned sixteen last February, she most definitely takes the adults' side. Margot's body has grown so womanly, too, while Anne still feels as shapely as a broomstick.

Margot exits into the corridor with the file, and Anne can hear her descending the steep, break-ankle stairway, but then she hears an exchange of greetings, and a second later, when the office door bumps open, Anne is delighted to see that it's Bep, the firm's typist. Thoughtful Bep. Bashful Bep, but cheery when she feels at ease. "I'm here," she announces. She's a slim girl, Bep, with an oval face and a high forehead. A barrette inserted in her wavy hair. Not, perhaps, a conventional beauty, but beautiful on the *inside,* Anne knows. Her papa is the foreman of the work crew, a trusted friend of Pim's and well known as the handiest man in the warehouse. Bep has his shy, gentle eyes.

"Hello, Bep," Miep replies. "Just in time. Would you mind brewing a pot of coffee for Mr. Kleiman?"

"Of course not," says Bep. "Happy to do it."

"*I* can brew coffee," Anne chimes in, but gets ignored for her trouble.

"Where is everyone?" Bep wonders, hanging up her hat and scarf on the coat tree.

"Mr. Kugler's on a sales call," Miep reports, "and Mr. Kleiman's in the private office."

"With a mof," Anne is compelled to insert.

"*Anne,*" Miep scolds with a half frown.

"Well, he *is* a mof."

"He's a representative from the Frankfurt office," Miep explains to Bep.

"And he's wearing a Nazi stickpin," Anne adds, putting two fingers to her lip to imitate the infamous Hitlerite mustache and flapping up her hand in a mock salute.

"Anne, *please,*" Miep corrects, obviously trying to contain her alarm. "This is not how we behave in the *office.*" It's a sensible warning, Anne knows, but one that she feels suddenly compelled to ignore.

"It's true," she says. "I'm not making that up."

"And neither are you being helpful," Miep can only point out. "Now, I'm sure Bep is not frightened of a stickpin. Just as I'm sure you have plenty of work to occupy you."

"It's all right, Anne," Bep tells her lightly. Bep's eyes are bright behind her eyeglasses, but something about her makes Anne wonder if she's forcing it a bit. Bep frets. They all know that. And today her smile strikes Anne as rehearsed. Anne, in fact, has made Bep a sometime project of hers. Trying to boost cheerful, sunny Bep to the surface more often. So what else can she do but investigate?

The telephone rings, and Miep picks it up. Anne surrenders to her desk work, but not for very long. As soon as she's convinced that Miep is deeply enough involved in her call, she makes her escape.

In the kitchen Bep and she often gossip together, mostly concerning the male of the species, Anne gabbing away on the subject of her many beaux and Bep on her up-and-down relationship with her boyfriend, Maurits. But now as she enters, she finds Bep with her back to the door, head down, and bracing herself against the counter.

"Hello again," says Anne.

Bep turns. A flicker of alarm is quickly overlaid by the smile she pushes up. "Oh. Hello again yourself," she says, opening the cabinet and bringing down the surrogate. But her eyes are slightly panicked.

"Mummy taught Margot and me how to brew perfect coffee. You must start with cold water, else it'll taste flat."

Bep nods but does not reply.

"Bep, is something the matter?"

Bep glares at the spoonful of peaty surrogate she is leveling off from the tin. "What makes you ask *that*?" she wonders.

"I have instincts for that sort of thing." This is what Anne likes to believe. "There's something on your mind, I can just tell."

A swallow, and then Bep drops a bomb in a whisper. "I think Maurits is going to ask to marry me."

Anne's eyes pop wide open. "Are you *serious,* Bep? *Maurits?*"

"Yes. That's the one." Bep's glance is shy as she replaces the lid on the tin of Hotel Koffiesurrogaat. Her eyes are cool lakes.

Anne feels a giddy grin on her face. "Oh, *Bep.* You must be *beside* yourself."

"Yes. I know I *should* be," Bep agrees.

And now Anne feels a tiny secret thrill. Bep getting a proposal of marriage is one thing. Bep *refusing* a proposal of marriage? That's something else again. She tries to trim the eager curiosity from her voice. "Are you thinking of telling him no?"

Bep plugs the percolator into the electric socket. "Maybe," she says, and then she stops and looks at Anne with blunt trepidation. "Would that be such a terrible thing?"

"Terrible? I—" Anne shivers. "I don't *know.* Are you sure he's going to ask?"

"Pretty sure." Bep nods. "I mean, I think he's hinting at it. He's saying things like at our age his parents were married with two children."

"Do you love him?"

"That's a complicated question."

"Is it?" Anne wonders. "I wouldn't think so." In Anne's mind this is the only question that truly matters. She suspects that her parents married less for love than for the requirements of society, and look what happened. Pim stuck in an arrangement for the rest of his life with Mummy. A respectful arrangement maybe, but still Anne can never *imagine* settling for something like that. She knows that love is waiting for her out there somewhere. A heart that will match her own in every detail. And she doesn't want Bep to settle for anything less either.

Bep, however, shakes her head. "He always tries to be good to me. Do I wish he had a little more ambition? That maybe he would want more than just a job as a laborer for a concrete company? I don't know. My father thinks he's perfect material for a husband."

"And certainly it's good that your father approves."

"And he does. Very much so."

"Though, on the other hand, your father is not the one who's going to be married to him," Anne points out. "*You* are."

"Funny," Bep says with her lips in a straight line. "That is exactly what I said, too. Though Papa didn't think it was so amusing. He says Maurits is honest and a hard worker and if he wants to marry me, shouldn't that be enough?"

"Yet I still can't help but return to the most important question: Do you *love* him, Bep?" Anne asks again.

This time Bep expels a heavy breath as the percolator begins to pop. "I don't know. *Yes.* In a way. Of course I do, in a way."

"But. Not in the way you want to," Anne suggests. "Not in the way you want to love someone you're going to marry."

Bep loops her hair behind her ears. "I'm *twenty-three*, Anne. I know you're only thirteen. You're probably still much too young to really understand the sort of pressure that puts on me. My mother is continually making her 'jokes' about her eldest daughter, the 'Old Maid.'"

"But certainly that's no reason to say yes if you're not sure. Because your mother makes jokes."

"Maybe not," Bep says dubiously. "But where exactly is the long line of suitors for me to choose from?" She locks her gaze onto Anne's. There is a certain small terror in her whisper. "Maybe Maurits will be my only chance."

Anne blinks. "Only chance?" She doesn't understand. "Only chance for what?"

"For a husband, Anne. A family. For happiness," Bep says, and then her eyes go bright with tears. A breath catches in her throat, and Anne can only step forward and embrace her like a sister, gripping her tightly, trying to absorb the shiver of Bep's sobs. "Bep, Bep," she murmurs. "Don't tear yourself to pieces. You will make the right decision when the time comes. Have faith in God that you will. Have faith in yourself."

Bep swallows her sobs, nodding, and Anne allows her to slip from Anne's embrace.

"*Yes,*" Bep agrees. "Yes, of course you're right. When the time comes," she says, fumbling for the handkerchief in the pocket of her shift, "I'm sure I'll know."

A voice comes from the corridor. "Anne?" Margot steps into the kitchen threshold and then stops as abruptly as if she's bumped into a wall. "*Oh.* Excuse me."

"That's all right," Bep replies quickly, clearing her throat of its thickness, hiding away her handkerchief. "Anne was just showing me how your mother taught you to brew coffee. Quite informative." She forces a smile.

Margot observes the scene for a moment, then says, "Anne, we should be going. It's almost time to help Mummy with supper."

"But it's still early—" Anne starts to protest, till Bep cuts her off.

"No, no," Bep insists, sniffing. "You go, Anne. I was so late back from lunch, I have plenty of work I need to catch up with."

For an instant Anne considers arguing the point, but then instead she reaches over and plants a loud kiss on Bep's cheek. "I'll see you soon," she tells Bep, who flashes her a sharply grateful smile as the percolator steams, a smile that vanishes as quickly as it appears.

Outside, Margot wants to know, "What was that all about?"

"What was *what* all about?" Anne replies with faux innocence. She does a quick survey of the street, a habit now, just to be sure that there're no fascist types ready to initiate hostilities over the yellow star sewn to her climbing jacket.

"You know exactly what. Why was Bep upset?"

"Just a personal matter," says Anne as blithely as possible. She always savors any opportunity to have one up on Margot. "I really can't say anything more."

On the walk home, though, she cannot help but wonder about something. The truth is that she has never drawn the same line as Bep has just done with such rock-hard assurance: husband, family, happiness. Of course, she assumes that regardless of what she might have had to say on the subject to fluster Mummy, she *will* have all those things someday. But even if she *doesn't,* even if she forgoes the first two, the third has always floated freely, independently, in her mind. She will fall in love, doubtless. Of course she will. The war will end—how can it last forever? Eventually the English will arrive and the mof will be kicked back to his dirty little abode across the border. Jews will be free again, to be simply themselves, and she will find the one out there somewhere whose heart beats as hers, that much she assumes. But *happiness*? She has never planned on happiness coming from marriage or motherhood, but from something else. From something special inside. Mummy said that in Hebrew her name means "Favored by God," and she believes it. She believes that God is keeping a unique secret for her; keeping it hidden from everyone including herself, until the time is ripe for her to discover it. The essence of Annelies Marie Frank.

―――――

One afternoon after classes, Anne enters the front office of her father's firm and finds another girl occupying Bep's desk, lounging on the telephone with a lazy voice, but when the girl spots Anne, she quickly cuts the call short.

"Hello," says Anne with polite curiosity as she sets down her book satchel and hangs her jacket on the coat tree.

"Hello," the girl answers with a not-unpleasant expression. "I guess you're one of the daughters. I know there's one younger and one older, so you must be the younger."

"I must be," Anne says. "My name is Anne."

"I'm Nelli. One of Bep's sisters."

"Ah," says Anne. And she sees it now. The resemblance. This girl looks to be a few years Bep's junior but has the same high forehead and the same rounded chin. The same pinkish, bow-shaped lips and fluffy waves in her hair. But her eyes are different. They are larger, bolder, hungrier. Searching through her handbag, she produces a packet of French cigarettes and leans her head to the side as she ignites the tip with a bullet lighter.

"I don't think Bep likes people to smoke at her desk," Anne informs her.

"There are plenty of things I do that Bep doesn't like," Nelli says. "Just ask her. I'm sure she can give you a list."

Anne looks around. All the desks are empty. "Where *is* everybody?"

"In the office down the hall," Nelli replies without interest, and blows smoke. And then she says, "So it's true. You're Jewish."

Anne feels her spine stiffen as she becomes acutely aware of the star attached to her blouse. "Yes," she answers calmly. "Why do you bring that up?"

Another shrug from Nelli. "No reason. Only that you're prettier than I expected. You could really pass, I think."

Pass? "For what?"

"For Dutch," says Nelli.

At that moment the office door opens and in steps Margot in a hurry. "Sorry I'm late," she announces, removing her coat. Anne glares at the star sewn to Margot's jumper, too, but Nelli now looks uninterested. "I agreed to tutor some of the younger pupils in French after classes. Where *is* everyone?"

"In Papa's office, apparently. Margot, this is Nelli, Bep's sister."

Only now does Margot seem to notice the girl. "Oh. Hello. I'm Margot."

"So I heard," Nelli replies, expelling smoke. "How nice to meet you."

"You know Bep doesn't like people smoking at her desk," Margot points out.

"Hmm." Nelli nods. "I think I read that in the newspapers."

Margot blinks, confused. "You what?"

But before Nelli says anything more, there's some noise down the hall as the door to the private office opens and voices tumble out. Bep is the first one to return to the front office. Immediately her expression purses into a frown. "Nelli! What are you *doing*? Put that *out*, please," she demands.

Nelli huffs sourly but does as she's commanded, crushing out the cigarette in the saucer of a teacup.

"Don't make a mess," Bep scolds. "Take that cup and saucer into the kitchen and clean them, please. What are you *up to* anyway? You should be working. Have you finished with those invoices I asked you to file? *No.* I see you *haven't.* I suppose, as usual, I must watch every move you make."

"A pity you haven't anything *better* to do," Nelli tells her sister as she begins to page listlessly through the stack of unfiled invoices.

"Well, if you want to get paid for your work here, then I suggest that *you* find something better to do than loafing with a cigarette. We have an image to uphold in the front office." Bep is gathering folders from the filing cabinet, and she slams a drawer shut as if to punctuate her sentence. Only now does she glance over at Anne and Margot. "So you've met my sister?"

"Yes," says Anne blankly.

Bep nods and cradles the file folders. "Miep has left some work on Mr. Kugler's desk for you two with a note." And then to Nelli she pleads, "I beg you not to make me regret bringing you in," before she marches back toward Pim's private office, her flat heels clomping on the wooden floorboards.

"She's not very large, but she still sounds like an ox in shoes when she walks, doesn't she?" says Nelli.

Anne is offended. "That's a terrible thing to say. Especially about your own sister."

Nelli only shrugs. "You're right," she says wryly. "You're right. I must be a terrible person."

"Anne, let's not dawdle," Margot intercedes, setting her school satchel down beside Anne's. "I want to be able to *finish* the work Miep left for us before we go home."

Anne blinks away from Nelli. "Well, *you're* the one who was *late*."

"And *you're* the one who likes to dawdle," Margot counters, heading under the arch toward Kugler's side of the office.

Nelli expels a breath. "Aren't big sisters simply an impossible pain in the rump?" she wonders aloud.

Anne can't disagree with this. But she finds that she doesn't want to agree with Nelli either. "Excuse me," she says formally, and follows Margot.

"I don't like her," Anne announces.

"Who?"

"That girl Nelli." They are in the kitchen at home, scraping carrots for supper.

"She's Bep's *sister*," Margot says.

"*So?*" Anne frowns.

"So make allowances. Why don't you like her anyway?"

"*Why?* You heard her. *She says awful things about Bep,*" Anne complains with some vehemence.

Margot only shrugs. "You say awful things about *me.*"

"I do not! And even if I do, I would never say them in front of strangers."

"I am so comforted by that, Anne," Margot replies, as if there were a sharp tack on her tongue.

Anne is exasperated. "You and I are *different*," she protests. "Anyway, that has nothing to do with anything. I just don't like her. I don't have to have a reason—I have instincts about people." A pot cover rattles on the stove as water comes to a rolling boil. "Mother, the potatoes are boiling," Anne calls out dutifully.

Their mother comes bustling into the kitchen in her starched linen apron, already in the midst of admonishing Anne. "Well, *turn down the fire,* then, if they're boiling, silly thing."

Anne ignores this. "Margot already did it," she replies, and scrapes another carrot.

Their mother raises the lid on the pot. "Did you put the salt in, Margot?"

"A pinch," Margot answers.

"Well, another pinch won't hurt. Anne, go set the table, please."

"But I'm scraping the carrots, Mummy."

"Margot can finish that. Now go do as I say, will you? For once without further resistance."

Anne huffs to herself. "Yes, Mummy," she concedes.

"Margot, I'll need you to check on the lamb in another five minutes, please. I'd like to go get changed before supper. And the two of you should, too. Mr. and Mrs. van Pels will be here at six o'clock."

"Is their blockheaded son coming, too?" Anne asks.

"Anne," her mother scolds. "Peter may not be as quick as you and your sister, but Mr. van Pels is a valuable partner in your father's business dealings. To speak of his son so is out of the question."

"Sorry, Mummy," Anne mumbles. "I won't call him a blockhead when he's here. At least not when he's in earshot."

Their mother sighs with dreadful resignation. "I simply don't understand you. Why must you be so harsh with people? What are you trying to prove?"

"Sorry, Mummy," she repeats, but this time she is obviously abashed. She remains silent after their mother leaves, listening to the scrunch of the scraper against the meat of the carrot, and looks over at her sister, who is slipping on a pair of quilted oven mitts. "You know, Margot, even if I *do* say awful things about you, I never really *mean* them," she says.

A glance from those lovely eyes behind the lenses of Margot's glasses. "I know that, Anne. And when I say awful things about you, I almost never mean them either."

"Ha," Anne snorts, though she cannot help but smile.

"Now go and do as Mummy said," Margot instructs. "And remember, when you're laying the place settings, the blade of the knife always faces inward."

Near the end of the week, they stopped by a shop to pick up provisions for the office kitchen. Surrogate sugar, surrogate coffee, a box

of surrogate tea, a box of soap powder. Margot performed the complicated transaction with their rationing coupons, but somehow
that made it Anne's job to carry the sack. When she steps out onto
the street, however, her heart thumps thickly at the sight of the GVB
electric tram that has bumped to a stop in front of them, its bell dinging. She can feel a pair of eyes stick to her. A girl on the right side of
pretty, firmly attached to a well-coiffed, cocky-looking fellow in a
German army uniform. The girl drills Anne with a stare that gapes
somewhere between unpleasant alarm and utter abhorrence, but in
any case there is not a trace of pity in it.

"It's *Nelli*," Anne says aloud.

"Who?"

"*Nelli*. Bep's sister *Nelli*."

Margot glances up. "Where?"

"On the streetcar with a *mof*." Anne tries to point it out, but by
now the tram is banging away down its track, casually tossing off
sparks.

Margot shrugs it off. "I think you must be seeing things." But on
their walk to the office, Anne is debating with herself. Should she talk
to Bep? Will it shock her to know that one of her sisters has been
publicly observed hanging on the arm of a mof invader? Anne doesn't
want to embarrass Bep, but what if Bep hasn't a clue about what's
going on? Maybe if Anne spills the beans, Bep can do something to
dissuade her sister from such shameful folly. On the other hand, if
Bep *already knows* and is too ashamed to mention it, then Anne risks
humiliating her further.

In the office Anne enters the kitchen to put away the provisions
and finds Bep there with her back to her. Anne calls her name, and
Bep twists around, her eyes burning behind her glasses. "*Anne*," she
says, and gulps.

Quickly Anne crosses, sets down her sack, and takes Bep gently
by her arm. "Bep, what's happened?"

For a moment all Bep can do is shake her head.

"What is it? Did you have a fight with Maurits?" Anne guesses.

And at the mention of his name, Bep's eyes fill. "No. Not a fight," she says. Bep seems to want to hold in her next words, but she can't, and they all come tumbling out. "Maurits has been called up for the Arbeitseinsatz," she confesses in a shaky voice.

The Arbeitseinsatz. This explains everything. The so-called labor deployment of Dutch subjects deported to Germany to keep the mof's war machine cranking. And now to think Maurits is facing daily life toiling in a German factory or some abominable work camp, it's horrifying! How can he suffer through such a nightmare? Under the moffen heel like a slave? And not only that, but what about the fleets of Allied planes they hear roaring toward Germany? What if the bombardiers drop their bomb loads on Maurits's head? Bombs can't make a distinction between a German and a Good Dutchman, Bep points out tearfully. They only fall and explode.

"There must be something that can be done," Anne insists adamantly, but Bep only shakes her head harder, yanking off her glasses to clear her eyes with the palms of her hands. "*No.* Nothing."

"What about Pim? Have you talked to Pim?" Anne asks. "Surely he can come up with some solution."

"No, Anne. *No.* Nothing can be done. Maurits has been called up, and if he resists, he'll be sent to a concentration camp. Or maybe simply taken to the dunes and *shot.*" This possibility is too much for Bep, and she breaks into pieces. Immediately Anne claps her in an embrace, gripping tightly and absorbing Bep's sobs. She can feel the tears soaking into the shoulder of her blouse as she pats Bep's back sympathetically, cooing her name. If there's really nothing to be done but hold Bep as she cries, then at least Anne can do that much.

When evening comes, however, she takes her first opportunity to explain Bep's tragedy at the supper table. Pim pauses with his knife and fork over his plate and shakes his head grimly. "Terrible news," he can only agree.

Anne presses for something more. This is her father, after all—a man of great competence. He's kept a family of Jews safe in the middle of the Nazi occupation. Surely he can help save one gentile from labor conscription. "There must be *something* you can do, Pim. Can't you?"

But it's her mother who answers, with a sharpness that causes Anne to wince.

"*Do?* Don't be *absurd,* Anne. What can your father possibly *do?* Don't you understand this yet? We are *Jews,*" she reminds her daughter, eyes filling. "We have no power any longer."

For an instant no one speaks, until Pim leans forward with an expression of eloquent sympathy. "Edith . . ." he says.

But not even Pim can stop Mummy from leaping up from her chair to make a weepy exit. "*Excuse me,*" she chokes out before vanishing from the room.

By now Anne feels herself on the brink of tears, too. "I didn't mean to upset her, Pim. Really I didn't."

Her father nods. "Of course not, Anne," he tells her.

Margot stiffens. "Shall I go after her, Pim?" She's ready to leap from her chair as well. But Pim tells her no.

"She'll be all right. It's just her nerves. Give her a while alone."

And this seems to be the case. By the end of supper, when it's time to clear the table and wash the dishes, Mummy is back, dry-eyed and acting her usual self. "Anne, be more careful," she says when Anne brings in one of the large platters. "I don't want any chips in my china. It survived the journey from Frankfurt without so much as a nick in a saucer. Is it too much to ask that it survive handling by my younger daughter?"

That night as she's lying in bed, Anne tries to visualize the reality of a German labor camp. She pictures Maurits hunched in a line of prisoners, clothes filthy, digging ditches as ugly Boche guards in steel helmets and hobnail boots watch over them with guns at the ready. But beyond that she draws a blank. It must be a place of pure horror, no doubt, yet what exactly pure horror looks like, what it consists of, she finds difficult to imagine.

~

Since they invaded the Low Countries two years ago, the Germans are everywhere. Feldgrau uniforms fill the cafés and restaurants. Caravans of Opel Blitz lorries plow through the maze of narrow city streets, crushing the pavement under their tire treads and drowning out all sound, disobeying even the most minor tenets of Dutch law and Dutch courtesy. Had packs of savage wolves been loosed across Amsterdam, it would not feel any less dangerous than after the advent of the mof. "Mof," that complicated word. It's a Dutch insult in a way that only the Dutch can be insulting. A sort of old-fashioned derogation with a definition akin to "grumpy and unsophisticated." Not much of a slight for a murderous army of interlopers, but the Dutch language does not naturally accommodate rudeness, so really it's the best, or the worst, that can be offered. The Dutch do so enjoy hurling diseases as swear words, calling a person a cancer or a canker sore. But if they wasted their most beloved insults on the Germans, then whatever would they call each other?

There is, though, no shortage of names to call a Jew. Yid, kike, sheeny, assassin of Christ—Anne's heard them all by now. There may be shortages of coal, meat, milk, and fresh produce, but there's no shortage of insults in that department. It hurts her because she so loves the Dutch. She loves *being* Dutch. She would rather take heart at the heroic story of the Dutch transport workers who risked their lives by striking in protest of SS razzias—the brutal roundups in the Jewish Quarter. But then her friend Lucia, whom she's known since Montessori school, appears dressed on the playground in the getup of the National Youth Storm and tells her that she's going to miss Anne's birthday party because her mother won't allow her to be friends with a Jewess any longer. Anne glares at Lucia's face after this announcement. The girl looks trapped. In pain. Lucia has always been dominated by her mother, but Anne has no sympathy to spare her. If she despises the Germans, she despises *even more* the Dutch collaborators and traitors to the queen who've joined the Nationaal-Socialistische Beweging. That gang of filthy-hearted fascists whose cohorts parade in the street with their shiny boots and newly adopted swastika banners, as if *they* are the conquerors instead of the moffen. She glares at the black-and-orange cap atop Lucia's head, adorned with a seagull badge. Anne adores seagulls, adores watching them reel above the canals, and suddenly she *hates* Lucia. *Despises* her for stealing the seagull for her dirty fascist insignia. Anne would enjoy spitting in the girl's round piglet face, but instead she replies in a lofty manner, "I'm sorry to hear that. You're going to miss simply the best party that has ever been thrown."

Anne continues to laugh and crack jokes as the day passes. Whispering to her friends in class and passing notes. Showing off her hopping skills on the playground in games of hinkelen. Playing Monopoly at Hanneli's flat. At supper she discusses the newest developments: that her favorite flower is now the rose instead of the daisy and that her friend Jacqueline has invited her to sleep over. She pleads with her parents to allow her to go, and, as usual, Margot is of no help. She wouldn't dream of leaving home overnight, says Margot, not with thousands of German troops billeted in Dutch houses.

Dutch houses but not Jewish houses, Anne corrects.

Still. Margot shivers at the thought of it.

Anne makes light. She says the moffen are too busy swilling all the good Dutch beer to cause any trouble after supper. Finally her parents concede, at which point she gushes with affection, hugging them both so tightly, even Mummy.

But at night Anne lies awake, tossing about until her covers are hanging all askew. "Margot?"

A drowsy reply. "Yes?"

"Are you awake?" Anne whispers.

"No," Margot whispers back.

"I can't go to sleep."

"Try harder. Think of the subjects that bore you in school. Think of algebra."

"That won't help."

"Did you take your valerian drops like Mummy told you?"

"*Yes,* I took them," Anne answers with a pinch of frustration.

"Then call Mummy and ask for a cup of chamomile tea."

"Margot, will you stop offering silly remedies, please?"

"Keep your voice down, Anne."

"This isn't something that chamomile tea or valerian drops can cure."

"Then you'll have to come out and tell me what's actually

bothering you, because I obviously can't read your mind." She has adopted her favorite tone of sisterly impatience, but perhaps she actually sounds a bit interested to know, too.

"My friend Lucia joined the Youth Storm."

"Ah," says Margot.

"At least she *used* to be my friend. Now she's been infected by this Nazi disease."

"Did she say something nasty?"

"Her mother did, and she repeated it. It just made me realize what can happen now that the Germans have taken over."

"I thought you said they drank too much beer to be of any trouble."

"Oh, that was only so I could get what I wanted," she says. "The truth is, they could kick in our door right now if it suited them."

"And why would it suit them?"

"Because they're *Germans*," Anne answers with exasperation.

Margot props herself up on one elbow. Moonlight has sneaked in through the window, casting bars across the rug from the window lattice. "Well, we were Germans once," she points out rather distantly.

"Maybe *you* were, but not me."

"You were born in Frankfurt, Anne."

"That means nothing. That was the past, before the whole country became populated by the enemy."

"So you think of all of them as the enemy?"

"We're just Jews to them now," Anne says, her voice oddly matter-of-fact about it. "Dirty yids, no better than rats."

Margot takes a breath and then exhales it lightly as she lies down. "I can't believe all Germans think that."

"No? *I* can believe it. I agree with Mummy."

"Well, that's a miracle in itself."

"They're criminals. Just look at the faces of the soldiers when they see the star on our clothes."

"I think you're being unreasonable, Anne," Margot decides. "And quite honestly, you're too young to know what you're talking about. An entire nation of people can't simply become criminals. Besides, there are plenty of Dutch who look at us that way, too."

Anne sees Lucia's round face under the black cap and relives the furious sting she felt. It makes her mad at Margot. "Is there some *reason*," she wants to know, sitting up straight, "is there some *reason* that you will *never* agree with me? Is there some *reason* that you must always argue for the opposite view?"

"I don't."

"You do. You even defend the Nazis."

"I do *not* defend the *Nazis,* Anne," and suddenly Margot's whisper is indignant, and she has shoved herself up firmly. "Take that *back.*"

"It certainly *sounded* like you were defending them."

"I said *take it back.*"

Anne feels a hard pinch of regret. Margot sounds suddenly so *angry.* Margot, whose temper is so famously under control at all times. Yes, it was just one of Anne's stupid, silly accusations, born out of her own fear, but the ferocity of her sister's reaction has shaken her. Though she tries to hide this, of course. Blowing a sigh of surrender toward the ceiling, she drops down on the davenport. "All right, all right. I take it back."

But Margot is not yet satisfied. "*Say* it," she demands.

Anne swallows. "I don't think you are defending the Nazis," she admits. "Margot Frank does not, under any circumstances, defend Nazis."

"Words have *power,* Anne," Margot instructs her sharply. "You should be more careful how you *use* them." And with that she flounces back down under the covers, socking her pillow into shape.

A certain quiet descends as the hushed burble of conversation from the next room settles between them. Anne concentrates on calming the beating of her heart. Once she found the sound of their parents' conversation at the end of the day comforting, but now it's not helping at all. She can tell that their words are purposely muted, though it's still easy enough to make out what they're talking about. The scale of the razzias is increasing. Massive raids in the Jodenbuurt. Hundreds of Jews hauled away by the SS and black-clad Dutch bullies of the Schalkhaar police. Pim says it's all a matter of making the right decisions. All a matter of staying together as a family, come what may.

And then Margot coughs sharply. A tickle in her throat, perhaps, but it brings conversation in the living room to a halt. Their door is open a crack. A moment later Pim pokes his head in just long enough to decide that his daughters may still be awake, and quietly closes their bedroom door completely. A gentle darkness wraps up the room. Margot clears her throat, and silence separates them as Anne stares up at the crack in the ceiling plaster. She can no longer see it in the dark, but she knows it's there. She lets her thoughts flow freely. Away from the war and the horrific events in the streets. She tries to think about herself. That's not usually something that's so hard for Anne Frank to do, but she finds herself thinking instead of Mummy. Of Mummy and the fretful debate at the supper table over the treatment of the Jews. Of how terribly bitter and anxious the war has made her mother and how bleakly Mummy seems to view the future now. Not like Pim. Not like Pim, whose hope is unyielding. "Do you think Mummy and Pim love each other?" she hears herself ask. Maybe she didn't really mean to speak the question aloud, but now she has.

Margot sounds indignant again. And maybe a tiny bit panicked. "*What?* That's a *ridiculous* question."

"I'm not so sure. I mean, if you were a man, would you love Mummy?"

"No *wonder,*" Margot huffs. "No *wonder* people can hardly stand to be *around* you sometimes, Anne. You can be such a terrible, terrible pain."

But Anne only shrugs to herself. "I'm not sure *I* would want to love her if I were a man. Mummy's always so disappointed with everyone."

"I'm going to sleep, Anne. You should as well, before you say something too awful to forgive."

This gets Anne's attention. It's been one of her fears, but also one of her curiosities—that it might be possible. That it might be *possible* to push beyond the boundaries of forgiveness. Mummy says God forgives everything, but Anne must wonder. Is God forgiving the Nazis? Even as she lies in her bedroom staring at the crack in the ceiling plaster, even as Margot is fuming under her covers, is God forgiving their enemy?

On the morning of the twelfth of June, Anne's thirteenth birthday dawns, and the bright business of daylight begins above the good

Dutch pantile roofs. Anne is awake at six but must lie there for another three-quarters of an hour till she can reasonably wake her parents. So while Margot slumbers, Anne is already off to the races, living the day in her head. There'll be presents in the living room. Then she'll take the cookies she baked with Mummy to school and pass them out to her classmates at recess. She loves doing this. She loves to be generous. Being generous makes it so easy to bask at the center of everyone's attention.

Her party is scheduled for Sunday, and there are simply gangs of people expected to attend. There will be games and songs directed by Pim. There will be pastries, cookies, and bonbons served on porcelain platters with doilies provided by Mummy. Lemonade in the punch bowl and coffee in a silver service for the grown-ups. Small gifts wrapped in colored tissue for all the children attending. And, of course, always a surprise. This year Pim has rented a film projector and a reel of the canine adventures of Rin Tin Tin. Her own birthday matinee! And if you think that happens at Ilana Riemann's house or Giselle Zeigler's house on *their* birthdays, then think again. Anne Frank, as everybody knows, as everybody must realize, is special.

Morning rises. Even though she knows what it is, even though she has picked it out herself, it is the first gift she opens among all the presents filling the coffee table, the bouquets of roses and peonies, the lovely plant, the Variété board game, the bottle of sweet grape juice that she can pretend is wine when she drinks it, the strawberry tart, specially baked by her mother—such a wonderful array, but they all will wait.

She unties the ribbon of blue silk and carefully tugs open the wrapping until it emerges. The red tartan daybook. She smiles as she opens it and runs her fingers across the creamy vellum pages. A confidante. That is what she intends her diary to become. Her one true confidante, from whom she will hide nothing. Alone in her room, before leaving for school, she sits at Mummy's French secretaire and uncaps her favorite fountain pen. Quietly she smooths her hand over the empty page and then watches the paper absorb the ink of the very first line she writes.

> *I hope I will be able to confide everything to you, as I have never been able to confide in anyone, and I hope you will be a great source of comfort and support.*

3

DIVING UNDER

Hiding . . . where would we hide? In the city? In the
country? In a house? In a shack? When, where, how . . . ?

—Anne Frank,
from her diary,
8 July 1942

1942

OCCUPIED NETHERLANDS

On a Thursday afternoon before supper, Margot is studying for an exam at a friend's and Anne is alone in the flat with her mother, busily snapping snow peas into a bowl, when her father comes home early from the office. Instead of removing his hat, he invites Anne out for a walk.

"But." A glance to her mother. "I'm helping Mummy."

"So I see, but a short walk won't hurt, will it, Edith?"

Her mother frowns nervously. "Go. Do as your father asks," is all she says.

It has been raining for most of the week, but today is dry, the afternoon warm and balmy, and the caretakers have taken the opportunity to mow the grass. Anne breathes in deeply as they stroll the edges of the Merry's central lawn. "I love the smell of freshly mown grass," she says, expecting her father to agree. But Pim's expression is grave.

"Anne," he says, "you should know that soon we will be leaving here."

Anne feels a jolt in her belly. *Leaving?*

"For some weeks now," Pim begins, but he must take a deeper breath to continue. "For some weeks now, we have been storing our more important possessions with friends. Your mother's silver, for example, about which you were so curious. The point has been to prevent our belongings from falling into the clutches of our enemy. And now," he says, "the time has come when we *ourselves* must act to avoid falling into his clutches."

Anne stops in place and looks directly into her father's face.

"We won't be waiting for the Nazi to haul us off at his convenience, Annelein," he tells her. "We are going into hiding."

Anne blinks. Honestly, she is surprised at how exhilarated she feels. Suddenly she is stumbling over her own questions. Where are they going? Is there a place in the country? A farmhouse with chickens and fresh eggs? A secret hideaway where cows low in the pastures above the river, where windmills creak and the mof has left not a single boot print? Or maybe a barge where they can drive to safety down the canals and rivers. But Pim will not say. His face has turned deadly ashen. His expression so somber that Anne begins to feel her excitement tremble toward fear.

"Does Margot know?"

"Yes. But outside the family you must keep this *secret*," her father tells her. "Not a word to a soul. Not even your closest friend. You must promise me, Anneke."

"I promise, Pim. I promise. But will it happen soon?"

"Soon enough. You let your papa fret over the details."

Suddenly she seizes Pim in an embrace. It makes her feel secretly proud to have such information in her possession. And she loves Pim all the more for trusting her with it. Pim, the man who has everything under control.

"For now stay cheerful," he instructs her, stroking the back of her head, "and try not to worry. Treasure these carefree days for as long as you may."

That night at bedtime, Anne sits at the narrow vanity table to perform her nightly routine. Before the curlers are fastened into place, she dons her combing shawl. A fringed cape of pale beige satin decorated with roses over her shoulders. But instead of picking up her hairbrush, she stares at her face in the mirror. Is this the soon-to-be face of an onderduiker? She's trying to be brave. All through supper she smiled and courteously passed dishes. And maybe she *can* be brave. So they are going into hiding? So what? Other Jews have it much worse. Herded into a ghetto in the Jodenbuurt and cut off from the rest of the town by barbed wire. Transported into Germany like slaves or arrested and shipped to some terrible camp. She should be grateful and courageous. And anyway, isn't there an element of adventure to consider? It will be an exploit of sorts. She can write about it, put it all down in her diary. Quietly, picking up the brush, she begins the ritual of nightly brushing, but when Margot appears in her nightgown, she slips the brush from Anne's hand. "Let me do this for you," she says.

Anne does not resist. "Pim told me," she whispers.

"Yes," is all Margot says. Stroke after stroke after stroke, Anne gazes at herself in the oval mirror. It's so soothing. She feels that Margot can brush away her fears, her anxieties, all the problems of the world hammering at their door. Her sister's hand stroking the length of her hair with the soft bristles. Suddenly she loves Margot. Not just abstractly but fiercely, with a full and merciful heart. "I adore you, you know, Margot," she whispers.

"Of course you do," Margot replies. "I'm adorable."

"No. I mean . . . I mean I love you. Whatever happens to us, I want you to know that."

Margot continues with her brushstrokes but then bends over and kisses her little sister on the head. "I love you, too, silly."

Anne closes her eyes. When they were little, Pim used to tell them the story of the Two Paulas. A pair of invisible twins who lived secretly in their home. Good Paula was always courteous, thoughtful, and obedient, and she never complained. But Bad Paula was full of mischief, often selfish, and easily angered. When Anne opens her eyes, she is caught by her own gaze. Sometimes she dreams that *she* is the flimsy mirror image and that the face reflected in the glass is the *real* Anne. The real Anne, who only *she* knows to be the *true* Anne. Not the difficult Anne. Not the fearful Anne. Not the know-it-all Anne. Not the Bad Paula, but the good Anne. The brave Anne. The Anne Favored by God.

At first Mummy tells her that it was Pim who has received the call-up notice, but her sister confesses the truth. An order from Die Zentralstelle für jüdische Auswanderung, under the stamp of the mof security police, arrived in the morning post. A form letter from an SS-Hauptsturmführer, bearing the official rubber stamp, demanding that the Jewess Margot Betti Frank report for labor deployment inside the German Reich. By the time Pim comes home, he has already decided that they must move into their hiding place weeks earlier than planned. It's hard to resist the urge to panic as the process accelerates into a fluster of preparation. Anne packs her curlers, her favorite books, her tortoiseshell comb, clean handkerchiefs, and a few crazy things, too. Old tickets from a skating party at the Apollohal in the Stadionweg, a painted dreidel her omi Alice had sent her for Hanukkah, her poetry album from school with all her friends' handwritten poems, her film-star photos and collection of postcards, her set of table-tennis paddles. Memories are more important to her than dresses, she insists. Of course, she also carefully packs her diary. The tartan plaid album that, as she hoped, has indeed become her favorite and most intimate confidante, to which she has confessed all the turmoil of the last few days. The letter they leave on the dining-room table is for their upstairs tenant to find. It implies that they have fled Holland to join Pim's family in Switzerland. By the next afternoon, the entire family has slipped off the map of Amsterdam and into the hiding place: the rear annex of Pim's office building in the Prinsengracht. "Het Achterhuis" is what Anne will call it in her diary. The House Behind.

4

THE HOUSE BEHIND

The Annex is an ideal place to hide in. It may be damp
and lopsided, but there's probably not a more comfortable
hiding place in all of Amsterdam. No, in all of Holland.

... Up to now our bedroom, with its blank walls, was
very bare. Thanks to Father—who brought my entire
postcard and movie-star collection here beforehand—and
to a brush and a pot of glue, I was able to plaster the walls
with pictures. It looks much more cheerful.

—Anne Frank,
from her diary,
11 July 1942

1944

The Achterhuis
Prinsengracht 263
Rear Annex

OCCUPIED NETHERLANDS

No one would ever suspect there were so many rooms behind that plain gray door. There's just one small step in front of the door, and then you're inside. Straight ahead of you is a steep flight of stairs. To the left is a narrow hallway opening onto a room that serves as the Frank family's living room and bedroom.

She is sitting on the steps, alone. Thankful to be alone to write. Knees together with her diary on her lap. Her eyes lift from the page in thought. She gazes at the door that separates her from the remainder of the world.

If you go up the stairs and open the door at the top, you're surprised to see such a large, light and spacious room in an old canalside house like this. It contains a stove (thanks to the fact that it used to be Mr. Kugler's laboratory) and a sink. This will be the kitchen and bedroom of Mr. and Mrs. van Pels, as well as the general living room, dining room and study for us all. A tiny side room is to be Peter van Pels's bedroom. Then, just as in the front part of the building, there's an attic and a loft. So there you are. Now I've introduced you to the whole of our lovely Annex!

Yours, Anne

There are eight of them in hiding now, fifteen months after the Frank family slipped off the map. Anne and her family have been joined by the spice expert Hermann van Pels, also known as Putti; his wife, Kerli; and their son, Peter; plus Miep's dentist, the lofty Mr. Pfeffer, who makes it a crowd in more ways than one. In Anne's opinion. In fact, most everybody is driving her crazy in one manner or another. She scribbles in her diary when she manages a few moments to herself.

Mrs. van Pels is always saying the most ridiculous things, and her Putti is often exasperated. But that's not surprising, because one day Kerli announces, "When this is all over, I'm going to have myself baptized" and the next, "As long as I can remember, I've wanted to go to Jerusalem. I only feel at home with other Jews!"

Time is measured in increments of fifteen minutes, punctuated by the Westerkerk's bell tower. Fifteen minutes, followed by another fifteen minutes, followed by another, until hours pass into days and then weeks and months of dull routine, peeling bad potatoes, shelling peas, enduring the murky stink of confinement, the airless rooms, the plumbing problems, and, sometimes worst of all, enduring the burden of one another's company. She's often so very bored, even with herself. She apologizes to Kitty for all the "dreary chitchat" as her pen scratches across the page of her diary.

Mr. Pfeffer makes up everything as he goes along, and anyone wishing to contradict His Majesty had better think twice. In Fritz Pfeffer's home his word is law, but that doesn't suit Anne Frank in the least.

Meanwhile the war is heavily pitched around them. Allied bombers roar above their heads almost nightly, accompanied by the drumbeat of Boche flak guns. Last week the RAF dropped three hundred tons of bombs on Ijmuiden. Three hundred tons! British planes droned above them for an hour or more on their way to their target. But this

Sunday there's a break in the war's thunder. It's a quiet afternoon, and Anne and Margot have escaped the confines of their onderduikers' hideaway and slipped down to their father's private office to address the mounds of uncompleted office paperwork. There are no workmen in the building to hear them on a Sunday, so they can chat as they sort through the piles of business ephemera.

"It's a way to keep busy," Pim explains, "only a bit of clerical labor. I think it's the very least we can do for our helpers, don't you? Give Miep and Bep a head start on their work? Without them where would we be?"

Well, how can the girls possibly complain once Pim puts it like that? It is the women in her father's office who've taken on the role of daily helpers. Miep and Bep. Of course, Pim's good Dutch business partners, Mr. Kugler and Mr. Kleiman, manage the affairs of commerce to keep money in the coffers. But as far as managing the shopping, finessing the ration coupons, negotiating transactions with reliable grocers and butchers, and then lugging it all through the streets and up the steep, ankle-twisting Dutch steps, *that* is the women. It is the women who find a sweater or a skirt for Margot and Anne as they outgrow their clothes. It is the women who scrounge bits of soap or a container of tooth powder, who order correspondence courses to relieve boredom, who remember flowers on birthdays, who raise spirits and dispense hope.

So to help them out, these women who risk their lives daily caring for those in hiding? How could Anne argue? She can't. And even though she'd suffered through another bad headache in the morning, she joins Margot filing sales receipts from Pectacon. Boring. She'd rather be studying her French or her English. She'd rather be reading that biography of Catherine the Great. She'd rather be playing cards or teasing Peter, who maybe isn't quite the dunderhead she'd first thought him to be and who actually has a very sweet smile. But this morning none of that is available to her. Only clerical drudgery, though at least it's a break from the bickering of the adults. Mummy and Mrs. van Pels are at war again, this time over whose dishes are being chipped by whose careless handling.

"Do you think Peter is handsome?" Anne asks. She has decided on a tone of idle curiosity for this question, as she has nothing at all invested in the answer. Do you think the moon might be made of green cheese, she might be asking, or do you think Peter van Pels might be handsome?

"Handsome?" Margot gives her head a slight toss. "I suppose he's not so bad-looking. He's certainly strong," she says.

"But do you think he's . . . I don't know. Peculiar?"

"I think he's shy," says Margot, stapling a stack of papers together. The *ka-thunk* of the stapler punctuates her reply. "But why are you asking *my* opinion?"

A sideways glance. "Why? Why not?"

"I don't know. You're the one who likes him."

Anne stiffens. "And what is *that* supposed to mean?"

"It means you *like* him."

"I never said *any* such thing."

"Oh, *please*. You don't have to."

Anne swallows a breath of panic. Is it that obvious? "All I wanted to know—all I *asked*—is do you think he's peculiar?"

"Yes, a bit. But so are you." Margot grins.

"Ha, ha," says Anne. "My sister is so humorous."

"And I *do* think he's handsome. In a peculiar way."

Silence for a moment. Anne turns several of the invoices over in her hand. "So you're not interested, are you?"

"Interested in what?"

"You know what." She grabs the stapler and *ka-thunks* it down onto the corner of a stack. "In Peter," she says.

At this, Margot adjusts her glasses, pressing her fingers against the sides of the frames as she considers her options. "Well . . . now that you *mention* it. I suppose he *is* the only boy available. . . ."

Anne's voice drops. "Are you teasing me?"

"Pfftt. Of course I'm teasing you. How could I possibly be interested in Peter van Pels? I'm a year older than him."

"*So?*"

"So the girl can't be older than the boy. It doesn't work."

"But the girl can be *younger* than the boy. That's what you're saying?"

"Oh, for heaven's sake, Anne. *Yes,* that's what I'm saying. You have my permission."

"I didn't *ask* for your permission. Your permission to do what?"

"To pursue Peter if that's what you want."

Anne pretends some small interest in the carbon copies of customer orders. "Mummy says it's unladylike for a girl to pursue a boy."

Margot is frowning over her work. "And since when have you cared about what Mummy says? Since when have you cared about *anybody* and their opinions, other than yourself and your own?"

Anne frowns, too. She keeps her faux attention glued to the pile of papers, but her eyes have gone damp. "That hurt my feelings," she says.

Margot looks up, distracted.

"I *do* have feelings, you know, Margot. I know that everyone likes to think the opposite, but I *do* have feelings."

Margot's face clears. "I'm sorry," she tells Anne in a simple tone. "You're right. That was a hurtful thing to say."

Anne shrugs and wipes her eyes. "Anyway. May we change the subject?"

"Up to you," Margot replies, getting up to address the filing cabinet.

"I've been thinking a lot about what's going to happen once the war's over," Anne announces. "And I've decided what I'm going to do."

Margot does not look up from her work at the filing cabinet. "Have you, now?"

"Yes," Anne confirms.

"And?" Margot pauses to examine the paper in her hand before slotting it into place. "What's the big surprise going to be?"

"I'm going to be a famous writer."

Now a glance. "A *famous* writer?" her sister repeats.

"You think I'm being ludicrous?"

"No. I think you're being you." Silence. And then Margot closes the file drawer. "So what kind?"

"What kind of what?"

"What kind of famous writer?"

"Oh, you know. The kind the world adores."

"Oh. *That* kind."

"Maybe a novelist," Anne says with a more thoughtful tone. "Or a journalist. Who knows?"

"An international success."

"That's right. An *international* success, with flats in Paris, London, and New York, *all three*."

"Famous writers can't live in the Netherlands?"

"Not me. I intend to *see* some of the world."

"Mm-hm. Hand me that file folder, would you?"

"Hand you?"

"The file folder, Anne. You have the stapler on top of it."

"Oh," says Anne. She removes the stapler and hands over the file.

"Thank you."

A beat before Anne asks, "So what about *you*?"

"Me?"

"What are *you* going to do?" Anne doesn't really expect her sister to answer this. Normally Margot is not one to pursue these what-if types of games. But to Anne's surprise, Margot pauses in her work, at least long enough to give it a thought.

"I think," says Margot, "I think I would like to go to Palestine and study to become a maternity nurse."

Anne stops short. *"Really?"*

"I haven't said that before?"

"If you have, I didn't think you were serious. You want to go to the *desert*?"

"Not all of Palestine is a desert, Anne."

"More of a desert than New York or London."

"So? Maybe I'm more interested in doing something for the good of our people."

Silence. Anne frowns at a stack of wrinkled invoices.

"What?" says Margot.

"Nothing," Anne tells her. "It's only, as usual, you're the selfless one. Delivering babies in Zion for the good of the Jews."

"I'm not always the 'selfless' one."

"Compared to me you are."

"Well, maybe you can be a *writer* for the good of the Jews," Margot suggests.

Anne blinks, frowns slightly at the paperwork. A writer for the good of the Jews. To lift the Jews from the depth of their suffering and show them in the light that God has always intended them to be seen, as examples of goodness. Is that too grand a thing for a girl to imagine? "Maybe I can be," is all she says.

At supper she tests out her desires on the assembled onderduikers. That is, to live in a far-flung capital. To become a famous writer of some sort, adored by the world.

"Oh, *my*," Mrs. van Pels comments wryly. "Doubt *she'll* be finding a husband anytime soon."

"*Mother*," Peter complains. His hair is its usual tousled mess. But his face is growing thinner, more manly. His jaw hardening.

"All I'm saying is the truth," his mother replies with a sly wink. She is getting thinner, too, but from twenty months of dwindling food quality. Her face sags now. Her rouged lips look waxy. "A *career* girl," she says with mocking significance.

"You'll have to learn better French if you intend to live in Paris," Margot tells Anne with a thin whisper of superiority. "Votre français est plutôt atroce."

Anne replies sourly, "Aller manger un escargot, s'il vous plaît."

"Well, *I* for one am happy to hear that Anne has ambition," her mother chimes in surprisingly. "Though, really, Anne. Paris? New York? Why should you need to go so far away? I don't understand."

"Maybe to get away from constant criticism," Anne says, more harshly than she intends to. It's just that she's so easily rubbed wrong by adults. Though now the table has gone silent, except for Her Majesty Kerli van Pels, who snorts at Anne's cheekiness.

"*Well.*" Mr. Pfeffer offers a snide look down his nose as he helps himself to more of Mrs. van P.'s overcooked potato casserole. "Not just a writer but a *famous* writer? *Really?*"

"You find that so difficult to imagine, Mr. Pfeffer?" Anne snaps back.

Pfeffer had been well groomed and a meticulous dresser when he first arrived. Now his collars and cuffs are frayed and his hair is a dismal swath of gray brushed carelessly back from his forehead. *"Difficult?"* he says mockingly. "It's only that writers must possess *talent*, mustn't they? By definition, that is, they possess talent for something *other* than making trouble."

Anne shoots to her feet, ready to shriek, but her mother is quick with a reprimand.

"Anne. Sit back *down,"* she commands. Her face has grown tighter, her features more pronounced, as if someone has been slowly whittling away at her. "Donnerwetter, child, we're in the middle of *supper.*"

"So you're just going to allow him to *speak to me* like that?" Anne demands to know.

"Anneke, please. Sit back down," Pim advises. "Let's not upset everyone's digestion."

Anne scowls but plops back down in her chair, pouting. Bep is seated beside her. She has joined the gang of onderduikers this evening for supper and looks up from her plate. "Well, *I* for one would love to see New York City," she says.

Mummy sounds puzzled by this. "Would you, Bep? *Actually?*" Perhaps she cannot imagine a young lady visiting so far from home. But Bep sounds eager.

"Oh, yes," she says. "I've dreamed about standing atop the tallest building in the world and gazing out at the horizon, high up as a bird."

"Good for you, Bep," says Pim, always willing to be encouraging. "New York is really the most astonishing city I have ever known."

"Pim was in New York when he was a young man," Anne explains happily. "When he was still a bachelor. He worked for a college friend, whose father ran a big department store. What was his name, Pim?" she asks. "I don't remember."

"Straus. Nathan Straus. But his friends all called him Charley."

"Maybe we should plan on going there *together,* Bep," Anne says, only too keen to plan the future. "Both of us could view the world from the top of a skyscraper."

"That would be wonderful, Anne," Bep replies, but this draws a grouchy response from Hermann van Pels.

"When I was a lad, my old man would have whacked me good with a rod if *I* were ever as mouthy as this one. So now you want Bep tangled up in your silly daydreams, too?" he grumbles. "That's—"

"They're not *silly*," Peter cuts in on his father's grumping. "Anne is very smart. *Very* smart," he defiantly declares, to which his mother responds with a snide grimace.

"There's an old saying, Anne, and I think it applies: You are smart, smart, smart—but you are *a fool*."

"*Mum*, that's an *awful* thing to say," Peter shoots back. "If Anne thinks she's going to be a famous writer in New York or Paris or wherever, then *that's* what's going to happen," he insists, prompting his father to roll his eyes.

"And who are *you*? Mr. Gypsy Fortune-Teller?" his father wonders loudly, shoveling some stewed onion into his big mouth. A touch on his arm from his wife.

"Putti," Mrs. van Pels reproves her husband lightly. "Let it go. They're young. Let them have their folly."

"*Excuse me!* But I *really* can't take another breath in this company," Anne announces sharply, pushing up from the table, feeling her eyes wet as she abandons the room.

Her mother calls after her, "*Anne!* Anne, come back here and clean your plate." But Anne has no intention of following orders.

"Let Mr. Pfeffer clean my plate for me," she calls back over her shoulder. "He can always find room for another helping!"

Mr. Pfeffer looks up innocently from his plate in mid-chew and swallows. "Now, what did I say to provoke *that*?"

Up in the attic, Anne has taken refuge, forcefully cradling Peter's cat, Mouschi. Mouschi is not a perfect angel like Anne's cat, Moortje, the poor abandoned thing, but he's still a warm beating heart. Outside, the branches of a lofty horse chestnut tree with a majestic crown of leaves brush the window glass. She has learned to find comfort in this tree. A tree that has stood for decades or more, still patiently allowing the breeze to rustle its branches. It calms her.

She wipes her eyes quickly when she hears someone climb the ladder and recognizes the voice.

"Anne?" Peter approaches her with a careful demeanor, as if she might detonate unexpectedly. She turns to Peter's cat for comfort, pressing her lips against Mouschi's soft, furry head. "Adults are impossible," she declares in a wounded tone. Wounded, but perhaps willing to be mended by a few kind words.

Peter stops and leans against one of the wooden posts. At first he sounds boyish and wounded, too. "My paapje is sure a pain in the rump. No doubt. He's always there to criticize."

"And what about your *mother*? She's not exactly blameless either," Anne feels compelled to point out. Maybe she should have been pleased that Peter had risen to her defense against his parents, but really she was slightly irked, because coming out of *his* mouth her dreams *did* ring a bit ridiculous. And now she's irritated that he sounds more like he's complaining rather than trying to actually comfort her. Can boys really be so dense?

"Mum's not so bad," he says with a shrug. "She doesn't *try* to be mean. It just comes out that way sometimes."

Anne is not at all sure she wants to agree with this. She finds his optimism painful but keeps her mouth buttoned. Finally Peter manages to find a spot on the floor beside her. The attic is lit by a heavy white moon that silvers the branches of the chestnut tree. She feels the presence of his body beside her like a magnet, but he's gone silent, so maybe it's up to her to break through. "You know, Peter," she says, "I'm very happy that you're here."

He seems surprised to hear this, but happily so. "You *are*?"

"Yes, of course. I really have no one else to talk to."

"What about your sister? You have her."

"That's different. Margot's my sister, yes, and of course that means something. But we're so often poles apart. I can't *truly* confide in her. I can't truly confide in *anyone*."

"Well . . ." he says, but seems to fumble around in his head for a path to finish that sentence.

Anne looks up at him directly and takes in those big, deep eyes and that shock of curls. "Well what?"

He looks at her, too, and shrugs, rubbing the cat's head with his knuckles. "You can always confide in me," he tells her. "If you want to."

Three weeks later, in the middle of April, Anne feels her heart purring as she scribbles desperately into her diary, her hand trying to keep up with her heartbeat.

> *I can't tell you, Kitty, the feeling that ran through me. I was too happy for words, and I think he was, too. At nine-thirty we stood up. Peter put on his tennis shoes so he wouldn't make much noise on his nightly round of the building, and I was standing next to him. How I suddenly made the right movement, I don't know, but before we went downstairs, he gave me a kiss, through my hair, half on my left cheek and half on my ear. I tore downstairs without looking back, and I long so much for today.*

5

RADIO ORANGE

Dearest Kitty,
   Mr. Bolkestein, the Cabinet Minister, speaking on the
Dutch broadcast from London, said that after the war a
collection would be made of diaries and letters dealing
with the war. Of course, everyone pounced on my diary.

—Anne Frank,
from her diary,
29 March 1944

Jews are regularly killed by machine-gun fire, hand
grenades—and even poison gas.

—BBC Home Service,
6:00 P.M. news,
9 July 1942

1944

The Achterhuis
Prinsengracht 263
Hidden Annex

OCCUPIED NETHERLANDS

The razzias continue. According to what Miep tells us, more Jews have been netted with every passing day, many of them family friends from the Merwedeplein. The Kaplans, the Levitskys, the Rosenblits. Eva Rosenblit was in the same class as Anne and always laughed at her jokes. Miep has even heard a rumor that Hanneli's father was arrested, and maybe Hanneli with him. Anne tries to picture it. Lies being driven through the streets and packed into the rear of a German lorry, helpless. At the mercy of monsters. But it's too terrible. She can't allow such a thought to take root. She must believe that God is looking after Hanneli as closely as he is Anne Frank.

Peter has constructed a "moffen sleeve" for the radio. A loop aerial made of wooden slats and doorbell wire that can sift out the Hun's jamming signals, so that the radio reception remains clear and unimpeded by mof interference. He gabs on and on about medium range and shortwave bands, which Anne finds both impressive and boring. Can that be? Anyway, according to the latest programs, there's plenty of action on the Eastern Front. The Red Army has retaken Odessa and is ousting the mof from the Crimea, but on the Western Front there is still no invasion. Mr. van Pels is constantly griping about the English "slowpokes" with their tea and crumpets. Pim, on the other hand, points out that even with the Americans in the war, it cannot be an easy task to mass the kind of force necessary to penetrate Hitler's so-called Atlantic Wall, much less prepare to transport it across the English Channel.

Anne tries not to listen too much. She does not feel brave enough to contemplate an unending occupation by the mof, but neither is she confident enough to live on hope for an Allied liberation anytime soon. Instead she wants to live in the moment, which is why it's always so nice to have Bep for supper in their stuffy little hideout. She anchors them all, in a way. A real person from the real world outside this building. Mummy loves to cook for Bep, always praising her for her good appetite, no matter what's dished onto her plate. The van Pelses quit their constant bickering around her and save their criticisms for another time. Bep takes it all in thoughtfully, as if Mr. van Pels may very well be right, even if it's absolute rubbish he's spouting. She offers Anne a secret wink as he announces how Bep is quite the intelligent young lady. Bravo, Bep! Even old Pfeffer has compliments for her, usually followed by a list of indispensables that Bep should do her very absolute *best* to obtain for him.

After supper, when the dishes are washed, Anne sometimes follows Bep down the steps as far as their side of the door, hidden by the swinging bookcase that is the line of demarcation between freedom and constraint. Between life in the actual world and this strange limited existence in hiding. They often confide in each other on this trip down the stairs, Anne and she, sitting on the lower steps, away from the listening ears. Anne tells her about the romance that has flowered with Peter. Shy but marvelous Peter van Pels, who as it turns out is not a blockhead after all but in fact the focus of her heart's desire. She tells Bep of kisses she has received from the boy. About the fluttery dreaminess that dazzles her when they touch and the humid, salty feelings she can taste after their nightly kissing sessions have concluded. And as the months pass and the slow undertow of disappointment eventually drains Anne's feelings for Peter, she tells Bep about that, too.

For her part, Bep confesses her fears for her boyfriend, Maurits, who went into hiding rather than report to the moffen as a labor conscript. It's been months and months, and their separation is taking a toll on them. They pass letters to each other, but there seems to be less and less to say in them. When she tells Anne this tonight, there are clear tears in Bep's eyes behind her oval-framed glasses. Anne puts her arms around Bep, who begins to cry harder.

"Bep? *Bep,* what is it?"

But Bep only shakes her head, wiping at her tears by pushing her fingers under her glasses. "I just worry so much about you. About all of you. I'm sorry, I know I shouldn't be saying this. But you've become so dear to me, and I can't help but fear for you. Out in the streets, the Germans have turned brutal. Even worse than before. Maybe they're getting scared that they're losing the war, I don't know, but all I need to do is see those awful lorries packed with the soldiers and bristling with guns." She swallows hard and shakes her head. "I'm terrified for you, for myself, for everyone. Even in the office, every time I hear a car squeak to a halt in the street, my heart practically jumps out the window."

"Well, *that* would be something to see," Anne offers, trying to cheer Bep out of her tears.

Bep hiccups a slim laugh and breathes in deeply, regaining herself as best she can. "And upstairs you're all so welcoming. You're living in danger daily, yet your mother makes me feel so at home at the table."

"She can do that on occasion," Anne is willing to admit. "But it's not us, it's *you.* You and Miep. Mr. Kleiman and Mr. Kugler. When you come upstairs, it's a breath of freedom for us all. Believe me, the minute you leave, we all revert back to our stifled, irritable old selves and the arguments and complaints are renewed with a vengeance." Anne says this with a smile, for Bep's sake, though she wishes it weren't so absolutely true.

A foot scuffs a floorboard above. "Anne?" She hears her mother calling from the top of the stairs. She doesn't sound cross, particularly, only fretful.

"Yes, Mummy?" she answers, knowing the fun's now over.

"Let Bep go home. It's time to come back up and get ready for bed."

"Yes, Mummy," Anne replies dutifully. She hugs Bep good-bye and glumly trudges up the steps. At the top her mother shuts the door and says, "I don't like you sitting down there. It makes me anxious."

What *doesn't*? Anne wants to reply. But she stops herself. "Mummy, I've been down to Papa's office a million times. Why should you worry about me sitting on the steps all of a sudden?"

"I don't know, Anne," her mother answers truthfully. "But I do. It's just a feeling I've been having. A kind of ominous feeling. I can't explain it. Your papa says it's just nerves that we're all undergoing because the end of the war could be close, and maybe he's right. I don't know. I only know that I feel what I feel. Do you think you can humor me?"

And for a moment Anne sees her mother without the sting of judgment. She sees the unfiltered candor in her mother's face. "All right, Mummy," she says. "If it makes you feel better. All right."

In her diary Anne turns herself inside out and stares into all her inner recesses. Splashing ink on the paper, sometimes boisterously, sometimes angrily, often critically, perhaps even artfully. She has learned to depend on words to see herself more clearly. Her demands, her frustrations and furies, her unobtainable ideals, and her relentless desires, all a reflection of the lonely self she confesses only to the page, because if people aren't patient, paper is. It is often a mess, filling line after line, until she runs out of room in her lovely red tartan daybook and has to resort to filling up whatever stray bits of paper Miep and Bep can scrounge. Then, at the end of March, they are all listening to *Radio Oranje* on a Wednesday evening down in the private office when the education minister from the exile government in London broadcasts a speech advising the Dutch people to keep their diaries as a record for after the war, and it strikes her: Perhaps her diary could be important to *others* as well. A record for the Dutch, a record for the Jews, a record for all who have felt imprisoned. The next day she begins to *rewrite*. Not as a child confiding her thoughts to imaginary friends but as a chronicler of wartime. A true writer. It gives her a vision of herself to broadcast. A vision of the woman she should become, molded by what she is already feeling in her heart: a terrible and ecstatic slavery to words. This is what she could never explain to anyone. Not Peter, not Margot, not Mummy. Not even Pim.

Now she finds that she zealously steals every minute she can from the daily routine of survival in order to reinvent her diary. To make it into something other than it started as, the unbosoming of a thirteen-year-old ugly duckling.

To make it a book.

By the end of the first week of revision after Mr. Bolkestein's message, Anne has rewritten seventy-one pages by hand on loose-leaf sheets of flimsy wartime paper. She finds that the craft required in rewriting can numb her to the fear that still often seizes her, as if even the worst of the brutality swirling about them can be managed.

> *If it's that bad in Holland, what must it be like in those far-away and uncivilized places where the Germans are sending them? We assume that most of them are being murdered. The English radio says they're being gassed. Perhaps that's the quickest way to die.*

6

BURGLARS

"Police in building, up to bookcase . . ."

—Anne Frank,
from her diary,
11 April 1944

1944

The Achterhuis
Prinsengracht 263
Hidden Annex

OCCUPIED NETHERLANDS

9 April

Anne is reading in the common area. At nine o'clock everyone begins drifting toward bedtime, when there's a noise from belowstairs. Faces rise but then settle back into place. No one pays much attention, since everyone knows that Peter likes to take his bath in Pim's office because he's too shy to do it elsewhere, and he often makes a bit of noise lugging the big metal tub about. But then Peter appears, fully dressed, and knocks with quiet urgency on the door to the common room. Anne does her best to prepare a smile for him, even though his appearance simply doesn't have the same impact on her as it did. Still, she doesn't want to snub him or hurt his feelings. But then she's surprised when the boy isn't there for her at all but instead asks *Pim* to help him with a difficult assignment in his English translations. Pim sets down his book, his head tilts with a thought, and then immediately he's up and out the door without a word, but not before Anne's suspicions are put on alert. "That sounds very fishy to me," she informs Margot. "Since when does Peter go out of his way to do his lessons?" And why did he so pointedly avoid eye contact with her? "This is obviously a ploy—they're hiding something," she says, but Mummy is on her feet, her face gone bloodless as Pim suddenly returns with a tight expression.

"Otto?"

"Not now, Edith, please," he instructs tensely, and rounds up the other men with a sharp whisper. "Mr. van Pels, Mr. Pfeffer, if you please," he says, and the next moment they're hastening downstairs, feet thumping down the steps to the front building.

"*Mummy? Mummy, what's going on?*" she asks, just as Mrs. van Pels skitters into the room dressed in her robe and old carpet slippers, obviously already scared stiff by the sudden commotion of the men's exit. Her voice low but shrill: "*What's happening? What's going on?*"

"*Burglars are breaking in,*" Anne answers in a panicked hiss.

"We don't *know* that," Margot insists.

"Girls, come away from the door and stay quiet," their mother commands, drawing them into a circle at the rear of the room, though they can't stay quiet.

"What do you think is *happening*?" Margot whispers.

"I don't know, but don't *worry,*" Mummy says. "I'm sure it's under control. Wouldn't you think so, Mrs. van Pels? If things weren't under control, we'd know by now."

"I can't hear a sound," Mrs. van Pels tells them. "Why can't we hear a *sound*?"

"Maybe they met the burglars head-on," Anne proposes. "Do you think they *could have,* Mummy?"

"Anne."

"Maybe they're fighting them off right now."

"We'd *hear* them if they were fighting," Margot maintains, but with more hope than confidence. "Wouldn't we, Mummy? Wouldn't we hear them?"

"Girls, this doesn't help. Scaring yourselves silly," their mother declares. "I'm sure that no one is fighting with anyone." But her tone is not exactly reassuring, and silence strikes them mute when a sharp bang sounds from downstairs, followed by the sound of Mr. van Pels shouting, "Police!"

No one says a word as the minutes pass, till finally they hear footsteps approaching from below. Pim appears first, his face tight with nerves. "Douse the lights," he instructs hoarsely. "And everyone upstairs as quietly as possible. Burglars have forced out a panel of the warehouse door."

Anne swallows hard. "*Pim,*" she gasps.

"They're gone now, frightened off. But we expect to have the police in the building very soon."

Up above where the van Pelses sleep beside the kitchen, Margot drapes a sweater over a bed lamp, providing a ghost light that pools on the floorboards. Waiting in the dark, no talking, only hearts drumming. No use of the toilet, too much noise, so Peter's metal wastepaper basket is substituted for the commode, for those who can't stand to hold it. The odor sours the air. But still no conversation, only dreadful whispers. Only breathing, one breath in, one breath out, anticipating the arrival of the police. *The police!*

When footsteps are heard coming up from below, time stops. A terrible racket ensues as someone rattles the bookcase, and Anne shivers brutally. For an instant she believes that they are about to die. "Now we're finished," she whispers to the air, to God, to nobody. One aggressive rattle and then another, bang, bang, bang!

But then nothing.

Nothing follows but the sound of footsteps descending, and *then* nothing but silence. A ripple of relief passes through the room.

But in the aftermath it's suggested by the fainter hearts among them that if the police ever *did* advance beyond the bookcase, Anne's diary would be a bombshell primed to explode. It would betray not only those in hiding but those who have risked all to help them. Anne is appalled when even Pim admits to the logic of this fear, which only encourages Mr. van P. to declare that, for the sake of all, it should be burned.

Burned.

Anne feels something plummet inside her, but at the same time she stands up. She hears a hardness in her voice that surprises even her. "If my diary goes," she declares, "I go, too."

Silence.

And then it's Mummy who speaks. Mummy of all people. "Never mind about that. Right now we should simply thank God," she instructs. "Thank God we have been saved."

7

THE FREEDOM OF SUNLIGHT

No one is spared. The sick, the elderly, children, babies
and pregnant women—all are marched to their death. . . .
And all because they're Jews.

—Anne Frank,
from her diary,
19 November 1942

"The Gestapo is here."

—Victor Kugler,
4 August 1944

1944

The Achterhuis
Rear Annex of Prinsengracht 263
The Canal Ring

OCCUPIED NETHERLANDS

Twenty-five months in hiding

It is a Friday, the fourth of August. A warm and muggy day. The closed rooms smell of wood rot and stale air. Anne and Margot are working on an assignment from their mail-order shorthand course when the Grüne Polizei barge into their lives in the form of a mof sergeant and his gang of Dutch cohorts from the NSB. The Dutch detectives are dressed like civilians and carry their revolvers loose in their coat pockets, but the sergeant in charge is an Oberscharführer in the SS Sicherheitsdienst. He wears a uniform of hunter green with a leather peaked cap that sports a death's-head. A Totenkopf. Anne keeps staring at it as he bellows his commands, the silvery skull over crossed bones. Is it staring back at her? Below the peak of his cap, the Oberscharführer has a sulky civil servant's face with a pouty frown. But *then,* as it turns out, he is *quite* the generous spirit. He permits them a full *hour* to pack their pitiful onderduiker belongings instead of the regulation ten minutes, after he finds that Pim had been a reserve lieutenant in the previous war. "Good God, man. Why didn't you come forward when you had the *chance*?" The Oberscharführer is mystified. It's obvious that the small tin soldier inside him has come to attention in the presence of a superior officer. "They would have treated you well," he insists. "You would have been sent to Theresienstadt with other Jews of worth." The mof is bewildered. But Pim has no answer for him. How can he possibly?

· · ·

In Anne's memory the day will be broken into shards. Folding clothes into her backpack. Wrapping her toothbrush in a handkerchief with a sliver of soap. Picking up her curling iron, then putting it back down. Folding the brassiere that Margot had given her, tucking it modestly under a pair of woolen stockings. Helping pack a bit of food into a bag while silent tears glisten on her mother's cheeks. The dreadful disbelief stamped on everyone's face.

But then there is the sunshine. Walking out from two years in hiding into the summer brightness. It was such a surprise to feel warmth on her face so directly. For an instant she had simply enjoyed the freedom of sunlight before being loaded into the rear of a dark lorry.

8

BOULEVARD DES MISÈRES

Ten thousand have passed through this place, the clothed and the naked, the old and the young, the sick and the healthy—and I am left to live and work and stay cheerful.

—Etty Hillesum,
letters written from
Kamp Westerbork,
10 July 1943

One is certain only of death.

—Jewish proverb

1944

Polizeiliches Judendurchgangslager
KAMP WESTERBORK
Drenthe Province
130 kilometers north of Amsterdam

OCCUPIED NETHERLANDS

**Former Jewish refugee camp now under the control
of the SS Security Police and SD**

After their arrest on that hot day in the first week of August, they are
confined in the cellar of the SD headquarters in the Euterpestraat,
before being transported to the House of Detention I in the Kleine-
Gartmanplantsoen. There they spend two terrible nights suffering
from the stench of a polluted canal before being taken to Centraal
Station under a Dutch police guard and boarded onto a scruffy passenger train with the shades closed and the windows nailed shut. The
train bumps down the tracks of the Staatslijn C with the carloads of
other captive Jews, branching off at Hooghalen to the final leg of
track leading to the so-called Polizeiliches Judendurchgangslager:
the Jewish Transit Camp isolated in the mosquito-infested moorland
of Drenthe Province.

This is Kamp Westerbork, a barbed-wire enclosure of more than
a hundred barracks. Once it had been a refugee camp for young, un-
married German Jews pouring over the border to escape their Fatherland. But when the Nazi occupation began, the SS were delighted
to find that such a facility had so conveniently been established for
them in the Dutch lowlands, and with only a few alterations in the
amenities, such as the electrification of the fencing, they transformed
the camp from a refuge into a prison.

In a large hall filled with the clatter of typewriters, the Franks wait in one of many long queues. They have, at the moment, lost track of the van Pelses and Pfeffer, but the family is still together. Anne notices that after so long in hiding, their skin has turned as white as bleached flour from lack of sunlight. They have become living ghosts.

"Mother," Margot suddenly announces, "you're shivering."

And so she is. Both Margot and Pim move to comfort her, but Edith takes a step away.

"Please don't," is all she can squeeze from her lips as she hugs herself, quaking, eyes boring into nothing. But she does not resist when Pim alone takes her into his embrace, and Anne is struck by a bolt of guilt. To see her mother so far from comfort, untouchable by her daughters. She cannot help but feel that she is responsible. How many times did Mummy try to get close to her, and how many times did Anne shove her away?

Their assignment vouchers are clear. The place where all eight of them are billeted is a barracks with its own barbed-wire enclosure, because all Jewish onderduikers are interred in the camp *within* the camp: the so-called S-Block. *S* for Straffe. The Punishment Barracks. Punishment for the crime of having tried to save themselves by going into hiding. Because, of course, in the eyes of the Grossdeutsches Reich, onderduiker Jews are criminal Jews. Criminal Jews are forced to wear red patches on their dungarees and rough wooden clogs instead of shoes. They are assigned to the dirtiest work details. Men have their heads shaved and dig latrines in labor Kommandos, while women are sent to Section XII to salvage depleted batteries, splitting them with a mallet and chisel. The battery tar sticks to Anne's skin. The carbon bars turn her fingers a muddy red color. Everyone chokes on the chemical dust; the coughing is like an underrhythm to their work. *But* at least there are people to talk to and jokes to tell. Sand blows everywhere, driven by the moorland winds. It grits her teeth, and the mosquitoes leave welts the size of pennies, but the air is fresh and the sunlight unrationed. It is livable.

Except for Tuesdays.

There is a long, straight road that bisects Kamp Westerbork—the only paved road in the flat mud plain. The Jews call it the Boulevard des

Misères, because of the stretch of graveled railbed that runs beside it.
Every Saturday a train of boxcars enters the camp, between eight and
eleven in the morning, and comes to a steaming halt on the track. And
there it sits until Tuesday morning, waiting to be filled with human
freight. The metal signs bolted to the side of the boxcars tell the story:

WESTERBORK—AUSCHWITZ
AUSCHWITZ—WESTERBORK

Inside the barbed-wire boundaries of Westerbork, the Jews administer
themselves. They police themselves. The Jewish Kommando charged
with keeping order is known as the Ordnungsdienst, or more simply
as the OD. They are often thuggish and brutal in their duties, these
men, but luckily the head OD man for the S-Block has a reputation for
decency, so Anne takes this as a good sign. Perhaps God is watching
over them still.

Men and women are separated during the night. The Frank women
share a three-tier bunk bed, with dirty burlap sacks filled with straw
for mattresses. Mummy is still speechless most of the time. Numb,
though she cried when a brute with a visored cap and the Magen David
on his arm stole her wedding ring. It must have hurt her so much to lose
that ring, and to think that it was another Jew who stole it from her!

One night after lights-out, Anne is struck by a nightmare even
though she is still awake. Risking the abuse of their barracks elder,
she slips out from the bottom bunk and presses her chin to the second tier, where her sister sleeps. A thin glow from the camp lamps
seeps through the poorly mended shutters on the windows.

"*Margot*," she whispers. She can feel needles of fear heating the
back of her neck. It will mean some very bad trouble if she is caught
out of her bunk. "Margot, wake up." Anne prods her.

Margot does not move. She wakes without any kind of a start or
surprise, her eyes simply open, reflecting a wet light. "What *is* it?" she
hisses at Anne.

"Margot, I'm afraid Mummy and Pim are going to die," Anne
breathes.

Margot's eyes widen enough to show that perhaps she, too, has had such a fear herself. "Anne . . ." she whispers.

"Promise me you'll stay with me, Margot," Anne begs her. "Promise me that whatever happens to us, you'll stay with me. I couldn't stand being alone any longer. I think I would die."

"I promise," Margot tells her, reaching out from under the dirty blanket and taking her sister's hand. "I promise I will always stay with you, Anne. I will always stay with you."

At that moment Anne loves Margot entirely. Loves her like she has never loved her before. Perhaps that makes it so much harder when the news comes. First as a rumor, then as a fact. There's to be special transport. Not on Tuesday but this Sunday. And so, on the night of the second of September, their barracks elder makes the announcement to the entire population of the S-Block. "On the orders of the SS-Obersturmführer und Lagerkommandant, all inmates of Punishment Barracks, men and women without exception, will assemble for transport tomorrow." Including Anne. Including Margot. Including Mummy and Pim and all the other former inhabitants of the Achterhuis.

Morning comes to the Boulevard des Misères. The OD Flying Column in their fluttering capes and brown coveralls are brusque but not exactly brutal, since it's known that the Herr Kommandant prefers to keep things orderly. No panic. No violence, no untidiness. The Herr Kommandant is oh, so very humane, you see. Oh, so very handsome is the Herr Kommandant. Oh, so very polite. He ranges up and down the length of track in his immaculate SS uniform, trimly tailored, perfectly coiffed, confirming that all is in order. All is well. Assisting the elderly. Handing an infant up to a mother. Waving to the children. Anne sees their little faces, the children from the camp school, lined up by their teachers, loaded into the rail cars by the Ordedienst, cooperative and unafraid, like good little boys and girls.

When it's their turn, two OD men lift Anne up like she is nothing, and she has the briefest sensation of weightlessness before she stumbles forward into the car. Margot is right behind her, and then Mummy, and then Pim, and then they are shoved deeper into the mass of people before the doors of the freight car are rolled shut and Anne hears the heavy, irrevocable clang of the lock.

Inside, she and Margot are huddled together, gripping each other's hand. Only the narrowest cracks of light interrupt the darkness that encloses them all. A day earlier they were eating thin but edible broth with a short ration of hard-crusted brown bread. They were walking in the open air, absorbing the sunlight. The precious sunlight. But now they are all packed into this murky darkness. With so many sardined inside a freight car, the communal act of breathing takes on the low-pitched rhythm of a bellows. Mummy and Pim are trying to protect them with their bodies from the crush of people, though Mummy is whimpering, and not even Pim can comfort her. There's a heavy rumbling noise. Metal clanks. The carriage lumbers forward, and Anne feels its sudden lurch in the pit of her belly. It grabs her like a hook, and a claw of utter, helpless terror snags her. The locomotive lets go with a high, mournful howl as it leaves the camp perimeters.

The journey will be hideous. No space, no air, no food, no place to use the toilet. The wailing. The stench of shit and vomit. The sobs and moans. A trainload of Jews rolling into the unknown horror. But in a gruesome way, Anne will treasure the memory. It will be the last time they are all together as a family. Pim, Mummy, Margot, and Anne. The last of the Franks.

Three days hence cars and cargo arrive at their destination, a converted cavalry garrison in the marshlands of southern Poland near a village that the Germans call Auschwitz.

9

A PRAYER

Sometimes when I stand in some corner of the camp, my feet planted on Your earth, my eyes raised toward Your Heaven, tears sometimes run down my face, tears of deep emotion and gratitude. At night, too, when I lie in bed and rest in You, O God, tears of gratitude run down my face, and that is my prayer. Amen.

—Etty Hillesum,
a prayer written in
Auschwitz-Birkenau
before her death in
March 1943

1944

"*Mummy.*" Her sister is frantic. "Mummy, we're going to *die* here, I know it!"

"*Shut up,* Margot," Anne bites out, shivering against their mother's body. "You can't say that!"

"I *can* say it, because it's *true!*" Margot shouts back, her anger raw and shredding, her face like a crumpled wad of paper.

"Quiet, girls, *quiet,*" their mother demands. The three of them are crammed in with seven others onto the bottom pallet of the hardwood koje that serves as their "bed," so the matted layer of straw they lie upon reeks like a latrine, since shit and piss can only travel south. They are all starved to madness, and freezing, but in this nightmare Mummy might have found her true self. Anne is astonished by the transformation. She feels shamed by all the enmity that once divided them and is so grateful for even a thin shield of protection. Separated from Pim, her mother has become a different person, one whose every word and action seems to reflect the strength of her single purpose: keeping her daughters alive. And even though her body is a shrunken glove of yellow skin stretched over bones, she's making them a promise. "We're going to make it through this. We *are.*"

"But, Mummy," Margot breathes, always the logical one, "how *can* you say that? How can you make such a *promise*? We're a step below the lice here," she says.

"Mummy, make her shut up!" Anne demands, firing her angriest look at her sister. "You heard what Mummy said! She said she is going to *protect* us!"

"Protect us from the *cold,* Anne? Protect us from *dysentery?* You think anyone can protect us from that? Stop being an idiot!"

"And *you* stop being a bitch!"

"*Anne,*" Mummy snaps at her.

"Well, she *is* a bitch, Mummy. She's a stupid *bitch!*"

But suddenly her mother's arm is wrapped around her with a tender power, enveloping her, as Anne hears her mother's voice burrowing into her ear. "It's *all right,* my child. My baby. It's *all right.*" Rocking her so slowly. Whispering, "My baby, my little girl. I know you're so angry. So very angry. And so very afraid. But we are here, and we are *together,* and we are *alive.* Both my girls are here with me and alive." Shifting, she scoops her children into the circle of her arms. "Both of you are here with me and alive," she says. "And for that I thank God. And I pray to him that *he* will protect you from the cold when I cannot. And that *he* will protect you from sickness when I cannot. And that *he* will guide us through this trial. I am so *proud,*" her mother whispers. "So proud of you girls. My beautiful Margot and my beautiful Anne. You are so strong. So very strong. And I know that God is watching over you. I *know* it. And that he will bless you and keep you whole."

Anne can feel the tears chilling her eyes as she clutches her mother's hand. "Amen, Mummy," she weeps. "Amen."

"Amen," her sister weeps.

"Amen," their mother whispers.

A prayer offered in the swamps of Poland.

In the cold of Barracks Block 29.

Frauenlager BIa.

Auschwitz II.

Birkenau.

10

HOPE

Where there's hope, there's life. It fills us with fresh courage and makes us strong again.

—Anne Frank,
from her diary,
6 June 1944

And so I was standing there in the cold, and I was waiting. And then suddenly, I heard somebody calling me . . . and it was Anne.

—Hanneli "Lies" Pick-Goslar,
recalling Bergen-Belsen in
Anne Frank Remembered, a documentary

1945

Konzentrationslager (KL)
BERGEN-BELSEN
Kleines Frauenlager
The Lüneburg Heath

THE GERMAN REICH

Twelve weeks before liberation

Clinging together, shivering, Anne and Margot are motherless now. The evacuation that followed the final selection in Birkenau has left Mummy behind in the infirmary and orphaned them. A forced march along icy roads, loaded with panicked Wehrmacht troops retreating in the face of the Red Army, was followed by a transport in a putrid boxcar without water or food before they were dumped onto this ghastly heath, the ground crisp with sleet, where they have been abandoned to the rawest elements. This camp has no gas chambers, but then, they're not needed. The SS stay healthy on their side of the barbed wire and let starvation, the bitter winter, and pestilence do the führer's work. The prisoner shacks teem with disease. Typhus travels in the barracks dust of every scuffle over every scrap of bread. Within the first six weeks, Margot has become so sick that she's too weak to walk. Her voice has been replaced by an entrenched cough. The massive tent, where they were first sheltered, collapsed under the hammering of a thunderstorm, and now they are billeted in a frigid, louse-ridden block, packed together on the bottom pallet of a wooden bunk. This is Bergen-Belsen, and here the angel of death has made his home.

Except. Except there is *one* spot in this wretched cesspool where life is permitted. It is the Sternlager, the Star Camp, the *Free* Camp, where the so-called privilegierte Juden are held. Jews whom the SS think might still be valuable as hostages. There's *food* in the

Sternlager, bad food but food nonetheless. The inmates wear their own clothes in the Sternlager, instead of Kazet stripes or castoffs from the dead; their heads have not been shaved, and whole families have been kept intact. The barbed-wire fence that divides this paradise from what's called the Kleines Frauenlager is tightly crammed with straw, but there are points of desperation where the straw has been torn away. Points where a portal has been opened between life and death.

It is through such a portal, no larger than a fist, that Anne has been reunited with her dearest Hanneli. Her dearest, *dearest* Lies. While Anne was snug in the Achterhuis, hidden from the German death grip, Hanneli had filled her nightmares. Her sleep had been shredded by dreams of her sweet Lies trapped behind the cruel barbed wire of a Nazi camp, her clothes in rags, freezing, starving, and begging for mercy while Anne slept tucked under thick blankets in an attic hideout and ate enough food to fill her belly. Anne had wept for her. Cried out her name. But in Bergen-Belsen nightmares are turned inside out, and it is Hanneli who receives Red Cross parcels and Anne who shivers in sickened misery on the opposite side of the wire.

A winter darkness bereft of stars. Anne stumbles across the snow-smeared ground toward the fence. It is so intensely wonderful to see Lies, and so intensely horrid. To find her alive, still a human being, Anne is enraptured. And for a moment, as she peers through the fence's portal at Hanneli's pale, oval face, she loves Lies with every inch of her being. Hanneli alive! But in the next instant, Anne's mouth runs bitter. They sob together as their fingers touch through the barbed wire, but Anne can see the horror reflected in Hanneli's tears. She knows what her friend sees. Anne has been reduced to a diseased animal, filthy, infested with lice and scratching herself bloody, her eyes swimming with fever, her head shorn, naked but for a horse blanket clutched around her body, her louse-infested rags discarded. Anne cries that she is freezing. That she is starving. That the lice are driving her *mad,* and Lies cries with her. For her.

"*Anne,* what are you *doing* in this place? Why aren't you in *Switzerland*?" Hanneli demands, as if maybe Anne has tricked her somehow. Anne can only cry as she admits the truth.

"That was only a ruse," she sobs. "Really we were hiding in the rear of Papa's office building. The whole time."

"Oh, my God. All this time in the middle of Amsterdam?"

"Until we were arrested. Lies, I am so *cold*," Anne moans. "And there's nothing to eat here. We've all been left to starve. Do you have some food you can share? *Please*, Lies. I'm so hungry. *So hungry*."

"Yes, yes, I'll get you something, I promise. Come back here to-morrow night, and I'll have something for you."

So a night later Hanneli has bundled up a parcel from the Red Cross packages and heaves it over the wire. But there are many rats on Anne's side of the fence, animal and human alike, and a very large specimen of the human variety scurries out of the darkness and snatches the bundle from Anne's hands. She screams, and then she weeps. She weeps not just because she is starving but also because Lies is so beautiful. Because her dear Hanneli has something that she will *not* share with her loving friend Anne. Something she *cannot* share.

Hope.

The next night when Anne meets her at the tiny hole in the fence, Lies has another parcel for her and manages to toss it over. This time Anne snatches it up before any rats attack, and she tears it open with a wild appetite. But there is no hope for her in Hanneli's offering. Only Red Cross rations. A few Swedish knäckebrod crackers, some dried prunes, and a hard cookie. Holding back the cookie for Margot, she sobs as she devours the rest in front of Lies, as her friend watches through the portal. She sobs. The angel of death is following her, she tells Lies. Stealing her life from her, person by person, until soon she will have no family at all. No one.

II

FURIES

This is the Site of
The Infamous Belsen Concentration Camp
Liberated by the British on 15 April 1945
10,000 unburied dead were found here.
Another 13,000 have since died,
all of them victims of the
German new order in Europe,
and an example of Nazi Kultur.

—Sign erected on the Lüneburg Heath
by the 11th Armoured Division,
British Army of Liberation

Your furies have passed over me; Your terrors have cut
me down.

—Psalms 88:17

1945

BRITISH-OCCUPIED GERMANY

It's still shocking. Every time she wakes from a fitful sleep and finds herself lying in an actual bed with actual sheets that are clean and bleached white, it's *shocking*. How can this be? How can she deserve such luxury? The makeshift hospital around her smells of chlorine disinfectant and diarrhea, and the flies, buzzing everywhere, are having their feasts. Yet there's a breeze wafting through the open window sash that's warm and hopeful, and a part of Anne cannot help but take pleasure from it. Her brain is often murky, so when it recognizes pleasure, it is the oddest sort of sensation, the joy of simple warmth touching her face.

There is a bottle of clear saline solution hanging from a rack dripping down through a tube into a needle that's inserted into Anne's arm. The needle is held in place with strips of white tape. Sometimes the bottle will capture the sunlight in the morning, and Anne will watch, in awe, as the silvery light is distilled into her veins. It is on such a morning, as the daylight invades the ward, that Anne Frank manages to make a request of the British Red Cross nursing sister, who has recently changed her linen after she inadvertently shit herself, since diarrhea is still such a close friend. The nurse is a small, compactly built young woman, wearing a triangular cap on her head and dressed in trousers and army boots under her white smock. Her face is plain, no cosmetics, no expression beyond that of blunt detachment, except for the brief moment when she was changing the bedding and Anne had glimpsed a flash of something like pity in the woman's eyes. Perhaps even something like compassion.

"Please, there is a mirror?" Anne asks. She knows that much English at least, enough to ask this question. The first time she speaks, however, the nurse does not seem to hear her, and could she really be blamed for going deaf to the constant drubbing of demands coming from her patients? Schwester, Schwester, Fräulein, bitte! A bowl. Sister, please, eine Pfanne. Ich brauche eine Schüssel geben, bevor ich mich scheißen. I must have medicine. Medycyna. Siostra, medycyna. My dressing must be changed. No, change *my* dressing first.

So the next time, Anne must strain to speak up. "Please, a *mirror*?" The nurse frowns back at her. Says nothing, only stares. Holding onto her frown, she swats blankly at a fly, and then, with a thump of her army-issue boots, she turns and marches away. Well, that's it, Anne thinks. That's it. No mirror for me. I must now imagine my face. There were a few girls with mirrors at Auschwitz, but Anne never had the clout required to obtain such an item. Even a glance into the glass was too expensive. A half crust of bread was the price. Four potato peels. A contraband cigarette. Who could afford it? Anne must stick to her memory of herself: the young girl in the mirror she remembers from their days in hiding. The dark-haired, ugly-duckling type who showed up in the glass above the lavatory sink. Though she knows that such a girl and such a face no longer exist.

A party of flies light on her blanket, while one more hops onto her forehead and then her nose, though she doesn't bother to brush it away. German flies, of course. The führer's flies, here to torment Jews. But really, flies are like dead bodies. She no longer takes note of them. In the barracks blocks, the flies were as thick as paste, even in the cold. Hundreds of women packed together, spilling shit and blood and fluids: it was a fly paradise.

Anne turns her head at the surprise of the tromping of boots. The Red Cross sister has returned. She has preserved her frown, of course, but perhaps because she is still young herself, this nurse, she knows the value of the small pocket mirror that she bears, even if it is split by an awful crack down the middle.

"Mirror," the nurse declares, as if confirming the definition of the word. But now Anne is hesitant to take it. A flash of fear sours her belly. How foolish of her to ask. How stupid! Why on earth should she want to see her face, when it can only be the face of a corpse? She should simply turn away. She should simply turn away and glare into dead space, and she is about to do just that when the Red Cross sister decides to help her out. Opening Anne's bony hand with her own, the young nurse places the cracked mirror in Anne's palm.

The split reflection that Anne meets in the broken glass is haunted. Skin blotchy with disease. Dark cauldron eyes retain the cruel hunger she no longer feels in her belly. Her head was shaved by the English this time, and lice scabs dapple her skull. Whatever beauty she might have grown into is gone. Stripped away. She is hideous. If she had the strength, she would fling the mirror to the floor and let it crash to pieces. But since she doesn't, she simply lets it drop from her palm and stretches her neck with a muted moan of disgust, oblivious to the buzzing squadrons of the führer's flies.

At night she finds Margot sitting on the edge of her bed, but she does not scream or shout out for help. For an instant the smallest pinprick of hope stabs her. But there's really no fooling herself. There is no life remaining in her sister's gaze. Margot has simply followed her from the mass graves into the hospital block. Her hair is matted, her lips cracked. A purpled rash from the typhus colors her neck, and her eyes hang open like swallowing caves. The yellow star is pinned to the dirty brown pullover that she wears over striped Lager britches. Oddly, the apparition is comforting. Typhus had broiled Anne's brain with fever and taunted her with such appalling hallucinations. The dead calling to her from the corpse pits. Grasping the air with their skeletal claws. Demanding food they could no longer consume. Demanding a future they could no longer comprehend. But now she gazes back at her sister's face.

You can't just lie here, Anne, Margot tells her. *You have to get up.*

Anne manages, carefully and very slowly, to prop herself onto her elbows.

They won't send you back home till you can walk.

"And where," Anne wonders dimly, "is home, exactly?"

Where? Don't be silly.

"Amsterdam? I should consider Amsterdam my home still? Without you, without Mummy, without Pim?"

You cannot be sure about Pim, Margot tells her. *There is still a chance.*

"No. Pim is *gone*," says Anne flatly.

You don't know that for certain.

"I *do*. How could he have lived through Auschwitz? He was *old*, Margot. Fifty-five years old. How could he *possibly* have survived a selection?"

So you're the authority on life and death?

"You know very well how things worked. The Germans made it perfectly clear—the only way out was 'up the chimney.' They probably gassed Pim on the very first night."

You don't know that for certain, her sister repeats more forcefully.

"And what do *you* know for certain, hmm?" Anne frowns. "You're dead."

I know this much: As long as you remain lying here in this bed like a lump of self-pity, you will remain a lump of self-pity. I know that you must stand up and walk. That's what I know.

Anne looks into Margot's face and feels a keen edge of loneliness saw into her. "Do you hate me, Margot?"

Hate you?

"For what I did."

But she receives no answer from her sister. There's a noise from down the corridor, a door slamming, and when Anne looks up, her sister has been reabsorbed by the dark of the room. A deep exhaustion creeps into Anne's heart, and she lowers her head back onto the flat pillow. For a moment she drills a look through the darkness above her, but then her eyes sink closed, serenaded by the gaping snores and tormented groans of the surviving remnant as it slumbers.

In the morning a clatter of bedpans wakes her. She breathes in deeply as she sits up on her cot and ever so gingerly slides her legs out from under the bedclothes. Her legs are little more than sticks, but she has feet that touch the wooden floorboards. She gazes down at herself. Her skin is pockmarked with scabs. The Red Cross nurse appears at her bedside and, clucking noisily, shifts her back under the covers. She is, of course, too weak to resist. She cannot conceive of resisting anything at all. But when the nurse exits the ward, she tries again. Slowly she grips the wooden headboard as firmly as she can manage. Her legs feel brittle, and her body burns as if her papery muscles might shred, but marshaling all her puny strength into the effort, she rises. At first it is too much. Twice she plops back down onto the hard mattress. The third time her arms shiver with the strain, but suddenly she feels a lightness fill her and she lifts herself from the bed, as if she is a balloon on a string floating upward. Her legs tremble as they take on even the negligible weight of her body, but they do not snap. A tingle of dizziness washes through her head, but then she feels the meek comfort of the warm floorboards on the soles of her feet.

She is standing.

12

SURVIVORS

There are many resistance groups, such as Free Netherlands, that forge identity cards, provide financial support
to those in hiding, organize hiding places and find work
for young Christians who go underground. It's amazing
how much these generous and unselfish people do, risking
their own lives to help and save others.

—Anne Frank,
from her diary,
28 January 1944

The reemerging Jews can thank God for the help they received in that form, and feel humble. Much better people
might have been lost because of it. . . . There can be no
doubt that Jews, specifically, because of German persecution, were able to enjoy great sympathy from the Dutch
people. Now it is appropriate for the Jews to restrain themselves and avoid excesses. . . .

—De Patriot,
Dutch newspaper,
1945

1945

LIBERATED NETHERLANDS

October
**Five months since the entry of the First Canadian
Infantry Division**

~~~

Arriving at Centraal Station

Amsterdam might have been liberated, but peace looks no different from war. The city's wartime face passes by the train compartment's window, the grim façades of buildings on dull parade. Hulking carcasses of locomotives rust on abandoned rail spurs. The clouds are as thick as mud, all part of the drab landscape that stretches from one end of the continent to the other, as if color is now rationed along with milk and bread and coal. A fretful rain speckles the window glass as the train creaks along, following its fractured timetable toward Centraal Station.

She has organized a notebook. It is only two cardboard covers sandwiching the thinnest, flimsiest, poorest-quality paper in the history of thin, flimsy, poor-quality paper, but it should still hold ink. And she has organized a fountain pen, too. Organizing is much different from stealing, you see. To organize something is to obtain a vital item to fill a vital need, and *need,* she has learned, trumps all. The pen is lovely. A sleek red Montblanc with a nice thick nib. However, there's a problem. It is being quite stubborn, this Montblanc, on one essential point: It refuses to form words. It refuses to even touch the page with its nice thick nib. The pen remains in her hand but suspended above the paper.

Once she believed she had a gift. To be a writer. She believed that God had a plan for her, and that plan centered on her diary. But all those words, all those pages, are gone. Lost, along with any belief in God's Grand Plan. Stripped from her like her ambitions when, on a clammy August morning, the Thousand-Year Reich came pounding up the steps of their hiding place. Surely she must realize that she's been so completely ruined since that day, that if she attempts to write a sentence, the pen will simply blot and smear the paper with a slur of ink.

The compartment is crowded, unheated, and it smells of the lack of soap. Bundled against the draft, passengers share the same blank stare, blind to the rain-speckled world passing by the windows. Battered luggage is jammed where it doesn't fit. Heads nod off, lulled by the tedious rhythm of the rolling stock. Everyone's ailing, it seems. Everyone's depleted. All of Europe is sick. She keeps her cardboard suitcase, closed with a belt, on the floor of the carriage, sandwiched between her knees. It's all she owns, though none of what's inside is really hers. A hairbrush, a toothbrush. A few clothes. The UNRRA issued her a rubber-stamped identity card with her thumbprints and a small photograph stapled to it that permitted her to cross the Dutch border. But to her it is a false passport. She knows that she has no identity beyond the number imprinted on her arm.

Gazing into her transparent reflection in the window glass, she can see how much her hair has grown in. Her face is fuller. Her eyes are alert and darkly tense. Sometime during her convalescence, she turned sixteen, though the date passed weeks before she realized it. Calendars have meant nothing for so long.

The train's chugging momentum slows, and she feels a hard pulse of anticipation in her body. However, it is not the joy of finally returning home but an interior drumbeat of terror. She no longer knows what home *is* now. Her family is dead. Without them how can such a thing as home exist?

She feels an odd sort of estrangement as the recognizable sights of Amsterdam roll into view. The roofs are missing tiles. The upper stories of squat Dutch buildings line a section of elevated rail with taped-over windows. The twin spires and baroque dome of the Sint Nicolaaskerk stand under a muddy sky. She is returning to a world she believed she would never again see, and it feels both familiar and horrifyingly alien.

Dropping her eyes, she glares at the clean, empty page of the notebook open in her lap. A tear wets her cheek, but she does not bother to wipe it away as she simply forces the pen's nib down onto the paper's surface, against its will, until a heavy blue dot appears like a blemish. She glares at the dot. And then, quite obediently, the pen begins to move.

Anne Frank was nothing but a Kazetnik, she writes. A creature of the camps. And if she is now a displaced person, it is not because her life has been displaced, it's because her heart has been displaced. Her soul and all that once constituted Anne Frank have been displaced.

The conductor pushes through the crowded corridor calling out the stop in a harried voice: "Centraal Station Amsterdam." Swallowing heavily, Anne joins the dreary bustle of passengers about to depart. Her heart is thrumming heavily in her breast. There were postcards printed in Belsen for the DPs. She wrote a note to Miep on one of them before piling into the rear of a British army lorry, but who knows if it was ever received? Words on paper, like people, are so easily erased. People are so insubstantial, too. Who knows what has become of Miep? Of Bep or Kugler or Kleiman? Who knows what has become of anyone?

The train lumbers past the carriage sheds and warehouses of the freight yard. Toward the tall, single-span glass canopy of the station. Then slots in between the concrete platforms and slows to a halt. The stink of the track grease and the coal smoke follows her down the steps of the platform and into the half dark of the drafty concourse as she grips the handle of her suitcase. The noise ringing in the station rafters is both overwhelming and comforting. People muddling about, lugging their bags. Porters pushing carts loaded with steamer trunks. Women with trailing children struggling to keep up. Off-duty

Canadian soldiers, the Liberators of Holland, smoking their cigarettes and whistling after Dutch girls in their patched-up dresses.

Rows of tables are assembled in the booking hall, and glum lines
of ragged people are assembled in front of them. Typewriters are
clacking. It's the Dutch Social Service Bureau trying to bring order
to the chaos of returnees. Trying to manage the confusion of desperate stories by filling out forms.

A squat little clerk, seated behind his typewriter, glowers at an old
man's papers and issues a burdened sigh. "Ah, another *Jew*. Wonderful. And how did they forget to gas *you*, Uncle?" he inquires, to be
polite, in an amplified voice just in case the old man is hard of hearing.
Anne feels her heart shiver and fights a fierce craving to shove forward and rap the clerk across the face with her knuckles. And she may
have done so, but for the fact that she is hearing her name. Someone
is calling her with frantic excitement. "Anne, Anne! *Anne Frank!*"

Turning about, she stares, blinking, at the woman hurrying toward
her. The woman with ginger hair swept back from her brow, with
thinned cheeks, a heart-shaped chin, a hooded gaze. Anne forces her
mouth to form around a name. *"Miep,"* she whispers. And feels something crack open inside of her.

"Jan, it's Anne!" Miep exclaims in disbelief. Hearing her name
shouted in public panics Anne, and she must resist the urge to run.
"Jan! Jan, it's Anne!" Miep exclaims again, as if it's just too impossible to believe. "It's Anne Frank!" she calls, and seizes Anne in an embrace. "Oh, *Anne*. To have you return. To have you *return*. What a
miracle," she whispers, like saying a prayer. It's a frightening thing,
Miep's embrace. Anne has not been touched with affection for a very
long time, and this embrace is so murderously joyful. Many prisoners
of Belsen were killed after liberation, not by bullets but by the rich-
ness of the food the Tommies handed out. They died with their faces
smeared with chocolate, Spam, and condensed milk. This is how
Anne feels about the wrap of Miep's arms. It's so rich that it might
kill her on the spot, so she forces herself free.

"Oh, my heavens, I cannot *believe* this." Miep is still grinning as if
the expression has been stamped onto her face permanently. "We've

come to the station every day since your postcard arrived. And now, *here you are*. Jan!" she sings out again.

In answer to his wife's call, a tall, gangly fellow with a high cox-comb of hair and glasses as round as a pair of ten-guilder queens comes trotting from the tables wearing a stunned expression. His white armband reads SOCIALE DIENST. *"Anne?"* he questions the air.

"Jan, can you *believe* it? It's a *miracle*," Miep declares again, and then she whispers with naked relief, "We thought we'd *lost* you." But then she is turning away, raising her hand and waving. "She's over *here*! Anne is here!" she is shouting.

At once Anne feels as if she is trying to contain an explosion. As if she is a bomb that will rip shingles from rooftops and blast bricks to powder if she is allowed to detonate. Her heart thunders at the sight of the tall, threadbare figure stepping into a stripe of sunlight from the concourse windows. With a thump the suitcase falls from her hand, and she is rushing toward him, calling out, *"Pim!"*

He's so wretchedly thin, as thin as a shadow, and he appears con-fused, softly dazed, but then something fierce seizes his expression, and he cries out with perfect anguish, "My *daughter*!"

Clamping her arms around his bony body, Anne listens to the deep elation of her father's voice as he chants her name again and again, "Anne, my Anne, my daughter, my dear, dear Annelies."

It should be a moment of pure bliss. But even now, even as she absorbs the flutter of his heartbeats and sobs deeply in Pim's arms, she feels something terrifying that comes unbidden and unwanted.

A bite of fury shocks her.

13

GRIEF

For in much wisdom is much grief: and he that increaseth
knowledge increaseth sorrow.

—Ecclesiastes 1:18

1945

Jekerstraat 65
Amsterdam-Zuid

LIBERATED NETHERLANDS

"It is only the two of us, Anne," her father says. His voice is cracked. Ragged. Smoke from the cigarette clenched between his fingers migrates upward. Of all of them from their hiding place, it is only Anne and Pim who have returned alive. "Only us."

This confirms what she already knew without being told, but she does not tell him this. He seems not to be speaking to Anne anyway, but to a void rooted within himself. His face is tightly shuttered, and he glares at the window as if he could see through all the way to the land of death, where his wife, his daughter, his friends now reside.

The sun is sinking away, too weak to hold itself in the sky any longer. Its fleeting light pinks the walls of Miep and Jan's kitchen. Anne discreetly surveys her surroundings. It feels so strange—so wrong—to be sitting in someone's home. There are well-swept rugs and well-kept furnishings. Lace doilies with tulip appliqués on the arms of the upholstered chairs and the cloying scent of floor wax in the hallway. A bottle of good Dutch apple brandy has appeared from the hidden recesses of Miep's bureau, and Jan is pouring it into short white tumblers made from hobnail milk glass.

"*Otto*," he says as he splashes the brandy into a tumbler, naming each one of them. Pim is sitting beside Anne, his arm hooked over the back of her chair. The closed mask he wore only a moment ago has been replaced by an expression of manic disbelief that hangs loosely from his face.

"*Miep*," says Jan as he pours.

"Only a taste," his wife instructs softly.

"And now *Miss Frank*," Jan announces with a flourish that makes

Anne uncomfortable. She is the guest of honor here simply for surviving the KZs. That has been her only accomplishment: to continue breathing despite what that cost her. She watches the honey-gold of the brandy pour from the bottle. To accommodate the electricity shortages in Amsterdam, Miep has lit a paraffin candle at the center of the table. Jan allows himself a moderate splash before sitting. And then a silence takes hold. The last of the sunlight has fled, and a purpled dark spreads. Pim lingers over the silence, then hoists his tumbler, managing to speak the only word left to him. "L'chaim," he toasts.

To life.

A few minutes later, he is on his way to the toilet when he collapses. A dull thud in the corridor, and Miep is calling, "Anne! Anne, your father!"

The doctor who arrives an hour later is a Dutchman known to Miep for his reputation as one who had provided medicine for onderduikers who'd fallen ill during the occupation. He has the troubled face of a ragged old lion. Miep and Jan have managed to haul Pim up from the floor and have carried him to the long velveteen sofa. "Help me with his shirt, please," the doctor instructs Miep. And Anne sees how thin, how transparently birdlike Pim's chest has become. She thinks she might see his beating heart, a bluish tint beneath his ribs. Her father's eyes are open, but he is staring blindly up at the ceiling as the doctor jumps the bell of his stethoscope about as if playing a game of checkers.

Suddenly Anne can't breathe. A ferocious terror is burning the oxygen from the room, and she must get out. She must flee to the street, where a greasy white light glows from a lone streetlamp. Her hands are clenched, her body is clenched, she is breathing in and out, fighting the urge to run until she drops. So she squats against the wall of the building, closing herself up in a ball.

"You must understand that I can't tell him," she says.

Can't you? Margot is beside her in her dirty Lager rags, wearing the pair of wooden clogs she was issued.

"Don't you see? He's so fragile. If I tell him," Anne says, "if I tell him what I did, it could kill him. His heart might give out."

But Margot vanishes when the door to the flat opens. The doctor trudges out onto the sidewalk, and Anne hurries to her feet.

"How is he?"

In reply the doctor proffers a thick frown. Is this the same face he wears whether the news is good or bad? "Your father should be fine," he informs her grimly.

"But. What happened?"

"What happened?" A shrug as the man mounts his rickety Locomotief bicycle.

"Was it his heart?"

"His heart? No." The doctor considers. "I wouldn't say it was his heart. I would say it was *nerves*. An attack of angst, it might be called. I've given him a sedative so he'll sleep. Is your name Margot or Anne?"

Anne tenses. "Why?"

"Because those were the names he was calling for. I just assumed," says the doctor.

She swallows. "My name is Anne."

A nod. "You should go in and see him, then. The sedative will not take long to do its work."

She finds that her father has been transferred to the tiny room off the parlor and is tucked under a blanket, his stocking feet sticking out at the end of the bed.

"Anne," he says drowsily, his mouth forming a smile but his eyes drooping. He raises his hand to her.

"I'm sorry," she says, kneeling beside him and taking his bony hand.

"Sorry? For what? It is I who should be sorry for spoiling your welcome."

"You didn't, Pim."

"Tumbling over like an old tree . . ."

"The doctor said you're going to be fine."

But Pim doesn't seem to be listening to this. Instead he is gazing at her face with a kind of broken gratitude. "What a miracle you are to me. The Red Cross . . ." he says, and he must pause and swallow painfully before he can finish his sentence, "the Red Cross listed you and Margot as among the dead. The *both* of you—" He stops, and his mouth flattens. "Carried off with thousands of others to mass graves." His face crumples as if he can see it all happening. The bodies of his daughters hauled away from him forever. He hisses air from between his teeth. "I lived with that as a fact for months, and I was only half a human being." But then, he tells her, came her postcard to Miep. To find that his Anneke was *alive*? He shakes his head. "I was so shocked and yet *transported* by joy. To have you *back*. Dare I believe in such a miracle after death had claimed you? I've never been a particularly religious person, Annelein, you know this. But to me it seemed that this was nothing short of the hand of God at work."

Something angry nips at Anne's heart. God's hand? But before she speaks another word, she sees that the doctor's sedative is at work here, and that Pim is softening into sleep. She watches as his breathing lengthens.

The electricity signals its return to the district as a floor lamp blinks to life. In the dining room, Miep has a plate with some rye bread and komijnekaas. Anne devours it all, stuffing it thoughtlessly into her mouth, until she spots the mix of sympathy and horror on Miep's face.

"That's the end of the cheese, I'm sorry to say," Miep apologizes. "There are many things that are still scarce even after the Germans have gone. But I have some soup I could warm up. I could give you a bowl."

Anne chews a mouthful of cheese and bread self-consciously, nodding, averting her eyes to the plate. When she's sure Miep is busy in the kitchen, she crams a bite of bread into her mouth and then stuffs the final crust into the pocket of her sweater.

"No meat," Miep informs her as she returns with a steaming soup bowl. "But. We maintain." Her version of the Dutch national motto: Je maintiendrai.

Anne picks up the spoon and starts to eat, trying to slow herself, but it's hard. She can hear how loudly she's slurping, but she can't help it. It's a lesson of the camps. When you have food, wolf it down. When the bowl is empty, she gathers in a breath and stares blankly. By the window is her mother's French secretaire that once stood in the corner of the bedroom Anne shared with Margot in the Merry. It presents itself just as it was. Its mahogany finish glows with urbane charm in a crease of lamplight, untouched by war and occupation, snatched out of time and placed here on Miep's carpet. It breaks her heart.

"Do you have a cigarette, Miep?" she asks.

Miep obviously must absorb this for a moment. Anne Frank smoking? But then she says, "I think Jan keeps some in a drawer, hold on." In a moment she returns with a box of sulfur-tipped matches, a black enamel ashtray, and a packet of Queen's Day cigarettes.

"Do you remember these?" she asks.

"The English dropped them," says Anne.

"So maybe they're a little stale."

No matter. Anne lights up, inhaling quickly. She feels a chomp of bitterness at the rear of her throat and sighs. "Thank you, Miep. I know cigarettes are valuable."

Miep shrugs. Valuable compared to what?

"Everyone else is dead," Anne says. "Everyone in hiding, except for Pim and myself. That's the story, isn't it?"

"Yes," Miep replies quietly, but without varnish. "That is the story."

Anne nods. She asks about Bep. About Mr. Kugler and Mr. Kleiman.

Miep lifts her eyebrows. "We all made it through, one way or another," she answers, as if advising Anne about the survivors of a shipwreck. "Bep and I did our best to maintain the office. There were still contracts to fulfill, and we felt we should do what we could to keep the wheels turning. But Mr. Kugler and Mr. Kleiman had the hardest time. After that awful day when the Grüne Polizei arrived, they were sent to the labor camps. Terrible places, yet they both managed to return in one piece. So now we're all back at the office along with your father. Amazing, really," Miep can only admit.

"He still goes to the *office*?" Anne's brow knits. She hears a certain petulance enter her voice, unbidden.

Miep either doesn't notice or pretends not to. "Every morning," she answers. "Though it hasn't been easy. Business is not so good, and there are certain problems that require sorting. It was quite difficult to keep fooling the Germans during the occupation, to convince them that the businesses were no longer Jewish owned. Things became knotty, and now they must be unknotted."

"So Pim sits at his desk shuffling papers?" says Anne. "He sits there using the telephone and giving dictation, just as if nothing has *happened*?" Why does she sound so incensed by this?

Miep only shrugs again. "What else would you have him do, Anne?"

"What would *I* have him do?" Anne frowns, her eyes rounding. "I would have him *shout,* I would have him *pound his fist,* I would have him rattle the *windows till they shatter.* I would *have* him, Miep, demonstrate his *outrage.*"

Miep exhales a breath. "Well," she says, "outrage. You know, Anne, that has never been your father's way."

Anne's eyes fly open. *"Margot!"* she calls aloud, her heart thumping against her ribs and her flesh chilled. Blinking at the silver of morning, she shakes her head back into the present. She must have fallen asleep on Miep's sofa. Her clothes feel rough against her skin. A blanket, which has been draped over her, sags onto the floor. Pim is slumped in a chair a few steps away, dozing, his head lolling with a rhythmic snore. For an instant he stirs, and his expression contracts as if he's been pinched. His face is paled by the daylight glazing the windows. Only the ruddy patches under his eyes retain color. He is dressed in overlaundered pajamas with faded blue and white stripes and a too-large flannel robe, his feet hooked into a pair of worn leather slippers. She blinks again. Around her the flat is as hushed as an empty room. *"Pim,"* she says with more intention, and watches him shudder into consciousness, blinking back at her with a hint of the same brand of empty panic she feels in her chest.

"Ah." He whisks a breath into his lungs. "So you're awake."

Anne sits up further, plants her feet on the floor, and sifts her fingers through her hair. "Shouldn't you be in bed? The doctor," she says.

"The doctor said rest, so I'm resting. But really there's no need to worry. I'm fine. Just a bit of excess excitement, that's all."

Anne looks at him, and he takes this opportunity to beam back at her in a fractured sort of way. "Ah, my Annelein. How *wonderful* it is simply to gaze upon your face. Thank God that you have been re-turned."

But Anne shakes her head. Lets her hair fall back across her face. "Miep said you just showed up at her door one day after the liberation."

Pim nods at this as if it is only too true. "I did. It was a long journey back from Poland. The Russians liberated Auschwitz in winter, but it wasn't till May that I could begin the journey home. I had to travel to Odessa and then board a boat for Marseille. And there was the matter of the French documents required. A Repatriation Card and other such nonsense," he says, and bats away the memory with his hand. "All in all, I didn't return to Amsterdam till June. Of course, others had long since occupied our flat in the Merwedeplein, and even if they hadn't, I could never have gone back there. Not to live. So what choice did I have but to show up like a beggar at Miep's door? She and Jan have been very kind to take me in. We owe them quite a lot, Anne."

"How did you do it, Pim?" she asks. "How did you manage to . . ." But the words won't form. Her father, however, can sense the question.

"How did I manage to stay alive in Auschwitz?" His expression drifts into a hollow spot. "*How?* It's a question I've asked myself again and again. And again and again, I come to the same answer," he says, and his eyebrows lift. "It was love."

Anne glares.

"Love and hope. Love of my family and hope that I would see them all again. That's what kept me alive, I believe." A shrug. "That is my only explanation."

"I was told," Anne says, and though speaking the next words is worse than dragging thorns through her throat, she forces out a clenched, almost shameful whisper. "I was told. I was told in Bergen-Belsen, by a woman who knew her, that Mummy died in the Birkenau infirmary. Of starvation."

A bleak nod of her father's head. "Yes. That is what *I* was told also."

"She was hoarding her bread for Margot and me."

"She was devoted to her girls," Pim concludes. But something in his voice betrays a reluctance to continue down this road. A small fidget runs through his body, and his hands tap restlessly against his knees. "Now come," he says, pushing up from the chair. "Let's have a cup of tea, the both of us." And as he advances on the kitchen, he tells her, "Tonight you will move into the sewing room. A young lady, I think, needs her privacy."

"But I'll be taking *your* bed, Pim. Where will *you* sleep?"

"Me? Oh, don't worry about the old man. There's a closet bed in the wall, which will be quite adequate for this old sack of bones."

And so it goes. That night Anne moves her suitcase into the sewing room. It's small, really just a closet with barely enough space to yawn between the four walls, yet to her it seems quite cavernous. Anne has never in her life had a room to herself. When the door is shut, the privacy feels soothing in a way, a spot where she can breathe. But also it's deep water. When she is alone, who knows where her displaced heart will lead her? She opens her suitcase and removes her contraband. A cardboard notebook of the world's cheapest and flimsiest paper and a fountain pen that has learned how to cooperate.

———

She wonders if she might not drown in her own privacy. In hiding she would run to Pim's bed when the English bombers came or when she was terrorized by her own dreams. But that's impossible now. Now when she feels the loneliness overcome her, she can only sink into it.

That's when I think of my diary, she writes on the page of her journal.

It is lost, of course. She remembers the pages scattered on the floor on the day of their arrest, but at the time she could not make sense of what she was seeing. Nothing seemed to matter in that instant. The Gestapo had breached their hiding place, and they were doomed. The shock was so horrific that even Anne's precious diary meant nothing to her. All her years of work were no more than scratches on paper, and she barely gave it a look. It wasn't until they reached Kamp Westerbork in Drenthe that she began to feel its loss. She remembers it now, she writes, as she might remember the closest of friends whom she has lost for good. But isn't it folly for her to mourn the loss of a possession? She should be spending her tears on the memory of her mother, of Margot. She should be weeping over the loss of Peter, and of his parents, and even that stuffy old mug Mr. Pfeffer.

But her eyes remain dry at the thought of them. What does that say about her, this Anne Frank, whose tears are for herself and no one else?

On the page she writes, Please do not answer that question.

1945

Amsterdam

LIBERATED NETHERLANDS

This much Anne has discovered by opening her ears: Most Amsterdammers think of themselves as the true survivors. They have survived five years of occupation by the moffen. They have survived the tyranny of the Nazi Grüne Polizei and the NSB collaborators. They have survived losing their bicycles, their radios, their businesses. They have survived losing their husbands and sons and brothers to prison camps and labor conscription. They have survived the Hunger Winter by scraping the scum from the bottoms of milk tureens or by swallowing a few spoonfuls of thin broth at a crowded emergency kitchen. And when the roads into the town were barricaded, when the moffen disconnected the propane lines and cut off all food supplies, when the bread and the beets ran out, they survived by boiling tulip bulbs for supper over wood fires. And when the tulip bulbs were gone, they survived losing their friends and their families and their babies to slow starvation. They are certainly in no mood to sympathize with a lot of bony Jews who babble on about cattle cars and gas chambers and God knows what kind of atrocities. Who could believe it all? Who would *wish* to believe it all?

She walks the streets still conscious of an invisible star sewn to her breast, even if it never shows up in a mirror. Many of the shops in town are boarded up, and those that aren't have precious little actual merchandise to offer. Even in the Kalverstraat, the store windows advertise empty packages above the signs that read VOOR SLECHTS VERTONING. For Display Only. The Vondelpark is bereft of foliage, because the city's trees were felled to their roots and chopped into pieces to warm the stoves of a freezing population. There's no rubber for tires, no sugar to sweeten the feeble tea and tasteless coffee surrogates, no butter, no whole milk, not much of anything, really. But at least now there is an acute shortage of Germans as well. Few are disappointed since *that* particular commodity went missing.

On the Day of Liberation, Canadian armored columns rolled across the Berlagebrug in Amsterdam-Zuid. The same bridge over which the armored columns of the Wehrmacht rolled five years earlier. Anne spent Dutch Liberation Day in a hospital bed of DP Camp Belsen trying to comprehend her *own* liberation, but she has since watched the newsreels in the cinema of the lumbering Churchill tanks strewn with flowers. The giant, grinning Canadian boys, tall as oak trees in their fatigues, still grimy from combat, clutching joystruck Dutch girls. She can only sit in hard silence when she watches the cheering, sobbing throngs of Amsterdammers on the screen, waving their tricolors and tossing streamers.

In the weeks since her return to the living, she has retrained herself to do small things, such as buying bread at a neighborhood bakery without gouging out a piece on the spot and stuffing it into her mouth. She has trained herself to resist dividing the crowd lined up for the streetcar into fives. Fünferreihen! Five in a row! As every Kazetnik knows, five in a row was the basic unit of measure of the KZ. It was one of the essential phrases of life and death.

Auschwitz-Birkenau distilled Anne's German vocabulary down to fundamentals. And even now that she has returned to Amsterdam, hell's lexicon is still fully entrenched in her mind. A camp is a Lager. Not a Konzentrationslager but a KZ—a Kazet. A Blockführerin is the female monster in SS uniform commanding a barracks block. The prisoner appointed to *imitate* the brutality of such a female monster is the Kapo. A Krema is one of the five crematoriums in Birkenau designed to incinerate huge populations of corpses after its gas chambers are emptied. The roll call for all prisoners, which lasts for hours upon hours in the drenching rain, the freezing sleet and snow, is the Appel. Appel! Appel! The Kapos still bellow in the darkness of her mind. Appel! Appel! Mach schnell!

Morning. The sun rises alone into a clear, cloudless sky. The window in her room faces a narrow cobblestone alley, which resembles a rubbish dump. Slag and wire and hunks of grimy machinery, a rusted stove, an old icebox, a broken toilet. She can hear voices from the kitchen, and then there's a knock at the door. It's Miep carrying a steaming cup of tea for her. Good Miep. Trustworthy Miep, dressed for the workday in a lavender dress and low heels, no jewelry, and only a touch of lipstick. "Your papa is at his breakfast, and I've left your plate warming in the oven," she explains to Anne. Then, with only a hint of caution, "I understand that you'll be joining us today," she says, "at the office."

"Pim thinks I should keep my mind occupied while he finds a school for me to attend."

"Probably a very good idea, don't you think?" Miep prompts, but Anne answers with silence, forcing Miep to fill in the empty space between them. "Well, I should be going," she reminds herself. But she lingers. "I'm sorry that this room is so small." She frowns lightly as she surveys the cramped space. "Perhaps you should put up pictures of film stars, like you used to," she suggests. "To liven it up."

But Anne can only gaze at the walls and absorb their blankness. "Yes. What a good idea," she replies without the barest drop of conviction.

When she peers into the kitchen, she finds Pim's beanpole figure alone at the table, his fork frozen in his hand as he sits under the spell of some heavy tome open beside his plate. A wrinkle of concentration crinkles the skin at the top of his head. In hiding, Pim would read his beloved Dickens aloud to her in the language of its author, along with the aid of his well-thumbed English-to-Dutch dictionary.

In Auschwitz the Germans marched men of his age straight to the ovens, didn't they? She was so sure he couldn't possibly have survived. But something in her father had carried him through to liberation. Was it really love and hope, as Pim insists, or was it the invisible survival instinct of Otto Frank? She gazes at her father quietly. Then steps out of the kitchen without alerting him to her presence.

Their mother had told them to find one beautiful thing.

Margot and Anne, that is. Find one beautiful thing. It was a day when the rain had churned the Women's Camp in Birkenau into a quagmire. Soaking wet, they'd been lugging chunks of broken cement on a work detail, and when Anne fell, the Kapo had slashed her viciously with a hard rubber truncheon. Every day find one beautiful thing, her mother told them. Margot approached it like a lesson to learn. Assignment: Find one beautiful thing. But Anne tied her last knot of hope around her mother's words. And that night in the barracks, she gazed at her skin, purpling from the Kapo's blows, and found beauty in the colors, like a bouquet of violets.

Find one beautiful thing every day, and they would survive even Birkenau.

Except they didn't survive. Only Anne is alive.

Her hair is growing back so thickly; it already hangs down onto her neck. In the mirror she can see that she is dressed not in lice-ridden camp rags but as a human being. The red cloth coat only slightly frayed at the hem. A skirt, a blouse. Even undergarments beneath. Actual undergarments. A shadow passes across the mirror's glass. Margot is peering over her shoulder in the reflection. Even after her death, her sister's cough is deep and corrupting. She gazes out from the glass, dressed as she was the last time Pim photographed them in hiding, wearing her ivory knit sweater with the short sleeves that Bep had given her and the green porcelain barrette she received from Mummy on her birthday clipped in her hair.

You have a spot on the collar of your blouse, her sister is compelled to comment.

Anne frowns. Absently rubs her thumb over the pale stain on the material. "It doesn't matter," she says.

So you don't mind looking like a ragamuffin?

"It's a spot. It doesn't matter."

No? You don't think so? You don't recall that the Nazis said Jews were slovenly?

"So now my spot is a mark against the Jews? It's a bleach stain."

I'm simply saying that as they judge one, they judge all.

"That's Mummy talking," Anne points out, and then glares deeply into her sister's reflection. "Maybe it should have been *you*," she whispers.

Margot gazes back from the thinness of the mirrored glass.

"I see the way people look at me," Anne breathes. "Those glances over my shoulder to the empty spot where you should be standing. You wanted to be a nurse, Margot. You wanted to deliver babies in Palestine. What am I doing with a future?" she asks, but no answer is forthcoming. Margot has vanished from the mirror's surface as their father knocks politely on the door.

"Anne? May I?"

"Yes, Pim," she answers, and gazes at her father's reflection that has replaced Margot's. He's wearing his wide-brimmed fedora raked at an angle, the brim shadowing his eyes. After his liberation from Auschwitz, her father resembles a poor artifact of himself. He wears a putty-colored raincoat that hangs like a sack. His mustache and the fringe of hair around his ears are well barbered but have lost most of their color. He stares into the mirror's reflection, catching Anne's eye until she turns away from him, feeling oddly embarrassed.

"*So,*" he begins with a vigorous note inserted into his voice. "Are we ready to go to work?" Work. Over the gate to Auschwitz, there was a legend wrought in iron: ARBEIT MACHT FREI. Work Will Make You Free. But this is not bloodied-knuckle slave labor she is headed for. Not digging trenches in the muck or hauling backbreaking stones. It's freedom through office work. Pecking out words on Miep's typewriter. Sorting index cards. Shifting papers into files at the Prinsengracht office, and all the while the upper floors of the annex, which housed them in secret for so long, concealed them from the moffen enemy for more than two years, sit vacant. Their hiding place, once the nave of their existence, now just empty space. She thinks of the lumpy cot where she slept, the wobbly table where she wrote. Her picture collection plastered across the walls—Shirley Temple, Joyce Vanderveen, Ginger Rogers—all part of their secret fortress above the spice warehouse. It often felt like a prison while she was in it, a young girl in love with glamour and talk. With boys and biking, swimming and skating. With freedom and sunlight.

"I've lost everything, Pim. Everything there is to lose."

An airless beat separates them.

"*Anneke.*" Her father pronounces her name as if it's a lead weight, his gaze thinning as he shakes his head. For a moment he breathes unevenly. His carefully crafted expression crumbling. "I can only imagine," he says, "how you and your sister suffered." His eyes drop, no longer part of his reflection. "*Alone.* Without your mother. Without *me.*" And now he turns his face away to wipe his eyes. "I'm sorry," he apologizes for the tears. Then stretches a lifeless smile across his face as he shakes his head at the mirror. "You are so strong, Anne. I must learn from you."

Anne stares. She feels herself go quietly rigid.

"What I want to *say*," her father tells her tremulously, "what I think is *important* to say, is . . ." He damply clears his throat. "*Grief.*" The word cracks as he speaks, but he clamps down on it with a frown. "Grief," he says, "is natural. But we cannot allow ourselves to be crushed by it. God has given us life, Anne. For reasons that only he can understand."

Anne stands motionless, but she feels a rising boil inside. "You think," she asks with a biting precision, "it was *God*?"

Her father blinks.

"You think," she repeats, "it was *God* who has given us life?"

"*Anne.*" Her father tries to interrupt, but she won't allow it.

"If it was *God* who has given us life, Pim, then where was he at Birkenau?" she demands. "Where was *God* at Bergen-Belsen?"

Her father raises his palm as if to deflect her words. "Anneke."

"The only thing God has given us, Pim, *is death.*" She feels the horror erupting inside her. "God has given us the gas chambers. God has given us the crematoria. *Those* are God's gifts to us, Pim. And *this*," she declares, exposing her forearm to the mirror's reflection. This is his mark." The indelible blue defilement stains her forearm. A-25063. The number that replaced her name. Sometimes she still feels the sting of the tattoo needle that etched it into her flesh. Sometimes she can still feel the ink burn under her skin. It was so obscene. A woman in stripes with a green triangle wielding the needle. So impossible to believe in what was actually happening to her. "God has *taken* our lives away, Pim. He's *stolen* them like a thief."

And now her father is only nodding rhythmically, eyes shut tight. When he opens them, he takes a gulp of air as if he has just escaped drowning. His face in the mirror pales with loss and fear. "Yes, Annelies," he says, "it *is* impossible to believe that God has chosen life for us. Chosen you and me among so many others who died. It's utterly impossible to comprehend, yet that is precisely what we *must* believe," he tells her, "if we are to survive."

Silence is all Anne can offer him.

The morning is bright and sharp as glass as they travel to the office. Her father keeps up a brisk pace as they walk to the tram. He is carrying a leatherette portfolio under his arm, a gift from Miep and her husband, Jan, as a replacement for the one stolen by the SS Grüne Polizei. They walk quickly and silently up the Waalstraat to the broad lanes of what had been the Zuider Amstellaan but is now the Rooseveltlaan, the new name painted across a large wooden signboard. People swarm the sidewalks with the quick pace standard to the Dutch, but many of them have their heads bent downward.

Pim's companies survived the war through a bit of a bureaucratic shell game, so now, after returning from Auschwitz barely more than a bag of bones, he can still sell pectin to housewives to make jam and spices to butchers for making sausages. Sales have plummeted, but Pim is not pessimistic. Oh, no, not Pim. Housewives may not yet have fresh fruits to preserve, but there's always a market for spices, and in any case it's only a question of time before the economy picks up. A year. Maybe two. "We can survive a year or two, don't you think?" he asks Anne, but does not appear to expect her to answer. "A year or two is not so bad."

There's a crowd of people waiting on a traffic median in the center of the Rooseveltlaan. Some of the town's trams are actually up and running again. The new GVB has managed to scrape up enough functioning cars to run limited service, in the mornings and afternoons, though the carriages are appallingly overcrowded and slow. Tramlijn 13 grumbles to a halt in front of the solemn crowd that's gathered. Anne and her father must elbow their way aboard, but shoving is a lesson learned at the camps by young and old, and she finds some eerie comfort in the jam of people. All those tram riders crammed together.

Her body is used to that kind of human packing from the cattle cars and barracks blocks and accepts it, going loose, boneless. Offering the crush of bodies no resistance. Her mind hangs blankly in her head like a stone. No thought as she inhales the smells of human grime and routine exhaustion.

Pim has begun a miniature lecture on the subject of food. How expensive it has become. "Miep and Jan have been very generous with us. But food is still quite overpriced. Just look at the cost of beans, *simple beans.* I will contribute, of course, when Mr. Kleiman agrees that the business is strong enough for me to take a salary again. But until that time we must be careful not to consume more than our fair share, Anne."

Anne says nothing. She glares at the buildings as they pass in a flat conveyor belt of tall brick façades and ornate masonry. Terra-cotta red striped with ocher or white ermine like the sleeves of royalty.

Maybe it's her body that remembers. The rumble under her feet of wheels on a track. The mob of humanity compressed. She is suddenly reliving the transport that carried Margot and her to the heathland of Bergen-Belsen without their mother. She can smell the septic odor of boxcar transport, feel the cold sickness in her belly. Margot's face was sticky with tears as they clutched each other. They had been separated from the men on the ramp in Birkenau, and the women were on their own now, utterly. But instead of their mother collapsing in despair, all of her fragilities had simply fallen away. She became a lioness, protecting and caring for her girls, even as starvation and exhaustion racked her body. Anne was shocked at the pride she felt for her mother. And the love. But now Mummy had become so sick that she'd been taken to the Women's Infirmary Barracks, so that when the selection was made by the SS doctors, Anne and Margot had been herded without her into the boxcars to be transported deep into Germany.

We'll see her again, Anne kept repeating to her sister. After this is over, we'll see her again.

But even as she spoke the words, she could not believe them. Somewhere in the car, a woman was chanting the kaddish in a croaking voice. A prayer of affirmation and a prayer for the dead. The cadence of the woman's voice merged with the clunking rhythm of the train wheels, and Anne knew that they had seen their mother for the very last time.

Leaving the tramlijn, she trails her father's pencil-thin shadow. They follow the path of the canal that flows between the tall, narrow brick faces of the old merchant houses. The street is lined with the skinny iron bollards bearing the trio of St. Andrew's crosses. Little Ones from Amsterdam, they're called. Amsterdammertje. When they were small, she and Margot would play a game, chasing each other through the rows, pretending that they were dodging a mouthful of teeth owned by some great dragon about to chew them up. She thinks of this as if she is remembering a fairy tale she once read, instead of a piece of her life.

Pim natters on about the length of the walk, tapping the dial of his wristwatch. She has noticed that on those occasions when they're alone, her father drums up some sort of efficient chatter about the schedule of street trams, the scarcity of spices, or the price of substitute ingredients. Anne tastes something foul at the back of her mouth.

"I can't do this, Pim," she says.

"Anneke, please. It's all right. It's only a building. Just an old building. You'll be fine once you get inside."

But Anne is shaking her head. "No. No, I won't be."

"Anne." Her father speaks to her softly. "Think of our friends. Our friends who cared for us so well while we were in hiding. Think of Bep and Mr. Kugler, not to mention *Miep.* They're all there waiting for you, Anne. They're all so excited to have you back with them. You don't want to disappoint them, do you?"

Anne stares darkly, as if their disappointment might be something to see hanging in the air. The truth is, she fears that they will all smell death on her the moment she steps into the office.

"Shall we go on, then?" her father wonders.

Tightly, she nods her acquiescence.

"That's my girl," Pim tells her. "That's my Annelies."

It rained the night before. A drenching downpour, drumming against the window glass and the roof tiles. But the sky is clear this morning and crisp. Sunlight lifts the faces of the old Grachtengordel canal houses into sharp, clean relief against the blue, rain-scrubbed sky. Those neat façades of pastel brick take the sunlight like paint. Anne gazes at them as she walks. Their scrolls and flourishes still stolidly thrifty in their adornments after three hundred years.

Closer. They're getting closer to the last home she'd known. Crossing the bridge arching the Leliegracht, Anne feels her stomach lurch, and a passing cyclist scolds her when she vomits greenish bile into the gutter. Pim hurries back with a handkerchief for her to wipe her mouth. "Only a little way farther. A few more minutes," he tells her. "Breathe deeply," he instructs, and she does. "Are you ready to keep going?"

Anne swallows. But she nods again, though she knows quite well that she is *not* ready. A few minutes pass until her father slows and removes a key from his coat pocket. Anne steps to the edge of the pedestrian walk and stops. Facing the set of battered and dingy wooden doors, her feet stick to the brick pavement. There is nothing extraordinary about the face of Prinsengracht 263. It is modest, un-embellished. The address placard is still in place. The names of the businesses are stenciled on one of the warehouse doors in block letters. A board has been tacked over the hole that was kicked in by burglars while they were still in hiding.

The restored carillon of the Westertoren chimes clearly. The same clang that punctuated their days in hiding. She had come to rely on them for their continuity, until the Germans removed the bells and melted them down for their bronze. On the sunny morning of their arrest, the belfry was silent as they were loaded into the rear of a dark green police lorry. No clarion chime as eight fugitive onderduikers were hauled away. The Gestapo had placed a bounty on Jews in hiding. Seven and a half guilders a head, half a week's pay for most Dutch workers, though Miep says that by the war's end the bounty had risen to as high as forty a head, paid to anyone willing to repeat a rumor or betray a secret. Anne wonders, rather distantly, about who betrayed them. How much they were paid? Was it someone they knew? Before this moment their betrayal had felt fated to her, part of an inescapable outcome. This is the first time she has wondered about a person with motives. But then her mind jumps, as it often does now, as her father has opened the door to the high office stairwell and is peering with concern in her direction. "Anneken?"

Anne stares at the impossibly steep steps leading upward from the open door and then asks a question that feels both terrible and matter-of-fact. "When you thought I was dead, Pim, were you relieved?"

Her father flinches as if she has struck him in the face. *"Anne,"* he manages to say. She is pleased to have hurt him, as if inflicting this wound can in a small way compensate for all the wounds she herself has suffered.

"I think you must have been a little relieved. I know I was never easy. Wouldn't it have been simpler if Margot had lived instead?"

Her father continues to stare at her with blank alarm. "Anne, that you could *say* such a thing."

But Margot, too, seems to be interested in an answer to Anne's question, for she has appeared beside the open door, dressed in the pastel blue shift that she so often wore during their years in the hiding place. Mummy had taken it in so that Margot could fit into it, which made Anne jealous, because everyone knew that particular shade of pastel blue looked much better on her than on her sister. She tries to forgive Margot for wearing it now. "Isn't it true, Pim?" she asks.

Her father advances on her. For a moment he glowers, gripping his briefcase, and then his finger pokes the air sharply. *"Never* say this," he commands, his eyes flooded by a terrified fury. "You must *never* ask such a question again. Do you understand me, Anne? *Never."*

Anne gazes back at him. She feels empty. Her father's anger sags, and his eyes are awash with pity. He grips her tightly enough to squeeze the air from her, and slowly she returns the embrace. He smells of a dab of cologne. She can feel the light stubble on his cheek, after he'd shaved with a dull razor blade. She can feel his bones through his coat. Margot maintains her questioning gaze, asking Anne when she will tell him the truth.

Prinsengracht 263 has suffered through a long war, too. Its paint is peeling in shreds. The sleek layered finish on the doors has been scoured away by five years of Dutch weather and five years of German occupation without paint or varnish for repair. She waits for her father to step into the building first. "They're all so thrilled to have you here. Really quite thrilled," he assures her as they climb the leg-breaking Dutch stairs, her father having assumed the role of the Unblinking Optimist. He opens the door, its frosted window stenciled with the word KANTOOR. Anne hears the chairs scrape and the voices rise happily in the light and airy space. Mr. Kugler lopes in from his office on the other side of the alcove. He is a tall man, Mr. Kugler, with sloping shoulders, a jar-shaped head, and valiantly melancholy eyes. He clasps Anne's hand in both of his and kisses her like an uncle on the cheek. "So *wonderful*," he tells her in a heavily heartfelt voice. "So *wonderful*." Anne feels oppressed. But then she sees Bep. Bep—Anne's darling Bep. She is thinner, her face sharper. She offers Anne a short, timid hug and a smile weighted by trepidation, eyes widened by the pair of rounded eyeglasses she still wears. Anne is confused. Is she now so frightful that her friend cringes at the sight of her? Miep's earnest embrace, on the other hand, is still too dangerous, still too alarmingly maternal, so Anne quickly breaks it off. A dusty light is filtering through the high, unwashed window marked with adhesive patterns from the tape used as protection against flying glass after a bomb blast. The room smells of the cast-iron coal stove in the corner, which, starved of coal, only whispers a rumor of heat.

Throughout this scene Pim has been standing aside clutching his briefcase, his wide-sweep fedora on his head, his baggy raincoat hanging on him as if he were a scarecrow, gently beaming with approval. But he takes his first opportunity to retreat, withdrawing to his private office down the corridor past the coal bin. A moment of awkwardness ensues as Miep sets Anne down at a desk with instructions about how to evaluate piles of papers. Office work after Auschwitz. The dry little details. Anne must struggle to focus. Really, she'd rather be breaking up greasy batteries, sticky with silver oxide. Really, she'd rather be hauling the barracks shit bucket. This is too clean. She repeats the details of her instructions back to Miep, who nods. "Yes. Absolutely *correct*," Miep tells her with obvious satisfaction.

Anne catches Bep's gaze for an instant, but Bep's eyes quickly drop.

Throughout the afternoon Anne crinkles papers. She wonders if the person who denounced them worked for the company, or even works there still, the name of the betrayer printed on one of these sheets she's pushing around the desk, secretly mocking her. Mr. So-and-So the wholesale spice trader or Mr. Such-and-Such the freight master. Maybe him, maybe not. She sorts invoices this way and that way and makes a stack here and another one there. But then she gets lost in the blunted light streaking the dirty windowpanes. Unlike the Germans, the Dutch do not believe in shutters. They believe in open windows that speak to the world. Honest citizens have nothing to hide and have no need to shutter their windows. But the grime of occupation has made Dutch windows opaque.

Don't rush so, you'll make mistakes, Margot tells her.

Anne ignores her.

I'm sure those invoice copies are not in the proper order.

She hears a long, plaintive mew and looks down at a scrawny black tomcat. *"Mouschi!"* she exclaims in utter amazement, and scoops up the slinky little thing in her arms with a desperate pulse of need. Peter's cat alive, *alive.* "Mouschi," she purrs against the soft peak of the cat's ear. "Mouschi, little Mouschi, you sweet, sweet boy . . ."

"For a while one of the salesmen took him home for his wife," Miep says, and gives the skinny tom a playful rub on his bony cat noggin. "But she sent him back because he wouldn't stop scratching the upholstery, the little devil."

"Of course he was scratching the upholstery. He knew that it wasn't *really* his home." Anne squeezes Mouschi against her breast and rests her cheek on his head, but she must be squeezing him too tightly, because the cat suddenly squirms free and pounces to the floor, padding away, leaving Anne with a sickly feeling of loss. Anne thinks of her own little Moortje, her beloved tabby, to whom she was so devoted. But Pim had insisted that she leave Moortje behind when they went into hiding. Anne had sobbed but had done as she was told.

And *then* Anne was so livid when she found that *Peter* had been permitted to bring *his* cat to the hiding place that she absolutely hated the boy. But now here is Mouschi again. At least God has deigned to spare a sooty black little mouser.

She leaves her desk to find Monsieur Mouschi a saucer of milk in the kitchen to coax him back to her, but instead she finds an unusual sight. Bep with a lit cigarette in her hand. *"Bep?"*

Bep reacts as if she's been caught in mid-crime, and there's a dash to extinguish the cigarette by tossing it into the sink and twisting open the tap.

"Bep, I'm sorry," says Anne. "I didn't mean to surprise you. Really, you don't have to hide a cigarette."

"Mr. Kugler doesn't like smoking in the kitchen. And I really have no taste for tobacco. It's just that sometimes it calms my nerves." She clears her throat. Once Bep's hair was a stylishly fluffy affair, which required extensive treatment by a hairdresser on the Keizersgracht. But now her hair is flat and lackluster. Her complexion is like clay. But more than her appearance has been altered. Where once there was warmth, there is now only this cold distance between them.

Anne says nothing at first, wondering what has changed. She can summon up only one possibility. "Bep," she asks, "do you hate me now?"

Bep responds as if she has been singed by a spark from the stove. "*Hate* you? Of course not, Anne. How could you think . . ." she starts to say, "how could you possibly *think* . . ." But her words fray to nothing.

"It's only that you've barely spoken to me all morning. Hardly a word."

Bep shivers. Shakes her head at the air. "*I'm sorry.* I'm sorry if I seem distant," she whispers. "But the truth is, it's all too much. I simply can't bear any more. I prayed to God for such a long time to make things right, but look what happened. Look what you went through in those terrible places," she says. "Your mother and sister. The van Pelses. Mr. Pfeffer. All gone. I have such horrible nightmares about it. It's too much, Anne. I know that sounds cowardly and unfeeling. But it's just all too much."

"It's not cowardly," Anne tells her, grateful for a glimpse of the old intimacy between them. "I can't bear it either. I try to tell myself to accept it. That I'm nothing special. That *so many* people lost everyone. Lost everything. Yet . . . I can't *think* . . ." She shakes her head. "I don't know how to *proceed.* The sun comes up, and I fill the day, but it means nothing to me, and I want so desperately for that to change," she hears herself saying. "I want so desperately to have a purpose. A *real* purpose."

She swallows. When she thinks of purpose, she can't help but think of her diary. Even if it was nothing but embarrassingly adolescent scribblings, it gave her purpose. It was the last innocent purpose that Anne had. "When we were in hiding, you remember, I had my diary," she says. "I know everybody thought it was a silly thing. Just childish doodling. But to me it was so important. It was all I had that was truly mine." And it's true. When she thinks of her diary now, she still feels the loss of it physically. As if a limb is missing. An arm or a leg. "But it's gone now, too." All that work. All those words. She blinks at that reality and drags her fingers through her hair. "At times I feel so guilty. My mother is dead. My sister is dead. So many dead, and yet I mourn a pile of papers. What does that say about me, Bep?" she wants to know. "What does that make me?" And for an instant she is truly hoping for an answer. But all at once the gate is closed. Anne has bared too much of herself. Bep has a very odd expression patched onto her face. Her mouth is closed by a frown, but her eyes are hiding something electric.

"What?" Anne asks her. "What is it, Bep?"

Bep only shakes her head tightly. "I must get back to my filing," she declares, and abandons the room.

Alone in the kitchen, Anne feels a thunderous wave of loss crash over her. She feels a greasy charge of nausea in her stomach and retches roughly into the sink, spitting bile over the remains of Bep's cigarette. Anne has lost her ability to be among people. She must learn to protect herself from them better. To protect them from her. Opening the drain, she washes the mess away.

If you're ill, you should tell Pim, Margot insists.

"Shut up," Anne replies. "Can't you just . . . *shut up*?"

Out in the corridor, Anne hears the low mumble of her father's voice on the telephone. Mr. Kugler opens the office door and then blinks dully at the sight of her. "Anne?" is all he says, but she is on the move and does not respond. *Where are you going?* Margot dogs her. *Anne, where are you going? Miep is depending on you to finish your work,* she complains, but Anne slips past the inner office's doors. She hears Mouschi on the stairs ahead of her. *Anne, you have work to complete,* her sister calls out. Mouschi glances back and then hops forward, shooting up the steep steps to a dust-shrouded landing above, where the windows are still plastered with opaque cellophane. Anne follows.

And then the bookcase confronts her.

Just a battered old thing, hammered together from scrap by Bep's papa. A three-shelf construction jammed into the corner near the window, loaded down with sun-bleached ledgers, their labels peeling, leaving crusty glue stains. Above it an old map hangs, tacked to the floral-print wallpaper.

But what remain hidden are the latch and the iron hinge. What's hidden is the wooden door behind it. All one need do is tug the concealed cord that lifts the latch and the bookcase will swing open, because it's not a bookcase. It's a gateway.

Mouschi curls around her ankle with a quiet purr as her hand reaches out. Her fingertips brush the rough wood. She stares at the shelf as if she can see through it, but then a voice startles her and her hand snaps back.

"Anne?"

It isn't Margot, it's Pim. Her father is frozen halfway up the steps, gazing at her with quiet concern. Kugler must have alerted him that his daughter had strayed from the office area. She glares wildly as he approaches her on the landing. "Anne," he says again, but then stops. Something in him takes a step back, she can see it. "You know," he tells her with a gentle distance in his voice, "there's nothing up there any longer. The Germans stole everything. Miep says they pulled a moving van up to the door and cleaned everything out. *Completely.* Not a tack remains."

Anne stares at the bookshelf, then back at her father. "Have you gone up there?" she asks.

His eyes empty. "Yes."

Mouschi meows drowsily in front of the bookshelf. "I want to go up, too," she says.

"No, Anne. Are you sure?"

Her jaw clenches as she steps forward. The hinge behind the bookcase still works. She hears the drab clank of the latch as she tugs the cord. Then the case swings forward as if it's floating, and she stares at the door hidden behind it. Slate-green paint. Her hand is on the doorknob, and as the door opens, Mouschi peeks in but then shoots away, retreating down the stairs, leaving Anne alone to peer into the short hallway. She bends quickly to snatch a small bean from a crack in the floorboards, clutching it in her fist. It was always Peter's job to haul the heavy sacks of dried beans they stored here up to the kitchen, and she'd been pestering him about something, just for fun, as he huffed away, when the seam split on a forty-five-kilo sack. It sounded like thunder as a tidal storm of brown beans came roaring down the steps, scattering into every crevice. Anne was standing at the bottom of the stairs, up to her ankle socks in dry beans, blinking back at the shock stamped on Peter's long, boyish face. Then suddenly he erupted into a gale of pure, unsullied laughter. It became a house sport afterward to find one or two slippery beans left behind after the cleanup.

Stepping into the hallway, she approaches the room to the left of the stairs. Hand on the doorknob, she shuts her eyes as she opens it. With her eyes closed, she can see it as it was. The mash-up of furnishings. The patchwork curtains that Pim and she had sewn by hand. The worn throw rug. This was the communal living room during the day and the bedroom for Mummy and Pim at night. For Margot, too, after the great tooth yanker Pfeffer arrived to steal her sister's bed and force her to sleep on a folding cot. On one side stood their mother's bed with the pale cream crocheted throw under the heavy walnut shelving. Mummy always kept her shoes under the bed, and Anne would have to crawl under to fetch one when it was accidentally kicked back too far. After Mummy's bed came the black stovepipe, followed by the table near the window with the embroidered cloth and mismatched chairs. And then came the wobbly old bed where Pim slept, its brass reddened with tarnish. When the English bombers arrived,

Anne would run to Pim's bed in terror, a child in search of sanctuary. Never to Mummy's bed. She can see Mummy now in her mind's eye, arranging the bedclothes in the morning, her pine-green cardigan threadbare at the elbows, her hair dulled by wisps of gray pinned into a bun at the back of her head. Anne feels a surge of joy at the memory, but a joy contaminated by loss and guilt. How blind she was to her mother's true courage and love. How foolish she was to have wasted so much time arguing. She had written such terrible, critical things in her diary in anger but had never thought to ask for Mummy's forgiveness, not even in Birkenau. In Birkenau it was hard for her to think of forgiveness, only survival. If only she had the chance now to open her eyes and find Mummy looking back at her.

But when Anne's eyes open, no one is there. There is nothing left. Only unswept floorboards, peeling paint on the window frames. She can hear the mice skittering away from her intrusion. Gloom drapes the room. The rags she and Pim had patched together those first days in hiding still shroud the windows. With a sweep she pulls them down, permitting the daylight to penetrate the room for the first time in years. She lets them fall to the floor and brushes off her hands.

The door to the next room stands open. This was her room. The room she shared with the eighth member of their household of onderduikers: le grand dentiste Pfeffer. Two lumpy beds, a meter apart, hers extended by a chair so her feet wouldn't stick out. A hook on the back of the door for her robe and nightclothes. A chair and a narrow wooden desk, and oh, how she had battled with that stuffy old bag Pfeffer for the privilege of that desk. It was one of the ongoing wars of the household. A battle so frustrating that she cannot seem to spare sympathy for Mr. Pfeffer's shadow in the crowd of dead memories that trail her. She thinks of the smirk of disapproval on the old fart's face and wants only to smack it away. When he wasn't shushing her or criticizing her, he was commandeering her precious desk space for his so very essential "work," the study of the Spanish language. Anne can still see him, his trousers yanked up to his chest, wearing a red dressing jacket and black patent-leather slippers, horn-rimmed glasses on his nose as he frowned, hunched over his orange-and-white-striped Spanish grammar, *Actividades Comerciales,* in the shrunken pool of light from her desk lamp. His lips moving in a whisper as he conjugated verbs. Me gusta el libro. Te gusta el libro. Nos gusta el libro.

It's your arrogance, Margot tells her. Her willfulness. She cannot forget. She cannot forgive.

But stepping into the narrow oblong space, she feels tears chilling her cheeks. The wallpaper is brown with water stains, and dust floats in the light that penetrates the filmy windows. In hiding she had pasted her postcard collection on the wall alongside the pictures of film stars she'd scissored out from issues of *Cinema & Theatre.* Deanna Durbin and Charles Boyer. Greta Garbo and Norma Shearer. She had adored movie idols and the European royal families. A young girl's infatuation with glamour. Incredibly, they have survived, these pictures. Some torn. Some ruined by splotching from roof leaks, but still here. She had traded with her friend Jacqueline for a postcard of the young princess of England. A pretty little girl smiling over the legend H.R.H. THE PRINCESS ELIZABETH OF YORK.

Once these pictures afforded Anne comfort, but now they mean nothing. She turns to the empty spot where her writing desk once stood. A rickety wooden table with a shelf and a gooseneck lamp. She recalls the sound of the chair scuffing the floor as she tucked her knees under the desk. Recalls the hard grain of the wood beneath her paper. Recalls how the desk wobbled slightly as she leaned her elbow on it. But mostly she recalls the deeply nurturing satisfaction she felt as she wrote, netted by the yellow lamp glow. The scratching of the nib of her fountain pen. The scrambling release to spill herself onto the paper.

A floorboard creaks, and she's back in her empty present. It's Pim. He steps up beside her, and his arm encompasses her shoulder. For a moment she permits this false comfort.

"*Anneke,*" he says, as if he's about to speak some difficult words, some disclosure of memory. "There's something. Something I should tell you," he begins, but whatever it is, she doesn't want to hear it. The weight of his arm is confining, and she breaks away. Wipes her eyes. The next door leads to the washroom and the delft-blue commode in the WC. The porcelain sink with its brass taps still shiny from use.

The large mirror hangs above it. She avoids its dark reflection and climbs the tall steps to the next floor, listening to the sound of her heels on the wooden steps, and enters the kitchen. There's a deep sink with a battered copper bottom and a goose-neck faucet. A long countertop below a few tiers of shelving.

When her father appears on the threshold, she blinks wildly at him, then turns away. "Do you remember the strawberries, Pim?" she asks, her voice strained by a manic joy over the memory.

"Yes," he replies quietly.

"*Bushels* of strawberries." How they all crowded the dining-room table, laughing as they cleaned piles of vivid red fruit, popping the fresh sweetness into their mouths. "I can almost smell them," she says, and feels herself smile. But then the smile simply floats away from her.

At night this room was where the van Pelses slept. Peter's parents, Hermann and Auguste. Putti and Kerli. He was a businessman, Mr. van P., but there was something rough about him, like unvarnished wood. He had a talent, though. He could name any spice, no matter how exotic, blindfolded, with only a whiff. And what can be said about Auguste van Pels? She liked to flirt and argue, both. Always ready to praise Pim's gentlemanly behavior and to go at it with Mummy about whose linen was being stained or china chipped. In hiding, she had begged so pitifully to keep her furs when her husband gave them to Miep to sell for food and cigarettes.

A short breeze clatters past the windowpanes. "We found Mrs. van Pels at Belsen," Anne says, staring at the empty room. "Margot and I." And for a moment she can see the woman, emaciated, all the happy conniving and farcical self-pity starved out of her. "She did her best to look after us."

"Well." Pim nods, his voice dropping into a pit. "For that I am grateful to her."

"She vanished, though. It was easy to do at Belsen. Do you know what happened to her?" Anne is aware that Pim has written letters, visited many offices. Obtained copies of camp records through the International Red Cross. She knows that he has become the repository for obituaries, but she hasn't asked for a single detail until now.

"She died," he tells her, "probably on a forced march to a camp in Bohemia."

Anne turns her ear to Pim, but not her eyes. "And her husband?" She hears her father exhale.

"I was with Hermann van Pels in Auschwitz up until his death," he says dimly. "I tried hard to keep his spirits up, but it was no good. He injured his thumb on a labor Kommando and made the foolish mistake of requesting lighter duty, but really he had already given up by then. The next day a selection claimed him. All I could do was watch as he was marched away toward the Krematorien."

Anne nods. People who simply gave up. Her fist clenches around the dried bean in her hand. She passes through the next door to the cramped enclave where Peter van Pels made his bed. She is halted for an instant by the emptiness of the spot but then moves toward the ladder leading up to the attic. She can hear the concern in her father's voice as he calls after her, but she does not care if the floor is unsafe or the ladder too rickety. In the attic there is nothing but dust and rot and debris to greet her. A rusty set of bedsprings, a few forgotten tins of UNOX pea soup, a pile of moldering barrel slats. Then through the dirty window she sees it. The horse chestnut tree. Its broad old branches, as tough as history, listing calmly in the breeze. A heartbeat swells in her breast. She feels, perhaps, that the tree can recognize her. That its leaves are whispering their grief, too.

The noise of Pim's ascension intrudes behind her. *"Anne,"* she hears him call, but she simply gazes at the tree's rustling branches.

"And Peter?" she asks him with a lifeless voice. "What became of Peter?" For a moment she remembers the two of them curled up together on the divan here in the attic. She remembers the athletic beat of the boy's heart as she rested her head against his chest, his arm hooked around her shoulder as the leaves of the horse chestnut tree gently trembled.

Mauthausen-Gusen. According to Pim that is the name of the camp in Germany where Peter died after the mof evacuated Auschwitz. "I *begged* him to stay with me," Pim says. "*Begged* him to stick it out in the infirmary barracks until the Red Army came. The Russians were so close. We could hear the boom of their artillery." But

Peter was headstrong. Even Auschwitz hadn't cured him of that. He wouldn't stay. "Of course, it was very easy to believe that the SS would simply murder everyone they didn't evacuate." Pim shrugs dimly. "Very easy to believe. Just as it was very easy to believe that compared to where we were, *anything* was preferable."

Anne stares. "He never liked to sit still for too long in one place," she says.

Pim nods. "I'm sorry, Anneke."

"Sorry?"

"I know that you had feelings for the boy in a special way," he says.

But Anne only shakes her head dully. "I thought for a while that I loved him," she says. "But that's a feeling that's hard for me to imagine now, Pim."

Her father leans against a wooden post, tall and lanky. The daylight is as soft as ashes, a spongy light that absorbs all brightness. Vast, full-bellied clouds scud across the sky. "Your mother was so worried," he says, "that something improper would happen between you and Peter up here. Unsupervised."

Anne narrows her eyes. "Nothing did happen. Not really." She wipes tears from her cheek thoughtlessly. "It's so strange, Pim. I think that's why I—" she starts to say but then shakes her head. "It's hard to explain. I think that's why I feel such *grief* over the loss of my diary."

"*Grief?*" Pim's posture stiffens at the shoulders, and his eyes narrow with a quizzical distress. "You feel *grief*?"

Anne shrugs, embarrassed. "It may sound ridiculous. It was scribbling on paper. I know that, and I know it sounds terribly absurd, and perhaps even terribly selfish. But 'grief' is still the word for what I feel. Maybe it's because if my diary had not been destroyed, they would all still be alive to me in some way. Not just in my memory but on the page."

Pim does not interrupt his gaze but expels a heavy breath. "Anne. There's something I must tell you," he says. "But I don't know how to *begin*. So I suppose the only way forward is to simply *say* it."

But before he can speak another word, there are footsteps below. Mr. Kugler calling Pim's name with an urgent tone. Pim crosses over and peers down the attic's ladder. "Mr. Kugler?"

"My apologies for interrupting, but . . . but there's a *gentleman* for you on the telephone."

"A *gentleman*?" Pim sounds puzzled and a bit irritated.

"Concerning the issue we were just discussing. I'm afraid it's rather essential that you speak with him."

Pim's sigh ends with a frown. "*Ah.* Yes. Yes, you're correct. Thank you, Mr. Kugler." Returning to Anne, he says, "I'm sorry. I must take this call."

"But what were you about to say, Pim? What were you about to tell me?"

Pim's expression turns circumspect. "We'll talk about it later, Anne," he assures her, his voice now gaining a velvety disinclination to say more. "I'm sorry, but I *must* go." He pauses. "Please, don't stay up here too long. The dust," he insists. "It's not healthy."

———

Jan is working late again, past supper. The demands of the Social Service Bureau in a chaotic time, Miep explains, so it's just them—Miep, Pim, and Anne—as Miep serves a tureen of thick beet soup. Pim is holding forth on an article he's run across in newspapers. As the First Canadian Army liberated the western Netherlands, young women would try to communicate with friends and relatives in towns still under occupation by chalking messages on the sides of Canadian tanks. Pim finds this not only ingenious but very heartening, apparently. "That these girls should have such faith in the future," he says with satisfaction. Anne doesn't seem to notice the bowl of beet soup in front of her; instead she stares at Pim. Her father's desire to leave behind the horrors they suffered is overwhelming. He is bent on returning to what he likes to call "ordinary life" and has no time to "belabor" the past. Anne finds this maddening.

"Anne, you're not eating," Miep observes.

Anne blinks. Stares down at the soup and then finishes it with steady strokes of her spoon. When she has sopped up the last traces of it with her bit of bread, she expels a breath. "So, Pim, who do *you* think betrayed us?" she asks, finally giving voice to the question that has been sparking about in her brain. Her tone is pointedly casual, but it's a question designed to force the past into the present. Pim's face goes blank. He rests his spoon on the edge of the bowl and enters a deep, momentary silence.

"I have no idea, Anne," he says finally, and gives his head a single shake. "I really have no idea." Only now does he meet her eyes, now that he has erected the wall of his response.

"You don't think it was one of our warehousemen?"

"Possibly," her father replies, now starting to stir his soup again with his spoon, signaling that he is finished with this topic.

"Mr. Kugler thinks it was the man who replaced Bep's father as foreman."

"He was troublesome, yes." Pim nods without commitment. "Especially after he'd found the wallet Mr. van Pels had dropped in the storeroom. But we have no proof that he is the culprit." He returns to his soup.

"Then what about the cleaning woman?"

Tapping the excess from his spoon against the rim of the bowl. *"Who?"*

"The cleaning woman told Bep that she knew there were Jews hiding in the building."

"Anne," says Miep.

"And how do you know about that?" her father inquires dubiously. "Did Bep tell you?"

"She told *Miep*," Anne answers. "I overheard them in the kitchen."

Miep frowns. "Anne, that was a private conversation."

"A private conversation," Anne repeats. "I'm sorry, but I don't think there should be anything *private* about this, Miep. Not about this particular subject. Do you think that Bep was telling the truth?"

"Of course," Miep replies, her voice stiffening. "You know that Bep would never fabricate. Not about something so serious. How could you even consider?"

"How should I know *what* to consider? She's stopped talking to me."

"Yes, well, she's having a very difficult time," Miep says in Bep's defense. "Please, you shouldn't take it personally."

"No? Hmm," Anne says. "That's an interesting point of view. I live

through three concentration camps, but I shouldn't take anything personally."

"*Anne,*" Pim jumps in, but Miep stops him.

"It's fine, Otto," Miep assures him.

Pim disagrees. "No, it's *not,* Miep."

"Thank you," Miep says, "but honestly, you needn't trouble yourself. It's true that I have no idea how Anne feels. I have no idea how either of you feel. After what you've suffered, I can only imagine."

"Only you *can't* imagine," Anne points out. "So what do *you* believe happened, Miep? Do you believe it was the cleaning woman who telephoned the Gestapo?"

"*Enough,*" Pim finally decides. "*Enough,* Anne. Just because a charwoman who occasionally ran a vacuum over the office carpet had suspicions that she voiced to Bep, that doesn't mean she was guilty of a crime. People gossip. Unfortunate things happened. The building was *burglarized,* for heaven's sake—how many times?"

"Three," Miep reports.

"*Three times.* Also, *we* made mistakes. Plenty of them, I'm sure. Windows were left open when they should have been closed. The front door was left bolted when it should have been unbolted. Curtains were peeked through in the middle of the day," he reminds her adamantly. "After two years I have no doubt that there were many people who harbored suspicions. But we don't have a shred of proof to indict any single one of them." Her father raises his spoon to his lips and slurps efficiently. Anne knows he is trying to close the discussion. In one way this doesn't surprise her. Pim is an expert at closing down conflict. But in another way it shocks her. How can he be so complacent? His wife died. His daughter died. His friends died. How can he simply sit there and slurp his soup?

"Why don't you want to *know,* Pim?" she whispers, her voice a thin knife blade.

"Anne," Miep breaks in again, but Pim raises his hand. He swallows and stares sharply into the hollow air.

"It will do no one any good," he says finally. "Vengeance? Reprisal?" His eyes lift to Anne's. They are heavy and darkly magnetic. "They only cause pain, Annelies. More pain."

"So the guilty deserve no punishment? The dead deserve no justice?" Anne asks. "Is that what you're saying?"

"I'm *saying* that I will not devote a single moment of the life I have remaining to retribution. And as for the dead? We live well, we love each other, and we keep them alive in our hearts. That is the justice they deserve, in my opinion."

Anne stares.

Margot is standing behind Pim, wearing her glasses, ready for bed, her hair brushed, dressed in a white, freshly laundered nightgown, just as their father must remember her.

That night Anne takes the Montblanc she had organized into her hand and touches the nib to the blank paper, producing a small dot of ink. But then the dot becomes a word, and the word becomes a sentence.

She once believed that being a writer would make her famous and that she would travel to the capitals of the world and be adored. Now she knows that this future is nothing but a fantasy. She will never be famous. She will never be adored. Her story is too badly poisoned by pain and death. Who could stand to read it?

14

THE TRUTH ABOUT DESIRE

I'm in a state of utter confusion: on the one hand, I'm
half crazy with desire for him, can hardly be in the same
room without looking at him; and on the other hand, I
wonder why he should matter to me so much and why I
can't be calm again!

—Anne Frank,
from her diary,
12 March 1944

1946

De Keiser Meisjeslyceum
Reinier Vinkeles Quay
Amsterdam Oud-Zuid

LIBERATED NETHERLANDS

Six months since Anne's return

The snow comes, the snow goes. Anne watches the frost dissolve from the windowpanes as a weak, sickly spring arrives. The weather warms, and the grass greens. Amsterdam rumbles along with the clumsy efficiency of one broken wheel on the wagon, patched too many times.

At Pim's insistence Anne is scheduled to appear at the office to help with the clerical work three afternoons a week. Also at Pim's insistence, she has begun attending the De Keiser Meisjeslyceum, a school for girls in the Oud-Zuid. It's not much more than an old brick pile, this place, with many of its windows cracked or boarded over, but Anne doesn't care. She is indifferent to her studies. Sometimes Margot appears in class to set a good example with her attentive posture, but her lice-infested rags and boiling sores spoil the intent. In Anne's mathematics class, her teacher is Miss Hoebee, a skinny Dutch mouse chalking numbers across a slate. But numbers make no difference to Anne. Algebra cannot hold her attention. At thirteen she was the Incorrigible Chatterbox who couldn't keep from gabbing and had to write an essay entitled "Quack, Quack, Quack! Went Mrs. Quackenbush." Now she simply falls into silences. To her, school is just another kind of prison camp.

There's a Jewish girl in her class. Griet, who was passed off as Christian during the war. She can astonish Anne by reciting the Apostle's Creed without a slip. Anne applauds as if Griet were performing a magic trick, which in a way she is. In the classroom Griet is as bored as Anne, but for different reasons. Griet has *always* hated school, she says, whereas Anne once loved it. After Birkenau, however, what is the importance of oblique angles? After Belsen what can the Pythagorean theorem mean to her? Anne watches Griet lazily doodling in her exercise book. Griet is not exactly brilliant, but Anne appreciates the girl's instincts to change one's nature when circumstances dictate.

Anne has organized a shell-shaped compact from one of her classmates, Hildi Smit, that obnoxious kattenkop, and used its soft pink puff to powder over the number on her forearm. She has considered more drastic solutions, such as staging an accident while cooking. But she also has no doubt that even as she might try to explain to Pim how the hot pan slipped and burned her skin, he would guess the truth and gaze at her with that sorrowful expression of sympathetic disappointment of which he is the master. And it doesn't help that he treats his own tattoo as a kind of shrine, which he folds back his cuff to reveal as the holy relic of his survival.

"What are you doing?" Griet wants to know.

"Nothing," says Anne, the notebook in her hands, finishing off a sentence with her Montblanc. They are outside, sitting on the short stone wall after dismissal.

"You're always writing in that thing now," Griet complains.

"Am I? Not that much."

"Yes you *are*. All the time." Griet does not like to write. She says it only makes her hand hurt. "What *is* it anyway?"

"It's just . . ." Anne hesitates. Since she began to commit words to paper again, she's been driven. Every night before sleep, every time she can steal a moment to herself, she is writing. Writing simply to *write*. "It's just a diary. Nothing important."

"And what are you writing about? Sex?" Griet inquires hopefully.

"Ha! Yes, since I'm such an *expert* on the subject," says Anne, closing the notebook. Then she squints at Griet. What she likes best about her new friend is that she makes no demands on Anne. Griet does not require her to be thoughtful or patient or grateful. Their conversations are relaxing, mindless, curious.

"Have you ever?" Griet asks her.

"Have I ever what?"

"You know. Done it with a boy?"

"Nope," Anne replies, closing her notebook and leaning forward on her knees. Sometime it's so pleasurable to be frivolous. To pretend that she's a young Dutch girl like any other. "Never even come close," she says, thinking of Peter up in the attic. His damp lips, their clumsy touching, all very tame. But the memory stings her so strongly that she dismisses it. She knows there is a boy named Henk whom Griet has taken up with. She's seen the two of them necking. "Have *you* ever?"

Griet frowns sheepishly. "Only sort of," she confesses. "I've let Henk do *some* things. Touch me places. But that's all." Henk's given her cigarettes and chewing gum and has even promised her a lipstick, since he claims that his older brother is in the black market. Also, he's a *goy*! Maybe Griet's become so accustomed to playing the role of a gentile that it's hard to go back to being a Jew in this world.

"And have you ever," Anne wonders, "touched *him* places?"

"Oh, you mean his lul? No, though he showed it to me once."

"Really?"

Griet snorts a small laugh into her hand and then drops her voice. "It looked like a sausage," she confides. "Like a weisswurst, only kind of purplish, and it stood up at attention. He wanted me to rub it, but I wouldn't."

Anne smiles. "Like Aladdin's lamp," she says, and laughs, delighted at the little crudity.

Griet grins back, devilish. "Until out comes the genie!"

———

Prinsengracht 263
Offices of Opekta and Pectacon
Amsterdam-Centrum

Pim has found her a bicycle, her first since hers was stolen during the occupation. It's an old black tweewieler with a worn brown leather seat and actual rubber tires, while much of Amsterdam is still riding on metal rims. After pedaling through a damp afternoon to the Prinsengracht office, Anne wheels her bicycle into the warehouse, because fingers are still generally too sticky for her to risk leaving it on the street. The noise of the milling machinery is loud, and the smell of the spices seasons the air. Cloves, pepper, and ginger. Monsieur le Félin Mouschi darts in a blur across the dusty floor, pursuing a rodent snack no doubt, leaving a trail of clover-shaped paw prints in the dust. Before the war Anne had looked forward to visiting the warehouse with Pim, especially when they were grinding nutmeg or cinnamon. The aroma made her feel giddy. And the older workers, softened up by the thought of their own kids, often gave her sweets. Licorice or sometimes honey drops. Mr. Travis showed her a magic trick with a coin that made her laugh, and she marveled at the mysterious warehouse slang the men barked at one another over the hum of the grinders. But all that changed once the Germans came. Mr. Travis had to take a job closer to the hospital when his son was badly wounded in the army. Mr. Jansen moved his sick wife to the country, where his brother had a farm. New men were hired. Unfamiliar names were written on the strips of tape above the coat hooks by the warehouse doors. "NSBers," she remembers Bep claiming in a dark whisper. Dutch Nazi Party men.

Anne squinted. *"Really?"*

"Some of them," Bep confirmed.

"And my father *knows*?" Anne had asked.

"It was *your* papa who told *my* papa they must be hired."

Shortly after they went into hiding, Bep's father, who was a chief participant in their secret, was struck by cancer and had to be replaced as workshop foreman. So with the family in hiding, the warehouse workers on the ground floor became a source of daily danger. If one of them heard something. If one of them saw something. If one of them suspected. They became the enemy in a sense, just as much as the moffen.

But now those men are gone. It's a new crew, free of traitors, but they keep themselves to themselves and have no interest in Anne Frank. Except maybe one of them. It's a Wednesday. Always a heavy day of milling to fulfill shipments for the end of the week. Propping her bike in the corner, Anne inhales the warm, nutty aroma of mace but can't help but notice that one of the workers gives her a direct look as he hefts a second barrel of spice onto a pull cart. He is a lean, sinewy youth with a hard, pale glare, and he muscles the large barrel into place as if he's showing off his strength. As if maybe he has something to prove to the dark-headed Joods meisje who's the owner's daughter. Anne peers back at him. The boy's hair is straw blond and uncombed. His clothes are patches sewn together. His jaw is square, and there's a heaviness to his eyes, as if something terrible and unalterable has settled in his gaze, turning his eyes the color of ashes. His name? She's never heard it, nor has she ever heard him speak. Something about the boy does not invite conversation. A second later the youth grunts and looks away like she doesn't exist, but he leaves Anne with a lift that starts just below her belly and spreads out into a breathy lightness that reaches all points of her realm.

That night in her room, she stares at herself naked in the wardrobe mirror and inventories her parts. Unlike Griet, with her voluptuous silhouette, Anne has remained quite petite in that department, and it makes her wonder what she would have looked like at this point if Christians had hid her as well. If she hadn't been starved to a cat's weight at Belsen. Would she have a woman's full body by now? Would the Canadian liberators call to her in the street in the same way they do to Griet?

In bed she pulls up the covers. Griet has tried to advise her on how to touch herself in a way that feels good, but it's a feat she has not yet managed to accomplish. She follows the instructions in her head, attempting to coax some kind of tingling reaction from herself. She imagines what it would feel like to have a boy's hand where her clothes hide her body. She thinks of the boy from the warehouse with the mop of blond hair. But then she's ambushed by a memory of Peter. Sitting with him up in the attic of the hiding place, sharing a bit of privacy while Mouschi purred in his lap, sprawled in a ridiculous paws-up position. Peter was three years older than Anne and spoke with an air of casual, clinical understanding as they discussed it all: Genitalia, both male and female. Sexual procedure. Preventive measures. Somewhat embarrassing at the time, but all highly informative. Her textbook understanding of the male organ had been confirmed—*verbally,* of course—as had her hunch that boys knew nothing whatsoever about the apparatus of the female. So she had explained. She had already educated herself on the various pipes and functions of a woman's plumbing and could give Peter a detailed lesson. He was impressed by her composure and comprehensive knowledge. But as she had confided to her diary, she had been a little perplexed when she'd explored herself in the privacy of her bath. She had been a little alarmed. How could a man ever penetrate such a tiny opening? Even more alarming, how could a baby ever be expelled *through* it?

What are you doing? Margot suddenly demands, as if thoughts of Peter have summoned her instead, and Anne practically jumps out of her skin, clutching the blankets up around her chin. "Damn it, Margot, what do you *want?*"

I want to know what you're doing, her sister replies, seated on the edge of the bed in her blue-and-white-striped rags and a lice-matted pullover. Her head shaved down to the scabs, her face colorless with death.

Anne frowns. "You *know* what I was doing," she insists. "You know very well."

And you think it's appropriate to do that with Miep and Jan in their bed right next door?

"Well, what do you think Miep and Jan do in their bed, dumbbell? Play tiddlywinks?"

Don't be crude, Margot instructs. *They're a married couple. You're just a girl with roaming thoughts. It's not healthy, Anne.*

"Oh, what? *What's* not healthy?"

You know, Margot assures her. *Just what you were doing. Touching yourself in that manner,* she says.

"How can that be so? How can it *possibly* be unhealthy?"

Because it . . . it unnaturally accelerates your development, Margot decides.

"Well, if that's so, then how come *you* were doing it?"

What? Margot squawks. *I was not.* She frowns.

"You *were,* I heard you. I heard you when we were in the same room before that old bag Pfeffer arrived. And it was *Mummy and Pim* in the room right next door," she adds with malicious relish. "You can't deny it, Margot. I heard what I heard. Maybe I was a few years younger than you, but I could still tell what was going on under your covers."

Don't make up lies, Anne, her sister warns, and Anne feels the anger surge freakishly through her body.

"I'm *not* lying. I'm not *lying*!"

Suddenly there is someone rapping fearfully at her door. "Anne?" Miep's voice calling. "Anne, are you *all right*? Anne?"

She is breathing frantically, sitting bolt upright with the blankets clutched to her chest, white-knuckled. But Margot is gone, leaving only empty space in her wake.

Anne assures Miep that there is nothing to worry about, using as few words as possible. She is oké. A word they have all adopted from their Canadian liberators. Oké.

But when she lies back down in her bed, she doesn't feel oké. She feels robbed. She feels frustrated. She feels shamed. It makes her think that desire can be a trap. A trap that once it snaps shut on you, keeps you trapped. Never to be completely free. That, she thinks, is the truth about desire.

15

JEALOUSY

I'm not jealous of Margot; I never have been. I'm not
envious of her brains or her beauty.

—Anne Frank,
from her diary,
30 October 1943

1946

Amsterdam

LIBERATED NETHERLANDS

Sitting on her bed in the light of her lamp, the notebook in her lap, she writes about a day in Birkenau during the last weeks Mummy was with them. There was a woman in their barracks, a Dutch woman, who for a ration of bread might organize something warmer to wear. The woman liked Margot because she was the same age as her daughter, or something like that. Anyway, Mummy traded a bite of their camp bread for a woolen pullover and gave it to Margot. Anne remembers it because she was just so insanely jealous. Wasn't *she* the sickly one? Growing up, wasn't it Anne who caught everything there was to catch?

The sweater was ugly and ragged along the bottom hem, and Anne had always despised the color brown, *but how she wanted it.* Wanted it because Mummy had given it to Margot and not to her. It made her feel very ashamed to be so overlooked. Margot got a pullover, and what did Anne get? Scabies.

Soon after her mother's trade for the sweater, there was a selection in their section of the Frauenlager, but not for the gas chamber. No, the rumor was it was for a work camp in Liebenau, far away from Auschwitz-Birkenau, and what luck! Margot and Anne and their mother were all three picked for the transport, but that's when the SS-Lagerarzt saw that Anne had the Itch. It was hard to miss, really; greasy red and black sores had spread over her arms and hands and neck. So instead of the sanctuary of an Arbeitslager, Anne was sent to the Scabies Block. After that her mother and Margot stayed, too. They didn't have to. They could have gone to Liebenau. There were no smoking chimneys there, just factory work. They could have survived. But because Anne had the Itch, they stayed.

Sometimes Anne can still feel the cold ground under her. Margot came with her to the Scabies Block just so Anne wouldn't be alone, which meant it wasn't long before both sisters were infected. They sat beside each other in the dirt, tucked under a blanket in the murky shadows of the block, not talking. Anne glared into nothing, listening to the groans of the sick and the squeak and patter of the rats. When a small scoop of light crumbled out from the ground beneath the wall, she didn't understand what was happening. Not at first. And then she heard Mummy's voice. "Is it working?" Mummy begged to know, and another woman answered, "Yes. It's working." Mummy and a lady from their barracks had managed to dig a hole from the outside. Anne heard Mummy calling their names and tried to call back, but she barely had a voice at that point, so she managed to rouse Margot, and they crawled over to the hole, where Mummy stuffed through a piece of bread. Margot tore it in two and gave her sister half. Anne can still taste the bitter roughness of that bread and remembers how desperately she swallowed it down. But even so at that moment, when she should have loved Mummy utterly, she felt a pinch of anger.

16

TRUST

I was born happy, I love people, I have a trusting nature,
and I'd like everyone else to be happy too.

—Anne Frank,
from her diary,
25 March 1944

1946

Amsterdam

LIBERATED NETHERLANDS

By noon a bright sun is bluing the sky, and Anne and Griet find they have had enough of school for the day. They hurry down the stairwell at the rear of the building and steal into the street. Only the circling gulls above the canal squawk with alarm at their truancy. On their bicycles it's twenty minutes to the movie house. The cobblestones have been lacquered silvery bright by the early rain, but Anne feels free riding her bicycle, darting and weaving in between pedestrians. She feels the thrill of the speed, the rough delight of her tires brisking along the streets. People scold her impertinence, but it only makes her laugh with a keen release, and she calls back to Griet to keep up with a wild brand of joy.

Canadian troops are occupying the newly opened pubs, dance halls, and café tables as the city slowly drowses awake. For months Canadian cigarette rations have stood as the standard currency across the town. Shopkeepers display printed signs in their windows written in English: NO CURRENCY ACCEPTED. CIGARETTES ONLY. The English language has invaded the movie houses, too, and Dutch has been relegated to the subtitles.

Anne and Griet buy their tickets and step into the dim auditorium, which is nothing but a roomful of chairs facing the whitewashed wall where the film will be projected. To advertise their freedom, their brash disregard, both girls have hooked their legs over the empty seats in front of them, causing their skirts to hike, uncovering their knees and showing off their calves.

The movie is a comedy. A short, fat man and a tall, skinny man are best pals, yet there's always something the fat one is doing to earn

him a slap or a punch. It's easy to see that the fat one is the funny man
and that his antics are driving the show. The skinny man is only there
to have jokes bounced off him and to administer hilarious punishment with a seltzer bottle or a bop on the noggin. The fat man is
chased by a tiny yapping lapdog. Chased by a Chinese cook wielding
a cleaver. Chased by a woman whose skirt has been ripped off. Everyone laughs. Anne laughs. She laughs as if she might never stop, as if
she might drown in her own laughter.

The girls are still laughing when they stagger out into the afternoon. They lean against the casements featuring the advertising
placards and huff smilingly at the air.

"Jezus *Christus,* that was too much," Griet moans.

Anne sighs a laugh and breathes through a smile. "I've never heard
you say that," she notices.

"Heard me say what?"

"Jezus Christus."

Griet only shrugs. "It's just a saying."

They hear a whistle as two of the Canadian soldiers cycle past
them. "Hey there, honeypot." One of them grins at Griet. "You look
like you're gonna bust outta your shirt." And then he says something
else that exceeds Anne's grasp of English, something that causes the
soldiers to chortle together loudly as they pedal off.

"What did he *say,* what did he *say*?" Griet is desperate to know.

"He said, 'Hello, you beautiful ladies—please marry us and come
live in our castles in Canada.'"

"Oh, he did not. *Did he?*"

"No."

"*Are* there castles in Canada?"

"I don't know. Maybe there are." She expels a breath. "I have to be
going."

"Aw, don't tell me you have to work in your father's dumb old office again."

"I do."

"It's not fair. You should come over to my flat. Nobody's home at
this time of day. We could do whatever we want."

"Tomorrow, maybe. Today, I promised my father."

"Promises." Griet shrugs. "Well, if you must. But before you go"—
she smiles—"I've got something for you."

Anne smiles back at the tube of lipstick that Griet produces from
her pocket. "Where did you get that?"

"Henk. He got a bunch of them from his brother," Griet whispers
mischievously as she unscrews the tube. Anne answers by shaping
her mouth into a bow. She feels the sticky, creamy flow of the lip
rouge, watching Griet shape her own mouth into an instructive oval
as she applies the color to Anne's lips. *"Perfection."* Griet's laugh is
impish. "Now you're irresistible."

But Anne's attention has been caught by a figure leaning against
the brick balustrade at the end of the canal bridge. It's the yellow-
haired boy from the spice warehouse. A loiterer, dressed in poor, ill-
fitting clothes, he gazes at them.

"Who's *that?*" Griet wants to know.

"I don't know his name. He works in my father's warehouse."

"Well. He looks very *interested* in *something*," she points out, and
gives Anne a nudge. "I wonder *what.*"

Curiosity. That's all it is. It's just for curiosity's sake that Anne walks
her bicycle up the Prinsengracht rather than riding it. At first she
camouflages her over-the-shoulder glances. Stopping to tie her shoe
and sneaking a peek. Another fleeting look as she allows an old man
to pass with his cane or to yield to a pair of cyclists dinging their bells
as they turn onto the Leidsegracht. Each time, she sees that he's still
behind her, hands stuffed into his trouser pockets, his shoulders
hunched with a purposeful stride.

She's both excited by this and a little frightened. The gulls are
swooping above her, crying. She can smell the diesel stench of boat
engines. By the time she passes the fat yellow advertising column at
the corner of the Rozenstraat, she quits trying to cover her backward
glances. Halfway across the bridge to the Westermarkt, she stops as
a canal boat putters beneath and leans her bike against the stone-
work. The boy hesitates for an instant. But then he walks toward her.

"You're following me," she accuses him blankly.

"Could be," he answers.

"Why?" She feels his eyes penetrating her bravado.

"Why do you think?"

"I'm sure I haven't the slightest," Anne insists.

"No?" A smile bends his lip. "I saw you coming out of the movie house. Do you like it when soldiers whistle at you?"

She feels a sudden heat. "It wasn't me they were whistling at."

"Oh. You mean it was your friend with the big boobies."

Anne's jaw clenches.

"Well, I like you better," the boy tells her.

"Oh, *do* you? That's *such* an honor." She frowns. Though, honestly, she's surprised at the bright sting of joy she feels.

"I like your face. I like watching you look at things."

"Things?"

"Things." He shrugs. "I liked the way you looked at *me*. But I wasn't sure."

"Sure of what?"

The boy gazes at her.

"Sure of *what*?"

Another shrug. "You're the owner's daughter. I'm just a broom boy. A piece of canal trash."

Anne stares back at him. "You're a gentile," she says, "and I'm Jewish." She says this and waits for his response. Waits to judge his response. But all he gives her is a lazy exhale. "That doesn't mean something to you?" she must demand.

"Well. My pap always said Jews are bloodsuckers. But my pap hated everybody. Me? I don't care if you're from the moon. I just want to touch your face."

Anne breathes in and then breathes out. The boy is so close to her. The maleness of him. She feels tension in the simple proximity of their bodies. She can smell his bitter sweat. Is it guilt that stings her? Margot is never going to stand so close to a rough-edged boy like this, with nothing but a heartbeat between them. Anne feels her attraction as if it's a type of pain.

"That's all you want?" she asks. "Just to touch my face?"

The boy's expression bends as he turns his head, unsure if he is being baited. She can see the hurt in his eyes. The uncertainty.

"Well, then," Anne prompts. "I'm standing here."

And now the boy straightens. His posture perks up, but his eyes are still hunted. "You mean . . . *now*?"

The carillon of the Westertoren chimes the quarter hour. The boy glances around, but the bustling Dutch citizenry are more interested in their own business than in how close together the two of them are standing. So he takes another step forward. She watches his hand rise and notices the dirt under his fingernails, but then she looks into his face as, ever so gingerly, his fingertips brush the skin of her cheek. It's just a whisper of a touch, but she feels it root her to the spot. For an instant the pain in his eyes has lifted. She swallows.

"Can I do it again?" he asks, but doesn't really wait for an answer. His fingers rise, and he strokes her cheek with a sudden intimacy that causes her heart to clench. Her lips part and her body moves, and in the next instance she seizes him, smothers her mouth against his. It is not a kiss, it's an attack. She wants to devour him at a single gulp. She snatches his hair as if she might rip it out. She wants to inhale him. She wants so much more than Peter's wet mouth could ever have offered her in the attic of the Achterhuis. She wants the boy's breath. She wants his blood. And when she bites his lip, she tastes it.

He yelps painfully as he breaks away from her. His eyes blinking with shock, he wipes his lips and glares at the stain of blood and lipstick on his fingers without comprehension. Anne gives him a wild gaze, her eyes flooding with tears, as she mounts her bicycle and launches her frantic escape.

Prinsengracht 263
Offices of Opekta and Pectacon
Amsterdam-Centrum

When she reaches the doors of her father's building, she is out of breath, still wiping away the tears as she rolls her bicycle into the warehouse. The air is thick with coriander, and a powdery haze hangs in the heavy sunlight. The men ignore her, too busy to bother with hellos, which is a relief. She climbs the steep stairs slowly and then pauses outside the office door, trying to compose herself. Wipes the lipstick onto a handkerchief, trying to compose a face to wear. She was once well known among her friends for her expressions of careless insouciance. But now her heart is a deep drumbeat in her chest, and she feels a terrible thrum of rage and hunger. She breathes in, she breathes out, her eyes shut tight, trying to suppress the painful surge of desire that she tastes in her mouth like the tang of the boy's blood.

"Sorry I'm late," she announces, breezing into the front room, her voice a panic of nonchalance. Miep looks up at her with blank anxiety.

"Late? Oh," says Miep, and then she shakes her head dismissively. "I hadn't even noticed. I think Bep has a stack of correspondence that needs filing."

Anne looks up, slips her book sack from her shoulder. Bep is watching her nervously from the opposite desk, then staples a selection of papers together with a quick bang.

"Where is everybody?" Anne wants to know. She noticed that her father's office door was closed when she climbed the steps from the warehouse, but it meant nothing. Pim has people in the private office all the time. Salesmen, advertising-agency people, spice distributors, a steady flow of municipal functionaries, all with their own particular rubber stamps that require inking. But now Anne wonders, "Where is Mr. Kugler? Where is Mr. Kleiman?"

A half glance from Miep. "They're in your papa's office."

Something about the sound of this is odd. The small intimacy softening Miep's voice. In the flat they share, Miep calls Pim by his given name, "Otto," but at the office it is always and only "Mr. Frank." Now it's suddenly "in your *papa's* office."

Bep is harried as she dashes off her explanation of Anne's assignment, and then she picks up the teacup and saucer from her desk. "I'm going to wash the dishes," she announces, standing. And before Anne can respond, Bep is bustling away, pausing only to collect an empty cup from Mr. Kleiman's desk before rattling off to the kitchen beside Pim's private office.

"Oh, *Bep*," Miep calls, holding up her own cup and saucer, but Bep is already gone. "Anne, I'm sorry, but would you mind taking this in, too?" she asks. Her voice is dim and distracted, hiding unspoken nerves.

"What's happening?" Anne asks.

"Nothing's happening."

"Yes. Something."

"I don't know what you're asking."

"There's something you're not telling me."

"Anne, please. The *cup*."

She takes it, pursing her lips. Passing her father's office, Anne can hear the weave of voices but cannot make out a word spoken. She slips into the kitchen behind Bep and sets Miep's cup and saucer on the sink. "Another cup, Bep," she says.

"Oh." A blank glance. "Thank you," Bep tells her with a thin smile, and returns to the teacup she is scrubbing.

Anne lifts herself onto the counter for a seat, legs dangling. "So who's in my father's office with him?" she asks as casually as possible.

Bep's glance is clouded. "Mr. Kleiman and Mr. Kugler are in there," she says. "And some other gentlemen. I don't know who they are. Honestly, no one is telling me anything." Bep frowns fearfully. "Not Mr. Frank, not Mr. Kleiman. Not even Miep." Her posture and expression are guarded, and the light of the flagging sun from the window turns her glasses opaque. Then, "Excuse me," she says, leaving the towel hung over the sink's faucet and returning the cups and saucers to the cupboard. "I should get back to my work. There's still so much to do."

Quickly, Anne drops her feet back to the floor, latching onto Bep's arm. *"Bep,"* she whispers. "Wait."

"I have to go."

"In a moment. Please wait for just a moment," Anne begs. Bep seems to freeze in place. "It's been hard for you, I know, with me around," Anne says. "And maybe one reason is that I should have said this to you sooner. So let me say it now: *Thank you*. Thank you, Bep, for all you did for us. Even if it all ended the way it did, you and Miep cared for us so well. You risked your own safety for ours."

Bep is still fixed in place, still staring, her eyes locked open behind the lenses of her glasses. "I don't need any thanks," she says tightly. "I don't want anyone to feel grateful to me."

"But I *am* grateful. You must let me be grateful, Bep. It's one of the few human things I can still feel. Grateful to you and Miep, Mr. Kleiman and Mr. Kugler. I can't explain it, but I need to be grateful."

Bep bites into her lower lip, shaking her head. "*No.* You don't *understand.*"

"I don't understand anything anymore," Anne admits. "I'm lost. So utterly lost. I need some purpose, Bep. I must *accomplish* something to justify myself. Why am I alive? Mummy's dead. Margot's dead. Why am I the lucky one? How can I deserve that?"

For an instant Bep looks at Anne with stark, pale terror. *"It's the police,"* she confesses suddenly, as if the words were too dire to remain unspoken a second longer.

"The police?" Anne repeats.

"The BNV. In your father's office."

Fear like a poke from a needle. Police? The BNV is the Bureau of National Security, and that only means one thing to Anne: arrest. She feels her throat thicken. "Why would you think *that*?"

"Because who else could it *be*? They've been here all afternoon. They called Miep in. For an hour she was in there. And when I asked her what was going on, all she did was tell me to stay calm and keep my head on. And then came *my* turn and all those dreadful questions. How *well* did I know the men working in the warehouse? How often did I talk to them? What was my contact with the man from the home office in Frankfurt?"

"The *mof*?"

"How many times did I speak to him over the telephone? How could I be expected to *remember* such a thing?" she exclaims. "I answered the telephone ten times a day." She bites down to steady the quiver of her chin, and then she whispers a dark conclusion to herself. "I think they suspect me."

Anne feels her neck heat with sweat. "Suspect *you*?"

A quick blink from Bep, as if for an instant she'd forgotten that Anne was there. Her eyes go wet. "Of betrayal."

"Bep," Anne breathes. "You're frightening me."

"I'm sorry, but what if it's true? What if they're planning on taking me into custody as a collaborator?"

And for the smallest fraction of an instant, Anne introduces that possibility into her brain: Bep as betrayer. A painful pinprick till she shakes it off. "No. That can't be true."

"*Can't it?* All I know is that the whole town's out for vengeance. Don't you know? It's 'Hatchet Days,' and I've *seen* what's done in the name of justice. Up close!" Eyes darting. "I'm sorry, Anne, but I must *go*. I really must."

"*Bep.*" Anne speaks her name as if trying to snag her with a hook, trying to latch onto Bep's arm again, but this time Bep won't permit it.

"I'm sorry, I'm sorry," Bep keeps repeating. "I'm sorry, but there's nothing you or I can do. Things will never be the way they were again, Anne. Not *ever*," she declares, and beats a tearful retreat, leaving Anne alone. Her eyes burn hotly. Her breathing shortens, and she feels she must force herself into her next breath.

Out in the corridor, Anne finds Mr. Kleiman lighting a cigarette outside Pim's private office, thin as a reed with short, silvered hair and round horn-rimmed spectacles. Because of his stomach troubles, Mr. Kleiman rarely smokes. Everyone knows that. But this afternoon he is inhaling the chalky gray smoke before he turns with a dismal gaze and observes Anne standing in the threshold of the kitchen.

"Goedemiddag, Anne," he offers with an unusual formality.

"Is something going on, Mr. Kleiman?" she asks him.

But Kleiman only shrugs as if to say, Who could explain it? His expression is pale and bleak. No more sunshine from Mr. Kleiman. Before the war he was a man with a cheery, sympathetic manner, who was known for his love of jokes, riddles, and tongue twisters. Now Mr. Kleiman is known for his sudden silences, as if he has been confronted by a riddle he simply cannot crack. A puzzle that will not be solved. He gazes at Anne through his spectacles; his expression looks bludgeoned and burdened by a deeply routine pain.

"Those men in there," she says. "Who are they? What do they want?"

His head shakes. "You'll have to ask your father about that, Anne," he answers simply. "It's not my place to say."

"Can I see him?" She takes a step forward, but Kleiman raises his palm to stop her.

"No. No, not now. Now is not good."

But Anne feels a rush of dark energy building up inside her. She quickly ducks past Mr. Kleiman and rattles the door handle.

"Anne!" Kleiman squawks. But the door is locked.

"Pim!" she demands, and in a moment the latch turns and the door cracks open, Pim blocking her entrance.

"I'm sorry," Mr. Kleiman is apologizing tensely behind her. "I had no idea that she would try to barge through like this."

"Anne," Pim says firmly. "This is no time for antics."

"What's going *on* in there? That's all I want to know." She tries to peer past Pim, but her father will not permit it.

"Anne, I'm closing the door."

"No! You can't keep any more secrets from me."

"I'm not. But some matters are private. There's a difference. Go back to your work and allow the *adults* to handle things."

"Oh, as if the *adults* have handled all matters so perfectly up till now."

"Anne."

"All the *adults* have done is raze half the world to the ground."

"Anne, do as you are *told!*" Her father's voice booms with an unnatural jolt of anger. "Do as you're told or there *will* be *consequences.*"

"Consequences? *Ha!*" she shouts back. "And what could those consequences possibly *be?* What can you take away from me that I haven't already *lost?*"

Pim simply doesn't answer her and simply bangs the door closed, relatching the lock. Anne bulls past Kleiman and storms away, but not to fume. Quickly, she dashes around to the landing and up the steps. Unhooking the bookshelf, she pushes it aside and enters the Achterhuis. The room creaks. Gulls squawk outside the windows, but she can hear a muffle of voices drifting upward from the private office beneath her. Once, after they'd gone into hiding, a big wheel from Pomosin-Werke in Frankfurt had traveled to Amsterdam to confer with Kugler and Kleiman over Opekta's financial health. Pim had been so anxious about missing this meeting that he'd lain down with his ear pressed to the floorboards to listen in. Margot, too, had been conscripted into lending her ear to the effort, trying to take notes in shorthand while prone on the hardwood. This worked for a bit, but when Pim had grown too stiff to continue, Anne had been drafted next. Now, down on her belly, she presses her ear to the floor. She can hear a strange tone enter her father's voice, stiltedly formal but also weighted by a hard anger and something else: fear.

"Please, allow me to finish my *point*," he is saying. "The survival of my family was my only concern. The businesses were secondary."

"That's irrelevant," she can hear one of the unknown men correct. "Regardless of your motives, Mr. Frank, facts are facts."

Anne, what are they saying? Margot wants to know, suddenly lying beside her, just as if they were still together in hiding, ear pressed to the wood. *I can't hear them, Anne. What are they saying?*

"*Quiet,* will you?" Anne hisses back. But she's missed what Pim has just said, and now the other man is talking.

"This will do for today, Mr. Frank. We'll keep you informed as necessary while we continue our investigation."

By the time Anne makes it back belowstairs in the front of the building, it's too late. Whoever the people were in Pim's office, they have made their exit. She can hear Kleiman's voice warning them to mind the steepness of the steps as they descend to the street. She thinks of trying to follow them, but before she can do so, Pim pokes his head out of the private office. "Anne. I want to speak to you, please," he announces darkly.

The private office was always considered very plush. The padded upholstery. The velvet drapes. The warm oak paneling. The well-polished desk and the brass fixtures. This was the spot where they would gather in hiding to listen to the BBC or Radio Oranje after the workers below had gone home. But now there is a forlorn quality to it. The brass has begun to tarnish. The furnishings show their many nicks and scratches.

The heavy drapes are dull with dust, and years of plumbing failures have stained the wallpaper.

"I cannot *conceive* of what made you feel *justified* in indulging in such an outburst."

"Who were those men?"

"Anne, I've told you. It's a private matter."

"There's nothing private about who betrayed us, Pim."

"Betrayed us?"

"Why is the BNV investigating Bep?"

"*Anne,*" says her father patiently as if naming a silly, irrational thing.

"They were interrogating her. She told me. Both her and Miep."

"Anne," he says again. "Those gentlemen are not BNV, and they were not *interrogating* anybody. You're letting your imagination run away with you. There were simply certain matters that needed to be cleared up. Certain questions that needed to be asked."

"Asked by *whom*? If you say those men are not BNV, then who *are* they?"

"Enough, daughter," Pim says firmly, his voice going ragged around the edges. "Please, *enough*. I've already told you everything you need to know."

"You've told me *nothing*," Anne protests.

"Untrue. I've told you it's none of your concern and that you should leave it be."

"Bep is very upset," Anne says.

"She had a difficult interview," Pim is willing to admit.

"Is she going to be dismissed?"

Pim huffs with an exhausted air. "No one is being dismissed. Bep is still a valued employee and a good friend to whom you and I both owe a great debt." At this point her father leans forward, hands clasping on his blotter. "So *please*, meisje," he says, adopting a sturdy calm, as he used to when he was soothing her agitations during a bombing raid. "Enough. I don't wish to argue any longer. I understand that you're confused. I understand that you're anxious. It's a very anxious world," he agrees. "But you must trust me to do what's best. For all of us."

. . .

Trust. Anne writes the word on the page. What an odd little word that has become to her. Anne should "trust" in Pim. She should "trust" in God. But how can she possibly?

Margot has appeared in her Kazetnik's rags, her face shrunk down to the bone by starvation and disease.

"What?" Anne demands to know. She is up in the Achterhuis, bundled in an old sweater, sitting with her notebook, her back pressed against the wall in the spot where her desk once stood. Margot's eyes are greasy with death in the light from the bare windows.

Have you really sunk so low that you could believe that a woman who risked her life for us could be a criminal? Bep? Bep of all people? You can't actually believe for a minute that she could have betrayed us, can you? That's lunacy.

"Maybe. Maybe it isn't," Anne replies dryly, flexing her writing hand. "Under the right circumstances, who is not capable of anything? Didn't the camps teach you that much, Margot?"

Margot answers her with a blunt glare. *Are you talking about Bep now or yourself?*

Anne glares back. "I'm *guilty,* yes. Is that what you want to hear me say? I'm guilty of the crime of surviving. That wretched sin. Bep must be able to see that. And who can blame her, really?" Anne wonders. Closing the notebook in her lap, she stares at nothing. "I *want* to trust Bep. Of course I do. But perhaps in a way it's easier to believe that she could have betrayed us rather than simply believe she's rejected me. That she can *see* that I am ruined and wants to put plenty of distance between us."

Anne speaks this aloud, but when she looks back at Margot, her sister is nothing more than dust motes drifting through the prying daylight.

───

Anne pedals through the damp afternoon to the Prinsengracht. At the Keizersgracht she climbs off her bicycle and walks in, just as she did the day the boy from the warehouse followed her, but there is no sign of him. Only people bustling to and fro, on foot, on bikes, as the seagulls mill above their heads. Does she *really* think he will still try to catch up to her? After she drew blood from his kiss? No, she doesn't think that, but she also hopes she's wrong. Maybe he's just gone to work, and she can catch his glance as he's lugging a barrel. When she reaches the warehouse, one of the workers holds the door for her, calling her "Little Princess." It's hard to know if he means it as a polite endearment or a casual jibe, but regardless, she nods courteously as she pushes her bicycle into the dusty storage room and leans it in the corner. No sign of a straw-headed boy, though. When she asks the foreman, Mr. Groot, about him, the man shrugs his heavy shoulders. "Didn't show."

At this point smelly old Mr. Lueders decides to chime in. "What you expect from his sort?"

Anne tilts her head. "What does that mean? His sort of what?"

"Fruit from a rotten tree," Lueders is kind enough to elaborate.

"All right, enough of that," Mr. Groot decides. "Sweep your own street, will you, Lueders?"

"What's his name? Can you tell me that much?" Anne asks.

Mr. Groot frowns as he lugs a heavy carton and dumps it on a wooden pallet. "We called him Raaf. But his father's name was Hoekstra. And Lueders is right. Not a good name around here."

"Not a good name?" Anne repeats.

The man shrugs, but it's obvious he's had enough of this conversation with the boss's daughter. "If you don't mind, miss? An end to these questions, please. There's work to be done."

Anne feels a queasy kind of disappointment in her belly as she begins to climb the stairs up to the office, when abruptly there is a clatter of footsteps heading down from above. It's Bep in her coat and hat, her handbag dangling from her arm. She's in such a hurry that she's rushing dangerously down the Dutch steps. Anne calls her name and starts to point this out when she realizes that Bep's face is a flood of tears. And though Anne's first instinct is to wedge herself against the wall, to clear the steps for trouble to pass, she resists the impulse and blocks the woman's way, forcing Bep to brace herself against the stairwell wall to halt her momentum.

"*Bep.* You're *crying.*"

"Anne." Bep is shaking her head, blotting her face with a handkerchief.

"What's *happened*?"

But Bep just keeps shaking her head. "I can't."

"Can't what?"

"Can't continue. I'm *sorry*," she cries, and then forces her way past. "I'm so very *sorry*."

"Sorry?" Anne freezes up for an instant. "Sorry for *what*? Bep? Bep, tell me what's happened! *Bep!*" she calls out as she follows the woman's path down the steps, but by the time she pushes past the door and bolts into the street, Bep is already hurrying along the pavement past the Westerkerk, and Anne is nearly run over by a cyclist who inquires if perhaps she's gone blind.

Clambering back up the stairs herself, she rushes to the kantoor window and bolts into the office, where a wall of stares meets her. Miep's eyes are red, and she frowns sadly back down at her typewriter. Kugler is seated at Kleiman's desk and surveys Anne's entry with a controlled melancholy, but her father is standing, with a sheet of paper hanging in his hand. His face silent.

"What's happened to *Bep*?" Anne demands, though she's really frightened to know the answer. "Why was she *crying*?"

Kugler draws a breath as if to choke up an answer, but her father hands him the paper and takes a small step forward.

"Anne, Bep has resigned," Pim says quietly.

Anne glares back. "What?"

"She's left the firm."

"But . . ." Anne shakes her head, as if to clear away such an unacceptable idea. "But *why*? What happened to her?"

Kugler and Miep both look up at this, as if they might be called upon to provide an answer, but Pim simply says, "There was nothing to be done, Anne. Bep's father is so very ill. The cancer has spread, and he needs care. We must accept that there are some circumstances that cannot be altered no matter how we might wish otherwise."

Anne clamps her mouth shut. Once she never would have imagined that Bep could possibly have betrayed them. But now? Perhaps she needed money for her father's treatment. Who knows what medicines cost on the black market while the mof still stood astride the world? Wouldn't Anne herself have sacrificed the lives of others to save Pim's life or even simply ease his pain?

She does not want to cry in front of Pim or Kugler, so she holds back till she can shut herself up in the WC, where she releases a knotted sob and allows the tears to flow. She's still losing people. Will that ever stop? Will she ever be able to truly count on someone's love again? Count on people's devotion without the fear of losing them? Without fear of their abandoning her, because even death is a kind of abandonment. How can she ever trust her own life not to crush her?

17

FORGIVENESS

Shouldn't I, who want to be good and kind, forgive them first?

—Anne Frank,
from her diary,
19 January 1944

From where do we know that it is cruel to not forgive?

—The Talmud
Bava Kamma 8:7

1946

LIBERATED NETHERLANDS

In the afternoons after school, Anne slips through the hidden door behind the bookcase to the confines of their former hiding place. Closing the door behind her, she feels as if she is shutting out the world. Shutting out the present. Up in the attic, she sits on the floor holding le chat Mouschi in her lap. They have cut a deal, she and he. Monsieur le chat Mouschi. She has cultivated his cooperation with treats of fish skin and bits of tinned tuna, and he is now a purring ball of fur for her to pet.

She breathes in and out. Once, she felt this place to be a sanctuary, but now its emptiness settles over her like the quiet storm of dust drifting in the sunlight through the window glass. The leaves flutter on the branches of the old horse chestnut. She has organized a pack of cigarettes from her father's desk and lights one with the scratch of a wooden match. Sweet Caporals supplied by the Canadian troops who liberated the city. A superior North American product. Before the war Holland was famous for the rich quality of the tobacco imported from its colonies, but now the dark brown shag of East Indian yield has been replaced by weak, fast-burning ersatz brands, so the punch of the genuine tobacco makes Anne's head swim. Canadian cigarette cards feature the members of the English royal family. The king, the queen, the princesses. Once those might have gone up on her wall, but now they simply go into the rubbish bin. She inhales a rush of smoke and feels it settle inside her. Once again they are depending on Miep, who has maintained her contacts in the Jordaan for essentials. Dried fish, Canadian cigarettes, potatoes, tinned meats and oats, plums and string beans, malt coffee, sugar surrogate, and even the occasional gristly beefsteak from a cooperative butcher.

Anne expels smoke and watches it waft like a thin ghost across the empty room.

Peter.

He was older than Anne but younger than Margot. Tall and solid, with a broad face and densely curly hair that often defied his comb. For a moment she remembers the feel of his body sitting beside her on the divan, up here in the seclusion of the loft. He was very male. So heavy with his strength, the inadvertent strength of his arm, its weight slung across her shoulder. At the time she'd had many girlish thoughts about the depth of his soul. On the outside he would have been a roughneck boy from Osnabrück, better at fighting than at talking. No religion beyond the work of his hands. Easily bored to laziness, ridiculous in his excuses, and absurdly morbid in his obsessions with imaginary diseases. Look at my tongue. Isn't it a strange color? But he also possessed a sweet, curious gaze that could settle on Anne with its guileless yearning. He had a good mind; she'd been so *sure* of it, but maybe that was more her desire than the truth. He preferred heavy work to too much thinking, so Anne had simply inserted the deep thoughts into his head for him. His silence she had taken for buried intensity. But really it was just the silence of a boy with nothing more to say. He was at ease with her. She listened to him when he jabbered on authoritatively, as boys do, or vented steam over his father's harsh disapproval. And with her head resting against his chest, she counted the beats of his heart after he'd run out of words, here in the gray attic.

Now she sits with his cat instead, for Peter van Pels is far beyond her touch.

I'm sure that he knew you still cared for him, she hears Margot say.

"Are you?" Anne shakes her head. She doesn't look at her sister's face but only hugs the cat. "I'm not." The cat struggles, suddenly uncomfortable in her arms. She must be gripping him too tightly. She does not attempt to calm him but lets him bound away. "I wasn't always very kind to him," Anne confesses, breathing in smoke from the smoldering Caporal she picks up from a red Bakelite ashtray.

You outgrew him, Margot points out, and Anne does not disagree.

"I always worried that it was painful for you."

For me? Margot sits on her heels, wearing a floral-print dress and the sweater Mummy had knit from cashmere wool. *Why for me?*

"You know why," Anne insists.

Anne. Now it's Margot's turn to shake her head. Her voice is meant to sound comforting, at least as comforting as the dead can manage. *I was not at all interested in Peter in that way. I told you that.*

"I didn't believe you."

Well. Perhaps at first I was disappointed, in a minor way, when I saw the direction in which his interests were roaming. But really, he was simply not my kind of boy. Nor was he your kind of boy. The only difference was, I was old enough to realize it, while you, she says, *you were so desperately romantic.*

"And lonely," Anne tells her.

Well. You didn't have to be. I was there. Pim was there. Mummy was there. If you were lonely, it must have been your choice.

"No, you don't understand."

Don't I?

"I'm not like you, Margot. I'm not like Mummy, or even Pim. I need something more in my life."

More? Margot asks. She blinks through the lenses of her spectacles. *Like what, Anne? What more do you need that none of us could supply?*

Anne shakes her head. "I can't explain."

Oh. You mean sex.

"You don't have to be so smug, Margot. And no, I don't mean sex. Really, I can't explain it."

Her sister shrugs. *If you can't explain it, then how can it be so important?*

The cat inserts a pause between them as he pounces on the cigarette pack left on the hardwood planking, but it's enough. Margot has not waited to hear Anne's reply and has dissolved into the gray daylight, leaving Anne with a hard itch of discontent. Or maybe it is this place. The attic. Their hiding place. The Achterhuis. Perhaps this hard itch is the only part of her former self she has recovered. The need to be something more. She had suffered so long from a secret loneliness, even surrounded by her chattering friends in the school yard, even as she laughed at jokes and flirted with the boys; there was an emptiness that she could never fill. And when they had slipped into hiding, the emptiness had followed her. Peter had been there for that. At least at first. In the small space in which they were trapped, his roughneck physique seemed manly. His boyish energy alluring. But then something changed. *She* changed. The satisfaction that Peter provided thinned. She realized he would never truly understand her and that, most likely, he didn't really wish to try. So what was left to her, trapped in this cramped and drab annex? She found that when she sat down in front of a clean page with her fountain pen in her hand, the emptiness was filled.

A sigh rustles through the branches of the horse chestnut tree outside as a burst of sunshine burns through the clouds. She watches the windowpanes brighten.

Tuschinski Theater
Reguliersbreestraat 26-34
Amsterdam-Centrum

The gorgeous deco towers are still standing. The Tuschinski Theater was a favorite before the war. Pim used to take them all to the matinees on Sunday afternoons and then to the Japanese tearoom on the premises for green-tea ice cream. Once on Pim's birthday, Mr. Tuschinski himself stopped by just to say mazel tov. When the moffen came, they called the place the Tivoli and showed anti-Semitic propaganda. But since the liberation, the Tuschinski name has been restored, though Anne heard from Pim that Mr. Tuschinski and his whole family went up the chimneys of the Kremas.

Inside, the palatial Grote Zaal is nicknamed the "Plum Cake," and even though the war has taken its toll on maintenance, it still looks rather scrumptious. The plush velvet, the confectionary swirls of the bric-a-brac. In the rear of the auditorium, Griet has just passed Anne a cigarette, but she draws a puff slowly, totally captivated by the screen as an American newsreel trumpets into the space. "This is *New York*," a narrator declares as an aerial view of soaring building spires circles in the reflection of Anne's eyes. "The greatest city the world has known!"

Anne's heartbeat swells. The subtitles are blurry, but who needs them? The sprawl of images is mesmerizing; Griet must nudge her twice in order to get her cigarette back. "The dazzling marquees. A glittering extravaganza," the narrator intones. "Crossroads of the world. Bright lights, the theaters, good food, and dancing to the music of the world's most famous orchestras." Something in Anne starts to expand. She can feel it rising from the pit of her belly. The Waldorf Astoria, the Starlight Roof, the Empire Room, Peacock Alley, Radio City Music Hall! Fifth Avenue from Washington Square to 110th Street. "The sidewalk cafés and towering apartment houses." People stream from banks of crowded elevators. The Empire State Building! "The tallest structure on the face of the earth." Sixty thousand tons of steel, ten million bricks, seven miles of elevator shafts going straight up. The never-ending view. "The turreted heights." The Statue of Liberty, a beacon of freedom! Anne's stare is steady. The force invading her feels like some kind of . . . *what*? Some kind of *destiny*, nothing less. Like a message for her alone from the future, or from fate, or maybe even from God himself. Could it be?

A hot dog with everything on it! On the screen a girl takes a huge bite in front of a street vendor. Grand Central Terminal! People streaming across a cavernous concourse, in sunlight pouring from massive cathedral windows. "This is New York," the narrator reminds with zest. "Where everyone's wish comes true. Where dreams come to life. Where the lights outshine the stars in the heavens!"

Squinting into the sunlight after the film, Anne feels as if the image of those towers has been singed onto the insides of her eyes.

This is New York. Where everyone's wish comes true.

Prinsengracht 263
Offices of Opekta and Pectacon

Two additions have been made to the office over the past few weeks. The first is a new typewriter. An Olympia Model 8. It's German-made war booty with a sleek military shape, a roll of vulcanized rubber, and a grin of punishing type bars. It boasts an assertive array of slate-gray keys, including a key for umlauts. It is a ruthless machine manufactured to type out arrest lists. To type out execution lists. Not so long ago, it was used to hail the führer's name at the close of every decree, in a clatter of steely type. Now it types out memos and correspondence advancing the sale of gelatin products to Dutch housewives. How humiliating for the Herr Typewriter. Such a demotion in rank.

Then there's the second addition. She is a well-built machine, too. A woman, with carefully managed hair, capable hands, and a profile as regally featured as the queen's head on a fiver. This is Mrs. Zuckert. Ostensibly it was Mr. Kugler who hired her as both a typist and a part-time bookkeeper, but Anne knows that nothing happens in the office without Pim's approval, and Pim certainly seems to approve. She's attractive for a woman of a certain age, handsome, with thick reddish curls, and a gaze as strong as hot coffee. And then there's the matter of her forearm, or rather what's tattooed upon it. Anne has only seen it once, as the woman stretched for a box of powdered milk surrogate on a shelf in the office kitchen. She's not very tall, and her sleeve was tugged away from her forearm, revealing a string of purple numbers.

In the kitchen, where the women address one another by their given names, Mrs. Zuckert explains that her mother named her Hadassah but directs everyone to call her Dassah. That is the name she answers to, she says. Everyone is polite, but there's a sense that Dassah is a creature that should be given a wide berth. There is something in her gaze that reveals the lioness at her core.

On the other hand, Pim appears quite eager in his approach

toward the lady. Suddenly he is spending time in the front rooms, just to look out the windows, he says, and absorb some good Dutch sunshine. Or he happens to remember a joke as he delivers a file to Mrs. Zuckert's possession. Mrs. Zuckert smiles appreciatively, regardless of the fact that it's a repeat of the joke from two days before. "Ah, yes." She nods, eyebrows arched. "Very clever, Mr. Frank," she responds in her good Germanic Dutch. "Very funny."

"Yes, Pim," Anne cannot help but cut in, "even *more funny* than it was the first time you told it."

"*Anne,*" Miep scolds her mildly. "Decorum, please. We're in a business office."

Tell *him* that, she almost answers, but buttons her lip. Pim, however, chuckles and takes his daughter's rudeness in stride. "Never mind, Miep," he says. "Anne has always had a talent for rudeness. God knows her mother, may she rest, tried to cure her of it, but . . ." He shrugs and allows the sentence to finish itself.

Anne feels her face blaze, but a terrible blackness overcomes her, so that she must look away. She must glare blindly at the small button keys of Miep's typewriter. Pim hands Mrs. Zuckert the file he carried in from the private office, along with a set of petty instructions, then strolls out in a businesslike manner as Anne seethes. To break up the concrete silence, Kugler begins to whistle. He's good, actually, and is whipping through a wireless hit from the Dutch Swing College Band. Anne's eyes rise and are caught by the pincer of Mrs. Zuckert's gaze. The message there is clear: Don't *like* me? Too bad. It's not your opinion that counts. Then, as a kind of counterpoint to Kugler's whistling, Mrs. Zuckert begins to rattle across the keys of the Herr Typewriter, spitting out her own impenetrable staccato rhythm.

"Have you talked to Bep, Miep?" Anne hears herself asking later in the afternoon, finding Miep in the kitchen fixing a cup of tea for Pim.

"A few days ago, yes," Miep tells her, turning off the fire under the steaming kettle. "She telephoned. Her father is back in the hospital."

"Did she say anything about me?"

"About *you*?"

"*Yes.* Anything, good or bad."

"Anne." Miep pronounces her name firmly and then takes a breath. Obviously to compose her words. "I'm not sure what you're *thinking*. But Bep was *overjoyed* when you came home. Just as we all were."

Anne says nothing more on the subject. Instead she says, "I'll take Pim his tea."

She knocks but doesn't wait for permission to enter, popping open the door to Pim's office. Pim glances up from the telephone with a wary expression. Anne brings in the tea and sets it on his desk but then doesn't leave. Instead she sits and waits, causing Pim to excuse himself from his call long enough to press a hand over the mouthpiece.

"Yes, Anneke?"

"I brought your tea," she tells him.

"I can see that, meisje, but I'm on a call."

"Yes, I can see that, too," Anne replies, but she does not budge.

Returning to the telephone with a half frown, he asks if he might ring the caller back. Setting the receiver on its hook carefully, he turns his frown on his daughter. "Is there something *wrong*?"

"Who were you talking to?" Her voice is neutral.

"When?"

"Just now on the telephone."

"Mr. Rosenzweig. My attorney."

"Why do you need an attorney?"

"Anne. Darling. I'm really rather busy."

"Why didn't we go to America?" she asks bluntly.

Pim blinks. Appears mildly stricken. "I beg your pardon?"

"Mummy's brothers were already there. You knew people in New York City. Mr. Straus," she says. "Why didn't we go there when we left Germany?"

"Why?" Pim lifts his eyebrows. "Well, it didn't seem necessary at the time. You must understand, Anne, when we emigrated, Hitler had only just been appointed Reichskanzler. It was *years* before any danger of war. And my first responsibility was to make a living and support the family. You and Margot were still so young. You were just a toddler then. So when your uncle Erich had an opportunity for me here in Amsterdam with Opekta, I took it." He curls his lower lip, staring for an instant at nothing. "We actually *did* consider the States, your mother and I, but it was so far away, an *ocean* away. Also, the Americans," he says. "They had very strict immigration quotas."

"For Jews," she says.

"Yes. For Jews." He doesn't deny it.

She swallows. Feels a rise of heat in her breast. "Do you ever hate the world, Pim?" It's a simple question to her, but it appears to shock her father. He shifts back in his chair as if to distance himself from it.

"The *world*? Of course not. How could I?"

"*I* do," Anne tells him. "Sometimes *I* do."

Pim looks back at her, pained. "Anneke," he whispers. "Please, it would break my heart if I thought that were true."

⁓

Biking over the Singel Canal bridge to the Rozengracht, Anne remembers the vulgarities once slopped in paint across the bridge wall. DOWN WITH THE JEWS! THE JEWS ARE OUR PLAGUE! They've since been whitewashed over, like many things, but they're still visible in her mind. However, she concentrates on other things. The stretch of her muscles as she pedals. The cool breeze ruffling her hair. The boy with the straw-blond hair. The touch of his fingers on her face. The salty taste of his mouth before she bit him. Another cyclist dings his bell as he passes her, breaking her reverie, and in the next instant she is skidding to a halt, gripping the handlebars, her knuckles bleaching white.

It's as if she has accidentally bicycled backward in time.

There's a man, rather scrawny, hatless, with a balding head and untrimmed chin whiskers, hard at work scraping yellow paint from a door, colored chips dusting his shoes, but the obscenity he's attempting to eradicate is still quite legible: KIKES PERISH!

Anne can only stare, rooted in place. She grips the handles of her bicycle, her palms going sweaty, her heart drumming in her chest, and she tastes a sickly-sour kind of fear in her mouth. How could this be? How can she still be confronted by such filthy scrawls?

The sign above the shop reads NUSSBAUM TWEEDEHANDS-BOEKVERKOPER. Nussbaum Secondhand Book Handling. A dowdy little place, the windows papered over with newsprint or boarded up. The scrawny man quits his scraping to take a breather and must notice her, because he turns about, still swallowing to catch his next breath. "I'm, sorry." He smiles. "May I be of assistance?"

No response.

"Are you a reader," he wonders, "looking for a good book?"

Her eyes blink from the door to the man, back to the door.

"Ah. Yes," he says. "Just removing an unfortunate eyesore. Someone's idea of a joke, I suppose." He says this with a slight frown but then returns to his smile, though his eyes are studying her now. "If you're looking for a book, you should come inside. I'm happy to make recommendations."

"Shouldn't you *do* something?" Anne demands.

"Do something? Well, as you can see I'm scouring off the paint."

"No, I mean, *do* something. Call the police."

A shrug. The police? "And what would they do, really?"

"You mean because you're a *Jew*."

A smile remains, but a bit of the life in his eyes goes slack. "I think I've had enough of scraping for now. My arms are getting tired. Why don't we step inside? We can share a pot of tea, and you can have a look at the shop. It's really much nicer on the *inside*," he confides.

A bell jangles above them as they enter. The shop has the comfortably musty smell that some bookshops develop after years of too many books packed into too small a space. The man is rubbing his arm as he goes to the hot plate sitting on a table behind the wooden sales desk. "I have no sugar or milk, I'm afraid. Not even surrogate." He speaks in Dutch to Anne, but she can quite definitely recognize the clipped accent of a Berliner.

"Is it because you're Jewish that you won't call the police?"

"No, it's because I see no point."

"So you should let them get away with it? Defacing your property."

"Someone slapped a door with a paintbrush." He shrugs. "Not exactly a capital offense."

"I'm sorry, it's only that—"

His eyebrows lift. "Yes?"

"I'm Jewish, too," she informs him.

The man shows her that smile again. "Yes, I rather surmised as much. But you needn't be sorry about it. It's not a crime any longer," he assures her, and then he observes Anne with a kind of gentle appraisal. "I'm Werner Nussbaum," he tells her, and leans across the sales desk to offer his hand. Anne stares at the hand for an instant, then steps forward and takes it.

"Mr. Nussbaum," she repeats, and examines his face more closely. A long, aquiline nose, slightly bulbous. A powerful forehead, balding across the crown, close-cropped curls, and a scraggly gray-white mustache over a vandyke beard. One eye droops as if it is simply too exhausted to open at full mast, though the core of his gaze is still probing, still eager.

"And you are?" he inquires.

"My name," she says, "is Anne Frank."

Mr. Nussbaum cocks his head slightly to one side, as if a thought has knocked it a bit off balance. "Frank," he repeats. "Well, that's a coincidence. I knew a man named Frank. German originally."

"We came from Germany," Anne admits. "Frankfurt-am-Main."

"Oh, no—this is too *impossible*," the fellow insists. "By any chance in the world," he wonders, "could you be related to an *Otto* Frank?"

Anne straightens. "Otto Frank is my father."

"Otto Frank. Who ran—*what was it?*—a spice business, I think, here in Amsterdam?"

"He still does," Anne answers.

"So you're saying . . . he *lives?*"

Now it's Anne who's feeling a bit off balance, thrown by this question that Jews must now ask one another. All she does is nod her head to answer, and she watches the man slump at the shoulders as if he had been working hard to keep his spine straight till this very moment.

"So miracles do persist. The mensch still lives," he declares, then looks back at Anne. "You must be confused. But I came to know your father quite well," Mr. Nussbaum explains gently, as he bares his forearm, revealing a tattooed number, "while we were guests at the same hotel."

When Mr. Nussbaum appears in the Jekerstraat flat, he begins to whistle Beethoven at the sight of Pim. Pim stands to his full soldier's height, his eyes flooding, and joins in whistling as well. This is how their reunion begins. All in all a teary welter, neither man able to control his emotions, and, watching them, neither is Anne. Pain strikes her, as if her heart has been thumped by a hammer, and she is forced to retreat to her room. Margot attempts to console her, or rather *interrogate* her, in her Lager rags. *Anne, why are you crying? Why are you crying?* But Anne has no answer for her. She cannot contain her own tears; she cannot control her own grief, though both seem to exercise perfect control over her. She is curled up in a ball on her bed when her father knocks.

"Anne?"

"Yes?" she calls, sniffing, staring at the wall beside her bed.

"May I come in?"

"I'm not feeling well," she answers, but Pim cracks open the door anyway.

"I'll only need a moment."

She rolls over and sits quickly, her eyes reddened. "Is Mr. Nussbaum still here?"

"No. He's gone for now," Pim tells her. "I'm sorry if our reunion was such a strain on you. Old men can get emotional."

"How did you meet?"

"How?" A small exhale. "At Auschwitz—we were billeted in the same barracks block. But I'm ashamed to say that the first time we met, I punched him in the face."

Anne blinks. "You *punched* him?"

"In the face, yes." Her father nods. "I don't even remember why now. Some measly dispute. But we were not the masters of our temper there."

"So you became friends because you struck him in the face?"

"No. We became friends because I heard him whistling 'Clair de Lune.' Terribly so, but with passion, as if every note he whistled were an affirmation that he was still alive. I knew immediately that I must ask him for his forgiveness. So I began to whistle it, too. After that"—Pim shrugs—"we became close comrades. We talked of music or art and literature. He had run a publishing company in Berlin before the Nazis stole it from him. He could recite Schiller, Heine, Goethe—especially Goethe—all from memory. It was quite inspiring. To keep using our *minds,* that was the thing. In the end, when I was truly on the edge of oblivion, it was he who brought one of the prisoner physicians to me. It's how I was admitted to the convalescent block of the infirmary, which probably saved my life. So I owe him a great deal. I tried to locate him through the Red Cross after liberation, but all I could determine was that he had been marched out of Auschwitz when the Germans were evacuating the camp. Honestly? Until today I assumed that he hadn't survived. So I must thank you, Anne, for returning him to me."

"I didn't do anything," she says.

"Perhaps you don't think so, but Werner tells me you made an impression on him."

"Did he tell you what happened? Did he tell you what they did to the door of his bookshop?"

"Yes," her father answers carefully. "He did. He also told me that he was struck by your spirit. And thought you were quite self-possessed." Pim says this, and then he adds, "*In fact,* he wondered if you might be interested in spending some time working in his shop."

Anne stares. "His shop?"

"Yes. I told him of your love of books," her father says. "He seemed eager to have you aboard. I'd still expect you to help out at the office, of course. But a few afternoons a week, shelving books after school . . . It's just him otherwise, so I think he could use another pair of hands. Does that sound like something that might interest you, meisje?"

Nussbaum
Tweedehands-Boekverkoper
The Rozengracht

The shop is not so very far from where Pim used to lease an office on the Singel. Anne now bikes there twice a week for a few hours before supper. She likes the place. She likes the smells of old paper and aging binder's glue and even the leathery stench of Mr. Nussbaum's cigar smoke. And of course she likes the shelves bursting with tatty old books of every size, shape, and color. Even when it's empty of customers, as it often is, there is still a comforting benefit from all those books, floor to ceiling, wall after wall. It's really quite gezellig, Anne writes in her notebook—a favorite word of the Dutch. A cozy den of books, she calls it. Her job is to categorize new arrivals, compiling them into stacks according to their type and then stocking the shelves. She loves handling the books and often forgets herself, opening the covers for a peek, only to lose herself in the pages instead of finishing her work. But Mr. Nussbaum doesn't seem to mind. He lends her this book and that and says, "Give this one a try," or "I think this is a story you might find either scintillating or preposterous. Or maybe both." And, of course, in addition to the books, books, and books, there is the cat. He's a hulking tortoiseshell lapjeskat with a lazy gaze, and Anne has named him Lapjes for his calico patches. He tolerates Anne's affection when he's in the mood, but he's a street cat by nature and only looks out for himself, lounging about in a spot of sun. Anne admires this ability of his but cannot seem to successfully imitate it.

"So tell me," Mr. Nussbaum begins. He wears a double set of sweaters, because, he says, he can never get warm, not with a hundred sweaters. Still, two are better than none. "Tell me, is it true?" he inquires. "Your papa says you have a talent with words."

Anne looks up from a heavy tome. Blinks. "Did he?"

"Oh, yes. He was adamant about it, actually. He said you were quite gifted."

Anne swallows. Turns back to the box of mismatched books she is unpacking. "Once I thought so," she answers.

"And what changed your mind?"

She looks up at Mr. Nussbaum's face. Is he making a joke? The man has a sly affection for irony, no doubt about that. But there's nothing ironic in his expression, only a humble curiosity.

"I was keeping a diary. When we were in hiding. I was going to write a book after the war. Maybe a novel or something. About our life. What it was like for us. For Jews," she says. "But it was all lost when we were arrested."

"And after that?" he asks.

"After?"

"After that you just quit writing altogether?"

Anne hesitates. "No," she admits.

"No."

"No, I still write. But it's not the same."

"Not the same, I see." He nods. He draws a thoughtful puff from his cigar and balances it, ember outward, on the edge of the sales desk, where there is a spot scarred black by many small burns on the varnish. "And why's that?"

"Because," Anne says. "Because it doesn't mean anything."

"No? Well, it must mean *something,* Anne," Mr. Nussbaum points out. "Else why would you be doing it?"

"I don't know," Anne confesses, turning away. "I suppose," she begins, but then shakes her head as she is displeased with her thoughts. "I suppose I'm simply compelled," she confesses, and picks up another book from the box.

"Hmm. That sounds like a writer talking to me."

"Do we really have to discuss this, Mr. Nussbaum?"

"Oh, no. No, not if you'd rather not," he says, opening up the thick sales ledger on the desk. "I only wonder . . ."

A beat. Anne looks back up. "Wonder what?"

"I only wonder," he says, perusing the ledger's contents, issuing her a brief but solid glance, "why you think your writing is worth less now than it was before? It's still your story. Isn't it?"

Anne stares.

"But you don't have to answer that question. Just something to think about," he says as he retrieves his smoldering cigar from the edge of the desk.

"Pim said that you owned a publishing house in Germany." Maybe she brings this up merely to block further interrogation on the subject of her writing, but a cloud scuds across Mr. Nussbaum's face.

"Yes, that's right," he answers. "My father's firm. It had been a small, scholarly, rather esoteric affair under him, but after he passed,

I took it over with the idea of building up the list of authors," he says. "Hermann Kesten, Joseph Roth, André Breton. Really it was quite a remarkable time."

"Until the Nazis," says Anne.

He agrees, his voice dropping into a quiet hole. "Until then." He shrugs almost imperceptibly. "I tried to start again elsewhere. I followed what had become the well-worn trail of literary exiles. First to Paris and then to Amsterdam. Amsterdam in particular hosted a constellation of German publishers at the time, so I dearly hoped I could make a go of it. But the money ran out, and, uh . . . life was not so easy. The magic in my world drained away."

Anne understands this. Even though Mr. Nussbaum is so much older, she feels a touch of pure kinship. A literary heart brought so low.

The next afternoon, when Anne arrives at the office, she finds that Mrs. Zuckert is yet again sequestered in Pim's private office with her steno pad.

"Doesn't it bother you?" she must ask Miep.

"Doesn't what bother me?"

"That she's taking over."

Miep shakes her head. "No one is 'taking over,' Anne."

At four o'clock Mr. Kugler goes into the kitchen, as he does at this hour every day for his afternoon cup of tea. Anne slips from her desk. "I'm getting a drink of water," she tells Miep, but doesn't wait for a response. In the corridor she can hear the laughter from the private office and then the chatty tone of their talk. What's worse, they're speaking German. *German!* The language of the executioners.

She catches Kugler in the kitchen gazing forlornly at the kettle on the hot plate as it builds steam. The air of talented modesty he once cultivated has been wrecked. Instead his expressions are often haunted or blank. She's noted that he's given to long, pointless stares while seated at his desk. He may rally then, he may rouse himself and become good old Mr. Kugler again, the man with all the answers. But she can tell that in his heart he has no answers any longer.

Slipping into the kitchen, she retrieves a water glass from the dish drain. Kugler looks up, but it's as if he doesn't quite see her for a moment. Then he takes a breath. *"So,"* he says without much conviction, "how is Anne today?"

"How am I?" she asks with a tone that asks, Isn't that obvious?

"School, I mean. How is school this year?"

But Anne does not answer his question. She walks to the sink and unscrews the tap, letting water rush into her glass. "She seems highly skilled," Anne points out.

"I'm sorry?"

"Mrs. Zuckert."

"Ah. Yes," he agrees. "Highly."

"I suppose she must have plenty of experience."

"She does," Mr. Kugler confirms, maintaining his mildly distracted tone. "Ten years as an assistant bookkeeper in an accounting firm. Before the war she helped out Mr. Kleiman from time to time."

"And *what*," Anne presses forward, "has become of her husband?"

Blankness. "Become of him?"

"Yes. What has become of *Mr.* Zuckert? Is he alive? Is he dead?"

Kugler looks suddenly alarmed. "That's really none of our business, Anne," he tries to convince her.

"No? You think not, Mr. Kugler? Well, I think it is." She takes a swallow of water and sets the glass down on the counter.

"Anne," Kugler breathes, "if you have questions, you must ask your father."

"That's what everyone keeps telling me, but my father says nothing. Listen to them in there laughing, the two of them. *Laughing,*" she repeats, as if naming a crime.

Kugler hesitates. His expression looks crushed. Finally he clears his throat and speaks grayly to the wall. "From what I understand," he begins, "her husband had been working in Germany before the Nazis. He was a Jew, but a Dutch-born Jew. So when they came to Amsterdam after Hitler, she sat for the test and became a Dutch citizen. The marriage didn't work out." A shrug. "I don't know why. But they were divorced, and he left for Canada. Or maybe it was Cuba, I don't recall."

Anne says nothing. But in her silence, Kugler's expression darkens, even in the sunlight from the kitchen's window. He stands when the teakettle's whistle stings the air, and he shuts off the burner flame. "You know, Anne, there's something I have noticed about you," he informs her. "I'm sorry, I hope you'll forgive me, but I have to say this. I've noticed that you often use your brutalization at the hands of the Nazis as if it's a weapon to wield. As if the pain and the awful sorrow you have borne have imbued you with a kind of unassailable righteousness," he says. "Of course, the stories your father told us upon his return . . . well, they were *horrific.* And I don't pretend to understand your anguish. But I must say that it wasn't easy for *any* of us. The SS sent Kleiman and me to one prison after another. First Amstelveenseweg. Then Weteringschans, where they held us for days in a cell with men condemned to death. Then finally to that godforsaken spot in the Leusderheide," he says despondently, as if he has stepped back behind the barbed wire in his mind. "Hard labor. Barely any food. Roll calls in the freezing rain. Kleiman would have died there, I'm sure of it, if it hadn't been for the Red Cross." He frowns, suddenly self-conscious, and shoots Anne a sliver of a glance. "Now, I know what you must be thinking," he says with a kind of miserable tension. "'*Poor Kugler.* He believes he's such a victim, yet he knows *nothing* about *true* suffering.' And maybe you're right. Maybe I cannot begin to conceive of the barbarities to which your people were subjected. Maybe Amersfoort and its ilk were not the same hell as those places to which Jews were deported. But I can testify, Anne, that neither were they holiday spas. I watched men die in Amersfoort. Good men, who should have been home with their wives and children, and I simply watched them drop over dead with shovels still stuck in their hands. Or worse. Clubbed to death in front of my eyes. Yet to hear you talk, it's as if you have utterly cornered the market on pain. It's the reason Bep left."

Anne stares at him in wordless response. And then, "No. No, *you're wrong.*"

"Oh, there's her father's illness, yes, if that's what you mean. But she has four other sisters, Anne. So if you want the *real* reason for Bep's departure, the truth," he says, "I'll tell you." He takes a breath and looks at her with blunt, deeply agitated eyes. "She could not face you any longer."

"That's not true," Anne insists.

"I'm afraid it is."

"No. *No.* I *know* the real reason Bep left—it's because the police suspected her of *betraying* us."

Kugler looks confused. Repulsed. *"Bep?"* And then he nearly laughs. "Don't be silly, Anne."

"I'm not. I know why those men were in the private office that day. I know that my father wants to keep me in the dark. He continues to tell me that it's nothing. A private business matter, but how can I believe that?"

Kugler is incredulous. "The greater question is, Anne, how can you believe that Bep could possibly be a *traitor*? How could you even *think* such a thing of a loyal friend?"

A loyal friend? Anne blinks at the question, feeling a cold pulse in her blood. For all his squawking on the subject, one might have imagined that Amersfoort would have taught Mr. Kugler something, but obviously he has refused to learn it. He has refused to recognize the insidious patience of betrayal. How it can infect the human heart without the knowledge of its host, until suddenly, one impulse . . . one moment's anger . . .

"It's not what *I* think, Mr. Kugler. It's what *Bep* thought," she insists. "It's the reason she left."

"No, Anne." Kugler shakes his head heavily. "No, Bep's leavetaking had nothing to do with any such thing. She left, quite simply, because she wanted a new life. She couldn't stand to confront the terrible past on a daily basis. She couldn't stand to face *you*."

Anne absorbs his words and feels a cold, weeping hole open in her chest.

"I'm sorry, Anne," Kugler says. "I am. I wish it *weren't* the truth. But it is."

Miep walks into the kitchen. "Mr. Kugler, there's a gentleman on the telephone for you," she says, and mentions the name of the gentleman. A Mr. So-and-So spice distributor from Antwerp.

"Ah," Kugler breathes, relieved. "I've been waiting for this call." Then he frowns. "Excuse me, Anne," he says, and quickly frees himself from the kitchen.

Miep waits for a moment, quietly examining Anne. "Is something wrong?"

But Anne has no words to speak.

In the attic of the Achterhuis, she sobs without hope, until quite suddenly the tears dry up as if the spigot has been twisted shut. She breathes until her chest quits heaving. Rubs her face, smearing away the tears. Dries her eyes on the sleeve of her sweater and ignites a cigarette, inhaling the acrid smoke. The branches of the chestnut tree nudge the window glass, touched by a whisper of wind.

Coming down the steps, she spots Pim by the door to his private office with Mrs. Zuckert. His hand is on her arm. And though Anne cannot discern what they are saying, she cannot miss the intimate tone of their murmur. She decides to make a noise. Scuffs a step loudly and watches how swiftly her father's hand disconnects from the lady's limb. His forehead prunes lightly as he calls upward, "Anne?"

"Yes, Pim. It's me."

"Your eyes are reddened. Are you all right, meisje?"

"I'm fine."

"You were up in the rooms again?" This is how he refers to the Achterhuis now: up in the rooms.

"Only for a few minutes."

"Anne, darling, I worry that you spend too much time up there."

"And I worry that you don't spend enough time, Pim."

An edge of silence like a knife, but Mrs. Zuckert ignores it. "Thank you, Otto," she says, her voice pleasantly relaxed. "I'll see you tomorrow." And then she smiles—"Good night, Anne"—but doesn't stick around for Anne to reply.

"You know, I can take dictation, too," she says to her father. "Don't you recall the mail-order courses?" Line-height parts, quarter-height parts, half-height consonants, the System Groote. "Margot and I completed them. Don't you remember?"

Another blink. Often the mere mention of Margot's name dampens Pim's expression. His poor Mutz, he always calls her.

"I could take dictation from you," Anne says, plowing ahead. "It would be good practice for me," she tells him with earnest intention. "So, really, you don't always have to rely on your dear Mrs. Zuckert."

For an instant Pim appears distressed. But then he quickly regains control and offers Anne his particular brand of pleasantly frowning agreement. "Hmm. *Well*," he says, matching Anne's earnest tone, "that sounds like a very compelling proposition." But during the fraction of a heartbeat in which he meets his daughter's eyes, she can spot the jolt of inflexible resolve behind the façade. The same resolve that must have enabled Otto Heinrich Frank to survive five months of KL Auschwitz.

Later, after the supper dishes are cleared and washed and Miep and Jan have gone out for their evening walk, Anne finds Pim sitting in a chair in the Jekerstraat flat with a book open. She watches him from the room's threshold. His body reedy and his face thin, but with a touch of color returning to his cheeks. His eyes look gentle and unhurried as he gazes down at the page, lost in words. It's Goethe he's reading this time instead of Dickens. The smoke from his cigarette curls softly upward.

He raises his eyes suddenly when he realizes that his daughter is watching him. "Anne?"

"So you know she's divorced?" Anne asks him.

His expression does not change, but the light recedes immediately from his eyes.

"Mrs. Zuckert," Anne says thickly. "Your favorite—" She begins to say, Your favorite in the office, but Pim's voice is level when he cuts her off.

"I *know* who you mean, Anne. And the answer is yes. I am aware that Mrs. Zuckert has been divorced. There is no need to stigmatize her over it. So she left a bad marriage. That does not make her a bad person."

"This is not about *her*," Anne lies, "it's about *you*, Pim. Why are you *doing* this?"

"Doing what, daughter? I'm not doing anything."

"Yes you are," she insists. "Yes, you *are*. It's obvious to everyone. She calls you by your given name, for God's sake."

And now her father expels a breath. He cheats a drag from his cigarette before tamping it out in Miep's Bakelite ashtray, which he's dirtied like a fireplace grate. "Anne," he says. Her name as a preamble. The beginning of a lecture or a sermon: *Anne, you have no idea what you're saying. Anne, you have no business interfering with adults. Anne, you are still only a child.* But what he says is, "Anne, I won't deny that I may have certain feelings in regard to Mrs. Zuckert. And I won't deny that she may, and I said *may,* harbor certain feelings for me." He pauses. Allows these words to sink in. "Now, of course I can understand that you might find it difficult to accept such a . . ." Such a what? "A *situation,*" he decides to call it.

"You *understand*?" All at once the fury in her breaks free. "You *understand,* do you? No, Pim. No, I don't think you understand a *thing.*"

Her father shifts uncomfortably in the chair and huffs a breath. "Really, it's always *this,* isn't it?" he says. "Always this anger. It's all you offer me, Anneke."

"Well, *perhaps*"—and her eyes are hot as she says it—"perhaps I'm angry because you're betraying my mother's memory."

"*No,*" Pim replies adamantly.

"*Yes.* You are. How long has your wife been *dead,* Pim? Fourteen months? Fifteen? No time to waste. Better get a replacement in the works!"

"*Stop it,*" he demands, running his fingers over the vein suddenly popping at his temple. "Just *stop it.*"

"Kugler says she used to do bookkeeping for the company. Is that when you first noticed her, when Mummy wasn't around?"

Her father leaps to his feet. "*I will not have this!*" he shouts, his face bleaching. "Don't you dare say such a thing!"

"She bore you two children. She made a home for us all. Even in a cramped hideout above a dirty warehouse, she made a home for us, and *this* is how you repay her? *This* is how you keep her memory? By chasing another man's wife?" Anne feels a surge of elation, as if provoking her father has proved that Pim is not so invulnerable to his own anger.

"Your mother and I," he breathes, and then he must swallow a heavy rock, blinking at the sharp tears in his eyes. "Your mother and

I had a long and very loving relationship. No matter *what* you think, Anne. No matter what you've so precociously surmised. I did everything I could to make her happy, and she did the same for me. In fact, *if* you recall, it wasn't *me* who criticized her. It wasn't *me* who always had a sharp tongue in his head for your mother. It was *her younger daughter* who so often left her crying," he says. "It wasn't *me* who complained so constantly and so vociferously about being so very misunderstood. It wasn't *me* who sought no value in your mother's solace—it was Annelies Marie Frank! How did you put it?" he demands suddenly of the air. "Let me see—it was something like, 'She means nothing to me. I don't have a mother! I must learn to mother *myself*!'"

Anne glares. A bright electric shock of realization has pulsed through her body at what Pim, in his anger, has just let slip. "*How*," she asks, "do you know that?"

"How do I know *what*?" her father demands, still quivering with anger.

"How do you *know*," she asks thickly, "how I put *anything*?"

And now a thin sliver of alarm inserts itself into her father's jagged expression. "I have no idea what you're talking about."

"*Yes* you *do*," Anne says.

"I think I've had enough. Enough accusations from my own daughter for one evening."

"You *read* it," Anne says with a heated mixture of indignity and mortification. "You read my *diary*. Otherwise how could you have known?"

Pim's mouth closes and is drawn into a straight line.

"*When?*" she demands. "I put it in your briefcase. For safekeeping. You *promised* me that no one would *dare* touch it there. I remember! But what you meant to say was no one but *you*."

Pim still has nothing to say. Only stares painfully.

And then an even more horrible thought strikes her. "Did you show it to Mummy, too?" she asks darkly. "Did *she* read it?"

"No." Her father speaks the single word.

"No? *Are you sure?* Perhaps you passed it around? Passed it around to the van Pelses? To that old fart Pfeffer? God, they were all such snoops, weren't they? Always prying. I bet they had such a good laugh at my expense. The tragic unbosoming of a know-it-all adolescent!"

"*No,* Anne," Pim protests. "No one else read a word. I can assure you of that. No one else."

"No one else but my father."

Pim swallows. His hands are squeezed into fists. His eyes wet.

And then suddenly, *"Anne,"* he whispers desperately, but before he can say another word, the front door to the flat opens and in come Miep and Jan, home from their evening walk. They are chatting and smiling until they freeze at the threshold of their own home, gazing in at the expressions of father and daughter. Miep sums it up quickly. "We're interrupting," she declares apologetically. But Pim steps forward, suddenly relieved.

"No," he corrects her. "No you're not. Not at all. Excuse me," he says, and yanks his fedora and raincoat from the rack. "I think I'm in need of some exercise." And with that he bolts from the flat.

1945

Konzentrationslager (KL)
BERGEN-BELSEN
Kleines Frauenlager
The Lüneburg Heath

THE GERMAN REICH

Final months of the war

The women's camp at Belsen is already packed to bursting by the time the wretched transport arrives from Birkenau. A tide of starving, freezing inmates is pouring into Belsen from camps all across the east, evacuated as the Red Army drums through Poland. No more room in the Belsen barracks, no more room in the sardine tins, so the Germans set up a Zeltlager. A tent city with perimeters drawn by ropes of barbed wire. It is November, and the tents billow in the bitter wind. This is where Anne and Margot huddle for warmth. But after four days the most vicious storm yet shreds the canvas and rips the tent wires from the ground. The screams of many hundreds of women are fused into a single shriek that is sucked from their bellies as the immense canvas roof collapses upon them like a shroud. How hard they fight to free themselves of it, Anne gripping Margot's arm by the wrist, shouting her name over and over. But beyond the tent is only the storm, frigid rain driving down like nails, like a shower of needles. Quickly, Anne and Margot join the women who have just fought their way free and climb back under the shroud for shelter. Those women who don't, die. Those who do, will die later. Those are the choices left at Bergen-Belsen.

The nights turn frigid. The living from the tent camp are condemned to the ramshackle wooden barracks of the Kleines Frauenlager, Anne and Margot among them. But they are billeted near the door, so that every time it opens, a punishing blast of icy wind bites into them. Close the door! they beg over and over. Please, close the door!

The latrines are overflowing with shit. The water is infected, and the dead are a swelling population. Bodies pile up. They freeze solid into grotesque sculptures.

By the time the snow comes, both Anne and Margot are boiling with fever. They pull apart old shoes in a work barracks. They suffer the unpredictable blows of the Kapos like everyone and stand for roll call until they can stand no longer and finally surrender to the sick block. But the Krankenlager at Belsen is not only putrid, it's an ice-house. Anne shivers, a frozen little animal. "At least we will be left alone here," she whispers to Margot, watching her breath frost. "We can be together and lie down in peace." But peace is elusive. Typhus kills Germans, too, so the moffen are afraid to come near them and leave the inmates of the Krankenlager to rot. Corpses are dragged to the edge of the burial pits or, if nobody has the energy, simply abandoned outside the doors of the barracks.

A grayness overcomes everything. Anne finally finds sleep on a pallet, curled next to her sister on the fetid straw. Margot has moved beyond words. Instead she communicates with shivering groans, glottal intestinal grunts, and her ruthless cough. The cough, that vicious, goddamned beast. Anne tries to cover both of them with her horse blanket, but really she's mad that Margot has shit on it again. Maybe it wasn't really Margot's fault—of course, no one can control their shitting in Belsen—but still she is mad, even while her exhaustion smothers her as she clings to Margot's bony body.

And then comes her dream.

A *wonderful* dream. Wonderful and dreadful. She is back in the hiding place and following Peter. They are running. *Laughing.* He has challenged her to a race up the stairs to the kitchen, and now he is threatening to eat all the strawberries before she gets there. She is *sure* she is going to beat him, though, *sure* of it. Until the stairs elongate and there are more and more of them, and soon Peter is far ahead of her. So far ahead that she can't see him at all. So far ahead that she can only hear his voice calling to her. Come on, slowpoke! Come on!

That's when something wakes her. It is Margot, or rather Margot's ghastly cough. She is coughing so loudly it's as if she's turning herself inside out, so sharply that it's like a blade chopping at Anne's ear, and all Anne wants to do is stay in that dream just a moment longer. Just a moment, because she is still so sure she can catch up to Peter. Still so *sure* she could, if it were not for Margot, who won't let her. Her sister's clawing cough has pried her from sleep and dragged her back to their filthy pallet.

Anne burns. "Can't you be *quiet*? Can't you for God's sake *shut up*?" She is shouting this in her head. It's hard to tell if it's actually coming out as a shout or if it's coming out at all, but it doesn't matter. She is so *angry* that Peter has surely finished every strawberry by now.

She bolts up, shivering, her nightdress soaked through with sweat, desperate to find her breath. Someone is rapping on the door and calling her name with a chill of panic.

"Anne, Anne!"

She is trembling, balled up on her bed.

"Anne!" her father calls.

But she does not answer him. Only rocks slowly forward, hugging herself, feeling the shudder of her heartbeat.

The truth is, she can't forgive him, because the truth is, she doesn't want to forgive. She despises forgiveness.

18

BREAD

Everything revolves around bread and death.

—Yiddish proverb

1946

Amsterdam

LIBERATED NETHERLANDS

There are nights when she cannot sleep. So at supper, and not for the first time, she steals bread from the table. Slips a roll from the bakery into a pocket of her apron dress. In her bedroom she closes the door and hooks the lock. Dropping onto her bed, she removes the roll and stares at it. She touches the rough texture of its yeast-swollen crest, thinly chalky with a residue of flour. Once it would have been impossible to save a bite of this bread. When bread fell into her hands, she could do nothing but devour it. Yet now she secretes it under her mattress.

She finds that she can sleep through the night knowing it's there.

Nussbaum
Tweedehands-Boekverkoper
The Rozengracht

Kneeling on the floor of Mr. Nussbaum's bookshop, she has spent an hour or more unpacking boxes. Mr. Nussbaum himself has just returned from a meeting with a dealer and is hanging up his patched-over coat and old felt hat. *"So,"* he says with a lively curiosity, returning to the sales desk to sort through a bundle of new acquisitions. "How is your *work* progressing?"

"Well, I've finished reorganizing the biographies," she tells him. "I think you'll be pleased."

A smile to himself as he tucks in his chin. "Yes, I'm sure I will be, but that's not what I meant. I meant, Miss Frank, how is your *writing* progressing?"

"*Oh.*" Her eyes drop. "All right, I suppose," she says, and removes a book from an open carton. Anne has continued to write since the day her pen discovered its words again. But though she once found meaning in her diary, in securing the events of the day on paper and molding them into an account of a life, her narrative is now fractured. She feels as adrift on the page as she does in this alien Amsterdam she's come home to, without a mother, without a sister, and with a father who continues to infuriate her with his vacant crusade to live in the present.

"That's *all*?" Mr. Nussbaum doubts. "Just all right? Not astonishingly well or appallingly badly?"

She grips the book in her hands. "I don't know what you want me to say, Mr. Nussbaum."

"I want you to say what you're thinking, Anne. What's your *plan*? Have you started that novel yet?"

"Novel?"

"Didn't you say you had a novel in the works? A book of some sorts?"

"No." Anne shakes her head. "It's not a novel. It's not anything."

"Well, it must be something if you're writing it," Mr. Nussbaum points out.

Anne draws a small breath and releases it. "Have *you* ever written a book, Mr. Nussbaum?" she asks to change the subject.

"*Me?* Oh, no. *God* no. I don't have the gift for that. When I was young, of course, I thought I was destined to pen a magnum opus. That it was only a matter of time before my name would be carved beside those of the greats. Tolstoy, Proust," Mr. Nussbaum says with a wry laugh. "But *no.* As it turned out, I was nobody's idea of Tolstoy." An affable shrug. "I *can* say this, however: I *did,* over time, become a rather decent editor. I even made a living at it. So I suppose the point I'm getting at is, if ever you would like to *show* me something, Anne, I'd be happy to give it a look."

Anne swallows. "Well. Thank you. I'll think about it," she answers, and tries to smile, but she feels suddenly vulnerable, maybe embarrassed by it all, so she begins sorting through a box of children's books that Mr. Nussbaum bought in an auction. "If I ever actually produce anything worthwhile." She says this, and then her face brightens, and she feels a lift in her chest. "*Oh!* Cissy van Marxveldt!" A swell of sweetness as she pulls out one book after the other. *The New Beginning, Confetti, Caprices, The Storms, A Tender Summer.* "I loved her books!" Anne exclaims. "I think I've read every one four or five times each."

"Then you should take them home," Mr. Nussbaum tells her.

"Oh, no. I *couldn't*. You can make a good profit on these. They're still in wonderful condition."

"All the more reason you should have them. *Profit?*" He waves the word away. "Unimportant."

"Are you *sure*?" She grips the top book in her arms.

"Positive." He puffs on his cigar. "Consider them your pay for the day."

"Thank you. But I'm sure they're much more valuable than that."

"Oh? Are you suggesting I don't pay you enough?" he jokes.

Anne feels herself smile again as she gazes back down at the book in her arms. Cracking it open, she skims through a paragraph. How joyful she was when she first read these treasures! At first, like all her friends, she wanted to *be* Joop ter Heul, that sprightly, fearless, madcap girl, always launching herself into the next adventure. It wasn't till she started her diary that Anne had realized it wasn't Joop the character but Joop's *author* she longed to become: The *Jewish* Cissy van Marxveldt! "Marxveldt's only her *pen* name. I don't remember what her real name is."

"It's Beek-de Haan."

Anne looks up.

"Did you know she was married to a Jew? A man named Leo Beek."

"No," says Anne, holding the book in her lap. She feels a pinch of inner dread. Married to a Jew? She knows what happened to Dutch Jews. Must even her girlhood adoration of Joop's exploits be tagged with sorrow now?

"I was quite friendly with them both, actually," Mr. Nussbaum tells her. "Many years before the war. The Netherlands was a large market for German publishers back then, have I said that? I used to visit Amsterdam regularly. But then all that ended." His eyes flicker at the memory. "Leo was executed by the Gestapo, I'm sorry to report. He was active in the resistance. They took him to the Overveen Dunes, like so many others, and shot him." He says this and then sees Anne's face. "I'm sorry, Anne, I've upset you."

"No, it's nothing," Anne says, and she sets the books down and shakes her head. "I'm sorry, Mr. Nussbaum, but I should go. I promised I'd help out at my father's office today."

"Of course," Mr. Nussbaum grants. "Just don't forget your pay," he says, lifting a smile and nodding to the books. "I'm quite serious."

"Thank you," Anne says, but suddenly she feels the desire to evacuate. She's not sure why, but she feels oddly trapped by Mr. Nussbaum's generosity, and when the telephone rings loudly, she has her opportunity. Mr. Nussbaum picks it up, and in the matter of a moment his expression has blackened. "*Yes, yes,* I received your so-called *correspondence* on this so-called matter. And I can only say that I am both insulted and appalled."

Anne gathers the books into her arms, but before she makes her exit, Mr. Nussbaum covers the receiver's mouthpiece with his hand. *"Anne,"* he says. "You know, we're still in touch, Cissy and I. I should try to arrange a meeting between you."

"A *meeting?*" She feels a shock of surprise. "Really?"

"Two great literary minds." Mr. Nussbaum grins but then must return to his scowling telephone exchange. Anne loads her "pay" into the basket of her bike and wheels it out the door with a wave that Mr. Nussbaum misses, his back to her now as he continues with his battle. Outside, she breathes the air in deeply. Stares at the stream of bicycle traffic passing her, then swallows lightly as she runs a finger over the cover of the top book.

These novels, Margot says. She has appeared, head shaven, wearing her KZ rags. *They were your favorites, weren't they?* Anne only shakes her head. "Do you think it's possible? Possible that I could actually *meet* Cissy van Marxveldt in person? That would be so wonderful." But when she looks up, Margot is gone. Anne climbs onto the worn leather seat and pedals out into the street.

The sun is shining, opening up the sky above the city into a cloudless stretch of blue. Light polishes the surfaces of the canals into pristine mirrors and brightens the dingy paint jobs of the houseboats bumping against their moorings. She navigates the streets of the Grachtengordel, pedaling harder over the bridges, and then breezing along, looping around a corner, racing the gulls. Her legs have gained muscle; her calves have gained shape, no longer matchsticks. She thrills at the breeze that combs through her hair and her clothes, at the speed of her turns and the bumpy terrain of cobbles under her tires. But mostly she covets the thorough clean sweep of her mind that riding her bike provides. No memories, no fears, just bright adrenaline pumping into her brain.

She's breathy and sweet with sweat when she arrives at the warehouse doors. One is cracked open, and a teasing whiff of spicy aroma wafts out into the street as she climbs from the bike's seat and adjusts her skirt, but then she stops. She freezes like the mouse that's just spied the cat—or exactly the opposite. It's *him*. The boy with the straw-blond hair, standing across the street at the edge of the canal. He stands with a watchful posture, back straight, shoulders tilted slightly forward, hands stuffed in the pockets of his patched-up trousers in a manner that almost makes him appear armless. His appearance adds urgency to her heartbeat, and she must swallow the impulse to call out his name or dump her bike against the side of the building and run to him. She feels herself take a step, but then a lorry rumbles between them, and when it passes, the boy is gone. The Westertoren chimes the half hour.

Taking the steep stairs to the office, she feels a disorienting itch. She glances over her shoulder halfway up, feeling as if the boy might be there behind her, but there's nothing, and she finds that her breezy physical elation has been depressed by something else. By the time she opens the door at the top of the stairs, she feels restless and unsatisfied. But when she stops again, it's because there's no one in the office. The place has a certain ransacked quality to it. The middle drawer of the filing cabinet stands empty, desktops are disheveled, and the drawers of Miep's desk are ajar. She feels a sharp pinch of panic, but then, with a noise of her shoe heels, Mrs. Zuckert enters the room. She faces Anne, and as if she is a mind reader, she says, "Nothing to worry about. Just a misunderstanding. Everyone's fine."

"But"—Anne stares—"what's *happened*?"

Mrs. Zuckert draws a breath and surveys the room. "Honestly, I'm not sure. Men from one of the state bureaus arrived. Your father said we were to be cooperative."

"Where is he?"

"With them at their offices."

"He's under *arrest*?"

Mrs. Zuckert frowns. "*Arrest?* No, of course not. Don't jump to conclusions, Anne. They came to collect records, that's all. Your father accompanied them, along with Mr. Kugler. Quite voluntarily, I should add. I'm sure it's nothing," she says, though her tone seems slightly unsure if that's so. "Simply part of the process. Come," she instructs, "sit down. Let me fix you a cup of tea. You look stricken."

And she is stricken. The thought of men from the state bureaus, rifling through the building, undoes her underpinnings. She feels suddenly fragile as she sits at her desk, glaring at the pale cup of tea that Mrs. Zuckert has delivered. "Do you know what they're looking for?" she asks, still staring blindly at the teacup.

"Do I?" The woman has pulled up a chair to the side of the desk. "No."

"You mean my father hasn't let you in on all the doings behind closed doors? I thought he would have."

"I don't know what you mean by that, Anne. But I can assure you, your father has told me nothing about any 'doings,' as you put it. Why would he? I'm just a secretary."

"*Ha*," Anne replies quietly, then turns to the tea, blowing ripples on its steamy surface. "You know you're more than that. We all know you're more than that."

And now Mrs. Zuckert expels a breath, her eyebrows arched. She stands and walks over to her handbag, usually stored in a drawer but now sitting out beside the Herr Typewriter. Anne watches her from behind, lighting up a cigarette. Highly unorthodox for the women to smoke in the office. "Would you care for one?" she asks, still with her back to Anne.

Anne pauses. "Yes," she says, and Mrs. Zuckert nods. Repeats the process and ferries a lit cigarette back to Anne along with Mr. Kleiman's red enamel ashtray. Anne takes the cigarette and draws in deeply. She watches Mrs. Zuckert return to the chair and adjust her skirt. Anne can see the machinery of the woman's mind churning before she releases smoke and fixes Anne with her eyes.

"All right. You're correct. I was being slightly disingenuous with you when I said I was just an office secretary to your father. You'll have to forgive me for that," she instructs Anne. "I wasn't sure what he has said to you and what he hasn't."

"He doesn't say much," Anne answers. "He's bent on treating me like a child. It's maddening."

Surprisingly, Mrs. Zuckert nods her agreement with this. "Yes, I can understand how it would be. Clearly you are no longer a child, Anne. *Clearly*," she repeats. "You've become a young woman. That's a very difficult time, I think, for any parent, and especially for a father. He's feeling lost. So he prevaricates. He avoids the issues or becomes suddenly authoritarian. But the truth is, he is completely out of his depth with you. Add the fact that you yourself are so implacably furious with the world, and, well . . . There's nowhere for him to turn."

Anne's gaze goes hot. "I was his child. He was supposed to *protect* me," Anne says. "He was supposed to protect us *all*."

"Yet he could not even protect himself," Mrs. Zuckert points out. "If he had died in Auschwitz, would you still find him so culpable?"

"But he didn't die."

"No, he didn't. And I'm thankful to God for that."

Anne says nothing. Mrs. Zuckert trims the ash from her cigarette on the rim of Kleiman's ashtray. She appears to be making some sort of internal choice. And then she says, "At Birkenau I was part of the Kanada Kommando. You know 'Kanada,' yes?"

Anne nods. Kanada was the name of the warehouse filled with the stolen luggage of prisoners. It was called such because Kanada was believed to be a land of great riches.

"I was assigned to the White Kerchief work group. Most of the women were Hungarian, and since my father was born in Budapest, I had a bit of the language. And there were advantages to be had as a Kanada Jewess. We all kept our hair. The work was not physically debilitating. The SS mostly turned a blind eye to our eating the food we found, so that was good, but still a horrific job in its own way. We had a direct view of the Krematorien as people were marched into the gas chambers, which pushed us all to the edge of insanity. We *heard* what went on inside," she says, "the screaming, the cries. And then nothing."

Silence. A tear dampens Anne's cheek, but she does not wipe it away.

"So I do understand your rage," Mrs. Zuckert tells her. "I do understand your grief."

"Why do you think *you* survived?" Anne asks bluntly.

The woman lifts her eyebrows. *"Why?"*

"I ask this question of Pim, and he tells me that it was because of *hope.* But how can I believe that? Because when I ask myself the same question, I have no answer. So now I'm asking you. Was it luck that sent you to the Kanada Kommando? Was it God?"

"God? I should be so presumptuous. Actually, it might have been nothing more than my ability as a typist. The SS were lazy, I found. They hated typing up paperwork, so I did it for them." She shrugs. "In the final months, I was transferred from Birkenau to the Siemens camp in Bobrek to work as a stenographer. The food was not as plentiful, but no Jews were gassed there, and I could keep my sanity."

"So. You are an excellent typist," Anne says. *"That's* your answer?"

Mrs. Zuckert gazes at her. "It's the only one I can offer." And then she says, "You know, Anne, we have all suffered. You, me, your father. But for me, losing everything has made it easier to embrace the idea of starting over. When you have lost everything, then you have nothing else that *can* be lost. Only gained."

The smoke from Anne's cigarette drifts upward.

Mrs. Zuckert draws in a breath before slowly releasing it as if she is drawing in strength. "Your father has insisted that I keep silent about this till he can determine that the correct time has come. And I'm sure that he'll be piqued with me when he finds out that I couldn't hold my tongue any longer, but *honestly,* when does the 'correct time' ever come? And I have never seen the point in surreptitious behavior. To me, if a thing *needs* to be said, it *should* be said. So I think you should know. I think *everyone* should know."

Anne still stares, though she is feeling a queasiness in her belly.

"Anne," the woman says, pronouncing her name as if it's a solid piece of iron. "Your father has asked me to marry him. And I have accepted his proposal."

Anne blinks. The room seems to have gone crooked. Then there's noise on the stairs, rising with a thumping urgency. The door shudders open, and it's Pim. He's winded. Shaken. Hunted. The sight of Anne and Mrs. Zuckert together at the desk shoves him backward a step.

"Otto," Mrs. Zuckert says, "Anne and I were just having a conversation."

"Yes?" he asks with a blighted anxiety. "Were you?" It's obvious he's guessed. It was obvious he'd guessed the second he heard her call him by his given name. He glances at Anne, who meets his eyes with steel.

"How did things develop with the bureau?" Mrs. Zuckert wants to know.

Pim breathes roughly. Shakes his head as his answer to her question. "It's still very complicated. There are still obstacles to be overcome, and the questions are endless. I'm quite confident that the matter will be properly resolved, but it will take more time than originally anticipated. I'm sorry," he says quickly, "but I stopped by only to pick up my spectacles."

"Your spectacles, Pim?" says Anne. "Since when do you ever wear your spectacles?"

"Anne, you shouldn't question your father," says her father's fiancée. "There must be something he needs to see clearly."

Pim blinks at them both. "Excuse me," he says, and exits down the hall toward his private office. A moment later he is out again and hurrying past the door, heading down the steps. For a man who's in his mid-fifties and who has endured ten months at Auschwitz, he can certainly move with clean agility when he decides it's warranted.

Mrs. Zuckert crushes out her cigarette in the red ashtray. "There are some customers who placed orders, Anne," she says. "They should be contacted about the delays this matter will cause. Perhaps you can help me make the telephone calls? We'll say that we're experiencing a temporary disruption of supply from our wholesalers. They probably won't believe us—news travels fast, especially when it involves the bureaus. At best they'll think we can't pay our bills, but then who among us can? In any case I've found that the Dutch are far too polite to ask embarrassing questions. So leave your father in peace and concentrate on work. It'll be better for you in the long run," she says. "Besides, you can always excoriate him at a later date."

"You don't feel guilty?" Anne demands.

"Guilty?" Mrs. Zuckert lifts her eyebrows again.

"Guilty at forcing my father to be disloyal to his wife's memory?"

"Oh, so now it's *me* who forces him, is it? Fine. The answer, I can *assure* you, is *no*. I feel no guilt over my feelings for your father. I feel no guilt, period. The dead are gone and lost to us now. And guilt is the worst kind of poison. That much, Anne, you should learn."

Suddenly Anne pushes herself up from the chair and bolts away from the desk. Away from Mrs. Zuckert, away from the office, down the stairs, and into the warehouse, where she mounts her bicycle and shoves off into the street. A squat little automobile scolds her with a toot, but she ignores it and pedals away, up the street and across the shaded Leidsegracht. Her heart is thrumming in her chest. Her muscles clammy. She is following the strongest of her urges, the urge to flee. To escape. Why she loses control is hard to say. Maybe it's because of a bump in the sidewalk, or maybe because her bike tires have lost too much tread, or because she has pedaled too close to the curb. Or maybe it's simply her own panicked anguish that derails her. The screech of a lorry's rubber tire is deafening, and then she is falling, nothing but a vivid helplessness between her and the pavement, until the impact of the fall slams the breath from her body. She sees a wheel wobbling above her and hears a voice swimming dizzily in her head. She can tell it's the driver of the lorry, who's out from behind the wheel, demanding to know if she's hurt as he's lifting her bicycle. She feels an uncomfortable throb in her leg, when suddenly Margot is there, trying to help her up, dressed in her school clothes, reporting on the accident. *Your knee. You've scraped up your knee.*

"I can see that," Anne answers flatly. But suddenly something's off. Through the dizziness she sees that it's *not* Margot helping her stand, it's the boy with the straw-blond hair. "Can you walk?" he asks her.

"I don't know. Yes, I think. Is my bicycle damaged?"

The lorry driver is a middle-aged Dutchman in a frayed cap, with callused hands and thick jowls. He lifts her bicycle to perform an examination. "Looks like the tire burst. And—I don't know—fender's a little bent. But it's not hard to fix. If you're not too bad off, I can put the bike in the rear of the lorry and take you to your house," he volunteers. "Where do you live?"

"In the Jekerstraat," says Anne. "But my father's office is just around the corner in the Prinsengracht."

"That'll do. Hold on." And as the driver makes room in the back of his lorry for the bicycle, Anne cannot help but be aware of the strength of the blond boy's arms and the salty aroma of his sweat.

"I saw you standing by the canal," she tells him.

"Did you? I saw you fall off your bicycle."

"I'm sure I can walk," she declares, though she's not sure that she wants to. Not just yet. Her leg *does* hurt, that's true. And maybe she's not quite ready to give up the weightless feeling of her body hung in the boy's half embrace.

"You smell nice," the boy offers, and Anne looks up at him, surprised. There's a kind of pale statement of fact in his eyes. The driver returns, yanking open the passenger door with a creak of hinges, and he and the boy load her into the passenger seat. The boy shuts the door behind her and steps away, hands stuffed back into his pockets.

The window is rolled down. Anne hooks her elbow over the door and leans her head out. "Your name is Raaf," she tells him.

"And yours is Anne," the boy answers.

"Why did you vanish?"

"I didn't vanish. I'm standing right here."

"But at the warehouse. You stopped showing up. Was it because of what I did?"

The boy almost grins. "Well. Usually when I wanna get bit, I steal a bone from a dog."

"I'm sorry."

The driver hops into the seat beside her and slams his door shut before revving the engine.

"Will you come back to work?" she asks the boy.

He shakes his head. "Nah. I got another job at a brewery house in the Lindengracht."

"But don't you miss the smell of the spices?"

"Never thought about it," the boy replies.

"Still, you're hanging about," she says, surprised by her own desire to flirt. "There must be *something* you miss about the place," Anne calls to him as the driver throttles the lorry into gear and shifts it forward. "I wonder what it could be?" she shouts out over the noise.

It's one of the warehousemen who helps her up the leg-breaking stairs. He's a short, stocky old snuiter whose name is Dekker, but the rest of the men call him "Duimen"—Thumbs—because he's so well known for dropping everything he picks up. "Don't you worry, though, little miss, I won't drop *you*," he tells Anne. He's also known as a bit of a schapenkop, a sad sack. A Simple Simon with room in his noggin for only one thought at a time. His smile is full of gaps, and his breath stinks badly of shag tobacco, but Anne can tell that he is trying to be kind to her, and so she does her best to arrange her face in an appreciative expression. At the top of the stairs, he knocks respectfully at the office door before pushing it open and calling out, "Halloo!"

Miep is back, and she stands up suddenly from her desk. "Oh, my heavens, what's *happened*?"

"Nothing. It's nothing. Really, I'm fine," Anne responds to the note of emergency.

"The little miss took a spill on her bicycle," Duimen reports diligently.

Miep is already across the floor assisting him in the minor burden of Anne's weight. "Let's get her in the chair, please, Mr. Dekker."

"Really, it's just a scrape. *Oww!*" Anne yelps when she must bend her knee to sit.

At this point Mrs. Zuckert returns to the room. "And what's happened here?" she demands blankly, a thick binder in her arms.

Miep pretends for a moment that she is deaf, inspecting the damage, leaving poor Duimen to respond, cap in his hands. "The little miss took a spill," he repeats with a trickle of anxiety this time. "From her bicycle," he adds, so as not to omit any significant detail.

Only now does Miep look up. "Mrs. Zuckert, there's a first-aid kit in the kitchen. The top drawer just under the sink. Would you mind? I think a bandage and some iodine are in order."

Mrs. Zuckert listens to this but remains where she is. "What about the bicycle?" she asks Duimen.

"Missus?"

"Is it badly damaged?"

"Oh, uh. No. I think it's not. The fender maybe, but I'm sure I can hammer it back into shape without much of a fuss."

"Good," Mrs. Zuckert approves. "Bicycles are impossible to replace." Only now does she turn back to Miep, who is sharing a glare of amazement with Anne. "Bandage and iodine. Top drawer under the sink," Mrs. Zuckert repeats, and then exits the room.

"Incredible," Anne whispers. "As long as the *bicycle* is fine, only then is it permitted to tend to my wound."

"I'm not quite sure that this qualifies as a *wound*, Anne." Miep is arranging a chair to act as a footstool. "More like a knee scrape. But you should keep it straight," she instructs before turning to dismiss Duimen. "Thank you, Mr. Dekker," she informs the man. "You've been very helpful."

"Yes, thank you, Mr. Dekker," Anne says, joining in, and Duimen is relieved to return to his toothless smile, giving a nod and flapping his cap back onto his bald head. "No trouble, miss," he tells Anne. "You just be careful now," he says, and out he goes, tromping noisily down the stairs.

"What exactly happened?" Miep wants to know.

"I'm not sure. My tire burst, and I slipped off the curb. Or maybe it was the other way around."

"No, I don't mean *that*," Miep says, her voice dropping ever so slightly. "I mean *here*. With Mrs. Zuckert."

Anne feels her jaw go rigid. "Why do you ask?"

"Because she says you threw a fit and stormed out when she tried to give you work."

"That's a lie."

"Well, then, what *did* happen?"

But the words are suddenly stuck in Anne's throat, and before she can possibly unstick them, Mrs. Zuckert has returned with the first-aid kit and a glass of something. "First-aid kit requisitioned," she reports to Miep, and then extends the glass to Anne. "Here. Drink this."

Anne stares at the glass and then at Mrs. Zuckert. She takes the glass but doesn't drink. It smells strong. "What is it?"

"Brandy," Mrs. Zuckert answers.

"*Brandy*?" Miep frowns with surprise.

"Drink it," she tells Anne again. "It'll calm your nerves."

"Where did you get brandy?" Miep wonders aloud.

"Oh, I thought you knew," Mrs. Zuckert replies. "Mr. Frank keeps a bottle of Koetsiertje in his office cabinet. To offer clients."

"But Mr. Frank . . ." Miep must take a breath before finishing. "He always locks the office."

"So he does, yes," Mrs. Zuckert agrees, "but he gave me a key. Now drink it," she orders Anne. And then to Miep she says, "You should take her back to your flat and put a cold press on her knee so it doesn't swell." She follows this order with a shrug. "Of course, that's just a suggestion."

Miep nods, standing. It's clear she's had enough. "Yes," she agrees archly. "What a good idea. Anne, drink the brandy," she commands. "I'll call for a taxi."

It does hurt. Her knee, that is. There's a slow ache in the joint. The iodine stings under the bandage, and the brandy burns, pooling in her belly. She is planted beside Miep in the back of a bicycle taxi, bumping along the street, following the noise of the gulls. The taxi man is a large fellow, with dusty gray hair bristling from under his cap and a metal livery badge hung from his coat. The air smells of motor traffic, and the morning sun has been clouded as it drags toward midday. "How worried should I be?" Anne asks.

"About your knee?" Miep says.

"About the bureau men collecting the office files."

Miep expels a weary breath. "I don't know, exactly."

"You don't like her, do you?" Anne asks.

"Who?"

"You know *who*. Mrs. Zuckert."

Miep looks directly at Anne and almost smiles. "No, I do not."

"Neither do I," says Anne. "So what does Pim *see* in her?" she complains to the air. "I shouldn't tell you this probably, but he's asked her to *marry* him."

Miep stiffens visibly. "Yes," is all she says.

"You know, *too*?"

"Yes."

"So Pim told everyone but me?"

"No. Your father said nothing about it."

"Ah. Then *she* told you. She must have taken great satisfaction in that moment. Don't you find it all too disgusting?"

Miep lifts her sharply tweezed eyebrows. Her eyes are blue oceans. "Your father is a very good man, Anne. One of the best men I've ever known. He's not perfect, as I'm sure he would be the first to admit. But he has sacrificed a great deal for the good of others. More than you know. We should not begrudge him a little happiness for a change. And if it's Mrs. Zuckert who makes him happy, then it's not for me *or for you* to criticize him. So I would advise you to bridle your anger. He deserves respect."

"As does my mother's memory," Anne points out.

"Then why don't you *grant* your mother's memory respect and stop insulting her husband? Do you honestly believe that she would have wanted your father to live in misery and loneliness for her sake?"

Anne, however, is not willing to answer this question. The taxi man shouts impatiently at a cyclist, and an auto horn sounds. A swift patter of rain peppers the taxi's canopy. Anne turns away to hide her face, pretending that it is the pain in her knee causing her eyes to well. Why should he be miserable or lonely? He *has,* after all, a living daughter.

. . .

It's late when her father returns to the flat. Miep and Jan have long since retired, leaving Anne sitting on the sofa, one stocking foot extended onto one of Miep's batik pillows, the open notebook on her lap. When the key grates in the lock and the front door opens, she can see, even in the room's waxy lamplight, that her father is slumped with exhaustion.

"Anne," he says with a kind of apologetic dread. A tone that matches the expression installed in his eyes. "You were injured."

"Injured." Anne repeats the word as if it has many sides to examine. "Yes," she answers, then shuts her composition book and stands with an overtly discreet grimace of pain. "My bicycle went off the curb. But that's unimportant." Tucking the notebook under her arm, she informs him with lifeless formality, "What's important is that Mrs. Zuckert has informed me of your plans. So let me be the first," she says, adding the absurdity of a half curtsy on her stiff knee, "to wish you every happiness in your new life."

"Anne," Pim repeats, more urgently, "Anne, *please*. Permit me a moment to speak with you." But Anne is making her exit with a small hobble, and shuts the door of her room behind her. Inside, she sits on the edge of her bed gripping the notebook, listening to her father's earnestly distressed knocking and the sound of her name on his lips. But she does not move.

So you're just going to shut him out like this? Margot asks. She is wearing the dirty pullover displaying the Lager star fashioned from yellow triangles. Her face is shrunken against her cheekbones, her glasses long gone, and her eyes popping like a starved animal's.

"He's shutting *me* out. He's shutting us both out."

"Please, Anne," her father keeps saying, "please open the door."

"I'm sorry, Pim," Anne calls back. "I'm undressed."

She hears him huff dryly. Disappointed in her resistance, disappointed in his inability to overcome it. "I see," he finally breathes. "Very well. Tomorrow, then, we can talk tomorrow. Good night, my darling."

"Good night," Anne calls back. And then to Margot she says, "She's got him now."

Got him?

"Do you really imagine that a woman like Hadassah Zuckert is going to permit his memory of either you or of Mummy to intrude upon her agenda?"

So you think she has an agenda, do you?

"Are you stupid as well as dead?" Anne demands to know. "She intends to claim him as *her own*, Margot. She wants to wash away any trace of his former life."

Oh, please. Margot frowns with a short roll of her eyes. *How could you possibly know such a thing?*

"How can you possibly *doubt* it? Every day it becomes harder for Pim to recall the details of Mummy's face. By now he must see her in the same way he looks at a musty old photograph."

And how can you possibly know such a thing?

"Because every day it's harder for *me* to remember Mummy's face. I mean, really *remember* it. To *see* it like I could touch her cheek as if she's still alive."

But Margot has no response to questions dividing life from death, and when Anne turns to her, the space on the bed where she sat is empty. She has not even left behind a wrinkle in the fabric of the blanket.

Late that night Anne tiptoes into the kitchen and opens the bread box. All she needs is a crust. Something to stash under her mattress. A barricade against the angel of death. She imagines Mummy for an instant, wasted to nothing in the Lager infirmary, squirreling away a stale sliver of camp bread under the fetid straw of her billet. Never forgetting her girls.

19

BETRAYAL

By the way, speaking of Jews, I saw two yesterday when I was peeking through the curtains. I felt as though I were gazing at one of the Seven Wonders of the World. It gave me such a funny feeling, as if I'd denounced them to the authorities and was now spying on their misfortune.

—Anne Frank,
from her diary,
13 December 1942

Dearest Kitty,
I'm seething with rage, yet I can't show it.

—Anne Frank,
from her diary,
30 January 1943

1946

Prinsengracht 263
Offices of Opekta and Pectacon
Amsterdam-Centrum

LIBERATED NETHERLANDS

A modest celebration is held at the official announcement of Pim and Dassah's engagement to wed. Pim has arrived in the front office with a bottle of Maréchal Foch. Everyone cheers at the pop of the cork. Everyone but his daughter. Wine burbles into the set of newly procured matched lead-crystal ware. Royal Leerdam, Pim laughs with a pleasantly incredulous note. How *does* she lay her hands on such things? he inquires of the air. He is referring, of course, to Mrs. Zuckert, his newly declared fiancée, who is standing beside him. He now continually calls her by his special nickname for her, Hadas, or, worse, sometimes the painfully more intimate Hadasma, as when he says, "Hadasma and I are so pleased that the people here in this room are the first to know of our intentions."

Anne sits and glares at the color of the wine that fills the glass on the desk in front of her. A dark purple with a tinge of pinkish light. One beautiful thing. But when the room toasts the happy couple, Anne does not move.

Mrs. Zuckert smiles at her. "Anne, you don't care for your wine?"

"Wine is too bitter for me," she answers with a blank tone. "It's my stomach, you see. I've always had a weak stomach—haven't I, Pim? Didn't Mummy always insist I had a weak stomach?"

Pim releases the thinnest sigh as he shifts a hand into the pocket of his trousers. "She did, Anne," he confirms. "That is true, she did."

A stumbling silence follows, until Kleiman pipes up. "So have you set the date?" he asks brightly, and Pim immediately offers him a pleasantly questioning blink.

"A date? Well. I'm not sure we have. Have we set a date?" he asks his fiancée.

"*Soon,*" Mrs. Zuckert replies as a joke, gripping Pim's arm. "Before he tries to escape," she says, and everyone laughs. Everyone but Anne Frank.

On a graying day, hectored by rain in the hour before sunset, Anne sits in a chair with her pen in her hand and writes that today Mr. Otto Heinrich Frank wed Mrs. Hadassah Zuckert-Bauer by civil procedure in the marriage hall of the Hotel Prinsenhof. The brief ceremony was held approximately one year and four months from the date of the death of Mr. Frank's first wife of blessed memory, Mrs. Edith Frank-Holländer, who perished of starvation in the infirmary of Auschwitz-Birkenau.

Mr. and Mrs. Frank are now slated to occupy a modest flat on the Herengracht, six days hence, where a single room, as adequate as any prison cell, will be provided for the new Mrs. Frank's freshly acquired stepchild, one A.F.

20

A KISS

Isn't it an important day for every girl when she gets her
first kiss?

—Anne Frank,
from her diary,
16 April 1944

1946

Amsterdam

LIBERATED NETHERLANDS

There's a brewery house off the Brouwersgracht, a dilapidated four-story canal house, chalky with decay, its ancient whitewash peeling from the bricks. Dingy houseboats bump against the canal walls, leaving paint scrapes like a little child left to color the walls with crayons. It's here she waits, leaning on her bicycle after school has been dismissed, smoking a cigarette, inhaling the odor of hops that drifts heavily on the humid air.

A breathy warmth floats above the canals, and the sun is thrust high into the sky like the eye of heaven. The brewery's rickety old lorry rumbles into view and shudders to a halt. A crew of workmen appear hustling out of the warehouse doors and start rolling out hefty ironbound kegs, which they proceed to usher up a ramp and stack onto the lorry's bed. He is wearing a stained canvas apron like the others, his blond hair bristling, uncombed. When he stops, he stands up straight and stares back at her until he gets a friendly elbow from one of the other workers. The keg in place, he hops down to the pavement and breaks into a trot, coming to a halt where only a meter or so separates them. His face is smudged with a half smile.

"You smell like beer," she says.

He shrugs. "You got your bike fixed."

"Yep."

"And your knee works."

"Can you take a walk with me?" she asks.

"A walk."

"Just a walk."

"Why?"

She swallows. "You know why," she answers, looking at him.

"I dunno," he considers, "you're kinda dangerous."

She doesn't disagree. "Does that mean you're too afraid?"

"No. But I can't. Not right now." One of the older workmen is already whistling for him to return to the job of loading the lorry. "I gotta work. But tomorrow," he says.

"Tomorrow."

"You'll be here?"

Anne gazes at him. Sweat makes his shirt stick to his skin. "Possibly," she says. And then she advances on him. Grabbing a handful of his shirt, she presses her mouth against his, attacking with a kiss, before breaking off with a pop of her lips. She feels her glare shove him onto his heels. "You'd better get back to work," she informs him as she mounts her bike, stabbing the pedal with her foot and pumping away.

The word she is not thinking, not admitting to thinking, is retaliation.

After supper her father springs his trap for her in the kitchen. She is washing the dishes and Miep is drying and setting them on the shelves when in comes Pim trailing the smell of Heeren-Baai pipe tobacco. "I'll finish up with Anne," he informs Miep, and Miep does not resist as she usually might when a man offers assistance in the kitchen.

Anne concentrates on dunking the supper dishes into the tub of soapy water, addressing them with a sponge. She brushes a strand of hair from her face with her wrist. Only after she plunges a soup bowl into the rinsing tub and then lifts it from the greasy rainbow of water does she glance at Pim. "Since when do you do kitchen work?" she wants to know.

"Oh, now, that's not very fair," her father responds amiably as he wipes the bowl with a faded cotton rag. "I used to help your mother quite often with the dishes. Don't you recall?"

Anne only shrugs and sponges another bowl.

"Can we discuss this, Anne?" Pim asks her, his tone dipping but still hopeful.

"Discuss what?" The bowl clinks against the rim of the pot as she rinses it and then hands it over. "Discuss supper dishes?"

"She makes me *happy,* meisje," her father tells her.

Anne frowns at the plate she picks up. "You've replaced Mummy. In the blink of an eye."

"No. *No,*" Pim corrects."I haven't. It's not like that. Hadas . . ." He speaks the name, then hesitates, eyes flickering as he works out the next sentence. "She offers me a different *kind* of happiness," he decides. "One that I never believed I could experience again."

"You mean in bed?" Anne asks ruthlessly.

Pim straightens like a whip crack, blinking over the top of his frown. "*Anne.* Shame on you for asking such an indecent question."

But Anne sighs drably over the sink. "I only wondered if that's what you meant."

"It certainly was not. What I'm speaking of is genuine happiness. Happiness of the heart."

Anne hands him a wet dish. "Oké," she says.

He accepts the dish and blankly runs the rag over it. "You're angry," he observes. "You're still very angry."

A glance from Anne, but no words.

"And whether or not you're willing to believe it, it's an anger I recognize, because I felt it, too. I *still* feel it. But I refuse to let it rule me. I refuse to, Anne," he insists forcefully. Then he puffs a breath and shakes his head. "Yet I see how it has you in its grasp. How it makes you suffer. Every day. Isn't there something I can do to help you be free of it, daughter? I continue to try but continue to fail."

And really before she knows she's done it, Anne has smashed the dish in her hand against the rim of the sink, shattering it into shrapnel.

Pim leaps back a step, gripping the bowl clutched in the dishrag.

"Oops," Anne announces, her eyes heating with tears as Miep comes hurrying into the kitchen to view the current catastrophe. "I'm sorry, Miep," Anne breathes, and strikes away a tear with her wrist. "Butterfingers."

Her father swallows deeply, wearing a pained expression, but he hands the bowl and rag over to Miep on his way out.

—◦—

The Grachtengordel
Amsterdam-Centrum

The street is narrow but thick with people trying to get a bit of shopping done on their midday breaks. In the doorway of an empty shop, Anne blocks the view of passersby while Griet strips off her socks and saddle shoes and slides on silk stockings. The stockings have seams that follow the calves of Griet's legs up her lovely thighs to the soft nether region under her skirt. A gift from her new Canadian boyfriend. Across the street is the Liefje cinema. "Love" cinema. The Canadians who take their Dutch girlfriends there like the joke.

"So I suppose this means you've dropped your sweetheart Henk?" Anne asks her.

A shrug. "Henk was just a boy. And it was never anything serious between us." Wriggling her feet into a pair of suede pumps, Griet says, "Albert is a *man*. And treats *me* like a woman."

"Does that mean you're doing it with him?" Anne asks bluntly, curious at what bonds men and women together.

Griet shrugs, bashful. "He says he wants to marry me."

And now Anne's brow creases sharply. Can the girl really be so foolish? "*Marry* you?"

"Yep."

"And you believe him?"

"I don't know. Maybe. Probably not."

"But you're still doing it with him."

"It's fun, Anne. It feels good. *Really* good."

Anne huffs dimly. "Isn't that him?" she inquires. A solidly built Canadian soldier in the standard beret and khaki fatigues. He wears a thick reddish mustache and is lighting his pipe in front of the cinema doors.

Griet can't help but grin. "That's him, all right. He's a lance sergeant, you know. In charge of a squad of riflemen."

"He's quite mature-looking," Anne must admit.

Griet gives her a look of defensive scrutiny. "You think I'm a whore, don't you?"

"No, and I would never use that word." Which is true. She hates the judgment in that word. But this talk of marriage, of commitment, unnerves her. Doesn't all commitment lead to eventual betrayal? "I'm only wondering," she says, "what happens if you end up with a baby in your belly?"

Griet shrugs this off. "Then I guess he'll *have* to marry me, like it or not. It wouldn't be so bad, I think. Being a Canadian."

"Unless he just leaves you in the lurch."

Griet frowns darkly, shakes her head. "He wouldn't do that."

"No?" Anne wants to make it clear she is not so sure about that. "Is he even Jewish?"

"Jewish?" Griet repeats, as if perhaps she has to concentrate to remember what that means. "I never asked."

"You never *asked*," Anne repeats, and looks at her friend more closely. "And does he know that *you're* Jewish?"

"He never asked me either."

"Oké. So he thinks you're a Good Christian Girl."

"Well, what if he does? Who cares? The war's over now, who cares?" It's obvious that she's sick of the conversation, and maybe a little sick of Anne, too. "Why are you always like this now?" she asks. "You didn't used to be so depressing about everything."

"I'm not. I'm sorry," says Anne, and maybe she means it a little.

Griet caps the lipstick she was using and slaps it into Anne's palm. "Here, take it. I've got plenty. Maybe you can paint a smile on that puss of yours." She grins, wagging Anne's chin playfully.

Anne only tugs away and puffs out a breath. "He looks impatient. You'd better go to him," she says, mounting her bicycle, "before he decides to marry the next Good Christian Girl with big boobies who comes along."

Griet blinks at her but then shrugs and follows her interest across the street. Anne watches for a moment as Griet approaches her Canadian, watches the smile pry open the young soldier's face as he spots her. The kiss in public, the lance sergeant's arm slung around her waist as they enter the cinema. It's a scene that reeks of the future. A terrifying future based on touch and joy and desire, she thinks.

The next day Anne escapes from school alone. She has slipped a set of ersatz pearls made from glass over her collar and powdered away the number on her forearm, as she's now in the habit of doing. Then, pedaling to the Lindengracht, she stops to apply Griet's tube of lipstick in the reflection of a garment shop's window so it will still be bright and fresh when he sees her. A passing lorryload of Canadian soldiers whistles and howls.

You don't think that makes you look a bit cheap? Margot inquires. She has filled the window glass with her Kazetnik's reflection, the Judenstern drooping from her pullover.

Anne glances at her as she puckers her lips. "Is it even?" she asks.

Margot squints without her glasses. *I suppose. But you still haven't answered my question.*

Anne dabs at the lip rouge lightly with a fingertip. "Maybe I don't mind looking a bit cheap. Did that ever occur to you?"

No, Margot must answer honestly. *No, is my response to that. I just hope you're not planning on throwing yourself at this boy.*

"Throwing myself? Whatever do you mean?"

You know precisely what I mean.

But Anne shakes her head, closing the lipstick tube. "You're just jealous," she says.

That's not true.

"It *is* true. You're jealous because I'm alive and you're not. Jealous because you never knew what it was like to be with a man, and I still can. You just want to deny me any sort of a normal existence."

That's not true, Anne.

"No? Well, if it's *not*, then why can't you just leave me alone? Why can't you just quit interfering and butt out?" A bell dings over the door as a stiff-faced Dutch matron steps out of the shop and shoots Anne a suspect frown before walking on.

Anne shakes her head. "Wonderful. Now I look like a lunatic thanks to you, talking to no one," she says, but Margot's reflection has vanished from the window glass.

When he appears from inside the brewery, Anne is waiting beside her bicycle. He comes trotting toward her again with his hands in his pockets, then stops as if an invisible wall divides them. "You look different," he tells her. His eyes are hooded and rather cautious, like a sleepy animal's.

"You don't," she replies. "And you still smell like beer." Maybe she overdid it, dressing up this way, trying to appear beautiful. Raaf is not exactly one of her beaux from school taking her out for ice cream. Maybe it's too much for him, this "beautiful" Anne, so she disguises any disappointment she might feel that he seems more confused than enchanted. But she doesn't disguise the fact that she is pleased to be standing so close to him, and she takes his hand. "Come with me," she says.

They walk to the spot Anne has mapped out in her head: the center of the Skinny Bridge off the Kerkstraat, straddling a narrow stripe of the sun-dappled water where leafy branches float calmly. She asks him for a cigarette as an excuse to stop, to anchor them to this spot, and is amazed to watch him hand-roll a pair of smokes so efficiently from a pouch of stringy black shag. He solders each into a tight little cylinder with a swipe of his tongue, offering her a light from a match that he ignites with a flick of his thumb. Halfzware, he calls the tobacco. She inhales its bitter tang that tastes like fireplace ashes cured in shoe polish. She says something to this effect, and he looks surprised at the sound of his own laughter.

She stands with the boy, sharing his hand-rolled shag, watching the smoke from it drift in the breeze that tousles their hair. This close she can't help but see that his face is caged. As if he's bracing himself for pain. He leans forward onto the railing, and she follows his lead so that their shoulders brush together. She presses her elbow against his and lets it stay. When he turns, she sees that the light has sharpened to points in the lazy blue of his eyes. His hand touches her cheek. And then his hand is slipping past her cheek, caressing her neck, and he is guiding her forward toward his mouth. Pressing her lips against the sudden dampness, she feels a shock of joy. In that moment the soft squish of their kiss quells the pang of her loss, releasing her from herself. Gentling the anger of her incompressible desire. In that moment her heart beats in a clean, strong pulse, as she seizes the un-combed hair at the back of his head and presses herself into him, ab-sorbing his heat. Her need fusing with his. Losing herself in a deep swim of stunningly guiltless pleasure.

When their lips separate, she gazes into the light of his eyes. It's steady and clear. His face is unlocked. "Raaf," she pronounces quietly.

"What?" His voice is close.

"Nothing," she replies. "I wanted to speak your name aloud." Raaf. Not Peter. A boy named Raaf with a thatch of straw-blond hair. She feels herself drawing him toward her, her arms slipping over his neck—she, opening her lips, opening herself to the messy, blissful in-vasion of human craving.

21

THE TRANSVAAL

And behold, thistles had grown all over it; nettles had covered its surface, and its stone fence had been torn down.

—Proverbs 24:31

1946

Amsterdam

LIBERATED NETHERLANDS

Her new room in the new flat has striped blue-on-white wallpaper and a creaking hardwood floor. With the window open, she can see the traffic passing on the canal—and often smell it as well. New furnishings have arrived for her father's new life, including a velveteen sofa and a tall Viennese wingback chair, plus a double bed for the newlyweds. Anne's lumpy old thing, however, has simply been transferred from her former room in the Jekerstraat. And her mother's French secretaire, which once adorned the corner of her room in the Merwedeplein, has remained behind with Miep. When Miep resisted this gift, Anne whispered, "Keep it, Miep. Please. I'd rather you have it than *her*."

～～～

De Keiser Meisjeslyceum
Reinier Vinkeles Quay
Amsterdam Oud-Zuid

After classes are dismissed, she initiates a shoving match by the bike shed with one of the other girls, a girl named Clare Buskirk, that scrap of carrion. But before it escalates, the normally all-too-jovial nature and health teacher, Mrs. Peerboom, comes galloping over to separate the combatants, her face two shades redder than a beet. "Goeie hemel!" she calls out righteously, with deep astonishment. "This is indecent. You're supposed to be *ladies*!"

"She'll never be a *lady,* Mrs. Peerboom," Clare spits, her ugly little face on permanent display. "She's just a *Jewess.*"

"And you're just a pile of shit!" Anne shouts back.

"*Quiet!*" Mrs. Peerboom barks. "Now be on your way, both of you, unless you want to explain yourself to the headmistress."

Anne goes silent, but her hatred is still loud in her ears. "I should have bashed her in the mouth," she tells Griet later, sharing a cigarette behind the school. "I should have squashed her like a bug."

But Griet is preoccupied, it seems. She is busy looking off in another direction.

"*What?*" Anne wants to know.

"What?"

"You're barely listening to me."

A shrug as Griet frowns at the cigarette between her fingers. "I have to tell you something."

Anne feels a sharp and immediate pinch of anxiety in her belly but tries to hide it with her impatience. "*Tell me?* Tell me *what*?"

"I don't want to say it."

"*Tell me*, Griet," Anne now commands. "You can't just announce that you have something to say and then say nothing."

Griet raises her eyes and stares.

"*Griet?*"

"I'm leaving school," the girl says.

Anne feels another pinch. "*What?* That's ridiculous."

"*Why?* You're always saying that it's such a waste of time."

"For *me*, not for *you*," Anne answers, trying to make a joke. "You need *educating*, lieveling," she says, rubbing Griet's mop of curls.

Griet smiles faintly and without mirth. "I'm getting married," she says.

Anne swallows. Repeats the word. "Married."

"Yep."

"Married," Anne repeats again, feeling a buzz of anger return. "To whom?"

"To '*whom*'? To '*whom*' do you *think*, Anne?"

"I don't know." Plucking the cigarette from Griet's fingers, she says, "Sometimes it's hard to keep track of the boys you're doing it with."

Griet's mouth hardens. "That's a shitty thing to say."

"Sorry," Anne says, without meaning it. "I guess you just took me by surprise. So it's the Canadian?"

"His name is Albert."

"Did he get you pregnant?"

"No. He just asked me, and I said yes. Why are you being so nasty? I knew I shouldn't have told you," Griet mutters to herself, standing and snatching up her book satchel. "I knew you'd react like this."

And suddenly Anne feels a bleak stab of remorse. "*Griet.* I'm sorry," she says, meaning it this time, but too late. Griet is already retrieving her bicycle.

"Griet, *please.*"

The girl stops, wiping away tears but refusing to look in Anne's direction. "Good-bye, Anne," is all she says. Then she mounts her bike and pushes off into the street. "I'll send you a postcard."

———

Dejected, Anne arrives at the bookshop, only to find no sign of Mr. Nussbaum. The door is bolted, shades drawn. She knocks tentatively and can hear Lapjes meowing like a big grump on the other side, but no Mr. Nussbaum. No note on the door, only the faint scour marks and chipped-paint reminder of the anonymous request for Jews to perish.

So now she is riding her bike, going nowhere, trailing the canals to let her mind drain to empty. No thought, no ambition, no feeling. But when she stops near a short metal bridgework to light a cigarette, it's Bep she spies stepping out of a sadly dilapidated old canal pub. Bep! She wants to call out the girl's name. She wants to run to her and hug her tightly. She wants to pour out the surge of affection she feels, but some internal drag of caution stops her. She thinks of what Kugler told her. That Bep could not tolerate the burden of Anne's friendship.

Bep buttons her jacket in the doorway and steps away. Anne considers following her, but then there's someone else stepping out of the pub. A lean-eyed girl wearing a kerchief over her short, stubby hair. She's gained a hard angle to her face since the time Anne spotted her on a tram on the arm of a mof soldier. And when she catches Anne's glare for an instant from across the cobblestones, all she offers is a hard blink before she turns in the opposite direction from Bep and walks away, head down.

"That's Bep's sister," Anne says to Margot, who is standing beside her in her Lager rags, her face livid with sores.

Really? Are you sure?

"Yes, I'm sure. You think I'm blind? That's Nelli."

She looked so broken, Margot observes. *Poor thing.*

"Poor thing? You expect me to have sympathy for her?"

Don't you?

"She was a bitch, Margot. A mof prostitute."

Why must you judge people so harshly? Mummy would never have called anybody such names. Didn't she always try to have a good opinion about people? Didn't she teach us to keep a good opinion of people, no matter what?

"Maybe. But Mummy has no opinions any longer about anyone," Anne answers. "She can't teach us a thing. She's dead."

So am I, Margot reminds her. *And yet here I am.*

"Yes," Anne must admit. "You're the only one who hasn't abandoned me."

The following day Griet is not at school, leaving Anne sitting beside an empty spot.

—————

The next day she pedals to the bookshop again, hoping this time to find it open, but the door is still locked tight. She raps on the window, cups her hands around her eyes to blot out the glare, and peers through the glass, but there's nothing to see except shadows. Back at the Prinsengracht, she knocks on the door to the private office and pokes in her head. "Pim?"

Her father is on the telephone, looking harried, but he waves her in anyway. She sits.

She's hesitant to involve Pim. She feels that the bookshop is *her* realm now. A small sanctuary, where, surrounded by books, she is insulated and protected by its quiet space. In the shop she can pretend to share the soul of the cat, that old calico rug, who lazes in the sunlight with a headful of cat dreams. Does she really want to open the door of that sanctuary to her father? Yet she's worried.

"When I arrived at Mr. Nussbaum's shop yesterday to work, it was completely locked up," she says. "No note. Nothing. I'm afraid that something's happened to him."

Is that a small flicker of caution she spots in Pim's eyes? "I'm sure he's fine, Anne. We spoke a few days back on the telephone, he and I. And now that you mention it, I do believe he said he had to do some traveling."

"So why didn't he tell me that? Why didn't *you* tell me that?"

"It didn't occur to me, Anne. Perhaps it should have," he is willing to admit, but meanwhile he's started slitting open the mail on his desk with a letter opener. Obviously attempting to send her the message that he's too busy to continue this discussion.

"Where is he traveling to?" Anne wants to know.

"I don't know, and he didn't say. Doesn't he travel for business on occasion? Estate auctions? That sort of thing?"

A spasm of paranoia strikes Anne. Pim and his barracks-block comrade. What else does Pim know that Anne doesn't? What else has Mr. Nussbaum been discussing with him? What sort of intelligence does he provide her father about the girl who works in his bookshop? "How often do you speak on the phone, the two of you?"

"How often? Not often," Pim answers.

"He's not giving you reports on your daughter's behavior? On her mental state?"

"Anne." Her father exhales. "You're being ridiculous."

"Am I?" She feels willing to believe this.

"*Yes*," he informs her in no uncertain terms. "Now, please, I'm busy. Aren't you? Doesn't anyone have work for you?"

Anne frowns. Her paranoia suppressed for the moment, her voice becomes lightly petulant. "There is nothing for me to do here. Miep's out on a sales call with Kugler. Mr. Kleiman went home with a sick belly."

Browsing through his correspondence. "Well, if you truly have nothing to do, then you can find something to clean. Isn't that what your mother would always recommend?"

The mention of her mother hardens Anne's expression. "I'd rather go out and have a bicycle ride," she says.

"Fine. Then do that if you must," her father concedes. "Only be sure you're not late. Remember your promise to help Hadas prepare for Shabbat supper."

"And since when do we observe the Sabbath anyway?" she asks with faint accusation.

Eyes lift from the letter in his hand. "So now you have an objection to the Shabbat?"

"No, of course not. Just curious. Are you becoming *pious*, Pim?"

"Please don't be rude, Anne. All I'm asking is that for once you do as I ask without argument."

"I'm not arguing. I was just wondering if maybe this is your new wife's influence."

"Anne, *really*," her father says irritably. "Why must you be so intentionally provocative? Is it so hard to accept that your stepmother should wish to celebrate the Sabbath in our new home?"

Home. Anne thinks about the word. What a weight it suddenly carries. Leaving the private office, she clambers down the steps to the warehouse, making an escape.

"Going out, miss?"

She takes hold of her bicycle. The door to the warehouse stands wide open for ventilation, and the scented air smacks of ground cumin. But old Mr. Nobody Lueders is looking up from one of the milling machines, his face grimy from the work but stretched out in anticipation of her response.

What's it to *you*, you ugly old plague? That's what she would *like* to reply, but instead she says, "Yes, Mr. Lueders. I am indeed going out. Just for a ride."

Lueders nods mournfully, his expression slumping into a frown. Since the advent of Mrs. Zuckert, this particular hireling has been happy to become her personal dog. Chasing after this stick and that one, with a tip of the cap. Sticking his nose where it doesn't belong.

Paying far too much heed to Anne's comings and goings. "Be careful, now," he adds as she mounts her bike and shoves off with a hard press on the pedal. "The town's still not what it used to be. Lots of rascals on the prowl."

The Skinny Bridge
Brugnummer 242
Amsterdam-Centrum

Her bicycle may look like a battered old piece of salvage, but even with its clacking gears and patched tires, Anne bustles over the cobblestones and whizzes past greasy old lorries to a narrow whitewood drawbridge off the Kerkstraat. This is the Magere Brug, cinching a narrow stripe of the muddy Amstel, but nobody ever calls it anything except the Skinny Bridge. Still half mounted on the bike, she's propped herself against the railing and has just lit a cigarette when she spots Raaf ambling toward her.

"You're late," she tells him.

"Late?"

"We agreed on half past."

"No we didn't. We didn't agree on anything. You just like to give orders."

"That's true," she admits. "But that doesn't mean you're not late. You must get a bicycle," she decides.

"Oh, yeah?" Raaf lets his eyebrows lift. "And how do I get one of those, huh? Are the Canadians giving away bikes along with chocolate bars?"

Anne chirps back, "I'll get you one."

And now Raaf's face contracts. She is getting used to this. His genial, thoughtful expression, crimping when she's embarrassed him about something. His clothes. His ridiculous haircut. The snort at the end of his laugh. She never intends to embarrass him, of course—it simply seems to happen.

"Females don't buy stuff for men."

"No? Is that how it works?" She's teasing him, slightly maybe, but also interested to know if this is true.

"At least not bicycles. Men earn their own money."

"Well, I wasn't talking about buying anything anyway," Anne explains. "I can pretend mine's been stolen, so my father'll get me another one."

"I don't need my own," Raaf says. "We can share yours."

"Oh, and how do we do that?"

"Here, give it over," he tells her, and she allows him to take her bicycle in his hands. "Now climb on in front of me," he says, offering his hand.

She feels herself grin.

Climbing on in front of him with only the smallest perch on the tip of the seat, feeling his arms stretched around her, his hands clamped onto the bike's handles, feeling the force of motion as he pedals harder, driving up the speed, it's all just so scary and delicious. The wild, unpredictable jolt of the bumpy cobbles, her arms stretched behind her, gripping his waist as her only anchor, on the edge of tumbling off. The thrill of it streaks through her like lightning.

"Stop! *Stop!*" she cries with eager laughter as they bump down the street.

At first he pretends to be deaf, still pedaling hard. "*What?* Can't *hear* you!"

"No. Stop up there at the corner," she commands. "There's something I want to do!" This time the boy obeys, skidding to a squeaking halt, at which point Anne twists about and seizes him for a kiss as if she is set on vacuuming the breath from his lungs. And oh, what a terror of desire she feels bubbling up in her. What a swallowing hunger she feels, the starving girl sharing her bicycle with too much boy. She glares into his face, her eyes vibrating. Drilling into his gaze with all the sharpness that is in her.

They sit in a grassy spot adjacent to the canal, filled with pale Amsterdammers eager to soak up a bit of sunlight. Cyclists glide past. Anne rests her head against his shoulder, smelling his sweat that's tinged with the aroma of boiled hops. She breathes him in and watches a squirrel scramble crazily across the grass. "Have you been with many girls?" she wonders. "Like this?"

"You got a lot of questions," he points out, but he still answers. "*Many* girls? I don't guess *many.*"

"You know I'm still a virgin," she says.

A small shrug. "Yeah, I figured."

Anne stiffens. "You *figured,* did you? How exactly did you *figure*? Am I wearing it stamped on my forehead?"

This makes him grin at the ground. "Nah. It's just the way you act."

Anne lifts her head and blinks. "I *act* like a virgin?"

"Don't get offended," he tells her.

"I'm not offended. I'm just very curious. Just *what* . . . just *how* do I *act* like a virgin?"

"Well, like *this,*" Raaf says, his grin crooked. "You get all fidgety."

"I get all fidgety," Anne repeats with a frown.

And now Raaf frowns, too. "I know I'm not saying it right. I just figured it out, is all. Don't get so ruffled. It don't bother me."

"*No?*" Anne says tensely. But she must admit to a small flare of relief in her heart.

"No, Anne," he tells her.

And at the sound of her name on his lips, she seizes him with a kiss. Diving deeply as he combs his fingers through the thickness of her hair and clutches the back of her neck, she gripping him tightly until a scold from a passing policeman on his bicycle separates them. "Hey, boy! Let's see some daylight between you two!"

Their lips part. "See now, you got me in trouble with the law." Raaf half grins.

She leans her forehead against his chin and breathes in the intimacy. "Of course. Blame the virgin."

Raaf picks up a stick, breaking it in two before tossing the pieces aside. Anne lolls her head against his shoulder and absently measures the size of her hand against his just for the sake of touch. That's when she notices that his finger is bent. The third finger on his left hand. Well, not *bent,* really, not like a bent nail, but definitely crooked. Why has it taken her so long to notice? "What happened to your finger?" she asks, and he snatches his hand away. "I'm sorry. Shouldn't I ask?"

Raaf flexes his hand in and out of a fist, as if he's trying to muscle out a cramp. At first he says nothing, but then he tells her, "It was my pap."

Anne blinks. "Your father bent your finger?"

Raaf shrugs. Picks up another twig from the grass to snap. "He was always kind of a canker, my pap," he says. "Always looking for a fight with somebody. But after Mam died, he got even worse. He did this," the boy says, flexing his hand again, "'cause I waved to a neighbor he didn't like."

Anne goes silent. She has learned about violence and plenty of it. She is not shocked by it, as she once was as a child, but it still saddens her.

"Pretty loopy, right?" Raaf grins painfully. "He's gone now. Dead. Got drunk and fell down the stairs last winter. Snapped his neck," says Raaf, snapping the twig absently.

"I'm sorry," Anne says, and means it. She's sorry because she can recognize the pain in the boy's face. The boy gives a glance at nothing and a shrug. "Did he beat you often?"

"Usually only when he was loaded. After I got bigger—quicker— I used to punch him back when my mam was around. To try to keep him off her. But then she died. Also, he was getting old, and his punching arm wasn't what it used to be. So when he started swinging, I'd just hit the street." He shrugs again. "I don't know. I hated his guts most of the time, the old pox."

Anne swallows quietly. "You have no brothers, no sisters?"

"Nope. After me, something happened to my mam. She couldn't give birth again. That pissed Pap off, too. He always said it was my fault there'd be no daughter to take care of him when he was old. Mam never seemed to mind so much, though." Tossing away the broken twig, he tugs out his tobacco pouch. "You want to share a smoke?"

"Sure." She watches him roll the shag. She's hesitant to probe further but then does so anyway. "May I ask you something else?"

"I guess." The boy seals the end of the smoke with a lick.

"How—" Anne starts to say, then stops and starts again. "How did your mother die?"

Raaf swallows. He lights up with a match. "I don't want to talk about her," he says. Then he says, "There's a place I want to take you today."

"A place?"

"Yeah. A place the rest of the world has forgotten."

The Transvaal
Oost-Watergraafsmeer
Amsterdam-Oost

During the Hunger Winter, when all of Amsterdam was crazy for wood to burn to keep from freezing to death, people started with the trees. The parks had trees, so why not chop them all down? Also, the wooden blocks in the tram tracks could be ripped out, so that's something, too. Furniture! Old Auntie's chipped Frisian cupboard! She won't mind if we burn it—she's in heaven anyway. And how about the empty homes of the Jews? Now, *there's* an idea, plenty of wood to be had *there*. Maybe Mr. Puls's removal company has hauled off all the furnishings, but there're still wooden beams, wooden floorboards, wooden stair rails and steps and spindles. Just tie a pry bar and a few hammers onto a sledge and you're on your way.

That was the thinking. In fact, it was so much the thinking that with all the wood stripped out, the walls of Jewish houses began to collapse for lack of support. Buildings crumbled wearily into brick piles. It was a mess. But so what? It wasn't as if the Jews were ever coming back. Everybody knew that.

They have crossed the Berlagebrug. Anne walks her bicycle through the streets, feeling a gritty disquiet grinding her belly.

Broken walls stand as ugly monuments. Rubble scattered. Signposts continue to boast the grand colonial names of streets: the Krugerstraat, Schalk Burgerstraat, De la Reystraat, the Paardekraal, and Tugelastraat. Street names of past imperial pride in what is now a precarious empire. The Spice Islands, Suriname, and the East Indies on the brink of revolution. The Kaapkolonie surrendered long ago, but here the names remain if nothing else. They are empty shells, these houses, the life husked from them. The vacant Pretoriusplein is surrounded by a square of debris and teetering façades, as if it has suffered under a rain of bombs. A playground for a residential park in the President Brandstraat that once would have teemed with children is now just an acre of mud. The empty corner of the Schalk Burgerstraat is boarded up.

This is the Transvaal.

Before the war it was a smart-looking enclave of workers' housing populated by Jews of a certain status. Maybe the old Jodenbuurt had been fed by the so-called Orange Jews—three centuries of Ostjuden fleeing the pogroms of the east—but the Transvaalbuurt had been built by the likes of the Handwerkers Vriendenkring to house a hard-working class of Jewish artisans. Cutters and polishers from the diamond district, neighborhood merchants, tailors, grocers, ink sprayers, and government clerks. Still far removed from the haute bourgeois Kultur bastions of the Merwedeplein in the Amsterdam-Zuid, perhaps, where pampered little girls like Anne and Margot Frank had lived, but the Transvaal had been home to Jews scrambling up the ladder. Les petit bourgeois juifs on their way up.

Now it's a wasteland. A designated "Jewish Quarter" by the moffen, it had been cut off from the rest of the town and emptied, trainload by trainload.

Anne stares up at the broken streetscape. A swirl of air catches dust and whirls it about as Raaf scoops up a chunk of brick and pitches it through one of the few unbroken windows.

"Don't do that, please," she says.

"Do what?"

"Break windows."

Raaf shrugs. "It was just a window. It's not like anybody was looking through it anymore." But Anne is not so sure of that. The swirl of dust could carry a thousand souls. Ten thousand.

"Come on," he tells her, and bounds ahead over a pile of slag.

A vacant block of flats on what was once the Louis Bothastraat. The front door is long gone, but she still pauses with her bike at the empty threshold, as if she should wait for permission to enter. Pigeons flutter out of the window indignantly as Raaf kicks at them shouting, *"Shoo!"* They've already splattered the windowsill with globs of blue-white droppings. There are no floors left. The floors have been taken down to dirt, but Raaf has dropped a few boards as a walkway, and he clomps across them like his own one-man army. "This way," he tells her. "You can leave your bike outside. There's no one here to steal it."

It was probably a bedroom at one point. He's covered up the windows with a sheet of dirty canvas, but there's light coming in from a hole in the ceiling. Here the floor is a slab of concrete. An empty crate marked CANNED PEARS turned upside down serves as a table. The actual pear tins are stacked beside it. There's a dirtied ashtray from a café called De Pellekaen sharing the crate top with an electric flashlight and a few half-burned paraffin candles. The bed is made from an old yellowed mattress covered by a patchwork of blankets. It's a hideout.

"So what do you think?" Raaf asks her with a crooked smile of pride at his digs.

"What is this place?" she asks, though really she already knows.

"It's my castle, where I am the king," Raaf tells her. "King Raaf the First!" he says with a laugh before flopping onto the bedding. Grabbing a pear tin, he applies an opener to the lid. "Want some?" he asks.

"No," says Anne. "Thank you."

"*Sure?* It's pretty good stuff. I like to drink the syrup first," he says, and then demonstrates by raising the tin to his lips and tipping it back. "Mmm. Sometimes I pour some schnapps into it, and then it gets even better."

Anne gazes at him from the doorless doorway.

"Aren't you gonna come in?" he asks her.

"I'm not sure," Anne answers. "Is this where you take them?"

Raaf tosses back another swig of pear juice from the tin and wipes his mouth with his sleeve. "Take who?"

"Your other girls," she says.

He looks back at her with that curiously broken expression he often wears. "Anne. There are no other girls."

"I bet," says Anne.

"No, it's true. Just you."

"I'm not your girl," she says.

"No?"

"No. I can't be."

"Because you're Jewish?"

"Because you're *not*."

"Then why do you let me kiss you?"

"Do you want me to *stop* letting you?"

"*No.*"

"Then shut up about it." She glances around at the walls. "This is what you call a castle?"

"I know it's not much." He shrugs at the truth. "I started coming here when my pap went on a bender. Or just when I kinda needed to get away from everything." Lighting one of the paraffin candles with a match, he then lights a cigarette. "So are you just gonna stand there?" he asks, and blows out smoke.

"I'm not going to do it with you," she assures him flatly.

Raaf sniffs. "Do what?"

"You know what."

"I didn't say you were," Raaf says simply. "So you still haven't come in," he points out.

Lying with her head resting on Raaf's chest, gripping his body like this, she feels as if she is holding on to a lifesaver in the middle of a flood. She listens to the slow bellows of his breathing. Listens to the unembarrassed thump of his heart. There are two buttons at the back of her blouse, just two below the neck. She feels him absently tug at the top button till it comes loose. One button and then the second.

"What are you doing?" she wants to know.

"Nothing."

"No, that's not true. You are very definitely doing *something*."

"I just want to feel your skin, that's all."

"You can feel the skin on my arm," she informs him, but doesn't complain any further when he continues to stroke the small patch of bare skin on her back.

"So it was two whole years?"

Anne does not move. She opens her eyes and glares at a crack in the plaster wall. "Was *what* two whole years?"

"You hid out from the moffen for two years."

"Did I say that?"

"I don't think I made it up."

"It was twenty-five months," Anne says without emotion. "Until the Grüne Polizei came."

"And you know who did it?" he wonders. "Who tipped 'em off?"

Anne lifts her head to look at him. To examine his face. His expression is blank.

"Why are you asking these questions?"

"I dunno. You ask me stuff all the time."

A blink before she lowers her head back to his chest. "There are theories," is all she tells him. She is surprised at how painful it is to discuss the subject. She is surprised that she feels not just the anger of the betrayed but also the shame of a victim. She rolls over on her elbow and gazes at Raaf's face. He's never been too curious before about what happened or how she survived the war. "Why do you want to know?"

"I *don't* really want to know," he answers. "I'm just trying to . . . to, I don't know. Be closer to you. To find out what you're thinking. It's not easy. I'm sorry I ever opened my trap," he says, and huffs out a sigh.

She looks at him, then lowers her head to his shoulder. "No. *I'm* sorry. I'm happy that you want to know more about me. I am. There are just some subjects . . . It's hard for me," she says.

The boy says nothing for a moment. And then when he speaks again, his voice is numb. "She starved," he says.

Anne raises her eyes.

"My mam. That's how she died. She starved." For a moment the boy holds on to a deep silence, then shakes his head. "It was like she shrank. Her body was just a bunch of sticks, except her belly was all bloated up. And her eyes," he says, "they looked like they might pop out of her head."

Anne feels her heart contract. "I'm sorry. I'm sorry," she repeats. Tears heat her eyes. She can feel his grief. She can feel the great weight of sadness he must carry, because she feels it herself. But her sadness is also bitter. She has refused to picture this moment of her own mother's death before, but now she sees it. The fragile body of sticks. The swollen belly, flesh tight against the bone. The popping eyes. And her mother's face.

The tears stain her cheek. She does not wipe them away. She feels the boy gently stroke the patch of bare skin at the base of her neck. She breathes in and out. Pigeons coo, a strange, hushed lullaby. An ersatz peace of a kind descends. More physical than spiritual, like a blanket for a pleasantly sleepy dip in the temperature. Anne presses her ear closer to his chest. He smells of toasted shag, of maleness. A heaviness that she can cling to. The beat of his heart, slowly descending into her subconscious, as her eyes drift shut. . . .

And then she is bolting upright on Raaf's lumpy mattress, smelling the stink of pigeon shit. Her skin is chilled, and a heavy shiver weakens her body. The light is drifting toward dusk as a drizzle of rain patters through the hole in the ceiling.

"*Raaf!*" She punches him in the shoulder with her balled-up fist, as hard as she can, and he bolts up beside her in confusion.

"Oww! *What?* What *is* it?"

"I'll tell you what it *is*," she answers furiously, wiping her eyes. "The sun is setting. The Sabbath's about to start, and you let me fall *asleep*! My father's going to be livid!"

The cloudy afternoon sky has given way to a leaden gray twilight, wet with rain. She is out of breath when she reaches the Herengracht, bangs in the front door, her clothes damp, her hair in wet ringlets on her brow as she stows her bicycle in the foyer. "Pim?" she calls, but what she finds is a shadow nested in the Viennese wingback.

"Hello?" she tries.

The figure sits motionless, and then the head rises.

"Hello, Anne." The voice is barely recognizable. It sounds dead somehow. Soulless.

"Dassah." Anne speaks the name.

"Do you know?" Dassah asks her slowly. She is wrapped in a

knitted throw. The light sketches across her face. "Do you have any *idea,* Anne, what time it is?"

Anne says nothing, glaring.

"When you didn't show up at the appointed time, he became worried. When you didn't show up an hour later, he was agitated. When you didn't show up at the start of dusk, he began to go a bit mad. I couldn't calm him," Dassah tells her. "It was impossible. He insisted on telephoning everyone he knew. Anyone who might know where you'd disappeared to."

"I'm sorry," Anne says with a swallow. She edges a glance to the dining table, laid with a white linen cloth and a trio of silver-rimmed porcelain place settings. A hand-embroidered cover for the challah bread. A pair of silver candlesticks holding two tall white tapers. The smell of something slightly burned coming from the oven. "I was . . ." she says, "I was with a friend."

"A *friend,*" Dassah repeats, a touch of wily bitterness in her voice. She raises a snifter and lets the brandy inside drift back. "Is that what you call him? A friend?"

"Where's Pim?" Anne asks suddenly.

"Probably sitting in the local police precinct by now, describing his missing daughter to the constable. He ran off with his faithful Miep at his heels an hour ago. Good and faithful Miep."

"Then I should go after them," Anne breathes. But she doesn't move. She feels stuck in place.

"I've never told you, Anne," Dassah says, "I've never told you the story of my daughter? My Tova."

A cold shock strikes Anne. *A daughter?* It's as if a frigid gap has opened up in the air. The presence of another daughter. Another secret kept from her.

"She was not a very pretty child. She had her father's looks, unfortunately. Smart enough, a good head for numbers like him, too, but a gullible nature. Sweet eyes, but a homely smile. Not like *you,* Annelies Marie. Not such a lovely princess. She never had beaux. She was shy and clumsy. Not like you. When there were parties, she was seldom invited. I told her that looks didn't matter. Popularity didn't matter. Only what is in your *mind* mattered. And she was a good daughter, so she didn't argue. I told her if *I* had worried about being invited to parties, I would have worried myself to pieces. Of course, the truth is that I was always invited to parties. The truth is that I was never shy or clumsy. And if I wasn't as pretty as some girls, I still had something special that boys liked to be around. You must be able to relate to that, Anne. Can't you?"

Anne does not answer.

"In any case, I didn't *really* understand my Tova's suffering. I didn't understand what it was like to be lonely, not yet. Not in the way Tova was lonely."

Anne stays frozen as the woman gazes at her snifter of brandy, then takes another swallow. "When the Boche came rolling in with their tanks and troop lorries," she says, "they were billeted in several of the houses up the street. All those strapping, fair-headed farm boys with their big black boots. They would jeer at my Tova on her way to school. A homely Jewish girl with the star pinned to her coat. They would jeer at me, too, of course, but not in the same way. It was harder for Tova. She took their insults inside her. That's when she began to have nightmares. *Terrible* nightmares. I told her to keep her chin up. I told her that she had to be strong, but she didn't know how. She didn't know how to be strong, not like you, Anne. In any case. One night she was late coming home. Very late. I was frantic. The razzias had started. Hundreds of Jews had already been rounded up in the public squares. I went to the police station, where they *laughed* at me. A missing *Jewess*? Who cared? There must be plenty by now. But when I came home, Tova was *back*."

She falls silent for a moment, Dassah, scowling into the pocket of a private shadow. "I knew immediately that something had happened, but Tova wouldn't tell me what it was. I kept asking her, '*Are you hurt? Did someone hurt you?*'" The woman shakes her head and then looks bleakly in Anne's direction. "It was a German. A soldier, she said, but that she wasn't hurt. I'll never know exactly how it happened. Did he force her? She wouldn't say a word. But as the days passed, I knew. . . ." For a moment she breathes in and out. "I knew that it was still going on. I could tell by the look on her face. I was so *angry*. So enraged. My own *daughter*—a moffenhoer. But she said to me, 'Mama, don't worry. We'll be safe now.' At first I didn't know *what* she meant. I just couldn't fathom it. And then I realized: Tova was *protecting* us. She said that the SS would never harm the mother of a German soldier's child." A pause as Dassah swallows bitterly. A smear of tears glosses her eyes. "I struck her when she said that," Dassah admits simply. "As hard as I could. I think in that instant I wanted to . . ." she starts to say, but cannot finish the sentence. "The truth is," she croaks, "the truth is that I wanted to *believe* her. Underneath all my fury, I wanted to believe that my Tova had actually made the right decision by *whoring* herself to a Nazi. Of course"—she shrugs in a small way and stares out into the air—"of course, that was a fantasy. When she was four months pregnant, there was a massive razzia in the Jordaan. The biggest yet. I wasn't there. I was in Amstelveen making arrangements with a man I knew, a Dutch Christian, who was willing to hide us for the right price. When I came back to our flat, I was told by the only neighbor who still deigned to speak to Jews that the Grüne Polizei had swept the neighborhood, street by street, house by house." She breathes out, as if she is finally ousting a breath that has been caught in her ribs for a very long time. "Tova was gone, and I never saw her again. As far as I have ever been able to determine, she was gassed during her first hour at Sobibor, as were *all* the pregnant women in her transport. She hadn't protected anyone by defiling herself. Just the opposite. Her childish scheme was her death sentence." She shrugs, but when she turns to Anne, a kind of dead fury is buried in her eyes.

"So now, my dear Annelies"—she glares—"you can imagine my concern when I hear that you are whoring yourself in a similar manner."

Anne's jaw tightens. "That's a lie."

"Is it? I know what you're doing, and I know with *whom* you're doing it."

Anne blanches.

"Oh, don't worry. I'm the *only* one who knows—for the moment. Your father still assumes you are pure, and I have no desire to create more pain for him. There's no reason for him to know that his daughter is desecrating herself."

"If that's what your spy Lueders is telling you, he's wrong." Anne swallows heavily. "I see a boy, yes. But I'm not doing *anything* with him," she declares. "At least not what you *think*."

"No? Well, then maybe I should test you. Shall I, Anne? Shall I ask you if he's touched you *here* or touched you *there*?"

"I've let him kiss me. That's *all*."

"Don't *lie!*" Dassah bursts out. "Don't lie, Anne. I *hate* lies. Lies are *worse* than the crime!"

"I'm *not* lying, and I haven't committed any *crime!*" Anne shouts back. "I'm not Tova, and he's not a Nazi!"

"*Oh, really?* Are you *actually* trying to tell me that you don't *know*?"

"Know *what*?"

"His father was NSB."

"No, that's not true."

"It *is* true."

"*No.* I know that his father was beastly and brutal, but that doesn't mean he was a Nazi."

"You must know that your father was forced to hire party men by the local NSB office?" Dassah informs her bluntly. "Well, he was one of them. A *Nazi,* Anne. For all you know, he could have been the one who betrayed you and your family to the Gestapo. The man who sent your mother and sister to their deaths!"

"No! *No,*" she repeats to Dassah. "*You're* the one who's lying!"

"If you *think* so, Anne, then ask the boy," Dassah suggests, "the next time he's got you on your *back*."

Anne seizes the nearest thing to her, a book that Pim has left on a shelf, and hurls it. Not really aimed at anything, but the crash of the porcelain vase bursts inside her head. She is sobbing with such wild anger as she charges out the door, not even seeing her father hurrying through the drizzle until she collides with him on the sidewalk.

"Anne! My, God, Anne, what's happened?! Where have you *been*? What's *happened*?"

But she has no explanations to offer. All she can do is try to swallow her tears without choking on them. "Let me *go,* Pim," she cries. "*Let me go!*"

"I will not. Not till you tell me what's happened."

"She's a monster!" Anne shrieks at him. "You've married a monster!"

"She insulted me, Pim." Smearing the tears from her eyes. "In a very hurtful way."

They are camped together in her tiny room. Pim's stooped figure folded onto the chair. A blanket around his shoulders. She has retreated to her bed, curled up against the wall, a fortress, refusing to look in her father's direction unless it's to offer him a volcanic glare. Rain dribbles down the window glass.

"If she said something harsh," Pim tells her, "I'm sure that she was simply speaking out of fear."

"You're *defending* her?"

"People often say regrettable things when they're afraid. They hide their fear with anger. You should understand that by now."

"Because I'm so well known for my cowardice?"

"Because you often let your fears get the better of you. Because you often speak without thinking things through. You can be quite hurtful at times."

"*I* can be quite hurtful?" she says. "*Again,* am I understanding this correctly? That according to my father, *I* am the one at fault?"

"So tell me, then, what did she say that was so evil?"

Anne starts to speak but then stops. Perhaps she does not exactly wish to explain it to Pim. "It was insulting," she repeats. "Terribly so. That's all I'll say."

"I'm not trying to assign fault to anyone, Anne," Pim insists.

Anne wipes at her eyes. "What else is new?"

"You think that's so bad?"

"I hate having to call her 'Dassah.'"

"What would you prefer to call her, then?"

"I would prefer not to speak to her at all."

"All right. That may be your preference. But it's going to make life quite difficult. Because the fact of the matter is this, Anne: Hadassah and I are married. Like it or not, she is your stepmother. I'm not saying she doesn't have her faults. Of course she does. We all do. But we have an opportunity here. An opportunity to become a family. To repair some of the ruin inflicted upon us. I cannot bring anyone back. Death has taken them, and that is all there is to say. I will always feel a terrible hole in my heart after losing your mother. And Margot, God rest her. My poor, poor Mutz," he says. "That hole will never be filled. My marriage to Hadas won't fill it. I know that. Even the return of my beautiful daughter Anne could not fill it. But I must try to find happiness again, and so must you. Otherwise what is the point of having survived? What is the point of living if we are to be poisoned by our own sorrow?"

Anne glares blindly at the windmill pattern on her bedspread. For a moment she feels her old love for Pim take hold. "You make it sound so very simple, Pim," she says.

"Oh, no. No, it is not simple, as tonight has proved. It will take work. Very dedicated work. But then what is our motto?" he asks.

"Oh, *God*, Pim."

"Come now, Süsse, say it for me, please. What has always been our motto?"

Anne frowns, rolling her eyes at the wall with a kind of flattened anger. "'Work, love, courage, and hope,'" she answers unwillingly.

"Exactly." Her father nods, his voice settling into a kind of imposed certainty. "Exactly. Now let us all try to make a new start, shall we?"

Silence. And then a knock at the door, which Pim opens, allowing Dassah to step into the threshold.

"I apologize," she says to Anne, "if I lost my temper tonight and spoke in anger."

"You see," Pim injects. Proof.

"I really should stay away from brandy when I'm tense."

"I'm sure it wasn't the brandy, Hadasma," Pim informs her. "I have no doubt that my *own* anxiety contributed greatly to the situation. When you didn't come home, Anne, I simply went off my head. Which reminds me, daughter," he says pointedly, "you haven't offered a single explanation. Exactly where *were* you?"

"Apparently," Dassah answers for her, "she went cycling with a friend from school. What was her name again, Anne?" she asks.

Anne blinks. "Griet," she answers blankly.

"Yes. Griet. That's it. They went cycling to the Vondelpark and stopped to rest but must have dozed off until the rain woke them. You remember how it can be, Otto. To stretch out on the grass in the late afternoon? It's better than a feather bed."

Pim draws a breath and slowly expels it as he nods. "I do remember," he claims. And it's obvious from his expression that he thinks this is a fine explanation, which he's quite willing to accept.

Dassah turns to Anne, cementing the falsehood between them. "So I hope you can forgive me," she says, "for speaking so roughly to you."

Anne stares.

Pim leans forward as a prompt. "Anneke?"

"Yes," says Anne thickly. "I forgive you," she lies.

"Wonderful," Pim breathes. "Thank you, Anne. Now you should change out of those damp clothes. You don't want to catch your death."

When Hadassah leaves, Pim huffs a breath of relief. "You have no idea, Anne," he says, "how much your approval means to her. Her only wish is for the two of you to become friends."

Anne glances over to the corner of the room, where Pim's poor Mutz is standing in her Kazet stripes, the filthy yellow star sagging on her pullover. She gazes back at Anne coolly.

At least, Anne, you will have some kind of mother again, she points out. *Isn't that better than none at all?*

Prinsengracht 263
Offices of Opekta and Pectacon

Anne is due at Pim's office after classes and dreading it. She spoke no more than two words to Pim this morning before stealing out the door for school and now feels the covert shame and anger from the night before pressing on her chest. When she arrives at the warehouse and stows her bike, she spots the foreman, Mr. Groot, stepping out to the edge of the street to roll a smoke. So instead of heading up the steps, she slips the strap of her book satchel over her shoulder and approaches him.

"Excuse me. Mr. Groot? Can I ask you something?" Groot looks a little undecided about that question, but Anne doesn't wait for him to say no. "That boy. Raaf Hoekstra, who worked here. You said he didn't have a good name."

"Did I say that?" Groot wonders.

"Does that mean he was NSB?"

"The boy? No. Not so much as I know."

"But the father, then. *He* was?"

Groot tends to his shag closely, glancing out at the canal.

"I *know* there were party men working here, Mr. Groot," Anne assures him. "I know it was my father who said they must be hired. It's not a secret, if you're worried that you'll be spilling the beans."

The man shrugs. Then nods his head. "Sure, old Hoekstra had a party number, all right. But it wasn't just that."

Another blockage.

"No?"

The man smokes.

"Mr. Groot?"

A glance in her direction, as if he's calculating odds. "Maybe you ought to ask your papa about this, miss."

"He doesn't like to talk about any of it. All that happened during the war," Anne says. "He thinks it's too painful. But I think it's important to know the truth."

"Maybe," Groot is willing to allow. "I just don't like spreading stories."

"*Please.* I won't say a word to anyone. I just want to *know.*"

Groot puffs out an elongated breath. "We had a problem with thievery," he says heavily. "This was back when van Maaren was still running things. Somebody was stealing from the spice inventory. To tell the truth, I always wondered if it wasn't van Maaren *himself*—but *he* said he had his eye on this *other* fellow we had. Dreeson was the name. Not the worst sort, Dreeson, when he was sober, but a boozer like Hoekstra. And Hoekstra and he had some kind of falling-out on the floor of the shop, over *what* I've got no idea. I think Dreeson had sneaked a few shots of kopstoot on his lunch break, and he said something that got Hoekstra angry. It came to blows, until I separated them and sent 'em both home. Then, the next day, Hoekstra showed, but Dreeson didn't. Not that day or the day after. It took a while for us to get the news, but it turned out Dreeson and his wife'd been hiding their boy from the Huns to keep him out of the labor conscription. Until the Grüne Polizei paid them a late-night call, and that was that. The whole family got hauled away."

Anne feels her throat thicken. "And you think . . . you think it was *Hoekstra* who betrayed them?"

"I don't *think* anything," Groot assures her. "But the truth is, Hoekstra liked to brag about his connections. He flashed around a pass he said he got from some Gestapo man in the Euterpestraat." A shrug. "Who knows if it was real? Who knows if any of it was real? He was a drunkard. It could've all been nothing more than big talk. But I do remember that fracas he had with Dreeson. And that Hoekstra could have the devil's own temper if you riled him."

"And what happened to him?" Anne wants to know. "To Hoekstra. After liberation?"

"Can't say. It was the last winter of the war. He started coming in for his shift drunk as a badger, so van Maaren finally gave him the boot."

"Still, you hired his son in his place."

"I didn't think it was fair to condemn the boy just because his father was a pox," says Mr. Groot. "So when he showed up looking for work, I gave him a chance." He tells her this, then yells over to one of the other workers and then turns back to Anne and stamps out the butt of his cigarette. "Excuse me, miss. Back to the job."

She has a difficult time forcing herself up the steps to the office. Halfway up, she stops, feeling herself teeter on the edge of a cliff. Panic swells inside her. She tries to focus on something, a crack in the wood of one of the steps. Counting backward from a hundred, she pinches her wrist, monitoring the surge of her pulse. Margot is there in her death rags. *So it's true,* she points out. *His father was a Quisling. A collaborator.*

The Transvaal
Oost-Watergraafsmeer
Amsterdam-Oost

The air is thick with humidity. She ducks out of school and bikes to the secret den in the Transvaal. Bumping across the Skinny Bridge. Sweaty by the time she turns onto the Louis Bothastraat. It's shocking to see the ruined buildings so overgrown, life insisting on life even in a graveyard.

When she enters Raaf's castle, she finds that the king is not in residence. Seized by an urge, she begins to search through the blankets, then raises the mattress, searching for some bit of evidence. Some connection to the Grüne Polizei. To betrayal.

Keep looking, Margot prods, appearing in her lice-ridden rags. Her skin ruddy with sores. *Keep looking. There must be something here to find. Some evidence.*

But Anne's afraid suddenly. Afraid that she *will* find something. Some evidence of guilt. Yet she can't stop searching. If the truth is ugly, then she must know it. She remembers the death's-head on the SD man's cap the day they were arrested. Is it still following her? Still watching her? Some nights she dreams it is. The Totenkopf keeping an eye on her. She feels her heart banging away in her chest.

"If you're digging for treasure, you're gonna be outta luck," she hears, and swings around with guilty alarm. Raaf is standing in the threshold, hands stuffed into his pockets.

She whips about but then straightens. Staring. "I was looking for matches," she claims.

Raaf points to the box of wax tips sitting in plain sight. "Matches," he says.

Anne frowns at them. Her belly churns, and she takes a step forward. Really, she is beyond pretense. The idea of continuing it is sickening. She will strike him with the truth as hard as she is able. "Your father was an NSBer," she declares.

The muscles along Raaf's jaw contract, and he turns his eyes away from her. "Who told you that?"

"It doesn't matter. But it's true. He was a Nazi."

Shaking his head with a frown. "I don't want to talk about this."

"Too bad. Because unless we do, I'm walking out and you won't see me again." She stares at him until he meets her eyes.

The boy looks cornered. Trapped. Finally he kicks the concrete with the toe of his shoe and huffs out an answer. "He needed a job," he says. Then seems to shake his head at the painfulness of what he's about to confess. "He used to be a real labor-pillar man, ya know? Always for the trade unions. *Always.* Even when I was just a little kid, he used to take me to the rallies and stick me up on his shoulders so I could see all the flags. Things were easier then. Pap did a lot of metal-work. For a while he was a welder for this shop in the Jordaan, but then he had some sort of trouble with the shop steward. I don't know what it was—maybe it was the drinking—but however it started, he made a grudge out of it. You were either *with* Pap or *against* him. Those were the only two choices he ever gave anybody. Anyhow, he lost his temper, the old dope, and ended up socking the steward in the snoot. Not only did he get the ax, but they put him on a list so he couldn't get a union job anyplace else. For a long time, he just kicked around. Doing one shit job or another, but there was never much food on the table. Then the war started and the moffen came. I guess he saw a way back to a payday."

"And my father was forced to hire him."

Raaf tilts a frown. "He wasn't a bad worker, Pap," he insists. "Most of the time. Sure, maybe he drank, but it's not like he was lazy or stupid just because he'd become a party man."

"But it must have been so . . . so 'unbearable' for him," Anne says. "So unbearable. A National Socialist working for a *Jew*?"

"He just needed to make a *living*," the boy repeats. "That's *all.* It's not like he wore the uniform or anything, or went around shouting 'Hou Zee!' to everybody on the street. He just went to meetings here and there. Why not? They had free beer. And I never heard him complain about working for a Jew."

"But you said he called the Jews 'bloodsuckers,'" Anne reminds him. "Those were your words."

"What are you trying to prove here anyway?" the boy demands.

"I just want to know the truth, Raaf. If your father was a Nazi, then I think I have the right to know. Was he a Jew hater? If he was still alive, wouldn't he be beating you for polluting yourself with a filthy yid?"

"Anne, you're starting to sound kinda crazy." He tries to put his hands on her shoulders, but she shrugs off his touch.

"He was a party member. I heard that he bragged about having connections to the Gestapo. That he had a pass from an SD man in the Euterpestraat."

Ask him now many Jews his father denounced, Margot proposes.

"How many Jews do you think he denounced?"

"Pap liked to feel big, but it was mostly all bullshit. That 'pass' he bragged about? He won it from some canker playing dice. He didn't know the goddamned toilet cleaner in Euterpestraat."

Don't let him hoodwink you, Anne, Margot warns, whispering in her ear. *His father was a Nazi. He's admitted as much. Who knows what crimes the man was complicit in committing? Crimes against our people.*

But Anne cannot completely ignore the pain in the boy's face. Carefully, she allows herself to sink down onto one of the crates. "Tell me the *truth*. I want to know. I want you to say it: yes or no. Was it your father who telephoned the Grüne Polizei?"

Raaf gazes damply at her.

"Was it your father who *denounced* us, Raaf?"

His gaze is unchanged. "What if I say no?"

"Is that the truth?"

The boy stares at her. "The last summer of the war. He wasn't drunk. He came home and wasn't drunk. Not that night," the boy says. "Instead he was talking to me like . . . like, *I don't know.* Like I was somebody *important* to him for once. Somebody to count on. He told me that he was going on a job. That he was going on a job and needed me along. Course I knew, I guess, what *sort* of job it was gonna be, but back then who *wasn't* pinching what they could? He said there was this place where he'd worked in the Prinsengracht that stored spices. Kegs full of spices worth plenty of poen. But that he couldn't do the job on his own."

Anne's eyes sharpen at this.

"My mam was still alive. There was nothing in the pantry, so I thought . . . *who cares?* Money's money. Who cares how you get it? It only matters what you use it for, and I thought I could use it for Mam. There were still half-decent pork shanks to be had on the black market then, *if* you had the cash. So I said who cares what I do in this klootzak of a world, you *know*? Who the hell cares *what* I do or how I do it?" He says this and stops. "Maybe I don't have to finish this story?" he says.

Anne does not speak, but perhaps the boy does not really expect her to.

"I mean, you *know* what happened next," he tells her. "You were *there*."

Anne gazes at him. "You smashed out a panel in the warehouse door," she answers.

"We brought the tools on a sledge. I used a pry bar at first and then just kicked in a plank. That's when I heard somebody yell for the police from inside."

Anne swallows. "That was Mr. van Pels. He was a spice merchant. After we were arrested, he was gassed."

Margot appears in her death rags to whisper in Anne's ear. *Now you must ask him the real question.*

Anne's mouth goes bitter. She would like to be sick. That's what she would like. But instead she looks at him and asks, "Was it *you,* then?"

Raaf gazes back at her with a drift of pain in his eyes.

"Was it you," she says, "who went to the Gestapo?"

He blinks, but the pain remains.

"Money's money. You said so. Who cares how you get it? Jews were worth forty guilders a head." Anne feels a flame ignite inside her chest. It burns up the oxygen in her lungs and leaves her searching for a breath.

"I would never do anything to hurt people. Not on purpose. You gotta believe me."

Slapping her hands over her eyes, she bursts into tears and collapses into herself, but when she feels Raaf's hands on her shoulders, she tears away from him. She hears a crack, feels a jolt in her palm, and it isn't until after the boy blinks at her with dumb shock and she feels the sting of her palm that she realizes she's struck him. A full-handed slap across the face. When she strikes him again, however, it's with real intention, her fists balled up with the force of her fury. The boy does not attempt to defend himself or deflect her rage, only allows himself to stand as her punching bag while she hits him again and again, until she's spent. Stumbling over the masonry lip of a doorway, she rips the knee out of one of her stockings as she falls and pukes. Pukes up the desire, the rage, and the poisonous grief being wrenched up from her belly, splattering her sleeves until she retches dryly. For a moment her hand trembles as she wipes her mouth with the palm of her hand. The boy is down there with her, but she bats his hand away. *"Don't touch me!"* she shouts, and then she is up, pushing herself clear of him. By the time she hits the street on her bicycle, she's pedaling with her blood pounding in her ears.

"Wait!" Raaf calls. He's shouting her name, but she is deaf to him. Deaf to him, deaf to her name, deaf to everything. The town passes by her in a welter of tears, the wind stinging her eyes. The door to the warehouse is open when she reaches the Prinsengracht. The men are loading up a lorry with barrels as she rushes past, abandoning her bike and banging up the ankle-breaking stairs, up, up, up, straight to the landing, the panic of her footsteps ringing in her ears. The bookcase squeals painfully as she swings it open and thumps up the steps into the embrace of the past. If her mother were there still, she would collapse into her arms, but her mother is at the bottom of an ash pit, so there is nothing and no one left to embrace her here in the dusty remains of her life. She lurches into the room where her desk once stood, finding nothing but the dry rot and the peeling magazine pictures stuck to the wall, and she drops to her knees and curls into a ball.

There the bells of the Westertoren summon her sister. Margot

with her hollow eyes and her filthy pullover. Yellow triangles forming
a star on her breast.

"Are you *happy* now?" Anne demands to know.

Am I happy?

"Isn't this what you *wanted*? *Me*, all to yourself. Never with a
chance to be with someone else. Just stuck to you forever! Isn't that
your *plan*?"

Anne. I don't have a plan. You know that.

Anne coughs miserably. Sniffs back her tears and wipes her eyes
with her palms. She feels like she has fallen to the bottom of a deep
well. "So now," she breathes, "so now I'm alone again." She shoves
her hair from her face. "I think maybe I'll *always* be alone as long as I
am here. It's why I want so badly to go to America. If I stay for Pim,
I'm afraid I'll never leave this room. I'll be a prisoner here forever,"
she says, staring into the air. Then she meets Margot's eyes. "Do you
think Peter ever thought of me?" she asks.

Peter?

"After we were separated on the ramp."

I think he must have.

"Do you?" A soft shrug to herself. "I didn't think of *him* that much,"
Anne confesses. "Hardly at all, until I came back to Amsterdam. Only
then," she says. And then her eyes deepen. "Sometimes I think it
would have been so much easier if I had just died with *you,* Margot. If
neither one of us had ever left Bergen-Belsen. Is that so terrible?"

She asks this question, but no answer comes. The spot where her
sister crouched is now empty. She is alone.

22

ANOTHER BIRTHDAY

Dearest Kit,
   Another birthday has gone by, so I'm now fifteen.

—Anne Frank,
from her diary,
13 June 1944

1946

Leased Flat
The Herengracht
Amsterdam-Centrum
The Canal Ring

At breakfast the telephone rings and Dassah answers it, but only to hang up a moment later. "Werner Nussbaum has returned," she announces to Anne and Pim at the table, pouring Pim a second cup of coffee. "Anne, he'll be expecting you at the shop this afternoon."

Anne stares back, above her plate of fried mush. She's relieved, but also a little miffed. "That's all? He's *returned* and expects me? No further explanation?"

Pim raises his coffee cup to his lips and takes a sip. "Anne, I'm sure you will interrogate the man when you see him," he says coolly. "For now eat your breakfast, please."

———

Nussbaum
Tweedehands-Boekverkoper
The Rozengracht

Mr. Nussbaum is pale. Thinner than he was. His smile looks waxy as Anne rolls her bike into the shop, leaning it against the wall. "And here she is," he announces with a brittle joviality. "The future of literature."

Somehow Mr. Nussbaum's friendly exclamation rubs her wrong. It sounds just too ridiculous. "I was afraid something had *happened* to you, Mr. Nussbaum," she tells him with undisguised reproach. "When I came to the shop and it was completely locked up."

The smile on Mr. Nussbaum's lips slips a notch. "Yes, well, I'm sorry about that, Anne. I am. I had to travel to the Hague, *unexpectedly.*

Apparently the government has determined that while I was imprisoned in Auschwitz, I was also accruing a substantial sum of unpaid taxes."

Anne feels her face heat. "That's obscene."

A shrug as he sets the kettle on the small hot plate. What else can be said?

"Is the same thing happening to Pim?"

"Isn't that a question for *him* to answer?"

A frown. "We're not exactly talking much these days."

"I see." He blows a spot of dust from the bowl of a china cup. "Will you have some coffee? It's only ersatz, I'm afraid."

"No, thank you," Anne replies, her voice subdued, thinking of Pim's chilly expression at breakfast. "It upsets my stomach."

Mr. Nussbaum nods. Begins measuring the ersatz blend into the tin coffee press. "I understand that you have a birthday approaching," he says. "You'll be seventeen?"

Anne has picked up the broom to sweep the grit from the front entryway. "Yes," is all she says.

"And there's a celebration scheduled?"

"Not my idea. But yes."

Mr. Nussbaum seems puzzled. "You're not looking forward to it?"

"So I'm seventeen, so what? It's not exactly an accomplishment. How many girls never lived that long?" she hears herself say. "Why am *I* owed a celebration?"

"*Anne.* You must never say that," he instructs her. "You don't have the *right* to say that."

Anne stops sweeping and looks up at the ghastly emptiness of Mr. Nussbaum's face.

"All those girls who *didn't* live?" he says. "You owe it to *them* to celebrate. Don't be so selfish."

She parts her lips but has no words to speak.

The kettle whistles a low note. Mr. Nussbaum removes it with a rag over the handle and pours the steaming water into the press. "I'm sorry. Perhaps that was uncalled for."

But Anne shakes her head with a twinge of humility, gripping the broom handle. "No. No, I *can* be selfish. Pim continues to remind me of that."

Another small shrug. Mr. Nussbaum sets the kettle back on the hot plate. "Everybody can be selfish, Anne. But if you're finding it so difficult to communicate with your father," he suggests, "perhaps you don't understand his needs very clearly. Perhaps his life has been more difficult than you're aware of. Can children ever properly comprehend their parents' hardships? I don't know. But I *do* know that regardless of the past he does his best to remain positive and to concentrate on what's *beautiful* in life."

Anne feels herself go still. *One beautiful thing,* she hears Margot whisper in her ear.

"And what's the most beautiful aspect of life to Otto Frank? The most important? *Family.* Being part of a family." The melancholy in Mr. Nussbaum's eyes is as dry as dust. "Maybe I shouldn't say," he tells her, "but if you want to learn something essential about your father, you should ask him sometime about the boy in our block in Auschwitz who called him 'Papa.'"

Anne feels an odd sting. "Papa?" How dare he ask someone else to call him that?

"I won't say more about it, but you should ask him."

Anne takes this and files it in the back of her brain, trying to swallow her jealousy. Can't she forgive Pim for finding a way to survive Auschwitz? But then that's the question, isn't it? *Can* she forgive him? Can she forgive *anyone,* Annelies Marie Frank included?

<hr/>

Wednesday, 12 June

Anne's birthday arrives, and a small party has been organized. Her chair at the dining table is decorated with crepe-paper streamers and ruby-pink dahlias that Miep brought from her window boxes. Dassah has taken a slagroomtaart from the oven, baked with sugar surrogate and dried fruit, and Mr. Kugler has hung up a handmade banner reading GELUKKIGE VERJAARDAG! Anne smiles, feeling on display, when, God knows why, Mr. Kleiman decides to lead the small assembly in a mortifying exhortation of "Hieperdepiep hoera!" in her honor. Swallowing a bit of panic, she accepts hugs and kisses from Miep and Jan and hearty handshakes from Kleiman and Kugler and three-cheeked kisses from their wives, though Anne and the new Mrs. Frank assiduously avoid any such tactile exchange. Pim, as always, reads a poem to the room, composed of the usual sugary paternal sentiment and daffy, awkward rhymes, all written on a scrap of paper he had to unfold several times and then peer at closely with his reading glasses on his nose. Applause follows. Anne permits Pim a peck on the cheek. But through it all she feels empty. She smiles as required, yet secretly there is nothing to fill her heart. Pim's pride in her, which had once been a gift in and of itself, has lost its value. It is all a charade.

Anne retreats to the kitchen to help her stepmother make the coffee. As a wedding gift, Miep and Jan have given Pim and his new wife a Kaffeegedeck-Set of good Meissen Zwiebelmuster with a delft-blue floral pattern. Dassah examines a small chip she's already made in a saucer. "I'm not used to owning such delicate things," she confesses. "My mother had an iron kettle she used for brewing and serving alike. To pour you had to place a piece of cheesecloth over the cup to filter the grounds."

Measuring the ersatz coffee makes Anne think of her mother as she fills the stainless-steel percolator from the tap. How particular Mummy was about the proper ritual, insisting the water always be cold. Screwing shut the tap, Anne releases a breath. This snag of memory, she finds, is like smelling a rose while being pricked by the thorny stem. She clutches it even as it wounds her. She watches the new Mrs. Frank slicing the tart into sections with a cake knife. How is this woman her mother now?

For a moment she is transported back into the past.

In the Achterhuis. It's another birthday celebration, but Mr. Pfeffer is complaining to Miep about the recent decline in the quality of vegetables. "I really don't mean to find fault. I'm sure it's very difficult, but *really,* it's often *barely edible* these days," he declares. The contingent of helpers from down below have been rather quiet throughout the party. Miep, Bep, Mr. Kleiman, and Kugler. It's as if they are clustered together as a visiting delegation from a foreign land. Miep clears her throat of whatever she would *really* like to say to old Pfeffer and replies in a well-managed tone, "Yes. It's barely edible *everywhere,*" she informs the good dentist. "The Germans are shipping all decent food into the Reich."

"Everyone, please," Pim suddenly pipes up with calm authority. "Enough about the unpleasant facts of daily life," he must insist. "We are all well aware of them. But today is a day for festivities. Our younger daughter has turned fifteen," he reminds the table, squeezing his wife's hand. "And," he announces with a wry smile as he draws a piece of paper from his vest pocket, "I have penned a humble poem in her honor."

"Yes!" Anne breathes happily. Pleased that she can count on Pim to remind everyone that *she,* by rights, should be the center of attention this afternoon.

Rising, he unfolds the paper and slips on his reading spectacles. "I must first thank my elder daughter for her work as a translator on this project, since I must still compose in German but prefer to recite in Dutch. Thank you, Mutz," he says to Margot with a bow of his head. "And now for the poem—and quite the work of art it *is,* if I do say so myself. *Ahem!*"

> "She does her best to be gracious and kind,
>   Yet that doesn't mean she won't speak her mind.
>   It is not a habit that's easy to keep
>   Without ruffling feathers whenever she speaks."

General laughter there from all assembled. Anne only bats her eyes comically.

> "Yet now that she's growing to woman from girl,
>   I know it's important her truths to unfurl.
>   And whenever her thoughts may be harsh or be fiery,
>   She keeps them secret in the pages of her diary."

A dull moan of agreement at this. "Oh, *yes,*" Mrs. van Pels half snorts, "Little Miss Scribbler!"

"And even though her days are cramped by small
        accommodations,
    And her actions often judged by grown-up observations,"

"Ha!" Anne tosses out.

"We know that her future will be a beautiful sight,
    As her star ascends, burning strong, burning bright!"

The applause is led by Anne, but everyone joins in. It's so obvious to her that the power of her father's affection has returned a dependable balance to the room. Even old grumblebelly Pfeffer is nodding with appreciation. Margot blinks at her in a silly way, as if to say, There she is! My sister the star! But when Anne catches her mother's eyes, there is such a glimpse of emptiness there. Not even sadness. Beyond that. Hopelessness.

Later, after she has set up her bed and changed into her nightclothes, after she has scrubbed her teeth with Margot at the washroom sink and pinned curlers into her hair, she goes to say good night to her parents. She feels the familiar scrub of a day's stubble on Pim's cheek as she kisses it. Feels the comfortable wrap of his arms, but when she turns to her mother, she feels suddenly shy. There is an urge to embrace her, but also a barrier. "Thank you for the lovely dinner, Mother," she says.

Her mother smiles without joy, not at Anne but at a pillow she is stuffing into a pillowcase. "Oh, it wasn't so much, really. Mr. Pfeffer is right. The quality of our food is worsening every day." She fluffs the pillow with a flat spank and drops it at the top of Pim's bed. "But it's kind of you to pretend otherwise," she says, now turning away to plump up the pillow on Margot's cot with the same little spank. "Happy birthday, Anne," she says.

"I'm sure they'll be here *soon*," Anne feels the need to blurt, just as her sister enters in her nightdress and slippers.

"Who will be here soon?" Margot asks.

"The English. I'm sure it won't be much longer, Mummy, before they push the Germans out."

Their mother shrugs. "We'll hope so. Good night," she says.

After the lights go out and Anne lies on her bed, too warm for a cover, listening to the heavy barge motor of Mr. Pfeffer's snoring, she stares up into the darkness above her. It's a deep thing, this darkness. Like a hole in the night.

"Anne, will you take the coffee service to the table?"

Anne blinks. Looks at Dassah. "Yes, I will," is all she says.

Carrying the coffee service on a tray, Anne places it on the table draped in worn linen. "Pim, will you ever retrieve Mummy's silverware?" she wonders aloud.

"Hmm?" Lighting up a cigarette, his forehead wrinkling.

"Mummy's silver," says Anne. "Didn't you say it went to friends for safekeeping?"

"Yes," Pim confirms.

"Did they turn out to be the kind of friends who are still keeping it safe, but now from *you*?"

"I've written a letter," Pim tells her, expelling smoke. "We'll get it back eventually. These things take time. Everyone was so badly displaced by the end of the war."

"That's your answer to everything," Anne points out, but if Pim hears her, he pretends not to. Instead he consults his wristwatch. "Mr. Nussbaum should be arriving soon. He told me he is bringing a special guest."

Anne is curious. "A special guest?"

"Haven't the slightest who," says Pim.

She tries not to show it, but Anne can't deny a thrill of anticipation. A special guest? Could it be—could it possibly *be* none other than her idol, Cissy van Marxveldt? What an astonishing birthday gift *that* would be.

The door knocker sounds. Anne can hear Dassah exchanging greetings with Mr. Nussbaum from the front room and hurries over, but she finds the man standing alone, bearing a gift wrapped poorly in newsprint. "Not very glamorous, I'm afraid," he confesses. "Just some jam and a bar of French army soap."

"Very nice. Thank you, Mr. Nussbaum," she tells him, trying to hide her disappointment by smelling the soap. But then she says, "You're here by yourself?"

He keeps smiling, but he looks diminished, as if he is slowly being erased, until not much more than his smile and the brightness of his eyes remain. "Yes. Unfortunately, I am."

"You know, I'm not sure *why,* but when I heard Pim say you were bringing a 'special guest . . .' You've talked so much about knowing Cissy van Marxveldt, I hoped it might be—"

"She couldn't make it, Anne," Mr. Nussbaum interrupts. "At the last minute. I'm sorry. I did want you to have the chance to meet her, but she lives in Bussum now, and I suppose she wasn't feeling up to the trip."

23

SACRIFICE

Performing charity and justice is preferred by God
to a sacrifice.

—Proverbs 21:3

1946

LIBERATED NETHERLANDS

School ends for the term, and the summer holiday begins. Anne's grades are terrible. Pim sits morosely at the breakfast table and examines her report as if it is a mournful thing indeed. He is quite disappointed by the low marks she received in classroom behavior. "It makes me sad to see you waste your education."

But she is surprised when Dassah speaks up. "Perhaps, Otto, Anne is no longer suited for school," she suggests. Sipping her coffee, she meets Anne's eyes starkly. "Perhaps she's ready for the world."

That morning Anne arrives at the bookshop but finds Mr. Nussbaum staring in a kind of trance at the window, unaware, it seems, that his cigar has gone cold. Unaware of her, it seems, as well. The pages of a newspaper lie on the floor, abandoned.

"Mr. Nussbaum?"

Nothing.

"Mr. Nussbaum?" she repeats.

And then, without breaking his trance, he speaks in a voice that is floating. Untethered. "Anne . . . have you heard?"

A dull pulse in her belly. "Heard?" She's seen him depressed before, yes, but this is the first time she's really seen him in the grip of despair. The first time, she thinks, that she's really seen his Auschwitz face.

"They're killing Jews again in the east," he announces.

Her heart tightens. Confusion strangles any response, but Mr. Nussbaum does not appear to notice.

"It's in the newspaper," he says. Anne glares back down at the discarded paper's headline. The word "Pogrom" stands out blackly. A favorite tool of the angel of death.

. . .

The blood libel. It's an ancient excuse for a pogrom. A small town. A gentile boy claims to have been "kidnapped" by a Jew, and the old rumors start swirling—Jews abducting gentile children for ritual murder! Siphoning innocent blood to consecrate their unholy matzo bread. Nothing new there. In any case, the shooting starts when the police arrive, but soon the mob takes over the murdering and the looting. By the next day, at least forty Jews—men, women, and children—are dead. Stoned, stabbed, shot, beaten to death. Including a Jewish mother and her infant son, arrested in their own home, robbed, and then shot "while trying to escape."

"That it still continues!" Anne laments.

Pim has finished his standard breakfast, toast and margarine with a powdered egg, and ignites his standard cigarette. He shakes his head heavily over the folded newspaper.

"Hideous," he declares.

Anne blinks. "That's *all* you have to say?"

Her father lifts his eyes to her, burdened pale things. "What else would you have me say, daughter?"

"Must I really *teach* you, Pim? Must I put the words in your mouth? You are a Jew who has suffered through Auschwitz. You should be outraged."

"I am long past outrage, Anne," he says with a sorrowful but maddening composure. "Such hateful violence. It's horrific. But as we have learned, the world of men can be a horrific place. I cannot allow it to drag me down."

"Really, Pim," Anne says, burning. "This is your response? The world is bitter, but we must rise above it? That's the type of thinking that sent Jews to the Kremas."

Pim's gaze grows deep. He surveys his daughter as if from a distance. "How can I help you, meisje?" he asks. "How can I help you?"

The question only makes Anne angrier. "You can *help* me, Pim—you can *help* me by waking up to reality!"

"Anne isn't wrong," her stepmother suddenly injects. Anne and Pim share the same surprise, turning their heads as Dassah enters the room with the coffeepot to refill Pim's cup. "Perhaps she's being overdramatic as usual. That's Anne. But I must agree, it would be foolish to abandon our caution."

Pim huffs, obviously feeling ambushed. "Hadas. Aren't *you* the one who said that one should have faith in God's intelligence?"

Pouring coffee into her own cup. "Of course. But that doesn't mean we should go blind. We should trust in God to keep us vigilant, not to tend us like sheep. The wolves are still hungry, Otto. That hasn't changed."

Pim stubs out his cigarette. "No, I'm sorry, but I refuse," he says, frowning. "I refuse to live in fear." He taps his lips with his napkin and stands, his tone resolute. "Live a just life. Do good when you can. That's the answer to the madness of such cruelties." Slipping on his suit jacket, he asks, "Anne, are you coming to the office with me today?"

Anne looks at a spot on the white linen tablecloth before she meets Dassah's cool eyes and says, "No, Pim. I promised Mr. Nussbaum."

At the bookshop Mr. Nussbaum reaches down behind the sales desk and pulls out a large, flat magazine, slapping it on the counter. Drawing a breath, he declares, "This is for you."

LIFE. It's the name of an American magazine.

Anne has Mr. Lapjes in her arms, the old furry rug, purring in a bored fashion. She takes a step forward. Looks down at the photo on the cover. "I don't understand."

"I found it in a lot I picked up from the library sale," he tells her. "And I've been saving it for you. For the right time."

The magazine's pages are so large, the size of America itself. She stares at it. On the cover is a jutting tower, piercing the cloud line with its steeple. The caption tells her it is the Empire State Building.

"So you see, Anne. What just happened in that village in the East? It made me realize the truth. We may pretend different, but Europe is dead. Dead for the Jews. Dead for you. *America,*" he tells her. "That's where you belong."

She looks back at him in silence.

"You should talk to your father. I know he prides himself on his faith in the future. It's one of the things that I admire most about him. But even *he* must see the truth. You should talk to him. Tell him you need to emigrate."

"Is that really what you think?"

"It's what I *believe,* Anne," Mr. Nussbaum tells her.

Anne shakes her head. "He'll never agree."

"He won't *want* to give you up. Of course he won't. He'll resist mightily, I'm sure. But even *Otto* must recognize the truth underneath it all. Even *he* must recognize that America is where a girl with your intellect and perception should find her future."

Biking home, she bumps over the uneven cobblestones, distracted by the images of America in her head. She has thought about it before in the abstract. She does have uncles there, her mother's brothers near Boston. They could sponsor her. And her father has his university friend running a big department store in New York City.

But the idea of emigration is both terrifying and gripping. She tries to picture herself in a café, ordering coffee in English. She imagines taking a bite out of a hot dog, as she's seen in the newsreels. She imagines herself exiting a crowded elevator, crossing the concourse of Grand Central Terminal, or at the top of a skyscraper, gazing out over the vigor of a vast and animated metropolis. In America there are no memories of the dead that must be pushed aside. There is only a spotless, uncorrupted future.

———

She uses cellophane tape on the oversize pictures she's scissored from the magazine and lines them up on the wall of her room.

"And what is *this* display?" Pim asks, failing to keep the iron in his voice from dragging this question toward criticism.

Anne looks over from her last taping job. "New York City."

"Yes, I recognize that fact. But where did it all *come* from, is what I'm asking."

"From a magazine Mr. Nussbaum gave me," she responds with innocence.

"I see," says Pim with a kind of neutral suspicion.

"I thought I might improve my English by reading the articles. But *really,* Pim, look at these pictures. Can such a place exist?"

"Oh, it exists, all right," her father replies, and his small frown confirms it. "Though, it's a very problematic city, New York, especially for foreigners. It's so large and really quite impersonal."

"Really? If I remember correctly, Pim, you once called it the most astonishing city you'd ever seen."

"Never mind," Pim says, his tone turning parental. "Didn't you agree to help your stepmother with the laundry?"

"I want to *go* there, Pim," Anne announces suddenly, not realizing until she speaks the words how deeply true they are. "I want to go to America."

What follows is a silence with many moving parts. She can see it rearranging Pim's expression in minute calibrations. The tic of an eye, the laxity of his mouth as it droops into the ruts of a frown. The decline of his shoulders and the tilt of his head toward conflict. A measure of hard fortification barricading his eyes. "I beg your pardon?" is all he says.

"I want to go to America," she repeats.

Pim releases a long breath and shakes his head. "These photographs. They may depict an exciting metropolis, but take my word for it, the place is so large it can easily swallow a person whole."

"Maybe that's precisely what I want, Pim," Anne replies. "To be swallowed whole."

"But how could that be so, Anne?" her father asks, obviously trying to calm his responses, obviously intent on maintaining the gentlest of possible tones. "You're young. Of course you have an urge to see the world. Perhaps we can think about a visit. Next year, maybe. I *do* understand the wanderlust of youth."

"No, I think you *don't,* Pim. I don't want to *visit* New York. I want to live there. I want to *emigrate.*"

Pim shakes his head, glaring at his shoes. *"Anne."* He speaks her name sternly. "I'm sorry," he says, abandoning any softer tone. "But that is not in any way, shape, or form a realistic possibility."

"Not *realistic*? My English is good. I hear the Canadian soldiers talk, and I can understand almost everything they say. Why is it not *realistic?*"

"How *could* it be? So you can speak some English? Do you think that's all there is to it? Do you imagine that a person simply packs a bag and boards a boat? Show me your passport, Anne. Where have you been hiding it?"

"Passports aren't the end of the world, Pim," she tells him.

"So says the world traveler. Emigration is an *extremely* difficult process, Anne. Immensely complicated," he says, "and expensive. So what about money? Where does the money come from for such an adventure? You think it can be pulled from a hat, do you, daughter? Even if the legalities *were* possible to sort through, where would the money for passage come from? You think that's cheap, Anne? It's *not.* Where would the money to *live on* come from? Thin air?"

"People get work, Pim," she answers. "People get jobs."

"Not seventeen-year-old girls. And that's another thing. Who would protect you? Who would keep you safe? *No.* My answer to this nonsense is *no.* I will not be drawn into further discussion," her father insists.

"What if I agree, then? The difficulties are *immense.* If you say so, I won't argue the points. But haven't you always taught me that difficulties are to be *overcome?*"

"It's *out* of the *question.*"

"*Why?* Mummy's *brothers* are there," Anne says. "And you still have your friend in New York. Mr. Straus."

"It's much more complicated than that."

"Always your answer to everything."

"*Because the world is not a simple place,*" Pim shoots back. "Your uncles entered the States *fifteen years ago,* long before the war. They were seeking *asylum.* The Gestapo had already imprisoned Walther once, and it was only a matter of time before both of them would land in a camp for good. So it was a completely different set of circumstances."

"Who cares how they got there? The point is they're still *there.* They could help us."

"Again—not so *simple.* Your uncle Julius is in poor health. And I say this in confidence, Anne—they're barely scraping by. They're workmen in a box factory, for heaven's sake. They couldn't possibly support more mouths to feed."

"But Mr. Straus isn't scraping by. He's rich. He must have connections."

"*Enough,* Anne. I'm not going hat in hand, begging, to Charley Straus. Not again. You have no idea what you're asking of me."

"So it's your *pride* that's stopping you, Pim? Is that what you're telling me? *Your pride?*"

Pim glares at her with red eyes. Then he turns his back and strides from the threshold, but Anne is still shouting after him. "You know what the proverb says, Pim! Pride is the mask of a man's faults!"

"Pride has nothing to do with it!" Pim halts and turns back to her. "We owe a debt, Anne, to the Netherlands. Has that ever occurred to you? We owe a debt to the Netherlands and to its people. Oh, there may have been some bad apples in the barrel—of course there were—but the Dutch welcomed us when few others did. And it was good Dutch people who risked their own lives to protect us. That cannot be forgotten. The Netherlands has become our home."

"You keep telling me that, Pim, but it's a *lie.* I have *nothing* here. Nothing *left.*"

"We have people who *care* for us, Anne. That's not nothing. We have people we can trust."

"But that's the point, don't you *see*? I don't know *who* to trust."

"Then trust in *me,*" he says, both a command and a plea. "I'm your father. If no one else, trust in me."

Anne goes silent, staring back. When she speaks, her voice is low, barely controlled. "Amsterdam is a haunted place. I don't *belong* here anymore," she insists.

"And you think you will belong in *America*? That's absurd, Anne. And even if it weren't, half of Europe wants to go to America. There are, however, quotas in place severely restricting immigration."

"You mean for *Jews*?"

"I mean for *everyone,*" her father answers. "For anyone. And we are *fine* just where we are. I have responsibilities here, Anne. A life to lead."

"*You* have a life!" Anne is suddenly incensed. "You! But what life do *I* have, Pim? What life do *I* have?"

"A life with the people who *love* you, Anne. *Isn't that enough?* You belong where your *family* is."

"My family is *dead*!" she hears herself shout.

"*I* am not dead!" Pim, angry now, ignites. "*I* am not dead, Annelies! *I* am your father, and I am still very much *alive*!"

"Are you *sure* of that, Pim? Everyone tells me that I have survived. What joy! Anne Frank has survived! Praise God in his heaven! But I don't *feel* it, Pim. I feel like this is an illusion and that I really belong in the burial pit with Margot!"

His eyes panic. "*Anne.*"

"Then, at the same moment, I want *everything*," she declares, her hands clenching into fists. "I want everything there is to *have,* and America *has* everything. That's why I cannot stay here. That's why I must *go.* With you or without."

Pim swallows. "I won't permit it."

"You think I *require* permission? You say I have no passport, but what does that matter? *This* is all the permission I need," she says, yanking up her sleeve. "*This* will be my passport."

She watches a shadow fall across Pim's expression as he gazes down at the number tattooed on his daughter's forearm. It's a radical transformation. His skin seems to shrink tightly across his skull. His eye sockets deepen. His mouth contracts into a straight line, and something terrible scalds the color from his eyes. She thinks perhaps this is his true face now. The face that meets him when he's alone with the mirror.

"Anneke," he whispers. The blunt rebuke in his voice has disappeared. He sounds hollow. "You must *realize* how much I *need* you here with me," he tells her. "How desperate I am to have you close by. I thought I had lost you both. Both my children. You cannot possibly comprehend the pain that a parent feels. For a father to lose his children? It's so tragic. So *unbelievably* tragic. But then *I found you.* I found you, and my heart found a reason to keep beating. *Please.* You're so young still. You need a father. And a father needs his daughter. Think about this. You *must.*"

Anne gazes back at him. Her mouth opens, but she has no words left to speak. The air is suddenly too thin. The walls too close. She shoves past him to get out. Out of the flat, out of the prison that the past has made of her present. She bursts into the street, and the open air swallows her. She runs. Runs until she sinks down on her knees in the grassy scrub beside the sidewalk. And there she remains, breathing in the tang of an approaching storm as a stripe of thunder unrolls above the chimneys.

Is this how you're going to behave? Margot inquires. She has knelt beside Anne, dressed in the dirty blue-and-red prisoner's smock they were forced to wear in the Westerbork Punishment Barracks. Her glasses are broken at the left hinge and repaired with a twist of wire.

Anne gives her a stare, then shakes her head. "So now *you're* judging me, too?"

No one's judging you, Anne.

"Liar."

Well, if I am, it's only because you're being selfish. Besides—since when has Anne Frank cared what other people think of her?

Gazing at nothing. "I'm not so impervious as everyone has always believed."

Then do the right thing, her sister urges. *Pim needs you. I can't help him, but you can.*

Thunder rolls through the clouds, and a sudden dash of rain starts to patter the sidewalk. Anne feels the rain as if it's nothing. In the camps they stood on the Appelplatz for hours in driving rain during the endless roll calls. The SS guards called the prisoners "Stücke." Pieces. Nothing human, only pieces. And pieces think nothing of the rain.

"I want so much, Margot," Anne whispers. "I want so *much.* Enough for ten lifetimes. How can I stay here? How can I possibly make this my life? I want to mean something. To be someone other than just a girl who did not die. I want to be a *writer!*" It's the first time she's actually spoken the words aloud since her return, even if she is only speaking to the dead. She glares into Margot's eyes, but the dead do not comprehend urgency. Her sister's eyes blacken into a pair of holes. *Mummy would want you to stay,* Margot tells her. *Think how she cared for us in Birkenau. Think how she sacrificed for us. Are you saying,* she asks, *that you can't now sacrifice a little for Pim?*

"Sacrifice . . ." Anne speaks the word as if it tastes of a burnt offering.

24

ENEMY NATIONALS

I love Holland. Once I hoped it would become a
fatherland to me, since I had lost my own.

—Anne Frank,
from her diary,
22 May 1944

1946

LIBERATED NETHERLANDS

"So I hear Bep is going to be married," Anne says.

Miep turns to her from across her desk, where's she's sorting through the morning post. "Yes," is all she says. "That's right."

"You're probably wondering how I found out."

"No, not really."

"I wasn't eavesdropping or anything," Anne lies. "But Mr. Kleiman isn't very quiet on the telephone."

"I see."

"I mean, it's not as if Bep actually *writes* to me. Did she tell you directly?"

"She sent a note," Miep answers. "I'm sorry, Anne, perhaps I should have mentioned it to you. But I wasn't sure. I didn't want your feelings hurt."

"Because I'm not invited to the wedding."

A small shrug. "I don't think they're doing much. Just a magistrate," Miep tells her mildly, with a certain insouciance, as if the matter really has no great weight outside an office chat. "She's marrying a fellow named Niemen. An electrician, I think, from Maastricht. They're having the ceremony there, so it's not actually close. I doubt any of us will make it."

Anne is silent, glaring at the stack of invoices she's been charged with ordering. She wants to be happy for Bep. She wants to forgive her for being so distant when Anne returned from Belsen. She wants to think of Bep as a sister again, but the awful question still nags at her. "Do you think it's possible, Miep?"

"Do I think *what* is possible, Anne?"

"Do you think it's possible," she repeats, "that Bep could have played a part in our betrayal?"

Miep does not react directly. She continues sorting the post.

"Miep?"

"Why would you *ask* this, Anne?" Miep wants to know. Her eyes have gone sharp. "Did someone put that into your head?"

"No." How does she explain that if it was anybody, it was Bep herself who put the idea into Anne's head when Bep was so panicked by the thought that the police had arrived to interrogate her. "No," she repeats.

"*Good.* Because anyone saying such a thing would be telling a *lie*," Miep informs her. "A grotesque *lie*. Bep," she begins, but then shakes her head as if mentioning the name is suddenly painful. "Bep would never have done anything to hurt you *or* your family. *You especially,* Anne. Above all people, you. You must know that. Bep is a loyal person. Right down to the bone."

"Mr. Kugler told me that it was my fault she left. That she couldn't stand to be around me any longer."

Miep huffs. Shakes her head. "I won't blame him for saying that. Mr. Kugler has faced more than his share of suffering, but he doesn't always know when to keep quiet."

"Are you saying that he was wrong?"

"I'm saying, Anne," Miep tells her, "I'm saying that he doesn't know the full story, and neither do you. Bep, after the war, she had a kind of nervous collapse. And it wasn't just because of what happened to you. It was because of what happened to everyone. *To her.* Her father's illness. The end of her romance with Maurits. There were many troubles. She couldn't hold up under it all. It was a tragedy," says Miep. "One of many. But it was no one's fault, Anne. No one's."

The fourth of August—Anne can feel the date looming like a ghost. It will mark two years since the day the Grüne Polizei entered the hiding place. Two years since they were arrested like criminals and force-marched toward the moffen slaughterhouses. The office at the

Prinsengracht has grown silent. Miep barely speaks. Kleiman has gone home with a bleeding stomach. Kugler has started smoking in the kitchen. Abovestairs in the House Behind, the past waits like a dreadful ghost. Pim grows tense. Easily aggravated. He's snappy on business calls, and for the first time Anne hears him argue with the new Mrs. Frank. Spats of temper over small things. Where has she put his shoes? His pipe tobacco? Why must she use so much starch in laundering his shirts? Tiny, petty accusations to exorcise his own guilt at marrying her? This is how Anne sees it.

At breakfast Pim announces that the best possible solution to the question of Anne's future is to send her to a school in the Oosterpark-buurt for a teacher's certificate.

"I don't want to be a teacher," is Anne's response.

"You would make a wonderful teacher, Anne," her father assures her briskly.

"No, you're not listening."

"I *am* listening. As a teacher you could make a life for yourself." His coffee cup clinks against the saucer as he sets it down. "As a teacher you could have a real impact. That's why you must study harder next term. Get better marks."

"That was Margot's fixation. Not mine."

"Anne." Pim glowers, his gaze bruised. You should speak more respectfully of the dead is the message in his eyes, but she knows he cannot bring himself to speak the words.

"School means nothing to me. It's all pointless."

"*Pointless?* That I should hear you say such a thing, Anne. It is not *pointless*. It is essential," her father retorts, and ignites a cigarette with a small nervous tic of his chin. He's started smoking day and night, she has noticed, blackening ashtrays wherever he goes. "Anne, you must understand," he insists. It's obvious that he's cross, but he's also simply perplexed by this unrecognizable Anne. What happened to the child he knew, the daughter who begged to be sent to school, who pined for it? "You must understand that I am still responsible for your future. You must trust me to make the correct decisions for you."

Anne stares blankly at him. "I cannot pretend, Pim, to be the person you thought I was. I cannot be like you. I can't sit behind a desk tidying papers into piles and pretend to myself that nothing has happened."

"Is that what you think I'm doing?" he asks. *"Pretending?"*

"Aren't you? This town is a haunted place. It might as well be a graveyard, and I simply can't live in a graveyard. It's too much, Pim. I don't *belong* here any longer," she insists. "Why can't I go to America?"

Her father releases the breath he holds in reserve for every time he hears her say this. "Again with this," he mutters. "Anne," he tells her forcefully. *"This* is your home. This is where you *belong*. And in the fall you will return to your classes. It's my responsibility to see to your education. It's what your mother would expect."

But Dassah suddenly offers a differing opinion: school isn't necessary for girls. "If she doesn't want to go, then let her get an actual job. By her age," says Dassah, "I was on my own. Nobody paying my way but me."

Anne is wary of this. Why is this woman coming to her aid? Not out of kindness, certainly. Perhaps only out of a desire to be rid of Anne, to be rid of the competition for Pim's affection. But whatever the reason behind Dassah's interjection, Pim has no desire to be trapped by this assault from both sides. He stands abruptly. "Excuse me. But I'm late for the office."

Outside, Anne pedals through the daily heat. The air stinks of canal trash. But when she arrives at the bookshop, she finds Mr. Nussbaum morosely engaged in a telephone conversation. He glances dark-eyed at her but makes no gesture of greeting. His tie is crooked and his shirt sweat-stained. The shop is airless. It reeks of old rot, old cat piss, and old pain. She tries to find comfort in Lapjes, scooping up the bulky bag of bones.

But then Mr. Nussbaum rings off. At first he simply glares into an invisible pit, his hand resting on the receiver.

"Mr. Nussbaum?" she asks, hugging the cat against her. "Is something wrong?"

His eyes flick to her. His face is as pale as soap. "What has your father told you?"

A swallow. "Told me?"

"About what's happening. *Here.* In our adopted country." His tone is bitter. Barren. "What has he told you?"

"Practically nothing," Anne answers. "He still pretends to be sheltering me from the ugly truths of the world."

"But that's not what you want any longer, is it? To be sheltered from the truth?"

"No," Anne says. Though suddenly she's not so sure that's true. The desolation in Mr. Nussbaum's face is frightening.

"Very well, then. You should know," says Mr. Nussbaum. "The sooner you get out of this country, the better, Anne. The Dutch have started deporting Germans. Even if they're German *Jews*."

Prinsengracht 263
Offices of Opekta and Pectacon

The door to the private office bangs opens. Pim and Kleiman look up as if she is a hurricane just blown in. *"Anne!"*

Anne glares. "How can I trust you when you don't tell me the *truth*?"

Silence strangles her father's voice for a moment. Then he forces out a breath and turns tightly toward Mr. Kleiman, who looks at her in a sickly way. "Mr. Kleiman, would you mind excusing us for a moment?" he asks.

Kleiman doesn't answer but stands with a dubious expression and slips past Anne.

"Close the door," Pim instructs her. "There's no use in the whole world hearing our business."

Anne keeps up her glare but closes the door. "I know everything," she says.

A terse swallow. The back of Pim's neck has gone stiff as he straightens a pen on his blotter. "Everything? And what does that entail?"

"When were you going to *tell* me?"

A strong frown at the desktop before he pronounces her name. "Annelies..."

"Is *that* what the bureau men are investigating? When were you planning on telling me, when they're at the door about to drag us away?"

An odd spark of confusion enters her father's expression. He blinks, and his eyes narrow. "I don't understand. What do you mean, 'drag us away'?"

"What do I mean? I mean when they come to stuff us into the cattle cars and deport us back to Germany."

"Anne, I have no idea *what* you're talking about."

"And how can that be true, Pim? *Mr. Nussbaum* respects me enough to *tell* me what's happening." And she repeats what she was told in the bookshop. How the government has done something "clever," as Mr. Nussbaum called it. In denouncing the Nuremberg racial laws, they have converted all German-born Jews back into German citizens— thereby branding them "enemy nationals." Enemy nationals subject to deportation back to Germany. "Don't pretend that this is a revelation to you, Pim," she says.

And now, to his daughter's deep chagrin, Pim leans back into his chair with a small laugh of relief. "Ah, Anne. Is *that* all this is about?"

The laugh, of course, incenses Anne further. Her hands are fists. "You think this is a *joke,* Pim? Those *men* who've come here to the office to interrogate you—how long will it be till they come with a lorry waiting outside to carry us away?"

"Anne," he says, his voice having regained its standard tone of confident control, "you're jumping to conclusions. This issue with the authorities. It's about *property.* Property and money. No one is coming to deport us."

"So you're saying that Mr. Nussbaum lied to me?"

"From what I understand, a handful of German factory workers have been expelled from the borderlands, but these were men who came during the war. It's only a bit of bureaucratic maneuvering on the government's part. A matter of territory, of business. And like any other business matter, it can be dealt with. That's all. We are safe, daughter. Let me repeat: No one is coming to deport us. That much I promise you."

"*Promise?* Now that's a funny word for you to use, Pim, *isn't it?* Didn't you also *promise* to keep us safe once before, and look how well that turned out."

All the light leaves Pim's face. "Anne . . ."

But she does not care if she has wounded him. That her words have cut him more deeply than anything she has done or said before. The risk is too great. "I *will not* be sent back to Germany, Pim," she bursts out, and bangs the table with the flat of her hand. "I will *die* first."

---

3 August

The next morning Anne tells her father that she has a sick stomach and should stay home. They have barely spoken since her outburst the day before, but Pim examines her with a hint of sympathy and nods. She waits until he and Dassah have both evacuated the flat, and then she fills up the tub and takes a bath. She washes her hair and puts on the best dress in her wardrobe, a robin's-egg-blue frock with a white velveteen collar that Miep found for her. She puts on her only pair of cotton stockings without mended holes and her suede shoes with the tiny silver buckles, and then she inspects herself in the mirror. Her final preparation before she leaves the house is to powder over the number on the inside of her forearm.

She has looked up the address in the newspaper. It's a hulking, redbrick merchant's mansion on the corner of the Museumplein. During the occupation it was well known as the office of the Reichskommissar's man in Amsterdam—a petty mof princeling named Böhmcker, most infamous for segregating the Jewish quarter from the rest of the city. His fiefdom was a fortified Sperrgebiet by the end of the war, but even if the air-raid bunkers remain fat earthen mounds, the hooked-cross banners are long gone, the trenches filled in, and the barbed wire pulled down. She expects there to be a guard at the door, or at least on the inside. A soldier with a rifle, but no. Instead there's a bustle of people heading this way and that and a slim, middle-aged woman seated at a carefully polished desk that's flanked by a flag. Red and white stripes, with stars on a field of blue.

"Good morning," Anne tells the woman in English. "My name is Anne Frank, and my wish is to emigrate to America."

25

PITY

Isn't there some old saying about love being akin
to pity?

—Anne Frank,
from her diary,
16 March 1944

1946

Museumplein 19
Consulate General of the United States
Amsterdam

LIBERATED NETHERLANDS

The fireplace in the landing hall is quite majestic. An imposing wooden mantelpiece is mounted above the hearth on stone pillars that are decorated with painted roundels, delft-blue tiles sporting windmills, canals, boats, and the like. The room itself is as spacious as a ballroom, richly appointed in the old mercantile fashion and paneled in elegant hardwood from the East Indies. It's a princely setting, but now packed with a herd of shabbily clad Dutch volk, all here for the same reason as Mam'selle Anne Frank, no doubt. She has written down her name, her address, the telephone number in the Herengracht for the lady at the desk before being shuffled into this room. No chairs left, so she finds a seat on the floor by the stone hearth. The room has taken on a very distinctively stuffy postwar odor of soap rationing and bad tobacco. Hours pass. She dozes off at some point and wakes in sweaty surprise when she hears her name called. Scrambling to her feet, she is greeted by a silver-haired gentleman wearing wire-rimmed glasses who introduces himself in lightly accented Dutch as Vice-Consul Aylesworth. "And you are Miss Frank?" He wears a fatigued expression as he offers his hand.

Anne shakes it with a damp palm. "I speak English," she is quick to mention.

"Do you? How nice," he continues in Dutch. "This way, please."

The room into which she follows Vice-Consul Aylesworth is quite a bit smaller. Just as elegantly paneled and papered, but the atmosphere is that of a harried functionary's office. Ashtrays are dirty with pipe litter. An electric fan oscillates gravely in front of an open window, teasing the edges of the papers stacked on the man's desk. "So," he begins. "You are here, as I understand it, because you wish to emigrate to the United States."

"Yes," says Anne.

"And you have a valid Dutch passport, Miss Frank?"

A swallow. "No."

"You have a valid passport of any nationality?"

"No. My papers . . ." she tells the man, "my papers were lost."

"Well, isn't *that* a common story," the vice-consul points out.

He thinks you're lying, Margot whispers in her ear, filling the empty chair bedside Anne with her Kazetnik's corpse.

"It's *true*," Anne protests. "It's really true. All I have is this," she says, and pokes forward the UNRRA pass from the DP camp. Her photo and thumbprint.

He glances at it but makes no effort to take it from her hand. Instead he frowns as she shifts in her chair, and then he turns the frown on her. "How old are you, Miss Frank? If I may ask?"

Anne swallows. "Seventeen."

"Seventeen. And are your parents aware of your visit here?"

"My mother is dead," she answers bluntly.

"Condolences. And your father?"

"He is alive."

"No, I mean he is aware of your plans?"

Tell the truth, Margot instructs.

"He's aware, yes."

"Then where is he?"

Anne struggles for an instant, deciding between a lie and the truth. "He himself has no plans to emigrate. Not yet," is what she says.

"So in the meantime you're here alone? Without him?"

Finally she decides on a stunted version of the truth. "He does not approve," she admits.

The vice-consul unhooks his wire-rimmed glasses and lets them hang from his fingers. "You understand, Miss Frank, that the application for emigration is quite demanding. The rules are very clear.

There are police reports required, references, sponsorships, not to mention the fees involved, which are not insignificant."

Anne stares.

Anne, what are you doing here? her sister suddenly demands. *Just apologize for wasting this man's time and go home.*

But Margot's admonishments only serve to agitate Anne further. They only serve to push Anne to the limits of her desperation. She has no required reports, no references or sponsorships, no money for fees. But she does have this single piece of evidence proving the profundity of her suffering, proving the righteousness of her appeal. She has yanked up the sleeve on her dress and is rubbing furiously at the smudge of powder there on her arm. "Please, look," she insists as she shoves out her arm to display the indelible number now visible. A-25063. "You must know what this means."

The frown crimping the man's features deepens, but her desperation does not produce any more noticeable effect. The bureaucrat only shakes his head. "Miss Frank," he says to her in English, "I'll need some time. Please wait outside."

Back in the crowded hall, Anne waits. She feels rather hollow. Rather emptied. Across the room a skinny Dutch mother is trying to amuse her bored children by singing to them.

> *"All the ducklings swim in the water,*
> *Falderal de riere, Falderal de rare."*

She has closed her eyes but opens them when she hears the creak of the door leading from the lobby. When the door opens, she feels a sharp whip of both anger and shame. Standing there in his baggy suit and his fedora raked to the side of his head is her father. The look of pity in his eyes is unmistakable as he removes his hat and speaks to her with weary patience. "Come, daughter. Shall we go home?"

The tramlijn is crowded. No seats vacant, so they stand as the carriage rattles down the track. Neither of them speaks. She did not toss a fit at the consulate when Pim arrived. What would have been the point? So she had gathered herself together and waited by the door as Pim spoke a few words to the vice-consul. Waited in silence as the two men finished with a handshake, the pair of conspirators in her entrapment. At the Rooseveltlaan stop, the tram creaks to a halt. In the midst of the jostling on and off of passengers, she feels Pim take her arm. Perhaps it's a fatherly thing to do. Perhaps he's hooking onto her in case she is tempted to escape. It makes no difference. Pim may think he is keeping her in her cage. But in her mind Anne Frank has already broken free.

When they return to the flat, Pim stays only long enough to drink a glass of water from the tap and turn Anne over to Dassah's charge.

Anne says nothing. She drops her bag and flops down into the Viennese wingback like a sack of rags, glaring. Dassah stands in the threshold to the kitchen, wiping her hands on her apron, evaluating the scene, her eyes as sharp as a fox's.

"I have to go back to the office," Pim announces numbly. "And I may be late coming home. Please don't hold supper for me," he tells the new Mrs. Frank, and gives her a distracted peck on the cheek. When Pim leaves, she turns to Anne and says, "Why don't you change out of those clothes? I could use some help with the potatoes."

Anne glares. But then pushes herself up from the chair.

Scrubbing the skin of the potatoes with a brush, she feels herself travel back in time. Standing beside Mummy, cleaning the potatoes for supper, listening as Mummy remembered doing the same thing with her own mother when she was young. The smile on Mummy's face at the memory. At the continuing thread.

Anne feels a tear slide slowly down her cheek.

Dassah does not acknowledge the tear. But as she picks up the paring knife to start peeling, she says, "He loves you. He does. But he's also terrified of you. Terrified that he'll lose you again."

Anne looks up from the scrub brush in her hand. Wipes the tear away with her wrist. "I'm not his to keep," she says.

26

THE FOURTH OF AUGUST

I was pointing out to Peter his mistakes in the dictation when someone suddenly came running up the stairs. The steps creaked, and I started to my feet, for it was morning when everyone had to be quiet—but then the door flew open and a man stood before us holding his pistol aimed at my chest.

—Otto Frank, quoted in
Anne Frank: A Portrait in Courage
by Ernst Schnabel, 1958

1946

The Achterhuis

LIBERATED NETHERLANDS

4 August

The day has come. That date that has been blackened on the calendar. Up in the attic, she remains a prisoner of the Achterhuis, smoking a cigarette. Craven A brand from the Canadians. The smoke is soft in her throat, which she finds disconcerting. She misses the small punishment of bitter shag. To be so comfortable inhaling smoke feels like a sin.

Mouschi is sulking somewhere belowstairs, so she has tried to capture the second warehouse cat, a brutish, hulking old mouser without a name until she called him Goliath. But Goliath is uninterested in affection. It is not his job to comfort Anne Frank, and he refuses to indulge any notions of cuddling that might interfere with his day. So she sits alone. A swift breeze wrinkles through the thickly leafed branches of the chestnut tree, and she listens to the familiar, untroubled rustle, closing her eyes. There are times when she wishes she could become a breeze. To be carried away into the sky. No memories. No past. No future but the open, endless air.

A waxy squeak of wood comes from the floorboards below. She recognizes the tread of Pim's footsteps; each step forward sounds a certain cautious optimism. She watches the leaves brush the window glass as he climbs the ladder and stands behind her.

"Anne?"

Anne says nothing, but her father doesn't seem to notice. "Anne, I'm happy to have found a moment alone with you. I'm happy because there's something I must tell you. I'm happy," he repeats, "but also *unhappy,* because the something I'm about to tell you is both good and bad." He shrugs, shakes his head at nothing. "I don't even know how to begin. So I suppose the only way forward is just to *say* it. Just to say it aloud." His voice is dense.

Anne looks at him stiffly, burying a secret and sudden desire to panic.

Pim turns, his head stooped, his hands hung on his hips, causing his elbows to stick out like wings. His face is a stone. "I have misled you."

He says this, but then further words on the subject are caught in a logjam. He must clear his throat roughly. A deep frown furrows his expression, and he blinks at the floor. "That's the bad part. But the good part is . . ." he tells her, "the good part is that your diary—the diary you kept all those many months while we were in hiding here . . ."

A chilly anxiety climbs lightly up Anne's spine.

"It was not . . ." he manages to say, his posture clenched. Blinking again, he forces his eyes to meet hers. "It was not lost," her father declares. "I have it."

She feels as if she cannot breathe, as if the weight of the silence that separates them is pressing down on her chest. The words make no sense to her, and neither do the dizzying surges she feels of both joy and rage. She feels confused by herself. Her mouth opens. Her heart triples its beat, but all she can say is, *"You?"*

Pim draws in a long breath through his nostrils and then releases it. "It was Miep who gave it to me," he tells her. "She and Bep had salvaged it from the floor the day the Gestapo arrived, and they kept it safe, waiting for you to return. But after . . ." he says thickly, "after we thought that you *wouldn't* be coming home . . ." His voice trembles as he yanks out his handkerchief to blot his eyes. "That was the day. That was the day," he tells her, "that my life ended as well, Anne. It was. But *then*"—he puffs breath into his chest, his lip quivering—"then comes Miep walking into my office with . . . with her arms *filled*," he says, wiping at his eyes and steadying himself. "She comes into my office and sets a stack of books and papers in front of me, saying, 'Here, Mr. Frank, is the legacy of your daughter Anne.'"

Silence.

Pim gazes pleadingly at her, begging her to understand as an empty space expands between them. "It saved me, Anne," her father whispers. "It saved my life. Because it brought you *back* to me." He sniffs, stuffs away his handkerchief, shaking his head in wonder. "Such a *gift,*" he tells her. "That was my thought. My daughter had *such a gift.* I was *stunned* by what you wrote. Stunned and humbled. And then, out of thin air it seemed, *you appeared.* You appeared, *alive,* and my heart *soared.*" He laughs, a sudden heave of joy in his voice.

"But . . ." says Anne, and she bites down on her lip before she can continue, "but you still kept my diary."

Once more Pim's face drops. He must nod his head to this, and he clears his voice of emotion. "I couldn't help but feel that it was," he starts to say, "*and you may not credit this,* but I couldn't help *feeling* that it was *mine* now. Can you make any sense of that?"

No reply.

"When you returned to Amsterdam," says Pim, "having survived such torture, you were so very different. No longer my little kitten. Of course, how *could* you be the same? How could *any* of us *ever* be the same? And yet I felt that the diary . . . it was all I had left of the Annelies I'd known. That child whom I had adored."

Anne stares. "So for all this time . . . you kept this secret. *Miep* kept it," she says, and swallows the first trace of anger in her voice.

"Please. Don't blame *her,*" Pim begs. "You owe our dear friend Miep a debt of gratitude," he instructs Anne. "It was *she* who saved your diary from oblivion—and at great personal risk, I might add. If the Gestapo man had returned, *as he had threatened he would,* all he would have needed to do was open the wrong drawer and disaster would have followed."

"What about your new *wife*?" Anne asks heavily.

"Anne."

"Has Dassah read it, Pim?" She feels a rush of humiliation, imagining her stepmother's eyes on the pages of her diary. Imagining Dassah reading all the judgmental complaints Anne had penned about Mummy, and Anne helpless to edit out a single painful memory, a single ugly thought.

"No one else but me has ever read a single sentence. I can assure you of that. Please. You must believe," Pim tells her, "that no one disrespected your privacy. You must see that Miep's intentions were always to keep your writings safe for your return. She didn't even tell *me* what she had. *Until*"—he shakes his head—"until we thought you were lost to us. And then afterward it wasn't Miep's or Bep's decision to keep it a secret from you." Her father scowls miserably. "It was *my* request that they keep silent. It was *my* request that they were honoring," he says. "Quite definitely against her better judgment, in Miep's case especially. She thought that I was doing you a great wrong."

"And *weren't* you?"

Pim's eyes widen. He sucks in breath and shakes his head. "I don't know," he answers. "Honestly, I never *meant* to keep it secret from you. Not really. Perhaps you're too angry to believe that right now, but it's true," he says. "There were many times, *many times*," he repeats, "that I *intended* to tell you. But I simply . . . I simply couldn't bring myself." Pim pauses. Puts his hand to the side of his head and runs his fingers gently over his hair. "I suppose in a manner of speaking I was *frightened*. Frightened that if I handed over your diary, I would be losing *you* all over again."

She stares at him.

"It still does frighten me," he assures her.

"Where is it?" is all she can ask.

Her father gazes at her face, then expels a breath.

In the private office, he shuts the door behind them. Sitting down at his desk, he produces a brass key from the pocket of his waistcoat and uses it to unlock the large drawer on the bottom left. She hears the scrape of the drawer as it slides open.

"So *here*, my dear, dear Annelies," her father says soberly as he plants the drawer's contents firmly on his blotter, "is your diary."

Silence blocks out any words.

They both stare at the stack of notebooks, one atop the other, the multicolored diary pages, loose-leaf. White, gray, salmon. Cheap wartime pulp, whatever kind of paper Miep and Bep could scrounge.

And then the red tartan plaid daybook from Blankevoorts. Anne feels a stillness enter her heart. How small it looks now. How light it feels when she picks it up.

"I hope," says Pim, "that you will be able to forgive an old man for his many mistakes." This is her father's prayer. But Anne cannot yet answer it. Gingerly unclasping the lock, she lifts the cover, and her eyes land on the snapshot of a dark-eyed child attached to the page of inky script. The girl she once was. The Anne who was once her. A horrific intimacy floods her breast as she reads the first line: I hope I shall be able to confide in you completely, as I have never done in anyone else before.

Her legs weaken, and she drops into the chair opposite Pim's desk, clutching the daybook. The tears are warm on her cheeks. "You were wrong, Pim," she whispers. "It was never yours. It was always only mine."

And as if he is struck by lightning, Pim bursts into a sob. He shakes his head, fumbling for his handkerchief. "I'm sorry, Anneke. I'm sorry," he says, wadding the handkerchief into his eyes. "I'm so sorry." Gently, he tries to mop himself up, saying, "I have made so many foolish choices. So many. There are times that I think there's been a terrible mistake. That God . . ." he says, and blows his nose into his handkerchief, "that God never intended that I should leave Auschwitz alive."

Anne gazes at him, still hugging her diary.

"I remember my poor Mutz, and I can't help but think," he says, "that it's your sister's spot I've taken. It seems to me that God would much prefer the children to have survived than an old man of limited worth." He sniffs, blots his eyes again, and refolds his handkerchief, clearing his throat with a thick rumble up from his chest. "But now. Now I must think not of myself but of my daughter, Anne. Her diary has been returned to its rightful owner, and I hope it will remind her of the girl I so adored. The girl she once was. The girl who she could become again. That," he tells Anne, "is my greatest prayer."

27

THE PAGES OF HER LIFE

I don't want to jot down the facts in this diary the way most people would do, but I want the diary to be my friend, and I'm going to call this friend Kitty.

> —Anne Frank,
> from her diary,
> 20 June 1942

It's funny, but I can sometimes see myself as others see me. I take a leisurely look at the person called "Anne Frank" and browse through the pages of her life as though she were a stranger.

> —Anne Frank,
> from her diary,
> 12 January 1944

1946

Amsterdam

Closed up in the private office. Sifting through her past. The notebook with the cardboard cover of malachite green. The sandy brown book of "Stories and Events of the Achterhuis." The long, stony gray "Book of Nice Sentences." Sorting the pile of multicolored pages. All of it swept up from the floor in fear of the Gestapo and then stuffed into a drawer—it's such a mess. But she reads.

> *When I think back to my life in 1942, it all seems so unreal. The Anne Frank who enjoyed that heavenly existence was completely different from the one who has grown wise within these walls.*

> *Do you think Father and Mother would approve of a girl my age sitting on a divan and kissing a seventeen-and-a-half-year-old boy?*

> *We were up at six yesterday morning, because the whole family heard the sounds of a break-in again.*

There are photographs, too, pinned to the pages. Photographs of Anne and Margot.

Do you remember that day at the beach at Zandvoort? Margot wonders. She is sitting on the bed wearing the green sweater that Miep found for her in hiding. Her eyes are large and warm behind her glasses.

"Of course I do. Look at you in that bathing suit. Already so well *equipped*, while I was still just a twig."

The air tasted salty, Margot says. *That's what I remember.*

"I remember rolling down the dunes. It was so much fun."

> *Last night Margot and I were lying side by side in my bed.*
> *It was incredibly cramped, but that's what made it fun.*
> *The conversation turned to the future, and I asked what she*
> *wanted to be when she was older. But she wouldn't say and was*
> *quite mysterious about it. I gathered it had something to do*
> *with teaching; of course, I'm not absolutely sure, but I suspect*
> *it's something along those lines. I really shouldn't be so nosy.*

Reading, she finds the ghosts of her dead still living on the page. All of them caricatured in ink. Dissected by her pen. Sometimes she can hear their voices in what she has written so clearly. It warms her and terrifies her, raising the dead.

> *Mrs. van Pels was so upset her face turned bright red. . . .*
> *The nonflushed mother, who now wanted to have the matter*
> *over and done with as quickly as possible, paused for a mo-*
> *ment to think before she replied. . . .*
> *Mother: "I didn't say you were pushy, but no one would*
> *describe you as having a retiring disposition."*
> *Mrs. van Pels: "I'd like to know in what way I'm pushy! If I*
> *didn't look out for myself here, no one else would, and I'd soon*
> *starve, but that doesn't mean I'm not as modest and retiring as*
> *your husband."*

〜

> *This morning I lay on Peter's bed after first having chased*
> *him off it. He was furious, but I didn't care. He might consider*
> *being a little more friendly to me from time to time.*

Night. Propped up by a folded pillow on her bed. No covers and sleeping in a rayon slip. The room is hot even with the window open. She reads in secret by candlelight so no one can see the gleam of a lamp under her door. In her hands is a stack of the cheap wartime loose-leaf she has shuffled together. Sometimes she thinks the pages are properly assembled, only to have an errant page confuse her until she picks it out and adds it to the pile beside her on the mattress. This entry in particular is a long one, July 1944, and she's had to deal with several pages gone truant from the proper order. She rubs the tension from her eyes. Ignites a cigarette and inhales smoke.

> *In everything I do, I can watch myself as if I were a stranger. I can stand across from the everyday Anne and, without being biased or making excuses, watch what she's doing, both the good and the bad. This self-awareness never leaves me. . . .*

And then there is another page out of order. She frowns as she starts to remove it, but then a string of words catches her eye.

> *It's difficult in times like these: ideals, dreams and cherished hopes rise within us, only to be crushed by grim reality. It's a wonder I haven't abandoned all my ideals, they seem so absurd and impractical.*

She feels something narrow within her. A tightness behind her eyes.

> *Yet I cling to them because I still believe, in spite of every-thing, that people are truly good at heart.*

If she had just been stabbed in the chest with a knife blade, she could not have suffered a sharper pain. There were those at Birkenau who would seize the electrified fence as a final escape. She often wondered how that freedom would feel. The high voltage ripping through your body. It's what she feels now in her small, flattened soul. The flash of electrical tremor as the pages fall from her hands, and she contracts into a keening knot.

28

THE CANAL

Amsterdam abounds in water, and even in the new quarters, we have not been able to suppress our hobby of canals.

—*All About Amsterdam,* official guide
published for the Canadian Army
Leave Centre HQ, 1945

1946

Amsterdam

It's a dreary, muddy-sky day. She has been compelled to go shopping with Dassah, since Anne is outgrowing what she has in her dresser drawers. Mostly underclothes. Much of the trip is a tersely mannered affair, but at a shop on the Kalverstraat, when Anne tries on a pastel green dress with a subtle floral embroidery, she shocks herself in the mirror. Her hair is past her collar now, thick and dark in a wave, and the dress, rather than hanging on her like a sack, fits her neatly. The reflection the mirror throws back at her is womanly. Even Dassah sounds surprised. "Lovely," her stepmother has to admit, and an oddly intimate expression touches her face. Her lips part as if she is about to speak again to Anne, but instead she turns to the shopgirl. "Wrap it up. We'll take it, please."

As they make their way down the sidewalk, Anne carrying the packaged dress against her breast, Dassah says, "You're not a child any longer, Anne."

And then they both stop dead in their tracks.

Anne grips the package tightly, her pulse beating in her belly. Sweat prickles on the back of her neck. The sight is painful. These people. Their clothes are rumpled and their faces grim and exhausted. They lug their valises or clutch bundles. Men, women, children in their mothers' arms or groping for their parents' hands, marched down the street by a squad of Dutch gendarmerie in khaki uniforms, rifles slung over their shoulders.

Some onlookers try to ignore the spectacle, stealing a glance before bustling onward with intentional blindness, but many stop and stare with heavy, blank expressions. A few decide it's funny and laugh, and a few more pitch insults. "Moffen animals!" they shout. "Back to your filthy burrow!"

A stooped, middle-aged man in a dusty coat shouts back in desperation from the guarded column. "We are Netherlanders! We are Amsterdammers!" But his words are met with boos and more insults.

Anne turns frantically to a stubby little fellow beside her wearing a ragged cloth cap. "What's happening? Who *are* those people?"

The little man gives her only the briefest of assessments before he replies, "Dirty krauts." He scowls. "And God willing they're being packed off to their rotten scumhole of a country." He cups his hand around his mouth and hollers, "Germans out! Netherlands for the Netherlanders!"

Suddenly Anne feels Dassah take her arm. "We should go," her stepmother whispers tautly. "We should *go*."

In the Herengracht, Anne wastes no time. They find Pim just home from the office, in his shirtsleeves, with his necktie loosened. "And how was the shopping expedition?" he's happy to inquire—and then his expression dulls.

"Pim, it's begun," Anne announces immediately.

"What? What's begun?" He looks to Dassah for an explanation, but Anne is pointing toward the window, as if it's all happening on the street outside their flat.

"The *deportations*, Pim. We *saw* them. People marched down the middle of the street under guard by soldiers with bayonets!"

"It's true, Otto," the new Mrs. Frank confirms. "We did see them. A dozen or so, not many. But it's true."

"Germans?" Pim asks.

"So it seemed," Dassah answers. "Of course, there was no way of knowing if any of them were Jews."

"Well, none of them were wearing the yellow star, if that's what you mean," Anne snaps. "At least not *yet*."

"*Anne*, please." Pim swallows heavily. "Don't *overreact*," he commands her.

But Anne will not be silenced. "We must *go*, Pim. We must all *go*."

"*No*, I am done," Pim replies, his expression stiffening. "I am done running, meisje. Amsterdam is our home, and here we will *stay*."

In desperation Anne turns to Dassah. "Surely *you* must see the danger," she breathes. "Surely *you* must."

But Dassah just gazes at her, silent and inscrutable, so Anne turns back to Pim, desperate. "Send *me,* then, Pim. Alone. If *you* must stay here, then at least let *me* go to America."

Pim breathes a sigh. "Anne . . ."

"I *told* you—I will *not* suffer through this. I will *not* be shipped like a beast back to Germany."

Pim regards her with a mixture of shock and pity. "Anne. It alarms me. It alarms me," he says, "to hear you say such things. That you could really feel so *alone* and frightened that you would have me send you off to a foreign country."

"Better America than the land of our executioners."

"I'm sorry. I'm sorry, daughter," Pim says, shaking his head. "I simply cannot conceive of *losing* you again. And I promise—regardless of what you may have seen today in the street—I *promise* you that we are in no danger."

"No danger," Anne repeats blackly.

"Whatever comes, we are better off *together* rather than apart."

Anne turns her glare on him. "I can only remind you, Pim, that you said the same thing before the war. Mother *told* us. She felt so guilty, but she told us there had been a chance to send Margot and me to safety in England. *You* prevented it," she says. "You prevented it because you were so convinced—so intractably *convinced*—that we were all better off *together.*"

The light in her father's eyes flickers out, and his expression shrinks tightly against his face. "I admit it, if that's what you wish me to do, Anne," he tells her. "I admit that I've made many mistakes in this life. Mistakes that have harmed the people whom I've lived for. And I understand how it may be hard for even my own daughter to trust me. To trust *any* adult, since we've made such a hash of things. But nonetheless that's exactly what I'm asking you to do."

"No, Pim. You don't understand. You don't understand *me.*"

Pim stares at her heavily, as if from a distance. "That I don't understand you? It may be true. Regardless of how close we have been in the past, Anneke, perhaps it's true that I have never really known you at all."

> *There's a destructive urge in people, the urge to rage, murder and kill. And until all of humanity, without exception, undergoes a metamorphosis, wars will continue to be waged, and everything that has been carefully built up, cultivated and grown will be cut down and destroyed, only to start all over again!*

Prinsengracht 263
Amsterdam-Centrum

The night goes, the day comes. In the Prinsengracht, Anne finds herself in the Achterhuis kitchen, where Auguste van Pels has her hair up in pins, drying the dishes that Mummy has just washed. Anne asks them if she can help, but Mummy tells her no. She says Anne is too much of a butterfingers and that soon they'll have no dishes left. Anne thinks she should be mad at this little jab on Mummy's part, but she's not. The two ladies are smiling at her from the sink, and Anne is smiling, too. The patchwork of curtains dulls the light in the room. She should just sit down, Mummy advises her. She must be tired. Isn't she tired? Mummy wonders. So Anne sits. She tries to tell them what's happened in the time that's passed since their arrest, since this place was their home, but neither of the women seems to understand her. They observe her with a comprehensive puzzlement. And then it's Mr. van Pels appearing in filthy Kazetnik garments. Two yellow triangles forming the Judenstern on his corpse's tunic. The teeth in the yawning hole of his mouth are rotting. "Anne, you be *quiet*," he warns. "Do you want those people down in the warehouse to hear us?"

And then she is suddenly terrified that she has given them away.

She hears a voice call her name from far off, but she doesn't answer because she must be quiet.

"Quiet? Ha!" Peter enters, his body emaciated in dirty KZ stripes, and laughs out loud at the very idea. "Anne Frank can never be quiet!" he says with a grin. But no one shushes him at all.

"Anne." She hears again this voice from a far distance, only now

it's closer, and her eyes pop open. It's Dassah in her pine-green office frock, standing in the threshold of the room, her hand resting on the doorknob as if she's prepared to slam it shut if required to protect herself.

Anne blinks roughly, bent into a jackknife on her knees; she shakes her head and glares at the floorboards. "Go away."

"Anne, are you ill?"

"Go away, *please*," she half commands, half begs.

"If you're ill, we should call for the doctor."

"Just . . . *go away*."

Dassah steps forward. She spreads a handkerchief on the dusty floor and carefully kneels down beside Anne. "These are the rooms where you lived, correct?" she asks, but she does not seem to expect an answer. "Incredible," she says. "This would have been considered a *palace* by most Jews in hiding."

But Anne is not interested in her stepmother's appraisal of the Achterhuis. "If you don't mind, please go to hell," she requests, and is surprised by the snort of Dassah's laugh.

"Well." The woman sighs. "I think I've already been there once, Anne," she says. "Have you forgotten?" And then she does something even more shocking. Gently, she turns back the cuff of Anne's sweater, exposing Anne's tattoo to the ghosts inhabiting the air. A-25063. Dassah lightly brushes her fingertips over the number as if she can feel it raised on Anne's skin. "This ink," she says, "is a poison. We have all been poisoned by it. Your father, you, me. But it has failed to kill us." There is something so lonely in her voice when she says, "You should remember that. We are alive. Not dead."

Anne gazes. Slowly, she draws her arm away from Dassah's hand. The woman takes a breath. Blinks a sheepish pain from her eyes. Her face has taken on a shadow of loss, but then she is Dassah again, her eyes shut off from pity. "Yet maybe you know that you're alive. At least maybe your body knows. Are you having intercourse?"

Anne glares.

"It's a question, Anne. A question that needs to be asked." Dassah frowns. "I hope not. I hope you are not so stupid. But if you are, please tell me that you are using the proper precautions. A condom," Dassah says to be blunt. "If you wish to live as a whore with that boy—" she is saying when Anne cuts her off.

"That's *over*."

A pause. "*Is* it?" She doesn't bother to ask why but only says, "So you finally came to your senses. Well, let us thank God for *that*."

Anne gazes at her blackly. "Why are you so horrible to me?"

"Oh, is *that* what I am? Horrible? You've already called me a 'monster,' so I suppose I shouldn't expect any charity from you. The truth is, Anne, you were terribly spoiled when you were a child. That much is obvious. It's made you weak and self-centered and eager to blame others for your shortcomings. Honestly, it's a wonder you survived at all. But since you have, you think that the world now owes you tribute. You've been twisted by your experiences into a kind of morose, self-absorbed little tyrant who demands that everyone worship her pain and loss as much as *she* does. And if they don't—if they refuse to give in to your egotism—then they are labeled 'a monster.'"

Anne smears at her eyes, glaring at the corner of her room where her desk once sat. "I *hate* you," she whispers bitterly.

"I can live with that," Dassah informs her. "But whether you can believe it or not, I am only trying to help you, Anne. I am trying to help you look in the mirror and see yourself as you are, because I have some very bad news for you. The world owes you nothing. You survived? So what? Millions didn't. Your sister didn't. Your mother didn't. But all your tears are for yourself, Anne Frank, the poor victim. And nobody loves victims. Victims are resented. Victims are reviled, that's the way things are. You must earn love, just as you earn respect. *That* is what I'm trying to teach you."

"If I'm such an awful human being, such a black spot, then why don't you help me get out of your hair? Convince Pim to let me go. He listens to you."

"Oh, you think so? Well, in some matters, perhaps. But Otto is still bent on keeping you sheltered. He is disinclined to give up on his sentimental attachment to you as a child. Disinclined to give up the memory of love that once bound you two together." Standing, Dassah retrieves her handkerchief from the floor and folds it into a square. "But what your father *really* requires from you now isn't love. It isn't even gratitude or respect, though he deserves all those things. It's *cooperation*. He won't admit it, but he's facing some serious trouble with the government, and the last thing he needs is *your* unrelenting attacks."

Anne only stares.

"Do you know how often I awake to find him standing in the threshold of your room, watching over you as you sleep? *You* are the star in his eyes, Anne," Dassah tells her. "I am his wife. We are partners now in this life, and he will always take my part. I know this. But no one has ever filled his heart like you."

<hr>

Miep has been the victim of a most common crime—a thief stole the tires from her bicycle—so she arrives on foot to pick Anne up for an afternoon movie matinee. A rain scarf covering her head, ginger bangs fringing her forehead. They board the Tramlijn 5 at the Koningsplein as it begins to drizzle. Anne watches people on the street convinced by the rain to pop open their umbrellas. Along the Leidsestraat many windows are still taped against air-raid bombs.

"Has he told you?" Anne asks.

Miep turns her head. "Has who told me what?"

"Pim. Has he told you what I did? That I went to the American consulate? Has he told you that I attempted an escape?"

A short intake of breath. "Well. That's a very harsh way of putting it."

"So he has told you. And what do *you* think, Miep? Do you think I'm a childish, self-centered bitch?"

"Anne, *please*. Language. It's not necessary."

"Do you think I'm a coward, wanting to desert him?"

Miep shakes her head. "No, neither of you is being cowardly. You're both being very brave, in my opinion. Trying to set things right. I'm only sorry that . . ."

Anne raises her eyebrows. "Sorry that *what*?"

"I'm sorry, Anne," she hears Miep say plainly, "that I kept your diary a secret from you. I haven't said that aloud to you, and I think I must. I'm sorry," she repeats. "It was against my better judgment, and I shouldn't have done it."

Anne swallows. Looks away. "You were only doing as my father asked."

"Yes. But that doesn't make it right."

"Maybe not," Anne agrees. "But, Miep, if it wasn't for you, it would have all been lost. *Actually* lost. Forever. So you don't need to apologize to me."

Miep blinks away a gleam of tears and swallows. "Thank you," she whispers.

Anne allows silence to separate them until, "You know, Miep, at first when I was writing in my diary—when I was thirteen—it was a kind of game to me. A fun way to pass the time. But then in hiding . . . in hiding, it became something very different," she says. "Do you remember the cabinet minister's broadcast over Radio Oranje? About all of us keeping wartime writings?"

"Yes, I think so."

"I took it to heart. I started to rewrite what I had already put down. All of it. I changed people's names. Gave them, you know—schuilnaamen," she says. Hiding names. "I thought I would sew it all together into a story I could tell."

"We all believed you had talent, Anne. I remember how you would read us bits and pieces. We all believed you had talent."

"Really?" Hearing Miep say this makes it sound true.

"Oh, yes."

"Even Mummy?" she asks.

"Of course. You think because she scolded you here and there that she wasn't proud of you? She *was*. She was immensely proud. It was only that . . ." Miep starts to say, but then she can't seem to finish the sentence. "She was so burdened. Her mind was so burdened." Miep frowns at her knuckles and shakes her head. "I tried so hard to help her, your mother. I couldn't blame her for feeling so pessimistic, of course. The world had become so brutalized."

Anne remembers her mother's eyes. The dim lights they had become after they went into hiding. Then their sharp, darting hunger, suddenly brightly displayed at Birkenau.

"So I tried to keep her focused on what was good and hopeful for the future," Miep says, and she must dig her handkerchief from her purse to dab at the tears she is obviously trying to resist. "But. To no avail," she can only conclude. "To no avail at all."

Anne recognizes the black onyx ring Miep has on her finger. A jet-black stone with a tiny gleam of white diamond. "You're wearing the ring from Mrs. van Pels."

"I am." Miep nods. "I thought I should begin to. It's such a lovely thing, you know. I can't help but think of what it would have been worth to the van Pelses on the black market. Yet they chose to give it to me as a birthday gift. It was really quite a beautiful gesture," she says, looking out at the rain. Then she turns her face back to Anne. Her mouth straightens. "If I may tell you something honestly, Anne, it was so hard for me sometimes. When you were all in the hiding place, it was so hard to climb the stairs and find everyone lined up, waiting for me. So desperate. So confined and so needy. There were days I wanted to scream. But then I knew I could always count on *you* to break the tension. Do you remember what you'd say to me every time I arrived?"

Anne reclaims a hollow brightness in her voice. "Say, Miep— what's the news?"

"That's *it*." Miep grins through her tears. "That's it exactly. It was always such a tremendous *relief*." Then the grin fades. She purses her lips and examines the frittering rain. "Impossible to believe that they're all gone. That only you and your father . . ." she says, but doesn't finish her sentence. "Impossible to believe that there could be such evil in people's hearts."

"People do wicked things," Anne replies. "Commit terrible crimes." In the reflection of the tram's rain-splattered window glass, she meets Margot's desolate gaze, glazed over by death. She stares at Anne with sad accusation. The conductor calls out the coming stop, and the tram hums to a halt. Passengers climb down; new passengers climb aboard with a routine jostling of shoulders. The bell rings, and the conductor sings out the name of the next stop.

"That's us," Miep says, obviously still disturbed.

"I killed Margot, Miep," Anne hears herself whisper.

But Miep is busy returning her handkerchief to her purse, sniffing back her sadness. Reassembling herself. "I'm sorry, Anne, but I didn't hear what you said."

Anne is glaring hard at the dirty floor of the tram. Staring at her scuffed saddle shoes. "Nothing," she says. "Nothing. I was just talking to myself."

De Uitkijk Bioscoop
Prinsengracht 452
The Canal Ring West

By the time they've exited the tram, the rain is coming heavily, settling into a solid drubbing of a downpour, so they must dash across the slippery cobbles from the tram to the cinema. Inside, some of the last remaining Canadians, still waiting to be shipped back to their homeland, lounge at the bar, off duty, bored with the Netherlands by now since nobody's shooting at them any longer. Their empty expressions say it. Bored of wooden shoes and windmills, of delft-blue chinaware and smelly summer canals. One of them is searching through the pages of a booklet entitled *All About Amsterdam*. He glances up and offers Anne a routine wink. She stares back at him without response. But in the auditorium a darkness is sweeping over her. The room is clammy with a sickly aroma of smoke and damp clothing. She feels all expression fall away from her face. An ugliness grips her belly. An oily guilt slithering through her.

An English newsreel begins with a fanfare of trumpets. The narrator's voice is a trumpet itself, as the images of the world flash past. Presenting the world *to* the world! Anne slouches deeply into her seat as crimes against humanity scorch across the screen and the camera pans across the piles and piles of corpses carpeting a scrubby expanse of mudflats. A bottomless hole opens under her. It makes her dizzy. She blinks. On the screen a few of the corpses are moving still, imitating the living as the narrator's tone drops into a righteously grim timbre. *"This,"* he declares, "is Belsen," and Anne feels her heart go rigid. "A city of the dead and the living dead." A woman squats as she sips from a bowl in the midst of the ragged debris of bodies. Skeletons stumbling in their rags, aimless faces gaping into the camera without comprehension. "What is impossible for film to communicate is the *stench,*" the narrator insists, but Anne can smell it. That putrid perfume of animal rot. She watches the SS women, still in their feldgrau frocks, rounded up by Tommies. Scowling and sneering into the camera. "Members of Himmler's female legion now required to bury the victims of their homicidal desires at the point of Royal Army bayonets." The bodies of the dead, decaying, shrunken limbs, sacks of bones, are being dragged to the burial pits, where they are tossed in like rubbish. The corpses tumble down, limbs akimbo— one more onto the dung heap. When Anne was in the DP hospital, she'd been so deeply gratified to hear that the SS had been forced to handle disease-bloated corpses with their bare hands. But seeing it now—seeing their disregard for the humanity of their bundles, seeing the grim repulsion stamped on their faces as they grip each corpse by wrists and ankles and heave it into the pit with the flourish of trash removers—it enrages Anne. The *obscenity* of it. The despicable handling of these naked dead, stripped and decaying.

"Anne, do you want to go?" Miep whispers, "Do you want to leave?"

Suddenly she can see Margot's face attached to every corpse. That one could be her. Or *that* one. Or *that* one sliding down the sandy bank into the massive open grave, that could be Margot.

She wants to scream. She wants to dive into the screen and shroud her sister's shameful nakedness with a blanket. She wants to bellow at those SS hags: Get your hands *off* her, you filthy cunts! And maybe she does, because the next instant she finds herself standing, her body clenched, her hands trembling, as the echo of her own voice thunders inside her head.

Quickly, Miep is up out of her seat and guiding Anne into the aisle. "You're safe now, you're safe," she's murmuring. "Anne, it's over, it's over," she tells her. But on the screen it isn't over. On the screen there's a soldier operating a bulldozer with a kerchief masking his face against the stench, the bodies twisting in the dirt as the broad blade digs in. "Let no one say," the narrator commands, "that these crimes were never real."

Tearing away from Miep, Anne runs, bursting from the cinema doors into the rain, desperate to outpace her panic. The bulldozer is behind her, plowing the corpses into the pit, its blade at her heels. She hears someone shout. A cyclist swerves on the slick cobbles; her body swivels out from under her. There's an instant of wild tumble, nothing but the air clutching her, until she feels the impact as she penetrates the surface of the water. Her body plummets as the canal receives her. She can feel her breath swell up from her belly and into her chest in thick bubbles. Eyes clamped shut, limbs thrashing as the tortured images of Margot's corpse are washed from her brain. If she doesn't fight, she will sink, so can't she just stop? Can't she? Please, please can't she just *stop*? The pressure of the depths grips her, trying to squeeze the final balloon of air from her breast as her feet flail against nothing. No floor to stop her, just a single plunge. The insistent downward draw to the bottom, where regrets end, where fear ends and pain dissolves. The panic of her body weakening. Her eyes flash open, her breath boiling from her lips. She knows the angel of death is waiting below. But before she can surrender, an intrusion. An intrusion! Margot is there, horning in, slinking down into the water, head shaved, her Kazetnik pullover ballooning around her arms, the Judenstern floating, her eyes wide and black. Not a single breath bubbles from her lips as she speaks. *Anne, if you die, we die with you.*

A jolt. A jolt to Anne's heart.

If you die, we die with you.

All she has left is a breath.

If you die—

A single breath.

—we die with you.

A single choice.

Margot liquefies into nothing, but with that last bubble of air in her lungs, Anne is pushing herself upward, fighting the drag of the darkness. Propelling herself toward a skim of light. A heave of desire, unbidden, but now shooting through her, animating her limbs, up-ward, upward, until she bursts into the air, and her eyes smart as the rain stings her face.

Her eyelids lift stiffly. She feels something cold, metallic, pressing here, pressing there. She can smell the scent of rubbing alcohol. There is a man bent over her. Thickly jowled, removing the tips of a stethoscope from his large ears that bristle with hair.

"I see you've returned to the land of the living," the doctor observes.

A dull ache creaks through Anne's body as she tries to move, so she stops and simply lies still.

"You have reached a verdict, Doctor?" Dassah inquires from the threshold.

The doctor replaces the stethoscope into his battered leather satchel. "The patient will live," he decides. "What you require, young lady, is *rest*." Grunting as he stands. "I'll give you a prescription," he says, and then, to Dassah, "Something to help her sleep."

When Dassah returns to the room after seeing the doctor to the door, Anne has rolled onto her side facing the wall. She has been dressed in her pajamas and feels now wholly exhausted, as if she has been running a race for days without an end in sight. But the cold shivers have finally vacated her body. "Where's Pim?"

"He'll be here soon," is all Dassah tells her dimly, stepping farther into her room. Her voice takes on a hard edge of interest. "*This* is where you want to go?"

Lifting her eyes to the photos of skyscrapers tacked on the wall, Anne observes the Kingdom of Manhattan. "Yes," is all she says.

Dassah nods, still gazing at the towers and concrete canyons. "You know I was born and reared in Berlin. A very large city. A very modern city. But *this*," she says, "this is a city from another world...."

"*Hello?*" Anne hears Pim calling urgently, and he appears, wearing his old raincoat and fedora. The skin of his face is bleached. Kneeling at the side of her bed, he takes Anne's hand in his bony grip. "My dear child," he says, as if beginning a prayer. "My dear, dear daughter."

"*Pim,*" she whispers, raising her arms for an embrace. "I'm sorry." Her cheek dampens.

"Annelein. There's utterly no reason for apologies."

"Yes. Yes, there is." She swallows. "I'm not the daughter you think I am, Pim. I'm not the person you think I am."

"Anne." He says her name and shakes his head softly. "You shall always be my darling daughter. No matter what. No matter how old you grow or what distance may come between us, you shall always be my child."

"No, you don't understand."

"I understand perfectly, Anne," he says.

"I'll leave the two of you alone," Dassah informs them.

"Thank you, Hadasma. Thank you," he says. And then he repeats himself, as if perhaps he is revealing a secret. "I understand perfectly. *Perfectly,* Anneke. I'm only grateful to God that I had the good sense to send you to swimming lessons when you were little. Those medals you earned have come in quite handy, I would say."

"No, Pim. Maybe you should *let* them send me back to Germany. Let the mof finish the job he started."

A dark breath exhaled. "Anne, it *grieves* me. It grieves me deeply when you say things like that."

Anne does not respond to this, but she guesses Pim might prefer her silence at this moment.

"Now, please . . ." He squeezes her hand. "Let's speak no more about such things," he tells her, as if tamping down the embers in a fireplace. "You should rest. It's what you need most. Shall I read to you? I would enjoy that, I think. Let me just put my coat and hat away."

He is gone for a few moments. Mouschi slips into the room, pushing through the gap in the door, and mews impertinently before leaping up onto the bed. Anne captures him in her arms, burying her nose in plush fur. She can hear the whisper of words between Pim and her stepmother. But then Pim returns, carrying a dog-eared volume. "I was just beginning again with *Great Expectations,*" he announces with a cautious joviality, and sinks down into the chair by the bed. "Dickens was a genius, I think, at portraying the essence of people. I've always admired this in his writing." He opens the book and places his eyes on the page. But then he says, "You possess some of that genius, too, Anne," he tells her, "when you write."

Anne's brow wrinkles.

"God has given you quite a talent. Perhaps I've never told you that," he says, musing aloud.

Anne can only reply with silence.

"Well, if I haven't, it was wrong of me. I *should* have told you. I should have, because it's *true*."

She does not know how to find gratitude in herself right now. But Pim does not appear to expect it in any case. He gives a sniff and clears his throat before beginning to read aloud. Anne leans back against the headboard, as if she is leaning back into the past, the father and his daughter at bedtime. Holding her purring cat against her breast, she presses her nose into the fur of his head as Pim ignites a cigarette and opens the book. She listens to the words but also to the drowse of his voice. Her eyes return to the magazine pages tacked to the wall. A city from another world.

29

MIEP'S TYPEWRITER

A few of my stories are good, my descriptions of the
Secret Annex are humorous, much of my diary is vivid and
alive, but . . . it remains to be seen whether I really have
talent.

—Anne Frank,
from her diary,
5 April 1944

1946

LIBERATED NETHERLANDS

She sits cross-legged on her bed with the stack of diary pages in her hand and can see the ugly reality of it by the candle's glow. It's juvenile. Poorly written. Nothing but adolescent rubbish. Or maybe it's just that it's so heartbreakingly personal. Humiliating, really. How stupid she was to be taken in by hopes and silly dreams of goodness.

In the office kitchen, Anne tells Miep the truth. "I wish you had never saved it, Miep," she says. Miep has just put on the kettle to boil the water for tea, igniting the burner with a match. Anne inhales a whiff of gas. "You should have let it be carted away into oblivion with everything else."

Miep gazes back at her. "I see," she says. "Well, if you're asking for my opinion on that, Anne, I can only say this: The ring that Mrs. van Pels gave me. You remember that I said how I couldn't touch it for a long time? It was simply too painful. But then I decided," she says with a breath, "I decided that I *must* wear it. Painful or not, I must honor the memory of her kindness. Of her gratitude." She swallows. "Your father was wrong in keeping the diary from you. He was," she tells Anne. "But it's no longer missing. You have it. It is in your hands. Isn't it your responsibility to honor the memory of those who have passed?"

Anne can only stare back at her, silent. Miep is silent, too. Then, suddenly, "Wait here," she says, and bustles out, only to return a moment later toting her old black portable typewriter, which she places on the countertop.

"So, Anne, here is a late gift for your birthday."

A blink. "My birthday?"

"This is mine, not the company's, and we have the new machine now anyway," Miep tells her. "So I want you to have it." Slipping open the case, she explains, "I keep it well oiled. There's a small toolbox attached."

Anne looks at Miep, confused.

"Writers need to write, don't they?" Miep asks. "And won't you benefit from equipment a bit more modern than a pencil?"

Anne can still only stare.

"If not for yourself," Miep says, "then do it for me. For me, Anne. For all of us who might want to remember those who never returned."

Anne feels an odd force rising inside her. The kettle on the stove begins to whistle with steam.

~~~

She has dragged the old wire table from the garden into her room and organized a board covered with paint stains as a desktop from the warehouse. On it she sets Miep's typewriter. Removes the case and gazes down at the button alphabet of keys. Pulling up her chair, she sits. Cranks a sheet of thin foolscap into the vulcanized-rubber roll. She's not much of a typist, but she places her fingers here and there, holds her breath, and taps out a line at the center of the page:

```
"Stories from the House Behind"
```

30

GOD'S COMEDY

Sometimes I think that God is trying to test me, both
now and in the future.

—Anne Frank,
from her diary,
30 October 1943

1946

At breakfast Anne has announced that she will refuse to return to the school when the new term begins in September. Pim is flummoxed, as she expected. But Anne is surprised, not by Pim's hangdog expression or his lecturing tone but by the new Mrs. Frank. Instead of raining down condemnation, she simply fixes her stepdaughter with a curious glare. "Well, Otto," she says. "It's not the end of the world. When I was sixteen, I already had a job as a stenographer with the Union Soap Company. So perhaps it's for the best. God must have other plans for Anne's future."

Dassah picks up the plates and takes them into the kitchen to scrub before work. Anne does not offer to help. In fact, Anne is still in her pajamas, which she has not bothered to launder, and they're starting to retain a hint of sweat and cigarette smoke.

Her father sips coffee from his cup and gives her a small look. "I thought you might come into the office today."

"No, not today," is all she says.

"And what about our friend Mr. Nussbaum? Doesn't he need help at the shop?"

She ignites a Craven A and whistles smoke. "What are you getting at, Pim?"

"I'm not getting at anything. I'm simply wondering if you're ever planning on leaving the house again."

"I've been busy."

"Really." He sounds skeptical. "Busy pecking at that typewriter Miep lent you?"

"She gave it to me. As a gift."

"Very well. As a gift, if you say so. But my point is—" he starts to say until Anne cuts him off.

"Your point is *what*, Pim? *What*? Why are you still sitting here? What is it you *want* from me?"

"It's nothing that I *want*, Anne," he assures her. "Only I hear you up half the night banging away."

"I'm *working*," Anne says. "I'm sorry if I'm disturbing your sleep."

"Not a question of that." He frowns. "Nothing to do with me. But you need your rest. It's not healthy. And now you come and declare that you're done with school."

"There are things more important than sleep, and there are things more important than school. I want to publish my diary, Pim," she announces. "I'm typing up a draft, that's what I'm doing. I want to turn my diary into a book." Pim's hands fall into his lap, and he drops a sigh like he's dropping a stone. *"Anne,"* he says with a light shake of his head, then repeats her name as if it alone sums up the entirety of the problem. "Daughter, *please*," he starts. "You must understand that what I'm about to say comes only from my desire for your welfare. You know," he tells her, "that I deeply regret having kept your diary from you. It was unfair and thoughtless on my part, I don't deny it. *But*," he says. "But the very idea that you would think of *publishing* it? As a *book*?" He shrugs sharply at the incomprehensibility of such a notion. "It's true, you have a gift for words. But really, Anne. I don't want to insult you, but . . . a young girl's *diary*? Who would publish such a thing? Who would want to?"

"There could be someone," she answers defensively. "If I put it in order. Work it into a real story."

"I'm just afraid that you're going to be hurt. That you're going to be dreadfully disappointed. Ask Werner Nussbaum, he was in publishing for decades. Ask him about how many would-be authors have their work rejected."

"Many, I'm sure. But that doesn't mean I shouldn't try. There could be *someone* interested in publishing it. Life in hiding from the mof."

"You believe that's what people want to read about now?"

"Everything I wrote *happened*."

"*Yes,* it happened. But consider what you're suggesting. I'm the first to admit it wasn't always a rosy picture during those twenty-five months. I don't imagine any of us would come off too well. You have a capacity for deep insight, Anneke, but also for harsh judgment. Even *cruel* judgment at times."

"Oh, so *that's* it. The truth comes out. It's not that you're afraid that nobody will publish it, you're afraid that somebody *will.* You're afraid I'll make you look bad."

"Not just *me,* Annelies. But may I ask? If you're so very *sure* that Jews are still being persecuted, even here in the Netherlands, is it *really* your intention to expose the most intimate moments of our life in such a public fashion?"

Anne frowns.

"Think of your mother," Pim tells her. "Consider the picture you drew of *her* in your pages." He gazes at her, not unsympathetically. "It was often very unpleasant and unfair. Do you really want the world to remember her as the critical, unsympathetic, and unlovable person you often made her out to be?"

To this, Anne has no answer.

Pim places his napkin from his lap onto the table. "I'm sorry, meisje. I returned your diary for your own private satisfaction, because it was the correct thing to do. But you have no right to expose the pain and suffering of those in hiding, since they are no longer alive to grant you consent. As a result I must be adamant. No publication of your diary."

Anne is suddenly on her feet, as if a fire has ignited in her belly. "How *dare* you, Pim?" she seethes. "How dare you act as if *my* diary was yours to return or not, to publish or not? I know that it frightens you. I know it! If my diary's published, then you'll no longer be in charge of what happened to us."

"I was never in charge of what happened to us, Anne."

"*Really?* You certainly pretended otherwise."

"That's *unfair!*" His face flushes pink. "That is completely, *completely* unfair. *Someone* had to assume a leadership role. You think it was going to be Hermann van Pels? You think it was going to be Fritz Pfeffer? Eight of us packed together, smothering each other day after day. I had no other *choice*, daughter. *No other choice.* And don't imagine it was *easy* either! Do you believe I enjoyed being 'in charge' as you would have it? The constant bitterness and bickering. The unending squabbling over *this* stupidity and *that* one. But someone had to play the peacemaker, so it was me. *Yes.* I will admit to that crime, Annelies. I took on the burden of that responsibility, and believe me, *burden* it was. But I tried not to complain. I did my best to stay impartial, to make decisions that were in the best interest of us all. When the toilet clogged"—he frowns—"who fished out excrement with a pole? The only person who volunteered. When Miep or Bep or Mr. Kugler was fed up with our complaints, who soothed their feelings? When you and Mr. Pfeffer locked horns over the use of the desk, who was the broker of compromise? It was hard labor keeping the roof on. Not to mention the fact that I was still trying to run a business to keep us fed and to educate you children—not just my own daughters, mind you, but Peter, too. In that respect I was father to you *all*," he declares. "*So,* my dear daughter, don't believe that I am frightened now by what you've written, because I am *not.* When I tell you that there will be no publication of your diary writing, it is not for my sake but for the sake of those who have passed before us—and for *yours.*"

Anne glares at her father's face, angry, his cheeks inflamed, then storms into her room. She hears him call her name but slams the door behind her.

There Margot is waiting in her typhus rags. *So now you're going to alienate Pim as well? Soon I'll be the only one you have left, Anne.*

"Shut up, will you?" Anne flings herself onto her bed and lights another cigarette, her hands still trembling with anger. "*You're* the one who said I had to *live. Remember that?* All I'm doing is trying to keep our story alive, too."

A cough rumbles through Margot's chest. *Is that really all?*

"I have no idea what you're talking about."

No? You complain that Pim withheld the truth from you. But aren't you still doing the same to him?

Anne turns, her face hot with tears. "I didn't mean to *do* it, Margot," she whispers desperately. "I didn't *mean* to."

But there is no one there to respond.

. . .

The next morning she ignores the knock on her door from Pim. She
pretends she cannot hear him speak her name but waits instead until
the flat is empty to go bathe in the tub. The water is tepid. She uses
the soap Mr. Nussbaum brought her. But then she stops. The tub is
so comfortable. So inviting. For a moment she slips beneath the surface, feeling the water envelop her. A few bubbles of oxygen. That's
all that stands between her and the angel of death. But then she rises
up, splashing, seizing her next breath of air.

***

Nussbaum
Tweedehands-Boekverkoper
The Rozengracht

> *. . . if I'm quiet and serious, everyone thinks I'm putting on
> a new act and I have to save myself with a joke, and then I'm
> not even talking about my own family, who assume I must be
> sick, stuff me with aspirins and sedatives, feel my neck and
> forehead to see if I have a temperature, ask about my bowel
> movements and berate me for being in a bad mood, until I just
> can't keep it up anymore, because when everybody starts hov-
> ering over me, I get cross, then sad, and finally end up turning
> my heart inside out, the bad part on the outside and the good
> part on the inside, and keep trying to find a way to become
> what I'd like to be and what I could be if . . . if only there were
> no other people in the world.*

She stops reading. Presses the pages against her breast. Mr. Nussbaum
is seated behind the sales desk in his bookshop, observing her with an
unreadable expression. For a moment he simply gazes at her, his arms
folded at an angle in front of him, a shadow across his face. Then the
chair creaks as he shifts forward, and he speaks quietly. "And how
old . . ." he begins, "how old were you when you wrote this?"

"Fifteen," she says. "I was fifteen. It was the last thing I wrote before the Gestapo came."

A blink and then a shake of his head.

"I know it probably sounds childish," she tells him.

"*No.* No, Anne. Not childish. Innocent, perhaps. A certain innocence. But not childish in the least."

"So," she breathes, "you think it's not so bad?"

He surprises her with a laugh, even though the shadow does not leave his face. "Not so bad? Anne, what you've read to me here today," he says, "it's been a privilege to hear it. *You,* Miss Frank, like it or not, are a writer."

Anne swallows. A flash of joyful terror shoots through her. "Well," she answers with gratitude, "thank you for saying that. But the truth is, I think, that I'm just some Jewish girl who the Germans forgot to gas."

"Now, you *see. This* is what I mean. *This* is why I told your father that he must allow you to go to America. So that you can be *free* of that awful stigma."

"You told him that?"

"I did. I told him exactly that. Unfortunately, he has his own ideas on the subject. But even Otto Frank can change his mind."

"Not very often," Anne says. She shakes her head. "And what if he's right? What if America would simply swallow me up?" She feels a rush of sadness. "The real truth is . . ." she starts to say, but her eyes have gone suddenly hot. "The real truth is, I'm weak. I am weak and frightened. And my so-called writing? All these pages? All the words?" She takes a breath. "I'm not sure I can recognize myself in them any longer." She blinks. Stares down at the floor. "The *me* I read about in my diary feels like a stranger. She can be frightened sometimes, and full of anxieties, yes, and childishly dramatic. But she's also sometimes so confident, so strong, so determined. So full of hope. I'm only a pale reflection of her now. A doppelgänger."

"*Anne.*" Mr. Nussbaum has left his chair as if to approach her, but she stiffens.

"No, please, let me finish." She smears at a tear and sniffs. "I want to be a writer, Mr. Nussbaum. I do. That hasn't changed. And maybe I *do* have some talent, but I'm frightened that it's not enough. I think it must be my *duty* to tell this story, because why else did I live through it all? But what if I've become too weak or too cowardly to face what I must face?" She is crying now, struggling through her tears. "There were eight of us in hiding. Only Pim and I came back. It makes it all so tragic, and I don't want to write a tragic story. I want to tell the story of our lives, not our deaths."

Now she allows herself the comfort of Mr. Nussbaum's embrace. It is a flimsy thing. So little left of him but a wrap of bones, yet she leans into it. "That's a very profound sentiment, Anne," he says quietly.

Anne only shakes her head. Swallows her sobs. She feels vulnerable, maybe embarrassed, as if she's given away too much. Separating herself from the embrace as gently as she can, she glares down at the rug, trying to reassemble herself. Returning her pages to their cheap cardboard portfolio. "No. I'm not profound, Mr. Nussbaum," she insists. "In fact, most of the time I'm very shallow. Pim may be right. Who would really want to publish *any* of it?"

"Well," Mr. Nussbaum says. "*Actually,* Anne . . ."

Anne raises her head. "Actually?"

"Actually, I have someone who is very interested in reading what you've written. Someone with much more substantial connections to publishers than I have any longer. And not simply connections here in the Netherlands, but internationally. France, Britain. Even, I believe, America."

Anne looks back at him tentatively.

"Can you guess who?"

"*Can* I?"

"Cissy!" he declares.

Anne draws a deep breath. Cissy van Marxveldt. The inspiration for her diary.

"I didn't want to say anything, of course," Mr. Nussbaum tells her, "until I was sure it would turn out. I know you were disappointed that she missed your birthday party, but I wrote to her afterward about you and just received an answer this morning. She's agreed to my sending her some of your work."

"*Is that true?*" Anne feels a little light-headed. She feels dizzied by the good news.

"It is true, Anne," he is happy to inform her. "No *promises,* of course.

But I think she will be interested. As a writer she appreciates the writer's *struggle*, you know? An artist's life can be isolating. Always up in your own head. But you should know that you are not alone on your journey. I am here to help you. And whatever I *can* do, I *will* do."

A heartrending tenderness stings her, causing her eyes to go damp. "I don't understand, Mr. Nussbaum," she whispers. *"Why?"* Anne wants to know. "Why do you care *what* happens to me or all my cat scratches on the page?"

Mr. Nussbaum's smile turns ghostly. "Why? Because, Anne, my dear, you are all the future I have left."

On Friday night Dassah has prepared a Shabbat supper.

Wearing a shawl, she circles her hands above the lit candles and covers her eyes before reciting the blessing.

"Baruch ata Adonai, Eloheinu Melech ha-olam, asher kidshanu b'mitzvotav vitzivanu l'hadlik ner shel Shabbat."

Anne has closed her eyes as well. Can she still pray?

Blessed are you, God, ruler of the universe, who sanctified us with the commandment of lighting Shabbat candles.

When she opens her eyes, she can see Margot in the flickering candle glow, wearing the pullover and the yellow star.

The next morning there's a knock on the door early. Anne, still in her pajamas, hears it in her bedroom. She is lying on the bed and staring at the small crack in the ceiling plaster when Pim speaks Mr. Nussbaum's name.

"I'm so sorry to intrude like this, without any notice," Mr. Nussbaum is apologizing, his voice tightly stressed. "But when this summons arrived for me in the morning post, honestly, I didn't know where else to go."

"What is it?" Anne comes hurrying into the room, throwing on her robe. "Mr. Nussbaum. What's *happened*?"

The man blinks in her direction, but his eyes don't seem to focus properly. Anyway, it's Pim who answers the question, glaring at the paper in his hands. "Mr. Nussbaum is being deported, Anne," he replies with muted shock. "Back to Germany."

An hour passes, and after a few telephone calls, one of Pim's kameraden is sitting on the chesterfield sofa that Pim had delivered from a furniture maker in Utrecht. It is the lawyer Rosenzweig. He's a lanky sort of mensch in an ill-fitting suit. Bald head. A straight, narrow face and large, hooded eyes behind round spectacles. The tip of a purpled camp number peeks from the edge of his shirt cuff. He's holding the coffee cup that Dassah has passed him on his bony knees. Anne has dressed and pinned back her hair with a barrette. She lights a cigarette and watches the smoke trail upward. Mr. Attorney Rosenzweig has come armed with details. According to his story, there is an internment camp in eastern Netherlands outside Nijmegen. A former army barracks now known as Kamp Mariënbosch. There the government has rounded up German refugees, newly branded as enemy nationals, including, as it happens, any number of German-born Jews. Rosenzweig says it's part of a land grab that the Dutch Committee for Territorial Expansion is advancing under the slogan "Oostland—Ons Land." East land—Our land. They want to annex their fair portion of German terrain and purge the ethnic Bosch.

"And this," Pim starts to say, but he must pause to lick the dryness from his lips. "This," he repeats, "is where Werner is going to be sent? To a *camp* again?"

Mr. Rosenzweig can only nod. "That would be the current procedure."

Anne feels a chill on her cheek. Cold tears. "How could this *happen*?"

But even now Mr. Nussbaum attempts to console her. "Anne. This place. Mariënbosch, if that's the name. It's just," he says, "it's just a detention camp. It is not a death sentence."

"*No?*"

"No," Dassah agrees more sharply. "So there's no need to be dramatic."

Pim turns his head to Mr. Nussbaum, his expression heavy but direct. "When are you due to report, Werner?"

"Report? Uh. In two days."

"Then, Hadas, you are correct. We still have time to work this matter through. I'm sure that Mr. Rosenzweig knows people he can contact," Pim says.

A frown says maybe Mr. Rosenzweig is not so sure about that, but he goes along. "There may be," he's willing to venture. "I'll see if there's anything that can be done."

"Good. Good." Pim nods and gives Mr. Nussbaum a soldierly pat on the shoulder. "We'll make a plan to meet again tomorrow. Until then we can always pray."

Pray, Anne thinks. Pray. She doesn't say it, but she thinks it: She prayed at Birkenau. She prayed at Belsen. For deliverance. For forgiveness. And she is still waiting for both.

"It's all God's comedy, isn't it?" Mr. Nussbaum says. But after Mr. Attorney Rosenzweig has taken his leave, Mr. Nussbaum says to Pim, "Otto. May I speak with you briefly? In private?"

Pim looks uncertain but forces a smile. "Of course. Hadas?"

Dassah turns to Anne. "Anne. Come take a walk with me."

They walk in silence. A lorry whooshes past, sending up a cloud of grit and exhaust. Anne coughs. Stops and leans against the concrete stairwell. The stink of the canal fills her nostrils.

"What is it? What's the matter?" Dassah is asking her. "Are you sick?"

Her pulse is mounting. She begins counting backward from a hundred in her head, trying to calm herself, but it surprises her when Dassah places a hand on Anne's forehead and tells her to *breathe*. Just breathe. In. And out.

For once she follows Dassah's advice without resistance. Breathing in, then out, until the panic in her heart settles.

"What do you think will happen to Mr. Nussbaum?" Anne asks. *"Really."*

"You mean what do I think free of your father's optimism? I would *like* to believe that it's all a mistake. That Rosenzweig can intercede with the right people and set things straight. But I don't know."

"What do you think he's saying to Pim in private?"

"I don't know that either. But if I were to make a guess, I would say that they're probably talking about *you*."

"What do you mean?"

"I mean he thinks that Otto should send you to America. An opinion that he's voiced over and over again until he's worn out your father's ear. You have quite a stalwart ally in Werner Nussbaum, Anne."

Anne swallows. "He told me that he would send some of my writing to Cissy van Marxveldt. The writer. She's very famous. He says he thinks she'll like what I've done."

When they return, Mr. Nussbaum is just taking his leave. Anne steps outside the door with him. A gull squawks overhead, circling in the high breeze above the canal. Mr. Nussbaum takes Anne's hand and pats it with affection. He is smiling, but something slips in his expression. A bright star of pain lights his eyes. "Good-bye, my dear," he tells her. "Wish me luck."

"I do, Mr. Nussbaum."

"Remember what I told you." But when he bends forward to kiss the side of her cheek, he whispers a single sentence. "You are not alone."

The day is ripped by a downpour out of the east, drumming on the domes of sprouted umbrellas, peppering the canals, beating wild rhythms against the good Dutch window glass. But by nightfall the windows are open, with only a tepid drizzle remaining. Anne is sitting on her bed, smoking a Canadian cigarette, staring at the sheet of paper cranked into Miep's typewriter. She has been trying to rework parts of her diary, to put together pages for Mr. Nussbaum to send to Cissy, when the telephone rings. She hears Dassah pick it up and then hears her call Pim's name with pointed alarm. Quickly, Anne is up from her chair, opening her door. The lamp near the door is lit, and she watches her father accept the telephone. She feels an itch of heat at the back of her neck. With the receiver pressed to his ear, his expression sags, the color draining from his face. "When?" is all he asks. A single word, burdened with the quiet necessity of loss.

Out of her room, Anne is insistent. "What is it? What's *happened*?" she's asking.

Pim only raises his palm for quiet. "Yes, yes, I see. I see. Yes, thank you, Mrs. Kaplan." Only now does he lift his gaze to Anne, as if eyeing an animal caught in a snare. "I'll take care of any necessary arrangements."

"*What*, Pim? *What arrangements?*" Anne demands, feeling her voice thicken in her throat as her father rehooks the receiver.

Pim takes a half breath. "Annelein," he says with a kind of sunken grief. "That was Mr. Nussbaum's landlady. She was at home when she received a visit from the police." A small fortifying breath. "I'm sorry," he tells her, and then his Adam's apple bobs as he swallows the words. His gaze goes bleak. "But Werner Nussbaum is dead."

A dull thump, like the blow of a mallet. "Dead." She speaks the word aloud, her eyes going wet. "No . . ." She can't comprehend this. "No. I just saw him. *How?* How can he be *dead*?"

"His body was found afloat in the Brouwersgracht," Pim informs her. "He must have slipped. The heavy rain. He must have slipped and fallen into the canal."

But the lie embedded in Pim's explanation is fooling no one.

Anne feels the room tilt. And then she is falling, too.

31

THE QUESTION OF
FORGIVENESS

We are not so arrogant as to say before you, "We are
righteous and have not sinned." Surely, we have sinned.

—Yom Kippur liturgy

1946

LIBERATED NETHERLANDS

The gravestones are spread across the dark green meadowland. Some are chipped and cracked with age or vandalism. Broken slabs of slate lie abandoned on the ground, lost in the untrimmed grass. There are no avelim attending Mr. Nussbaum's burial. The rabbi has had to conscript men from his community just to assemble a full minyan of ten for prayers. Pim seems to know some of them. His comrades. He is not the only pallbearer whose tattoo is showing as they ferry the plain pine coffin over the cemetery's terrain. Anne stands with Dassah behind her, watching the coffin as it's lowered into the earth. The tears are hot on her skin as the kaddish is recited.

Perhaps she should be cross with him for taking his own life. Perhaps she should shed tears of anger as well as loss. But really she feels so drained of tears that all she can do is say good-bye. Good-bye to Mr. Nussbaum. Good-bye to her stalwart ally. Good-bye to the man who understood her as a writer, who wanted to promote her work. Good-bye to all that. Good-bye to the man who said that he depended on *her* future for hope but could not find hope in his own.

Another mourner has appeared. Margot stands with the minyan, her head shaven, flaunting the dirty yellow star on her pullover. All eyes are on the casket as it descends, except hers, which are fixed on Anne.

———

Leased Flat
The Herengracht
Amsterdam-Centrum
The Canal Ring

At the flat, Anne dips her hands into the basin of water on the sideboard by the door, just as if she really could be cleansed of the dead. Dassah has prepared food and set it out on the table with the snow-white linen. The Meal of Condolence. But Anne has no appetite. She sits smoking on the chesterfield. She hears the crush of leather as someone sits beside her. It is the rabbi. Souza is his name. He wears a dark serge suit and reveals a plain black satin yarmulke when he removes a roll-brimmed fedora. He's young, maybe in his middle thirties, gaunt, with a clean-shaven face. He looks calm, a man who is comfortable inside his own skin. Anne catches a glance from Dassah as her stepmother dishes out a plate of holishkes for one of the pallbearers.

"I'm sorry, Rabbi," Anne tells him firmly.

The rabbi lifts his eyebrows. "Pardon me? Sorry for what?"

"I'm sorry, but you're about to waste your time with me."

A small shrug. "Well. Kind of you to say so, Anne, if I may call you by your given name. But I don't know what you mean."

"I know that my stepmother is used to getting her way. I'm sure you think you're doing her a favor."

"You're sure?"

"I don't need to be tended to."

He pauses for an instant and sets his plate on the mahogany coffee table. "Perhaps your stepmother is worried about you?"

A short breath escapes her. "That's a laugh."

"You resent her concern?"

"You could say that," Anne replies, staring at the ember of her cigarette.

"I take it that you were close to Mr. Nussbaum, may his name be a blessing."

"I don't want to talk about him."

"No?"

"Maybe you're not aware, Rabbi. Didn't anyone tell you the truth about what happened? He jumped into a canal. He committed suicide. Isn't that a sin?"

"It is, but who can really know what happened?"

"He was going to be deported back to Germany. You don't need to *guess* what was going through his head."

The rabbi shrugs lightly. "One might consider all possibilities, I suppose. You're feeling hurt, Anne?" he wonders. "Hurt by him?"

She swallows. "'Hurt' is not the word."

"Abandoned?"

She breathes in deeply. "Please. I don't want to talk about this."

"Even though it was you who started the conversation? It might help to talk, don't you think? I think at heart he was a very good man."

But this sets Anne's teeth on edge. "I thought so, too, Rabbi. He encouraged me to write. He said he wanted to see my work published. And yet he decided to drown himself instead." She says this and feels a terrible swell of guilt. "I'm sorry, I must sound very selfish. I *am* very selfish. If you don't believe me, just ask anyone. Ask my stepmother. Ask my father. *Ask them.* They'll tell you."

But the rabbi does not seem to be interested in asking anyone such a question. He removes a packet of cheap Dutch cigarettes from his jacket and lights one from the brass table lighter. "We knew each other, Werner and I," he says. "In Auschwitz."

Anne raises her eyes at the mention of the name.

The rabbi shrugs. "Four months I spent in that place." The smoke he expels merges with Anne's and hangs heavily above them. "We were on the same labor Kommando once, digging drainage ditches outside the wire. When I fell, it was Werner Nussbaum who stood me back on my feet. Saved me from the lash of the Kapo. Shared his bread with me. So I *do* know something about the man and the content of his heart."

"I'm sorry," Anne says, tasting shame. "I'm sorry, no one told me."

"No need to apologize. It was a place of cruelty. I don't have to explain that to you. But it was also a place of deep humanity." He takes in smoke and then releases it. "May I ask you, Anne? Are you also angry with your father?"

Anne stiffens. Says nothing.

"I think you must be," the rabbi tells her. "Suffering through such hell. Your father should have protected you, correct? I mean, isn't that what fathers are for? So you blame him."

"Not just him," Anne answers tightly.

"Oh, yes." He nods. "Yes, yes. Would you be surprised if I told you that I, too, know something about assigning blame?" the rabbi wonders. "I lost my wife and my two brothers, zekher kadosh livrakha. My brothers to Mauthausen. My wife to the gas straight off the train into Birkenau, because she was pregnant."

Anne is sobered by this. The rabbi breathes out smoke.

"Yet *you* survived," says Anne.

"I did," the rabbi admits.

"Why?"

"I don't know."

"You think it was God?"

"Maybe."

"You're a rabbi."

"Many rabbis died. Most did."

"Maybe God just overlooked you."

"You think God was making the decisions at Auschwitz?"

"You think he wasn't? Isn't he the Master of the Universe?"

"I can't blame the gas chambers on God," he says. "It was men who built them. Men who operated them."

"So you don't think that there was a *reason* that *you* survived? When all those other rabbis didn't? You don't think it was because there was something important you had yet to do?"

"Perhaps it was to talk with you."

Anne shakes her head. "That's not funny."

"It wasn't meant as a joke, Anne. How should I know? I would like to *think* that God saved me. *Me,* in particular, Armin Souza, for an unseen purpose. It's very flattering. But I have no proof that my survival wasn't utterly random."

"Do you know why *I* lived?" she asks.

"Are you going to tell me?"

"No. I'm asking a question. What if it was a mistake? What if God picked the wrong Frank girl?"

"Again, I cannot explain his thinking. I cannot comprehend his purposes. It's not for us to know. But what I *can* tell you is this: Now that you have survived, you have a duty."

"To the dead," she says.

"No. To the living. To yourself. To *you*. Your family dies, and you blame *them* for dying. You blame God, you blame your father, you blame yourself. I *know*. But you cannot keep it up. You cannot live on rage or grief. As much as you'd like to believe it's possible, it is not. You cannot live with the joy draining out of every day that passes. You survived the camps? Thank God. Now you must survive the rest of your life. More than survive. You must learn happiness, Anne. You must learn forgiveness."

Anne smokes, says nothing for a moment, until, "My sister," she says. "Her name was Margot. She wanted to make aliyah. She wanted to become a maternity nurse and deliver babies in the promised land."

"And you thought that was . . . what? Admirable? Ridiculous?"

"Both, maybe," she says. "I don't know. It's just another reason that she should have been allowed to live."

"Instead of you?"

Anne has no reply.

"I would have traded *my* life for that of my wife," he says. "If I could have snapped my fingers or clapped my hands. I would have done it. How much simpler would it be to be dead. To be relieved of the responsibility of carrying on. But that's not the way of the world, Anne. As you must know. Others die. We live. The best we can hope for is to make something of ourselves. To help others. To resist anger and fear and guilt and to move forward with the business of living."

"But what . . ." Anne swallows. She stares into the smoke of her cigarette. "What if I can't *do* that, Rabbi? Get on with the business of living? You make it sound like an easy choice."

"Have I?" the rabbi asks. "Then I apologize. It *is* a choice," he says.

"But I never intended to make it sound easy." He crushes out his cigarette. "When I think of the future, I do my best to compromise. It shall be as God wills *and* what we make of God's will." Rabbi Souza blinks slowly. "Are you familiar, Anne, with the notion of tikkun olam?"

Anne says nothing.

"Tikkun olam," the rabbi repeats. "It's something of a mystery. But I have come to define its meaning as 'repairing the world.'"

Anne shakes her head. "How is such a thing possible?"

"Repairing the world is a Jewish obligation," the rabbi says. "How? That's the question we must all ask and answer for ourselves, Anne. This much, though, I can say: We must learn to conquer our anger. We must put our faith in the sheer beauty of God's creation and practice repentance and forgiveness. Even if we don't want to. Even if we don't feel it in our hearts. *Especially* then. It is our duty to repair the damage we have done and therefore repair the damage done to us."

Anne eyes her smoldering cigarette, the ember glowing red. Repairing the world? She is unwilling to reveal it, but the rabbi's words have pierced her in an unexpected way. And some hidden part of her responds with a soupçon of hope.

That night she dreams of Belsen, and there Margot is waiting for her. They are spooned together on the filthy pallet, desiccated by typhus. Her sister coughing away the last moments of her life.

"Forgive me," Anne whispers. "Please, forgive me," she begs.

32

TRUTH

The truth is a heavy burden that few care to carry.

—Jewish proverb

1946

LIBERATED NETHERLANDS

Anne dashes around to the landing and up the steps, unlatches the bookshelf, and pushes it aside to enter the Achterhuis. She is pulling off her shoes so the squeak of the floorboards won't give her away. The anonymous men in dark suits have appeared once again and have been admitted into the private office. She can already hear the indistinct murmur of voices below her as she lies down and presses her ear to the floor so she can listen in. Margot appears beside her, her ear pressed to the floor as well. Her Kazetnik rags crawling with lice, she complains urgently, *Anne, I can't hear them. I can't hear them. What are they saying?*

Anne's eyes have gone wet with the shock of rage that has gripped her by the heart. "They're *saying*," she whispers hotly, "that our father is a collaborator."

For now the men in the dark suits have finished. But as Pim sees them off at the top of the stairs, Anne slips into the private office and fills one of the chairs, the cushion still warm. When Pim returns to find her there, he stops dead. His breath shortens. Maybe the soldier in him has just detected an ambush. "Anne?" He speaks guardedly. "Anne, what's wrong?"

"I heard everything," she tells him, staring blankly.

Pim pauses. "And what does that mean, exactly? You heard *everything*?"

"You know what it means," she insists. "I heard the *truth*, Pim. I was upstairs with my ear to the floor, and I heard the truth. All this time you pretended that it was just a simple business matter. A bureaucratic problem."

"And it always was."

"I was afraid they were going to deport you because you were German, but that was never the reason they were here, was it, Pim? They were here because you were selling goods to the German Wehrmacht."

Pim swallows. After quietly closing the office door, he sits in his padded chair with a careful creak of leather, as if he might be sitting on a land mine to keep it from exploding. His eyes dampen. "Anne..." he whispers. A plea.

"How *could* you, Pim?"

Her father draws a shallow breath and holds it as he repeats her name. "Anne, please. You must try to understand. It was wartime."

"How can that be any kind of *justification*? You. A Jew. *A Jew!* Yet you profited by selling to the *murderers of our people,* Pim! The murderers of our neighbors. Of our family!"

"*Anne,* don't say something you'll be unable to take back," Pim warns her bleakly. "The truth is that this sort of transaction was commonplace. The occupation authority was in control and had an army to supply. If they were interested in doing business with your company, then you simply accepted their price concessions and put your signature on the contracts. We were given no alternative. It was either supply them or be shut down. And we couldn't afford *that* possibility," he says thickly. "Business was terrible. Nonexistent. We *needed* the Wehrmacht's money coming in—*please, can't you understand that?* Maybe it was just a trickle, but it was enough to buy food to feed us in hiding."

But Anne's anger is not slackened. "You made us *war profiteers,* Pim. *Criminals.* Taking money from those who planned to slaughter us. And now the government's going to put us on the list for *deportation.*"

"*No,* Anne."

"They did Mr. Nussbaum. And he was *innocent*! Of *any* crime."

"Werner Nussbaum made his *own* troubles," Pim insists heatedly. "I warned him to simply *pay the taxes,* as abhorrent as they might be, and not to make unnecessary enemies. But he was stubborn. He was stubborn from the day I met him in the barracks block, and he wouldn't listen."

"At least he was true to his own *convictions*."

"Did I make a *mistake,* Anne?" Pim bursts out, his ears pinking with anger. "*Perhaps I did!* But at that critical moment, I believed that what I was doing was best for us *all*. Selling the Wehrmacht pectin? A few hundred barrels of spices? I believed I was *protecting* us, Anne. And if I was wrong—if that was a *sin*—I cannot change that now. Our regrets may be strong in our hearts, but none of them are strong enough to alter the past."

"And did *Mummy* know?" she asks sharply.

Her father stops. Stares before he answers simply, "I never kept secrets from your mother."

A sharp knock at the door, and in steps Dassah, a scolding expression clamped onto her face, one that she seldom wears at work. "What is going *on* here? We can hear your voices raised all the way in the front office."

"What about *her*?" Anne demands. "I don't suppose you keep secrets from *her* either. Does *she* know all about your dealings with the mof assassins?"

For once Anne seems to have actually taken Dassah by surprise. Her stepmother blanches. Steps in and quickly secures the door behind her. "You told her this?" she asks Pim pointedly.

"Hadas, please. No need for you to tangle yourself up."

"No? I think there's every need," says Dassah.

"Daughter," Pim says, and Anne shouts back.

"*Don't call me that!* I don't want to be your daughter any longer. Don't you understand that? I'm not your daughter any longer!"

If she had pulled out a dagger and plunged it into his heart, Pim could not look any more horrified. His face goes white.

"*Get out,*" Dassah tells her in a lethal tone. "*Get out of here.* You want to be free? Then go! *Be* free. But don't you dare say another word."

But before Anne can react, she hears a quick knock and the door pops open a crack, just wide enough for Miep to stick her head into the space. "I'm sorry for the interruption," she says. "But, Anne, there's a lady here to see you."

"A *lady*?" Anne's eyes are sharp.

"Yes. I think you should see her."

With her heart still thumping, Anne abandons her father and follows Miep out into the front office. There, standing by the door, is a woman, tall and thin with a swanlike neck. Her hair is a dark bob, peppered with gray, and she is wearing a long beige raincoat, her right hand tucked into the pocket. Her eyes smile, though there is a weariness in them. "*Ah*. You must be Anne," she decides, and steps forward. "I'm Setske Beek-de Haan," she says. "Though I suppose you might know me better by my pen name. Cissy van Marxveldt."

33

ATONEMENT

Rebuild the ancient ruins and lay the foundations for ages to come; you will be called the "repairer of the breach" and the "restorer of streets to dwell in."

—Isaiah 58:12

1946

Café Wildschut
Roelof Hartplein
Amsterdam-Zuid

LIBERATED NETHERLANDS

Sunlight spreads across the square, gleaming down the length of the tram power lines suspended over the street. The rose-brick building forms an elegant L.

Is this God's hand? Could it be that after such a horrendous row with Pim, God has decided to give her a way out? Why? Perhaps she's simply worn him down. Perhaps the Master of the Universe is simply so sick of hearing her kvetch that he's decided to step in by sending her this angel in the form of Cissy van Marxveldt. *Could* it *be*? Her heart is thumping.

"Mrs. Beek," Anne starts to say.

"No—please—call me Cissy."

"Cissy," Anne says. "I don't know what to say. Mr. Nussbaum said you were friends. But honestly. Honestly, I sometimes wondered if that was just a dream."

Cissy breathes a sigh. "I'm so saddened by the loss of our friend Werner," she tells Anne. "What a *heartache* that it should end for him so. I know that I missed his funeral. I intended to be there, but when the time came, I simply could not bring myself to . . ." Her words trail off. "He was a very kind man. There was a time before the war that Werner was quite encouraging to me. I often sent him drafts of my work, and he was always very gentle. Very *candid* in his assessments, mind you." She smiles. "He didn't suffer any laziness or half efforts. But he was always very gentle. I think he felt most useful to the world when he was working with writers. Writers like myself at times, who'd already experienced a modicum of success, but most especially with the young and talented variety who were just starting out." Cissy says this and then looks into Anne's face. "He thought you were quite the find, Anne."

This takes Anne aback. Perhaps up until this moment only half of her believed that Mr. Nussbaum's encouragements were real. Her other half suspected that they were born out of pity or out of his comradeship with Pim. But to have proof that he truly *was* discussing her with one of Anne's literary heroines . . . well, it's absolutely *startling*.

"He was always full of superlatives when it came to you. So much so that, to be perfectly truthful," Cissy tells her, "I had my doubts. How could such a young girl possibly possess the necessary maturity to produce the level of work he was describing? I thought he *must* be exaggerating. Until I read your pages," she says.

Anne tilts her head. "My pages?"

"Yes. From your diary." Picking up her purse, Cissy opens it in her lap. Anne watches her withdraw a kraft paper envelope bearing an Amsterdam postmark, then watches her open it and remove the contents. Anne gazes with blank shock at the stack of neatly typed pages Cissy is holding. "This passage especially struck me: 'In spite of everything I still believe that people are really good at heart. I simply can't build up my hopes on a foundation consisting of confusion, misery, and death. I see the world gradually being turned into a wilderness, I hear the ever approaching thunder, which will destroy us too, I can feel the sufferings of millions and yet, if I look up into the heavens, I think that it will all come right, that this cruelty too will end, and that peace and tranquility will return again.'" Cissy looks up and expels a small sigh. "Astonishing. Wonderful, and terrifying, and astonishing."

"*Where?*" Anne practically gasps. "Where did you *get* this?"

"Where?" A half smile, mildly perplexed. "What do you mean?"

"Who gave you these pages?"

"Well, they came in the post. From your stepmother. Hadassah is her name, isn't it?"

Anne can barely speak. "Yes," is all she can manage.

"She wrote me a note explaining that Werner had given her my postal address and asked her to forward a sample for me to read."

Anne says nothing more, though she can feel her pulse in her throat.

Cissy leans over and brushes the envelope with her fingertips. "Now I must ask you. The events you describe in these pages, they are all perfectly true?"

Anne blinks. "Yes," she answers.

"This is your diary of life, as you recorded it. Nothing imaginary added."

"Nothing," she answers.

"*Good.*" Cissy takes a breath of satisfaction. "Good, because it must remain what it is and nothing more. The diary of a girl trapped by the darkest of circumstances. But also the diary of a girl who rises above the danger," she says, "even as it overcomes her."

Anne can only stare. Her eyes have gone damp.

"Werner was right. Your work is a treasure, Anne." Cissy smiles gently. "Now. Let's discuss a plan. Shall we? As luck would have it, I've recently come in contact with a very eclectic publisher from overseas," she says. "They specialize in youthful literature, and I think that they might be quite interested in you."

"You said 'overseas'?"

"Yes, an American firm."

Anne feels her heart thump.

"One of the senior editors expressed an interest in having some of my books translated into English," Cissy tells her. "But that can wait. Because with your permission, Anne, I'd like to send him this typescript of your diary. What do you think?"

———

Leased Flat
The Herengracht
Amsterdam-Centrum
The Canal Ring

She finds Pim napping over his newspaper in the Viennese wingback. His spectacles have slipped down onto the bridge of his nose, the hair at his temples has gone quite white, and his lips flutter mildly with a cooing snore. She forgets sometimes that he is aging.

In the kitchen she finds Dassah washing up after the midday meal, a large cast-iron soup pot clunking against the side of the sink. Dassah turns her head. "So. She has returned."

"You sent Cissy my pages," Anne says.

"You make that sound like a crime, Anne. Isn't it what you wanted? Isn't that what Werner promised he'd do?"

"How do you know *what* Mr. Nussbaum promised me about anything?"

"Because he *told* me, Anne. How else? He told me the day before he drowned himself in the canal." A shrug as she scours the bottom of the soup pot. "It was simple enough. He gave me the woman's address. I borrowed the pages from your room for an afternoon, retyped them at the office, and dropped them into the post."

Anne swallows. *"Why?"*

"Ah. You don't enjoy feeling indebted to me, I suppose."

"All I asked you is *why?* You've always made it clear how much you despise me."

"Actually, you have that the wrong way around. It's *Anne Frank* who's always made it clear that I am despised by *her*. But no matter. I do what I think is best. What I think is best for *me*, best for your *father*, and best for *you*." She pulls the pot out of the sink and sets it down to dry it with a dish towel. "This diary of yours. I knew that Otto had it in his possession. I never read a word of it at the time, mind you, but I didn't have to in order to see that it was an anchor chain around your father's neck, pulling him down. I can recall him clutching the small plaid book as if he were clutching his own heart in his hands. He couldn't accept that the girl in its pages was gone. Which is why he couldn't give it up, even though it tortured him to keep it from you. He simply *couldn't* relinquish that memory. But then came the day his daughter was fished from a canal," she says. "And I thought enough is enough. He could not keep it from you any longer without his own guilt eating him alive."

Anne frowns. "You're saying it was *you* who convinced him to give it back to me?"

"Me? I don't convince your father of anything, Anne. He agreed because he knew it was the right thing to do. And also . . . well, he might have hoped to distract you. To silence your *constant* pestering about America. At least for a while. At least so he could sleep a night or two in peace." She says this before a heavy, apprehensive voice comes from behind them.

"What's going *on* here?" Pim wants to know.

Dassah's eyes flick from him to Anne. "All right. No more of this war between the two of you," she says. "Sit down at the table, please, *both* of you. We are going to either untie this knot or cut it."

Cigarette smoke drifts through the sepia-colored afternoon light slanting through the windows. Around the table an embattled hour has passed. But finally it comes down to *this* in Pim's opinion: "You decided you're finished with Amsterdam. With your home here. With your family and your friends. With me. With everything. And you intend to abandon your past and go to America in order to *publish* the most intimate memories of people who are passed, so that anyone—Jews, not Jews, taxi drivers, rubbish collectors, grocery clerks, housewives, and schoolgirls—can pick up a copy for a few pennies and pass judgment on us all. All our foibles and shortcomings. All our petty feuds and human failings. All of it. On public display."

"Otto—" Dassah says, but Pim cuts her off.

"No. *Please,* Hadas. I'm speaking to my daughter directly because, like it or not, you *are* still my daughter, Annelies, and will always be so. Have I summed up the situation correctly?" he wants to know. "Those are your intentions?"

Anne sits. Her hands clenched together in her lap. Her back straight. "Yes," she replies without blinking. "Those are my intentions."

Pim glares silently, as if the entirety of the universe is balled up in this moment. His hands resting in fists on the tablecloth. His back straight as well. His eyes like caves. "Well, then. Who am I to stop you?" he says. "*No one.* Just an old man whose judgment and opinion have lost their value." Standing slowly, his unbuttoned waistcoat hanging open, his necktie slightly askew, he seems to have aged a decade in a moment. "I think I require some air," he informs them.

Dassah gives Anne a look from across the table. It's a pointed look, even slightly pained, but for once it is devoid of criticism. Then she stands without a further word and follows Pim to the door. Anne watches them. Pim buttoning his waistcoat, slipping on his old tweed jacket and brown fedora from the hall tree. Helping Dassah into her cardigan, then bending forward to allow her to straighten his necktie and brush a bit of lint from his shoulders. The door opens. Light floods the threshold. And then the door closes and they are gone.

So, says Margot, who has appeared in the chair beside Anne, clad in her tattered Judenstern weeds. *Now you are free?*

That night Anne sits on her bed, her red tartan diary in her hand, tracing the pattern of the plaid cover with her fingertip, when she recognizes the knock at her door.

"Come in, Pim," she tells him.

He opens the door and pokes in his head. "Good night, daughter," he says mournfully. "I hope you won't stay up too late."

"Pim," she says. "Wait."

He hesitates but then pushes open the door just far enough to step in.

"Before he died . . ." Anne says. "Before he died, Mr. Nussbaum told me that I should ask you about the boy in your barracks block at Auschwitz. Do you know who he was talking about?"

Again Pim hesitates. But he slips his hands into the pockets of his dressing gown. "What exactly did Werner tell you?"

"Only that I should ask you about him. He said if I wanted to understand my father, I should ask him about the boy in Auschwitz who called him Papa."

Pim remains silent.

"Please, Pim. Tell me. I want to understand."

A long breath, in and out, as if resurrecting such a memory is a feat of heavy labor. Glancing to the floor, he shakes his head. "He was alone at Auschwitz, you see. This lad. Not much older than Peter, but he had no one with him. No one at all." Then his eyes rise to hers, and he swallows. "In the best way I could," he says, "I tried to look after the boy. I remember that the others around us, all they could *talk* about was *food*. Nothing but food, day and night, and so I said to him that we must get away from such talk or else go insane. Instead we talked of music. The great symphonies, the great composers. He was a fervent fan of the classical composers, the boy. In particular Schubert. It became a routine between us. Whenever we could, we would recall the melodies of our favorite pieces. I think we both began to depend on it, really. Then one evening in the barracks, I asked him. I asked him if he would consider calling me Papa." Pim lifts his eyebrows over this memory, obviously returning to the barracks, returning to the moment in his mind. "I suppose I'd been thinking of it for some time, but it stunned me a bit that I actually had—if you'll pardon the expression—that I actually had the chutzpah to ask him. He must have been a bit stunned, too, this young man, because at first he resisted. He said that he was indebted to me but had to point out that he already *had* a papa who was still very much *alive* in hiding." A small shrug. "So I tried to explain. I tried to explain to him," says Pim, "that I was a man who *must* have someone to call him Papa, or else . . . or else I wouldn't know who I was any longer."

Anne feels her eyes dampen. "And did he?"

"Did he?"

"Call you Papa?"

"He did. He called me Papa Frank till the day we parted after the liberation."

Anne looks at Pim, says nothing.

"I suppose," Pim tells her, "that Werner hoped this story would help you understand how difficult it is for me, a man of my age, to alter the image of himself inside his own head. Even when that image has been obviously proved false." He swallows, his eyes wetting brightly. "I *failed* you, Anne. I could not protect you. I could not be *your* papa, the papa you needed when you were suffering at Birkenau. Or the papa who could rescue you and your sister from Bergen-Belsen. It's a terrible thing," he says, and shakes his head. "A terrible thing when a man who has defined himself for so long in a certain way finds that he is powerless to protect the very ones who have loved and trusted him the most. The ones who *depended* on him the most. His own *family*," he says, swallowing back his sorrow. "I know that you have been enraged by the fact that I engaged in commerce with the enemy. And perhaps with good reason. But please, daughter, try to understand that regardless of my choices, good or bad, I did what I did," he says, "sacrificing my own principles to keep us all alive and fed." Removing his handkerchief from the pocket of his robe, he dabs at his eyes. "All I've ever hoped for, Anne. Since you and I were reunited. Since you and I survived. All I've ever hoped is that you would understand that and forgive me my weaknesses."

A silence. Anne lightly hugs her diary to her chest, and she feels a tear on her cheek. "So *now,* Pim," she decides, "now it is *my* turn to tell *you* a story." She breathes in. "It's the story of a girl who once believed that God only wished for people to be *happy,* a girl who believed that if a person had courage and faith, then any hardship could be overcome. A girl who believed that despite all the evidence to the contrary, people were *good at heart.*"

"Yes." Pim nods. "I think I know that girl."

But Anne only shakes her head. "She's dead, Pim. That girl? She didn't survive."

"But how can that be true, meisje? How can that be true? I look at you and see such spirit. Such resolve. You have been so badly hurt. So unfairly scarred, yes. I know that you think I've been blind to what has happened to you. *Willfully* so, and maybe I've pretended to be," he admits. "But really, I'm not so foolish as to imagine that you could *possibly* be the same girl I recall as a child. The same girl who called me in to hear her prayers, even if sometimes I might have convinced myself otherwise. Or *wished* to do so. And if you believe that I have tried to trap you in your former childhood in order to avoid having to face my own failings, then I won't lie and say that there is no truth in that. But it is only a partial truth," he says, wadding his handkerchief into a ball. "I am a man who must feel useful. I am a man who thinks he can understand the workings of the world. But I am baffled by my own daughter. I want so desperately to help her. To be useful to her. But I don't know how."

"If you don't know how, Pim," Anne says, her eyes heavy, "then perhaps you should ask her. Perhaps you should simply ask *her.*"

Pim's gaze goes level as he inhales a long breath. "So perhaps I will." His eyes sharpen. With pain? With fear over the answer to the question he has not yet asked. "How, Anne? How can I be useful to my daughter?"

"You can let her go, Pim," his daughter replies. "Just that. You can let her go."

~~~

The day is bright. Outside, the smell of wood smoke hangs heavily in the air. Up in the Achterhuis, Anne stares out the window of the attic, stroking Mouschi, who is a ball in her lap. The leaves of the chestnut tree are turning.

Tomorrow is Yom Kippur, says Margot, kneeling beside Anne in her lice-infested rags.

"Yes," Anne says, listening to the cat's purr.

"Are you going to temple?"

"You think I should?"

You have to answer that question for yourself, Anne.

"Do you think I should fast?"

It's not for me to decide.

"Hunger pangs are something I'm familiar with," Anne points out. "You don't think I've fasted enough for one lifetime?"

I think you should do what you believe is best.

"Since when?"

Since always.

"You think I must make atonement?"

Silence. Anne looks over at her sister, but her sister is gone. There's a squeak of wood from below as Pim climbs the ladder from the landing and steps into the attic behind her. Anne looks at him, hugging the cat. He is dressed in his overcoat, his fedora raked to one side of his head. He glances about the shabby room. "It's so drafty up here, daughter," he points out. "Don't you feel it?"

Anne does not answer this question, however. "Dassah wouldn't say where you'd gone."

Pim draws a breath and expels it. "I was attending to some

business," he tells her. "You may wish to know that our business practices have been cleared by the government. I've received a letter from the Institute for Enemy Property Management that serves as a clean bill of health."

Anne looks up but says nothing. Pim is obviously surprised by her silence.

"Nothing to say? I imagined you would have a stronger reaction to this news," her father points out. "All restrictions on the business—on us—have been *lifted*. All fears of deportation over. I thought you would be relieved."

"Tomorrow is Yom Kippur," she tells him.

"It is," Pim agrees.

"Are you going to temple with Dassah?"

"I am."

"Are you going to fast?"

"We are. She and I."

"Are you going to make atonement?" Anne asks her father.

"As a Jew, what else can I do?" he asks, and draws an elongated kraft envelope from inside his coat pocket.

"What's that?" she asks him.

He frowns thoughtfully as he considers the envelope, tapping it against his fingers. "It's the result of much work by many people in a short period of time."

Anne grips the cat hard enough to elicit a mewing complaint.

"It's what is known as an affidavit in lieu of a passport," he says of the envelope, his eyes going bright with tears. "And it will permit entry into the United States by one Miss Annelies Marie Frank."

Anne is stunned. The tears come, freely drenching her cheeks as she still grips the cat.

"I understand dreams, Anneke," her father tells her. "Youth does not have the monopoly on hope." And then he asks thickly, "So you can forgive an old man?"

"*Pim,*" she breathes, but the tears get the better of her. A sob chokes her, and, dropping the cat, she runs to him, just as she did before the war, when she was still a girl favored by God.

Pim whispers, "You are a brave young woman, meisje, who's been unjustly brutalized by forces far beyond your control. My only prayer is that if you can forgive me, perhaps you can begin to forgive the world as well. And, more important, forgive yourself."

But even before she opens her eyes, Anne knows that she will see Margot there. Waiting. Waiting for her to atone.

34

THE DIARY OF A YOUNG GIRL

Seriously, though, ten years after the war people would find it very amusing to read how we lived, what we ate and what we talked about as Jews in hiding.

—Anne Frank,
from her diary,
29 March 1944

1961

Waverly Place and Mercer Street
Greenwich Village

NEW YORK CITY

Dear Miss Frank,

I think I must be one of your biggest fans. I've read "The Diary of a Young Girl" six times! The library at my school only has one copy of it, and I keep checking it out over and over again. Sometimes, though, Mrs. Mosley (our librarian) says I should give somebody else a chance to read it, and makes me check out a Nancy Drew instead, which is O.K. I like Nancy Drew books, but I like your book better. You are so smart, and Nancy Drew has never had to escape Nazis or hide in a secret annex with nothing very good to eat.

Maybe this isn't nice to tell you, but once after somebody else had checked out your book, I found mean things written in the margins about Jewish people. If it had been in pencil, I would have just erased it, but it was in pen, so I had to scratch it out. This got me in trouble with my Granny Flynn, because she saw me scratching it out and said I should NEVER write with a pen in a library book for ANY reason. But I still think I did the right thing. I hope you will think so too.

Warm regards,

Edwina C. Buford (Winnie)

P.S.—Grampa Flynn says that he doubts your whole story is really true. He says writers like to make things up. But I told him that I think it is ALL true. It is, isn't it?

Dear Winnie,

It made me very happy to receive your letter.
You are so kind to have checked out my book so
many times. And there is certainly nothing
wrong with reading Nancy Drew either. Though I
will have to admit that I read several Nancy
Drew books when I first came to America and
couldn't understand what the heck was
happening! That was probably because I was
still so new to this country and never felt
like I understood what the heck was happening
inside or outside of the books I was reading.

And as far as what mean things people choose
to think about Jews, I'm sorry to say that
there's nothing very new in that. Though I
believe you are quite brave to try to do
something about it. I can't tell you if it's
worth getting in trouble with your grandma over
it, though. That will have to be your decision.

Your friend,

Anne Frank

P.S.: I am sending you an autographed copy of
"The Diary" in the mail. This way you'll never
have to borrow it from the library again. And
you can assure your grandpa, or anyone who asks
you, that it is true. All of it is true.

Dear Miss Frank,

*My name is Sally Schneider, and I am in the sixth grade
at William Howard Taft Elementary School. (We just call
it "Taft.") I am a very big fan of your diary, but I feel bad
sometimes, because my last name is Schneider, which is
German. My grandmother came from Germany before*

*World War II, but I still feel sorry for what the Germans
did to your Jewish people. My mom says it's none of our
business what happened in Europe and that I should be
proud of my German heritage. Which I am. There's a
festival every fall (called Oktoberfest), and I always help my
nana make the "Baumkuchen." She won't talk about World
War II or Germany at all, because she says she is a good
American now. Which she is. But I still felt sad reading
your book, although I also really liked it. It's confusing,
isn't it?*

*I hope you are happy being an American now too.
Maybe one day we can meet if you ever visit Cincinnati
(Ohio).*

Yours truly,

Sally Schneider

Dear Sally,

It IS confusing. Yes! But you don't need to
feel bad because you are from German stock. It
took me quite a long time, I'll confess, but I
can honestly say I am no longer angry with the
Germans simply for being German. And I could
never think of blaming you for your ancestry.
That is the same thing the Nazis did to the
Jews, blamed children for the blood that flowed
in their veins.

I have to disagree with your mom, however, if
you don't mind. What happens in the world is
everybody's business, especially when it comes
to attempting to murder an entire people.

Thank you for sending me your letter, Sally.
I hope I have explained how I feel on the
subjects you broached. I am happy being an

American now, though I often miss being a "Niederlander" in Amsterdam.

Enjoy your time at "Taft."

Anne Frank

Dear Miss Frank,

Our teacher gave us the assignment to write to our favorite author, so of course I picked you! All the girls in my class have read your diary, and we all really, really love it!

My mom got me "The Diary of a Young Girl" for my birthday, and I must have read it ten times already. And every time I finish it, it makes me feel good, even though what happened to you is very, very sorrowful.

Thank you for letting us read about your life during World War II. My teacher says you must have been very courageous, and I agree!

Your fan,

Judy Borstein

Township Middle School
Morristown, New Jersey

Dear Judy,

Thank you for your lovely letter. It was very kind of you to pick me as your favorite author. I'm very honored and happy that you are a fan of my diary. Is it okay that it makes you a little sad after you finish it? I think it should. I think it should make everyone a little sad.

Sincerely,

Anne Frank

Dear Miss Anne Frank,

We both have the same name! Though I am Presbyterian, and my last name is "French." Also, I don't have an "e" on the end of my first name, which is "Ann." I am in the seventh grade at Hillbrook Junior High School in Ft. Clarkson, Michigan. My English teacher, Mrs. Parsons, gave me "The Diary of a Young Girl" to read, because she said she thought I could "handle it." (Though she says I'm still not old enough to read any of your other books yet.) Anyway, I read your diary, and she was correct! I could handle it, though it made me cry sometimes. It was so good and so sad at the same time. But I loved it so much that I have read it over and over again! Though I'm really sorry to hear that your sister and mom died after your diary ended.

My mom died too. It happened last winter, though my mom died in a car accident coming home from the grocery, which I know is so different than what happened to yours. I still miss her so much, sometimes in the middle of the day, or even when I'm playing volleyball in gym class. It just comes over me for no reason. It's hard to explain. But somehow your book has made me feel better. Thank you for writing it.

Best wishes,

Ann French

Dear Ann (without an "e")

Thank you for sending your kind words. I'm very touched by them. I'm so very sorry to hear your mother passed away. You are correct; mine did, too, when I was fifteen. She died in a concentration camp the Nazis ran in Poland. That was a long time ago, but I still miss her. I'm sure I will always miss her. Things do, however, become easier, even if the pain of missing her never goes away, which I doubt it ever will. At least it has not yet for me.

I hope you like the autographed copy of "The
Diary" that I am sending you. I wrote you a note
on the title page.

All my best and heartfelt wishes,

Anne (<u>with</u> an "e")

Dear Miss Frank,

*Even though I am a teenager now (my birthday was last
week), I still loved reading your "Diary of a Young Girl,"
even if my sister (who is fifteen) teased me. She says she's
reading "ADULT" books now, not "SEVENTH-GRADE
STUFF." But if you ask me, I would rather read your book a
hundred times, instead of "Lord of the Flies" once.*

*I did get into an argument with my brother, though, about
your book. (He's seventeen, and keeps telling our mom that
he's going to join the Army instead of going to college, which
makes Mom crazy!) But he says that the Jews should have
fought back when the Nazis came for them. He says HE
would have fought back, why didn't the Jews? I told him that
they were probably afraid. He said, "You mean they were
CHICKEN?" I said no, not like "CHICKEN" afraid. But
the Nazis had guns, including machineguns, and the Jews
didn't. I hope I gave him the right answer.*

*Anyway, I still love your "Diary" and will keep it forever, so
that I can give it to MY daughters to read (once I get married.)*

Sincerely,

Diane McElroy

11 June 1961

Dear Diane,

I am so very pleased that you have enjoyed my
work so much, and you should tell your sister

that Anne Frank says her diary is not simply
"seventh-grade stuff." Though "Lord of the
Flies" is pretty good, too.

Also, you may tell your brother that many
Jews DID fight back. It is very hard to explain
to you, though, the reason why many more did
not. You're quite right, that it was not because
of cowardice. My father and mother offered no
resistance when the Germans arrested us, not
because they were afraid for themselves but
because they feared for their children. They
thought that the best way to protect my sister
and me was to obey orders. Who could have
conceived what was really in store for us all?
That's a poor answer perhaps, but it's the best
I can do.

Thank you for writing. I hope your children,
daughters or sons, will read what I have
written someday. And maybe their children, too.
One can only hope.

Yours,

Anne F.

She's late, but when is she not? Standing in a white Vanity Fair rayon slip, she sorts madly through the mess of cosmetics on her dresser top. You can pick up Ideal brand Summer Poppy for fifty cents at Rexall, but she'd splurged for Revlon's Super Lustrous Fifth Avenue Red at a dollar ten, even though UNICEF assures her that there are still plenty of hungry children in Europe and Asia. At the mirror she uncaps the bullet of lipstick in her hand and inhales the lush, rosy, waxy aroma. But when she puckers her lips, she is captured by her own reflection. It's definitely Jewish, this mirror, unlike the flattering mirrors in the department stores, paid to please. It refuses to soften her face and shows her every angle. The sharpness of her jaw. The dusky light in her eyes that thickens into shadows. She follows the shape of her mouth, Lustrous Fifth Avenue Red flowing as bright as blood.

A meow. Her Majesty Wilhelmina. Her orange tabby winding around her ankle, begging for attention.

"I'm late," she says. "I don't have time for you." But she's not actually speaking to Ihre Majestät Mina. She's speaking to Margot, who has appeared as a face in the background of the mirror, wearing her rotting blue-white Lager stripes and yellow six-pointed star fixed to the pullover.

You don't need lipstick, her sister tells her.

Bending forward, she pops her lips to smooth the color and then lightly mouths a Kleenex to blot the excess, leaving behind a perfect kiss. "I do. My lips have no color."

You're beautiful without cosmetics.

"No. *You* were the beautiful one," Anne insists, lacing her lashes with a touch of mascara. "I'm thirty-two. In America thirty-two means cosmetics." Grabbing up her brush, she attacks the cascade of her hair stridently. The shelves of the medicine cabinet are crowded, and she has to rearrange everything to find the tin of Johnson & Johnson Band-Aid Plastic Strips. Look . . . Feel . . . Flex Like a Second Skin.

What's that for?

A glance. "You know what it's for," she insists, popping the tin open. She tears away the paper sleeve from one of the strips, peels off the backing, and positions it over the blue scrawl of tattoo ink on her forearm. A-25063.

You're still ashamed of it? Margot wants to know.

"*No,* I'm not ashamed. How many times do we have to have this discussion?"

It's just a question.

A huff. "I'm not ashamed of the number, Margot. I'm ashamed by the pity it provokes. Besides, I don't want to scare the girls." She opens the mirror to replace the tin, and when she closes it again, Margot has vanished from the glass.

Riding the IRT

June is hot this year. The subway is humid with body heat. Electric fans rage impotently, their hornet buzz drowned out by the steel of the tracks. Advertising placards line the car above the heads of passengers. ARE YOU SMOKING MORE NOW BUT ENJOYING IT LESS? HAVE A REAL CIGARETTE—CAMEL! YOU'LL ENJOY THE FASCINATING FLAVOR OF JUICY FRUIT GUM. IT'S DIFFERENT, DELICIOUS— AND FUN TO CHEW! ALERT TODAY—ALIVE TOMORROW! ENROLL IN CIVIL DEFENSE.

An obese fellow with a crew cut fills one of the pink fiberglass seats in the opposite row. He frowns over his paper, sweating. A MONSTER! the headline of the *Daily News* bellows. EICHMANN STANDS TRIAL IN JERUSALEM! She stares blankly at the photo of the little man with the horn-rimmed glasses, seated in a glass box. He has no face, she thinks. He has no face.

East Twelfth Street and University Place
Greenwich Village

The Fourteenth Street station is a mess of people as she leaves the train. But at least she can breathe again when she hikes up the dirty steps into the open air. She starts running as fast as she can in heels on East Twelfth, but the world seems to be packing the sidewalks to slow her down, and by the time she reaches the synagogue, she is sticky with sweat. The building displays an anonymous façade across from the Police Athletic League. The only clue to its identity is the discreet line of Hebraic lettering over the door. This is a new kind of synagogue. A postwar synagogue. A post-Auschwitz synagogue. Gone is the rich Jewish Deco. At street level it is less of a temple and more of a bunker.

"Ann," she hears her agent, Ruth, call as she steps in through the door. In America everyone calls her *Ann*. On the opposite side of the

Atlantic, the *e* at the end of her name had afforded her the small nod of a vowel, an echo of the biblical Hannah. But here the pronunciation has long ago been mashed into a single syllable. *Ann*. She is permitted to keep the *e* only if she agrees to silence it. Or she is permitted to keep the vowel note only if she replaces the *e* with an *a*. So there is her choice: misspell her name or mispronounce it. She has chosen to mispronounce it, laying the short breath of the vowel to rest while privately depositing it into the deep vault where all her silenced elements are stored.

"*I'm sorry,*" she breathes.

"It's okay," Ruth tells her.

"I just couldn't get out of the apartment."

"It's okay. Just relax. Cool off. Sit down, have a drink of water."

As meticulously dressed as always, sporting white gloves, a mauve-colored blouse, and a stylish chapeau, Ruth smiles with authority at the mothers and daughters filling the synagogue's basement hall. She is a person who likes to take things in hand, and Anne is happy to allow her to do just that. Dear Ruth. Her father was Zalman Schwartz, who first published Anzia Yezierska in Yiddish and whose uncles, aunts, and a raft of unknown cousins perished in the gas chambers of Treblinka and Chelmno. *So,* Ruth explains with a sort of blighted enthusiasm, she has made a career out of representing Jewish refugees for the same reason that she's such an eggbeater for so many Jewish charities. "*Guilt.* What else?" Ruth confesses. "After all that came to pass in Europe? The millions?" A shrug. "What else could it be?" she asks Anne with only the tiniest spark of hope that Anne might have a different answer in mind. But Anne has no answer at all. Not for Ruth. Not for the millions.

Draining her water glass, Anne fills it again, concentrating on the quiet burble of liquid traveling from the pitcher to her glass. Find one beautiful thing, their mother told them. Giant bulletin boards festooned with year-end notices and handicrafts from Hebrew school dominate a wall. A dozen colorful Stars of David, cut from felt and held together with library paste. "Form a line, if you please," Ruth is instructing as Anne sits down at a trestle table draped with a clean linen cloth. Anne breathes in, drinks from her glass, leaving a bright ghost of lipstick on the glass's rim as Ruth dispenses directions with firm charm. "For those of you just arriving," Ruth announces, "please see the lady with the cashbox, Mrs. Goldblatt, to purchase your copies before having them signed. And remember, one dollar from every sale will be donated to support the International Jewish Orphans Fund."

Books are purchased. Mrs. Goldblatt makes change from the cashbox, squinting through her thick glasses and often mistaking quarters for nickels. But a line is formed, and Jewish orphans are properly supported. This is Ruth's congregation. Her husband, Gus, was chair of the Building Fund. She maintains a certain pride in her contributions to the community's success, if pride in one's accomplishments can be accepted as a forgivable transgression against halakhah.

There's a hardcover on a small wooden easel facing out. Neat stacks are arranged beside Mrs. Goldblatt. It's been out in paperback for more than a decade now, Anne's diary, and that's where the royalties come from, but these are specifically from the small inventory of hardbacks kept in print to satisfy the demands of Hanukkah and the blossoming bat mitzvah craze across Morningside Heights and the Upper East Side. She has written four books in ten years. *Answer the Night* was even nominated for the National Book Award, but this is the book she knows she will be remembered for, no matter what else she might produce. This is the book that will eternally define her.

Her publisher had balked over her title. *The House Behind*? Behind *what*? The verdict was that it was just too confusing for the young American girls who were *most certainly* going to be the book's market. So instead they devised something simple, a title to which they were sure any twelve- or thirteen-year-old could relate.

The Diary of a Young Girl.

And who could argue with that?

A photo that she had tucked away in her diary features Anne, the schoolgirl, on the dust jacket. A child's eyes staring up at her. The thick wave of hair. The full, girlish lips. The gaze resting in shadow. So many years after publication, she should be accustomed to it by now, but the sight of herself in all her innocence can still poke her in the heart. That girl with hooded eyes, gazing out from the past.

Sometimes Anne searches the mirror for her, but she has yet to find her there.

Ruth drops a few copies off at the table, one for a Mrs. Fishkin's daughter, Elizabeth, who's in California but a big, big fan; one for the rabbi's daughter, Sarah with an *h;* and one for the rabbi's niece, Zoë, living on a kibbutz in the west of Israel. Anne uncaps her fountain pen and puts it to work. A Conway Stewart Blue Herringbone, with a fourteen-karat, chisel-edge nib. A nice thick nib. She likes her nib thick. It centers her.

A grinning adolescent girl is first in line, with two copies for Anne to sign. Susan Mirish is her name, and she's an incredible fan. She hopes Anne will sign one copy for her and one for her dearest, dearest cousin, Isabelle, who's also, as it happens, an incredible fan. Anne obliges, looping the dedications across the frontispieces of the books and swooshing through her signature twice. Next in the line, Adele Spooner is more circumspect. She read Anne's diary in seventh grade and wants to know just exactly what Anne was *getting at* when she wrote that she still believed that people were good at heart. But fortunately, Adele's mother is impatient. "Adele, *enough.* You think you're the only one on line? The lady's signed your book—let's *go.*"

"To *Deborah,*" says a tall, skinny woman with a floral hat who speaks with a nasal Flatbush accent. "My daughter," she explains. "She was so depressed that she couldn't come today, 'cause she's so crazy for your book it's ridiculous. But of course she breaks her leg, the nudnik. Honestly, what are girls doing these days, can you tell me? I never climbed a tree in my life."

Anne offers her smile as a response. Under Deborah's dedication she writes, "Get well! Climb more trees!" and makes sure she shuts the cover before Deborah's mother can catch it. She feels a certain lift from these girls. Their freshness lightens her heart. Their clean, untroubled adoration provides a shot of joy. She is astonished sometimes at how much they do *adore* her diary. It makes her think that perhaps people *are* good at heart. Or might be. Or could be.

She signs another for Samantha, who goes by the name Sammi. With an *i* at the end, the girl instructs her. When Anne looks back up, she sees that Ruth is busy chatting with the wife of the congregation president, but she also sees a woman without a child to usher, standing in the line. A woman—maybe in her middle forties—wearing an inexpensive jacket and a blue floral scarf on her head.

Anne looks back at the girl in front of her. "What was your name again, liefje?"

"Natalie," the girl replies.

"Natalie," Anne repeats, and she concentrates on the pen moving in her hand. Next in line is Rebecca, who says that she gets in trouble with her mom for reading with a flashlight under the blankets past her bedtime. Anne smiles back at this, and then she feels her heart jump and quickly leaps to her feet.

"Hello, Anne," the woman in the jacket begins, in a voice that carries an accent from the old country.

Anne does not know if she should believe her own eyes. Can this be true? *"Bep,"* she whispers with joyful alarm. "Bep, is it really *you*?"

1961

The Empire State Building
Fifth Avenue and West Thirty-fourth Street

MIDTOWN MANHATTAN

The brochure calls it the Eighth Wonder of the World, and really it's
the only one that still carries clout, isn't it? The Pyramids? The Colossus of Rhodes? The Hanging Gardens of Babylon? All those corny
ancient achievements, now nothing but dust or rubble. Only this
most modern of cities can boast of the number-one tourist attraction
of the twentieth century. It has 102 stories above the ground. It climbs
1,454 feet straight up into the air like an unchallenged dream. It is the
Empire State Building, maybe the Greatest Wonder of Them All, at
Thirty-fourth and Fifth.

Bep carries a plastic Brownie in her purse. Anne shoves back her
hair with her plastic sunglasses and snaps a shot of Bep posing on the
observation deck, smiling blankly, one hand resting on a coin-
operated telescope. A lock of Bep's hair, an escapee from her scarf, is
worried by the crosscurrent of wind. Her eyes squint into the light.
As a backdrop New York has provided what a million visitors have
proclaimed to be the world's most spectacular view. But Bep looks
like an ashen shadow in the brightness of the day. In Amsterdam her
face was as plump as a peach, but now it has gone sallow. Her eyes are
nervous and shy of contact behind her cat-eye glasses. Anne hands
back the camera after snapping the shot, and Bep turns away toward
the vast scope of buildings and sky. At this altitude New York is an
open jewel box. The broad sprawl of the city is awash with azure under the clouds. The view of West Thirty-fourth Street, a straight ar-
tery dividing Macy's from Gimbels, runs to the Hudson River, and
has soaked up the river's watery blue. A gritty, diamond-encrusted

cityscape runs east-west, north-south, buildings stacked like drag-on's teeth, tall and small, on the city's grid. Cars stream like ants. People are reduced to specks. And off past the jutting piers, where the ocean liners nestle at their moorings, off to the west across the river, the landscape flattens and smears into a blue-pebbled map of crowded townships, and then the world beyond New York levels off and blurs into a band of slate-colored horizon.

Bep's explanation of her life since she left the Prinsengracht in tears is thin.

She and her husband emigrated to the States in '48. Children? Yes. Two boys. There is a picture in her wallet of all of them together, stand-ing in front of their small brick suburban house outside Philadelphia. Is she still an office worker? Sometimes. Her husband owns a hardware store. She helps out with paperwork. But mainly she's a housewife. Een huisvrouw, she says. Only now does Bep find Anne's eyes directly. "Do you think about it often?" Bep asks her. "The days in Amsterdam?"

"Every day. I think about them every day," Anne replies. She stares out at the horizon, allowing the wind to tease her hair across her face. Bep joins her in this long stare, and they share the silence high above the city's hubbub. A mesh of wire fencing in a seriated fringe has been installed below the observation deck to discourage jumpers.

"Anne, I have something to tell you," Bep says thickly. Her voice has now exposed the full urgency that she's been trying to hide. "But I don't know how to say it." Anne feels a cold weight in her breast. "Do you . . ." Bep begins to ask her, "do you recall my younger sister, Nelli?"

A pause. "I remember her," is all Anne says.

Bep expels a difficult breath. "It's about *her*," she explains, "this thing I have to tell you. It's about her." Bep's eyes fall, tearless but stricken. "She was a collaborator."

Anne feels her back stiffen. "Landverrader" is the word Bep has used in Dutch. A homeland traitor. A homegrown Quisling.

"There was a German soldier she fell for." Bep's fingers twist around the handle of her purse. "They were lovers throughout the occupation."

Anne says nothing. Only waits.

"Somehow . . ." Bep informs her, "somehow she knew the truth. About the hiding place." Bep shakes her head at a dead spot in the air. "I don't know how she found out. I swear I never told her a thing, I *swear it,* Anne. But somehow she found out anyway. I knew because once we were having a terrible row over her . . . over her *relationship* with this German, and she shouted at me, 'Why don't you forget about me and just go back to your *Jews*?'"

Anne is now staring. Staring at the movement of Bep's lips as she forms words.

"It was *her,* Anne," Bep confesses. "It was Nelli who rang up the Gestapo and betrayed us all. It wasn't one of the warehousemen, it wasn't the charwoman. It wasn't anybody but my sister."

Anne says nothing. She can say nothing.

"I mean, I have no documents to offer as proof," Bep admits. "No letters of confession. Nelli was very roughly handled at the end of the war. They shaved her hair off in the middle of the street and painted her head orange. Even so, she has never owned up to anything. She still blames others for her troubles. Regardless, I know it to be true. I know it to be true in my heart that it was *she* who denounced you."

What she feels first surprises Anne. Not anger, not shock, not even relief, but a pinch of regret. It's true that many theories have been offered, but inwardly, Anne has assigned this crime to Raaf. Raaf, that straw-haired boy with his hands stuffed in his pockets. And now if this is *true*? All these years blaming Raaf in her heart to discover now that she's been *wrong*? It hurts her.

"I'm sorry, Anne," Bep says. "I'm so very sorry. I should have told you long ago, but I couldn't bring myself to. I just couldn't."

Anne blinks at her and stares. "Why? Why would she *do* it? What had we ever done to *her*?"

Bep looks down. Shakes her head. "I have no good explanation. She was angry. Papa was so sick, and it was terrible. The cancer was taking him slowly and with great pain. She was angry and grieving and wanted to lash out. At me, at anyone she felt had judged her. That is my only explanation as to why. That and maybe because we were young and child-foolish in the middle of an ugly time. I don't know. All I can say for certain is that a kind of cruelty simply consumed her."

A kind of cruelty, Anne thinks. Can it finally make sense? Why Pim always resisted investigation. Why he always refused to pursue the subject of their betrayal, clinging obstinately to the parody of forgiveness he had constructed. How could he do otherwise? Bep's *sister*? He could never be party to dragging Bep through such public disgrace. Not after the dangers she risked in caring for his family and friends. "My father knew, didn't he?"

A swallow. Bep brushes away the forelock of hair that's escaped her scarf. "I never told him directly. I've never told anyone directly until now. But I always believed he knew, yes." A shrug. "I know you won't credit this, Anne, but I *do* believe that in a sense Nelli didn't really understand what she was doing. That she didn't really know about those terrible places where the Nazis sent the Jews."

"No. No, of course not. *Nobody* knew, after all. *Nobody* had the slightest clue, did they? Whole populations were nothing but innocent dupes, even though the BBC was *broadcasting* across the continent that Jews were being gassed. It was just English propaganda, wasn't it?"

Bep shrivels into a slump, her shoulders disappearing. "I knew you would be angry. Of course. You have every right to be angry. You have every right to hate me."

A sharp sob strikes Anne in the chest. She grabs her forehead, eyes squeezed tightly shut. She can feel the thump of her heart dictating her reaction, but she resists it. Shaking her head, she blinks open her eyes and wipes them roughly with the palms of her hands. *"No,"* she answers, though her voice shivers. "No, Bep. I don't hate you. I could never hate you. You risked your life to keep us safe. And what your sister did?" A heavy breath stops her. "What your sister did or didn't do," she says. "You bear no responsibility for that."

Bep gazes back at her. Her eyes are dark with suffering, wounded, begging forgiveness. When she breaks down in tears, Anne hesitates but then steps forward. She gathers the woman into her arms, her own tears wetting her cheeks, and stares past Bep at Margot's thin shadow, her Belsen death rags hanging from her body as she gazes back at them with blighted sympathy. Clouds move. The envelope of light drains of color. Drains of anger. Empties itself of regret and reprisal. What can Anne possibly do but embrace an exhausted forgiveness, along with her lost friend?

Bep breathes in and out as they separate. Opens her purse for a handkerchief and mops her eyes. "I have something for you, Anne," she manages to say. Replacing the handkerchief, she draws out a small, flat package, wrapped in brown paper and closed with Scotch tape. "Something that was yours many years ago. I took it because . . ." says Bep, but then it's hard for her to explain why she took it. She shakes her head. "I wanted a memento of you. It was an impulse, but once I had it, I was too embarrassed to give it back."

Anne gazes at Bep, who nods at her to accept it. Her gaze drops to the package as she takes it into her hands. The package is soft. Pliable. Carefully, she tugs open the tape that binds it and stares at its contents. "My combing shawl."

"I found it on the floor that awful day. And I took it. I thought I would keep it for you until you came back. But I suppose it's taken me a long time to return it."

Odd how such a small thing, such an insignificant item from her girlhood, has such an effect. "I would wear this over my shoulders every night. And I remember how sometimes Margot would brush my hair for me," she says. "We could be arguing all day, but that special moment would overcome all of it. It made me feel so close to her that it was impossible to feel anything except love. *More* than love," Anne says. "I felt as if we had something magical that only sisters could share." She looks past Bep, to the spot where Margot should be standing, yet it's nothing save empty light now.

"Anne—" Bep starts to say, but Anne breaks in, the words coming unbidden, unplanned.

"I killed her," she announces. A thin shiver passes through her body.

Bep squints at her, confused. "You . . . you *what*?"

"I killed her. I killed her, Bep. I killed my sister at Bergen-Belsen."

Bep opens her mouth. "I don't . . ." she begins, but then she shakes her head as if to shake the words away. "Anne . . ." she whispers.

"It's not my guilt speaking," Anne says. "That is, my guilt at surviving when she did not. I *do* feel a terrible guilt over that. Survival? That is its own kind of crime. But my crime is something different." Rolling tears begin to ice her cheek, but she does not wipe them away. "We were..." Anne tries to continue, but her words die in her mouth, and she must start again. "We were in Barracks Block 1 in Belsen, Margot and I. Both of us had been brought into Germany from Birkenau. The weather was freezing. The camp was overflowing with disease. Typhus, dysentery, scurvy," she recites the list. "Both of us were dreadfully, dreadfully sick. And I had been suffering from these ... these *horrible* visions—rats the size of dinner platters crawling over us. Blinded cats, their eyes gouged out, shivering and mewing in agony, but when I tried to pick them up, they would spit at me and bite my fingers until I was bleeding. I suppose it was the fever. I felt like my eyes were slowly boiling inside my skull, and I was *so, so* horribly exhausted. All I wanted to do was sleep. To fall into the deepest sleep ever conceived and never, ever wake up. But the barracks block was noisy. And Margot was coughing so loudly. We were lying close beside each other on the same pallet. There were lice in the straw. Lice in our ears and under our arms. Lice everywhere. In every crevice and pit of our bodies. I couldn't sleep no matter how exhausted I felt, because *everything* itched so badly, my whole body. I just wanted to tear my skin off. And Margot was *still coughing*. I remember how I shouted at her, 'Be quiet! Can't you be *quiet*?' But she just kept coughing. I only wanted to sleep," she tries to explain as the tears flood her eyes and cling to her lashes. "I only wanted to *sleep*."

She sees it all again. The disease-rotted barracks. The pallet on which she lay beside Margot. She can smell the stench of the filthy, lice-infested straw. The stink of bodies. The noise of Margot's cough. She feels the impulse to shut her up. To heave her away. A beat. She swallows something hard and heavy. "So I shoved her," she confesses. "She was lying with her back to me, and I shoved her from behind. I only wanted her to stop. *Just stop coughing so loudly, so I could sleep.* I didn't mean to shove her ... to shove her so *hard*." Her voice diminishes. "So hard that she would roll off the pallet. But I *did*. I *must* have. And when she fell, it was too much for her. She was so weak. We were both so weak. The impact was too great a shock for her body." The slowest beat. "She was *dead*," Anne whispers. And then her sister is on the ground. Limbs akimbo. Her body motionless. Eyes open but her gaze stolen. Anne can feel the scream clog her throat, but she is too weak to release it as those around her begin to strip the corpse of its value. The dead have no need for socks on their feet. They do not require a woolen pullover.

Bep stares, her eyes raw. And then slowly she says, "Anne. Anne, I want you to listen to me, please." She wipes her eyes, but a strange calm has transformed the woman's face. "Will you? Will you listen to me? What you just told me—what you just told me you *think* happened," she corrects. "You should consider it nothing more than a nightmare. Do you *hear* me, Anne? You were so ill. So fevered. It was simply—I'm sure of it—simply another *hallucination*."

Anne gazes at Bep heavily. "Hallucination," she repeats.

"You were so young," Bep tells her. "Just a helpless child. You must believe me when I tell you that you have no right to take on the guilt of your sister's death. The blame for that lands squarely on the men who perpetrated these crimes. *Not on you,* do you understand that?"

Anne is shaking her head, swiping at the tears on her face. "I know what I know."

"But you *don't* know, Anne," Bep insists sharply now. "You *don't* know. You think that you were *strong* lying there in that hideous place? Do you really? If Margot rolled off the pallet and died, then it was because she was coughing so violently. Not because of any kind of pitiful shove on your part. Not because of *you*."

Anne can't find any words. All she can do is concentrate on drawing in a breath against the tears and grip the flat package against her breast until it's Bep who embraces her.

With forgiveness.

With love.

Like a sister.

35

REPAIRING THE WORLD

If God lets me live, I'll achieve more than Mother ever
did, I'll make my voice heard, I'll go out into the world and
work for mankind!

—Anne Frank,
from her diary,
11 April 1944

1961

Waverly Place and Mercer Street
Greenwich Village

NEW YORK CITY

The apartment is dark but for a yellowish glow from the street that defines the edges of the room and the furniture. So Anne doesn't bother turning on a lamp till she reaches the kitchen table by the fire-escape window. Miep's portable typewriter is stationed there. A battered old thing by now, with a sheet of onionskin cranked around the rubber platen.

She keeps photographs on the wall.

When her diary was published in Hebrew, a letter came from Tel Aviv. In it was a picture of Hanneli and her husband with a baby on her lap. Both had thought the other dead, but now there is this photo of life. Beside it a small frame from B. Altman's encloses a snapshot of Miep posing with Anne in her cap and gown after she was graduated from Barnard. Then there's the fading color shot of Pim with his arm around Dassah, the ancient architecture of Jerusalem behind them. Pim is squinting, smiling into the desert sun, and Dassah is shading her eyes.

And Margot? The photo of Anne and Margot on the beach at Zandvoort more than twenty years before is locked in a sterling silver frame. Locked in time.

She opens her purse, plucking out the combing shawl. A flag of silk unfurls, and she feels her pulse quicken. Pale beige fabric decorated with roses and small figures. She gathers it to her nose to see if she can still smell the past clinging to it, but the sachet of her adolescence is long gone and she can only smell a musty trace of memory.

Sitting at the table, she lights a Camel. Her tawny cat, Mina, curls around her ankles and then struts away. "Odd after all these years, to know the truth," Anne says, and stares into Margot's eyes. "I thought I would feel something more. But really I don't." She nearly laughs. "I find," she says, wondering if this could really be *true*, "that it makes no difference. So it was Nelli who betrayed us. So what? Even if it's true, no one comes back to life."

Margot is sitting beside her at the table, a young schoolgirl with a yellow Judenstern sewn neatly to the breast of her sweater. Resting her cheek against her hand, she observes Anne from behind the lenses of her glasses with half a smile. Anne gazes back at her. She realizes just how young Margot still is. Just a teenager, never to be any older.

Do you feel unburdened?

"Unburdened?" Anne considers this. "Bep made her confession. I made mine. But I doubt I will ever feel *unburdened*."

But she could be right, you know. Bep. Belsen was so hellish, Anne. We were both so sick. We were both so weak. I fell from the pallet. Maybe it wasn't your fault at all.

A shrug. Who knows? Who will ever really know? "There are times when I feel so lonely, Margot. So separate from the rest of the world. As if I don't actually exist. As if I'm just a shadow," she says. "Like you." Exhaling smoke, she watches Margot dissolve quietly in its cloud.

The telephone gives a chilly ring, and she crosses the room to snap the receiver off the wall. On the other end, she hears the voice of an old man. "Er is er een jarig, hoera-hoera. Dat kun je wel zien dat is zij!" An old man's happily croaking birthday song. "Zij leve lang, hoera-hoera, zij leve la-ang hoera!"

"Hello, Pim," she says. "You know it's actually tomorrow."

"Oh, yes, I know that." He speaks to her now in English. "Of course I know. But waiting for another day was too much. Hadas said I must wait, but *I* thought, 'No. I must sing my daughter her birthday song right this moment.'"

"Pim," Anne says. "Pim, you'll never guess who appeared today."

"Who *appeared*?" he asks, as if perhaps his daughter is describing a magic trick.

"Bep," Anne says, swallowing quietly.

"*Bep?*"

"Yes."

"*Our Bep?*"

"Yes. We went to the top of the Empire State Building. Just as planned when we were in hiding. Do you remember?"

"Of course. Of course I remember," he says, though a slight vacancy in his tone makes her doubt that he really does.

"And what did Bep have to say for herself?" Pim wants to know.

Anne pauses. The smile that has half formed on her lips stiffens.

"Anne, are you still there?"

"Yes. Yes, Pim. She said she's lived here in America for years. She said her husband owns a hardware store. And she has two children."

"Well," Pim replies with a satisfied tone. "That is wonderful. Wonderful to know. I am so very glad to hear that she is happy."

Anne's eyes have gone damp with tears. She starts to speak, but as it happens, all she can speak is silence.

"Anne?"

"Pim. This call. It must be costing a fortune. I should let you go before you have to take out a bank loan."

"Take out *what*?"

"Nothing. Nothing, Pim. I should let you go. I mean, I should say good-bye."

"Happy birthday, meisje," he tells her. "I think of you daily."

"Me, too, Pim," she says. "Me, too."

And sets the phone's receiver back on its hook.

In the bedroom she has changed into her kimono and sits in front of the vanity mirror, gazing deeply into the shadowed eyes contained in the circle of glass.

When she peels off the Band-Aid strip, her secret number is revealed. She brushes the spot with her finger. A-25063. The ink has faded to a tender shade of violet.

One beautiful thing.

Draping the pale combing shawl over her shoulders, she straightens the fringe hanging from its edges and picks up her brush from among the scattered lipsticks, eyeliners, and bits of crumpled Kleenex smudged with eye shadow. Combing her fingers through her dark curtain of hair, she applies the brush, stroke after stroke after stroke. The long ritual. And then, for a moment, she pauses. Leans forward toward the face in the glass.

Could it all be nothing but a vivid flash? Her life, she wonders. Could it be no more than a blink in the hectic desire of a dying girl's thoughts? A moment's hesitation before the angel of death collected her into his bundle of sticks? This life, now contained in the circumference of a vanity's mirror, is it real? Can it be real? A life for a girl who should have *had* no life beyond the mudflats of Bergen-Belsen. If she blinks, will she feel her last breath constricting her body? She cannot help but test it.

A blink.

And yet she breathes.

If it is all a dream, then she is dreaming a life that did not end. A life that demands the purpose that is coloring her gaze. Why does she have such a life? Who can say? But she has it and must therefore put it to use. Where will it take her? How will she pursue it, this woman she has become, this Annelies Marie Frank confirmed by the proof of her reflection?

Tikkun olam, Rabbi Souza had told her. Her duty to repair the world.

How? By living. By putting words on paper.

She steals another breath. She steals another breath as she counts another brushstroke, just as she counts another heartbeat, alone with herself, a survivor, a beating pulse, a living inheritor of all that has passed, advancing into an unfixed future, the chatterbox, the bundle of contradictions, Anne favored by God, surrounded by the hope of the dead.

Author's Note

In writing this book, my priority has been to honor Anne's story with honesty and accuracy, so I have remained loyal to the facts wherever possible. I've read deeply, delving into Anne's diary as well as Holocaust histories, biographies of Anne Frank, and transcripts of interviews with people who knew her. I've traveled to Amsterdam twice in researching *Annelies*. While learning about the Jewish experience in Amsterdam during the war, I've visited the old Jewish Quarter, the Resistance Museum, the former Diamond District, and the Jewish enclave in the Transvaal, once left in ruins by a freezing population desperate for firewood. And specifically in relation to Anne Frank's life, I've seen the bookshop where she likely picked out her tartan plaid diary, the Jewish Lyceum where she and her sister, Margot, were sent to school during the occupation, and the former Gestapo headquarters where the Franks and their friends were detained after their arrest. I've explored the Frank family apartment in Amsterdam. And, of course, I've spent hours inside the Anne Frank House itself. I've followed Anne Frank's path from Amsterdam to the remains of the transit camp Westerbork in the northeastern Netherlands; to Auschwitz-Birkenau, where they were all shipped by the Nazis on September 3, 1944; to Bergen-Belsen inside Germany, where Anne and Margot died of typhus months later. Through continued study and access to these resources, I have done my best to portray the historical backdrop against which the Franks lived with veracity and respect.

The story I tell in *Annelies,* though, is not history; it is a piece of fiction based on my research and my understanding of Anne's diary. The prewar section of the novel is a fictionalization of actual events, although the timeline has been slightly adapted to accommodate the drama and the dialogue of the characters largely imagined. Anne's parents *were* in fact already planning to go into hiding in the annex behind Otto Frank's business when the process was accelerated by Margot's unexpected call-up into the German labor service.

Anne Frank's experiences in the concentration camps of Westerbork, Birkenau, and Belsen are also imagined, but based on survivor accounts of conditions in the camps and on the accounts of people who had contact with Anne and Margot in those places. For instance, the scene in which Anne meets her friend Hanneli at the barbed-wire fence in Bergen-Belsen is based on an actual meeting often described by Hannah Pick-Goslar, who survived Belsen and lives today in Israel.

The story of my character Anne returning to postwar Amsterdam is of course completely imagined. According to the testimony of survivors, Margot Frank died of typhus inside Belsen in February or March of 1945. It's said that she rolled off the pallet where she was lying, and the shock of the fall killed her. Anne Frank died a few days later, and their bodies were taken to mass graves.

In reality, of the eight residents of the House Behind, only Pim— Anne's father, Otto Frank—returned. I have based my character Pim on my reading of Anne's diary, on my research, on interviews of Otto, and on my dramatic imagination. Miep, too, is based on a real person—the indomitable Miep Gies, the woman who actually saved Anne Frank's writing from the floor of the hiding place on the day of the family's arrest by the Gestapo. My characters of Bep, Kugler, Kleiman, and Jan are all based to some degree on the Dutch individuals who supported the Franks in hiding. So are Anne's friend Hanneli and the others hiding out in the House Behind; Anne's mother, Edith; Augusta and Hermann van Pels; their son, Peter; and Mr. Pfeffer. My characterizations of them are dramatic constructions based on my reading of the diary, related books, documentaries, and my own imagination.

The important characters who are *entirely* fictional are the Dutch boy Raaf, the bookshop proprietor Mr. Nussbaum, and Anne's stepmother, Dassah. Anne's father, Otto, was indeed remarried in the 1950s to a quite wonderful and generous woman who was also a survivor. So the character of Anne's stepmother, who for dramatic purposes is portrayed with a darker side, is *purely* a product of my creativity and is in no way based on any actual person. All such completely fictional characters were developed to fulfill the dramatic requirements of the plot, though I did my best to make them realistic within the historical context.

I believe in the importance of historical accuracy in fiction and have endeavored to create a postwar world in which Anne might have lived, one that is anchored in fact. At times, as I've mentioned, I took the names of actual people whom Anne Frank knew and assigned them to fictional characters instead of simply creating characters completely from whole cloth. But I did so only when excluding them from the story would be too significant an omission. In creating these characters (including the character of Anne herself), I tried to synthesize the results of my research with the portrayals of people in Anne's writings.

I also took care not to draw conclusions about the question of the Frank family's betrayal, to which history still lacks definitive closure. During my research for this book, I was surprised by how many theories are still being generated. The question of who betrayed Anne Frank seems to be one surrounded by a multitude of conjectures but with no real answer. As the author of the novel, I try not to come down on the side of any one particular speculation but simply present different possibilities. The only character who overtly declares her belief concerning the identity of the betrayer is the character Bep in her scene with Anne atop the Empire State Building. Here Bep expresses her conviction that it was her sister (Nelli) who betrayed the Franks to the Gestapo. This is based on a theory advanced by a book coauthored by the son of the actual Elisabeth "Bep" Voskuijl, published in the Netherlands in 2015 and entitled *Silence No More*. The book is premised on the testimony of Diny Voskuijl, another of Bep's sisters, and Bep's wartime fiancé, Bertus Hulsman. It's the conclusion of the book's authors that Nelly Voskuijl was a Nazi collaborator during much of the German occupation of the Netherlands and that it was she who was likely the culprit. But even in this case, I try to make it clear that this is what my character believes, not an endorsement of the theory's validity.

As I wrote this story, I was constantly aware of the fact that Anne

Frank was a real person, a person who wrote one of the defining books of the twentieth century before dying tragically. In imagining a life for her had she survived, I hope to accomplish two things: to give Anne the life she was cheated of and, through telling the story of one girl, to tell the stories of all the Annes, thereby underscoring the lost potential of the millions who perished and reminding us of what we are missing in our world today because of their loss. Anne Frank's legacy is one of hope, and it is *my* hope that if I can offer a reminder of what we have lost, we can dedicate ourselves to making a better future.

Acknowledgments

Sitting at a laptop, tapping away at the keyboard, can be isolating. But thankfully there have been many more people involved in the creation of this book than simply myself, and I owe them all my gratitude and deep appreciation. I hope I have made that clear to them over the years it has taken to complete this novel, but I'd also like the opportunity to do so in print.

I must thank my incredible agent, the best of the best, Rebecca Gradinger of Fletcher and Company, whose hard work and devotion made it possible for me to continue over the long journey of the soul this project became. Her commitment, patience, and insight through multiple drafts kept me focused and on track, and honestly I could not have written this book without her. Additionally, many thanks to Christy Fletcher, founder of her amazing agency, and to Veronica Goldstein for her professional support and excellent management of the myriad details.

My deep appreciation goes to my wonderfully patient and simply outstanding editor, Sarah Stein, who did the detailed in-the-trenches editing that balanced the narrative flow and kept the story lean and the prose well polished. Thank you, Sarah. Your dedication was immense, and I owe you a tremendous debt of gratitude.

Thank you to Viking editor in chief Andrea Schulz for her devotion to the book and for her essential work in shaping the novel's contours. And my thanks to Viking publisher Brian Tart for his commitment, as well as to all the other incredible professionals at Penguin Random House with whom I am honored to work. I'm so grateful to assistant editor Shannon Kelly, whose hard work and great dedication to the project have been invaluable; to Maureen Sugden, whose copyedit was so sensitively and skillfully done that it felt like a true collaboration; to production editor Bruce Giffords; to Nancy Resnick, interior design, and Brianna Harden, whose cover design is perfect; to marketing director Kate Stark and Mary Stone, title marketer; to publicity director Lindsay Prevette and Louise Braverman, publicist; and to the entire Penguin Random House sales staff, who have dedicated long hours of heavy lifting to bringing the book to readers. Thank you all for getting *Annelies* to its audience.

My gratitude goes also to Amy Einhorn, who published my first novel, *City of Women*, under her imprint, and who originally bought the Anne Frank book. Thank you, Amy.

I want to extend my appreciation as well to those who supported me along the way. Thank you to my writing consultant, Carol Edelstein of A Gallery of Readers, who acted as a valuable sounding board for the work, and to Ans van der Graaff of Ans van der Graaff Vertaalservice in Middelburg, Netherlands, whose translation skills were so helpful to me in my research. Thank you to my fellow writers Pat Stacey and Charles Mann, who listened to me go on and on about this book and continued to be supportive throughout. I also greatly value my social media connections with fellow writers Jillian Cantor, Lyndsay Faye, Kathleen Grissom, Judy Hooper, Pam Jenoff, Erika Marks, Paula McLain, Julie Ries, Erika Robuck, Kate Whouley, and Andria Williams.

In my research, I had vital assistance from several sources. I must offer immense gratitude to the Anne Frank House in Amsterdam for allowing me access to areas of the house not normally available to the public, such as the office kitchen and the private office, both spots where important scenes in the book are set. Also, I would like to pay my respects to the memory of Cornelius Suijk, who passed away in 2014 at the age of ninety. In his youth, Cor was a member of the Dutch resistance. He was also a friend of both Otto Frank and Miep Gies and served the Anne Frank House as a board member and as a director. Cor, it is an honor to have known you.

My gratitude goes as well to the Ymere Corporation and communications adviser Andre Bakker for a tour of the Frank family flat in the Merwedeplein in Amsterdam South. Andre was quite generous with his time and expertise, and extended his tour beyond the Merwedeplein to a number of spots of historic interest across the town, including the former Jewish Quarter and the building that housed the so-called Joods Lyceum. He was a tremendous resource for me. But, at his request, I must also mention that he did his best to persuade me not to write about Anne Frank. As he pointed out, there were many Jewish families such as Anne's in Amsterdam who suffered under the Nazis and came to tragic ends in places such as Birkenau and Belsen. And wouldn't it be of greater benefit to explore their struggles instead? This was, he explained, the position of the Ymere Corporation, and why he had extended his tour beyond Anne Frank's story, to the larger tragedy that engulfed the Jewish community during the war. My only response is that, though I both understood and deeply respected this point of view, that was not the book I was writing, and I hope that other writers take up his challenge and do justice to all the other stories that comprise the tragedy that befell Amsterdam's Jewish population.

Finally, I cannot forget my family, who not only supported me throughout the process but provided me with respite and encouragement: my mother, Marcia Gillham; my sister, Lisa Gillham; and my boys, Cameron Gemmell and Alexander Pavlova-Gillham.

And as always, I must thank, from the depth of my being, my life's partner and wife, Ludmilla Pavlova-Gillham, who is still my touchstone in all things.

A PENGUIN READERS GUIDE TO

ANNELIES

David R. Gillham

AN INTRODUCTION TO
ANNELIES

Annelies is a powerful and deeply humane novel that asks the question: What if Anne Frank survived the Holocaust?

It's 1945, and the war is over. Anne Frank is sixteen years old and has survived the concentration camps. But with her survival comes a host of new challenges, and her struggle is far from over. As she reunites with her beloved father, Pim, in newly liberated Amsterdam, she finds that returning to her life is more difficult than she could have possibly imagined.

Anne has lost her mother, her sister, and the beloved diary that housed her dreams during her years in hiding. As she and Pim attempt to piece their lives back together, she finds that she has lost herself as well. Gone is the lively, curious child who dreamed of becoming a writer. In her place is a woman haunted by the horrors she's experienced, and most painfully by the memory of her sister, Margot. While her father works to build a new life after loss, Anne is adrift.

But as the people of Europe begin the slow process of rebuilding after the war, Anne finds herself once more accessing the hope that inspired her in the Secret Annex and uses her writing to amplify the voices of the lost, in the hope that they may never be forgotten.

In *Annelies*, Gillham has created a powerful narrative of what might have been. Anne Frank's words have become a beacon of hope amid tragedy, and she has come to represent the senseless horror of the Holocaust. Gillham's lyrical prose gives life not only to the icon but to the human being, as she grows from adolescent to woman in the wake of tragedy and rediscovers hope.

3

A Conversation with
David R. Gillham

Annelies *is a work of historical fiction that asks the question: What if Anne Frank survived the Holocaust? What sparked your interest in reinventing the life of such a treasured writer?*

Anne Frank's story has always been a story of hope, and hope is the common thread of my writing, especially under conditions where it's hard to imagine that such a thing can survive. Probably the most famous passage from Anne's diary is dated in July 1944, and in it she writes that, even in the face of war and persecution, she still believes in the basic goodness of people. But the question has been asked, could she still have believed this after experiencing the horrors of Auschwitz and Bergen-Belsen? It is a challenging question, and one that I wanted to try at least to answer. This novel is my attempt to do so.

How did you approach writing about a Holocaust victim? How are you able to provide validity to Anne's story?

As I wrote this story, I was constantly aware of the fact that Annelies Marie Frank was a real person, a person who wrote what would one day become an important addition to world literature. And yet she died tragically as one of millions of unknown faces. In imagining a life for her had she actually survived, I hoped to accomplish two things: to give Anne the life she was cheated of and, through telling the story of one girl, to tell the stories of all the "Annes," thereby underscoring the lost potential of the millions who perished. Anne Frank's legacy is one of hope, and it is *my* hope that if I can offer a reminder of what has been lost, we can dedicate ourselves to repairing the world.

How did you set about researching the novel? How did you use your talents as a novelist to imagine Anne's story?

In writing this book, my priority has been to honor Anne Frank's story with honesty and accuracy, so I have remained true to the facts as I understood them. I've read deeply, delving into Holocaust histories, biographies of Anne Frank and her father, "Pim," memoirs and transcripts of interviews of people who knew her, as well as studying her diary itself. I've traveled to the Netherlands twice in researching *Annelies*. To be better educated in the Jewish experience in Amsterdam, I've visited the old Jewish Quarter, the former Diamond District, and the former Jewish enclave in the Transvaalbuurt, once left in ruins by a freezing population desperate for firewood. And specifically in relation to Anne Frank's life, I've seen the bookshop where she likely picked out her tartan plaid diary, the Jewish Lyceum where she and her sister, Margot, were sent to school during the occupation, and the former Gestapo headquarters where the Franks and their friends were first detained after their arrest. I've explored the Frank family apartment in Amsterdam's Merwedeplein complex. And, of course, I've spent hours inside the Anne Frank House itself. I've followed Anne Frank's path from Amsterdam to the remains of the transit camp Westerbork in the northeastern Netherlands; to Auschwitz-Birkenau, where all the inhabitants of the "House Behind" were shipped by the Nazis on September 3, 1944; to Bergen-Belsen inside Germany, where Anne and Margot Frank died of typhus months later. Through study and access to these resources, I have done my level best to portray the historical backdrop against which the Franks lived with authenticity, sincerity, and respect.

The portion of the novel set during the period before the Franks went into hiding fictionalizes a chronicle of events recorded in Anne's diary, although the timeline has been slightly adapted to accommodate the drama, and the dialogue of the characters largely imagined. The dramatic action of the novel after the return of my character Anne from Bergen-Belsen is completely fictional, of course, though the background of events against which the action unfolds is based on my research in actual postwar history.

Your last novel, City of Women, *was also set in World War II. What attracts you to writing historical fiction, specifically in this time period?*

I've always been drawn to the past and consider myself a lifelong student of history. I think that history offers many lessons to the present and that, as a novelist, I am drawn to portraying the parallels. As far as the Second World War is concerned, it seems to me that its sheer scope and tragedy continue to exceed our ability to understand it. So we keep trying. Certainly there have been other brutal and scarring calamities in the length of human history, but few, if any, have so irrevocably changed the face of the world and still resonate so widely and deeply. We are living today with the consequences of that war.

One of the most important relationships in the novel is between Anne and her father, Otto "Pim" Frank. How did you develop this father-daughter relationship, both before and after their traumatic experiences?

Dramatically, Anne and Pim represent two different approaches to redemption after trauma. One approach (Pim's) refuses to dwell on the tragedies of the past and looks only toward a better future. The other approach (Anne's) refuses to relinquish those tragedies and, by facing them, must try to overcome anger and guilt. Both paths may to lead to redemption and forgiveness. Both are valid, even when in conflict, because both are fueled, in the end, by the power of hope. Hope is at the heart of *Annelies.*

In developing the fictionalized relationship between my characters Anne and Pim, I read biographical and historical works such as those produced by Melissa Müller, Carol Ann Lee, and R. W. Jansen. I watched dramatic performances based on Anne's experiences. I studied accounts of their father/daughter relationship and their personalities left by friends such as Miep Gies. I watched and rewatched postwar film interviews given by Otto Frank and listened to the stories of the late Cor Suijk, who knew Mr. Frank personally. But really it was Anne Frank herself, in the pages of her diary, who provided me with the contours and depth of their relationship, which I have attempted to portray and from which I have extrapolated.

Did any other writers inspire you while writing Annelies?

I had not actually read Anne Frank's diary before I read Philip Roth's novel *The Ghost Writer*. In it Roth's protagonist, Nathan Zuckerman, imagines that a young European woman in her twenties whom he meets is actually Anne Frank. It's only a moment's fantasy, really, and Nathan quickly realizes that it's his willing imagination at work. But it was *The Ghost Writer* that inspired me to pick up Anne's diary and read it. I was thunderstruck—not just by her insight and humor, but by her subtle brilliance as a writer.

And then, of course, there are the many writers who experienced the Holocaust and bore witness, including Eli Wiesel, Isabella Leitner, Primo Levi, and Etty Hillesum (the Dutch writer whose journal and letters were published after her death in Auschwitz). Also, there are the memoires and reminiscences of those who knew Anne Frank personally, such as Hannah Pick-Goslar, Eva Schloss, Nanette Blitz-Konig, and Jaqueline van Maarsen. And many, many more survivors, on whose courageous testimony we have come to depend to form our understanding of what cannot be understood.

What do you want people to take away from reading Annelies?

That hope can survive. That in the face of all obstacles, in the face of destruction, in the face of despair, hope can abide. In fact, it must abide. That is the message of the book. And that, I think, is what Anne Frank tried to tell us.

QUESTIONS FOR DISCUSSION

1. In *Annelies*, Anne and her father, Pim, often have a thorny relationship as they cope with the trauma of surviving the war in different ways. How would you describe their different approaches in attempting to rebuild their lives?

2. Perhaps the most famous passage in Anne Frank's diary concerns her belief that people are basically good at their core. How do you think the novel *Annelies* addresses this? Does the fictional character Anne believe this to be true, even after her horrific experiences in the camp?

3. The relationship between the character Anne and the boy Raaf is fraught with contradictions and danger. Why do you think Anne propelled herself into this relationship?

4. How do you think the Jewish concept of *tikkun olam*— "repairing the world" and taking moral responsibility for the welfare of others as well as one's own—helped Anne repair herself?

5. Anne feels a tremendous amount of guilt surrounding the death of her sister, Margot. Do you think her guilt is warranted? How well do you think the character Anne resolves her feelings of guilt by the end of the novel?

6. The real Anne Frank has become an international symbol of the loss perpetrated by the Holocaust, and a powerful voice of hope through her diary. In what ways has she become mythologized? Did reading *Annelies* change the way you thought about her?

7. *Annelies* focuses on how anti-Semitism was still very present in Europe despite the fall of the Nazi regime and the liberation of the camps. Did that surprise you? How is this aspect different from other World War II novels?

8. When you first picked up this book reimagining Anne Frank as having survived the Holocaust, what did you think of that starting place? Did your opinion change after finishing the book?

9. At the end of the book, the author includes a list of fictional letters from readers responding to *The Diary of a Young Girl*. How did you think the young letter writers in the book experienced Anne's diary differently than we do?

10. This novel is based on real people and events. Did knowing that transform your reading experience? Do you read differently when characters are purely fictional?